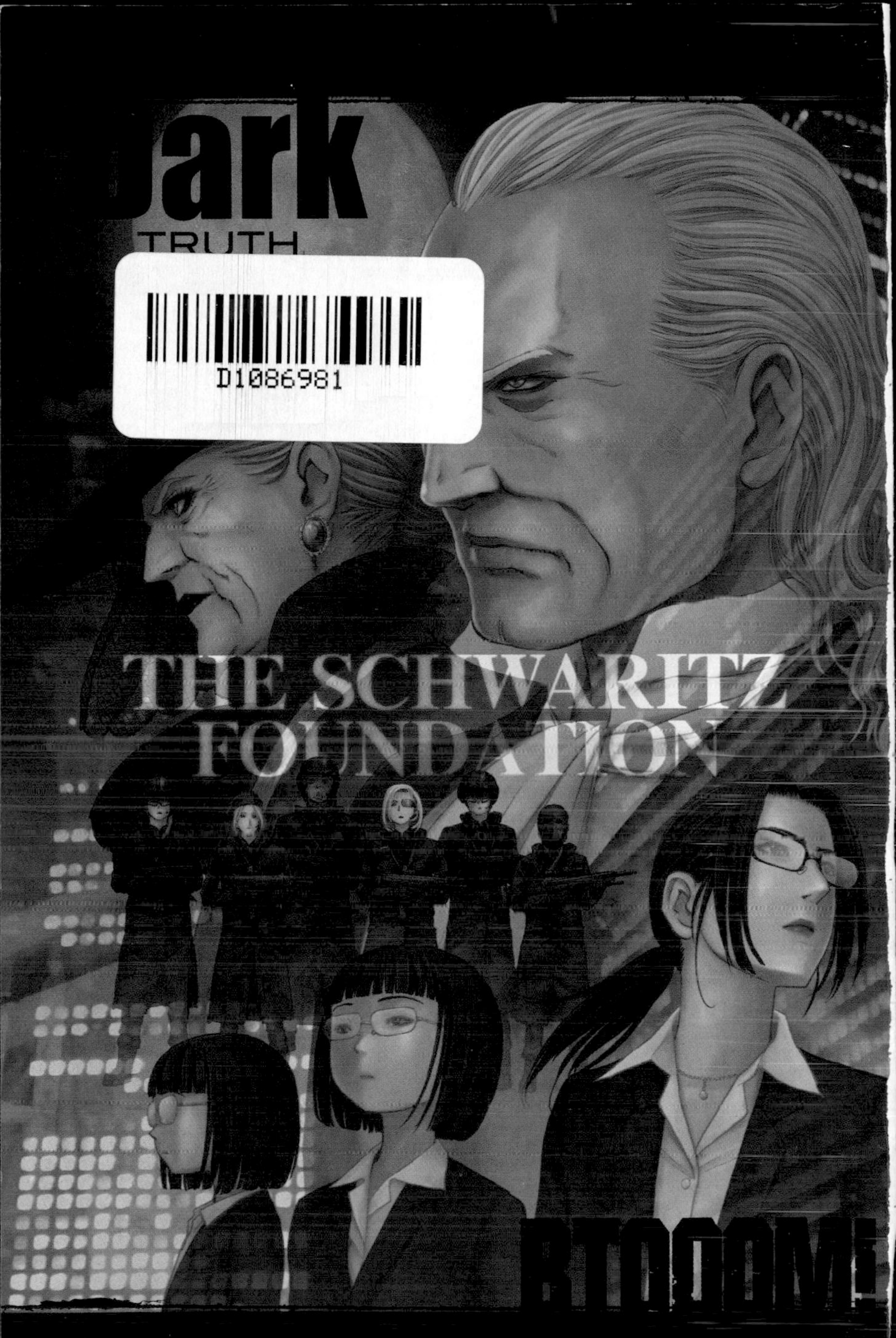
Dark
TRUTH
THE SCHWARITZ
FOUNDATION
BTOOOM!

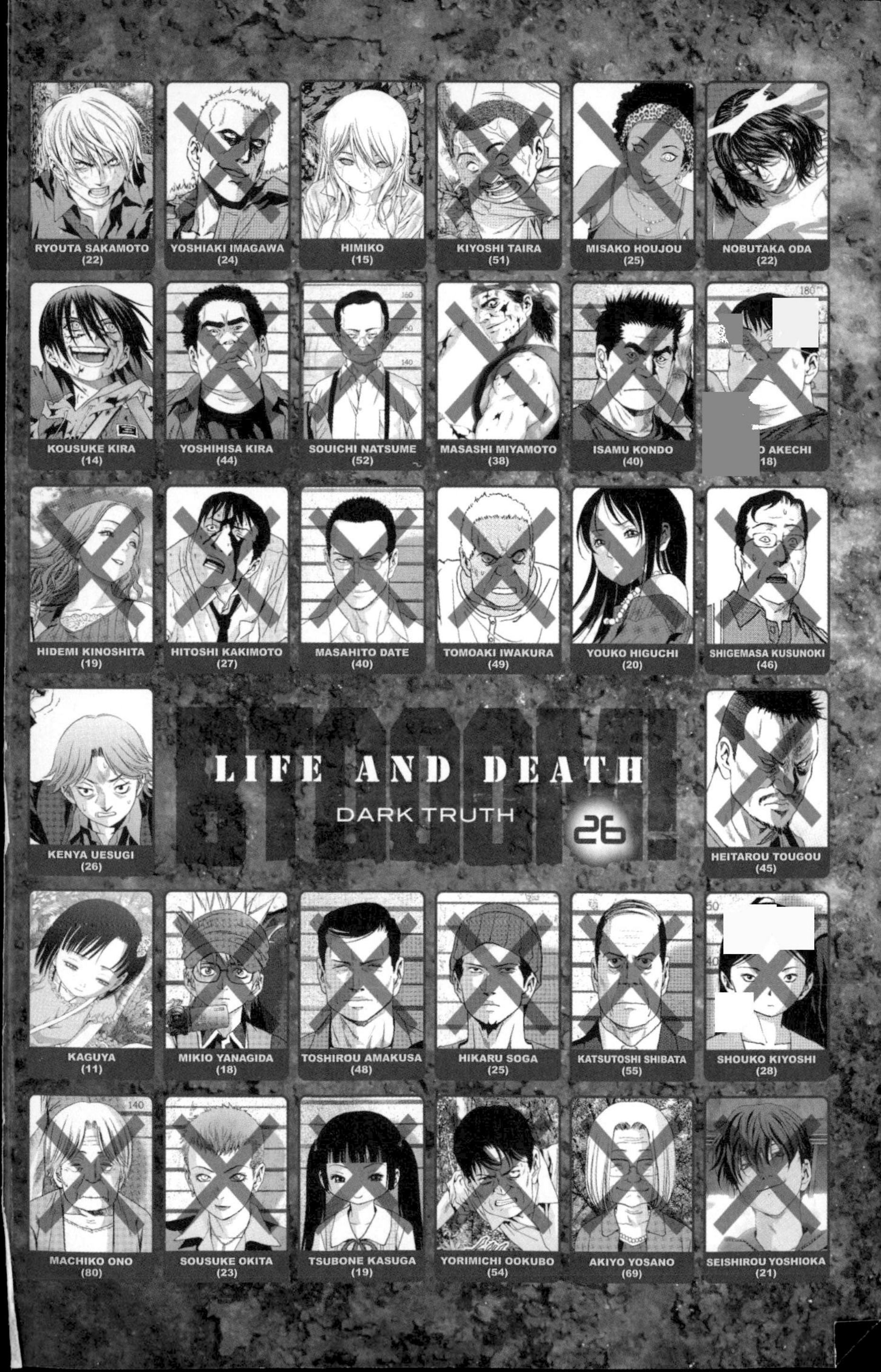
RYOUTA SAKAMOTO (22)
YOSHIAKI IMAGAWA (24)
HIMIKO (15)
KIYOSHI TAIRA (51)
MISAKO HOUJOU (25)
NOBUTAKA ODA (22)
KOUSUKE KIRA (14)
YOSHIHISA KIRA (44)
SOUICHI NATSUME (52)
MASASHI MIYAMOTO (38)
ISAMU KONDO (40)
O AKECHI (18)
HIDEMI KINOSHITA (19)
HITOSHI KAKIMOTO (27)
MASAHITO DATE (40)
TOMOAKI IWAKURA (49)
YOUKO HIGUCHI (20)
SHIGEMASA KUSUNOKI (46)
KENYA UESUGI (26)
LIFE AND DEATH
DARK TRUTH
26
HEITAROU TOUGOU (45)
KAGUYA (11)
MIKIO YANAGIDA (18)
TOSHIROU AMAKUSA (48)
HIKARU SOGA (25)
KATSUTOSHI SHIBATA (55)
SHOUKO KIYOSHI (28)
MACHIKO ONO (80)
SOUSUKE OKITA (23)
TSUBONE KASUGA (19)
YORIMICHI OOKUBO (54)
AKIYO YOSANO (69)
SEISHIROU YOSHIOKA (21)

BTOOOM!

Dark
Reality Version

JUNYA INOUE

26

CHARACTER

NOBUTAKA ODA

GENDER: Male
AGE: 22
BLOOD TYPE: AB
JOB: Restaurant manager
HOME: Tokyo

Sakamoto's biggest rival and an old classmate of his from high school. His elaborate plans and surprisingly daring athleticism have helped him procure chips at a rapid pace as he plans for his own departure from the island. Engaging in life-or-death battles with his former best friend Sakamoto, he has demonstrated himself to be an unequaled master at combat.

HIMIKO

GENDER: Female
AGE: 15
BLOOD TYPE: B
JOB: High school student
HOME: Tokyo

A foreign high school girl who has teamed up with Sakamoto. She harbors a deep resentment against men after a sordid experience in her past, but after surviving some battles thanks to Sakamoto, she begins to trust him. Her character in the online version of "BTOOOM!" is actually married to Sakamoto's character, and she has fallen in love with the real Sakamoto too.

RYOUTA SAKAMOTO

GENDER: Male
AGE: 22
BLOOD TYPE: B
JOB: Unemployed
HOME: Tokyo

After spending every day cooped up in his home gaming online, he suddenly finds himself forced to participate in "BTOOOM! GAMERS," a killing game taking place on a mysterious uninhabited island. As a world ranker in the online third-person shooter "BTOOOM!," he uses his experience and natural instincts to survive and concoct a plan to get off the island with his comrades, only for it to end in failure. At the Sanctuary, he teams up with Kaguya and Soga to beat Torio.

KAGUYA

GENDER: Female
AGE: 11
BLOOD TYPE: AB
JOB: Grade schooler
HOME: Tokyo

A mysterious little girl who came across Sakamoto when he washed ashore. She doesn't speak and uses a tablet to communicate. She's the figurehead of the Order of Moonlight, a religious cult, and can see dead people. In the Sanctuary, she worked with Sakamoto and Soga to defeat the real villain behind the tragedies, Torio.

KENYA UESUGI

GENDER: Male
AGE: 26
BLOOD TYPE: AB
JOB: Office worker
HOME: Tokyo

A cowardly and easily flattered young man who used to dream of becoming an actor. He was almost killed by Kira, but he escaped thanks to Higuchi's lie-detecting ability. He was previously a part of Tougou's team.

KOUSUKE KIRA

GENDER: Male
AGE: 14
BLOOD TYPE: AB
JOB: Junior high student
HOME: Tokyo

This junior high student harbors a dark, brutal, murderous past. On the island, he blew up his own father and is genuinely enjoying this murderous game of "BTOOOM!". He's always been a big fan of the online version of the game, and his dream is to defeat "SAKAMOTO," a top world ranker. Unfortunately, he keeps failing at it. Tougou's death makes him realize for the first time ever how precious life is.

BTOOOM! 26

LONGER SCHWARITZ

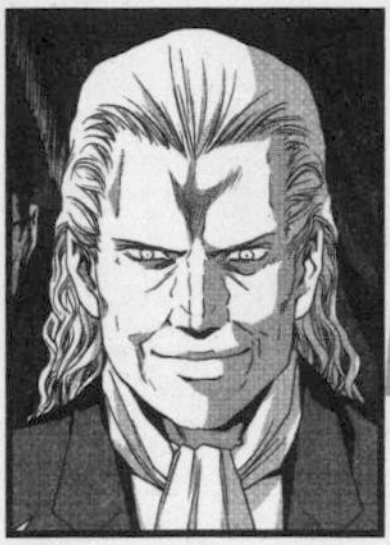

GENDER: Male
AGE: 77
BLOOD TYPE: O
JOB: Capitalist
HOME: New York

A descendant of European aristocracy, he is a man of power who controls the world behind the scenes with his considerable capital. In order to more thoroughly control the online realm, he founds the THEMIS project and has high hopes for "BTOOOM! GAMERS."

XAVIERA FRANCISCA

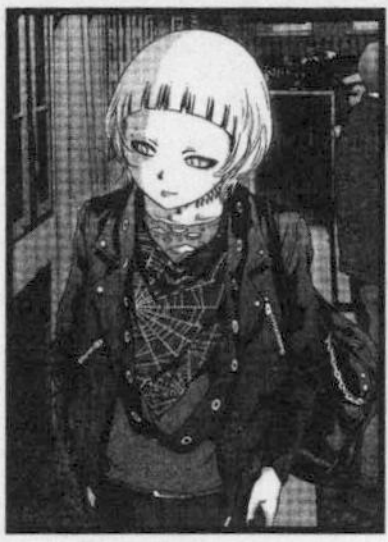

GENDER: Female
AGE: 22
BLOOD TYPE: O
JOB: Freelancer
HOME: Washington

The operator of the drone that dropped the medicine case down on the island. Instead of BIMs, she attacks the players with a machine gun. Her skill is universally acknowledged, and in the online version of "BTOOOM!", she is the reigning world champion. However, she's never beaten Sakamoto, so she's obsessed with doing so.

TAKANOHASHI

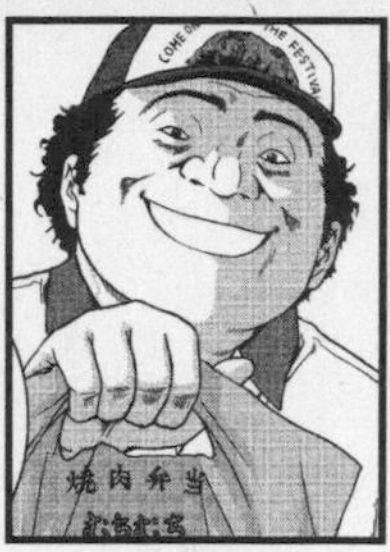

GENDER: Male
AGE: 45
BLOOD TYPE: AB
JOB: Game planner
HOME: Hokkaido

An executive staff member at Tyrannos Japan, he is the leader behind all the development of the online and real-life versions of "BTOOOM! GAMERS." He considers Sakamoto a valuable player and debugger. As a result of Sakamoto's plan to hijack the helicopter, Takanohashi's precious game was almost forced to come to a premature end.

HISANOBU

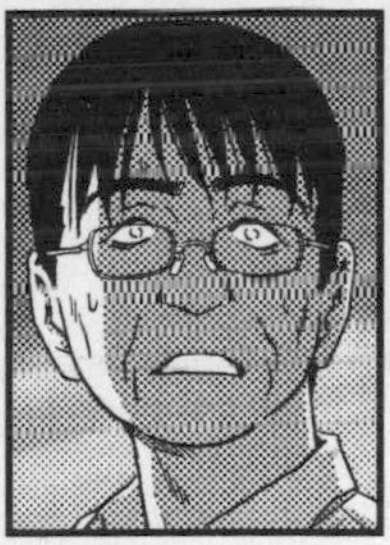

GENDER: Male
AGE: 55
BLOOD TYPE: A
JOB: Unemployed
HOME: Tokyo

Yukie's new husband and Sakamoto's stepfather. He's worried about how much time his stepson spends up in his room and scolds him, only to be attacked. Having just been laid off, he racks up debt because of his praiseworthy efforts to preserve his family's lifestyle. However, Yukie is frail in body and mind and attempts to kill herself. Fate has dealt him an unfair card in life.

TSUNEAKI IIDA

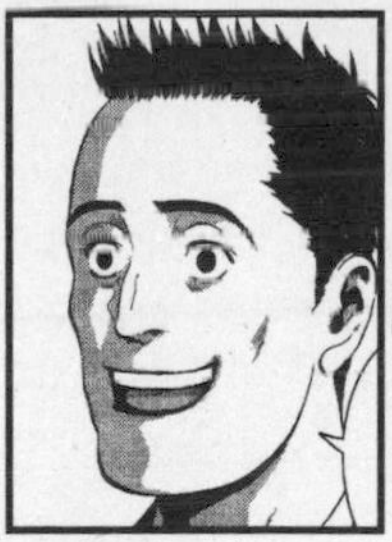

GENDER: Male
AGE: 24
BLOOD TYPE: A
JOB: Programmer
HOME: Tokyo

An employee at Tyrannos Japan and Sakamoto's senpai from college. He's an excellent programmer and works under Takanohashi on the development of "BTOOOM! GAMERS." But he doesn't agree with the inhumane nature of the game and approached Sakamoto with the proposal and strategy to put a stop to the game's development, only for the plan to fall apart.

MATTHEW PERRIER

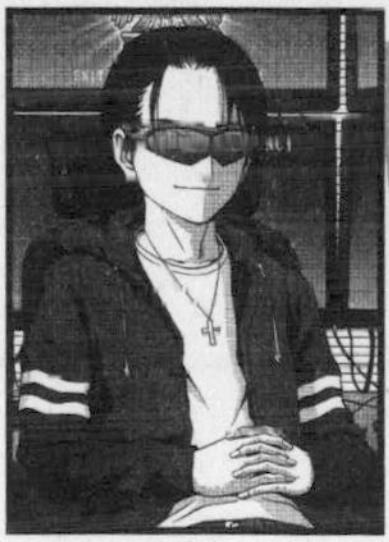

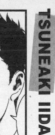

GENDER: Male
AGE: 27
BLOOD TYPE: O
JOB: Ex-NSA programmer, political refugee
HOME: Washington (location unknown after exile)

A former programmer with the NSA (U.S. National Security Agency), he's a capable hacker and curbed a number of cyber-crimes while with the NSA. But after learning about the government's darker side, he made off with sensitive data about the THEMIS project—in a way, the evidence of their nefarious plans—and defected to another country.

INTRODUCTION Dark REALITY

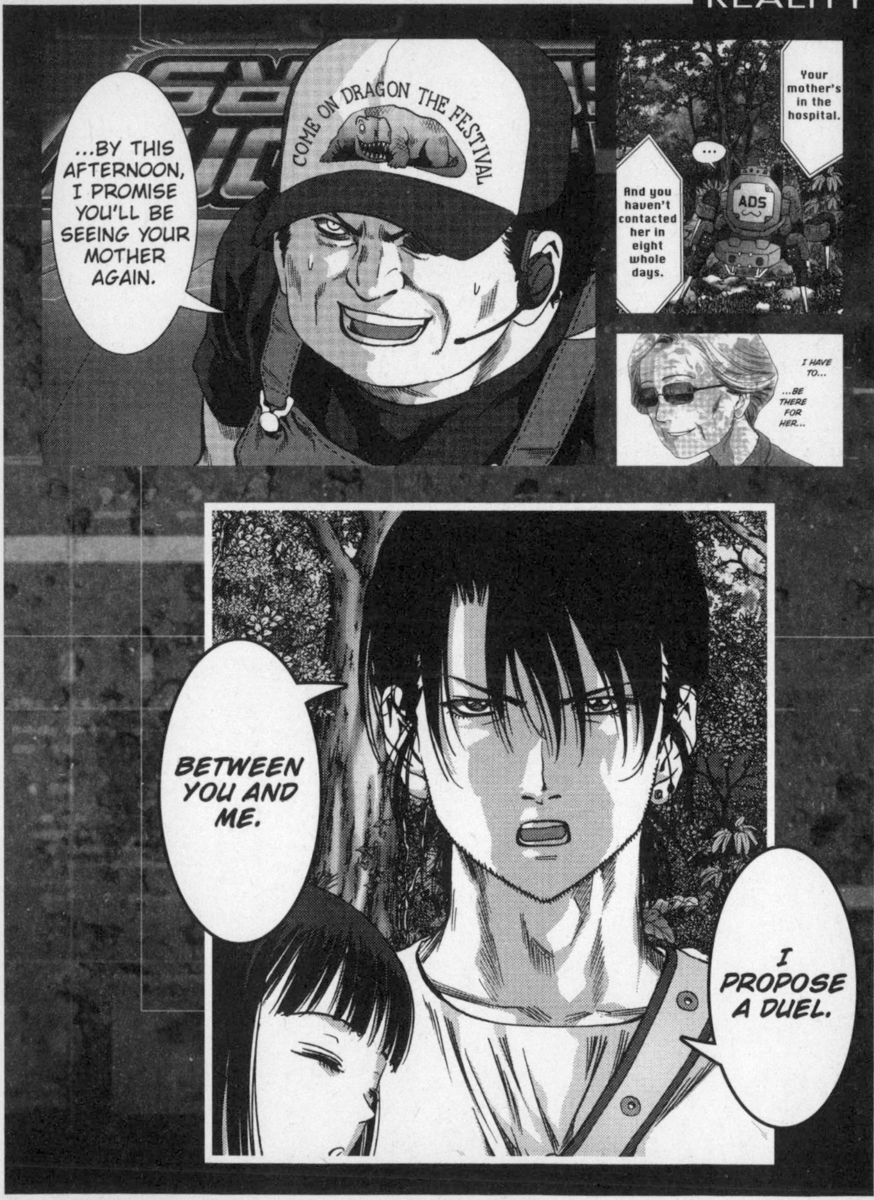
Your mother's in the hospital.
...
And you haven't contacted her in eight whole days.
I HAVE TO...
...BE THERE FOR HER...
COME ON DRAGON THE FESTIVAL
...BY THIS AFTERNOON, I PROMISE YOU'LL BE SEEING YOUR MOTHER AGAIN.
I PROPOSE A DUEL.
BETWEEN YOU AND ME.

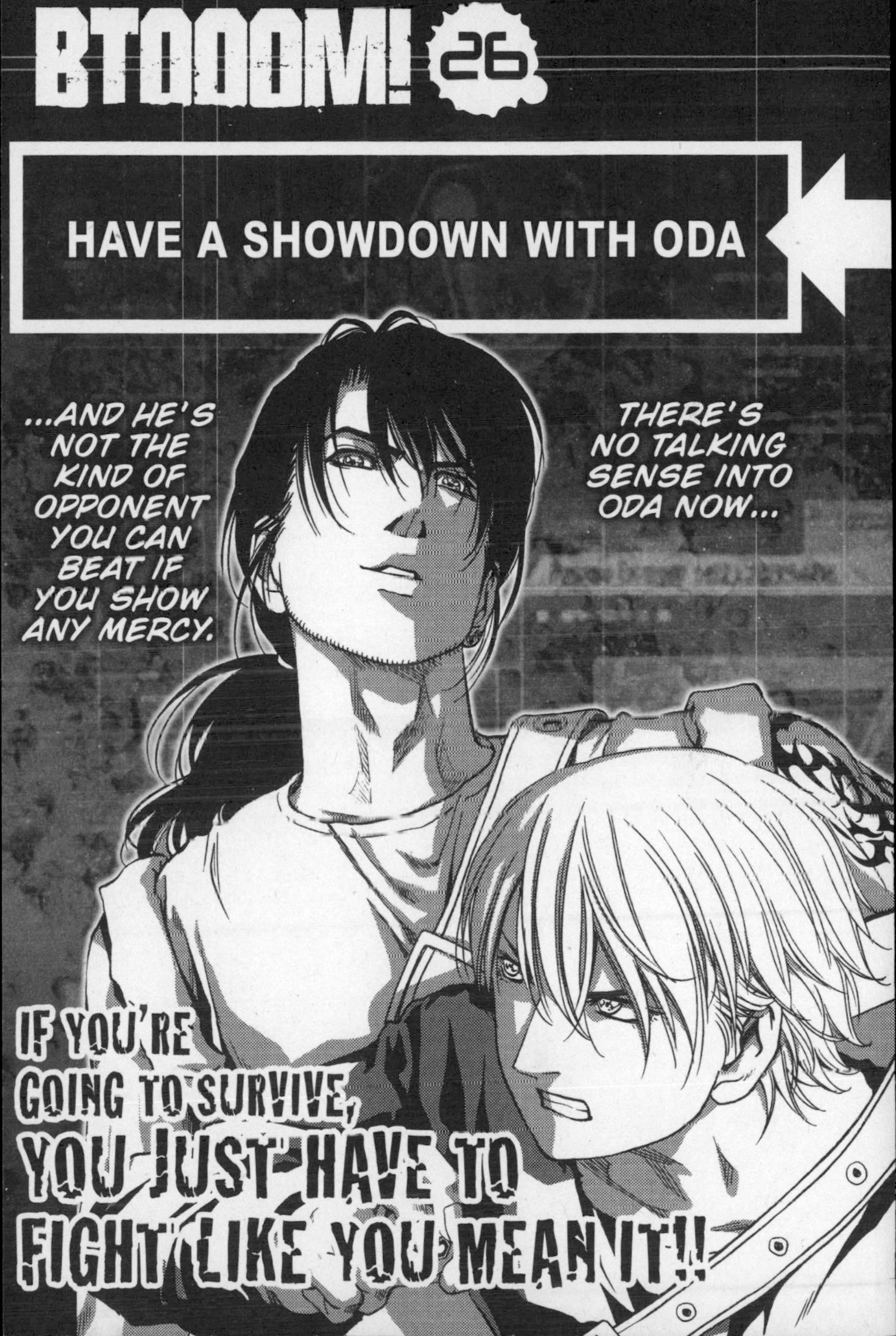
BTOOOM! 26
HAVE A SHOWDOWN WITH ODA
THERE'S NO TALKING SENSE INTO ODA NOW...
...AND HE'S NOT THE KIND OF OPPONENT YOU CAN BEAT IF YOU SHOW ANY MERCY.
IF YOU'RE GOING TO SURVIVE, YOU JUST HAVE TO FIGHT LIKE YOU MEAN IT!!

Dark REALITY

CONTENTS

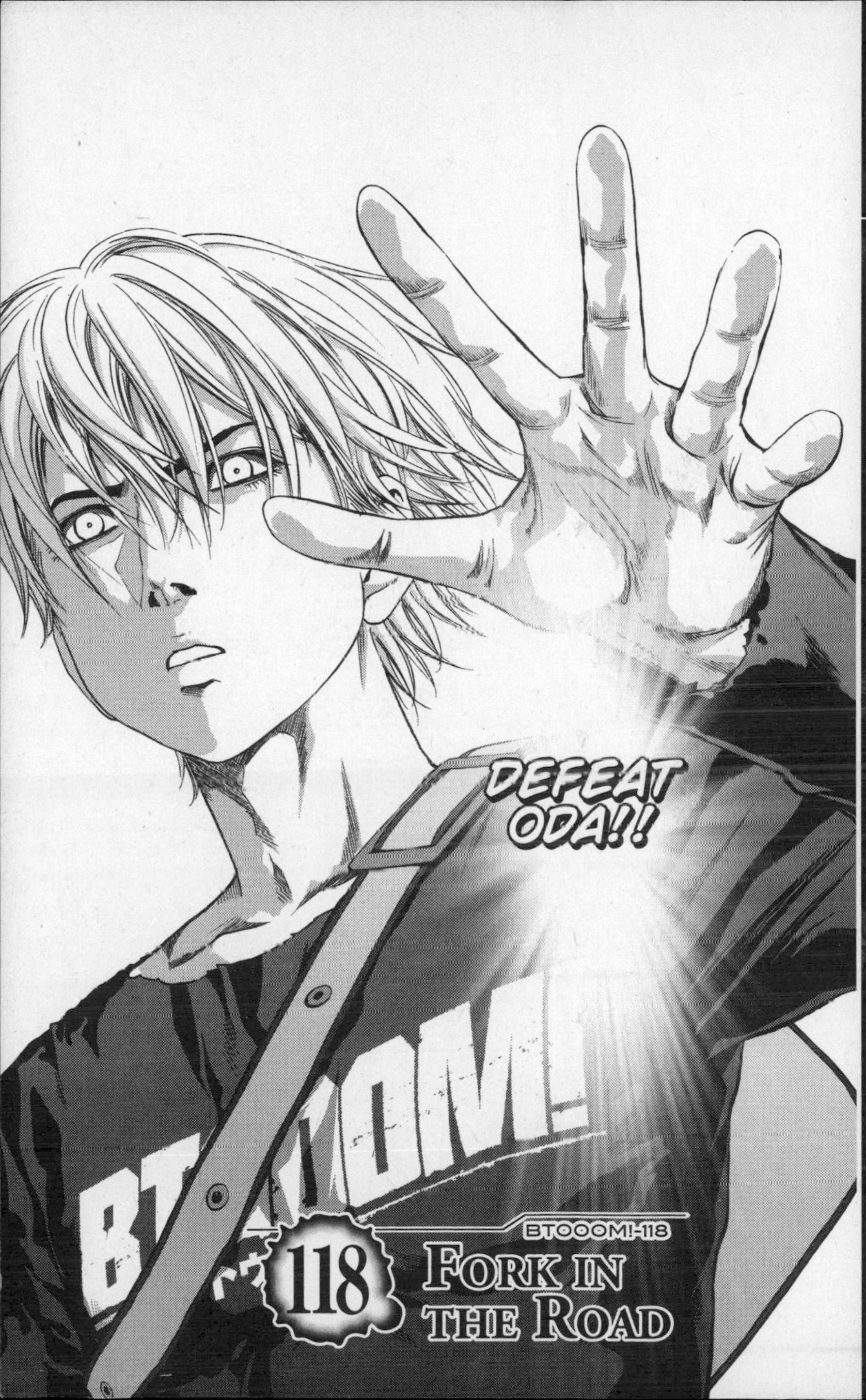
DEFEAT ODA!!
BTOOOM!-118
118
FORK IN THE ROAD

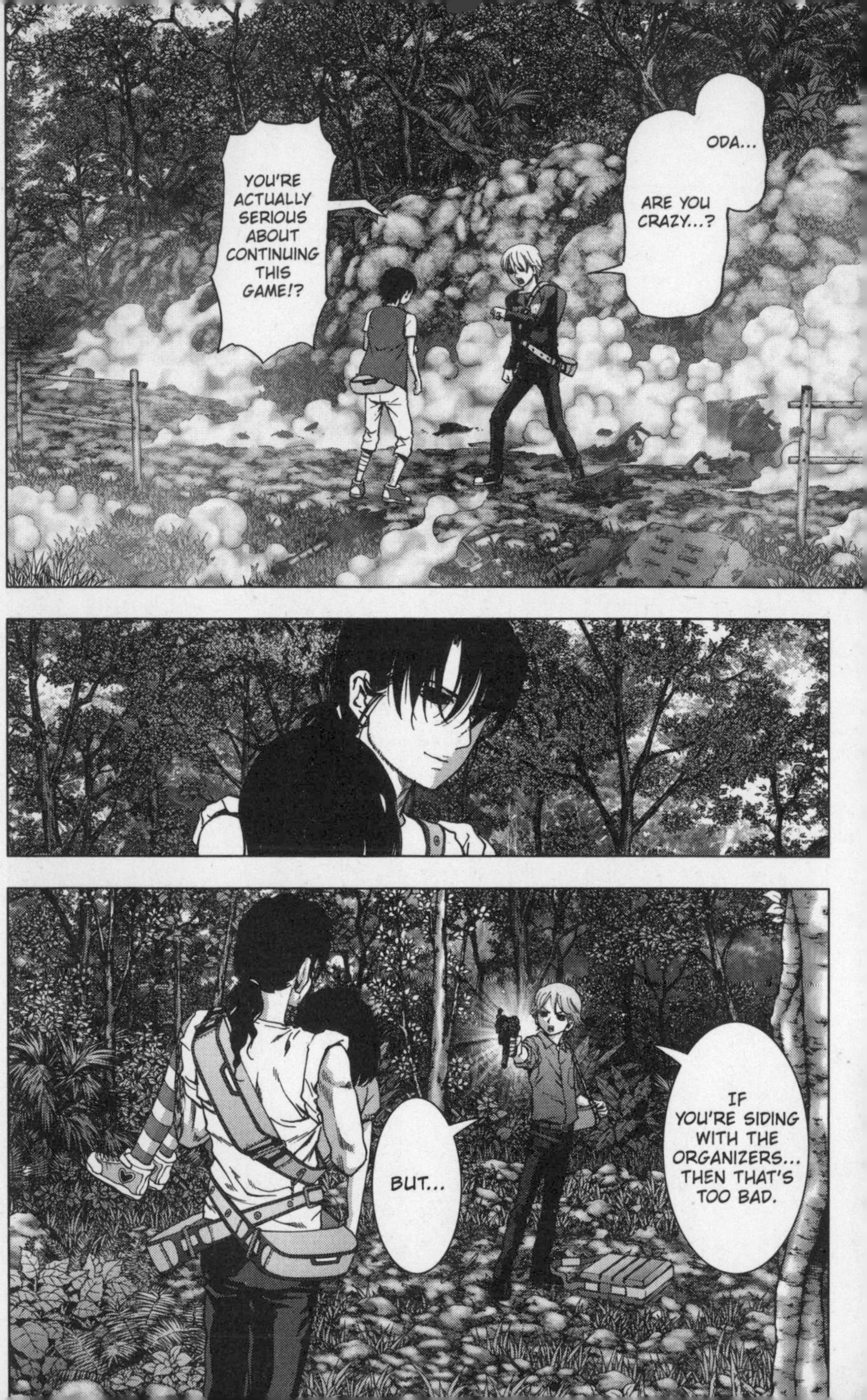
ODA...
ARE YOU CRAZY...?
YOU'RE ACTUALLY SERIOUS ABOUT CONTINUING THIS GAME!?
IF YOU'RE SIDING WITH THE ORGANIZERS... THEN THAT'S TOO BAD.
BUT...

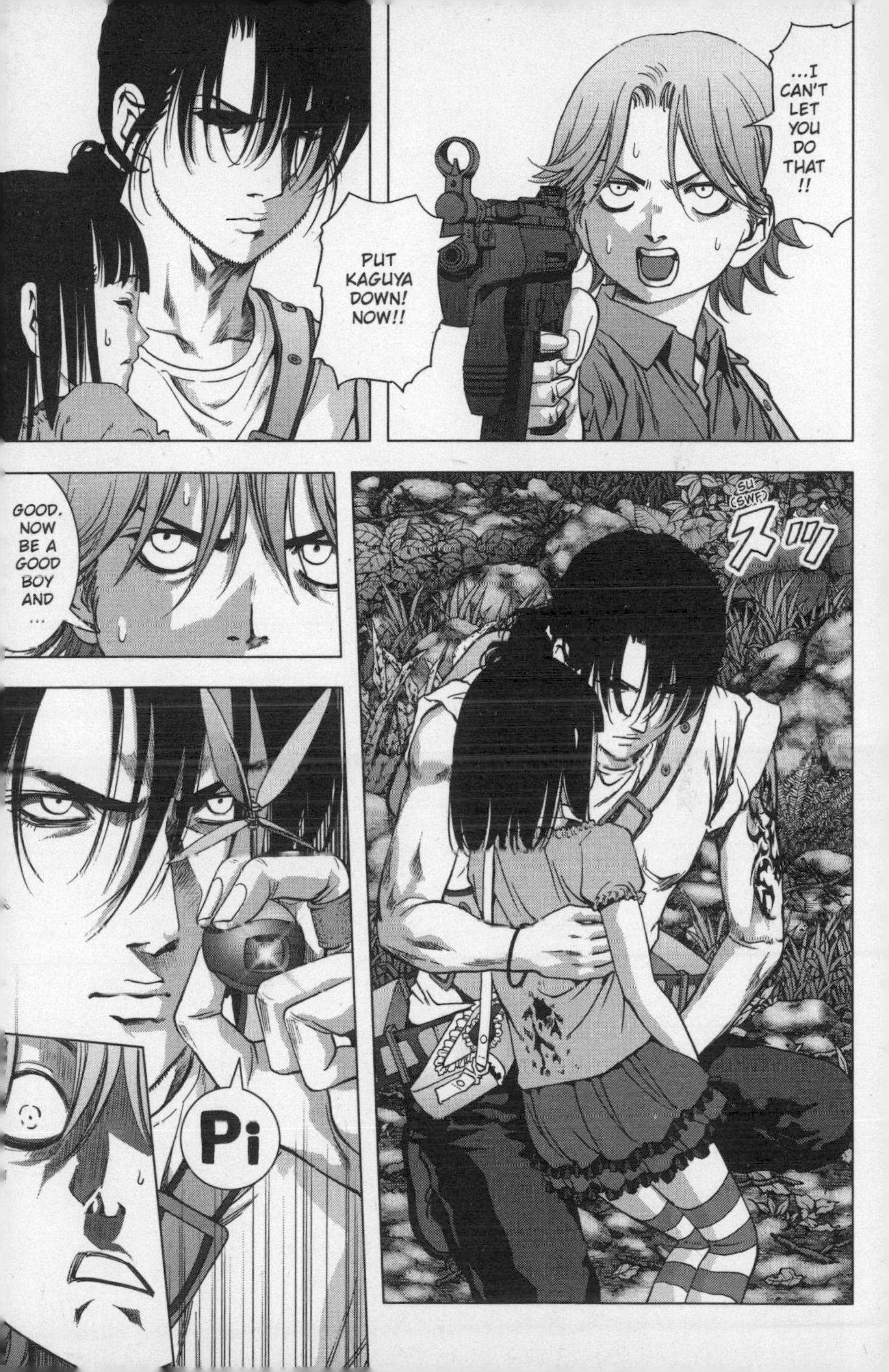

...I CAN'T LET YOU DO THAT!!
PUT KAGUYA DOWN! NOW!!
SU (SWF)
スッ
GOOD. NOW BE A GOOD BOY AND ...
Pi

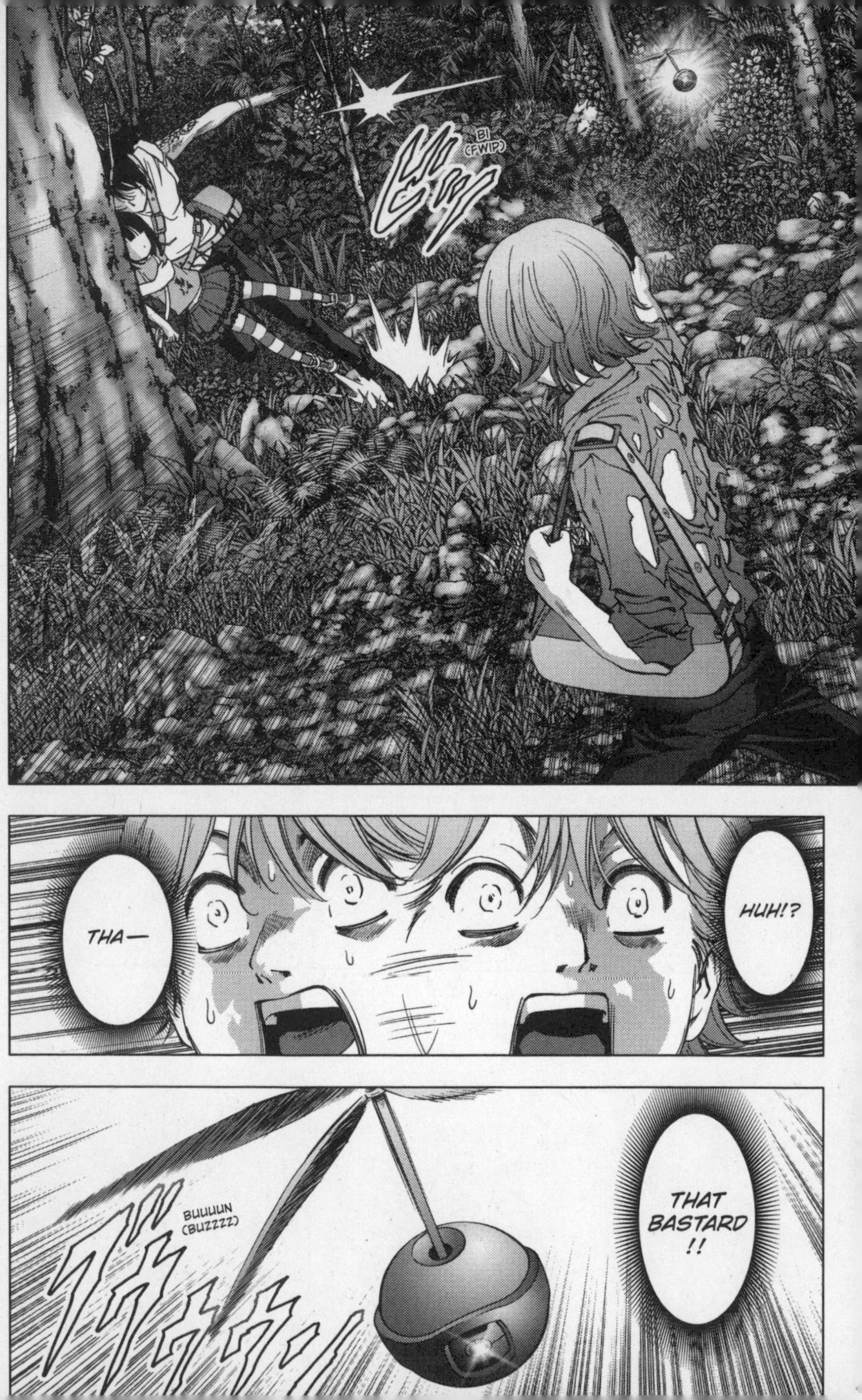
BI (FWIP)
HUH!?
THA—
THAT BASTARD !!
BUUUUN (BUZZZZ)

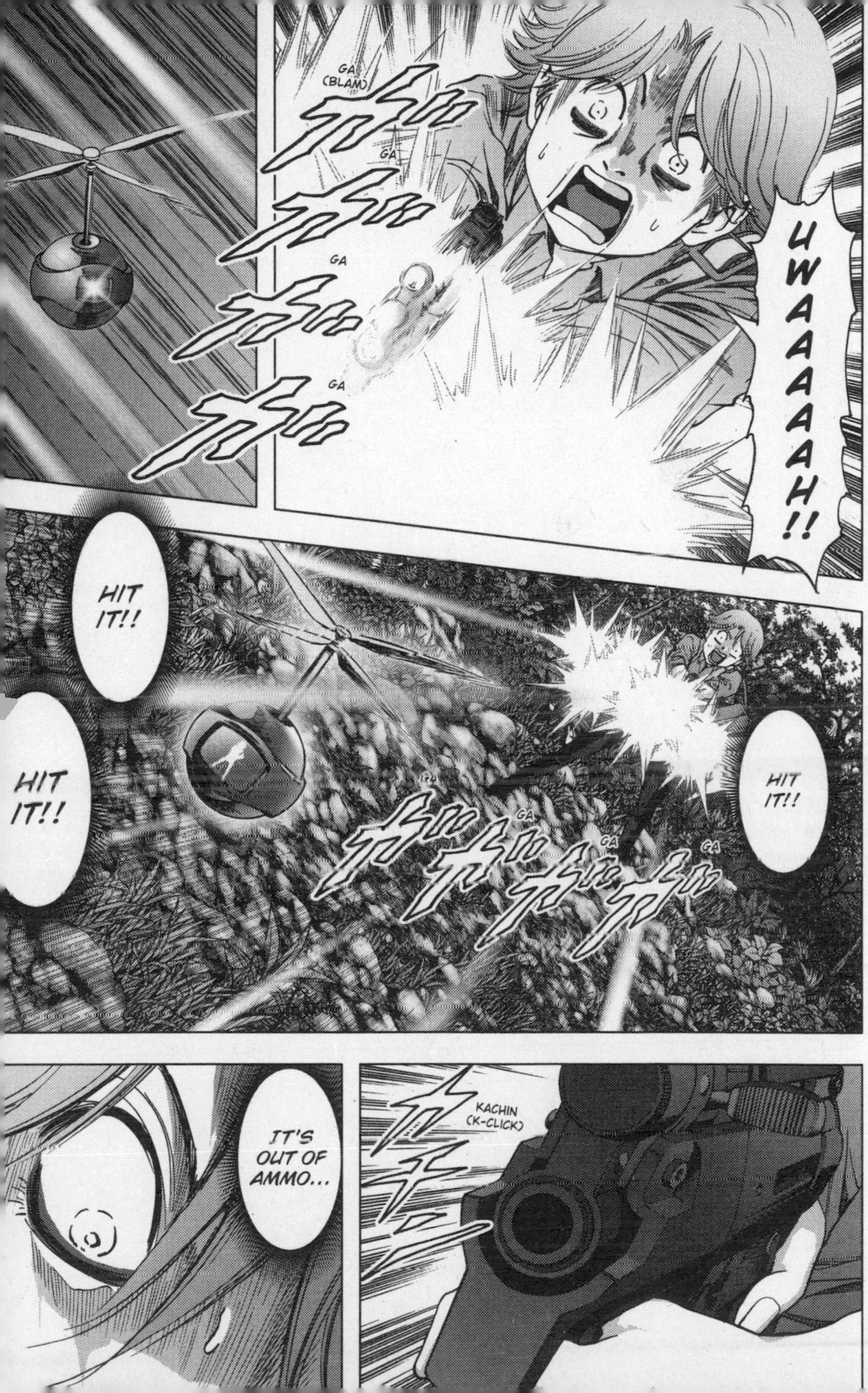
GA
(BLAM)
GA
GA
GA
UWAAAAAAH!!
HIT IT!!
GA
GA
GA
GA
HIT IT!!
HIT IT!!
KACHIN
(K-CLICK)
IT'S OUT OF AMMO...

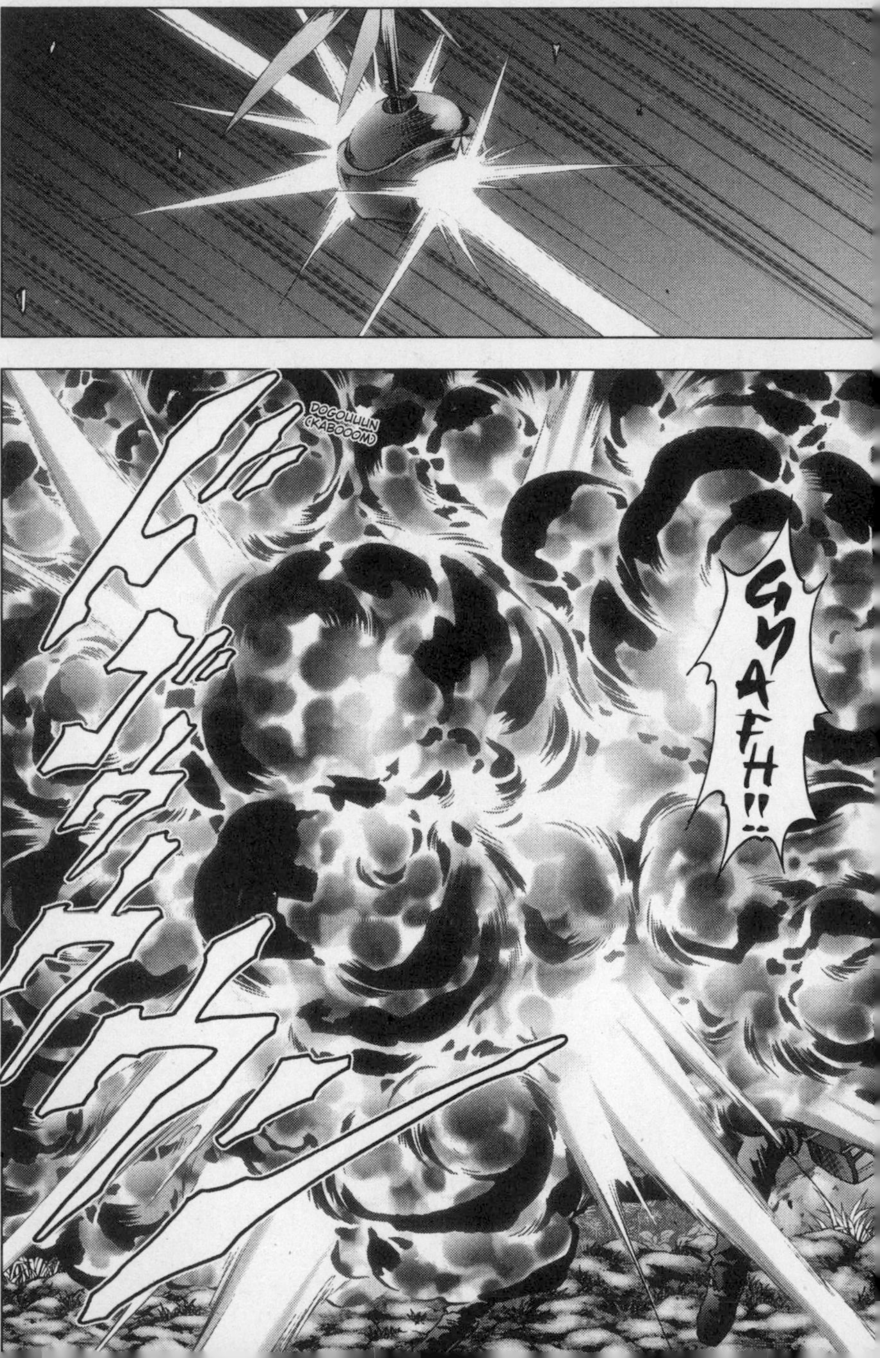
GYAFH!!
DOGOUUUN
(KABOOOM)

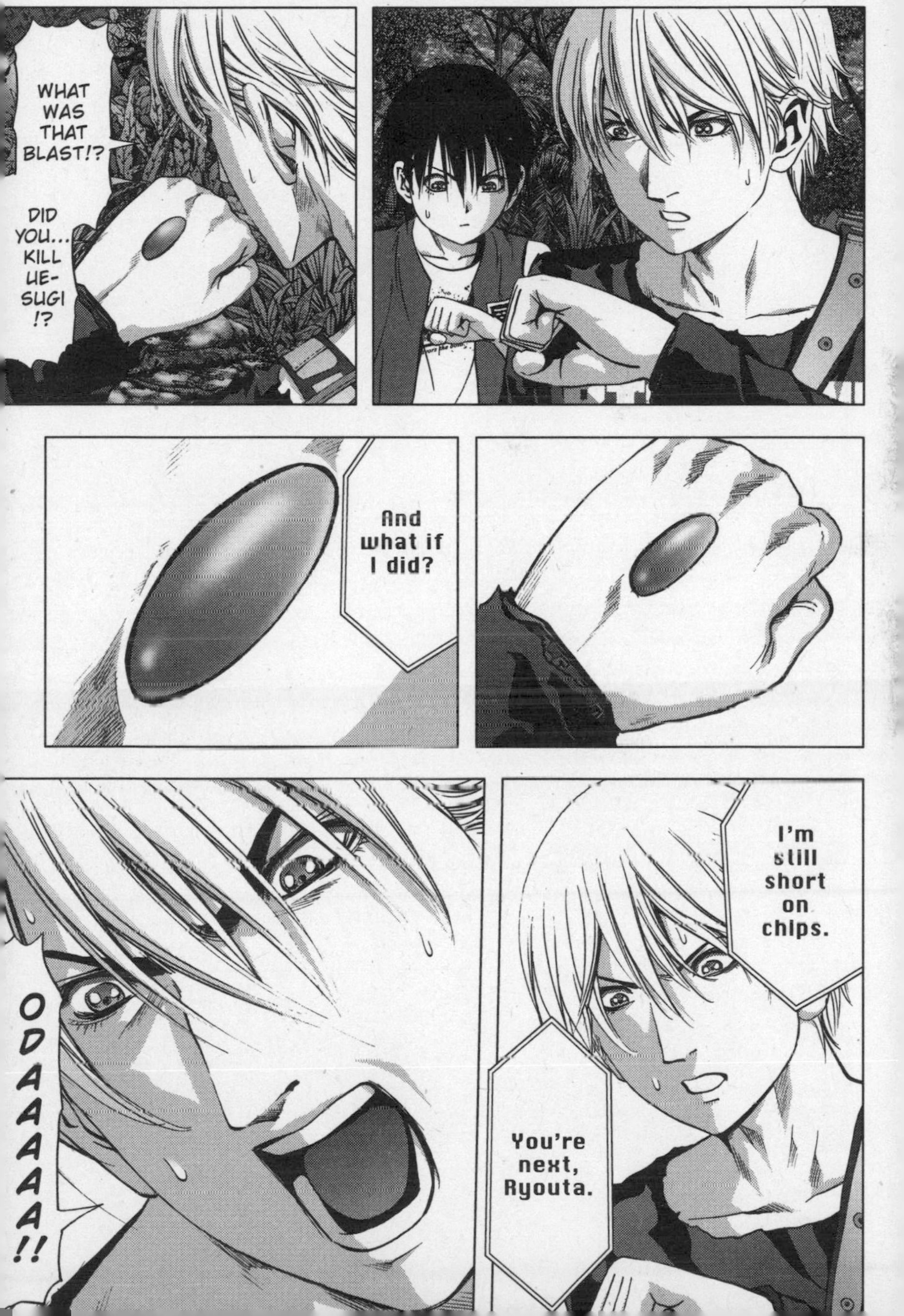
WHAT WAS THAT BLAST!?
DID YOU... KILL UE-SUGI !?
And what if I did?
I'm still short on chips.
You're next, Ryouta.
ODAAAAAAA!!

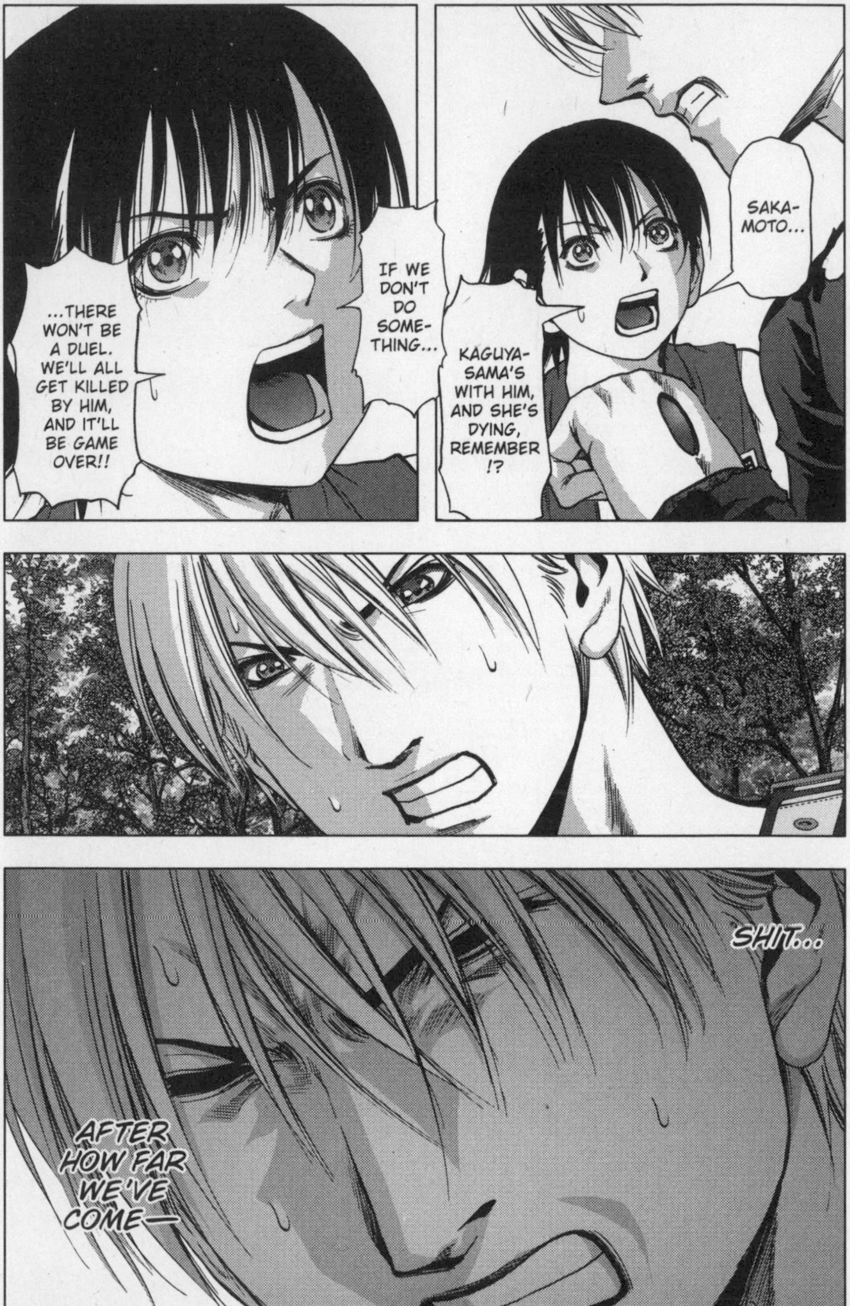
SAKA-MOTO...
KAGUYA-SAMA'S WITH HIM, AND SHE'S DYING, REMEMBER!?
IF WE DON'T DO SOME-THING...
...THERE WON'T BE A DUEL. WE'LL ALL GET KILLED BY HIM, AND IT'LL BE GAME OVER!!
SHIT...
AFTER HOW FAR WE'VE COME—

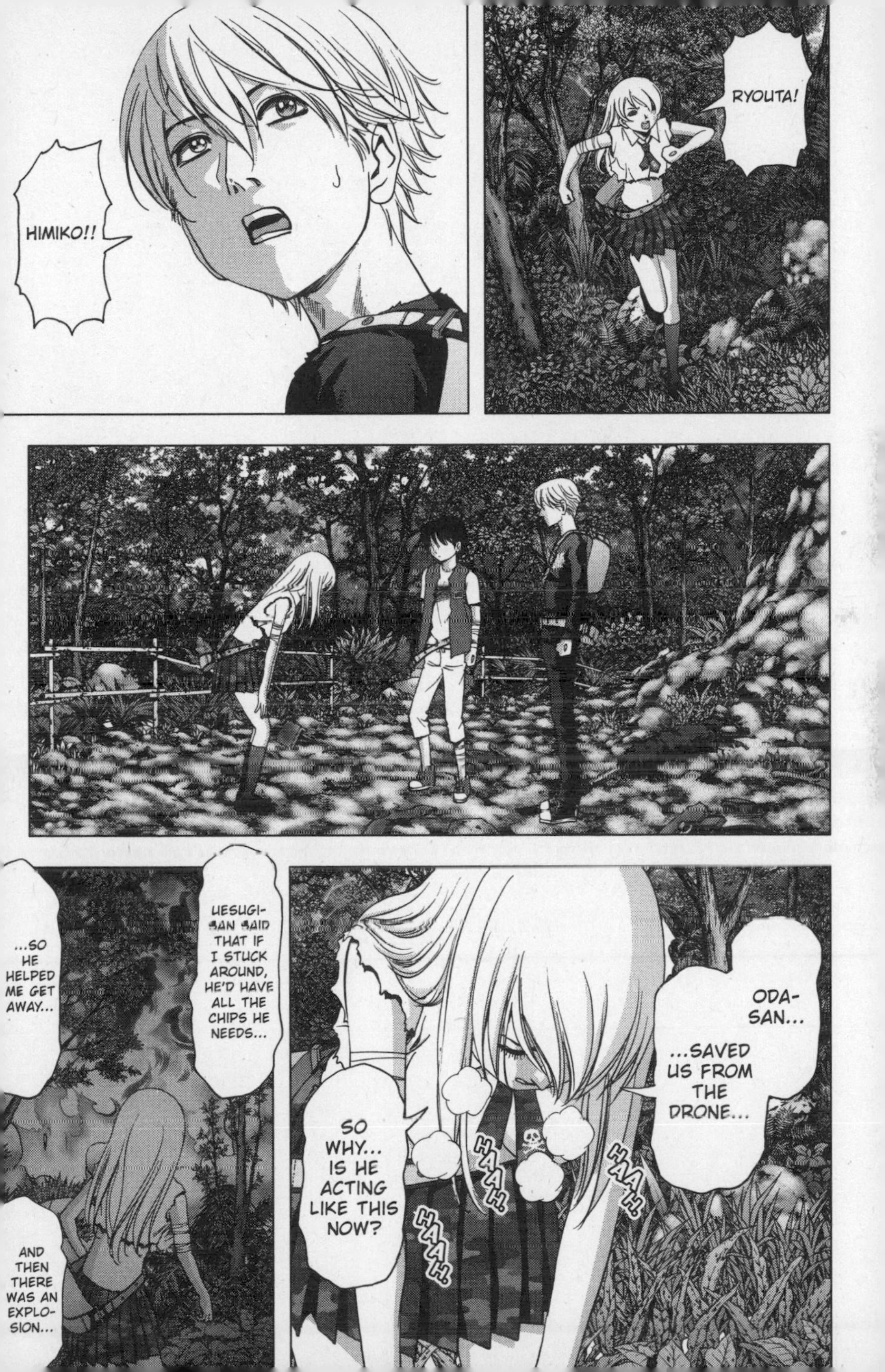
RYOUTA!
HIMIKO!!
ODA-SAN...
...SAVED US FROM THE DRONE...
HAAH.
HAAH.
SO WHY... IS HE ACTING LIKE THIS NOW?
HAAH.
UESUGI-SAN SAID THAT IF I STUCK AROUND, HE'D HAVE ALL THE CHIPS HE NEEDS...
...SO HE HELPED ME GET AWAY...
AND THEN THERE WAS AN EXPLOSION...

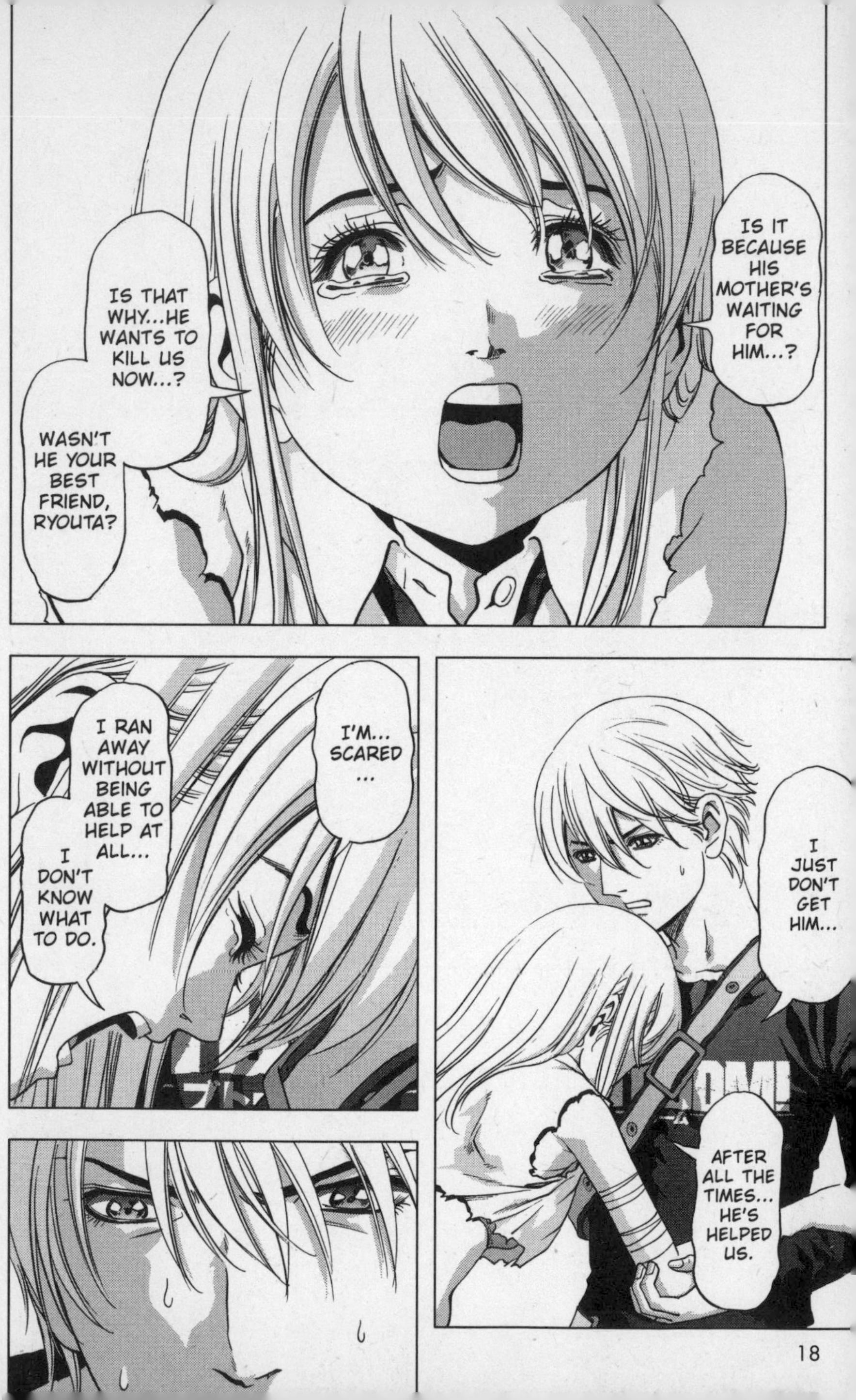
IS IT BECAUSE HIS MOTHER'S WAITING FOR HIM...?
IS THAT WHY...HE WANTS TO KILL US NOW...?
WASN'T HE YOUR BEST FRIEND, RYOUTA?
I JUST DON'T GET HIM...
AFTER ALL THE TIMES... HE'S HELPED US.
I'M... SCARED...
I RAN AWAY WITHOUT BEING ABLE TO HELP AT ALL...
I DON'T KNOW WHAT TO DO.

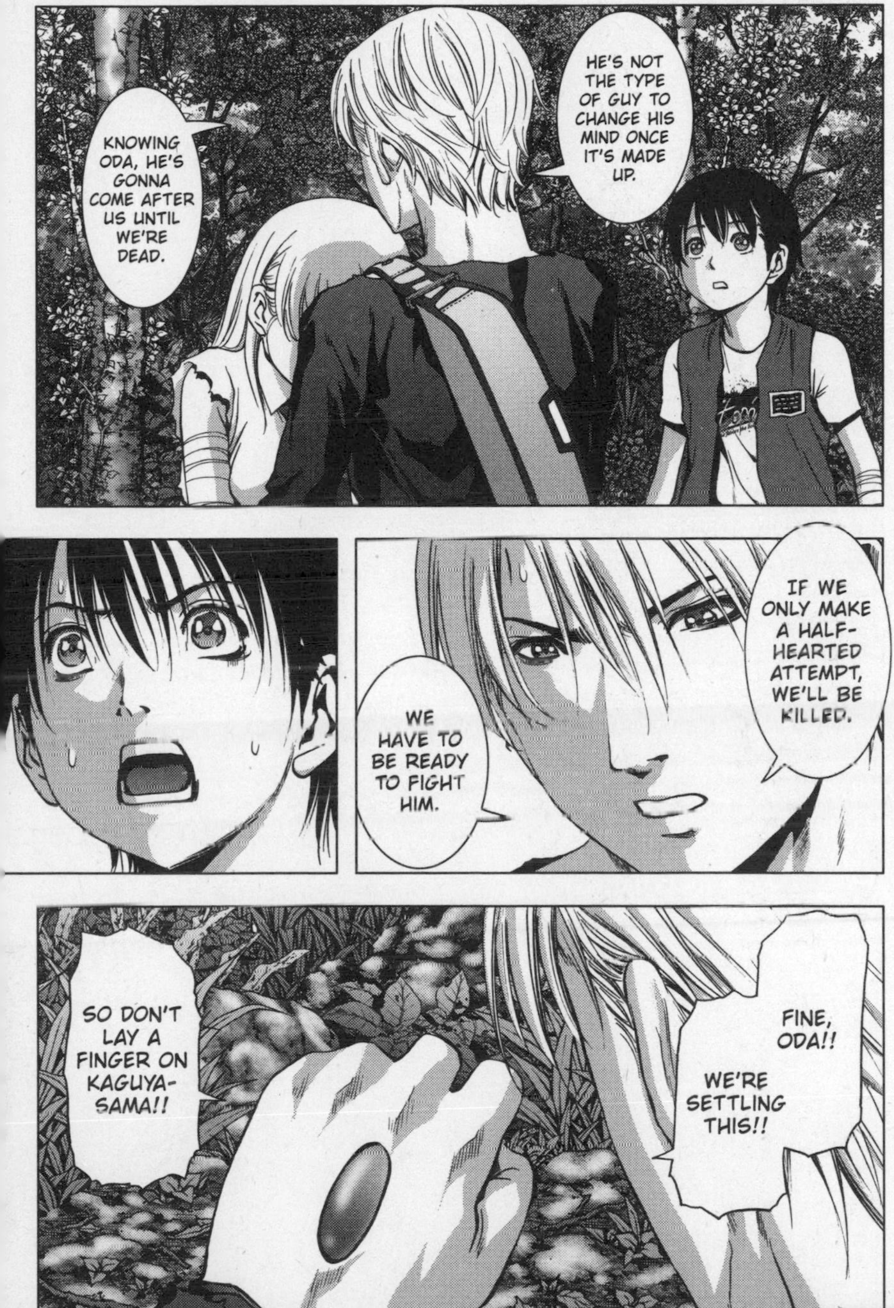
HE'S NOT THE TYPE OF GUY TO CHANGE HIS MIND ONCE IT'S MADE UP.
KNOWING ODA, HE'S GONNA COME AFTER US UNTIL WE'RE DEAD.
IF WE ONLY MAKE A HALF-HEARTED ATTEMPT, WE'LL BE KILLED.
WE HAVE TO BE READY TO FIGHT HIM.
FINE, ODA!!
WE'RE SETTLING THIS!!
SO DON'T LAY A FINGER ON KAGUYA-SAMA!!

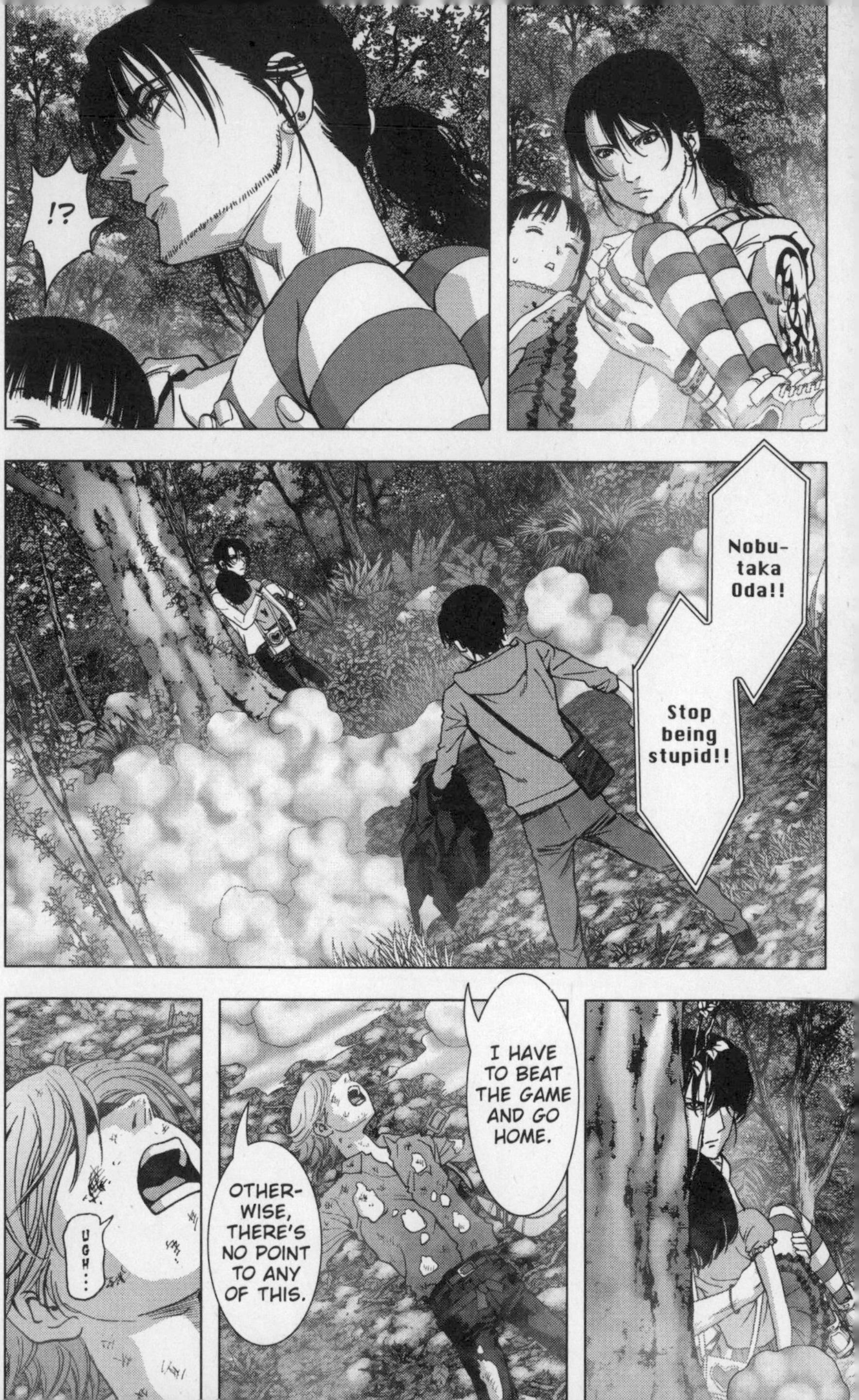
!?
Nobu-taka Oda!!
Stop being stupid!!
I HAVE TO BEAT THE GAME AND GO HOME.
OTHERWISE, THERE'S NO POINT TO ANY OF THIS.
UGH...

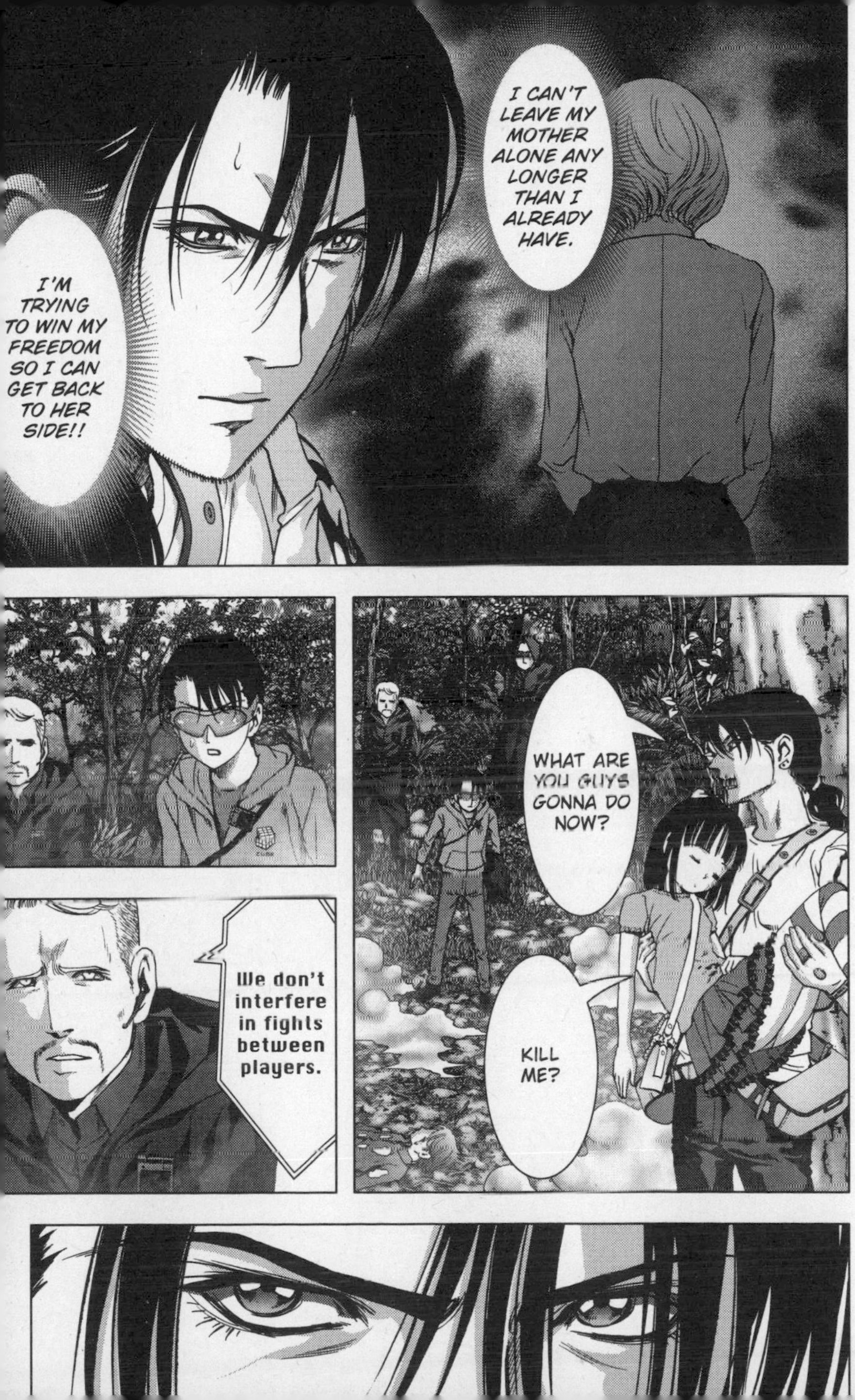
I CAN'T LEAVE MY MOTHER ALONE ANY LONGER THAN I ALREADY HAVE.
I'M TRYING TO WIN MY FREEDOM SO I CAN GET BACK TO HER SIDE!!
WHAT ARE YOU GUYS GONNA DO NOW?
KILL ME?
We don't interfere in fights between players.

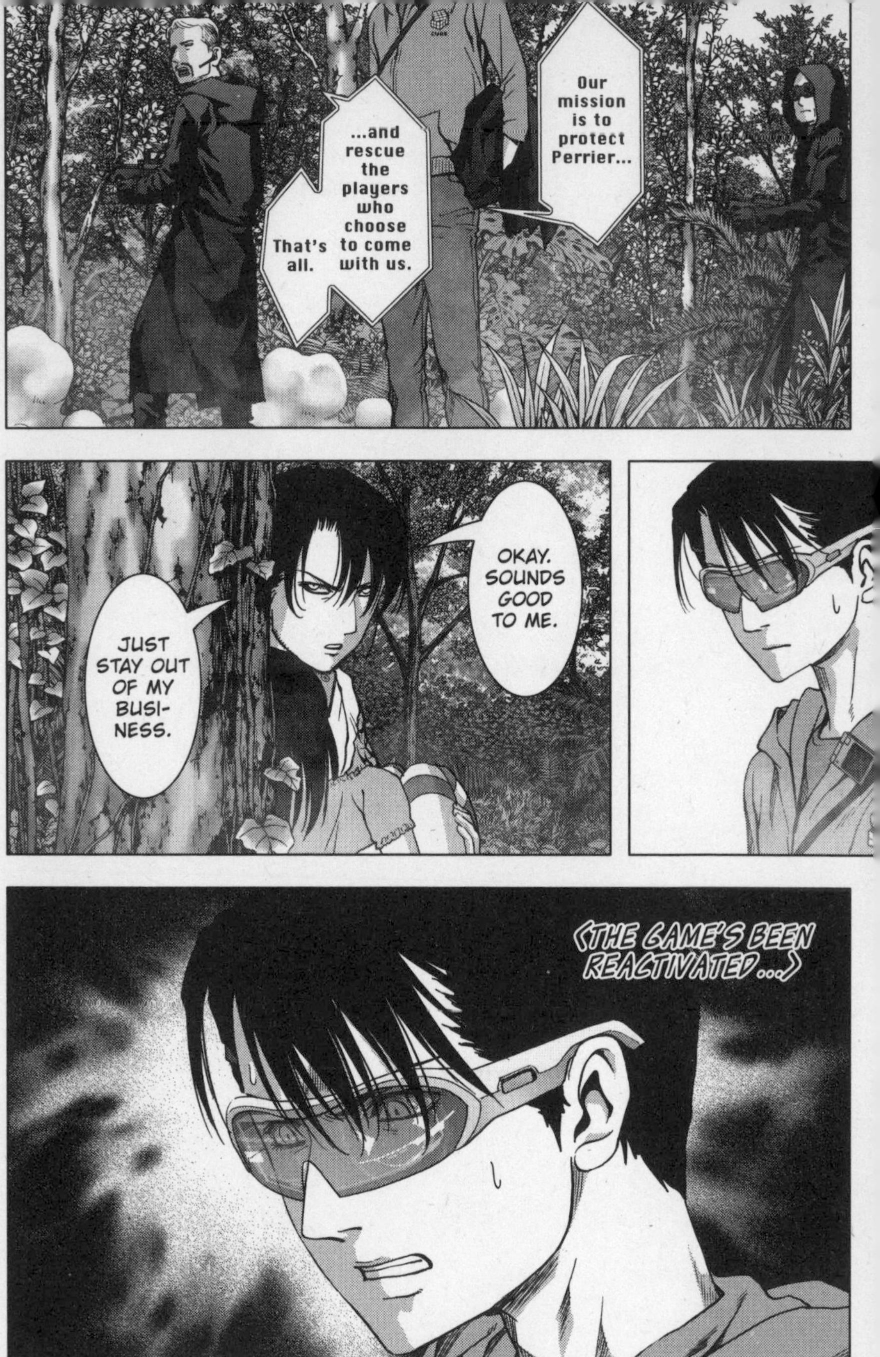
Our mission is to protect Perrier...
...and rescue the players who choose to come with us.
That's all.
OKAY. SOUNDS GOOD TO ME.
JUST STAY OUT OF MY BUSI-NESS.
<THE GAME'S BEEN REACTIVATED...>

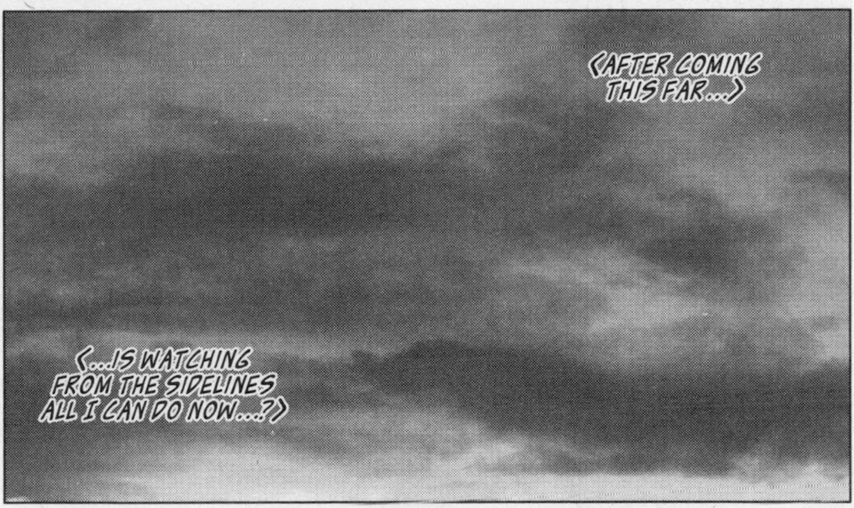
〈AFTER COMING THIS FAR...〉
〈...IS WATCHING FROM THE SIDELINES ALL I CAN DO NOW...?〉

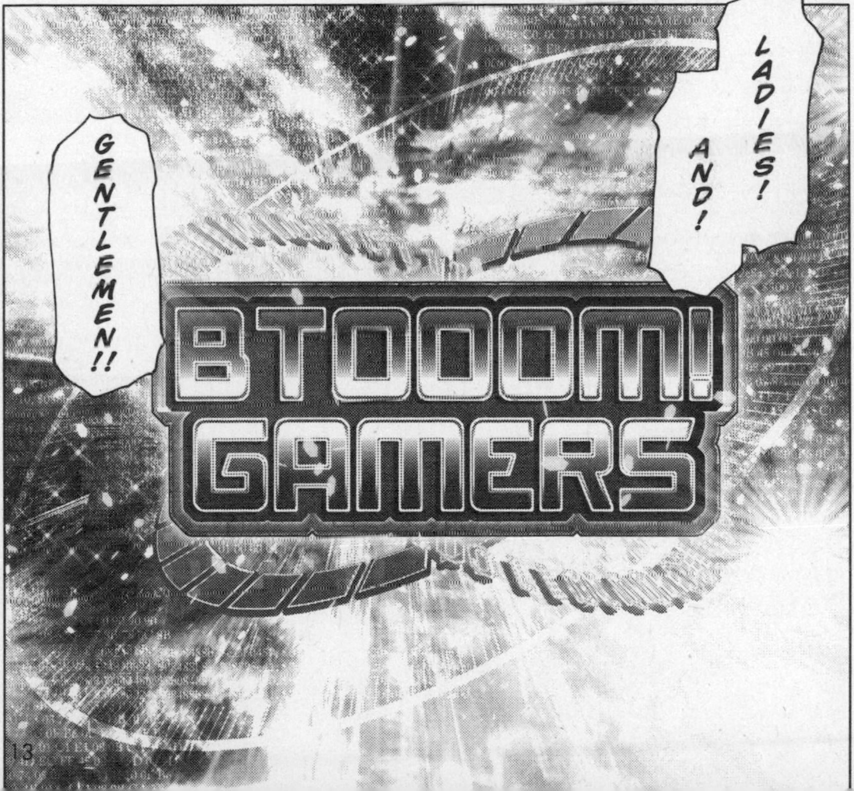
LADIES! AND!
GENTLEMEN!!
BTOOOM! GAMERS

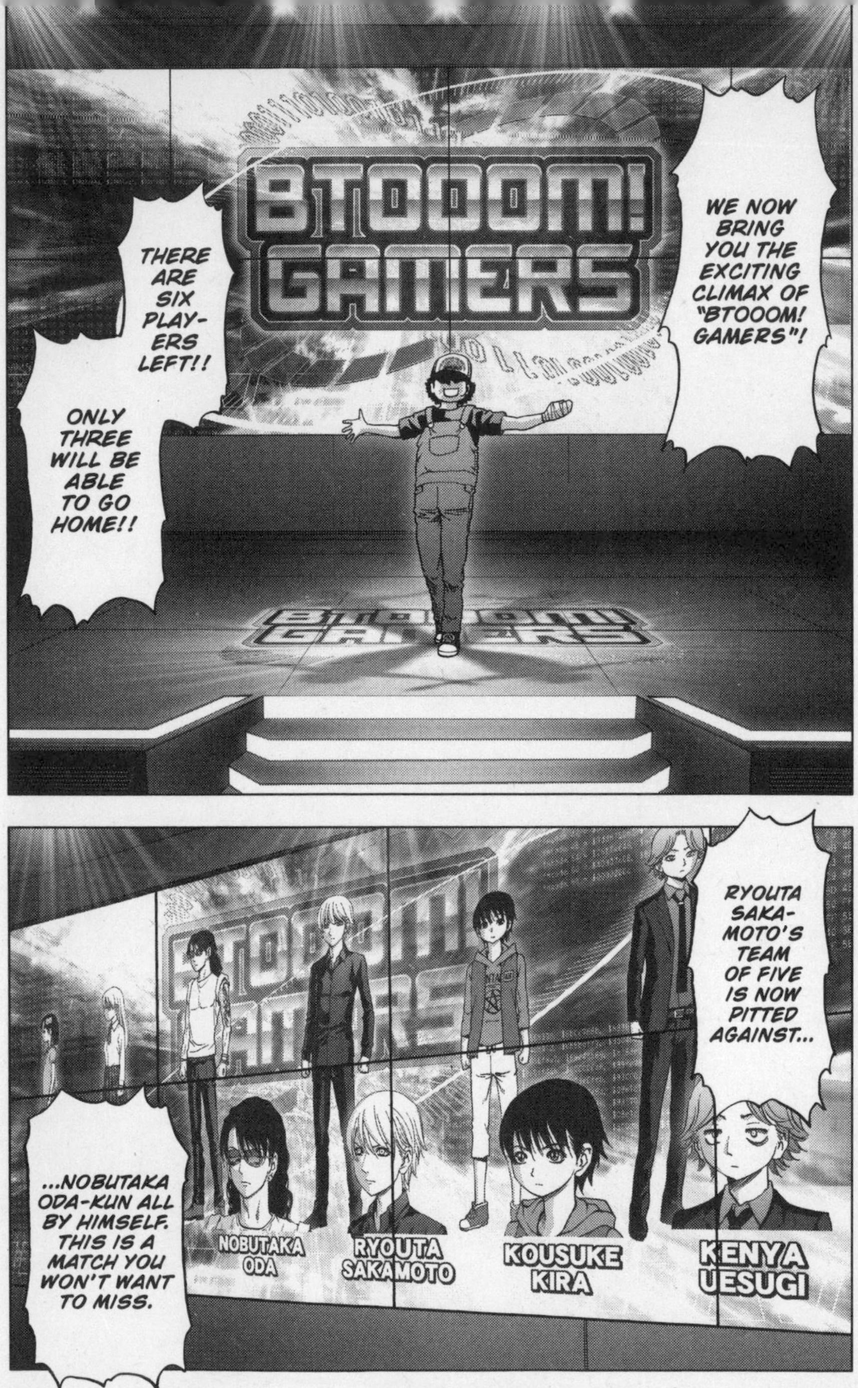
BTOOOM! GAMERS
WE NOW BRING YOU THE EXCITING CLIMAX OF "BTOOOM! GAMERS"!
THERE ARE SIX PLAY-ERS LEFT!!
ONLY THREE WILL BE ABLE TO GO HOME!!
RYOUTA SAKA-MOTO'S TEAM OF FIVE IS NOW PITTED AGAINST...
KENYA UESUGI
KOUSUKE KIRA
RYOUTA SAKAMOTO
NOBUTAKA ODA
...NOBUTAKA ODA-KUN ALL BY HIMSELF. THIS IS A MATCH YOU WON'T WANT TO MISS.

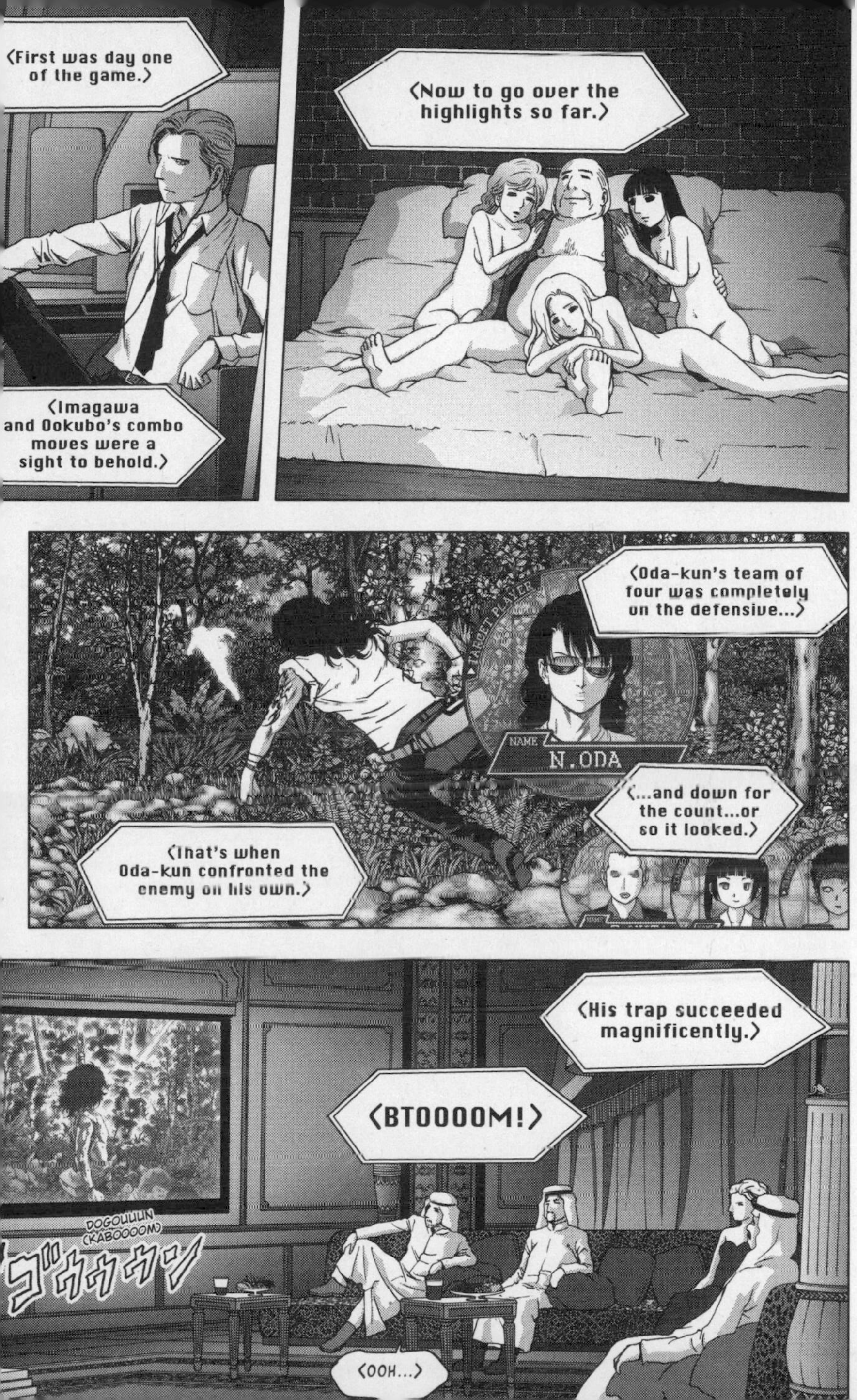
⟨Now to go over the highlights so far.⟩
⟨First was day one of the game.⟩
⟨Imagawa and Ookubo's combo moves were a sight to behold.⟩
⟨Oda-kun's team of four was completely on the defensive...⟩
NAME
N.ODA
⟨...and down for the count...or so it looked.⟩
⟨That's when Oda-kun confronted the enemy on his own.⟩
⟨His trap succeeded magnificently.⟩
⟨BTOOOOM!⟩
ゴゥゥゥン
DOGOUUUN (KABOOOOM)
⟨OOH...⟩

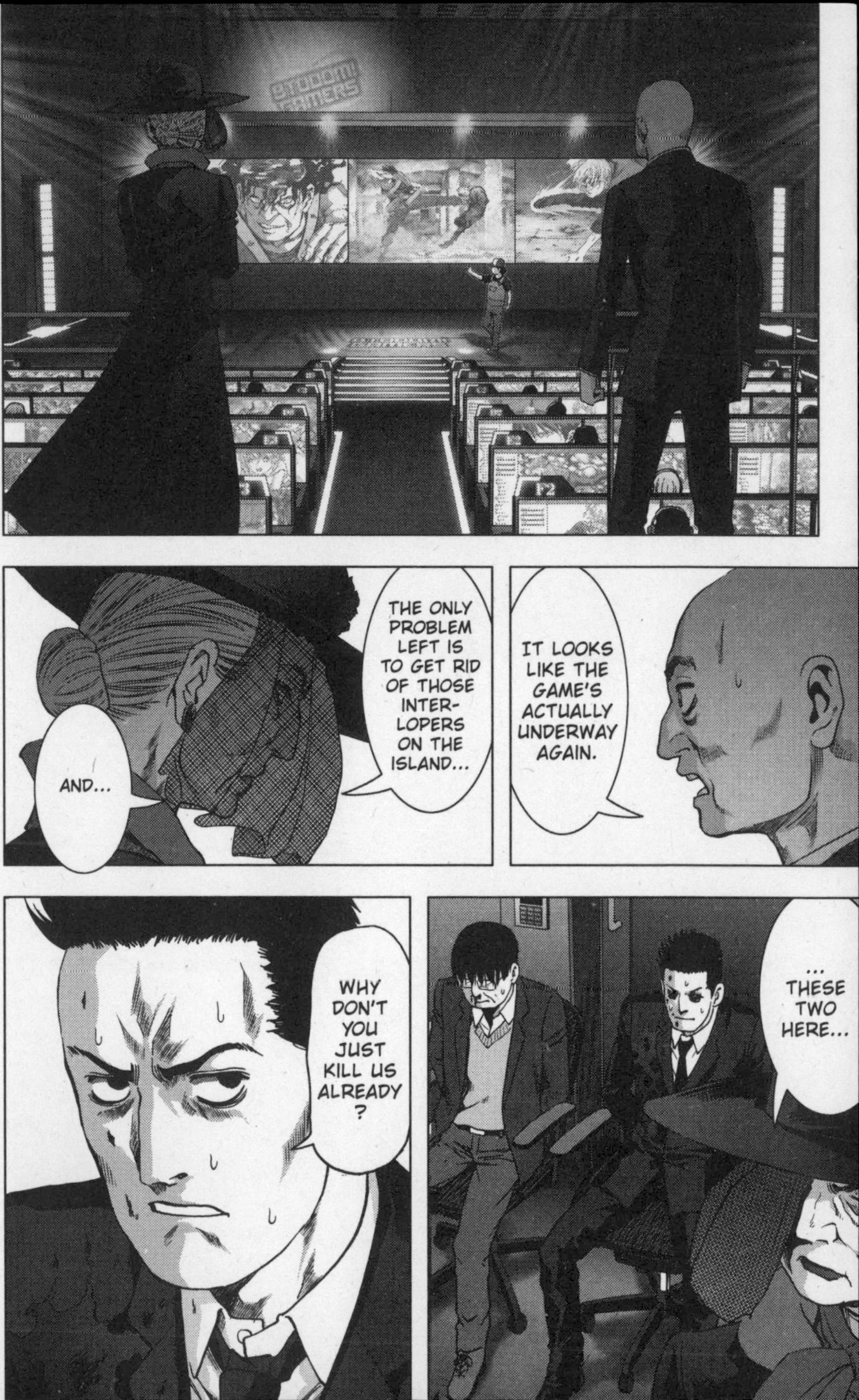
IT LOOKS LIKE THE GAME'S ACTUALLY UNDERWAY AGAIN.
THE ONLY PROBLEM LEFT IS TO GET RID OF THOSE INTER-LOPERS ON THE ISLAND...
AND...
...THESE TWO HERE...
WHY DON'T YOU JUST KILL US ALREADY?

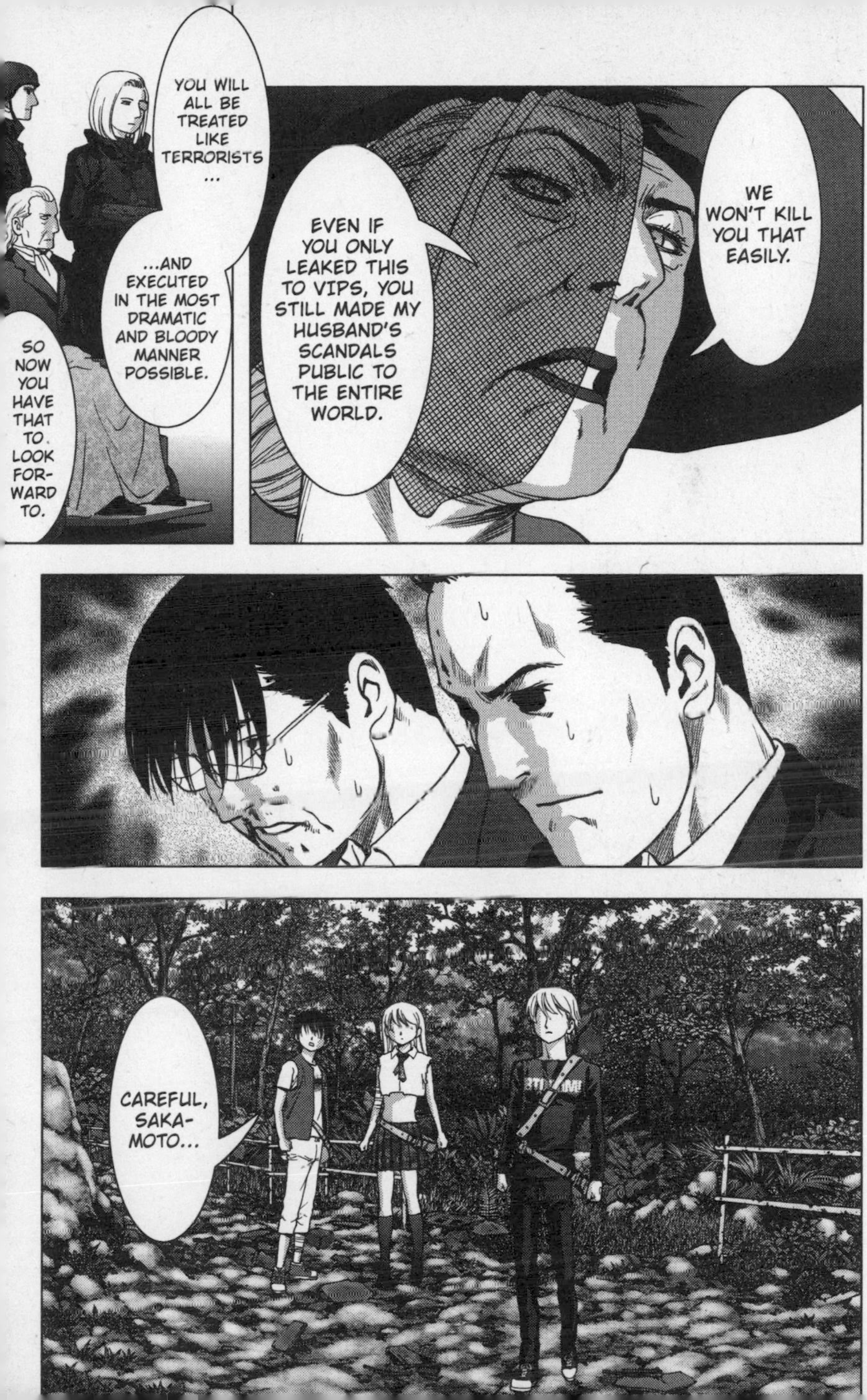
WE WON'T KILL YOU THAT EASILY.
EVEN IF YOU ONLY LEAKED THIS TO VIPS, YOU STILL MADE MY HUSBAND'S SCANDALS PUBLIC TO THE ENTIRE WORLD.
YOU WILL ALL BE TREATED LIKE TERRORISTS ...
...AND EXECUTED IN THE MOST DRAMATIC AND BLOODY MANNER POSSIBLE.
SO NOW YOU HAVE THAT TO LOOK FOR-WARD TO.
CAREFUL, SAKA-MOTO...

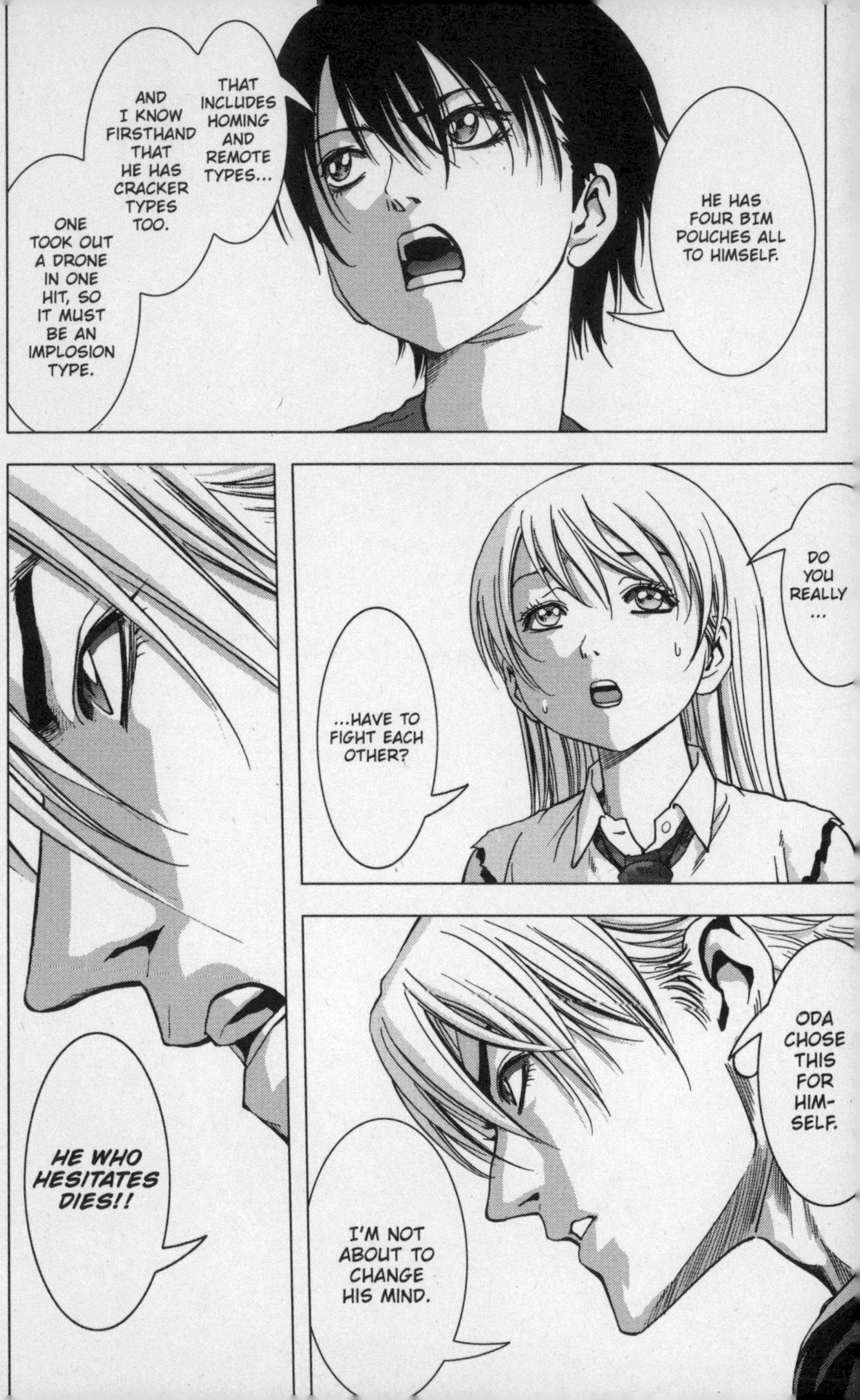

HE HAS FOUR BIM POUCHES ALL TO HIMSELF.
THAT INCLUDES HOMING AND REMOTE TYPES...
AND I KNOW FIRSTHAND THAT HE HAS CRACKER TYPES TOO.
ONE TOOK OUT A DRONE IN ONE HIT, SO IT MUST BE AN IMPLOSION TYPE.
DO YOU REALLY...
...HAVE TO FIGHT EACH OTHER?
ODA CHOSE THIS FOR HIM-SELF.
I'M NOT ABOUT TO CHANGE HIS MIND.
HE WHO HESITATES DIES!!

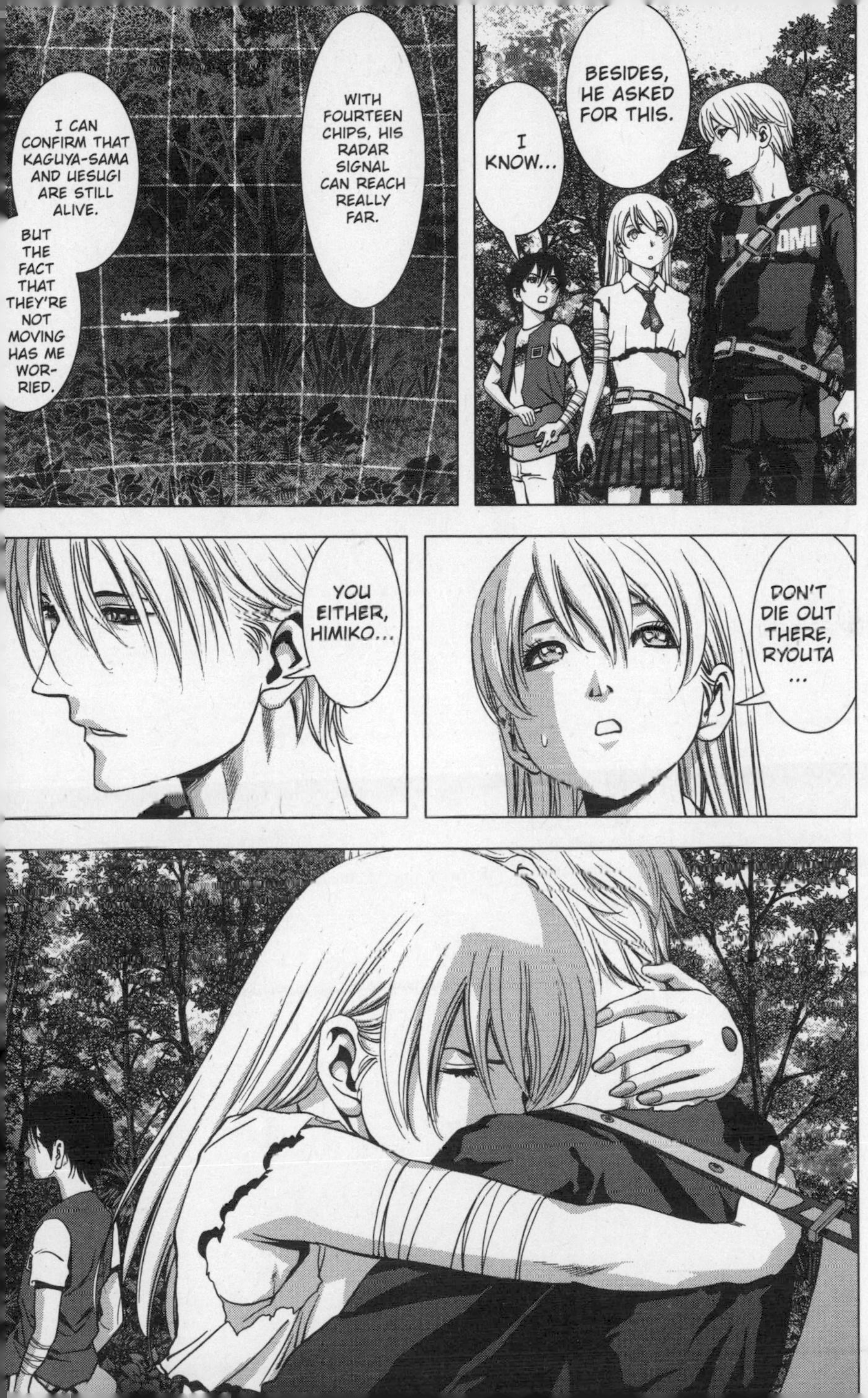
BESIDES, HE ASKED FOR THIS.
I KNOW...
WITH FOURTEEN CHIPS, HIS RADAR SIGNAL CAN REACH REALLY FAR.
I CAN CONFIRM THAT KAGUYA-SAMA AND UESUGI ARE STILL ALIVE.
BUT THE FACT THAT THEY'RE NOT MOVING HAS ME WOR-RIED.
DON'T DIE OUT THERE, RYOUTA ...
YOU EITHER, HIMIKO...

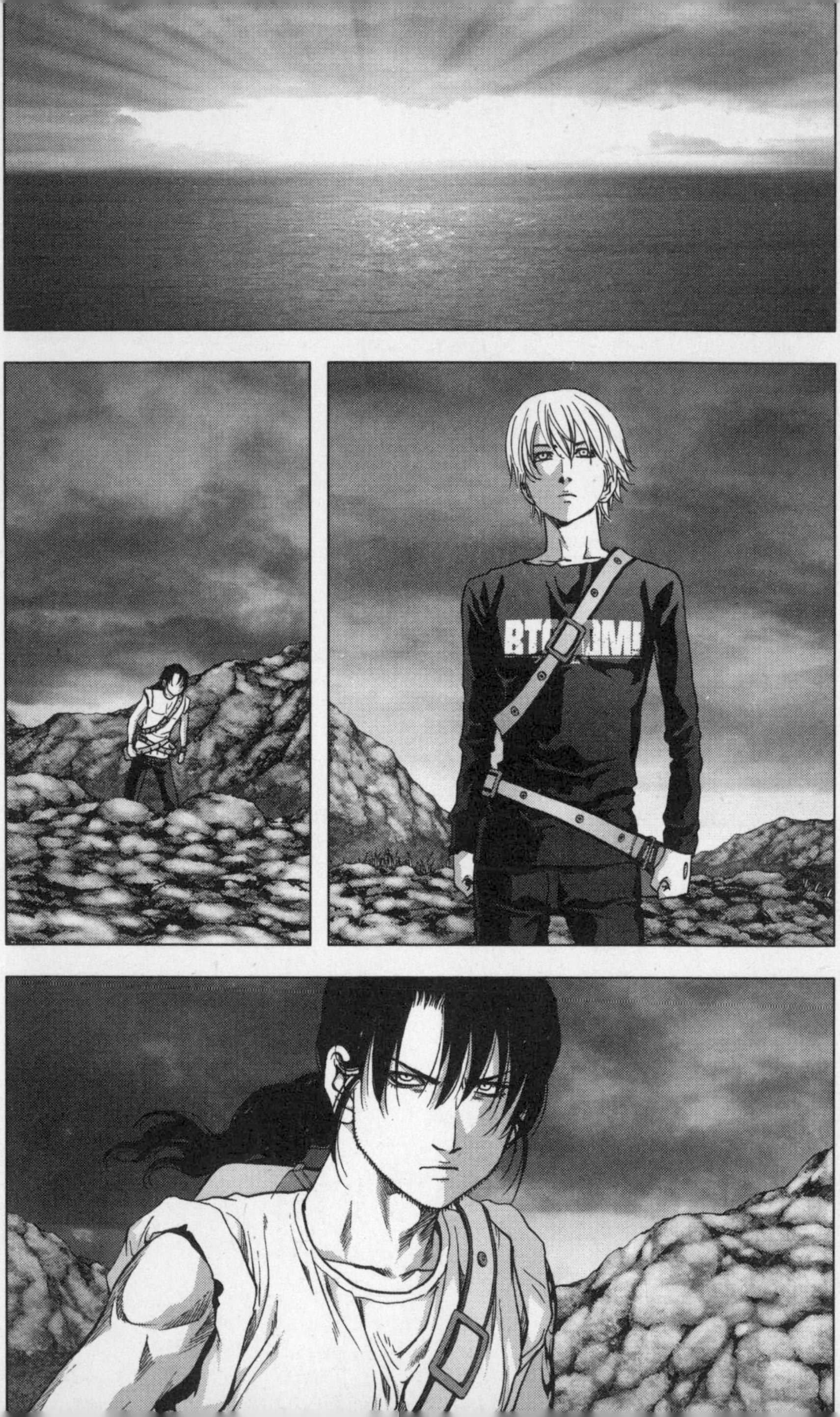

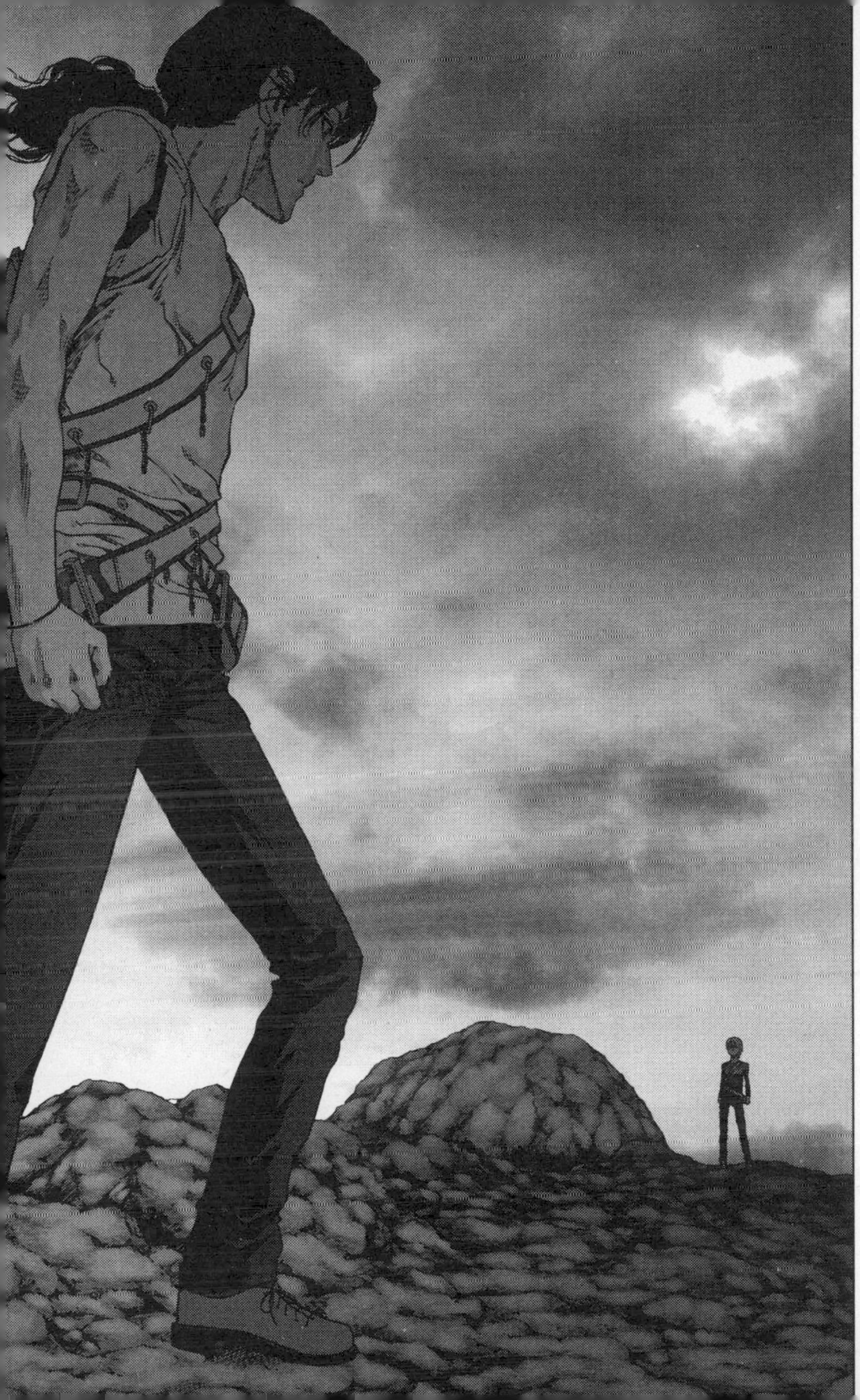

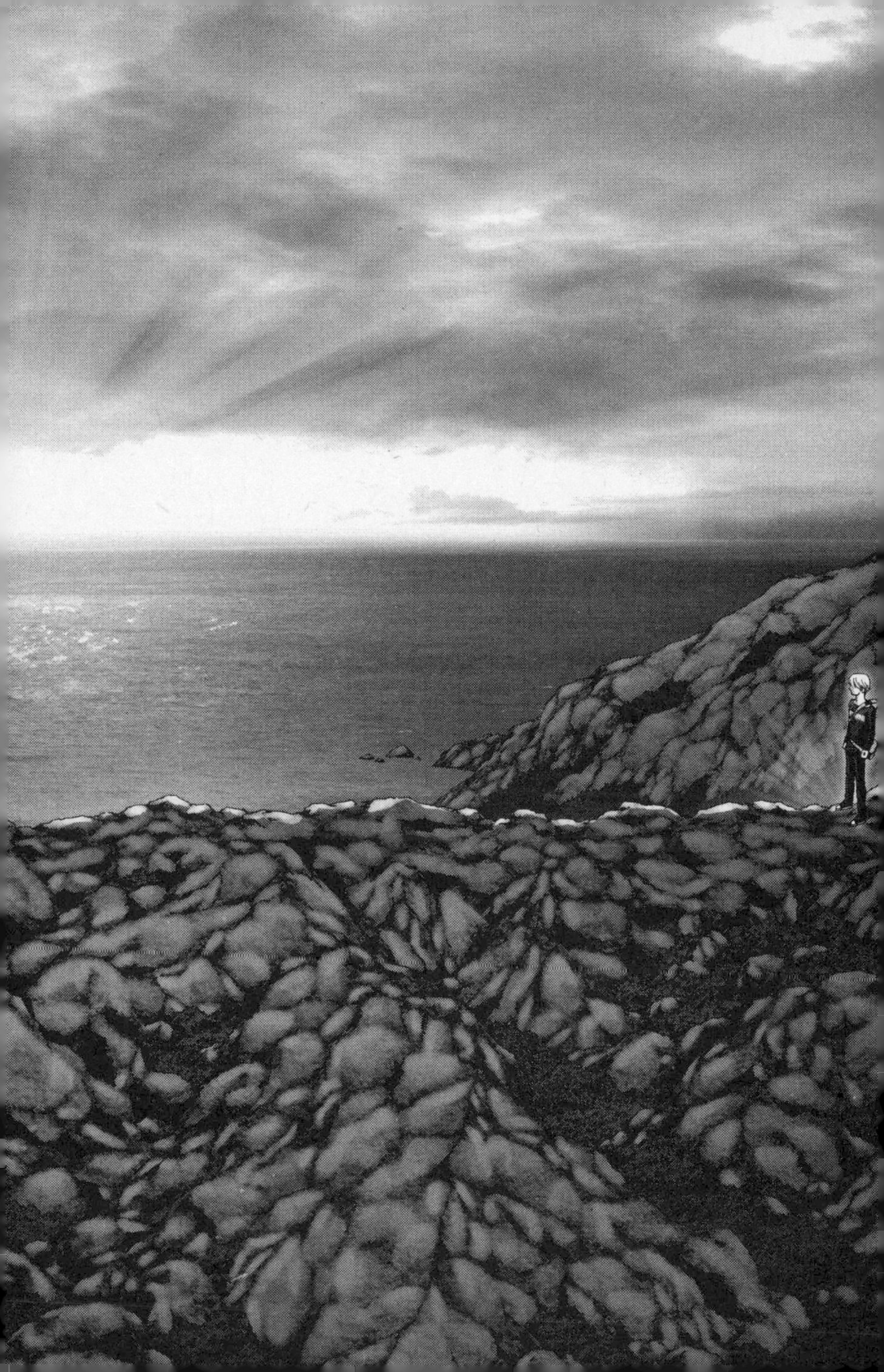

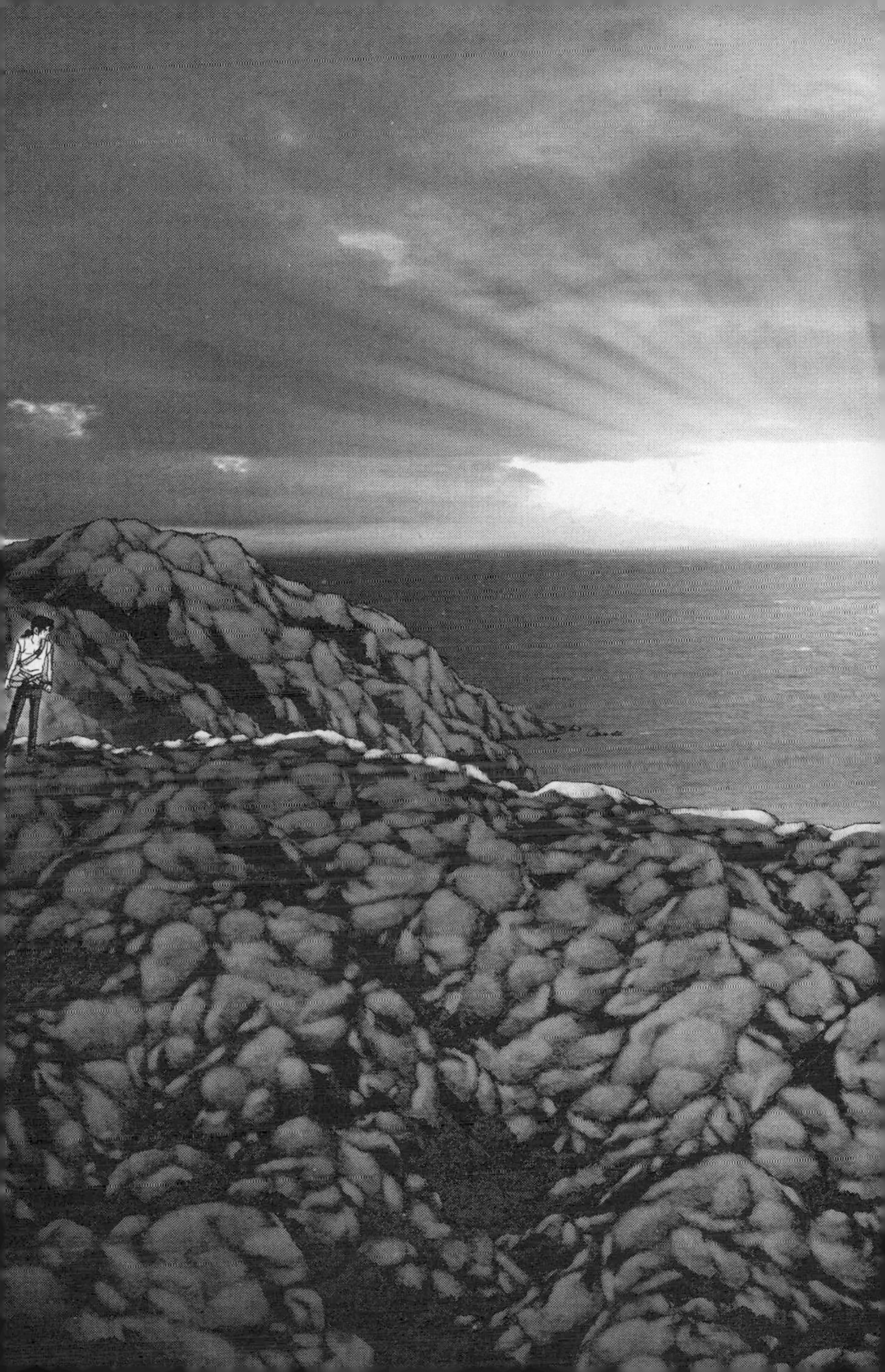

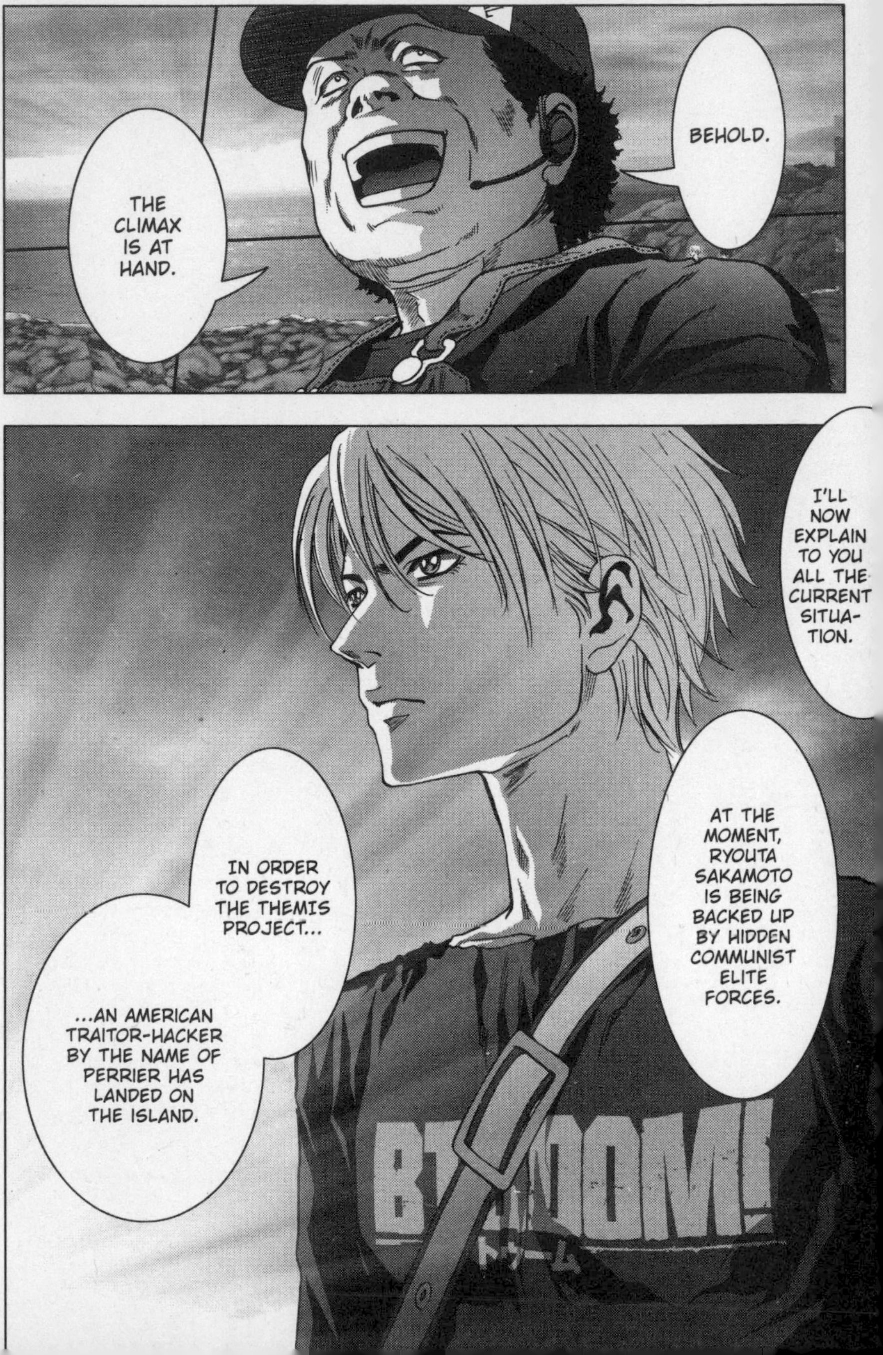
BEHOLD.
THE CLIMAX IS AT HAND.
I'LL NOW EXPLAIN TO YOU ALL THE CURRENT SITUATION.
AT THE MOMENT, RYOUTA SAKAMOTO IS BEING BACKED UP BY HIDDEN COMMUNIST ELITE FORCES.
IN ORDER TO DESTROY THE THEMIS PROJECT...
...AN AMERICAN TRAITOR-HACKER BY THE NAME OF PERRIER HAS LANDED ON THE ISLAND.

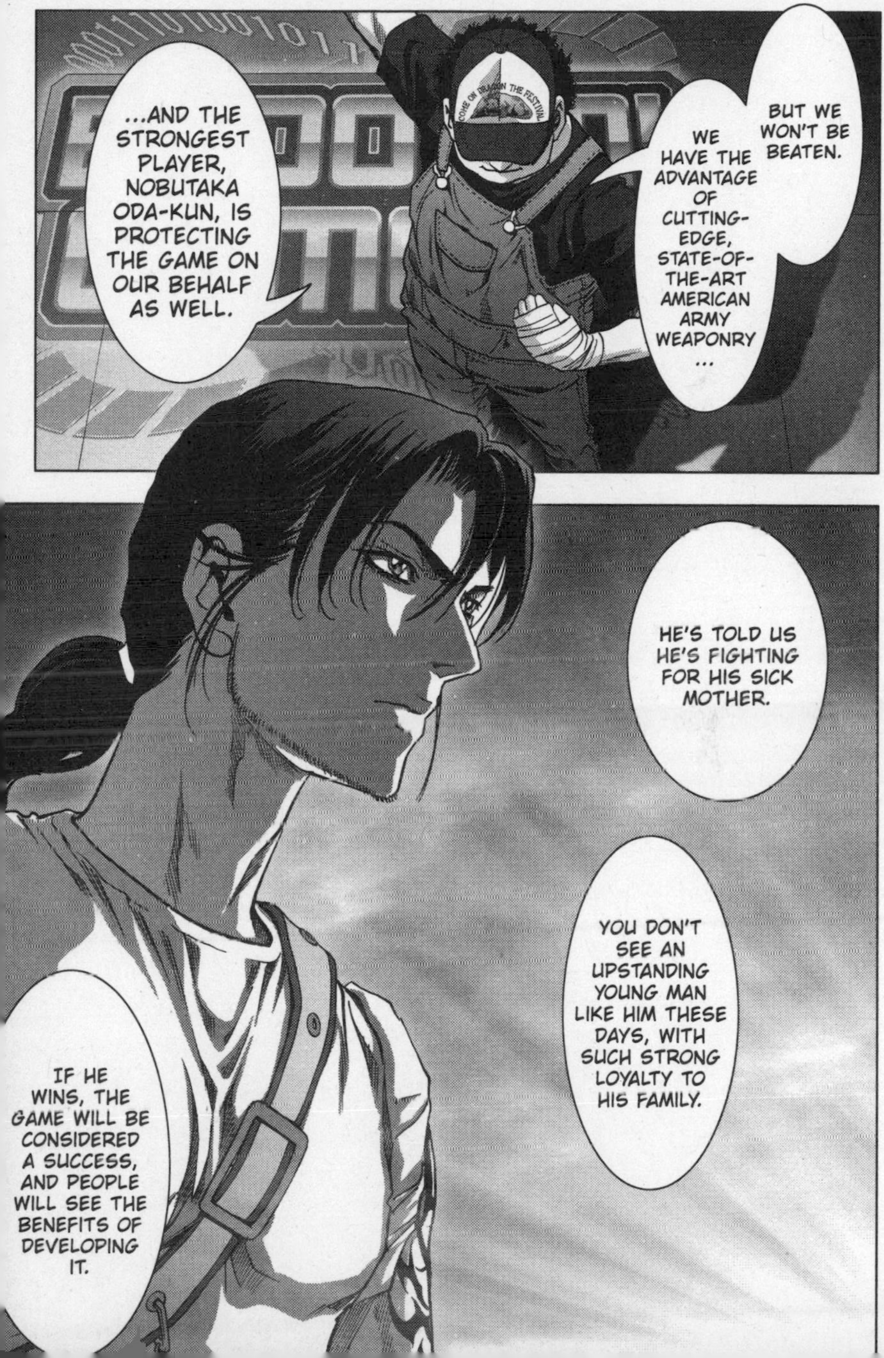
BUT WE WON'T BE BEATEN.
WE HAVE THE ADVANTAGE OF CUTTING-EDGE, STATE-OF-THE-ART AMERICAN ARMY WEAPONRY ...
...AND THE STRONGEST PLAYER, NOBUTAKA ODA-KUN, IS PROTECTING THE GAME ON OUR BEHALF AS WELL.
HE'S TOLD US HE'S FIGHTING FOR HIS SICK MOTHER.
YOU DON'T SEE AN UPSTANDING YOUNG MAN LIKE HIM THESE DAYS, WITH SUCH STRONG LOYALTY TO HIS FAMILY.
IF HE WINS, THE GAME WILL BE CONSIDERED A SUCCESS, AND PEOPLE WILL SEE THE BENEFITS OF DEVELOPING IT.

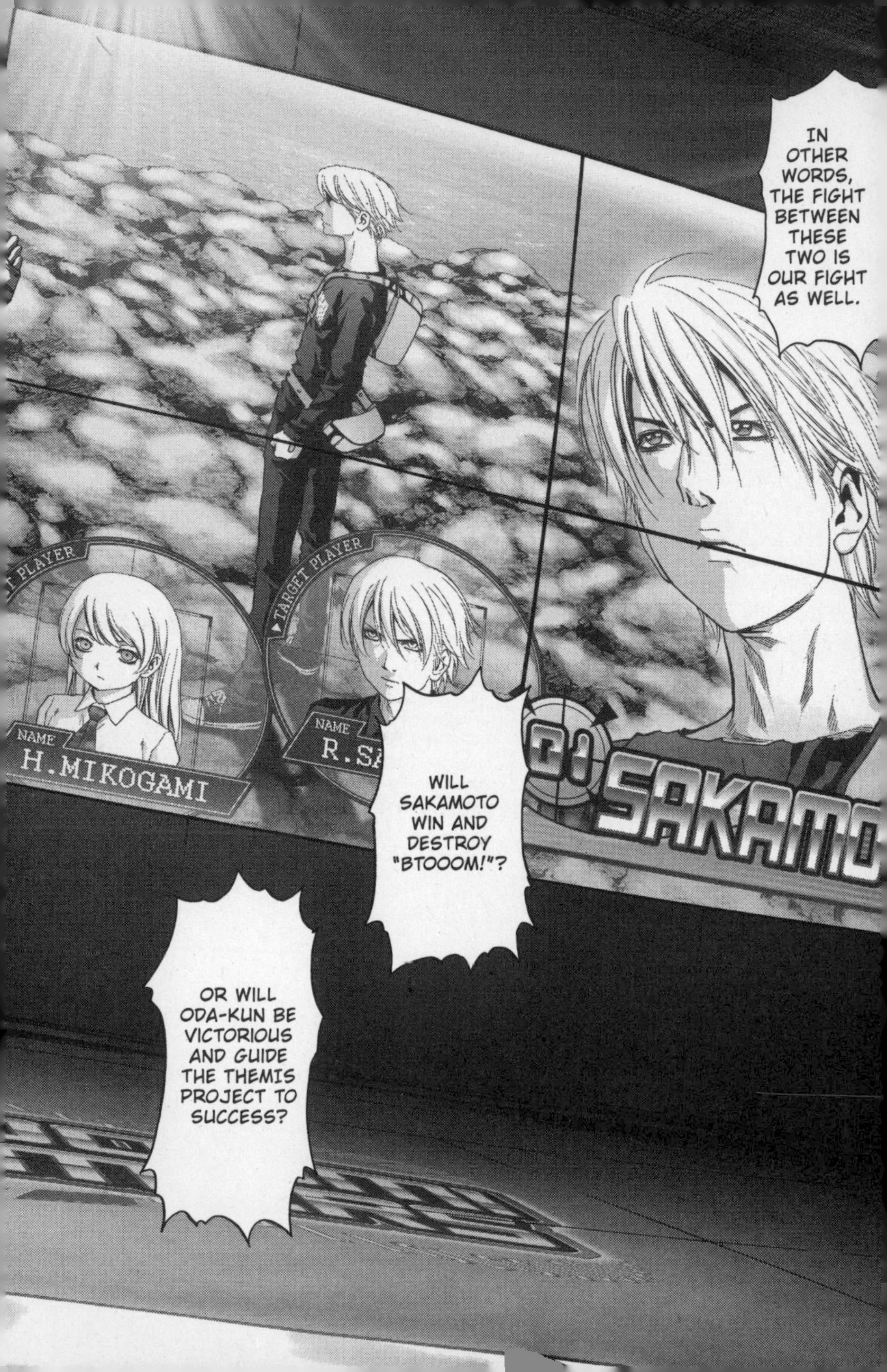
IN OTHER WORDS, THE FIGHT BETWEEN THESE TWO IS OUR FIGHT AS WELL.
TARGET PLAYER
NAME
H.MIKOGAMI
TARGET PLAYER
NAME
R.SA
SAKAMO
WILL SAKAMOTO WIN AND DESTROY "BTOOOM!"?
OR WILL ODA-KUN BE VICTORIOUS AND GUIDE THE THEMIS PROJECT TO SUCCESS?

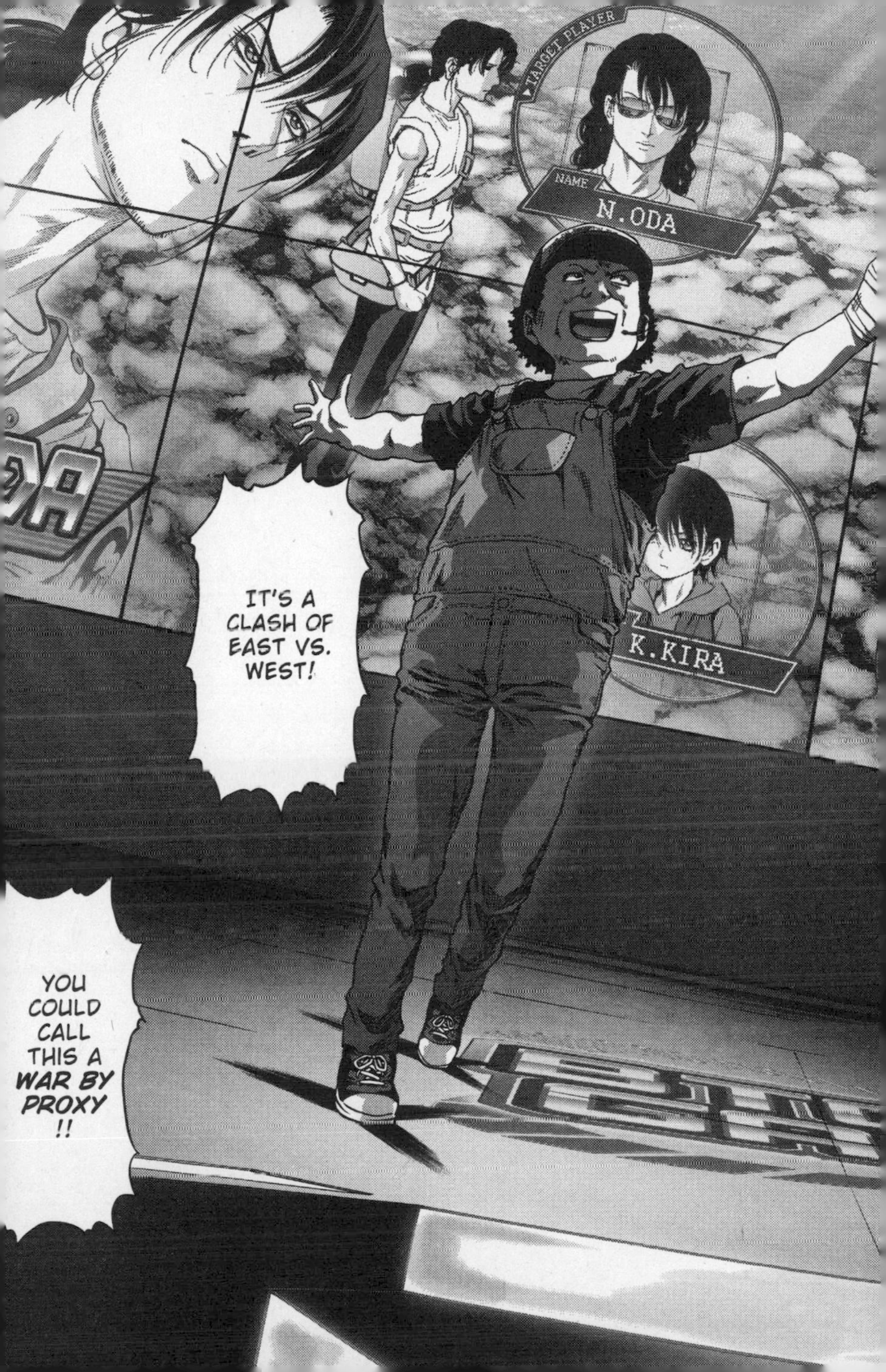
TARGET PLAYER
NAME
N.ODA
K.KIRA
IT'S A CLASH OF EAST VS. WEST!
YOU COULD CALL THIS A *WAR BY PROXY* !!

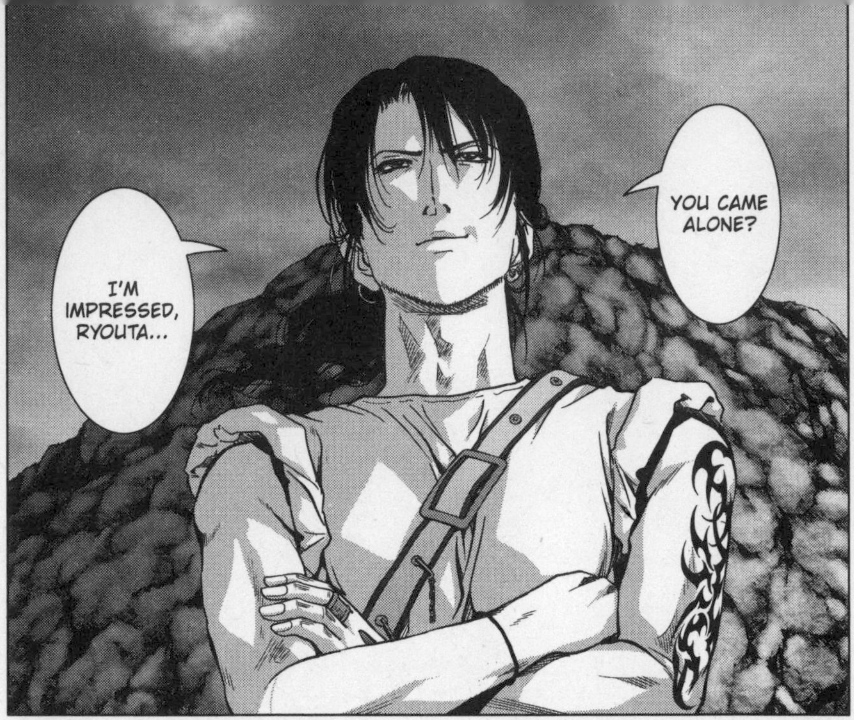
YOU CAME ALONE?
I'M IMPRESSED, RYOUTA...

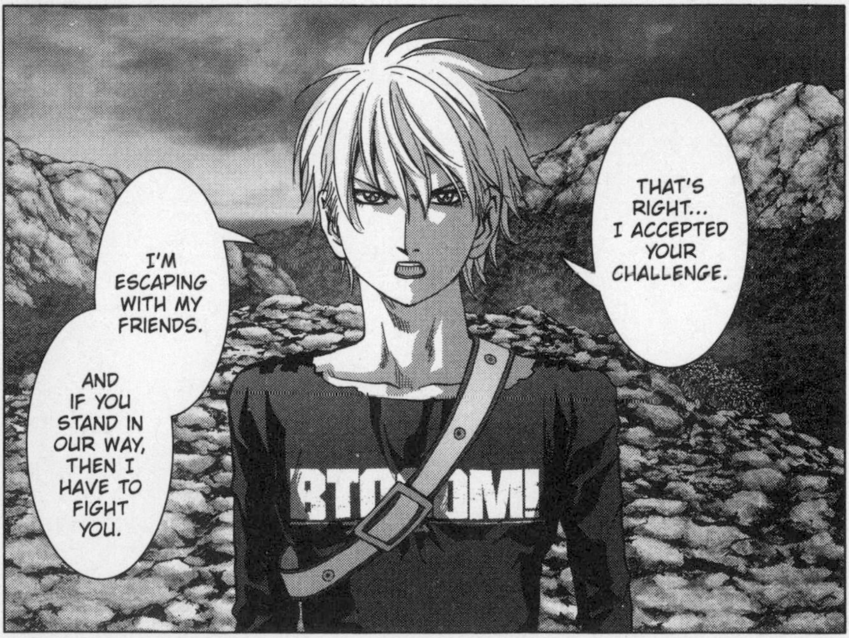
THAT'S RIGHT... I ACCEPTED YOUR CHALLENGE.
I'M ESCAPING WITH MY FRIENDS.
AND IF YOU STAND IN OUR WAY, THEN I HAVE TO FIGHT YOU.

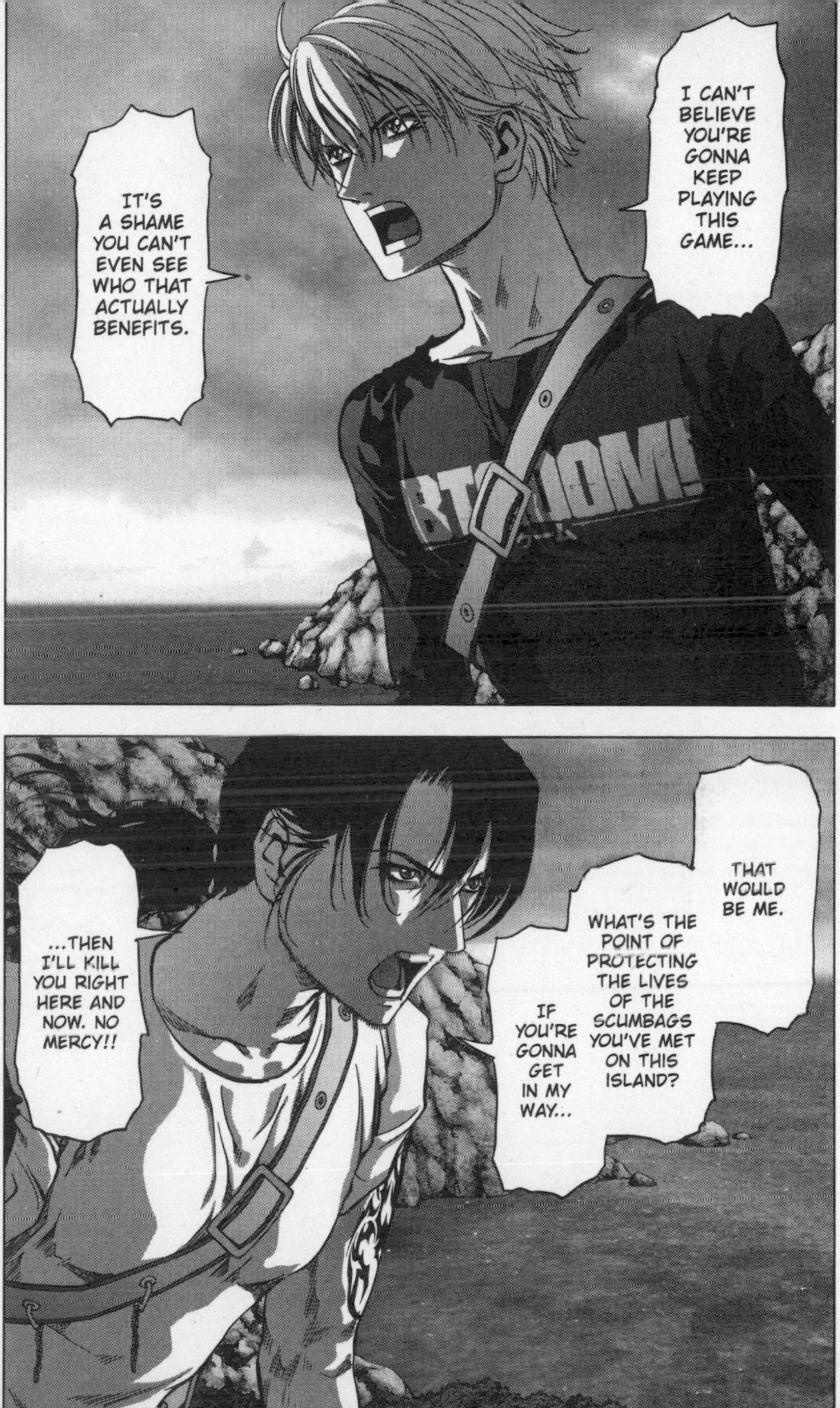
I CAN'T BELIEVE YOU'RE GONNA KEEP PLAYING THIS GAME...
IT'S A SHAME YOU CAN'T EVEN SEE WHO THAT ACTUALLY BENEFITS.
THAT WOULD BE ME.
WHAT'S THE POINT OF PROTECTING THE LIVES OF THE SCUMBAGS YOU'VE MET ON THIS ISLAND?
IF YOU'RE GONNA GET IN MY WAY...
...THEN I'LL KILL YOU RIGHT HERE AND NOW. NO MERCY!!

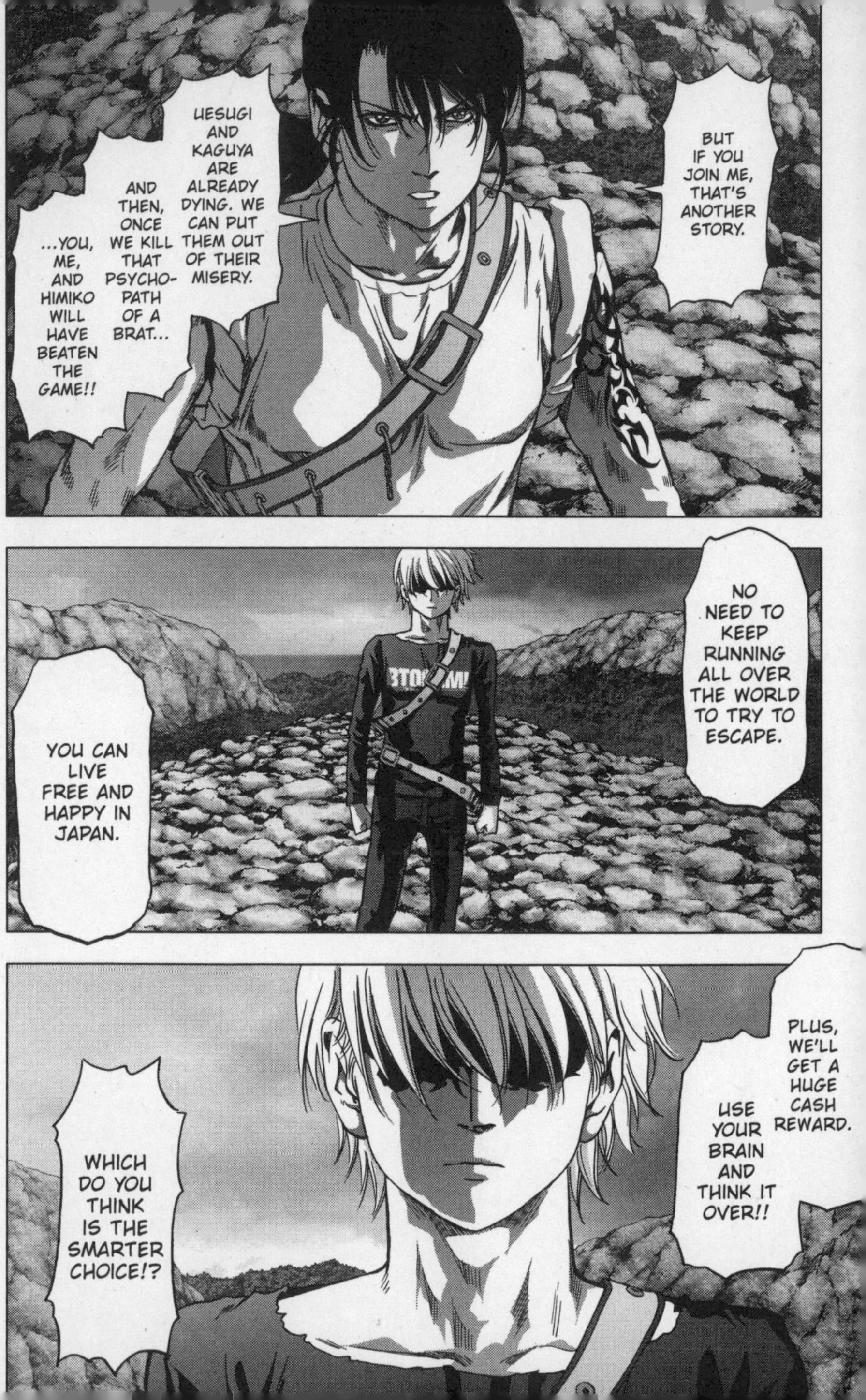
BUT IF YOU JOIN ME, THAT'S ANOTHER STORY.
UESUGI AND KAGUYA ARE ALREADY DYING. WE CAN PUT THEM OUT OF THEIR MISERY.
AND THEN, ONCE WE KILL THAT PSYCHO-PATH OF A BRAT...
...YOU, ME, AND HIMIKO WILL HAVE BEATEN THE GAME!!
NO NEED TO KEEP RUNNING ALL OVER THE WORLD TO TRY TO ESCAPE.
YOU CAN LIVE FREE AND HAPPY IN JAPAN.
PLUS, WE'LL GET A HUGE CASH REWARD.
USE YOUR BRAIN AND THINK IT OVER!!
WHICH DO YOU THINK IS THE SMARTER CHOICE!?

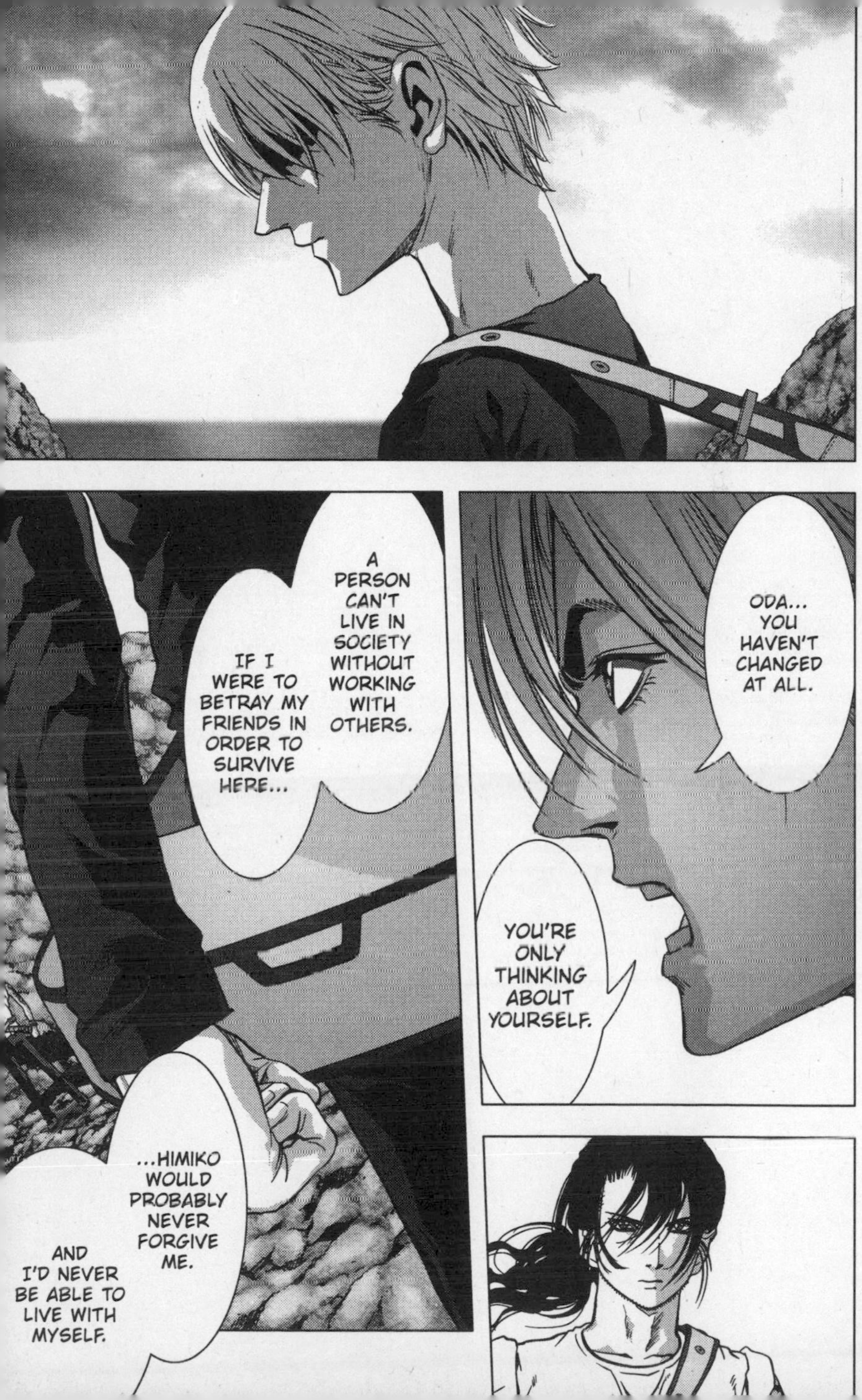
ODA... YOU HAVEN'T CHANGED AT ALL.
YOU'RE ONLY THINKING ABOUT YOURSELF.
A PERSON CAN'T LIVE IN SOCIETY WITHOUT WORKING WITH OTHERS.
IF I WERE TO BETRAY MY FRIENDS IN ORDER TO SURVIVE HERE...
...HIMIKO WOULD PROBABLY NEVER FORGIVE ME.
AND I'D NEVER BE ABLE TO LIVE WITH MYSELF.

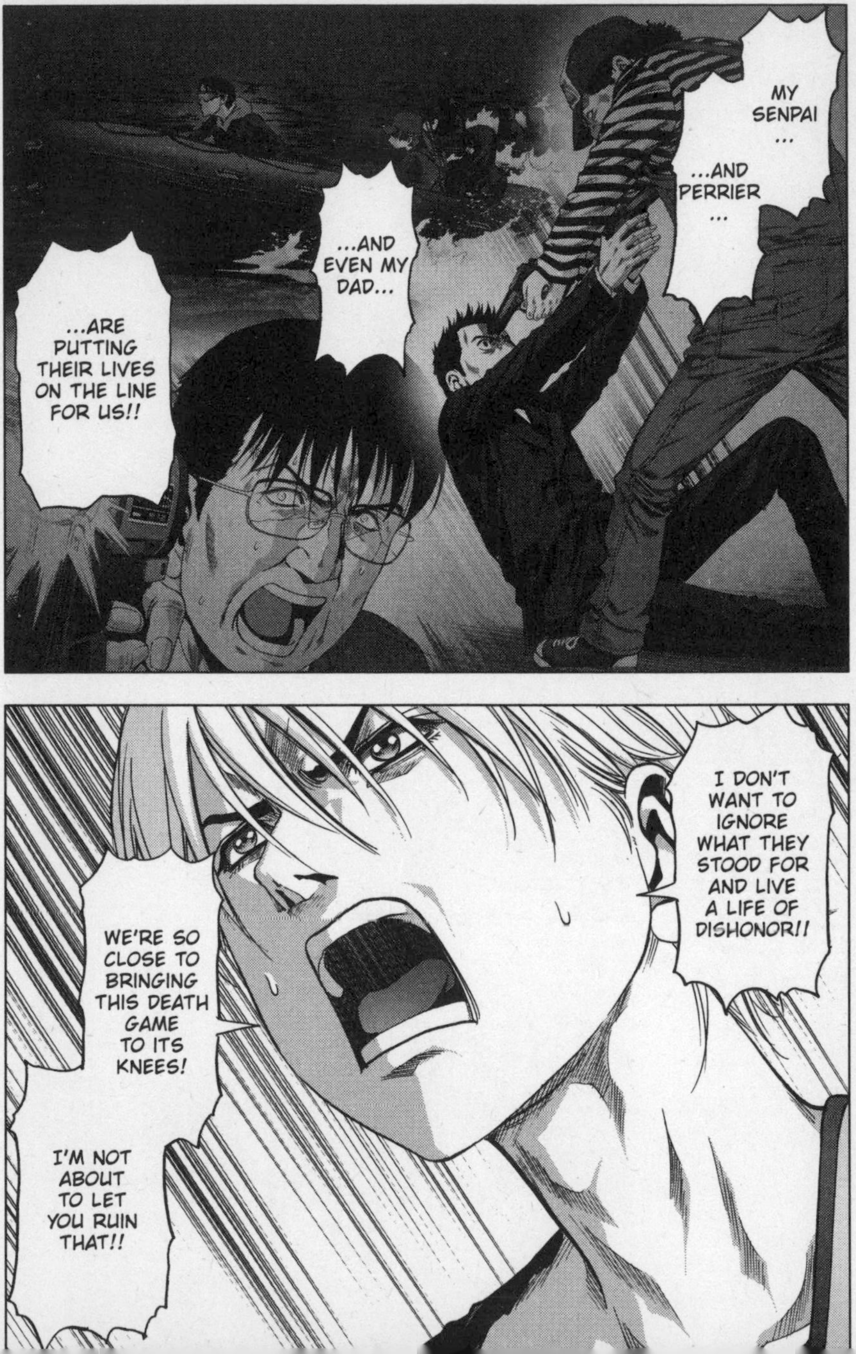
MY SENPAI ...
...AND PERRIER ...
...AND EVEN MY DAD...
...ARE PUTTING THEIR LIVES ON THE LINE FOR US!!
I DON'T WANT TO IGNORE WHAT THEY STOOD FOR AND LIVE A LIFE OF DISHONOR!!
WE'RE SO CLOSE TO BRINGING THIS DEATH GAME TO ITS KNEES!
I'M NOT ABOUT TO LET YOU RUIN THAT!!

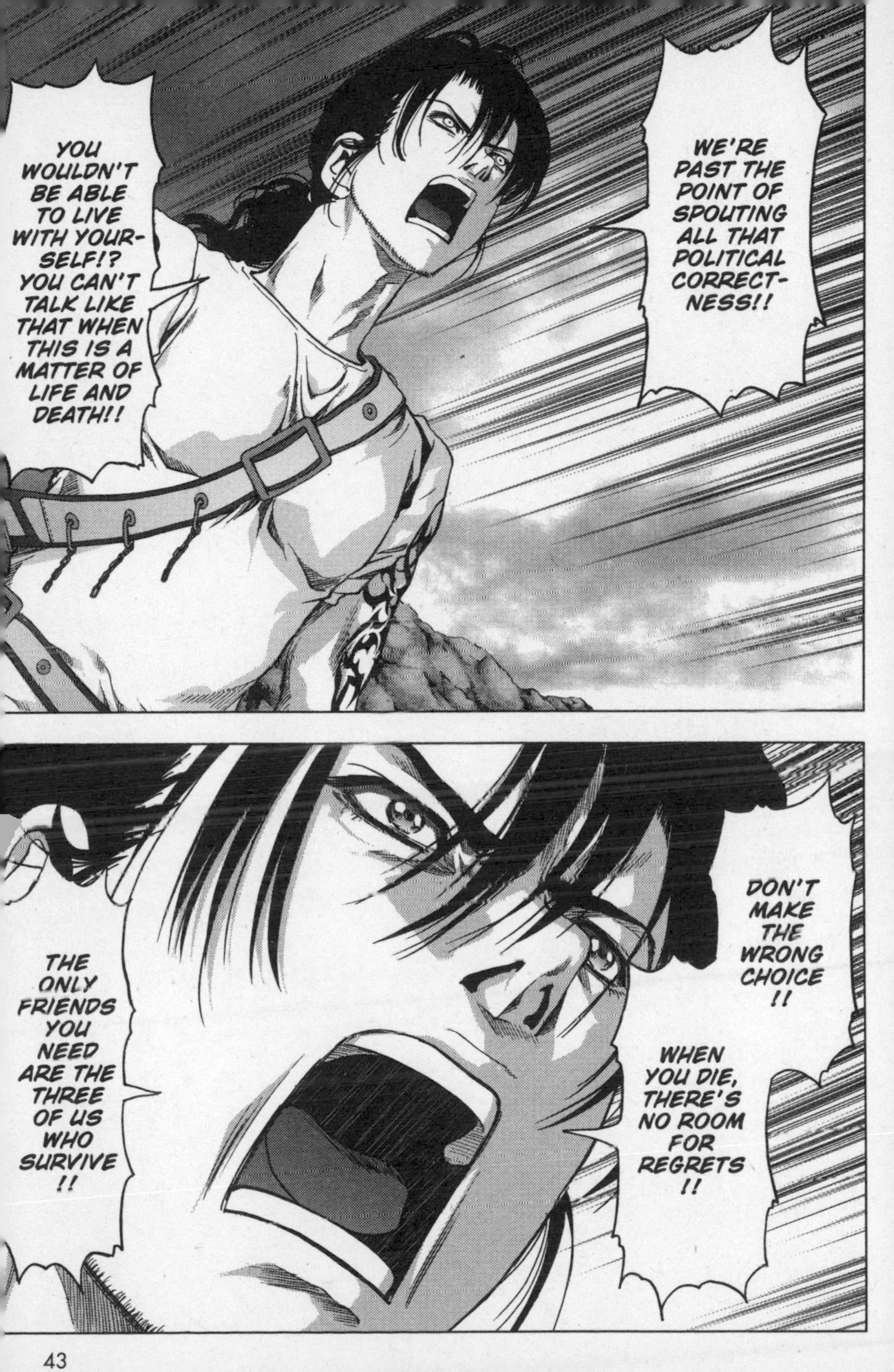
WE'RE PAST THE POINT OF SPOUTING ALL THAT POLITICAL CORRECT-NESS!!
YOU WOULDN'T BE ABLE TO LIVE WITH YOUR-SELF!? YOU CAN'T TALK LIKE THAT WHEN THIS IS A MATTER OF LIFE AND DEATH!!
DON'T MAKE THE WRONG CHOICE !!
WHEN YOU DIE, THERE'S NO ROOM FOR REGRETS !!
THE ONLY FRIENDS YOU NEED ARE THE THREE OF US WHO SURVIVE !!

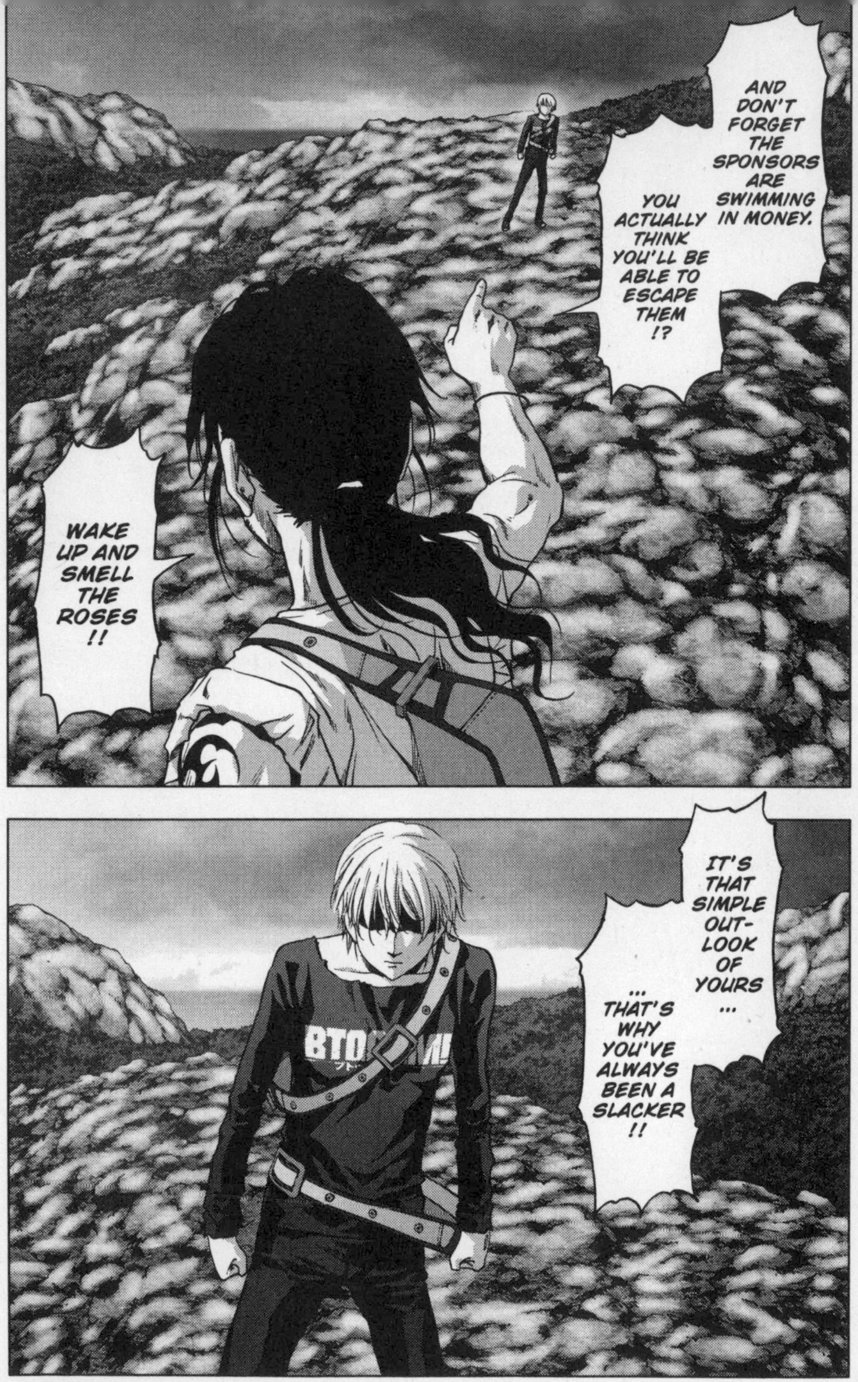
AND DON'T FORGET THE SPONSORS ARE SWIMMING IN MONEY.
YOU ACTUALLY THINK YOU'LL BE ABLE TO ESCAPE THEM !?
WAKE UP AND SMELL THE ROSES !!
IT'S THAT SIMPLE OUT-LOOK OF YOURS ...
... THAT'S WHY YOU'VE ALWAYS BEEN A SLACKER !!

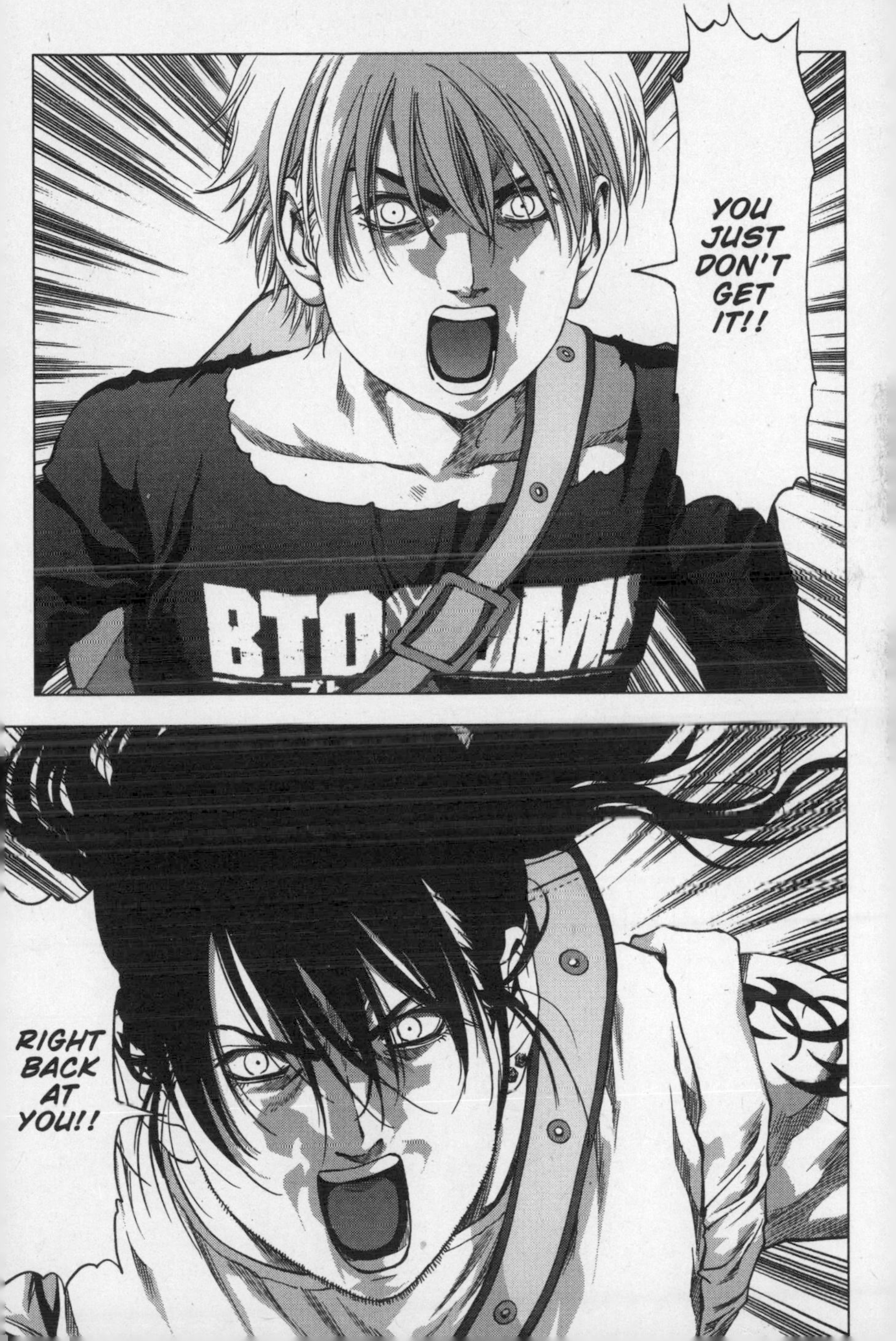
YOU JUST DON'T GET IT!!
RIGHT BACK AT YOU!!

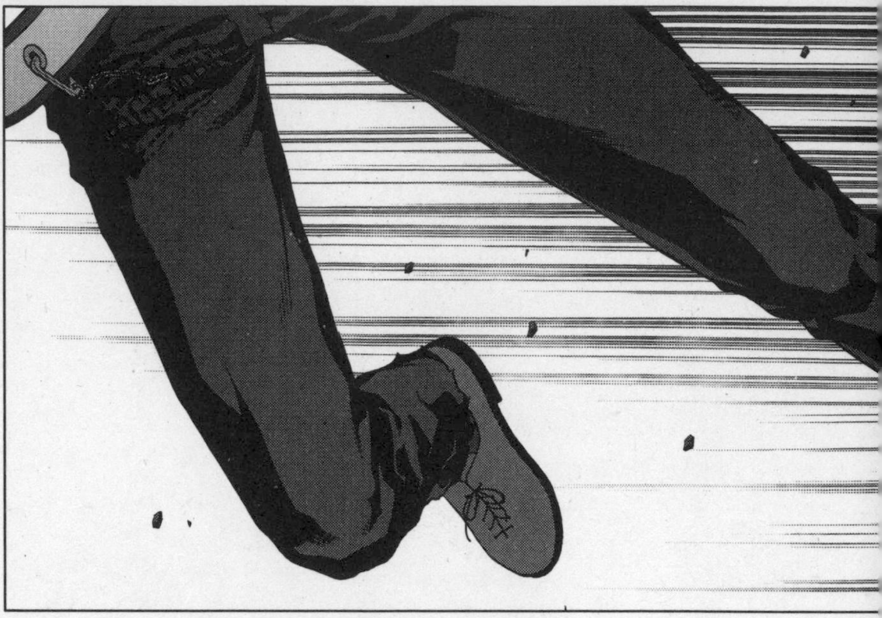
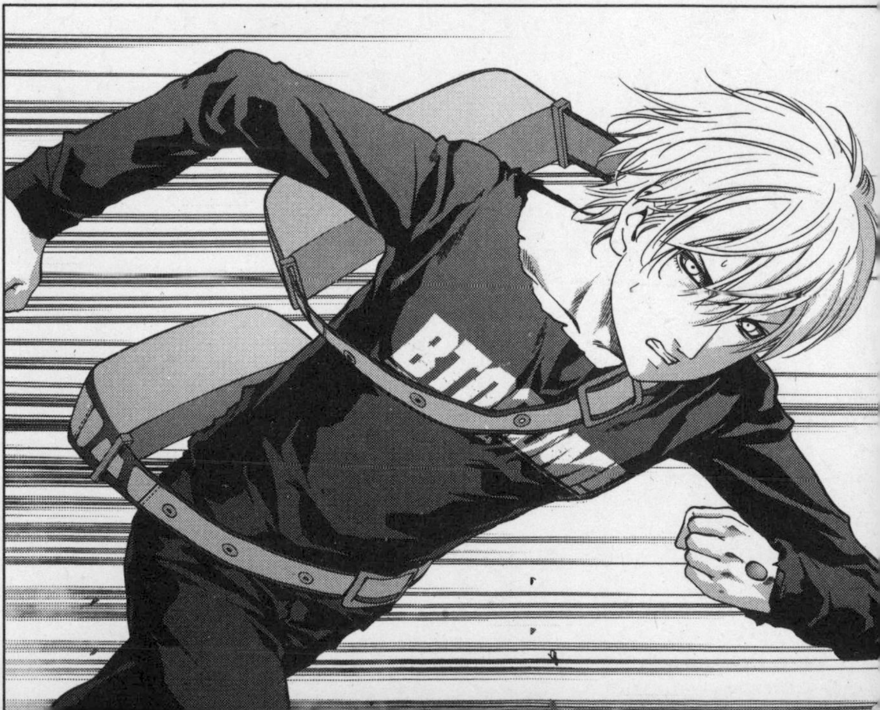

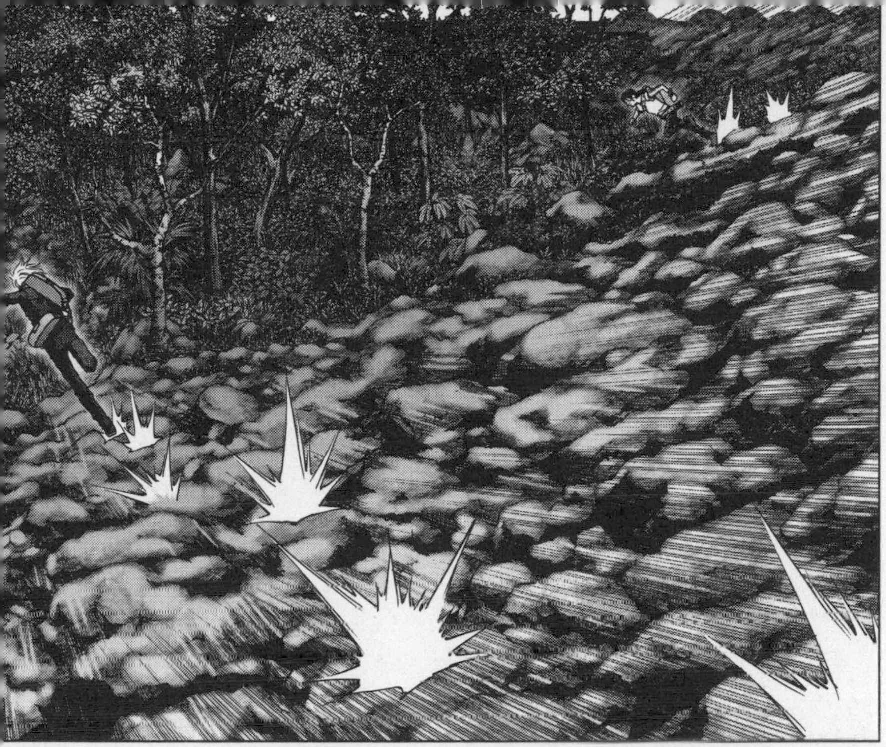
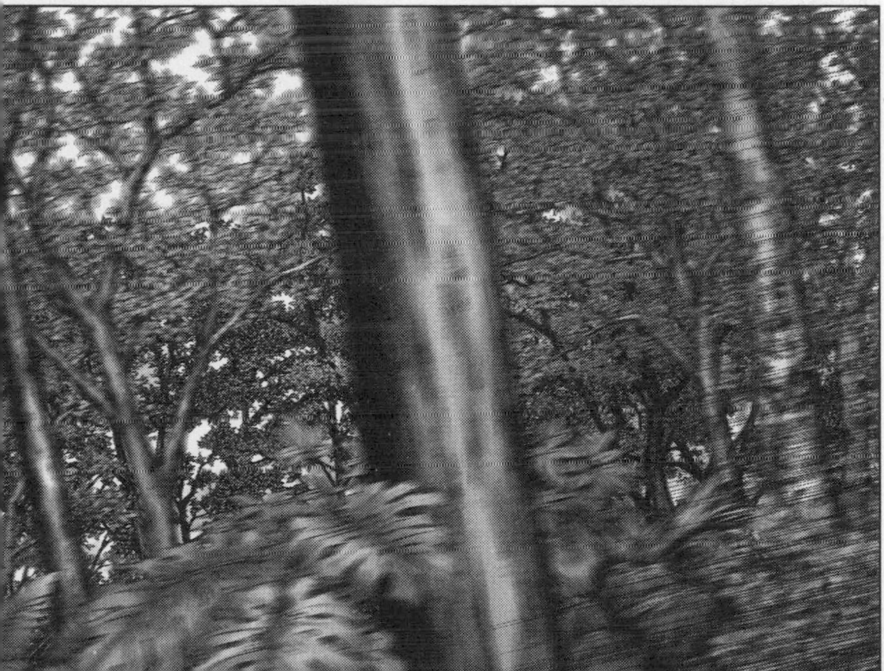

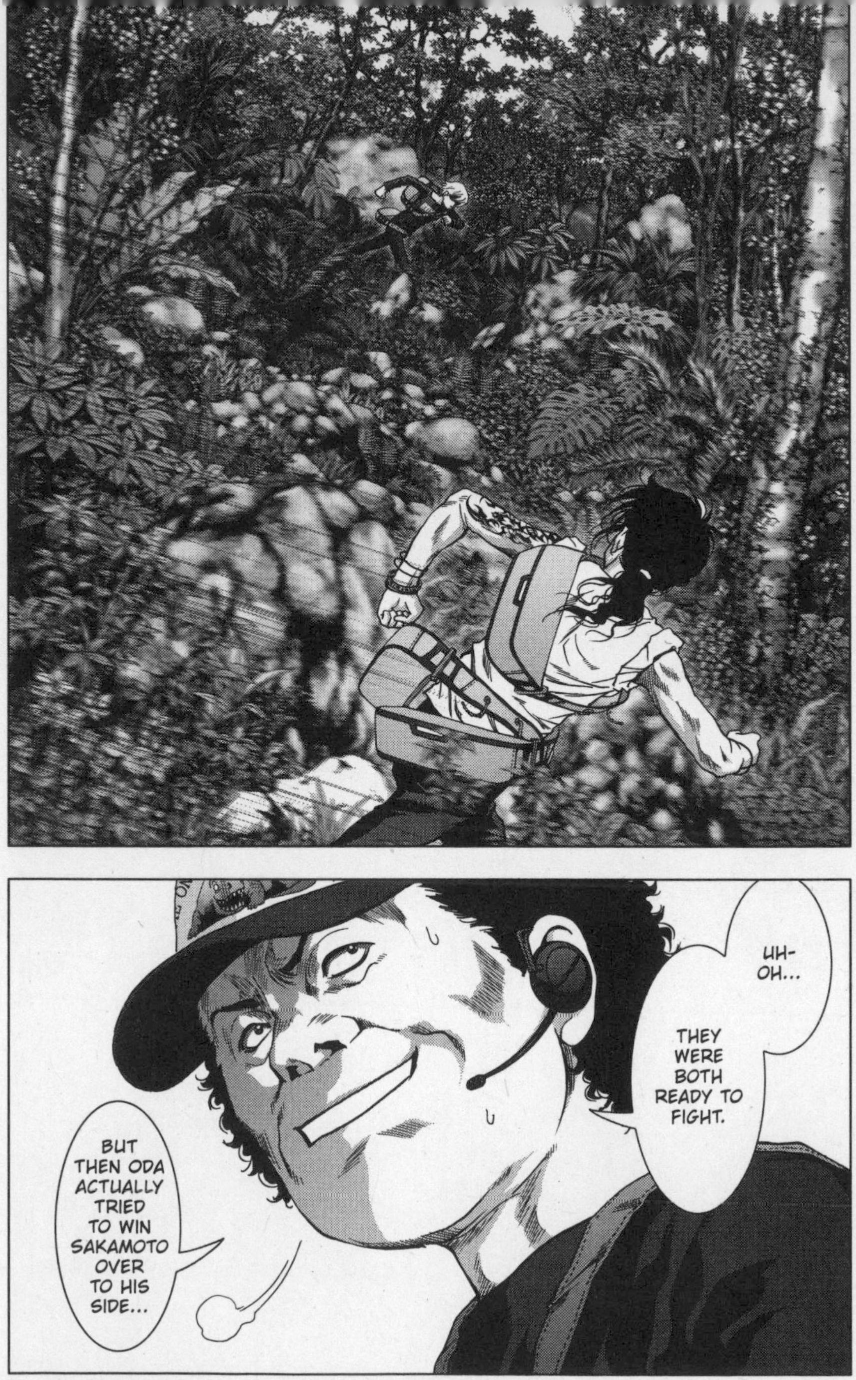
UH-OH...
THEY WERE BOTH READY TO FIGHT.
BUT THEN ODA ACTUALLY TRIED TO WIN SAKAMOTO OVER TO HIS SIDE...

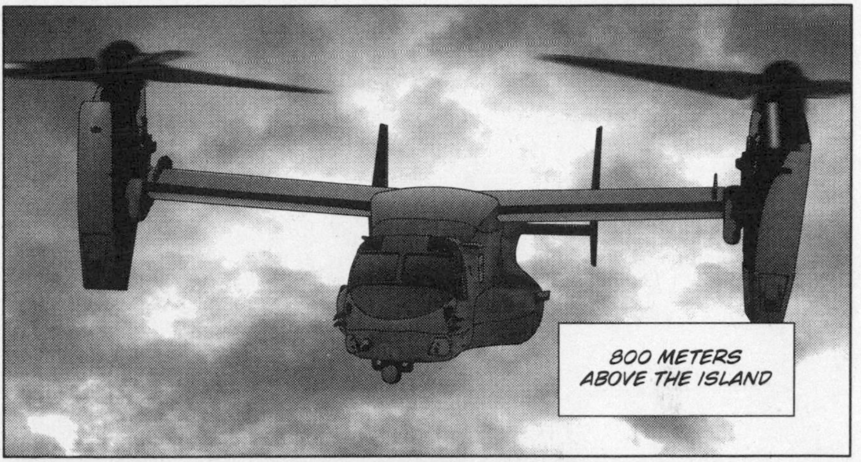
800 METERS ABOVE THE ISLAND

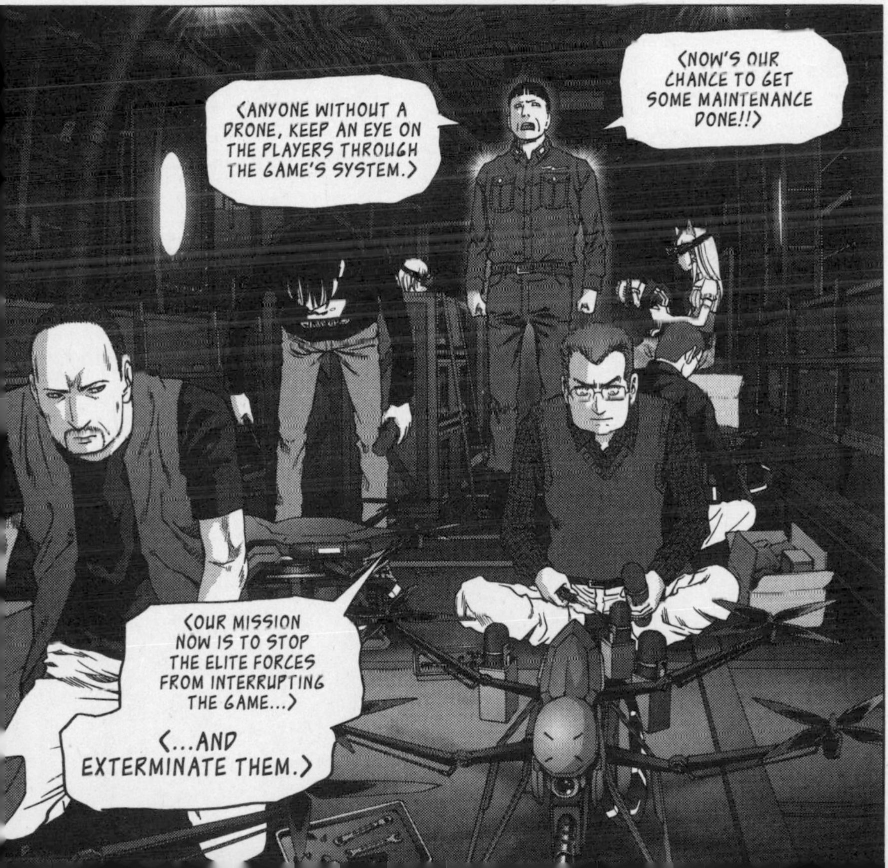
<NOW'S OUR CHANCE TO GET SOME MAINTENANCE DONE!!>
<ANYONE WITHOUT A DRONE, KEEP AN EYE ON THE PLAYERS THROUGH THE GAME'S SYSTEM.>
<OUR MISSION NOW IS TO STOP THE ELITE FORCES FROM INTERRUPTING THE GAME...>
<...AND EXTERMINATE THEM.>

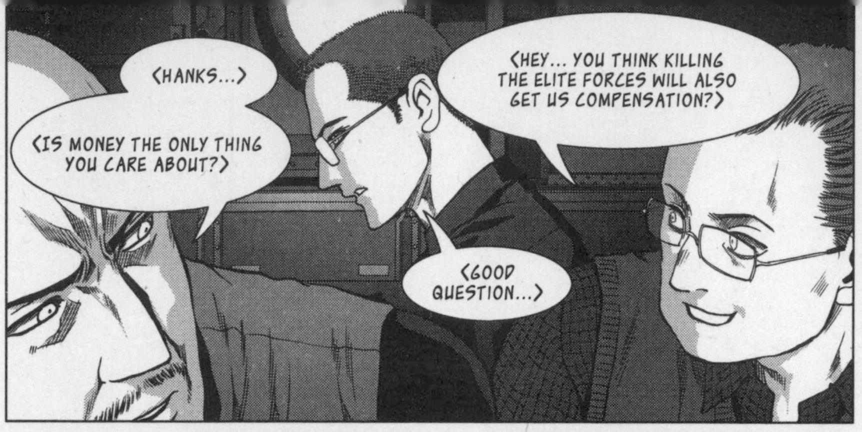
<HEY... YOU THINK KILLING THE ELITE FORCES WILL ALSO GET US COMPENSATION?>
<HANKS...>
<IS MONEY THE ONLY THING YOU CARE ABOUT?>
<GOOD QUESTION...>

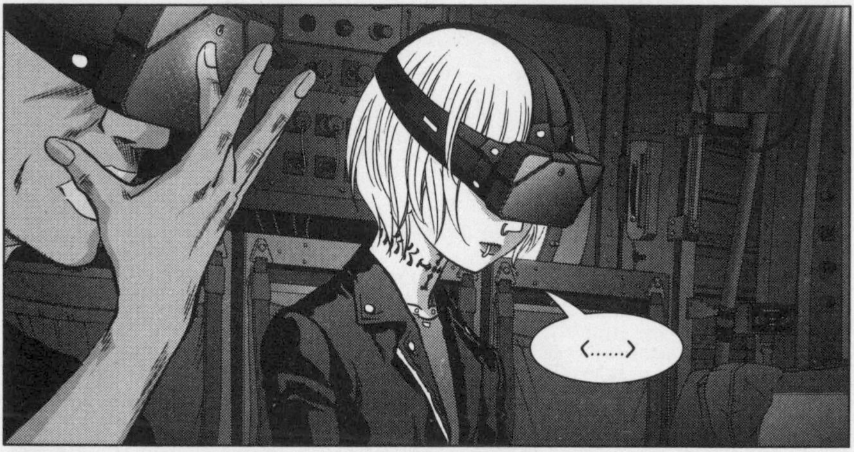
<......>

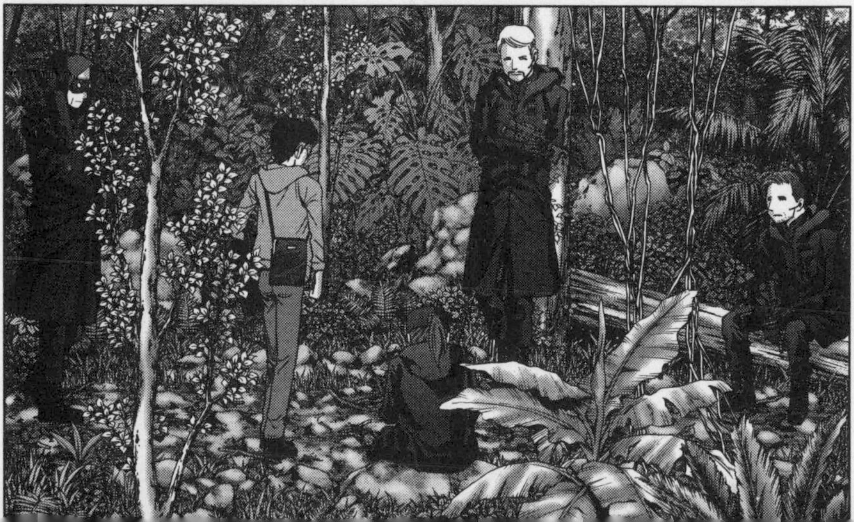

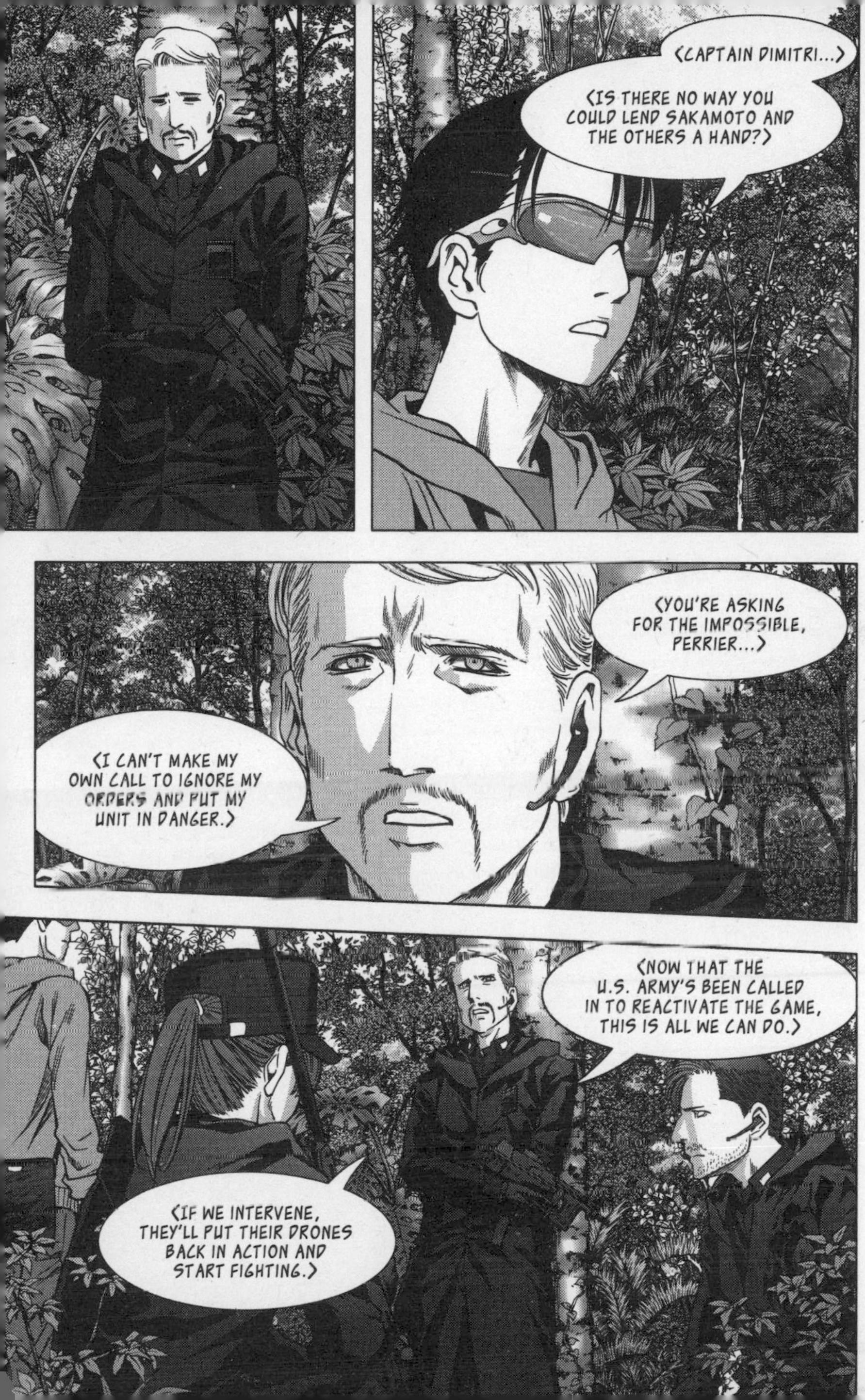
<CAPTAIN DIMITRI...>
<IS THERE NO WAY YOU COULD LEND SAKAMOTO AND THE OTHERS A HAND?>
<YOU'RE ASKING FOR THE IMPOSSIBLE, PERRIER...>
<I CAN'T MAKE MY OWN CALL TO IGNORE MY ORDERS AND PUT MY UNIT IN DANGER.>
<NOW THAT THE U.S. ARMY'S BEEN CALLED IN TO REACTIVATE THE GAME, THIS IS ALL WE CAN DO.>
<IF WE INTERVENE, THEY'LL PUT THEIR DRONES BACK IN ACTION AND START FIGHTING.>

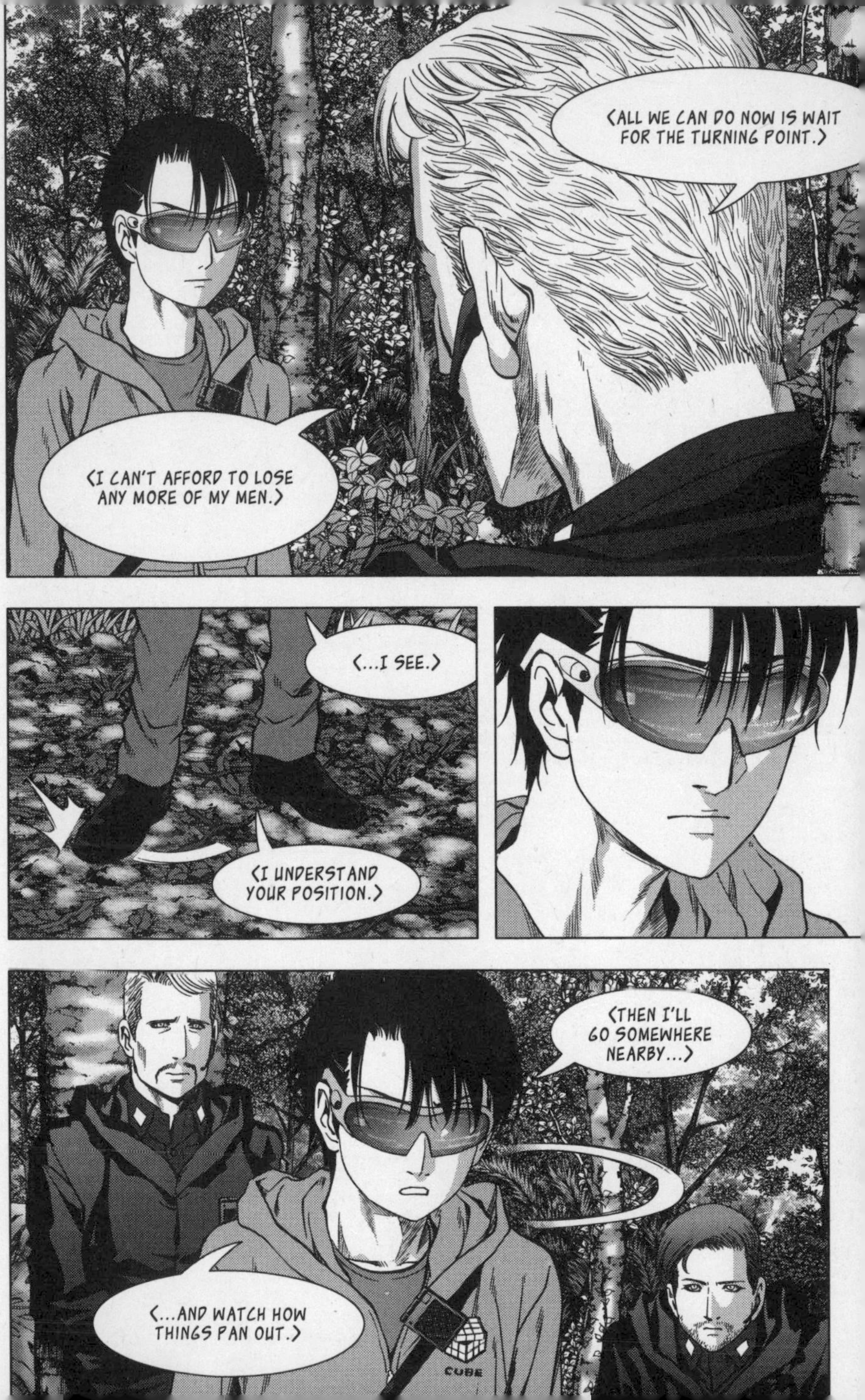
<ALL WE CAN DO NOW IS WAIT FOR THE TURNING POINT.>
<I CAN'T AFFORD TO LOSE ANY MORE OF MY MEN.>
<...I SEE.>
<I UNDERSTAND YOUR POSITION.>
<THEN I'LL GO SOMEWHERE NEARBY...>
<...AND WATCH HOW THINGS PAN OUT.>
CUBE

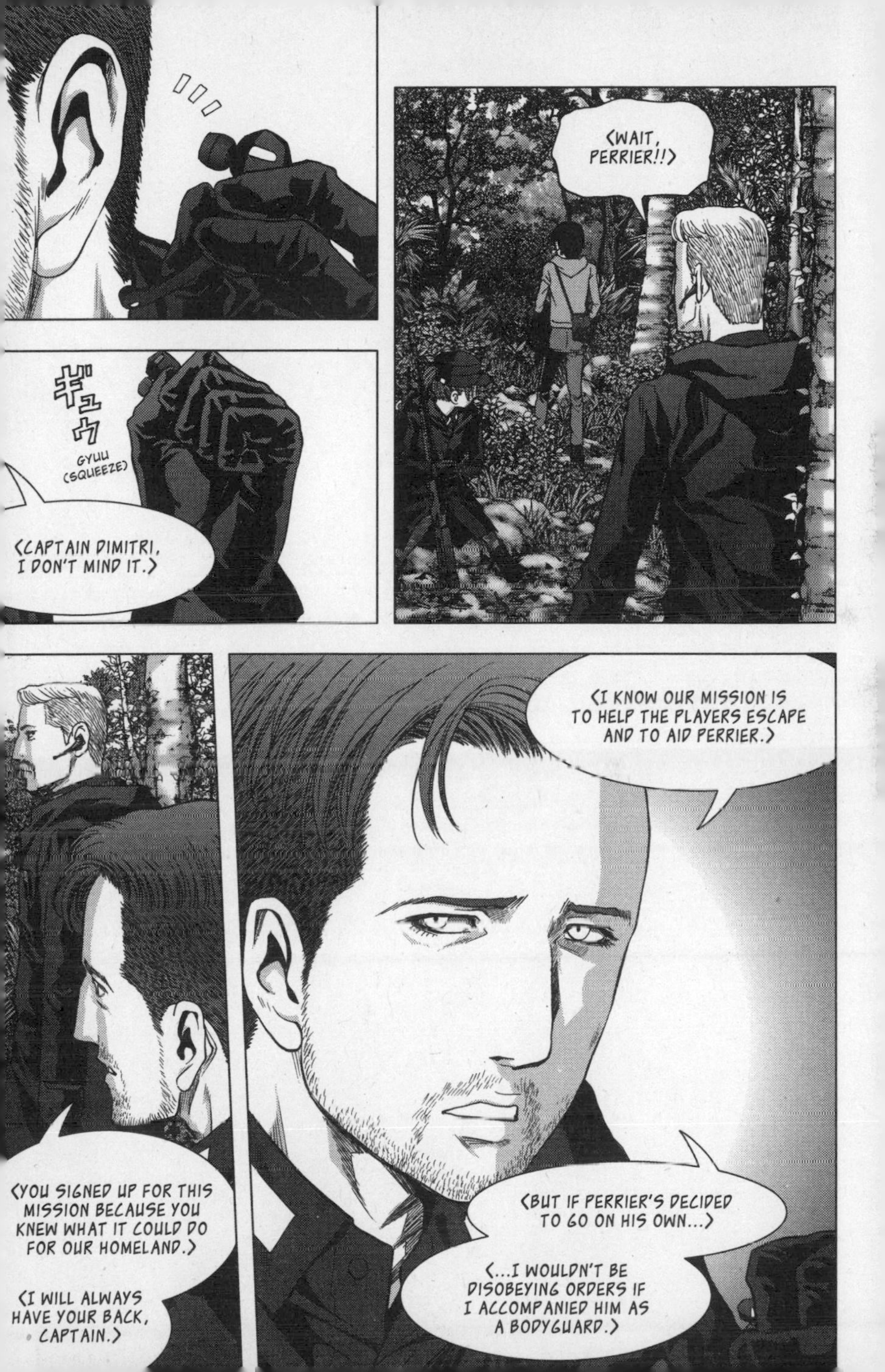
<WAIT, PERRIER!!>
ギュウ
GYUU (SQUEEZE)
<CAPTAIN DIMITRI, I DON'T MIND IT.>
<I KNOW OUR MISSION IS TO HELP THE PLAYERS ESCAPE AND TO AID PERRIER.>
<BUT IF PERRIER'S DECIDED TO GO ON HIS OWN...>
<...I WOULDN'T BE DISOBEYING ORDERS IF I ACCOMPANIED HIM AS A BODYGUARD.>
<YOU SIGNED UP FOR THIS MISSION BECAUSE YOU KNEW WHAT IT COULD DO FOR OUR HOMELAND.>
<I WILL ALWAYS HAVE YOUR BACK, CAPTAIN.>

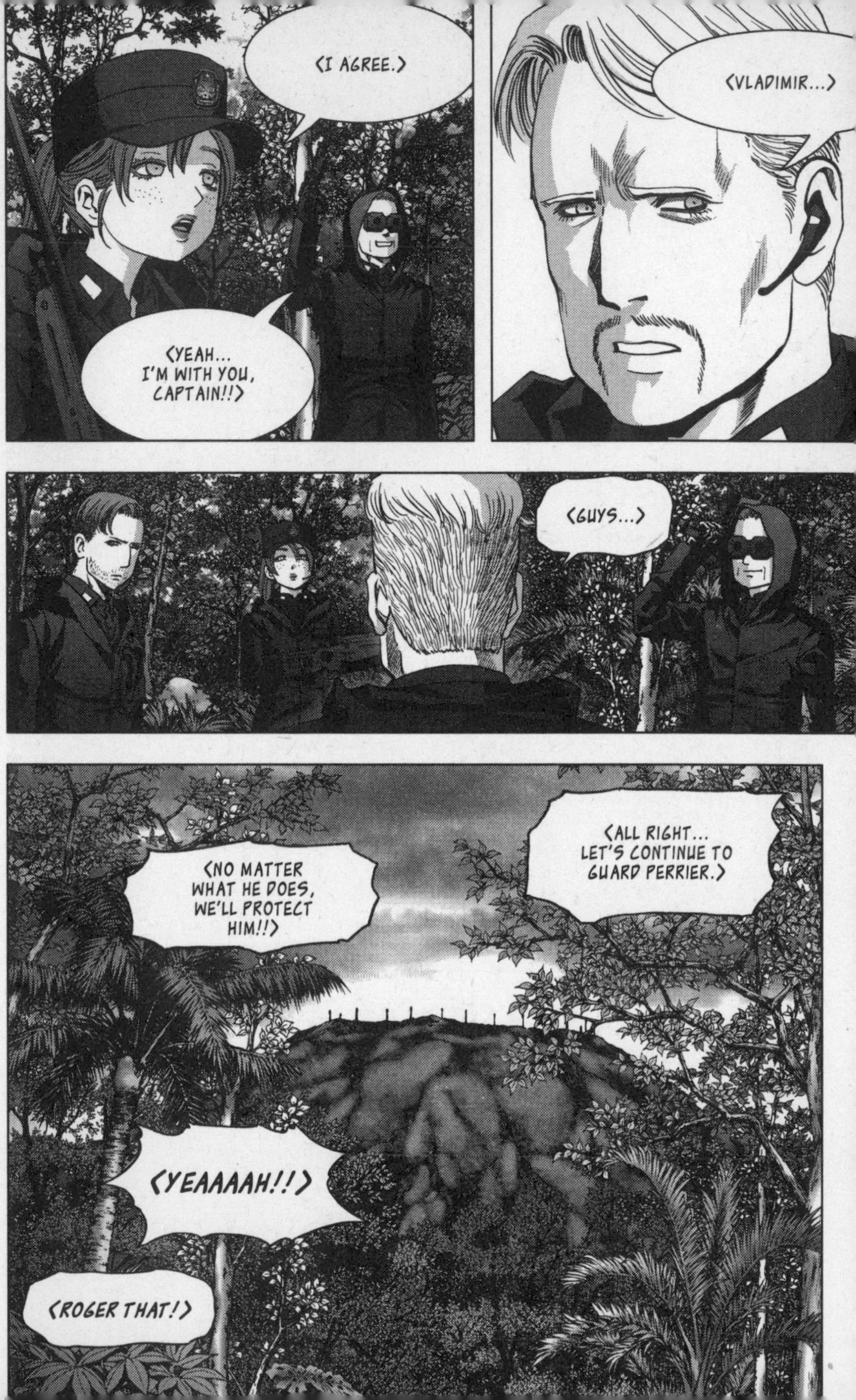
<VLADIMIR...>
<I AGREE.>
<YEAH... I'M WITH YOU, CAPTAIN!!>
<GUYS...>
<ALL RIGHT... LET'S CONTINUE TO GUARD PERRIER.>
<NO MATTER WHAT HE DOES, WE'LL PROTECT HIM!!>
<YEAAAAH!!>
<ROGER THAT!>

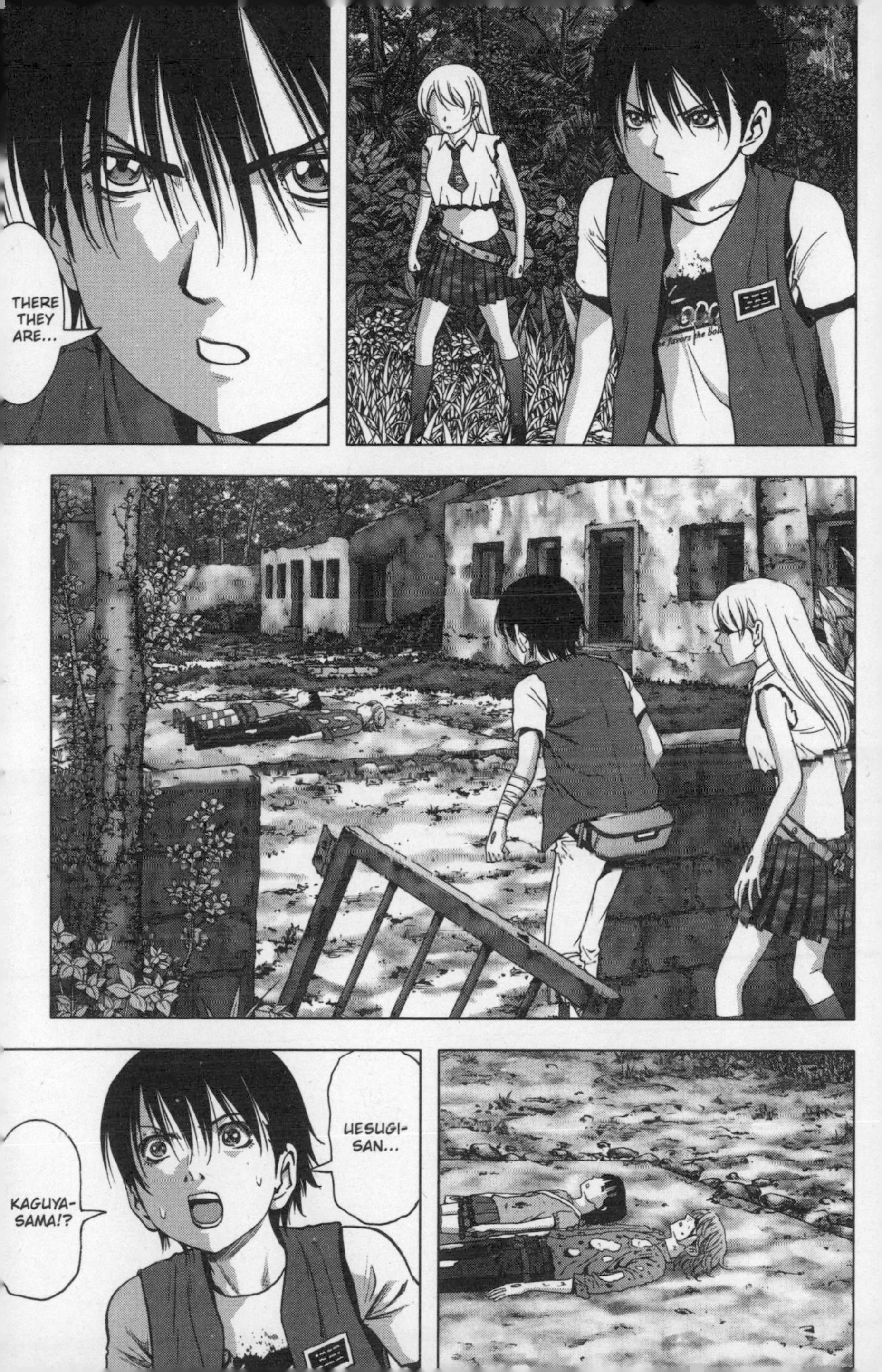
THERE THEY ARE...
UESUGI-SAN...
KAGUYA-SAMA!?

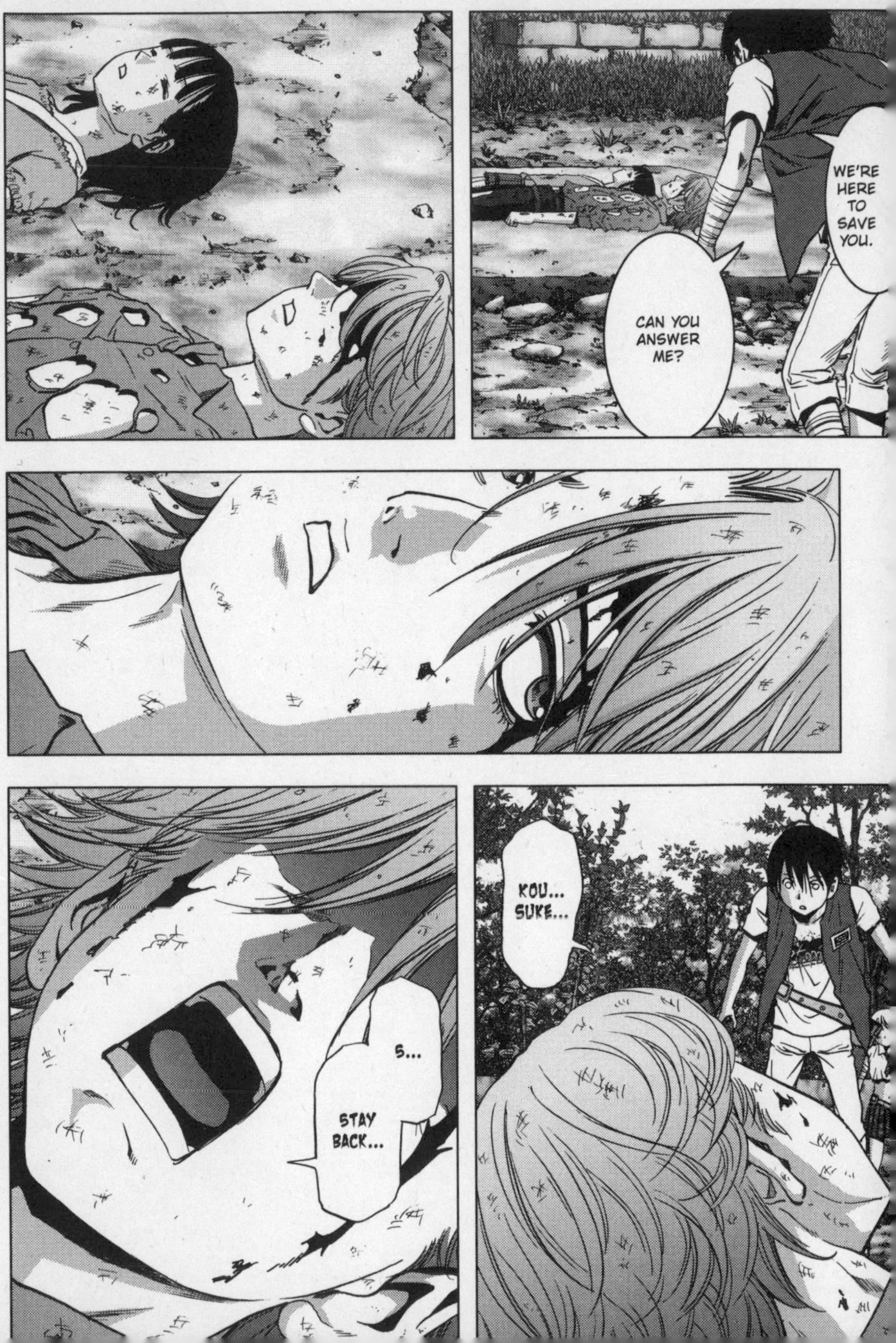
WE'RE HERE TO SAVE YOU.
CAN YOU ANSWER ME?
KOU... SUKE...
S...
STAY BACK...

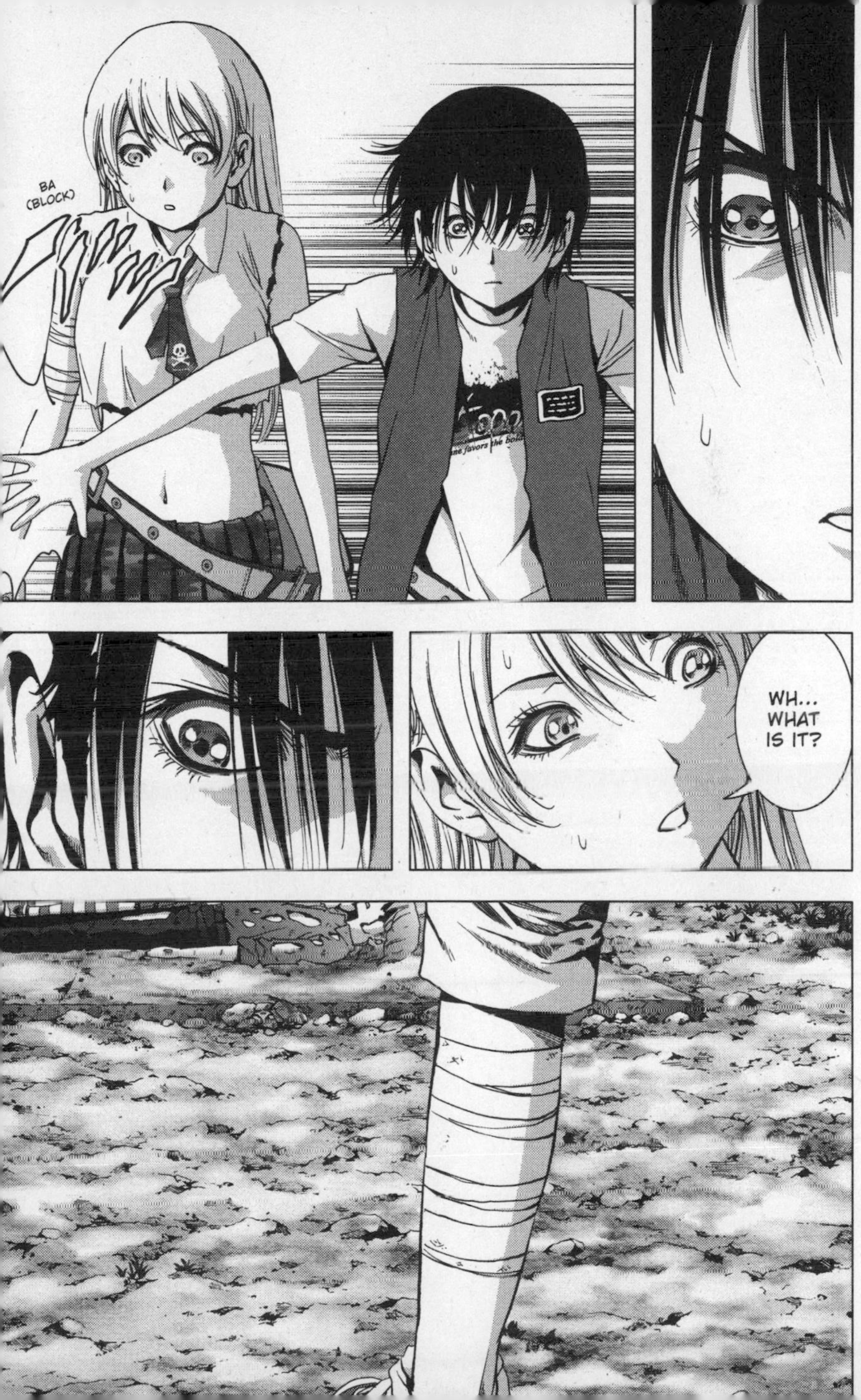
BA (BLOCK)
WH... WHAT IS IT?

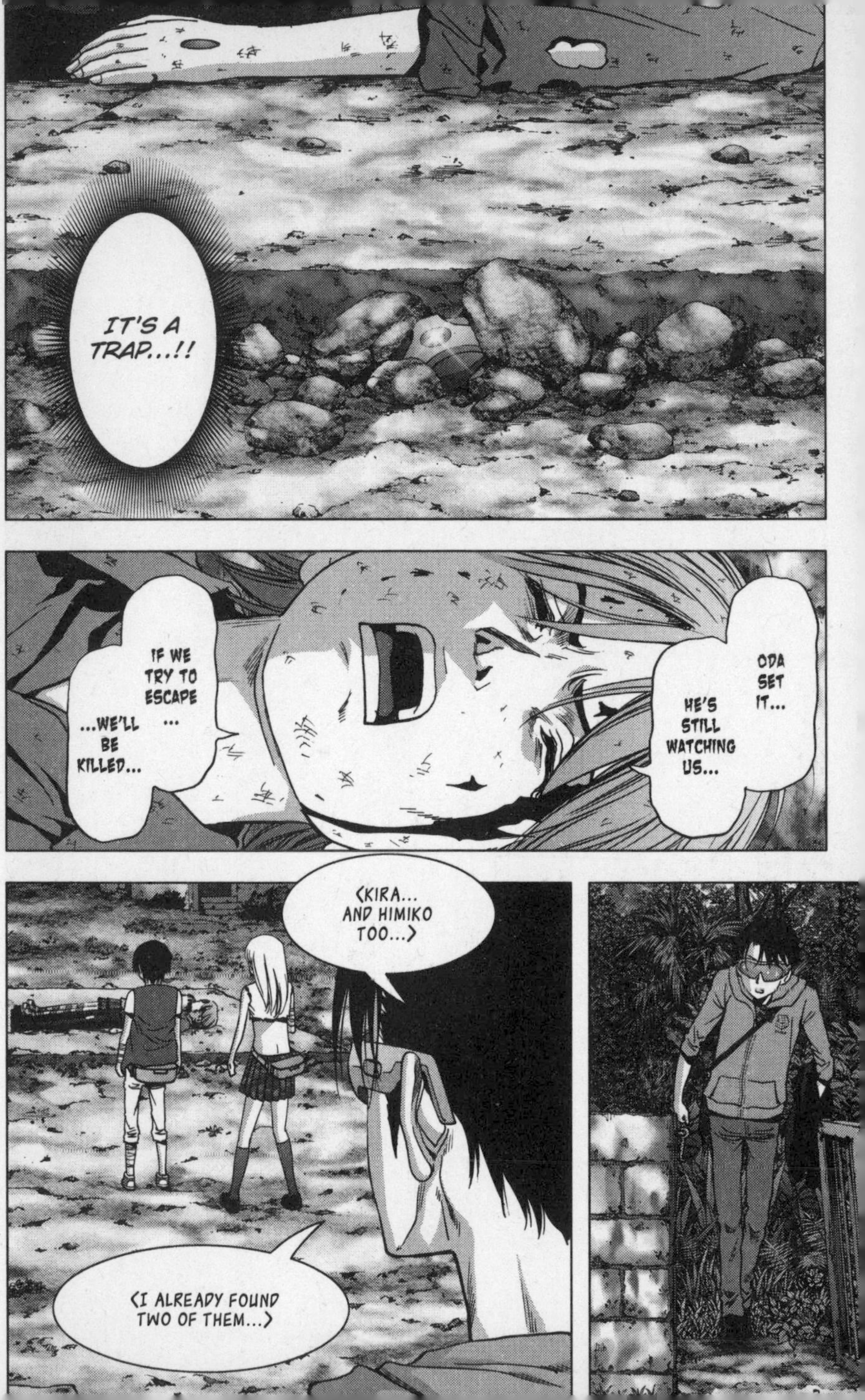
IT'S A TRAP...!!
ODA SET IT...
HE'S STILL WATCHING US...
IF WE TRY TO ESCAPE ...
...WE'LL BE KILLED...
<KIRA... AND HIMIKO TOO...>
<I ALREADY FOUND TWO OF THEM...>

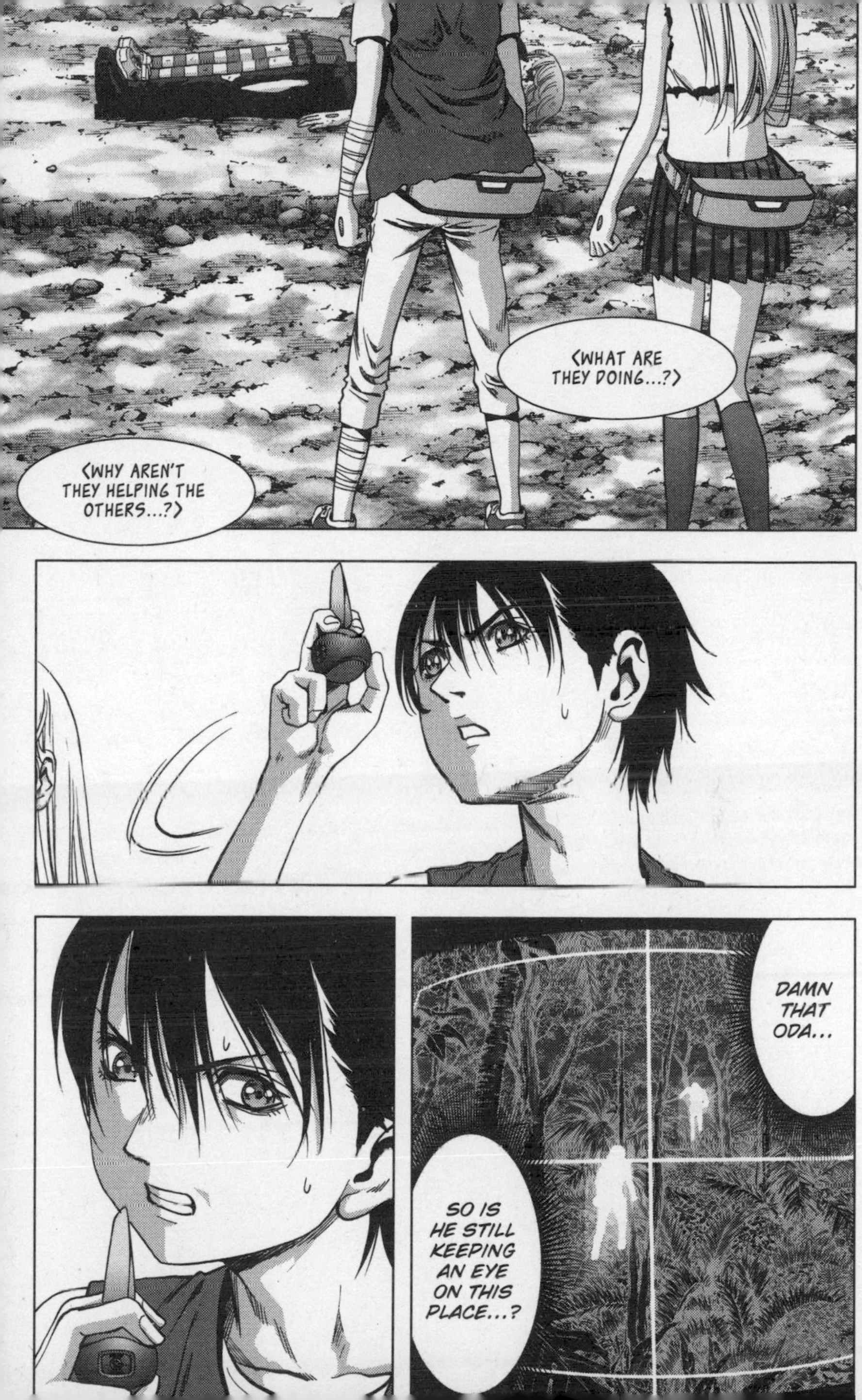
<WHAT ARE THEY DOING...?>
<WHY AREN'T THEY HELPING THE OTHERS...?>
DAMN THAT ODA...
SO IS HE STILL KEEPING AN EYE ON THIS PLACE...?

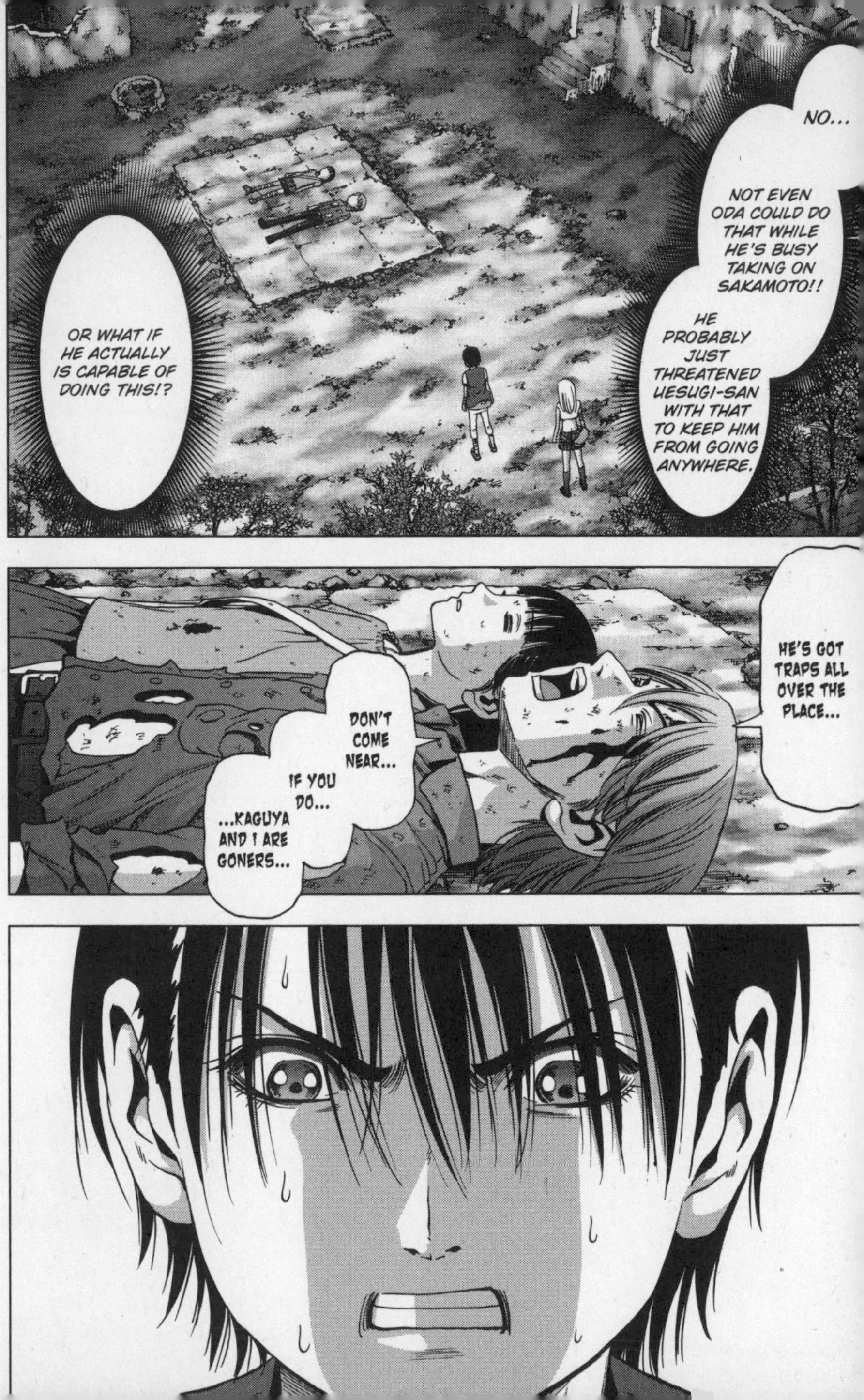

NO...
NOT EVEN ODA COULD DO THAT WHILE HE'S BUSY TAKING ON SAKAMOTO!!
HE PROBABLY JUST THREATENED UESUGI-SAN WITH THAT TO KEEP HIM FROM GOING ANYWHERE.
OR WHAT IF HE ACTUALLY IS CAPABLE OF DOING THIS!?
HE'S GOT TRAPS ALL OVER THE PLACE...
DON'T COME NEAR...
IF YOU DO...
...KAGUYA AND I ARE GONERS...

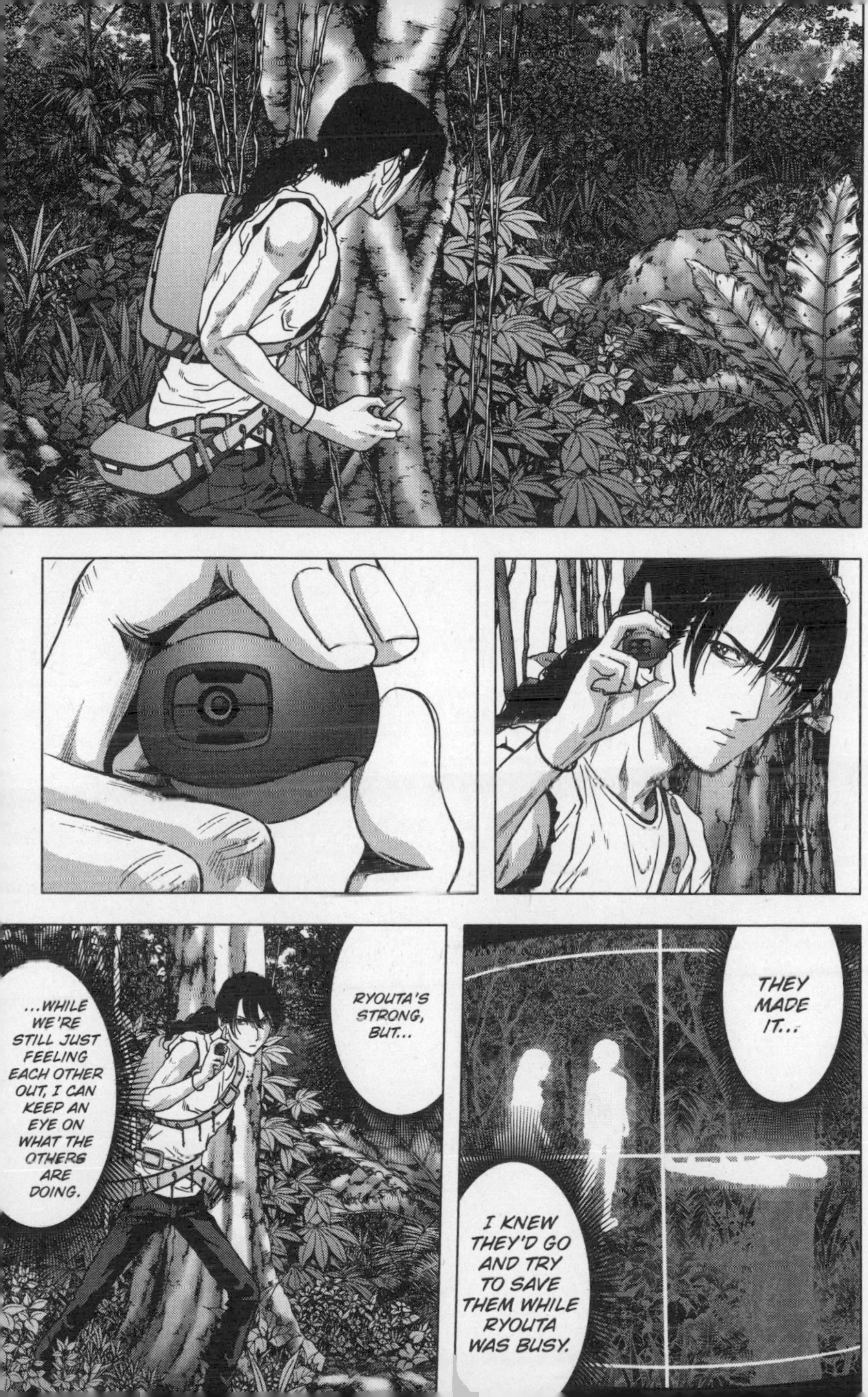
THEY MADE IT...
I KNEW THEY'D GO AND TRY TO SAVE THEM WHILE RYOUTA WAS BUSY.
RYOUTA'S STRONG, BUT...
...WHILE WE'RE STILL JUST FEELING EACH OTHER OUT, I CAN KEEP AN EYE ON WHAT THE OTHERS ARE DOING.

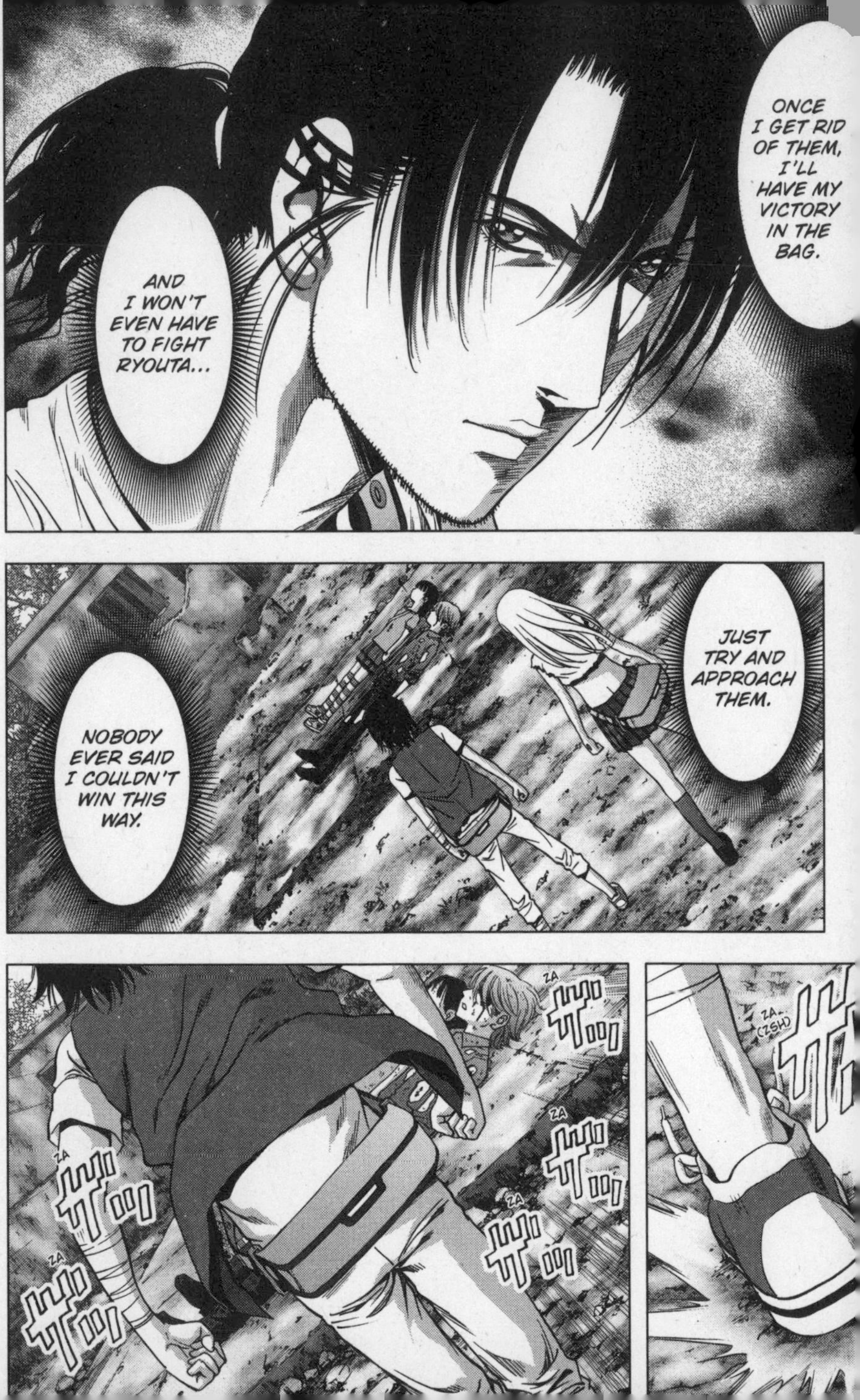
ONCE I GET RID OF THEM, I'LL HAVE MY VICTORY IN THE BAG.
AND I WON'T EVEN HAVE TO FIGHT RYOUTA...
JUST TRY AND APPROACH THEM.
NOBODY EVER SAID I COULDN'T WIN THIS WAY.
ZA (ZSH)
ZA
ZA
ZA
ZA
ZA

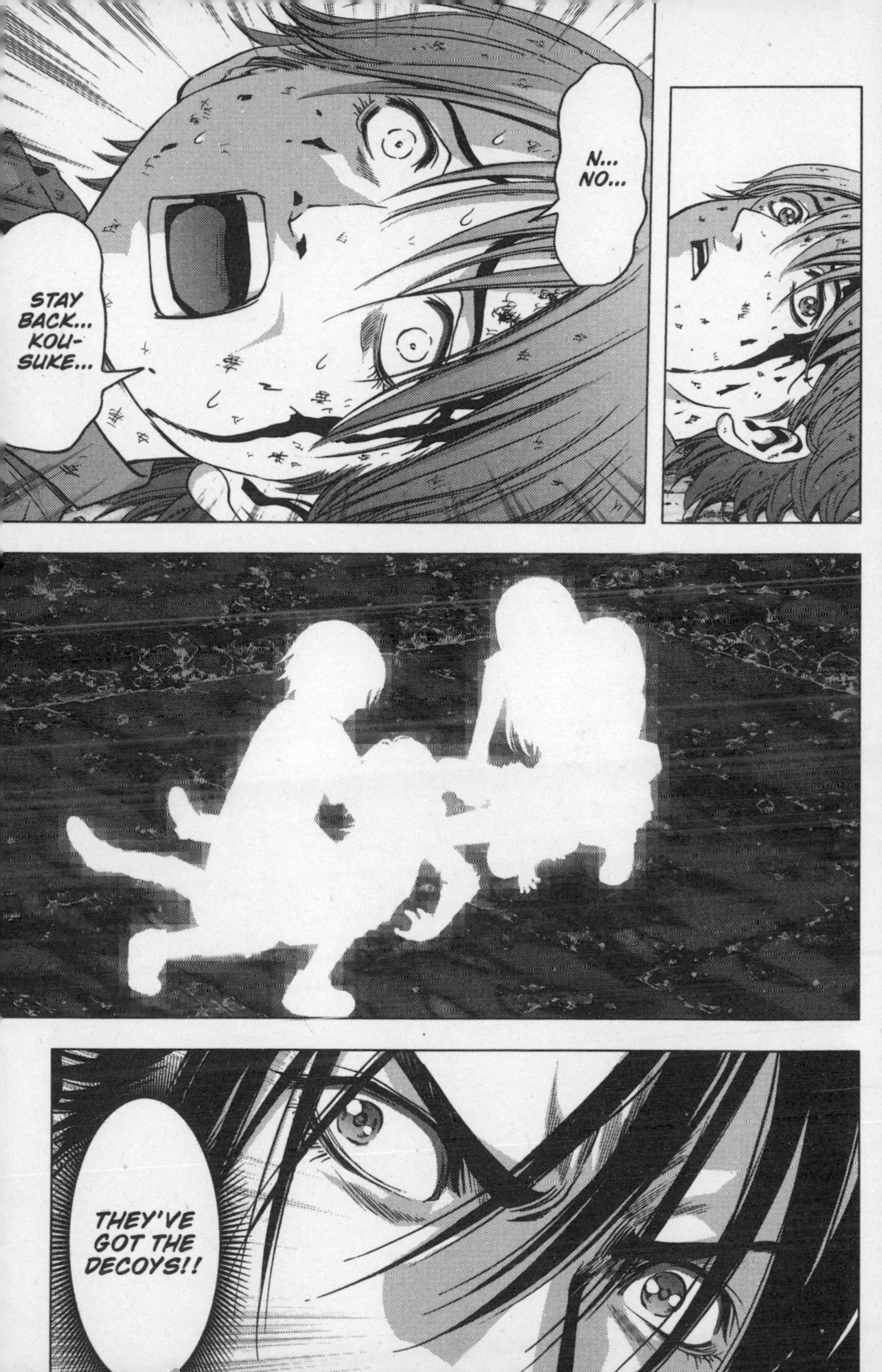
N... NO...
STAY BACK... KOU-SUKE...
THEY'VE GOT THE DECOYS!!

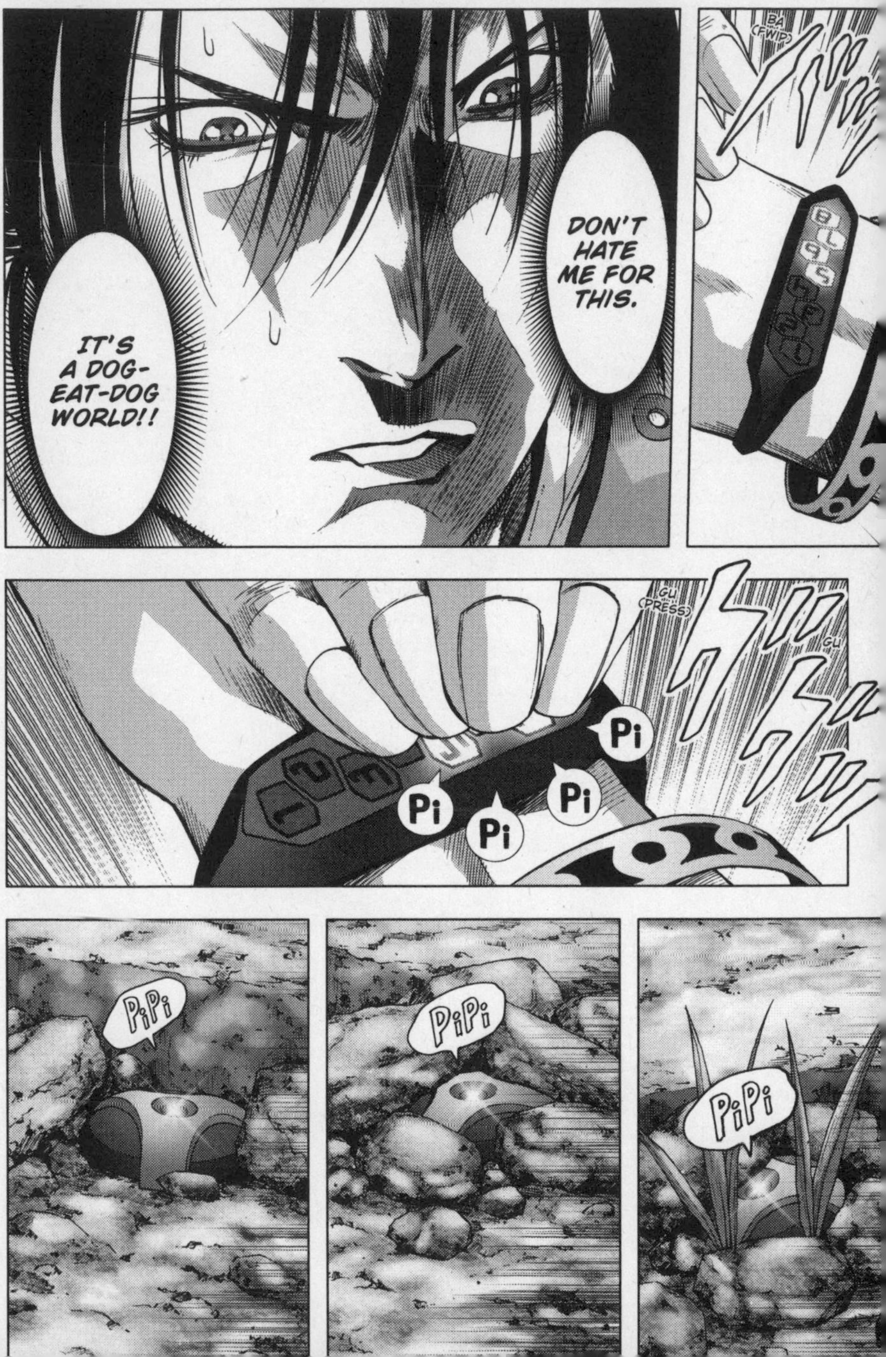
BA (FWIP)
DON'T HATE ME FOR THIS.
IT'S A DOG-EAT-DOG WORLD!!
GU (PRESS)
GU
Pi
Pi
Pi
Pi
PiPi
PiPi
PiPi

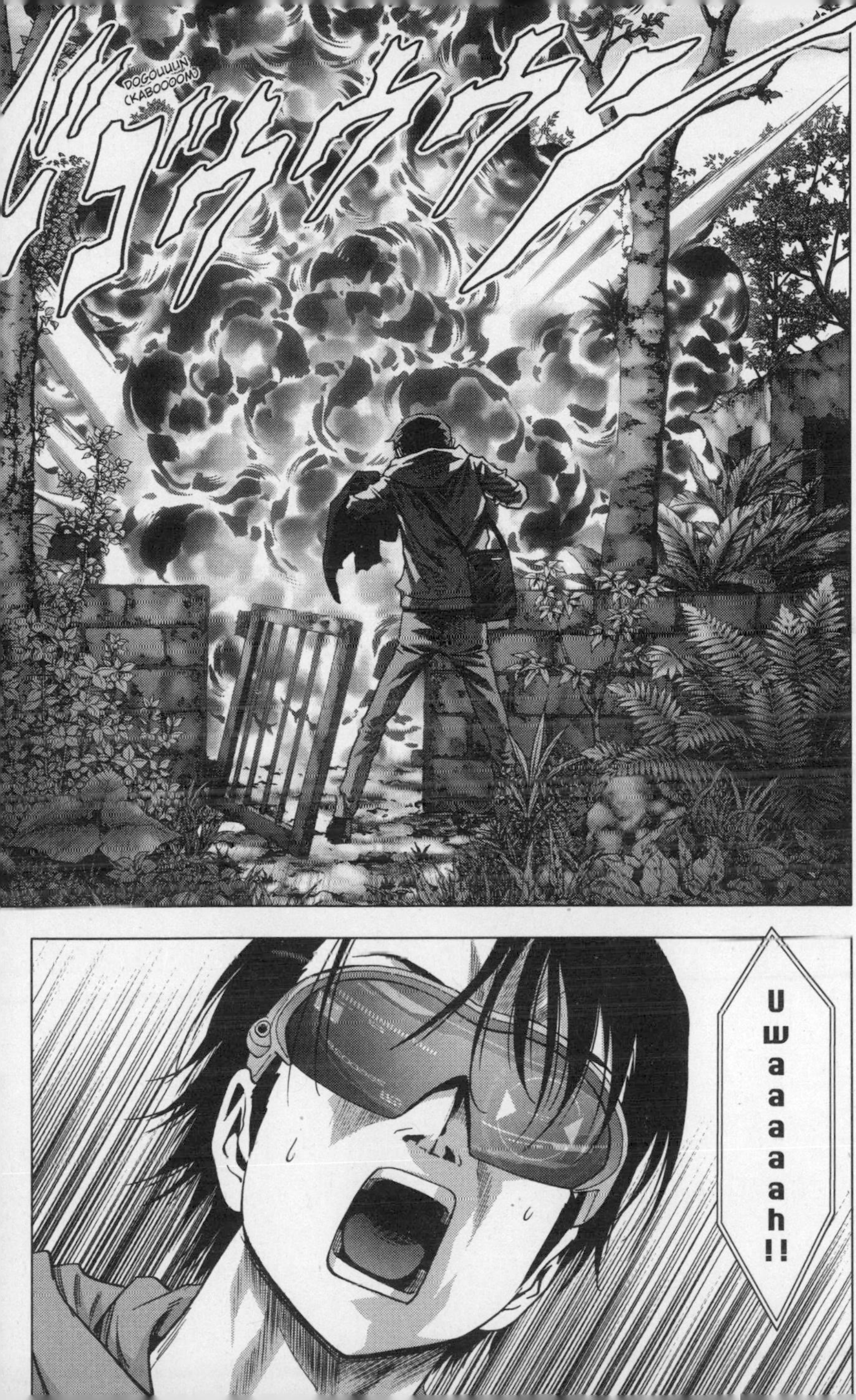
DOGOUUUN (KABOOOOM)
Uwaaaaaah!!

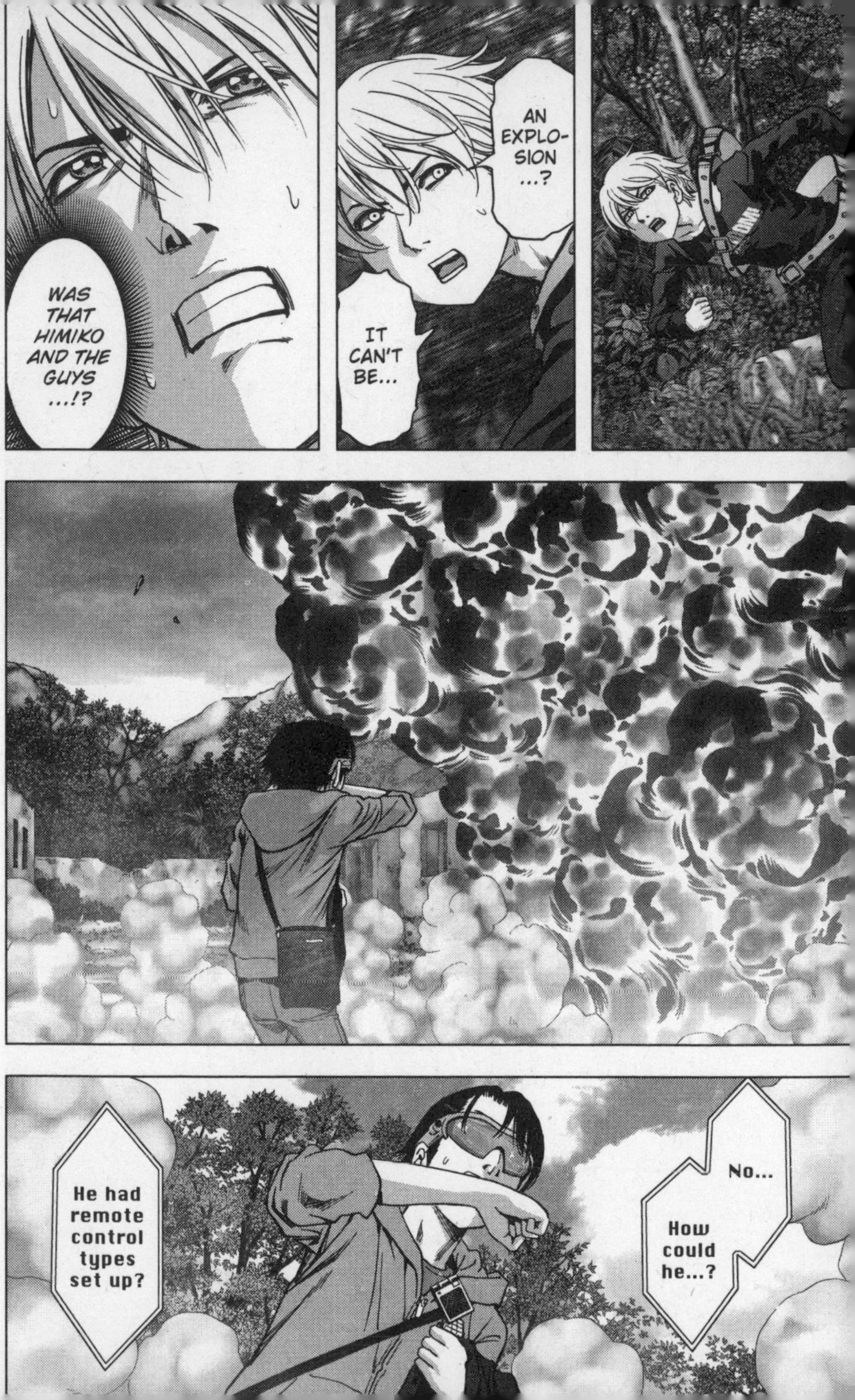
AN EXPLO-SION ...?
IT CAN'T BE...
WAS THAT HIMIKO AND THE GUYS ...!?
No...
How could he...?
He had remote control types set up?

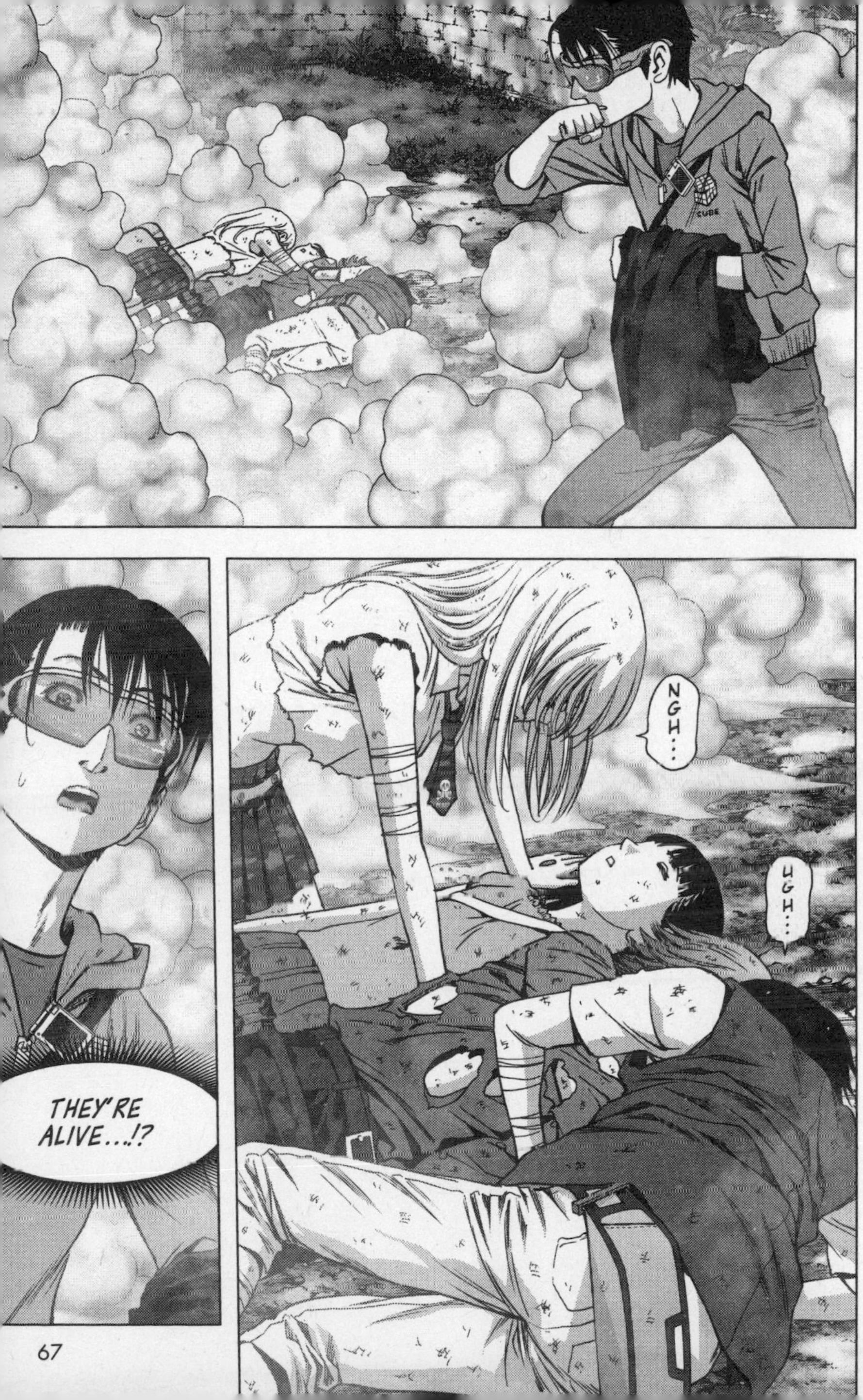
NGH...
UGH...
THEY'RE ALIVE...!?

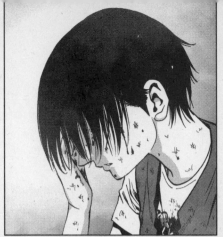

IS EVERY-ONE OKAY...!?

HOW DID YOU SURVIVE THAT!?

I DIDN'T KNOW WHEN HE MIGHT SPOT US AND DETONATE HIS BIMS...

SO IT WAS ALL IN ONE SECOND...

I MADE A GAMBLE ON ONE SINGLE SECOND.

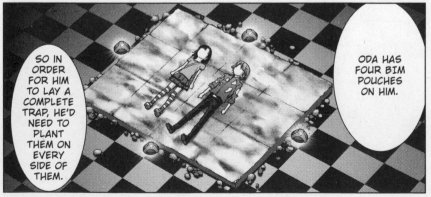

ODA HAS FOUR BIM POUCHES ON HIM.

SO IN ORDER FOR HIM TO LAY A COMPLETE TRAP, HE'D NEED TO PLANT THEM ON EVERY SIDE OF THEM.

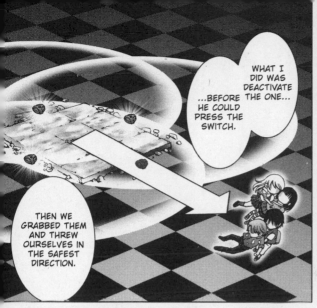

BUT ONCE I FOUND ONE OF THEM, I WAS ABLE TO SECURE A SAFE ROUTE FOR US.
PiPiPu-!
WHAT I DID WAS DEACTIVATE THE ONE...
...BEFORE HE COULD PRESS THE SWITCH.
THEN WE GRABBED THEM AND THREW OURSELVES IN THE SAFEST DIRECTION.
ONLY NUMBER FIVE IS STILL BLINKING...
DID IT GET DEACTIVATED AHEAD OF TIME...!?
I DID IT...
I FINALLY SAVED A LIFE...

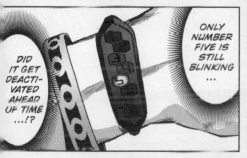

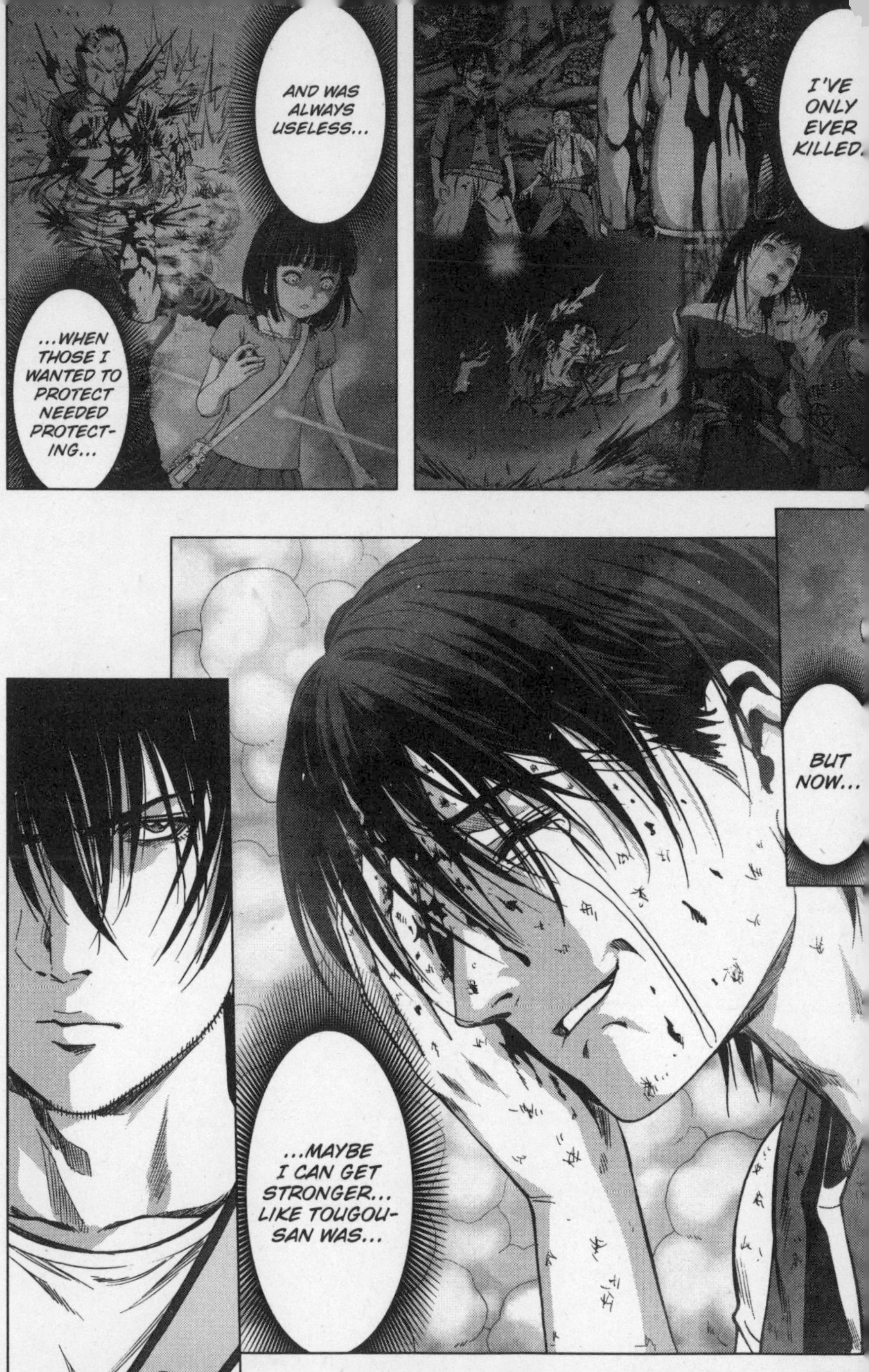
I'VE ONLY EVER KILLED.
AND WAS ALWAYS USELESS...
...WHEN THOSE I WANTED TO PROTECT NEEDED PROTECTING...
BUT NOW...
...MAYBE I CAN GET STRONGER... LIKE TOUGOU-SAN WAS...

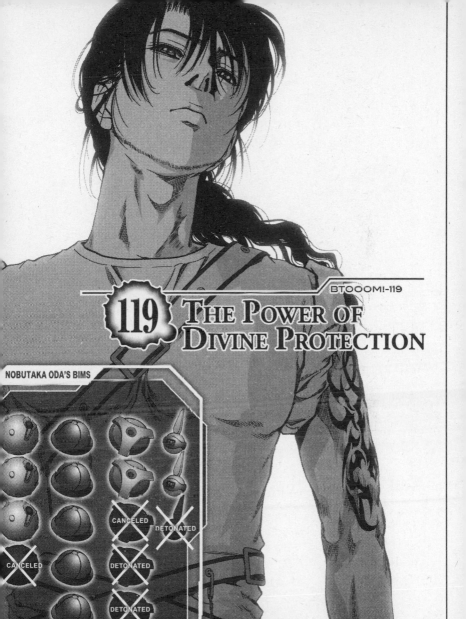

119 THE POWER OF DIVINE PROTECTION

NOBUTAKA ODA'S BIMS

CANCELED

DETONATED

CANCELED

DETONATED

DETONATED

DETONATED

ESTIMATE

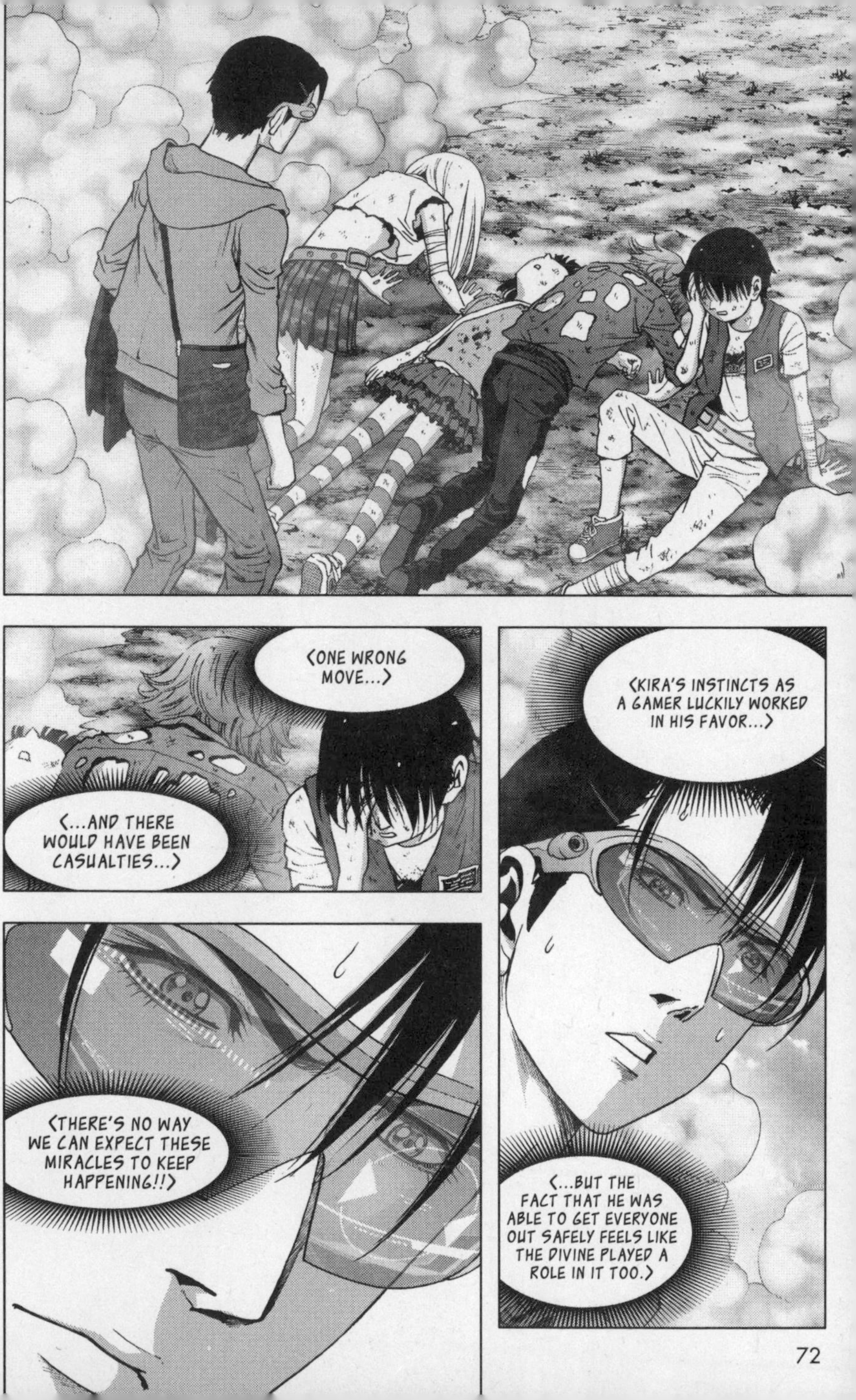

⟨KIRA'S INSTINCTS AS A GAMER LUCKILY WORKED IN HIS FAVOR...⟩
⟨...BUT THE FACT THAT HE WAS ABLE TO GET EVERYONE OUT SAFELY FEELS LIKE THE DIVINE PLAYED A ROLE IN IT TOO.⟩
⟨ONE WRONG MOVE...⟩
⟨...AND THERE WOULD HAVE BEEN CASUALTIES...⟩
⟨THERE'S NO WAY WE CAN EXPECT THESE MIRACLES TO KEEP HAPPENING!!⟩

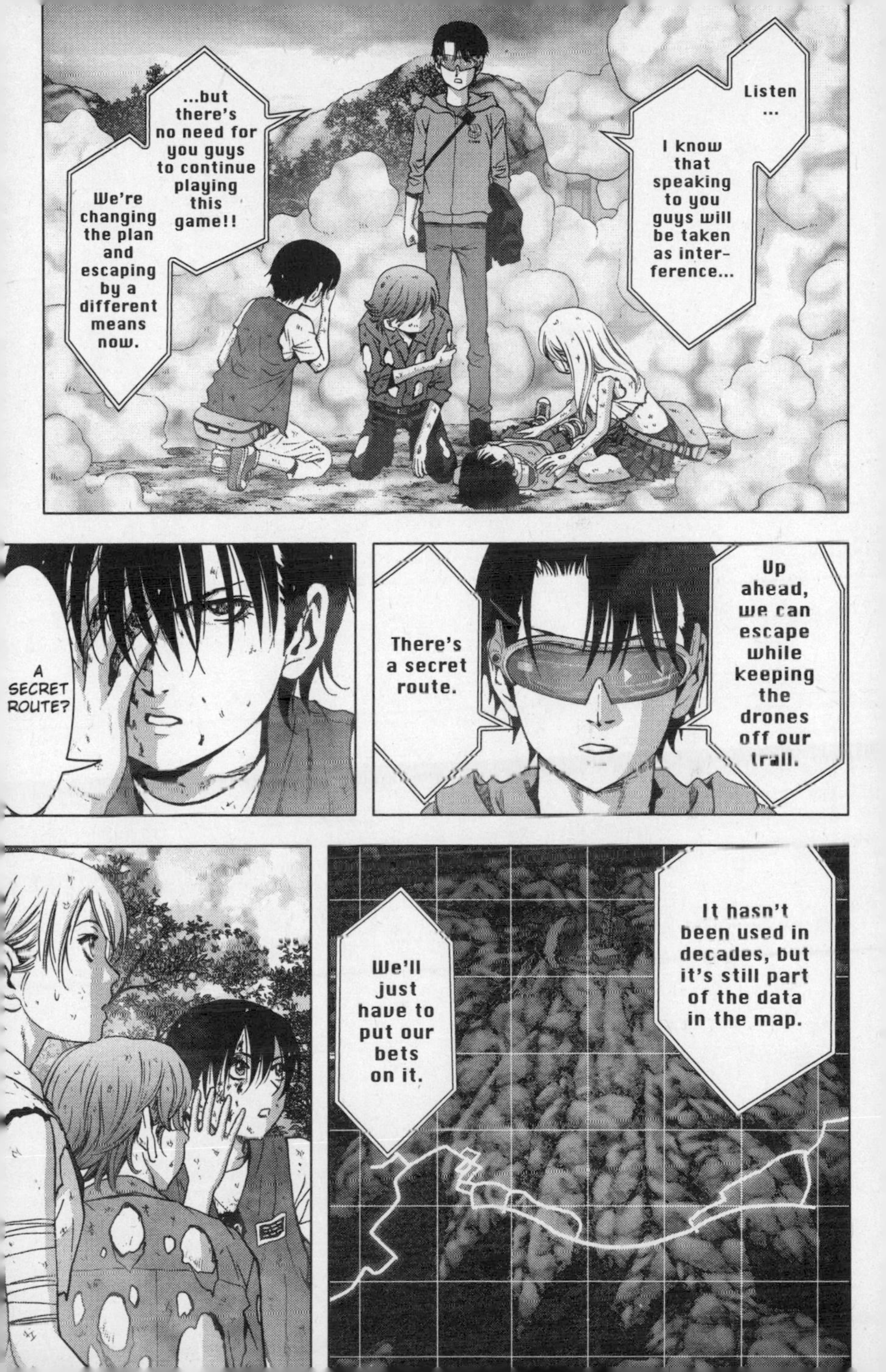
Listen ...
I know that speaking to you guys will be taken as interference...
...but there's no need for you guys to continue playing this game!!
We're changing the plan and escaping by a different means now.
Up ahead, we can escape while keeping the drones off our trail.
There's a secret route.
A SECRET ROUTE?
It hasn't been used in decades, but it's still part of the data in the map.
We'll just have to put our bets on it.

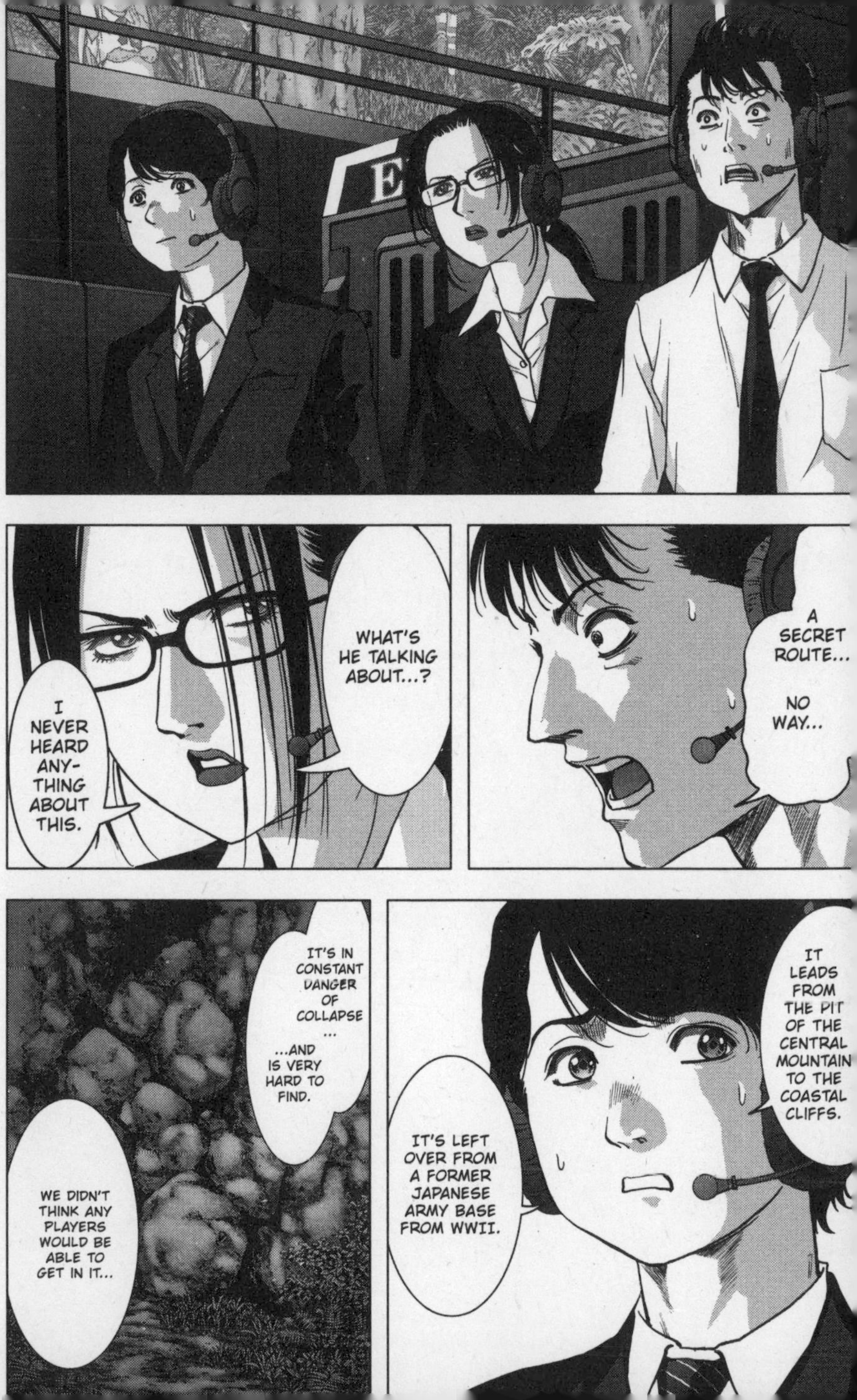
A SECRET ROUTE...
NO WAY...
WHAT'S HE TALKING ABOUT...?
I NEVER HEARD ANYTHING ABOUT THIS.
IT LEADS FROM THE PIT OF THE CENTRAL MOUNTAIN TO THE COASTAL CLIFFS.
IT'S LEFT OVER FROM A FORMER JAPANESE ARMY BASE FROM WWII.
IT'S IN CONSTANT DANGER OF COLLAPSE...
...AND IS VERY HARD TO FIND.
WE DIDN'T THINK ANY PLAYERS WOULD BE ABLE TO GET IN IT...

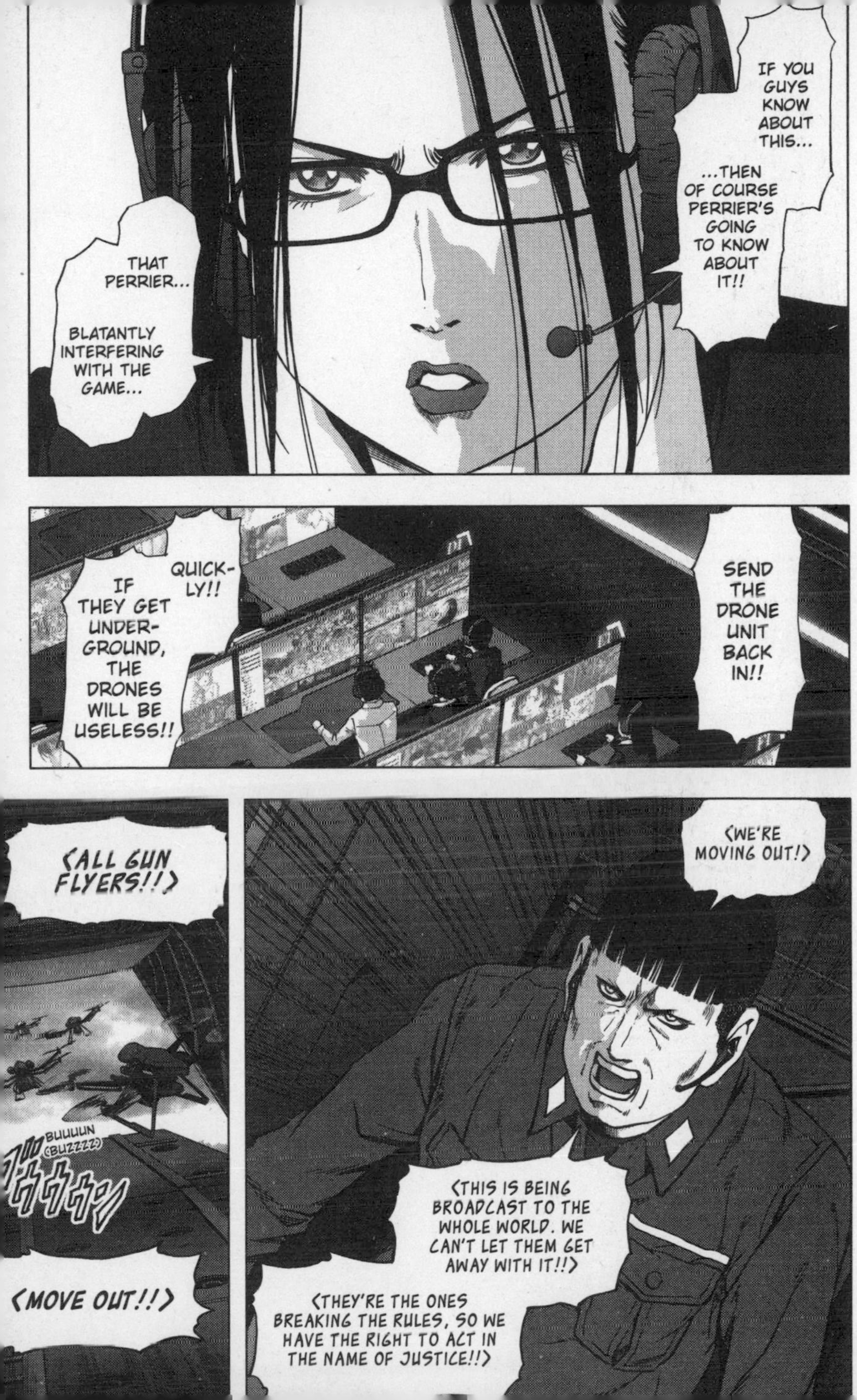
IF YOU GUYS KNOW ABOUT THIS...
...THEN OF COURSE PERRIER'S GOING TO KNOW ABOUT IT!!
THAT PERRIER...
BLATANTLY INTERFERING WITH THE GAME...
SEND THE DRONE UNIT BACK IN!!
QUICKLY!!
IF THEY GET UNDERGROUND, THE DRONES WILL BE USELESS!!
〈WE'RE MOVING OUT!〉
〈THIS IS BEING BROADCAST TO THE WHOLE WORLD. WE CAN'T LET THEM GET AWAY WITH IT!!〉
〈THEY'RE THE ONES BREAKING THE RULES, SO WE HAVE THE RIGHT TO ACT IN THE NAME OF JUSTICE!!〉
〈ALL GUN FLYERS!!〉
BUUUUN (BUZZZZ)
〈MOVE OUT!!〉

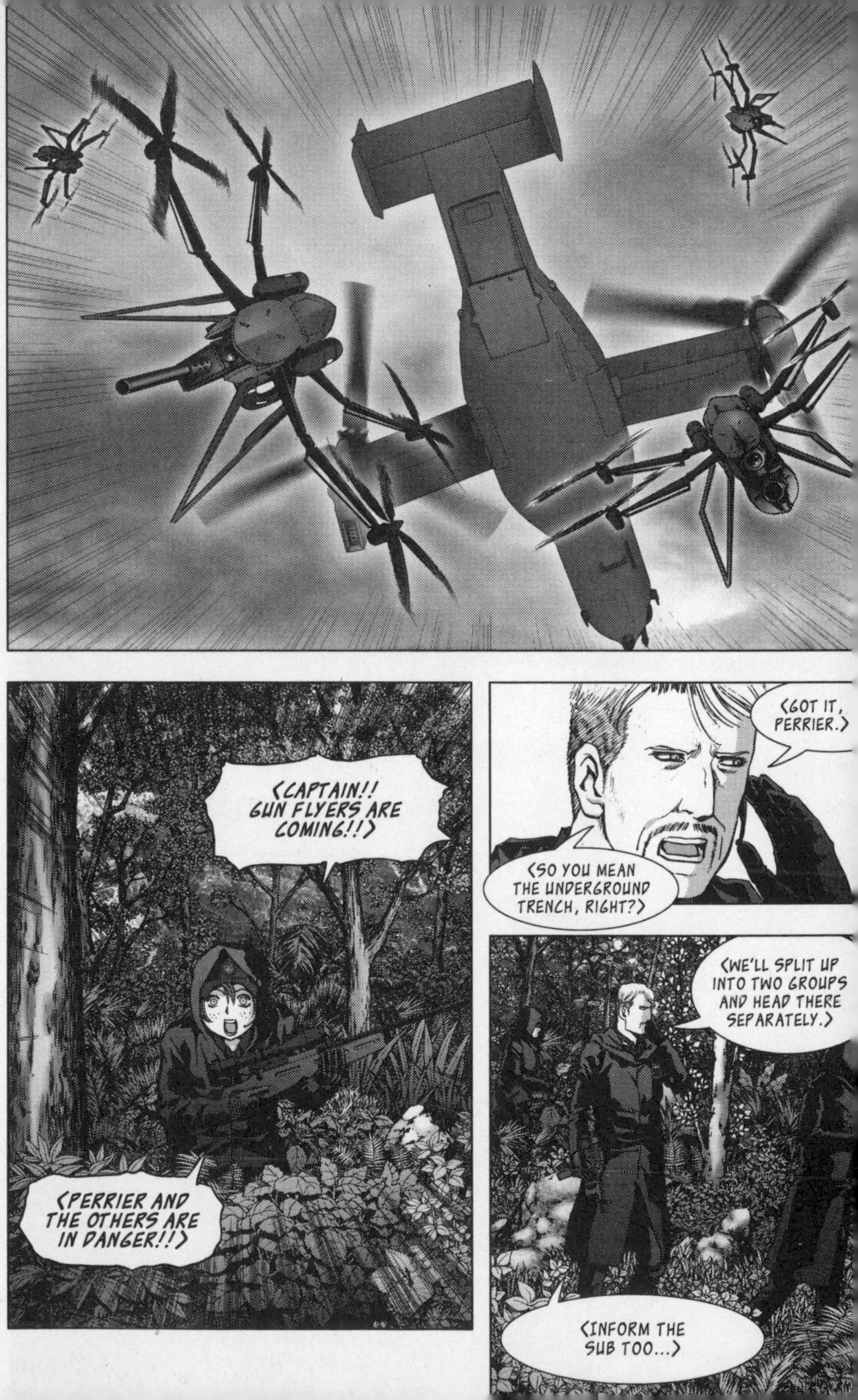

⟨GOT IT, PERRIER.⟩
⟨SO YOU MEAN THE UNDERGROUND TRENCH, RIGHT?⟩
⟨WE'LL SPLIT UP INTO TWO GROUPS AND HEAD THERE SEPARATELY.⟩
⟨INFORM THE SUB TOO...⟩
⟨CAPTAIN!! GUN FLYERS ARE COMING!!⟩
⟨PERRIER AND THE OTHERS ARE IN DANGER!!⟩

⟨WHAT!?⟩

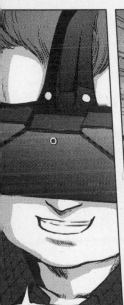

ブゥゥゥン
BUUUUN
⟨BUZZZZ⟩

⟨PERRIER HAS
BEEN SPOTTED!!
THOSE TEN
MILLION DOLLARS
ARE MINE!!⟩

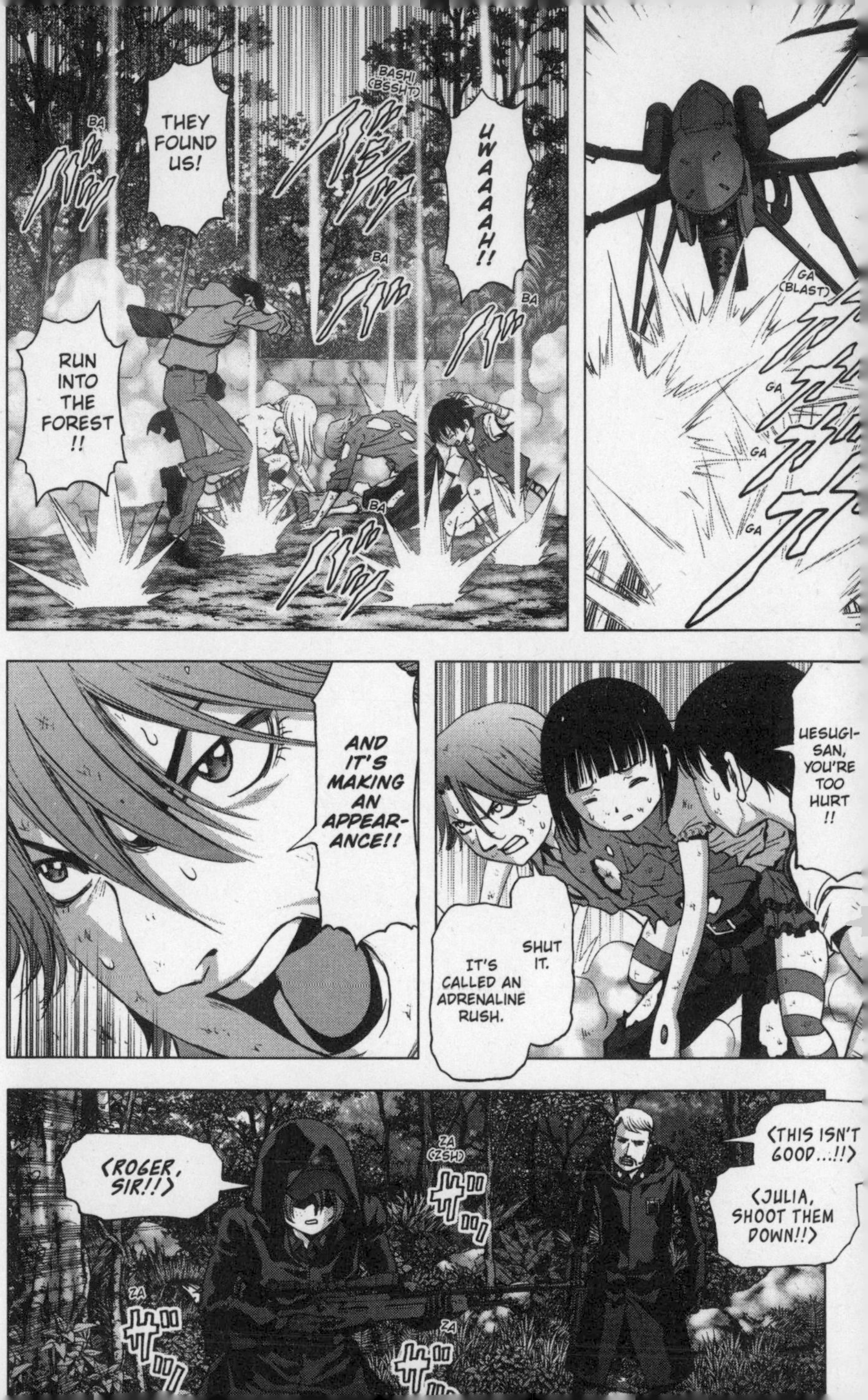
GA (BLAST)
GA
GA
GA
BASHI (BSSHT)
UWAAAAAH!!
THEY FOUND US!
BA
BA
BA
RUN INTO THE FOREST!!
BA
UESUGI-SAN, YOU'RE TOO HURT!!
SHUT IT.
IT'S CALLED AN ADRENALINE RUSH.
AND IT'S MAKING AN APPEARANCE!!
<THIS ISN'T GOOD...!!>
<JULIA, SHOOT THEM DOWN!!>
ZA (ZSH)
<ROGER, SIR!!>
ZA
ZA

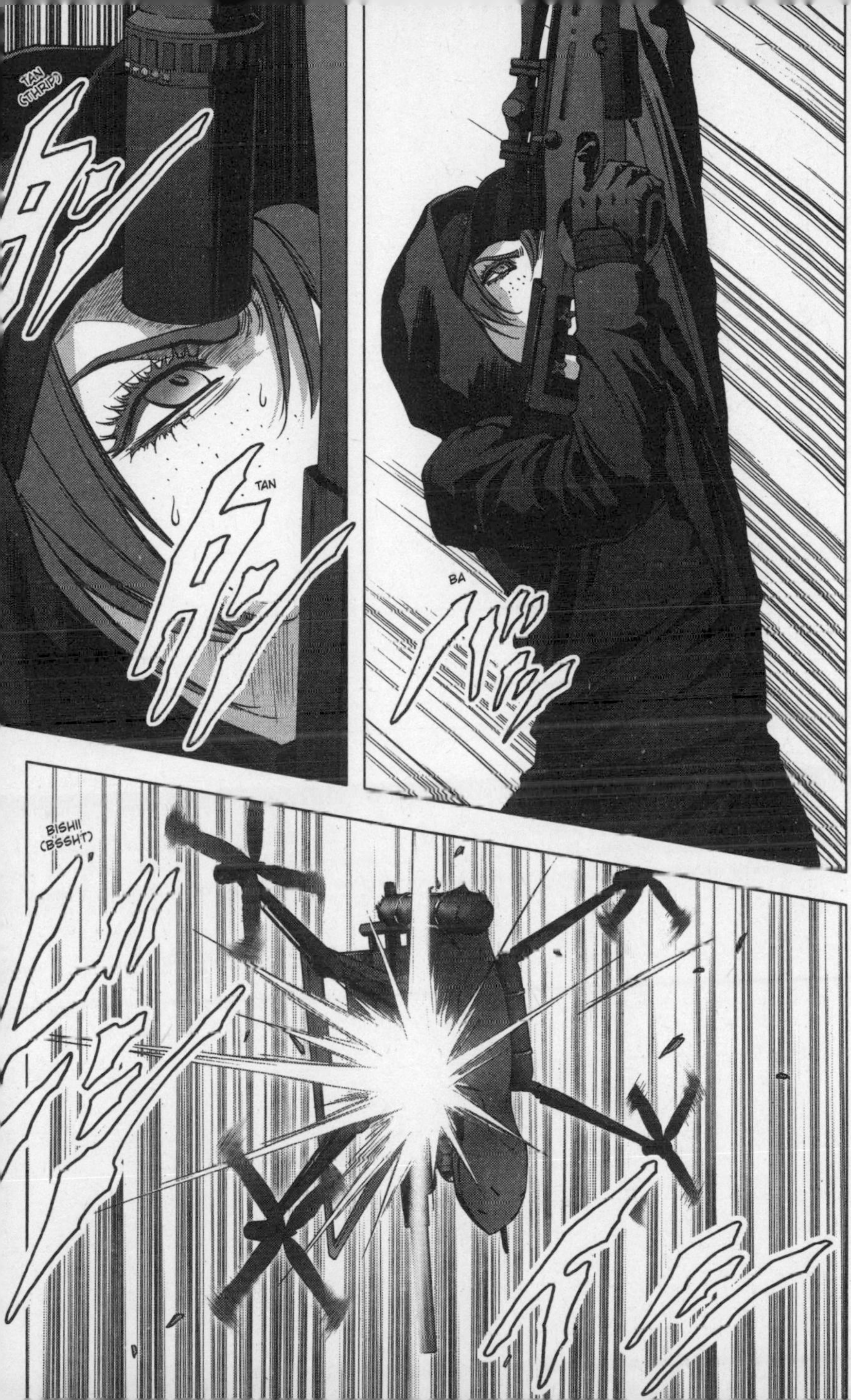
BA
TAN
(THRIP)
TAN
BISHI
(BSSHT)

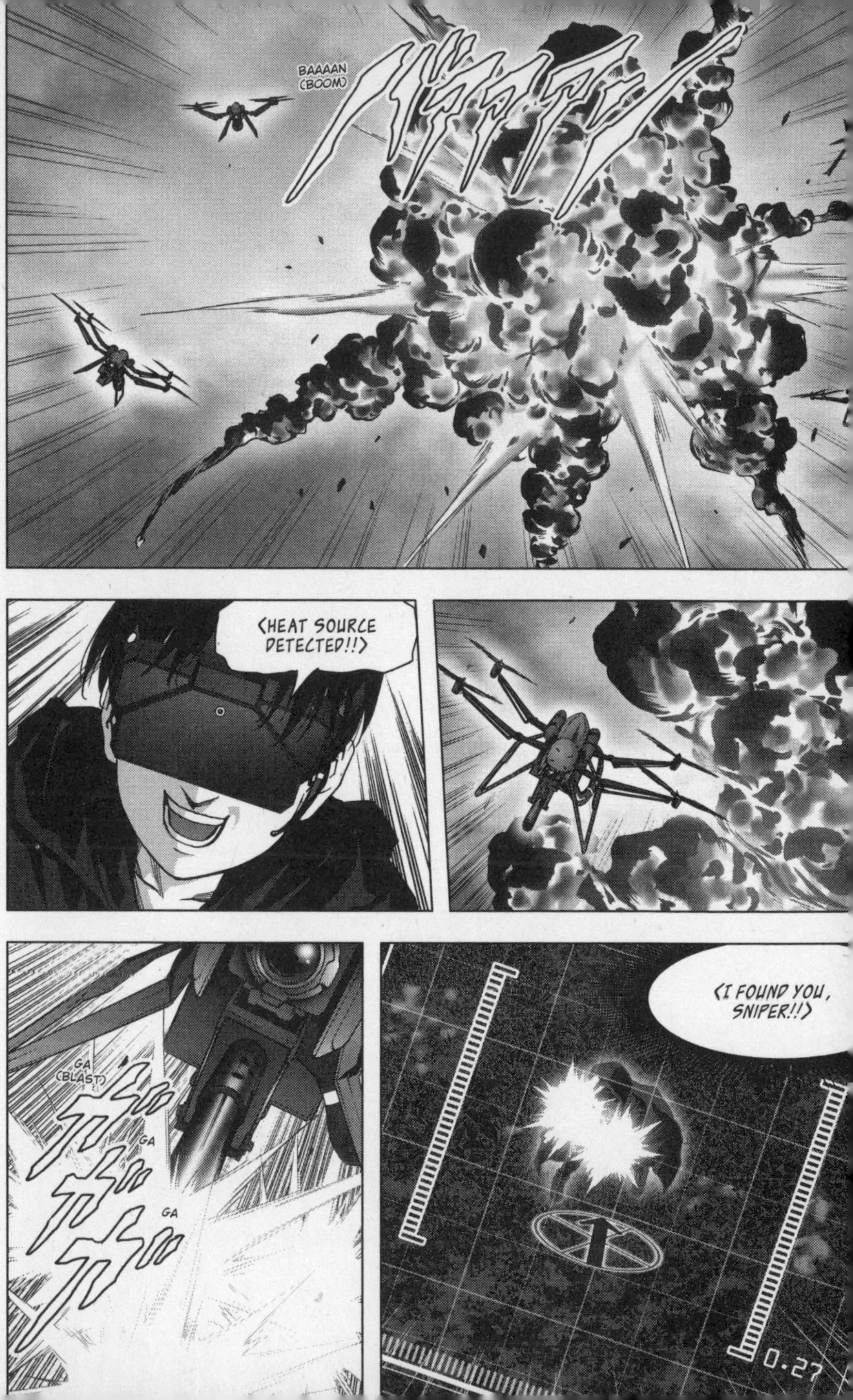
BAAAAN (BOOM)
<HEAT SOURCE DETECTED!!>
<I FOUND YOU, SNIPER!!>
0.27
GA (BLAST)
GA
GA

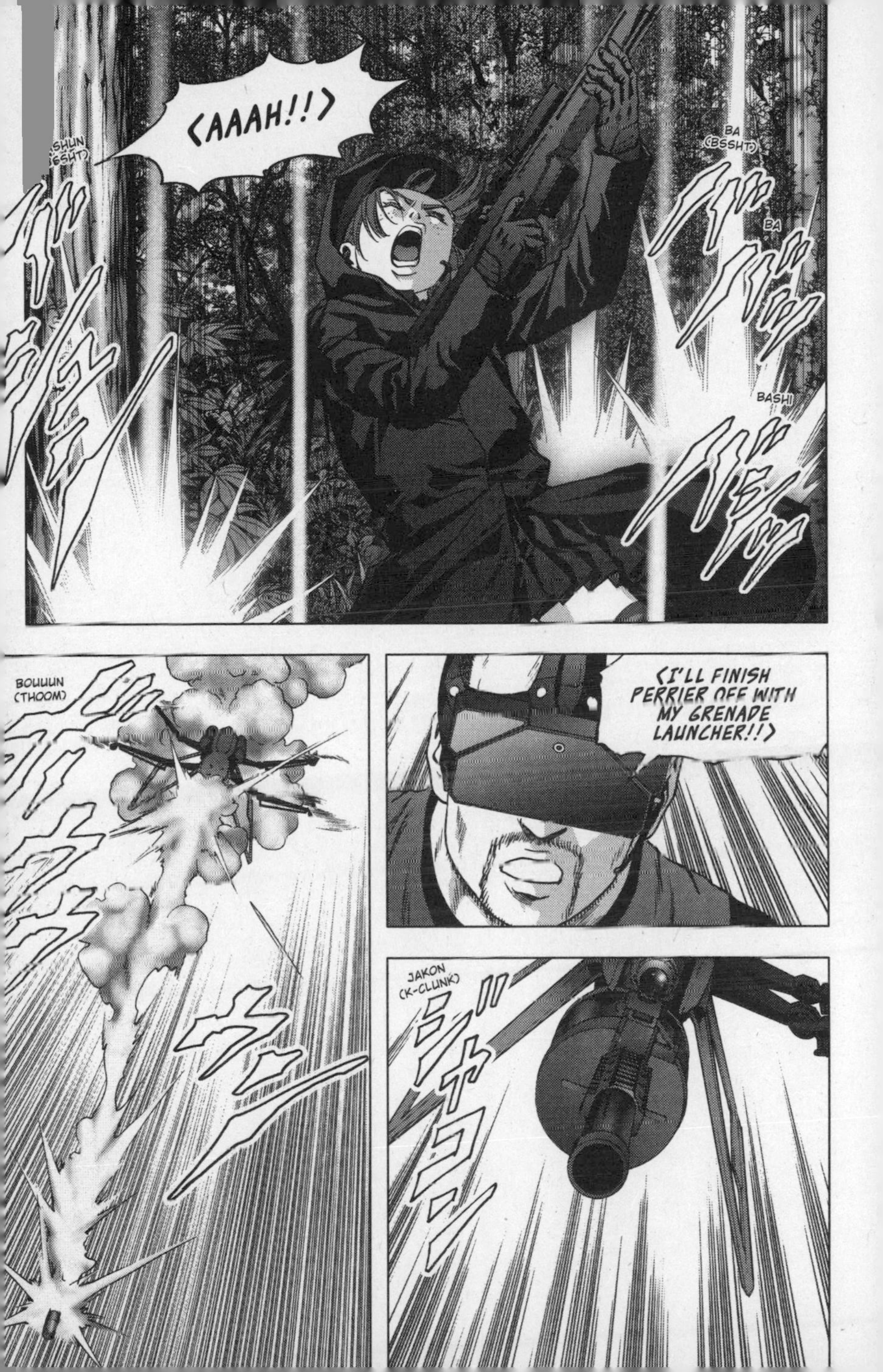
BA (BSSHT)
BA
BASHI
<AAAH!!>
ASHUN
SSHT)
<I'LL FINISH PERRIER OFF WITH MY GRENADE LAUNCHER!!>
JAKON (K-CLUNK)
BOUUUN (THOOM)

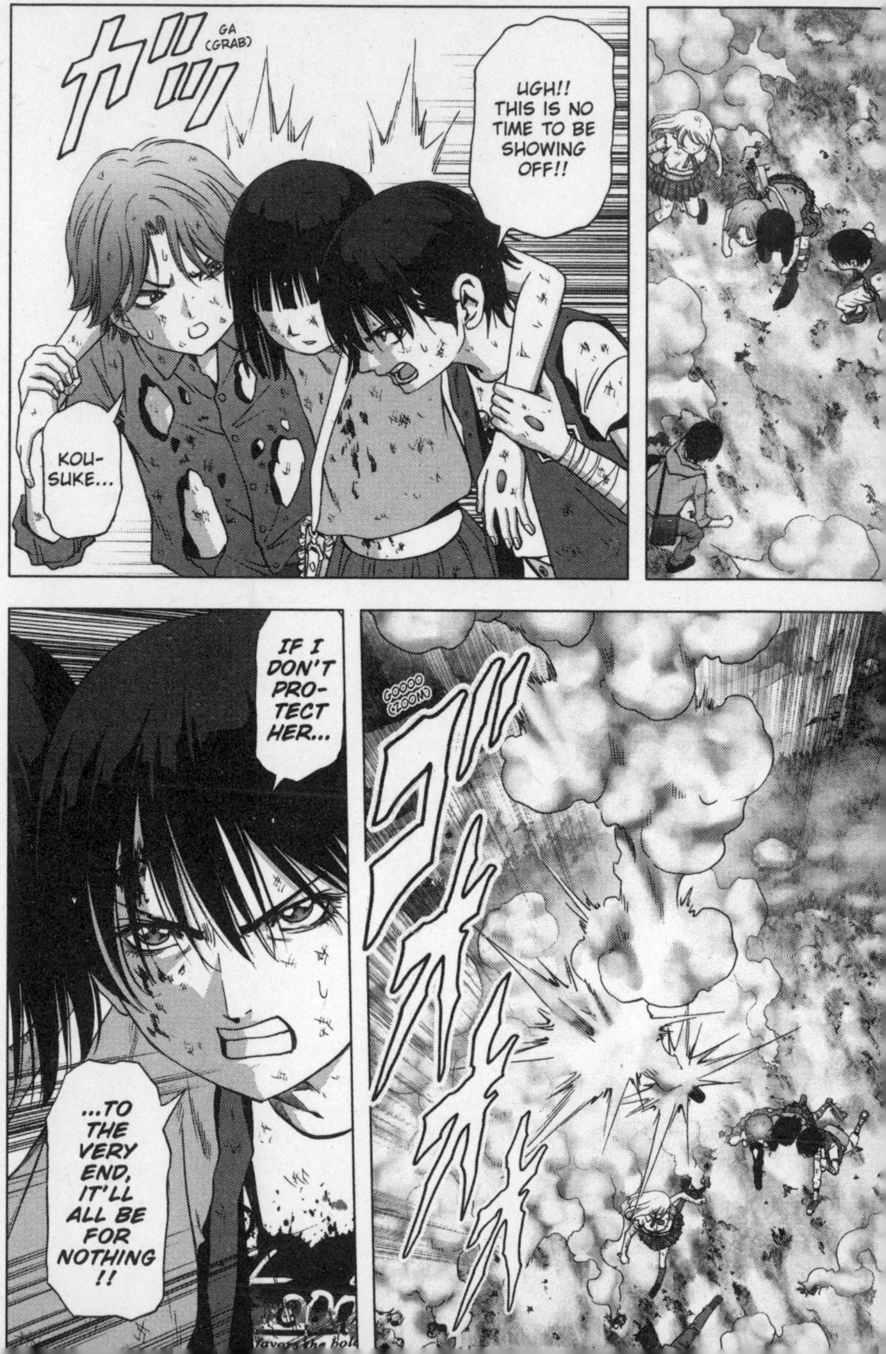
GA (GRAB)
UGH!! THIS IS NO TIME TO BE SHOWING OFF!!
KOU-SUKE...
GOOOO (ZOOM)
IF I DON'T PROTECT HER...
...TO THE VERY END, IT'LL ALL BE FOR NOTHING!!

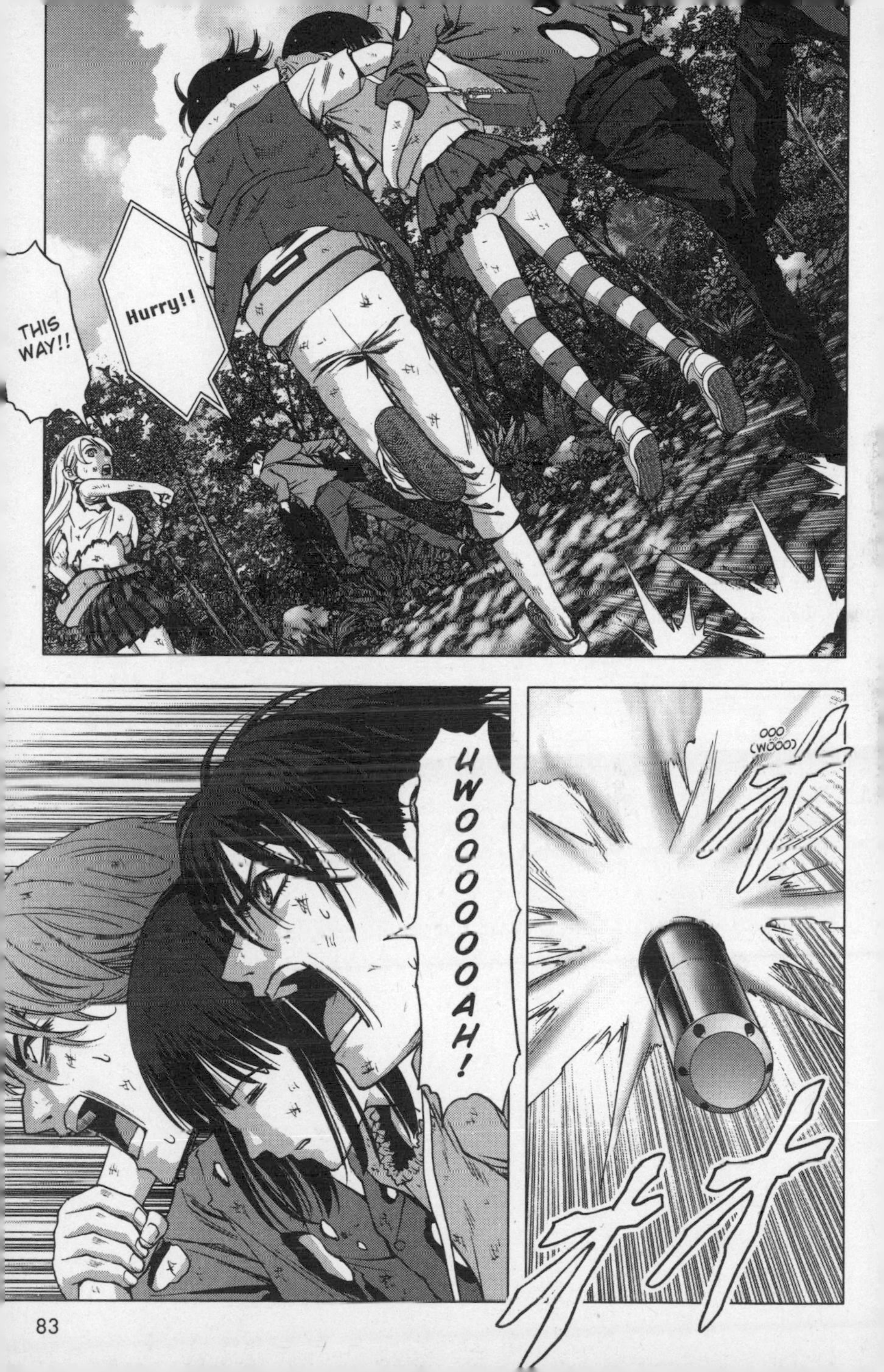
Hurry!!
THIS WAY!!
OOO
(WOOO)
UWOOOOOOOAH!

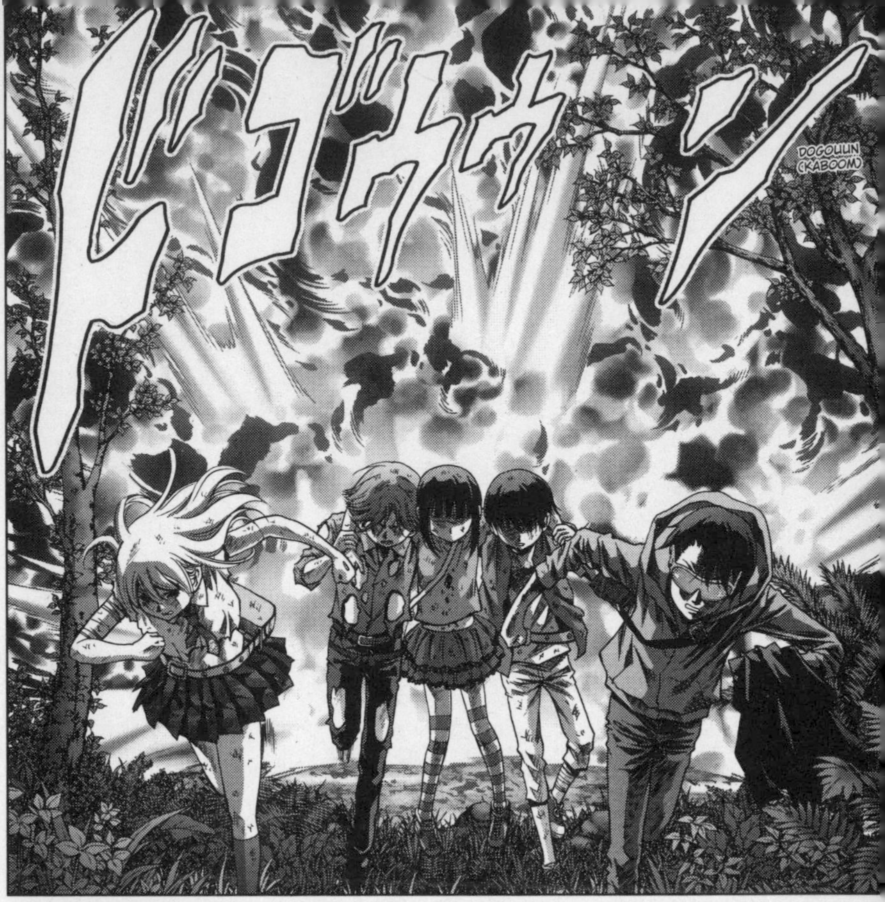
DOGOUUN (KABOOM)

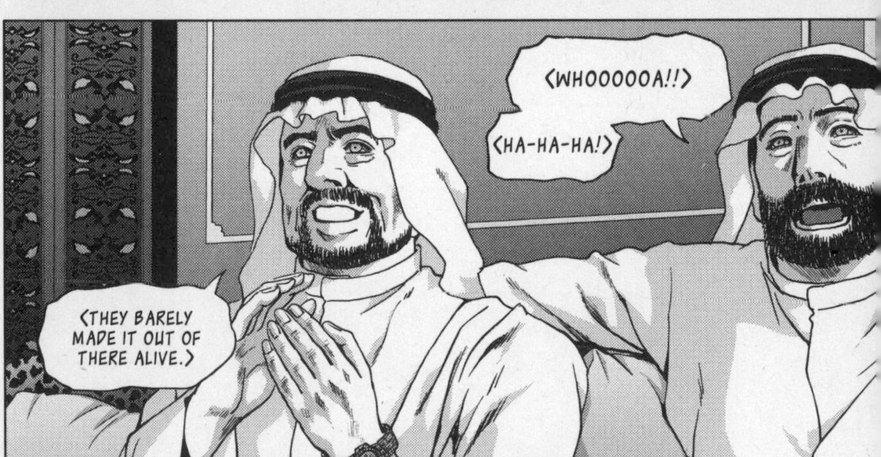
⟨WHOOOOOA!!⟩
⟨HA-HA-HA!⟩
⟨THEY BARELY MADE IT OUT OF THERE ALIVE.⟩

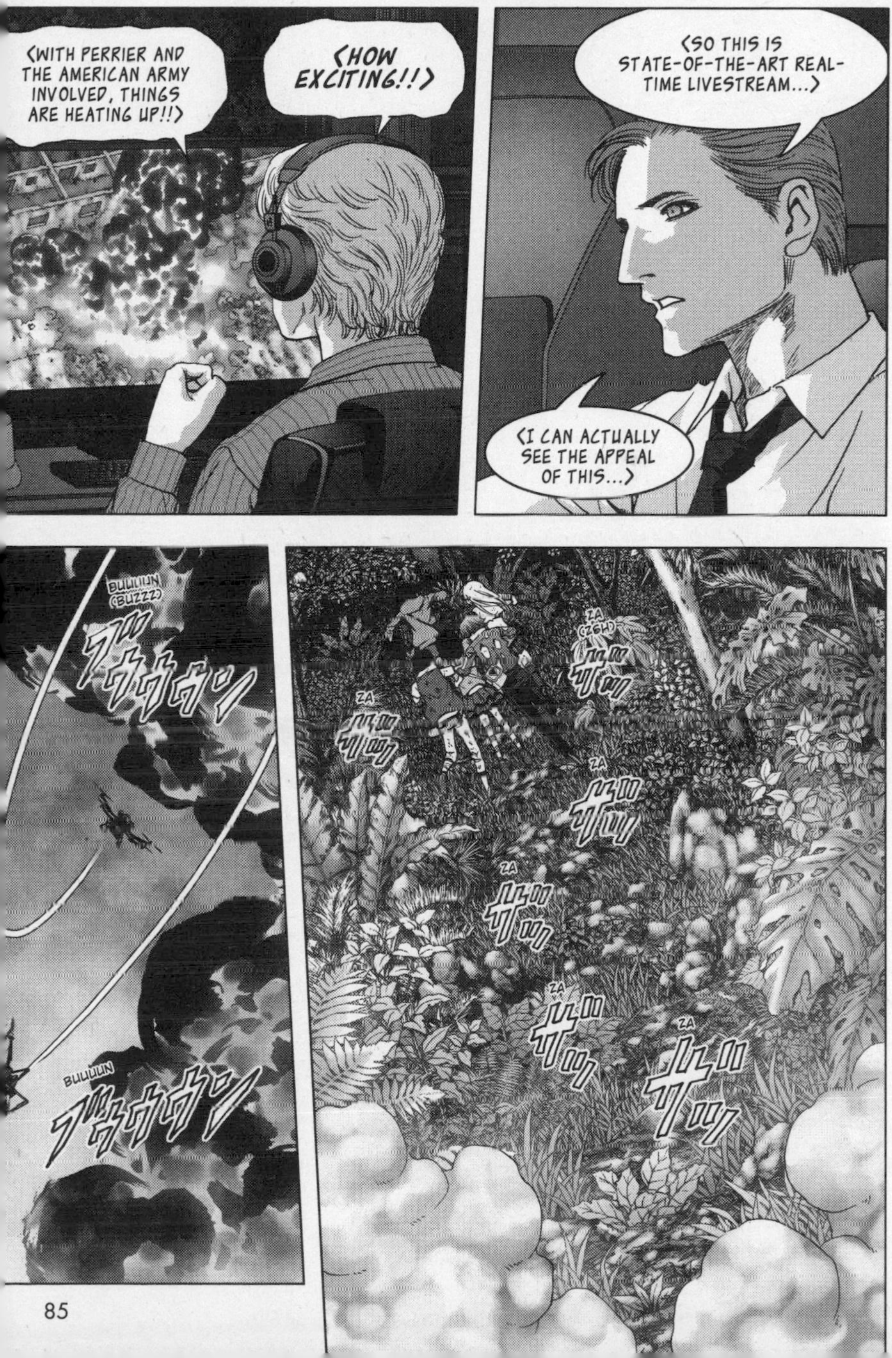
⟨SO THIS IS STATE-OF-THE-ART REAL-TIME LIVESTREAM...⟩
⟨I CAN ACTUALLY SEE THE APPEAL OF THIS...⟩
⟨HOW EXCITING!!⟩
⟨WITH PERRIER AND THE AMERICAN ARMY INVOLVED, THINGS ARE HEATING UP!!⟩
ZA (ZSH)
ZA
ZA
ZA
ZA
ZA
BUUUUN (BUZZZ)
BUUUUN

〈THE SITUATION'S DIRE.〉

〈WE'RE HEADING FOR THE ENTRANCE TO THE BASE NOW.〉

〈GOT IT!! I'LL SEND JULIA AND VLADIMIR YOUR WAY.〉

〈LEAVE SAKAMOTO TO ME.〉

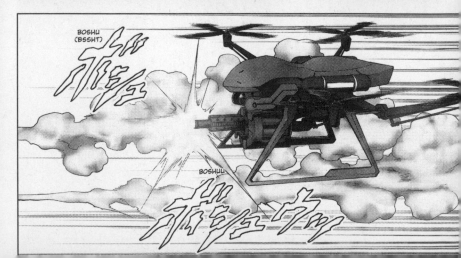

BOSHU
(BSSHT)

BOSHUU

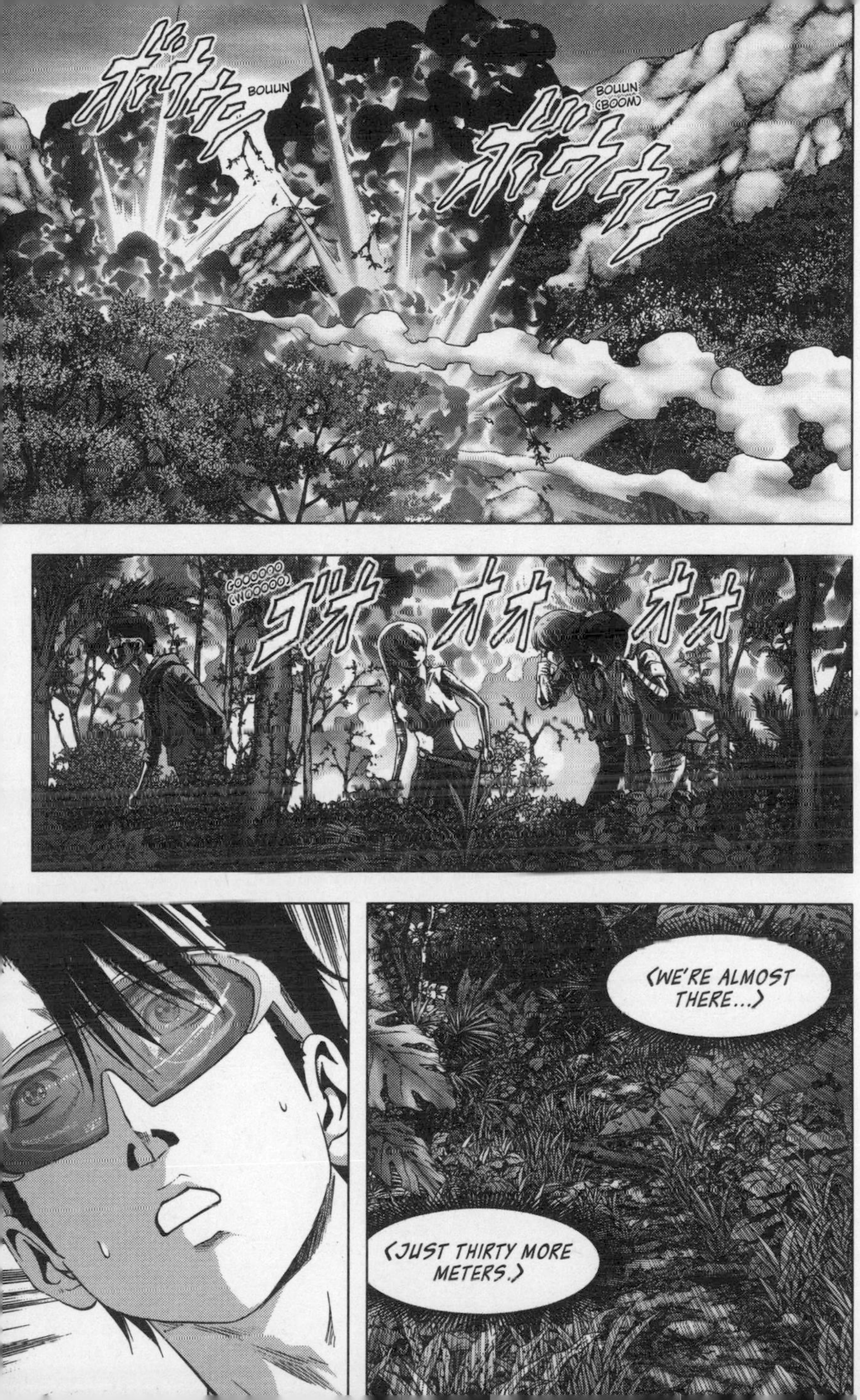
BOUUN (BOOM)
BOUUN
GOOOOOO (WOOOOOO)
‹WE'RE ALMOST THERE...›
‹JUST THIRTY MORE METERS.›

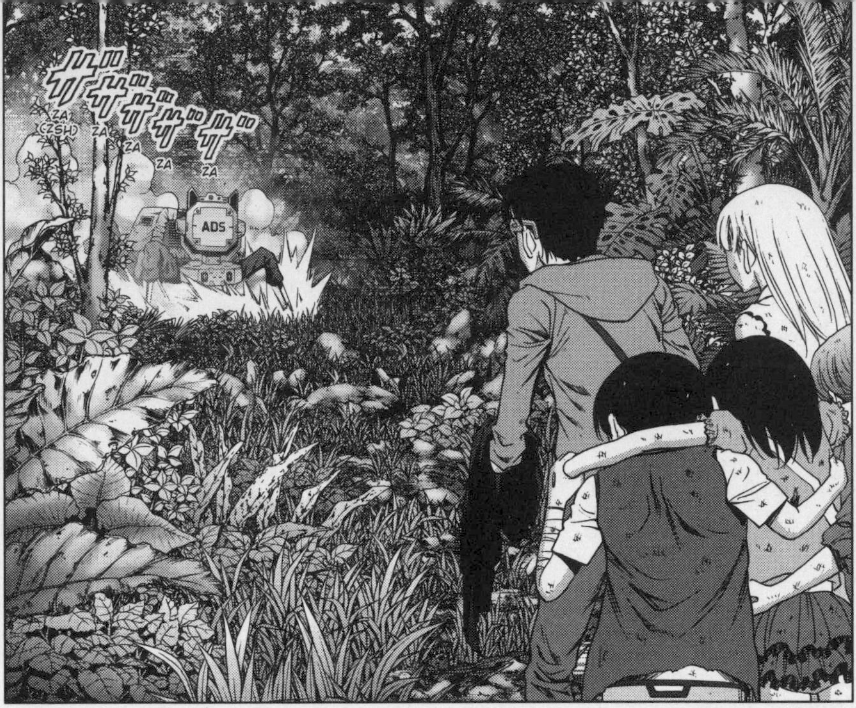
ザザザザザ
ZA (ZSH) ZA ZA ZA ZA
ADS

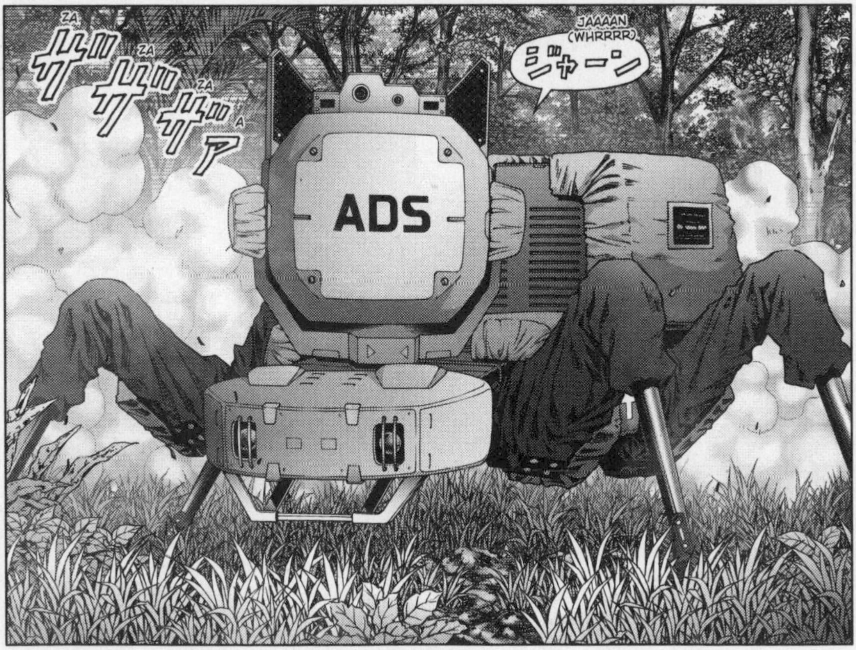
JAAAAN (WHRRRR)
ジャーン
ザザザァ
ZA ZA ZA A
ADS

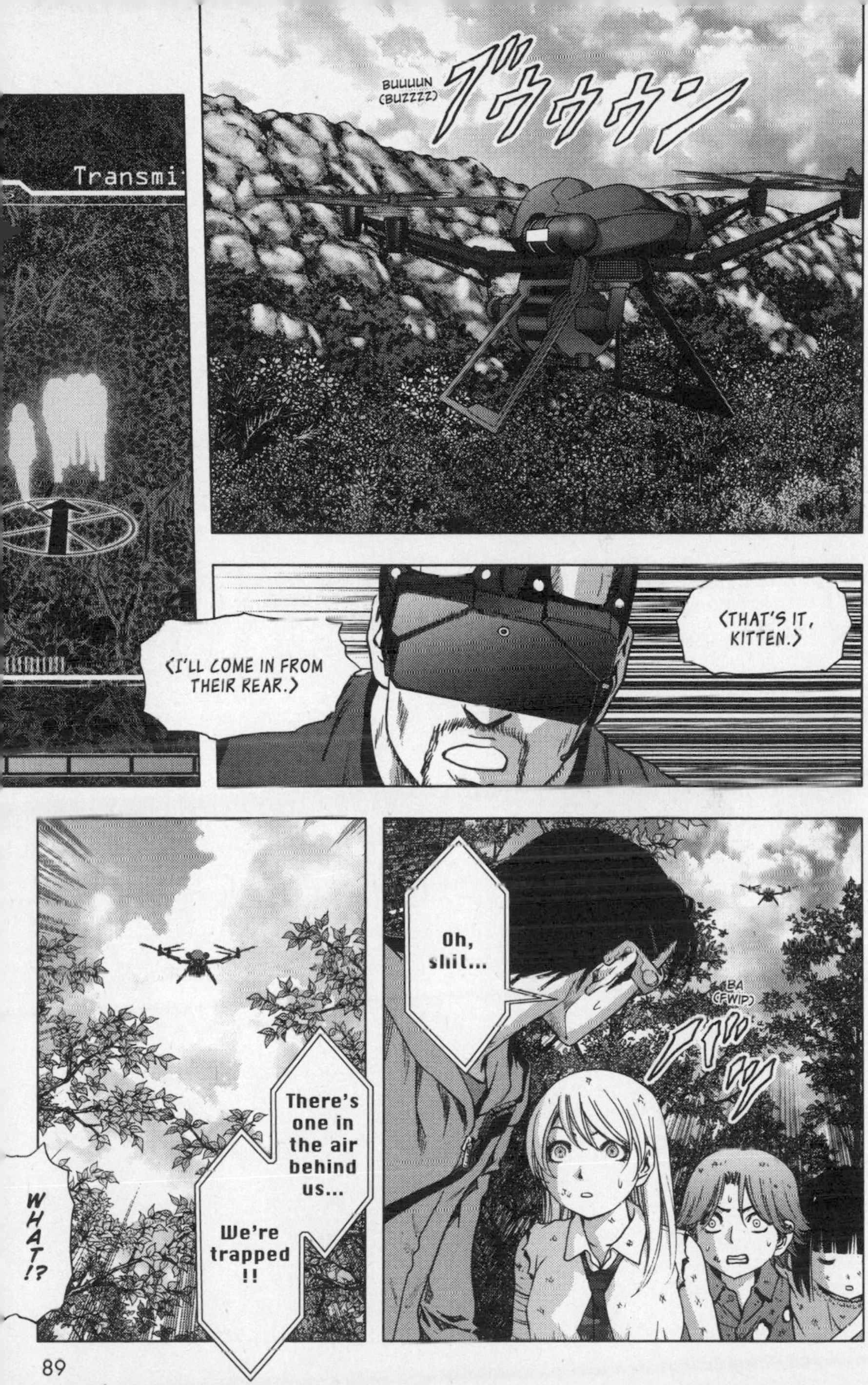
BUUUUN (BUZZZZ)
〈THAT'S IT, KITTEN.〉
〈I'LL COME IN FROM THEIR REAR.〉
Transmi
Oh, shit...
BA (FWIP)
There's one in the air behind us...
We're trapped!!
WHAT!?

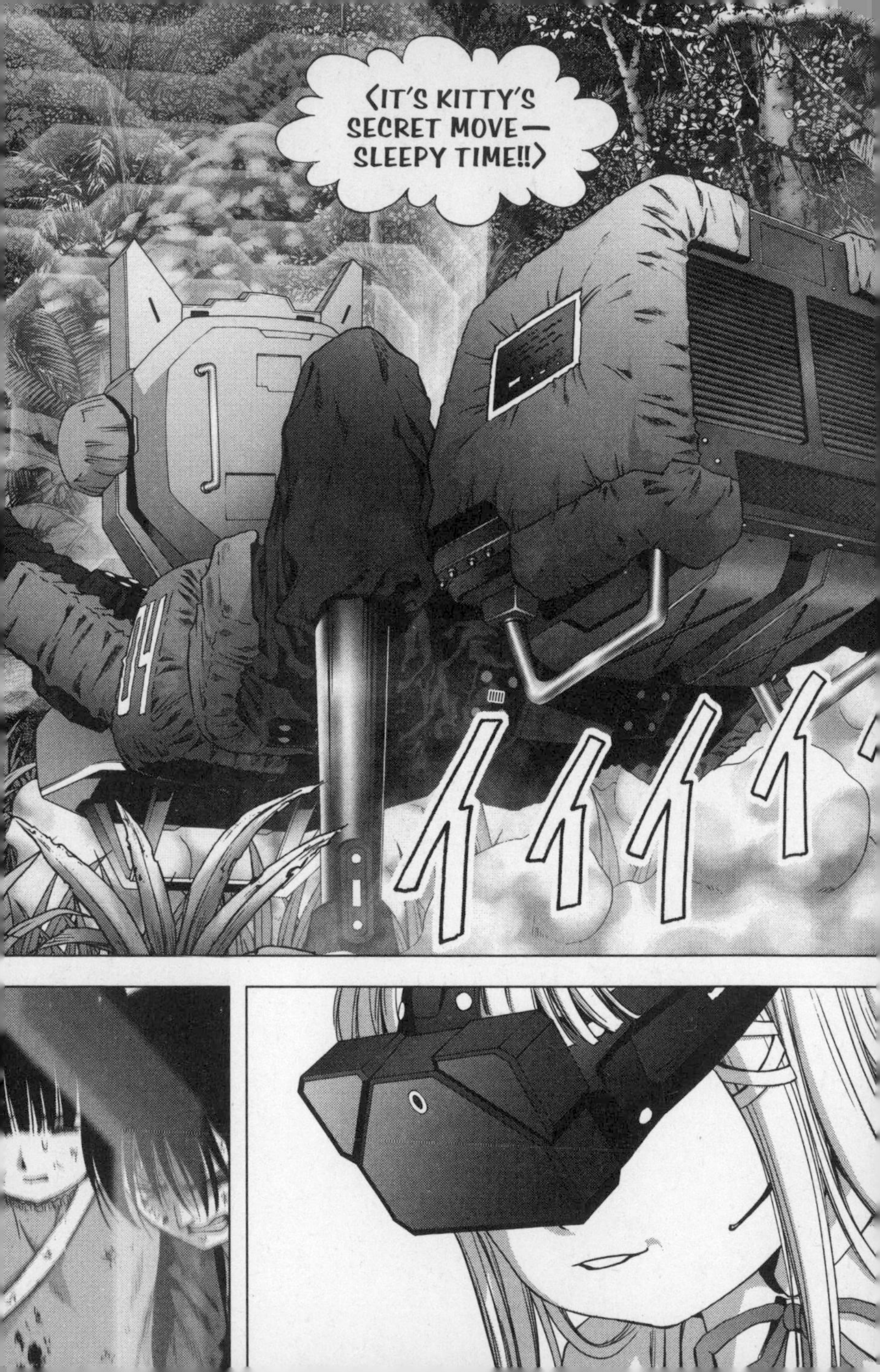
〈IT'S KITTY'S SECRET MOVE—SLEEPY TIME!!〉

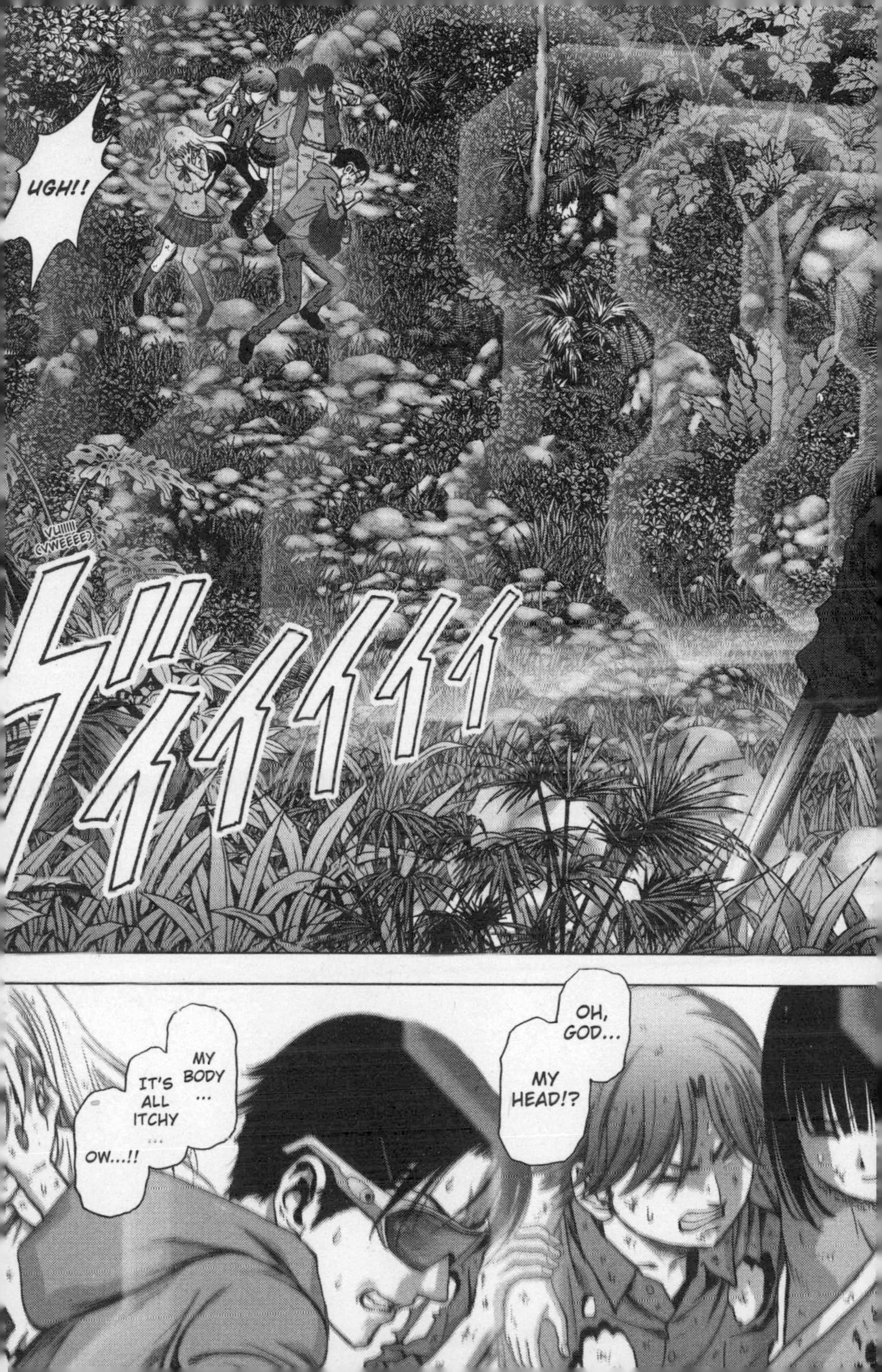
UGH!!
VUIIIII (VWEEEEE)
OH, GOD... MY HEAD!?
MY BODY... IT'S ALL ITCHY... OW...!!

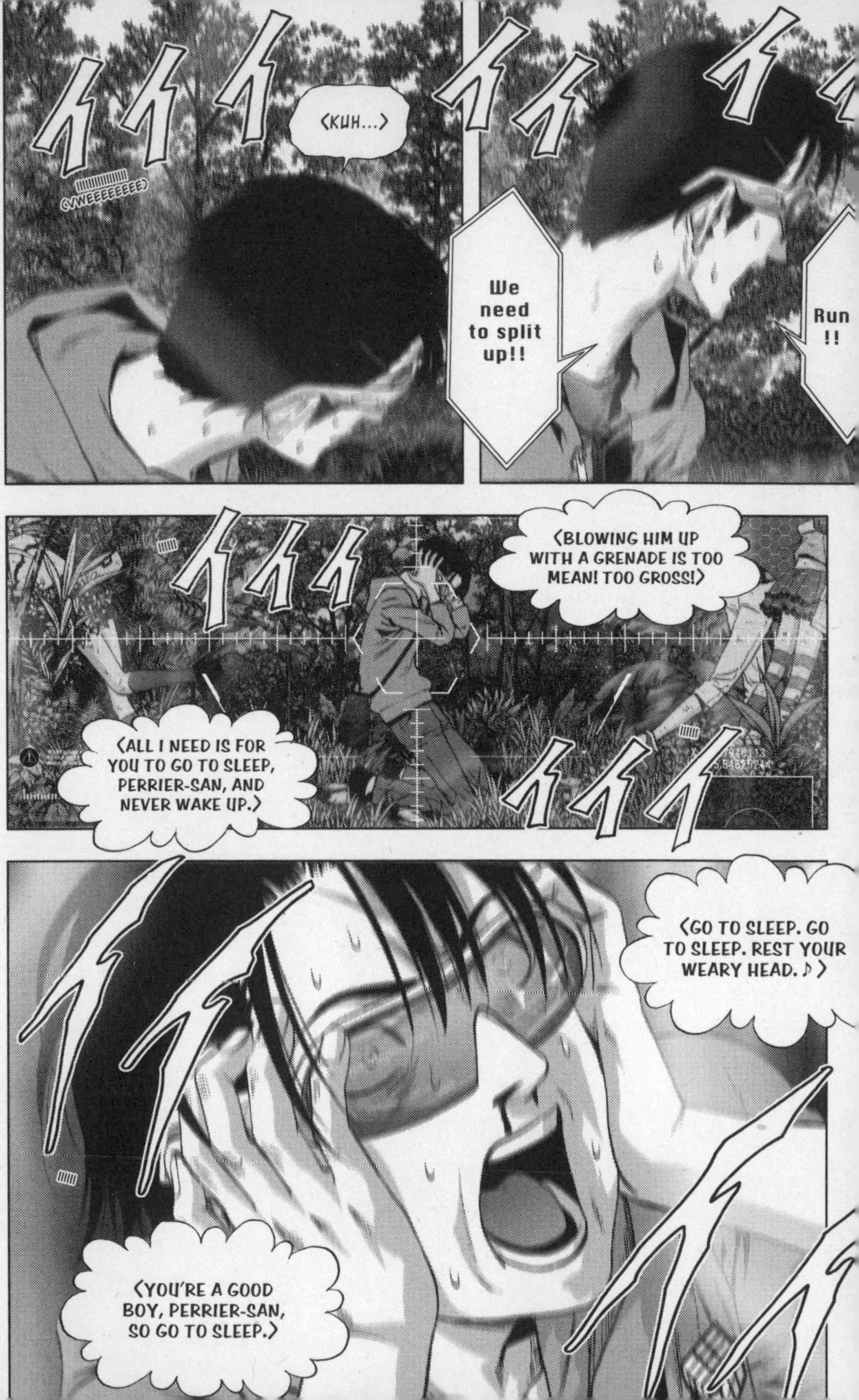
Run !!
We need to split up!!
〈KUH...〉
(VWEEEEEEEE)
〈BLOWING HIM UP WITH A GRENADE IS TOO MEAN! TOO GROSS!〉
〈ALL I NEED IS FOR YOU TO GO TO SLEEP, PERRIER-SAN, AND NEVER WAKE UP.〉
〈GO TO SLEEP. GO TO SLEEP. REST YOUR WEARY HEAD. ♪〉
〈YOU'RE A GOOD BOY, PERRIER-SAN, SO GO TO SLEEP.〉

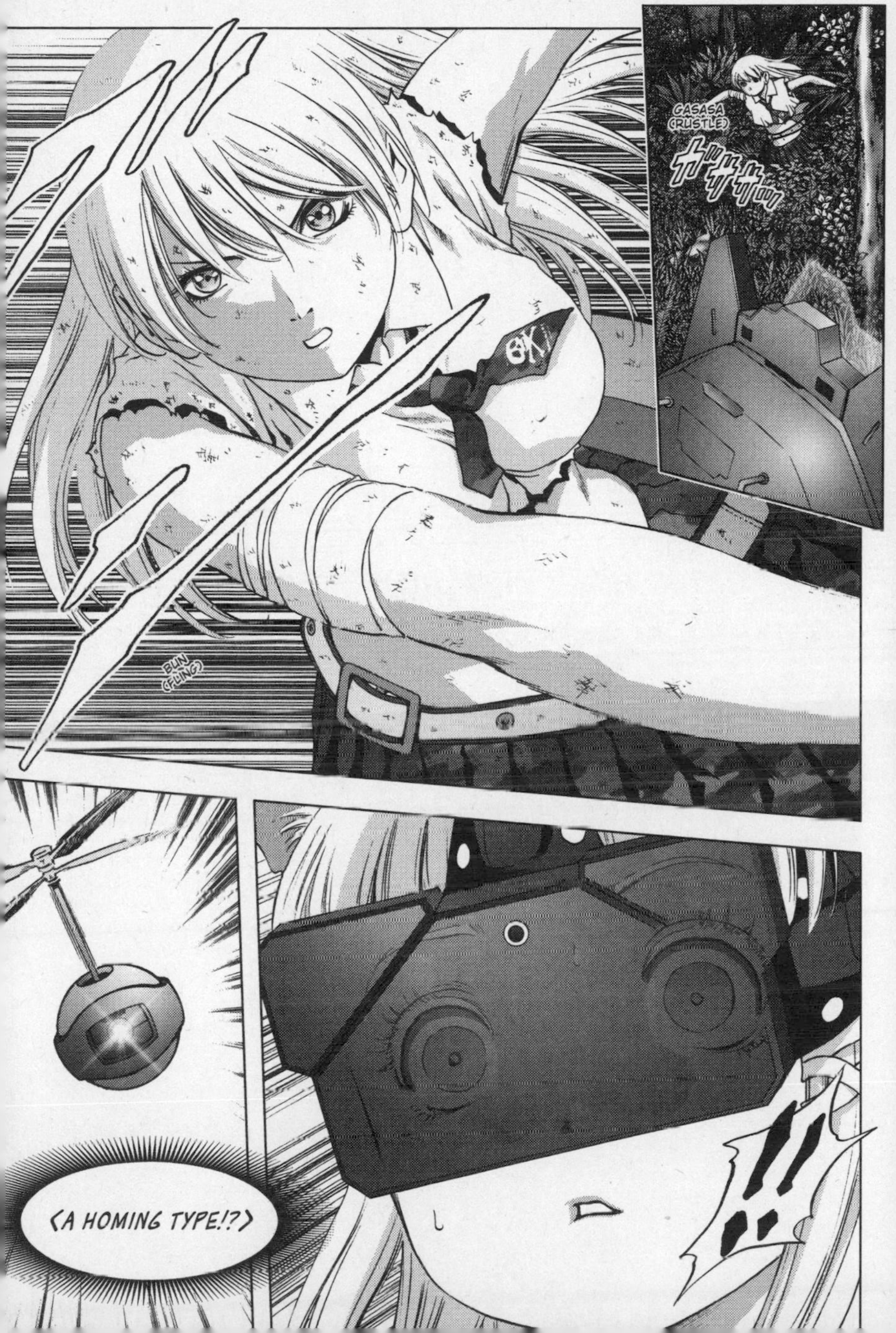
GASASA (RUSTLE)
BUN (FLING)
!!
<A HOMING TYPE!?>

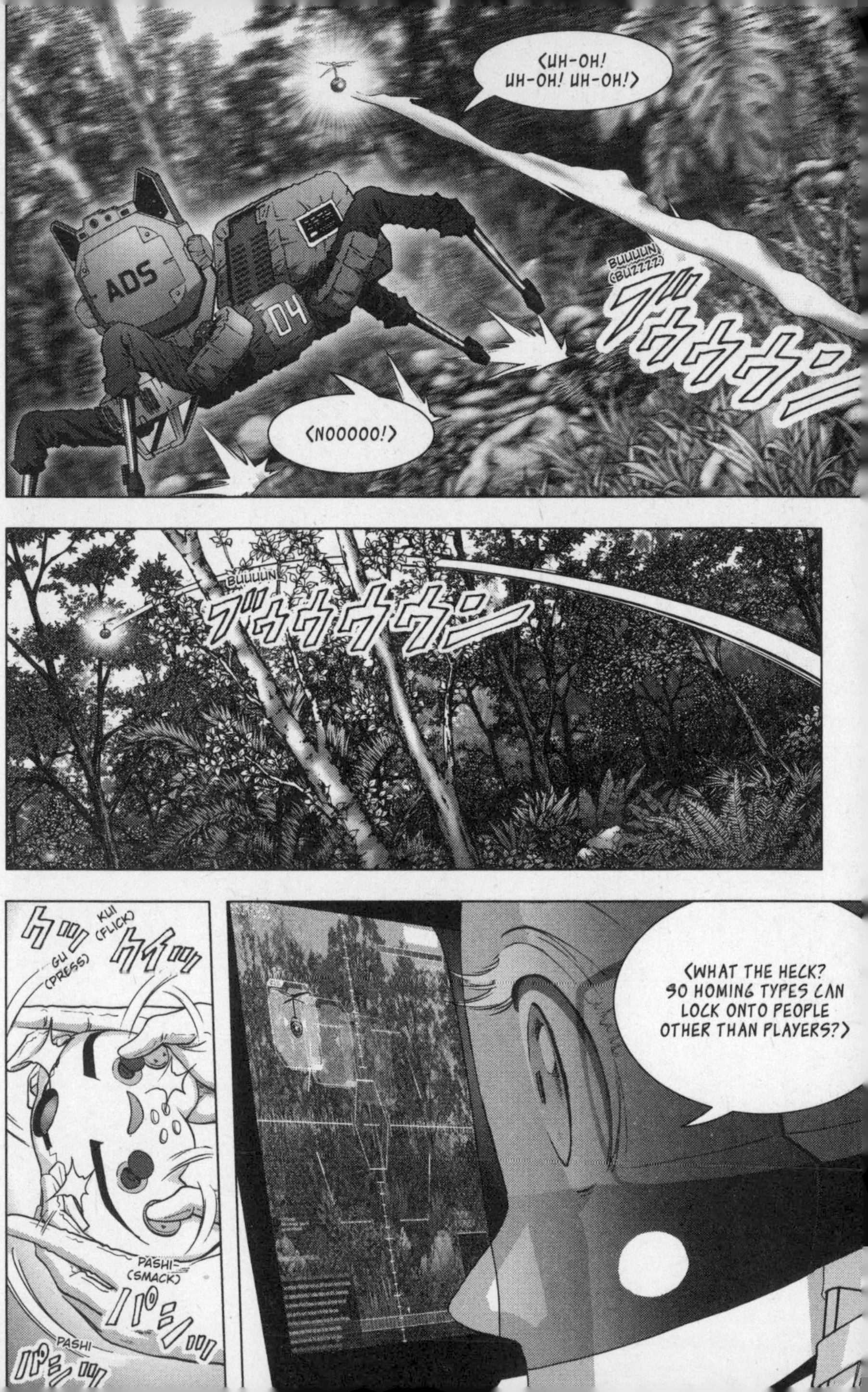
<UH-OH! UH-OH! UH-OH!>
BUUUUN (BUZZZZZ)
<NOOOOO!>
BUUUUN
<WHAT THE HECK? SO HOMING TYPES CAN LOCK ONTO PEOPLE OTHER THAN PLAYERS?>
KUI (FLICK)
GU (PRESS)
PASHI (SMACK)
PASHI

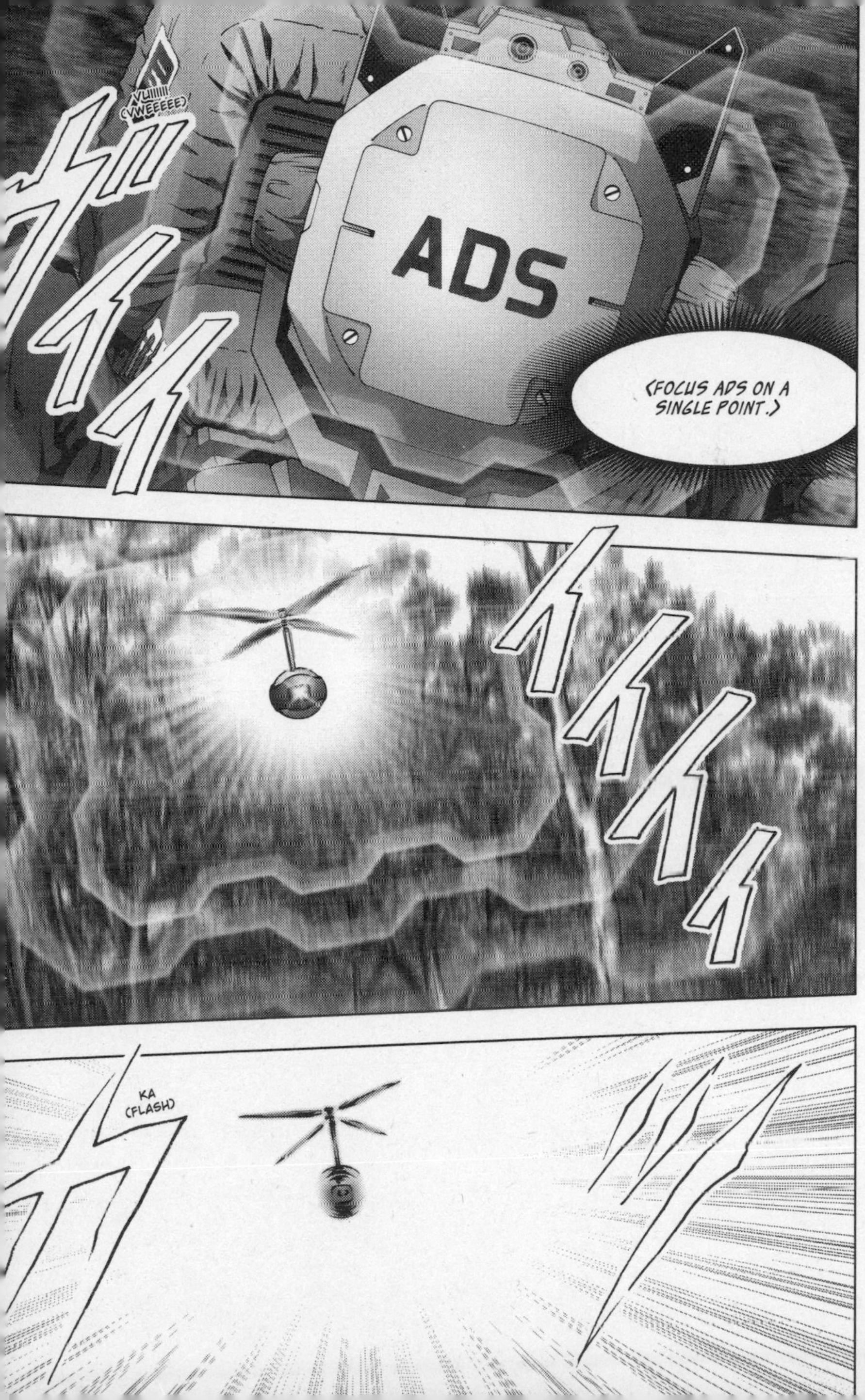

VUIIIIII (VWEEEEE)
<FOCUS ADS ON A SINGLE POINT.>
ADS
KA (FLASH)

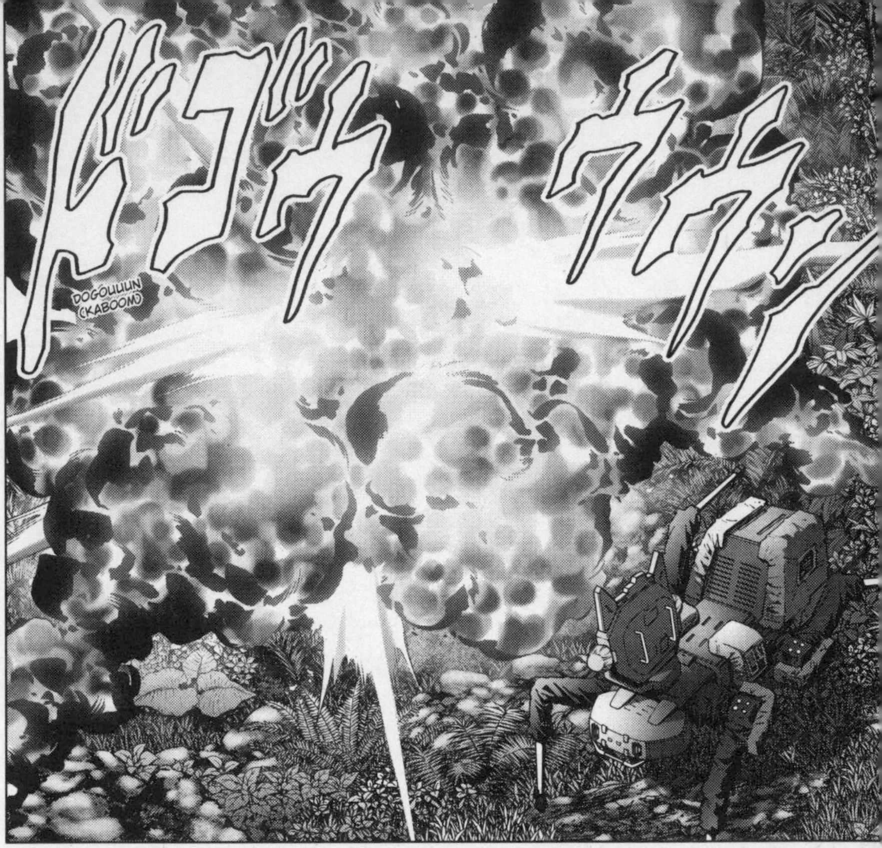
DOGOUUUN
(KABOOM)

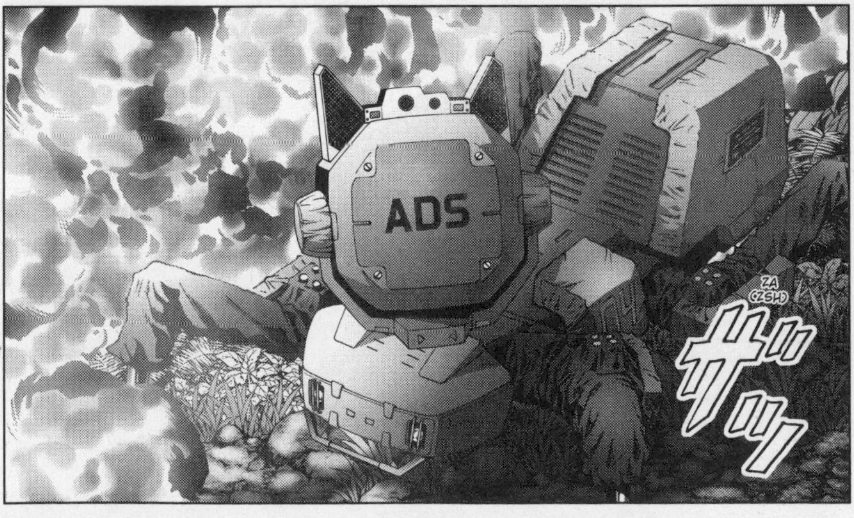
ADS
ZA
(ZSH)

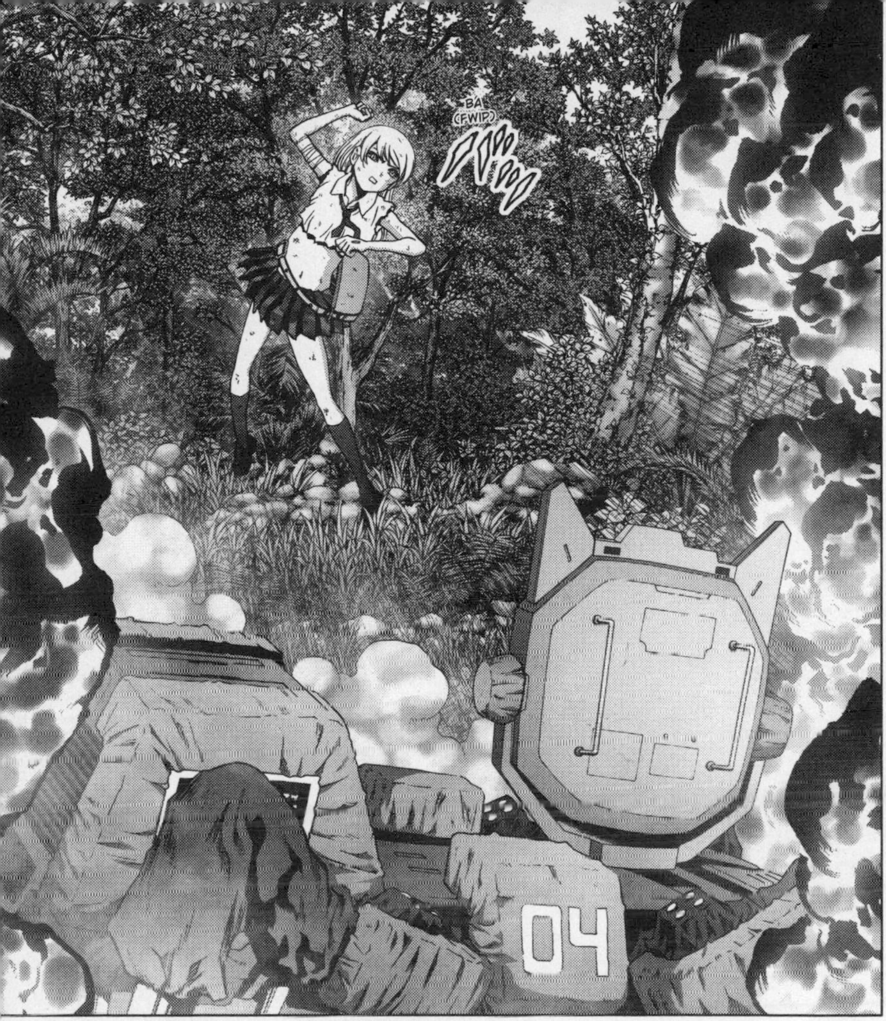
BA
(FWIP)

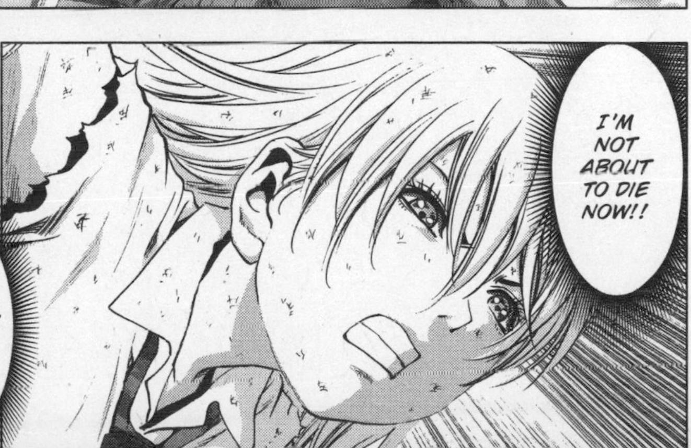
I'M NOT ABOUT TO DIE NOW!!

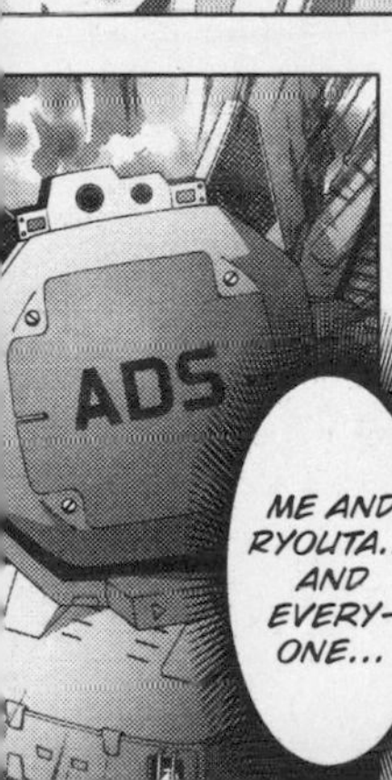
ADS
ME AND RYOUTA... AND EVERY-ONE...

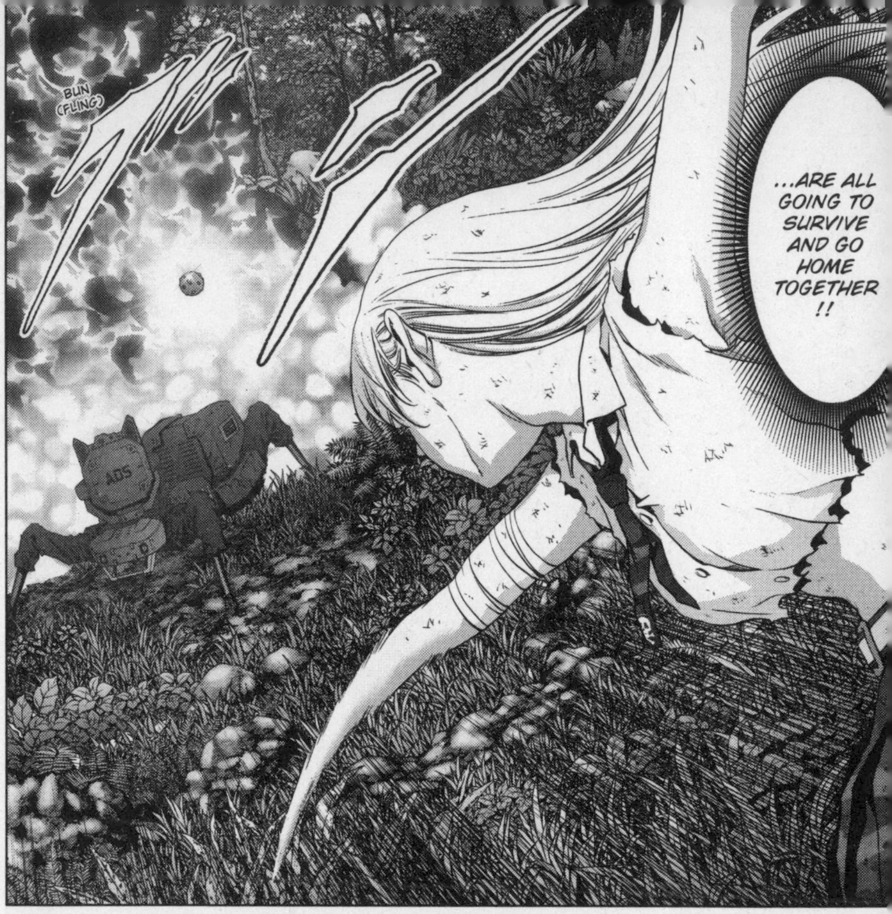
...ARE ALL GOING TO SURVIVE AND GO HOME TOGETHER !!
BUN (FLING)
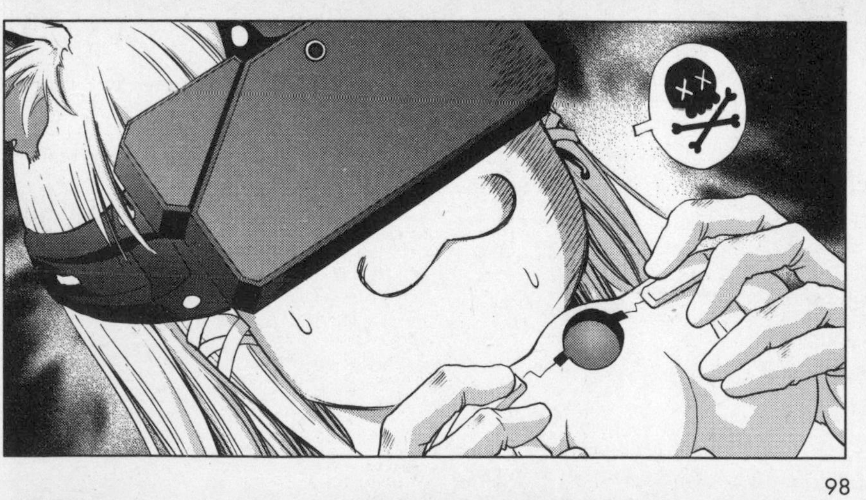

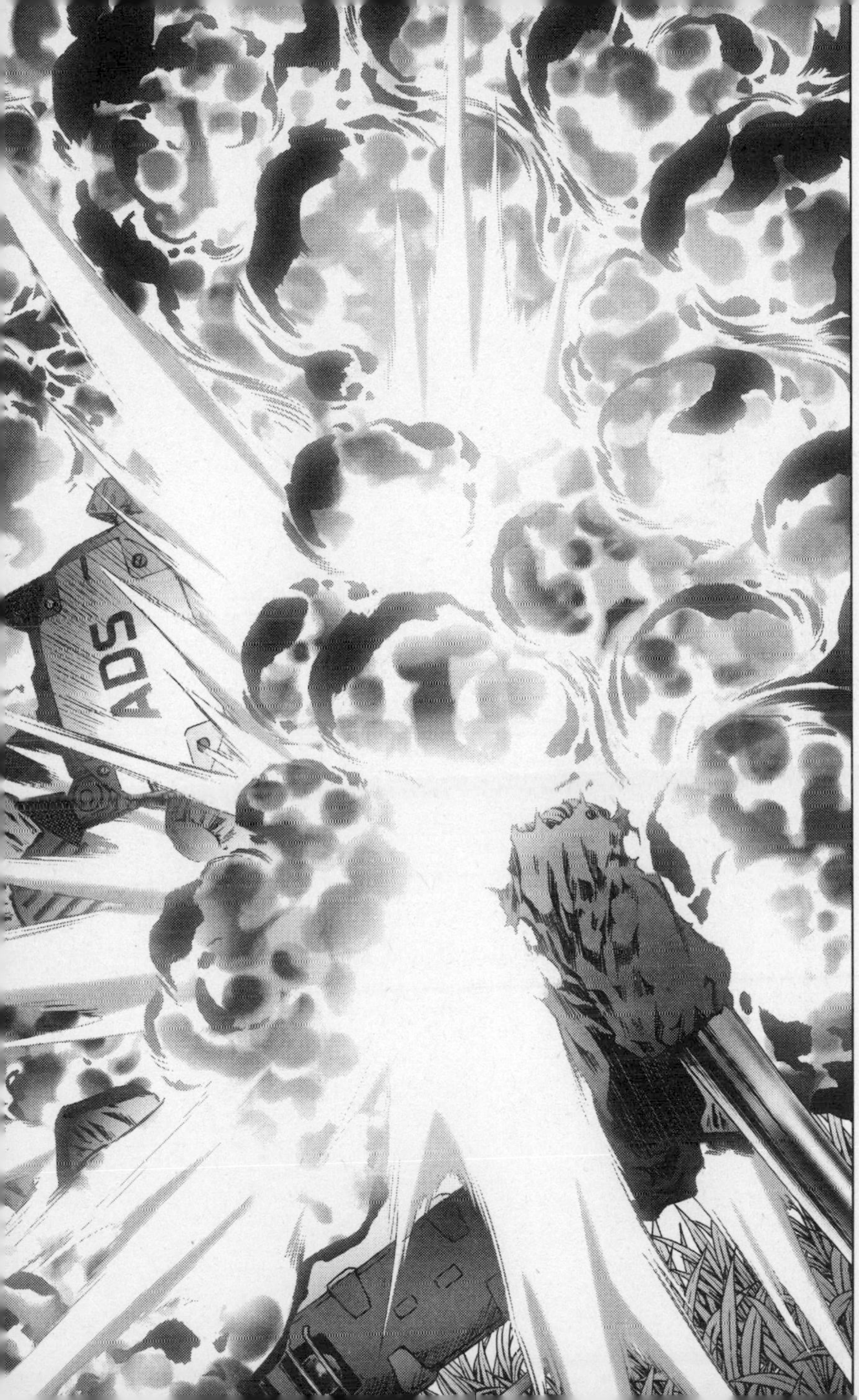
ADS

〈KITTEN, YOU'RE SUCH A NOOB...〉

〈DIDN'T YOU REALIZE THAT'S A BEGINNER-LEVEL FEINT SHE PULLED?〉

GOUIII (ROOOOAR)

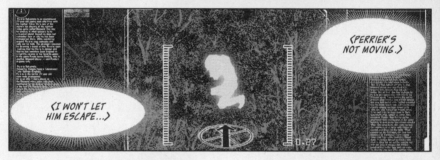

〈PERRIER'S NOT MOVING.〉

〈I WON'T LET HIM ESCAPE...〉

0.27

BOUU (BOOM)

BISHII (BSSHT)

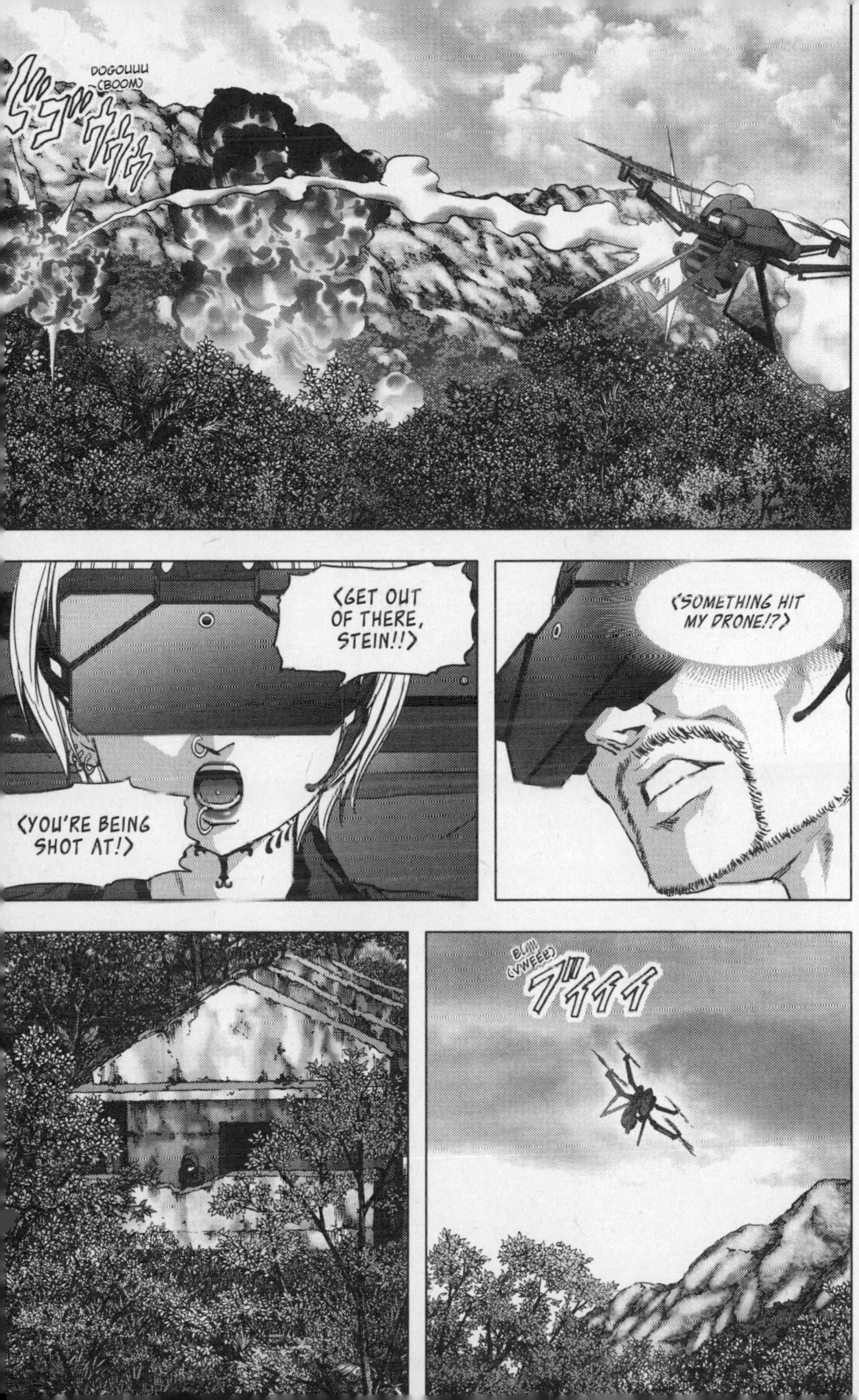
DOGOUUU (BOOM)
‹SOMETHING HIT MY DRONE!?›
‹GET OUT OF THERE, STEIN!!›
‹YOU'RE BEING SHOT AT!›
BUIII (VWEEE)

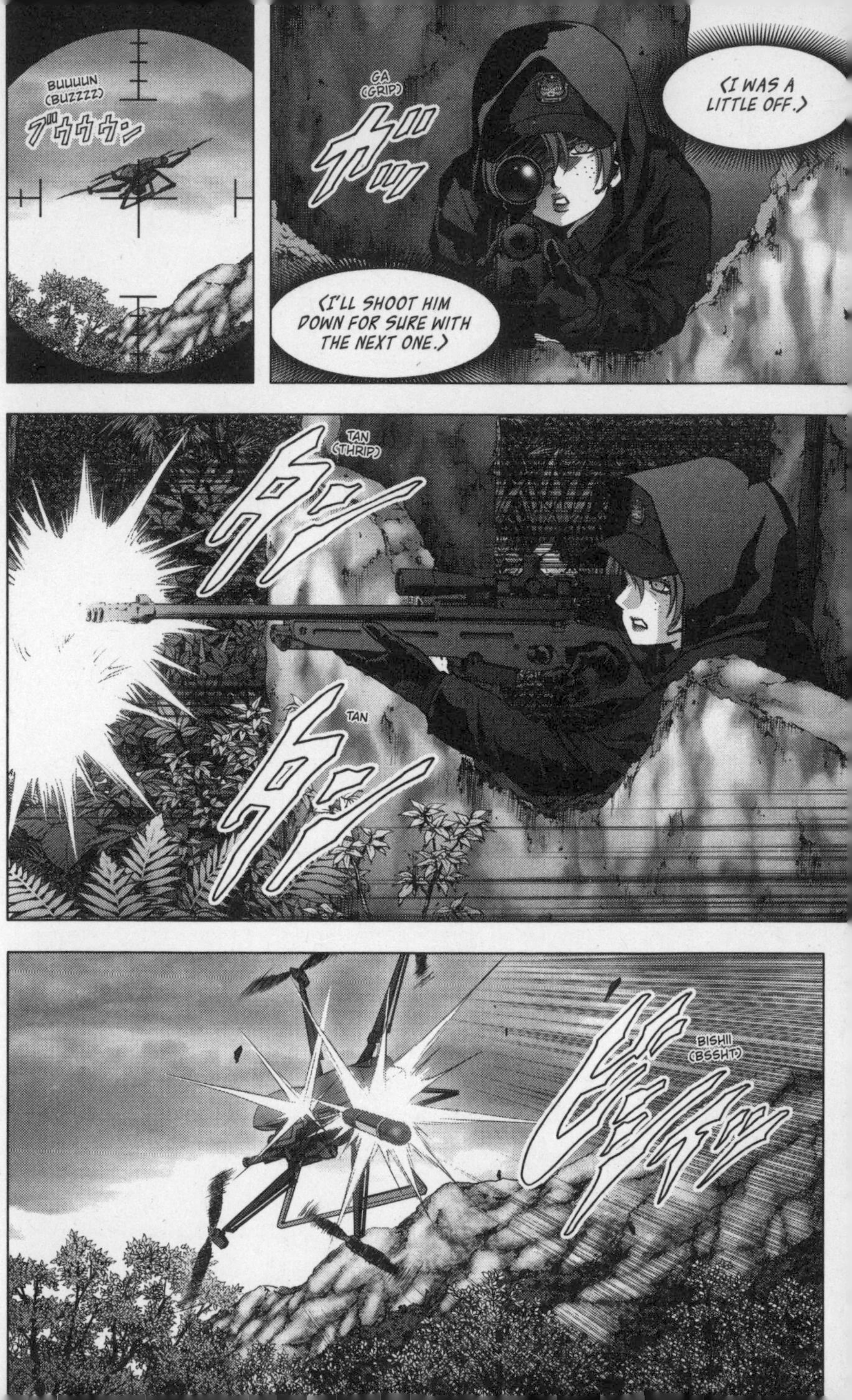
<I WAS A LITTLE OFF.>
GA (GRIP)
ガッ
<I'LL SHOOT HIM DOWN FOR SURE WITH THE NEXT ONE.>
BUUUUN (BUZZZZ)
ブウウウン
TAN (THRIP)
タン
TAN
タン
BISHII (BSSHT)
ビシィ

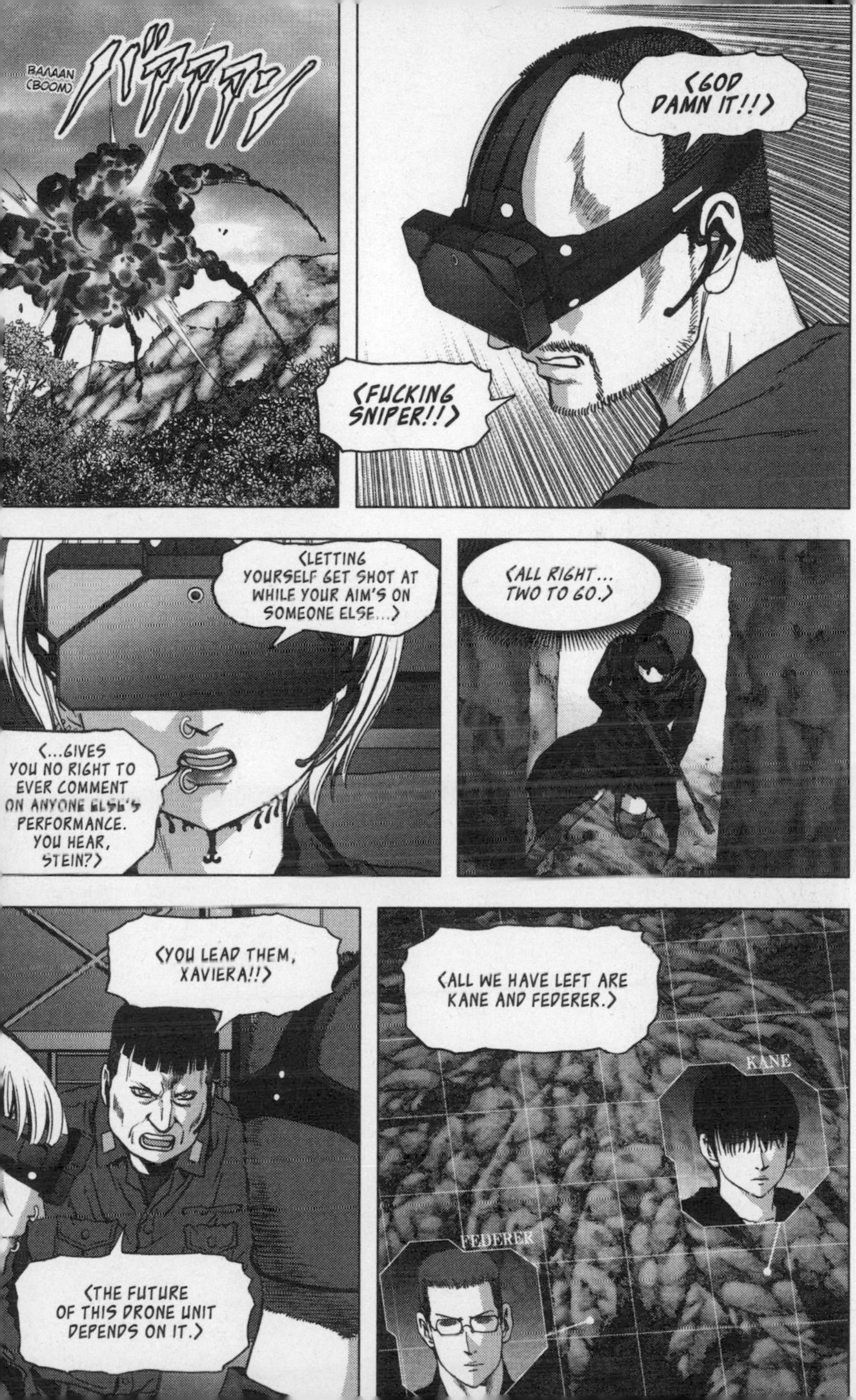

<GOD DAMN IT!!>
<FUCKING SNIPER!!>
BAAAAN (BOOM)
<ALL RIGHT... TWO TO GO.>
<LETTING YOURSELF GET SHOT AT WHILE YOUR AIM'S ON SOMEONE ELSE...>
<...GIVES YOU NO RIGHT TO EVER COMMENT ON ANYONE ELSE'S PERFORMANCE. YOU HEAR, STEIN?>
<ALL WE HAVE LEFT ARE KANE AND FEDERER.>
KANE
FEDERER
<YOU LEAD THEM, XAVIERA!!>
<THE FUTURE OF THIS DRONE UNIT DEPENDS ON IT.>

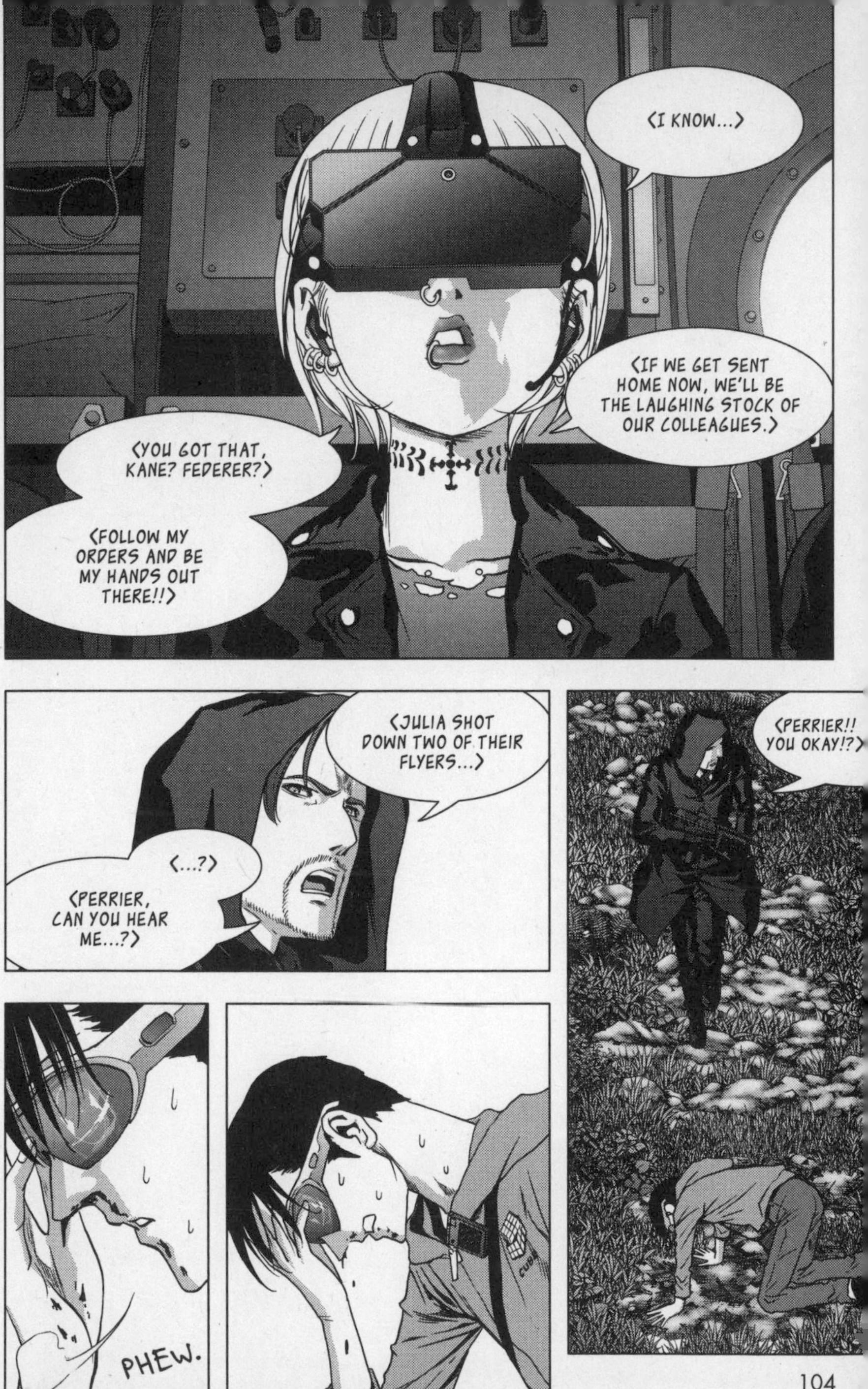
〈I KNOW...〉
〈IF WE GET SENT HOME NOW, WE'LL BE THE LAUGHING STOCK OF OUR COLLEAGUES.〉
〈YOU GOT THAT, KANE? FEDERER?〉
〈FOLLOW MY ORDERS AND BE MY HANDS OUT THERE!!〉
〈PERRIER!! YOU OKAY!?〉
〈JULIA SHOT DOWN TWO OF THEIR FLYERS...〉
〈...?〉
〈PERRIER, CAN YOU HEAR ME...?〉
PHEW.

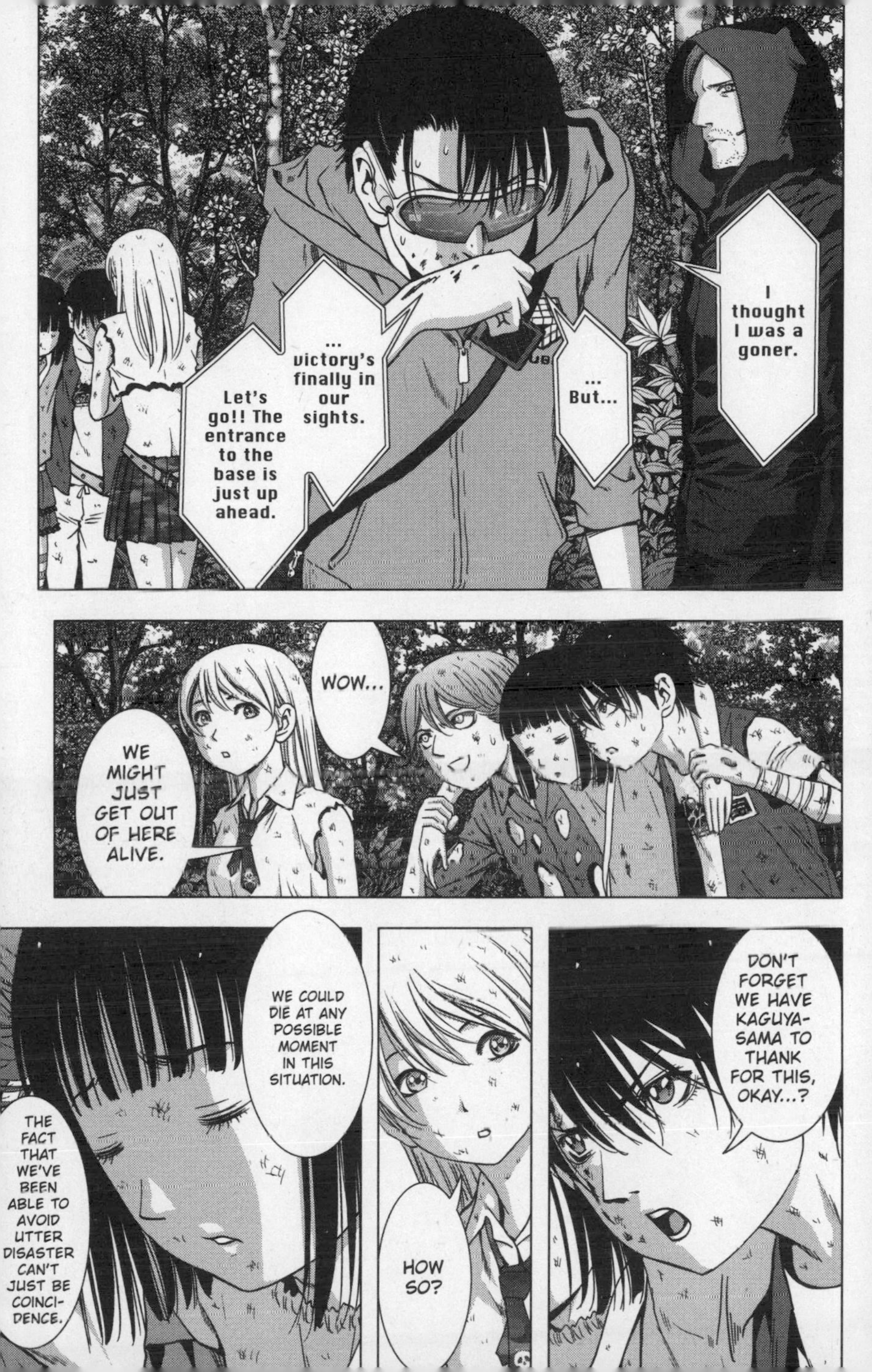
I thought I was a goner.
... But...
... victory's finally in our sights.
Let's go!! The entrance to the base is just up ahead.
WOW...
WE MIGHT JUST GET OUT OF HERE ALIVE.
DON'T FORGET WE HAVE KAGUYA-SAMA TO THANK FOR THIS, OKAY...?
HOW SO?
WE COULD DIE AT ANY POSSIBLE MOMENT IN THIS SITUATION.
THE FACT THAT WE'VE BEEN ABLE TO AVOID UTTER DISASTER CAN'T JUST BE COINCIDENCE.

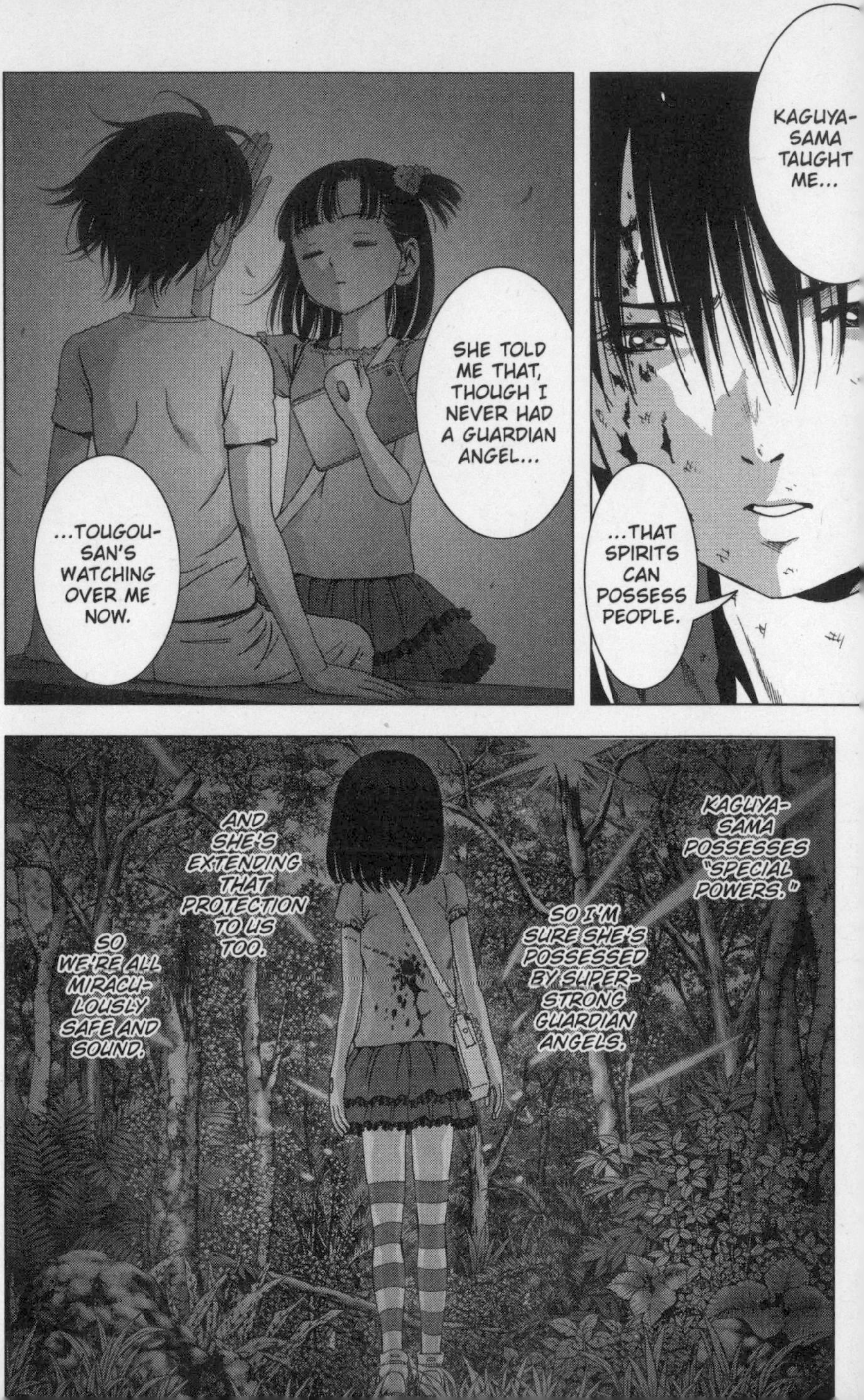
KAGUYA-SAMA TAUGHT ME...
...THAT SPIRITS CAN POSSESS PEOPLE.
SHE TOLD ME THAT, THOUGH I NEVER HAD A GUARDIAN ANGEL...
...TOUGOU-SAN'S WATCHING OVER ME NOW.
KAGUYA-SAMA POSSESSES "SPECIAL POWERS."
SO I'M SURE SHE'S POSSESSED BY SUPER-STRONG GUARDIAN ANGELS.
AND SHE'S EXTENDING THAT PROTECTION TO US TOO.
SO WE'RE ALL MIRACULOUSLY SAFE AND SOUND.

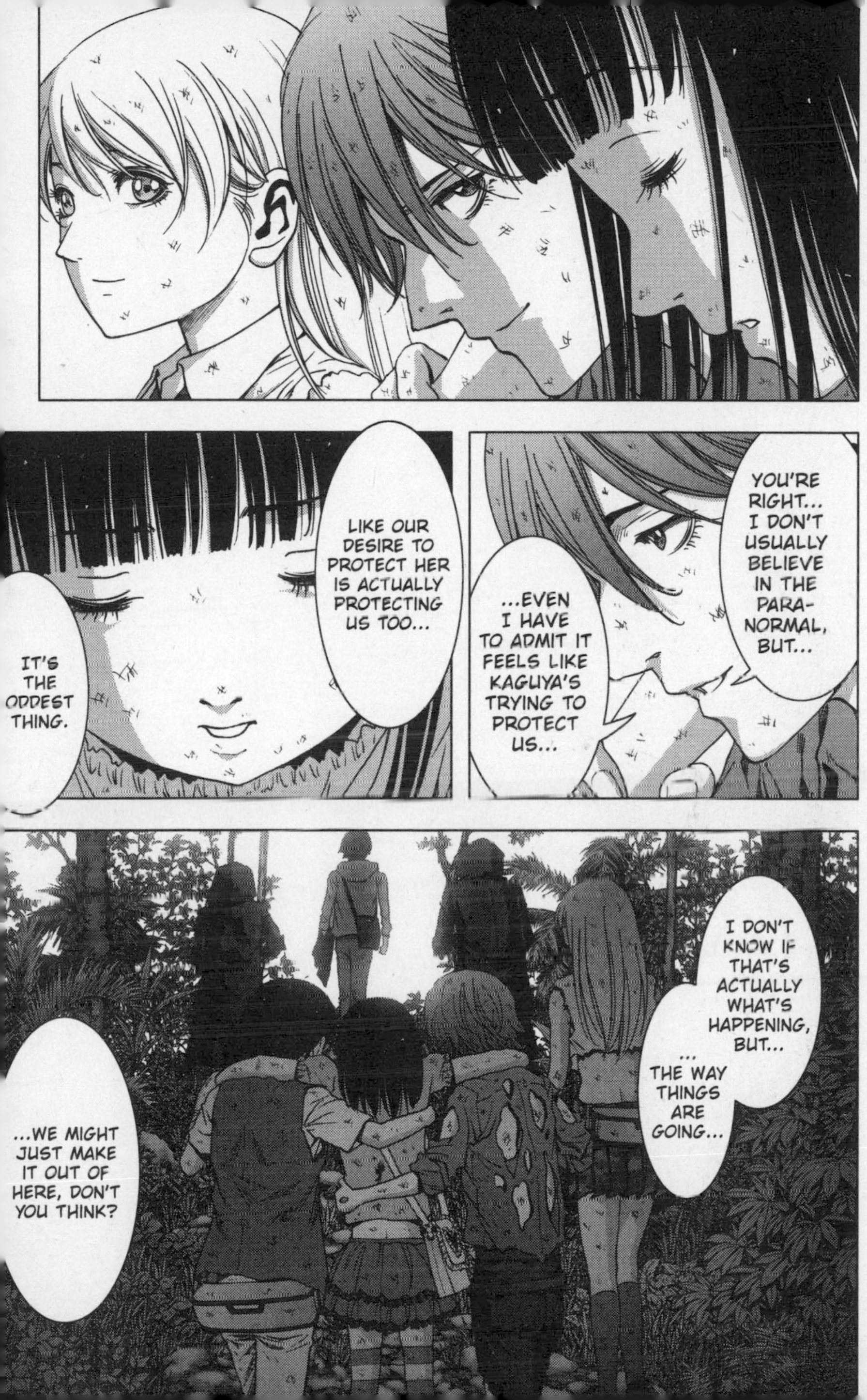
YOU'RE RIGHT... I DON'T USUALLY BELIEVE IN THE PARA-NORMAL, BUT...
...EVEN I HAVE TO ADMIT IT FEELS LIKE KAGUYA'S TRYING TO PROTECT US...
LIKE OUR DESIRE TO PROTECT HER IS ACTUALLY PROTECTING US TOO...
IT'S THE ODDEST THING.
I DON'T KNOW IF THAT'S ACTUALLY WHAT'S HAPPENING, BUT...
...THE WAY THINGS ARE GOING...
...WE MIGHT JUST MAKE IT OUT OF HERE, DON'T YOU THINK?

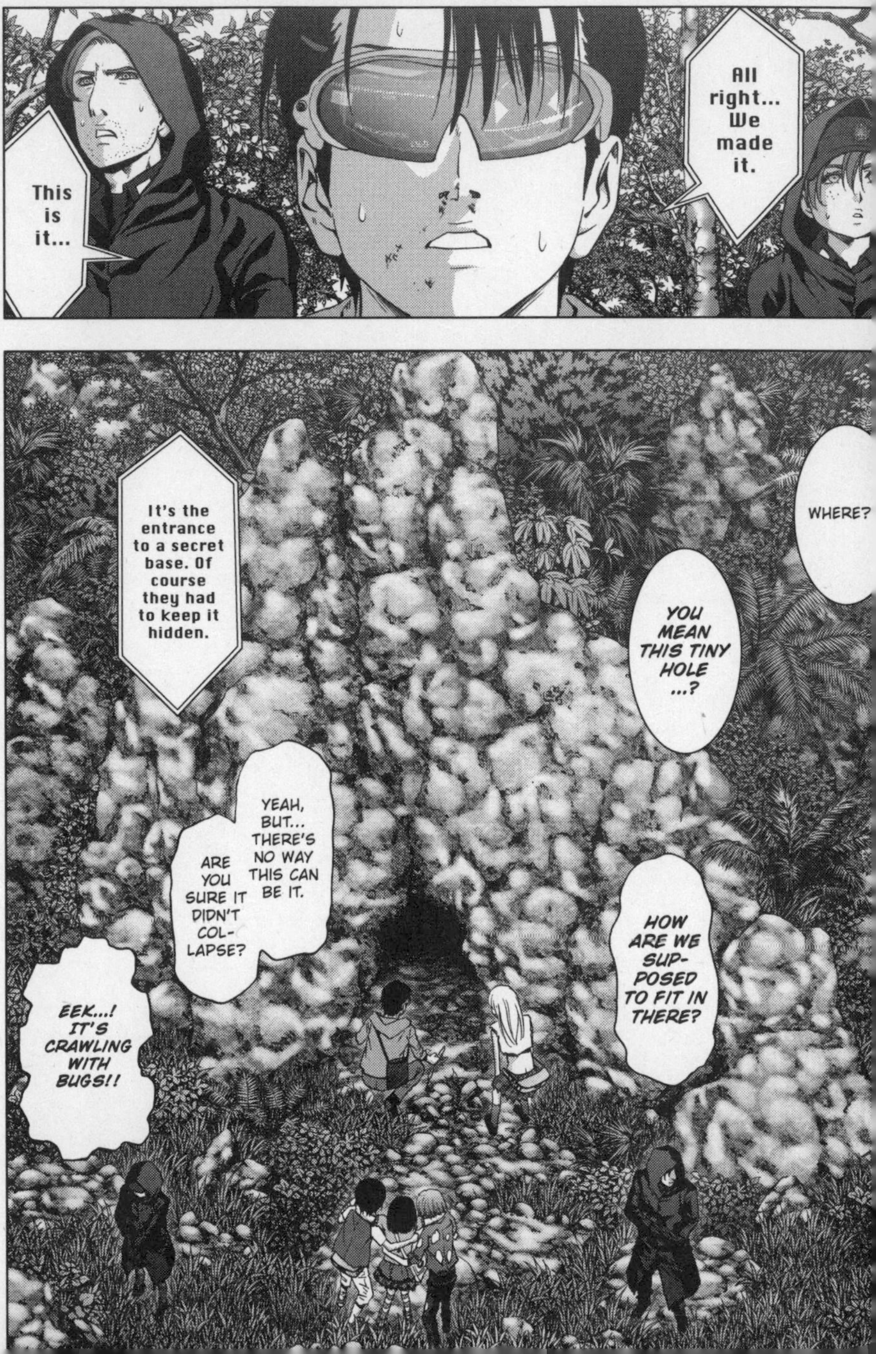
All right... We made it.
This is it...
WHERE?
YOU MEAN THIS TINY HOLE ...?
It's the entrance to a secret base. Of course they had to keep it hidden.
HOW ARE WE SUP-POSED TO FIT IN THERE?
YEAH, BUT... THERE'S NO WAY THIS CAN BE IT.
ARE YOU SURE IT DIDN'T COL-LAPSE?
EEK...! IT'S CRAWLING WITH BUGS!!

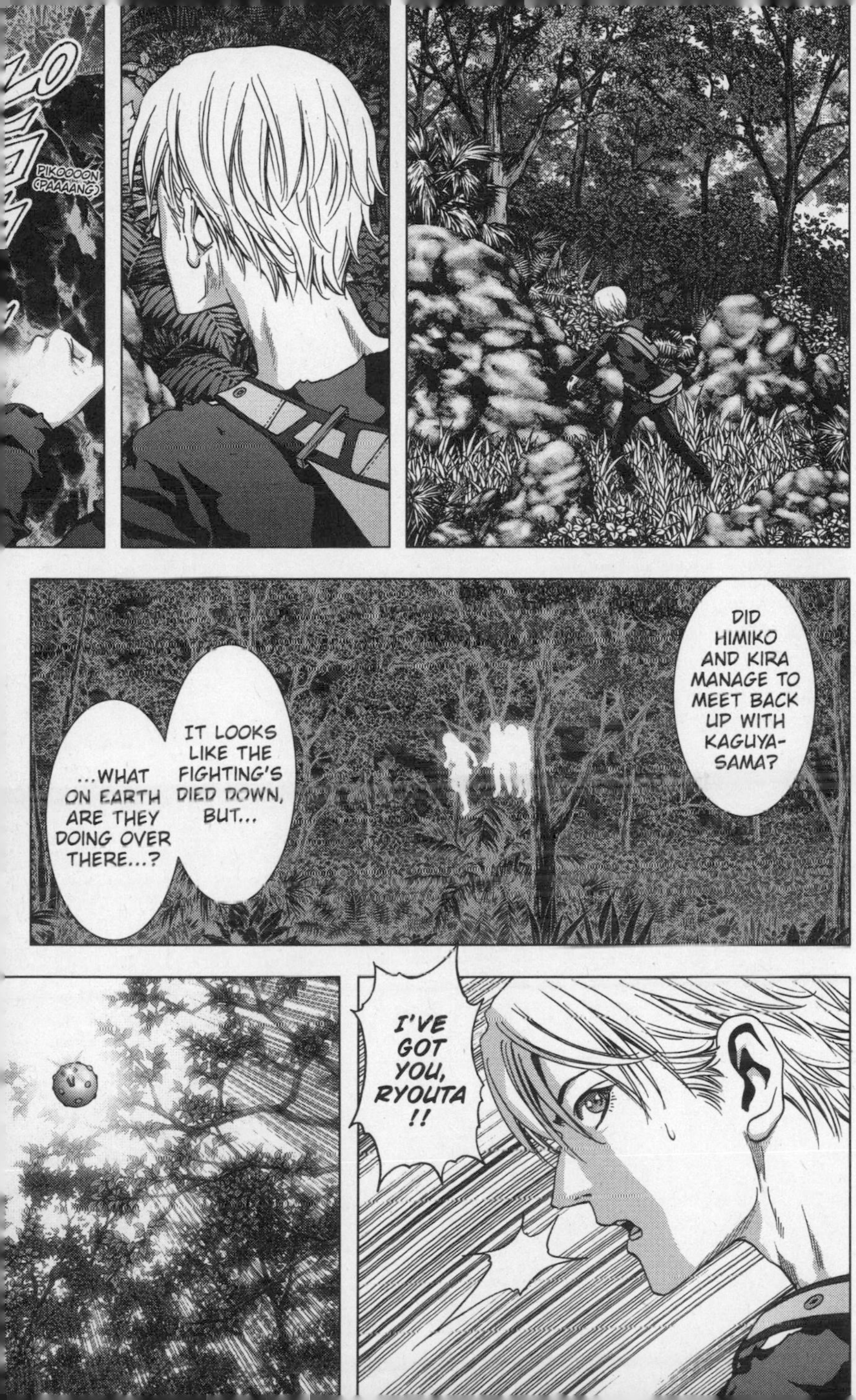
PIKOOOON (PAAAANG)
DID HIMIKO AND KIRA MANAGE TO MEET BACK UP WITH KAGUYA-SAMA?
IT LOOKS LIKE THE FIGHTING'S DIED DOWN, BUT...
...WHAT ON EARTH ARE THEY DOING OVER THERE...?
I'VE GOT YOU, RYOUTA!!

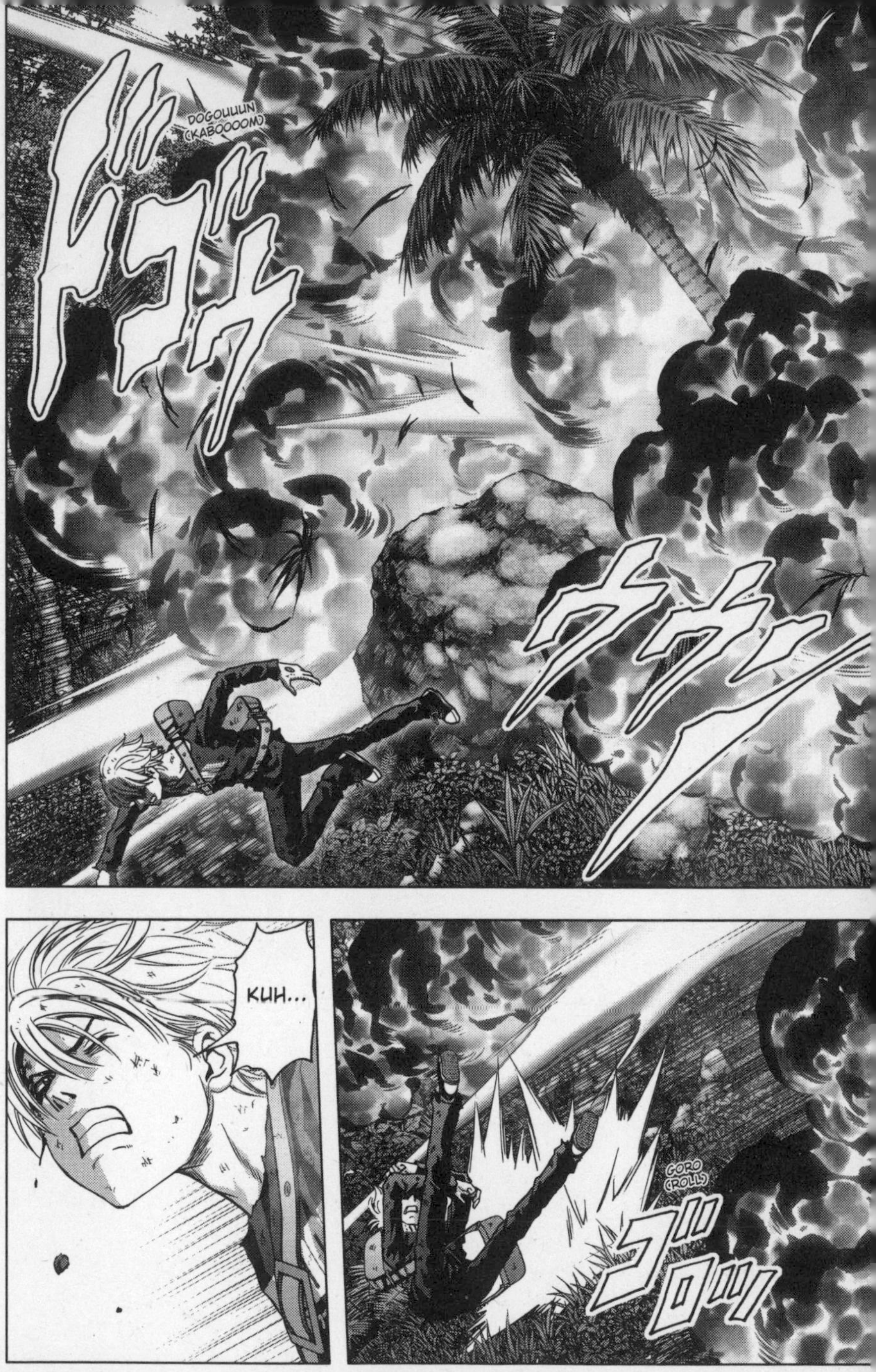
DOGOUUUN
(KABOOOOM)
GORO
(ROLL)
KUH...

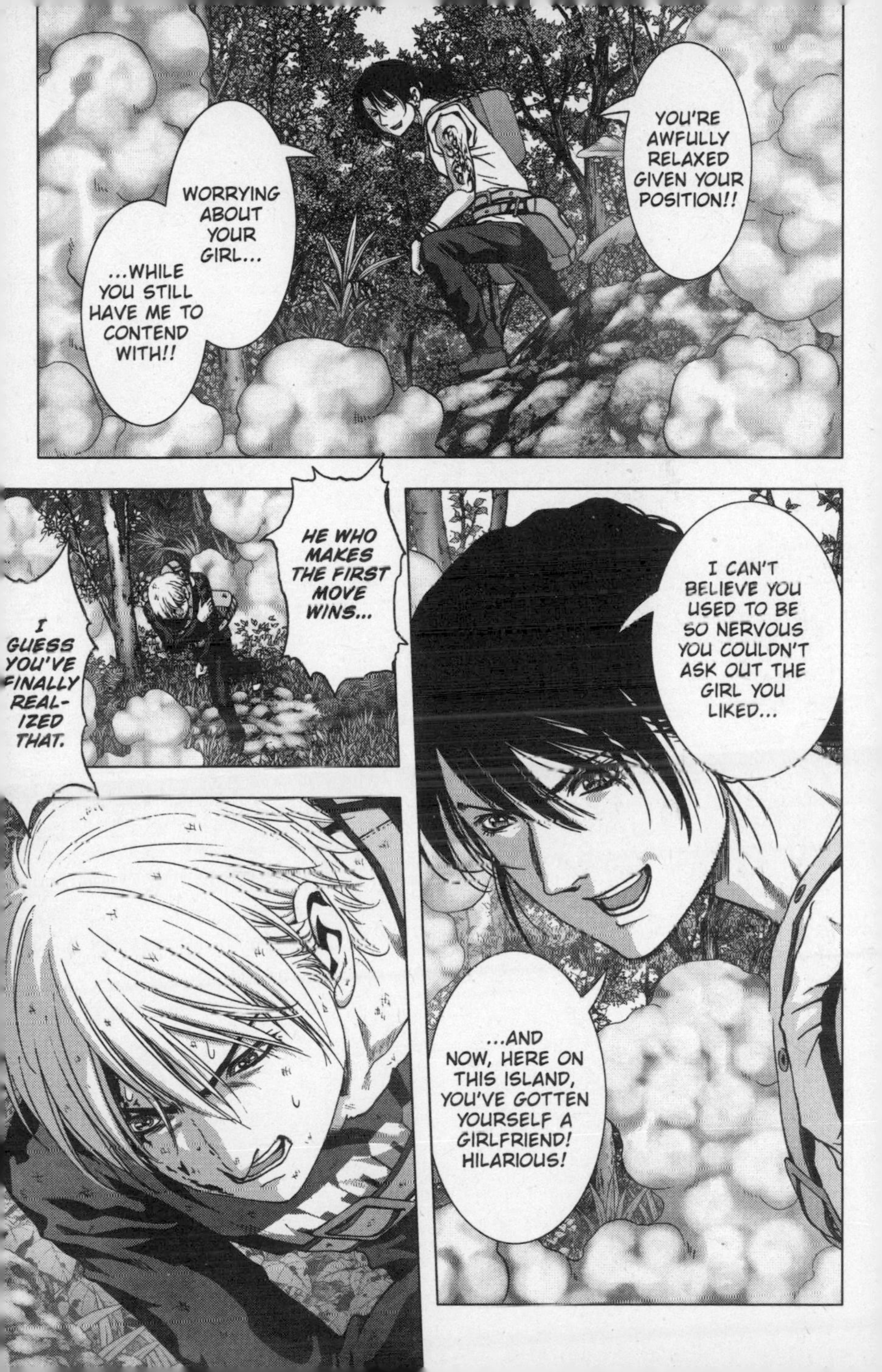
YOU'RE AWFULLY RELAXED GIVEN YOUR POSITION!!
WORRYING ABOUT YOUR GIRL...
...WHILE YOU STILL HAVE ME TO CONTEND WITH!!
I CAN'T BELIEVE YOU USED TO BE SO NERVOUS YOU COULDN'T ASK OUT THE GIRL YOU LIKED...
...AND NOW, HERE ON THIS ISLAND, YOU'VE GOTTEN YOURSELF A GIRLFRIEND! HILARIOUS!
HE WHO MAKES THE FIRST MOVE WINS...
I GUESS YOU'VE FINALLY REAL-IZED THAT.

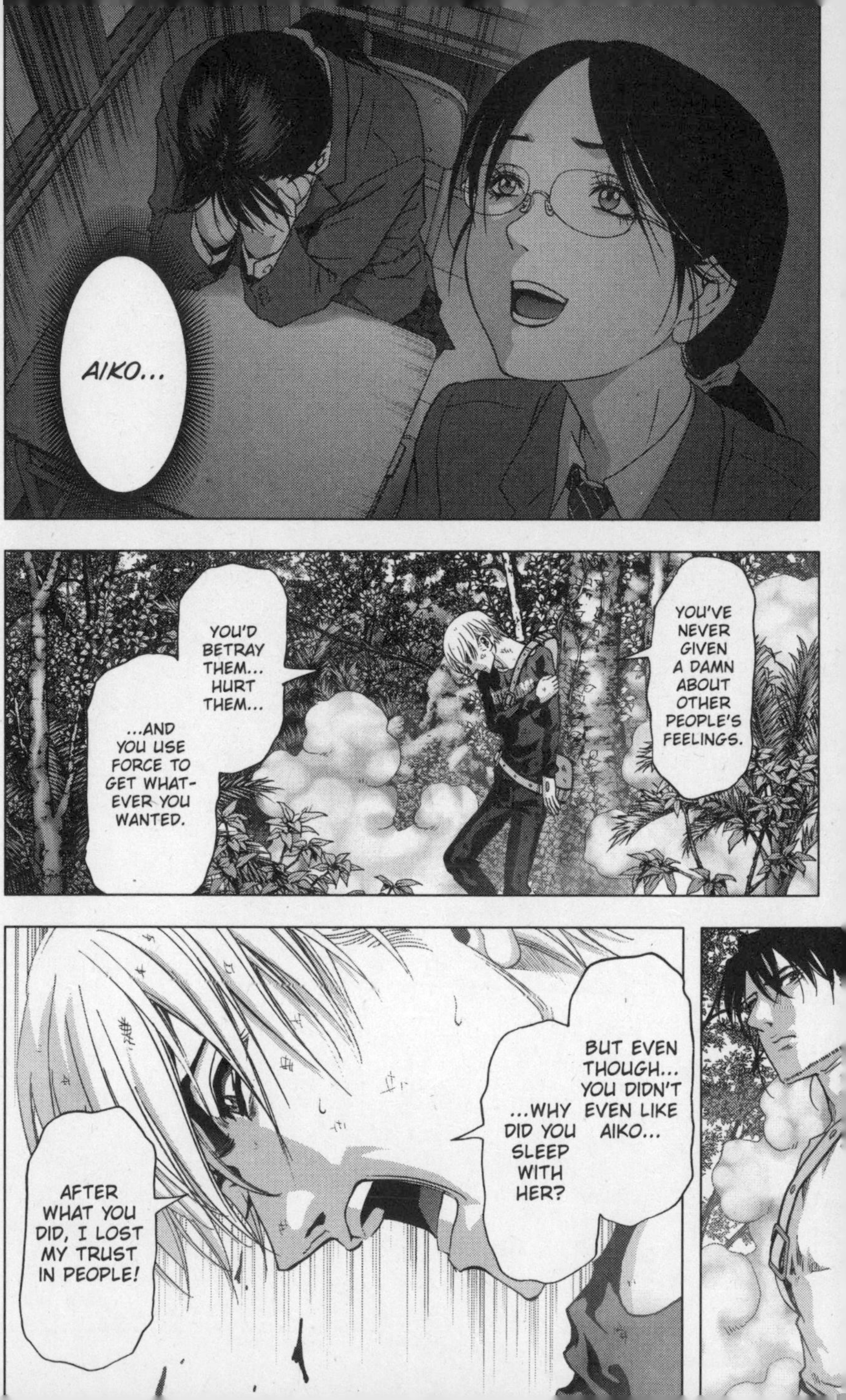
AIKO...
YOU'VE NEVER GIVEN A DAMN ABOUT OTHER PEOPLE'S FEELINGS.
YOU'D BETRAY THEM... HURT THEM...
...AND YOU USE FORCE TO GET WHAT-EVER YOU WANTED.
BUT EVEN THOUGH... YOU DIDN'T EVEN LIKE AIKO...
...WHY DID YOU SLEEP WITH HER?
AFTER WHAT YOU DID, I LOST MY TRUST IN PEOPLE!

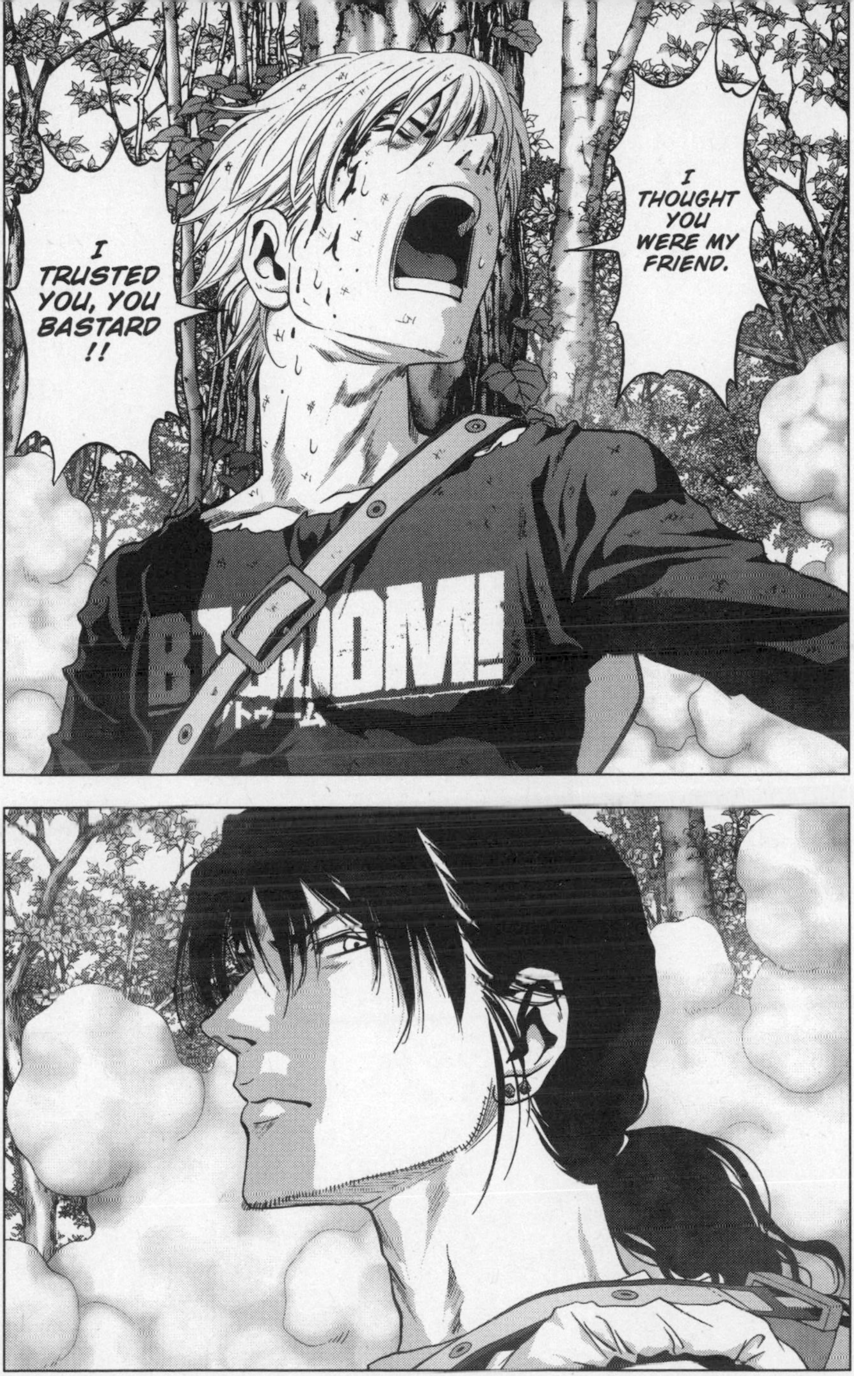
I THOUGHT YOU WERE MY FRIEND.
I TRUSTED YOU, YOU BASTARD!!

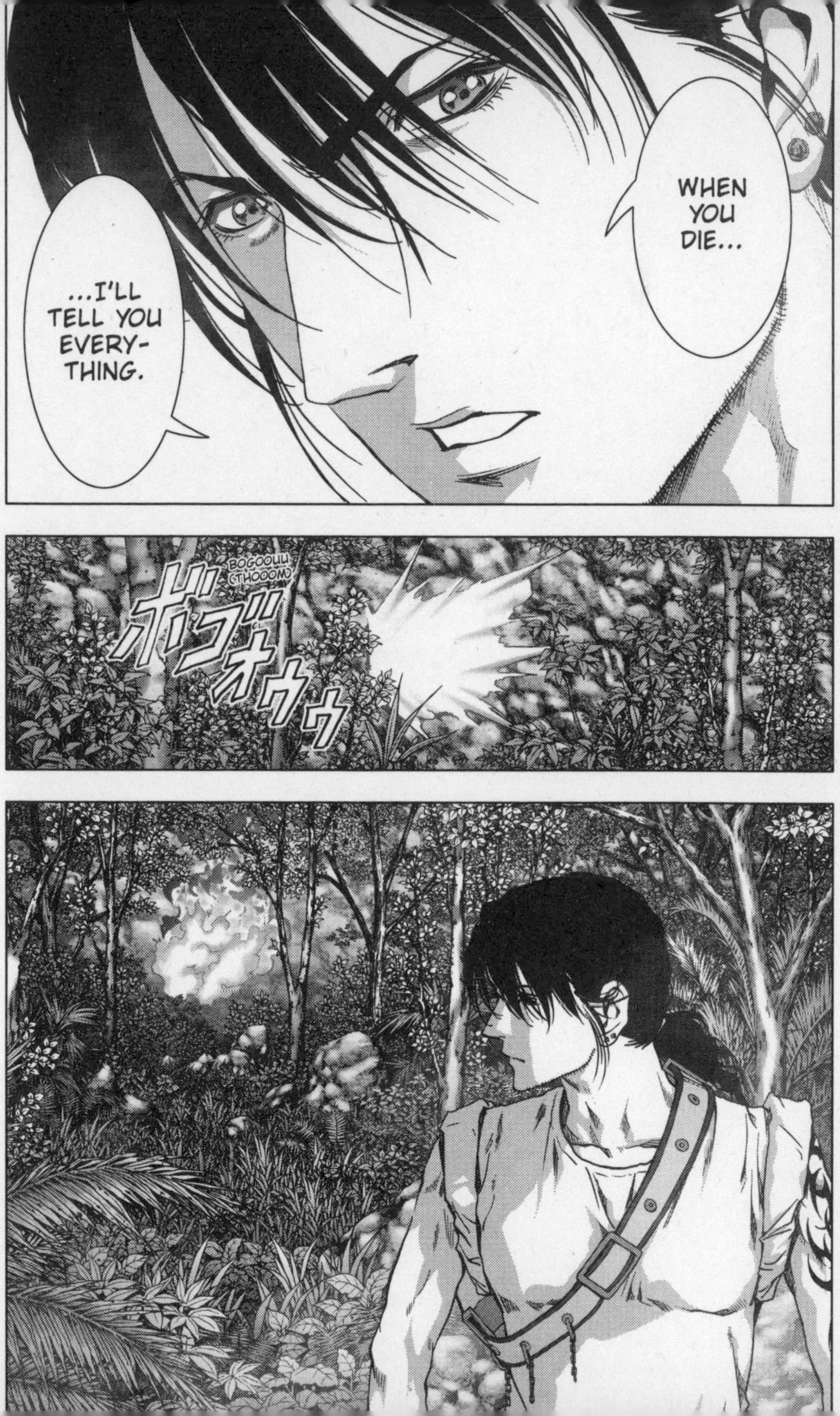
WHEN YOU DIE...
...I'LL TELL YOU EVERYTHING.
ボゴォウウ
BOGOOUU (THOOOM)

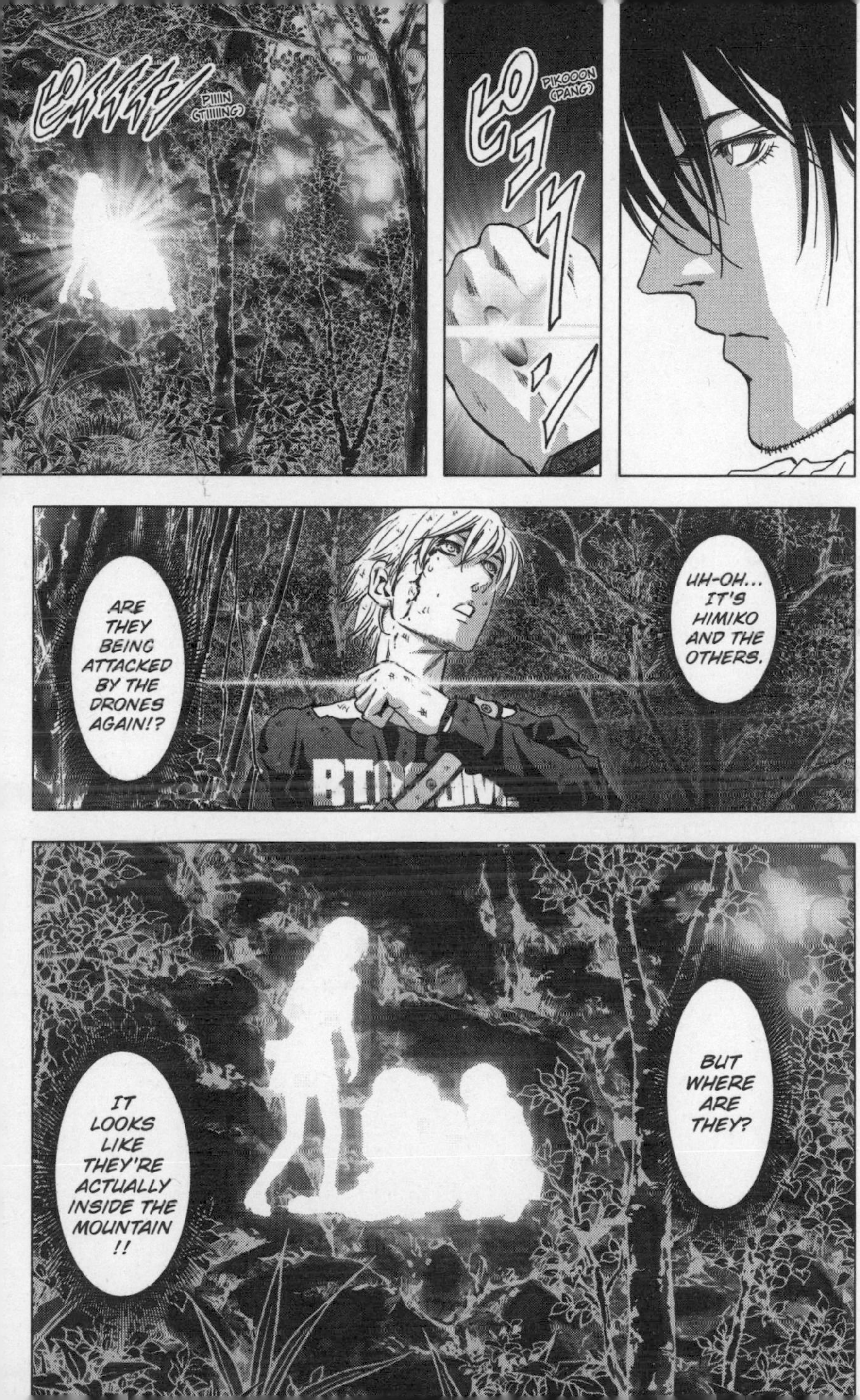
PIKOOON (PANG)
PIIIN (TIIIING)
UH-OH... IT'S HIMIKO AND THE OTHERS.
ARE THEY BEING ATTACKED BY THE DRONES AGAIN!?
BUT WHERE ARE THEY?
IT LOOKS LIKE THEY'RE ACTUALLY INSIDE THE MOUNTAIN!!

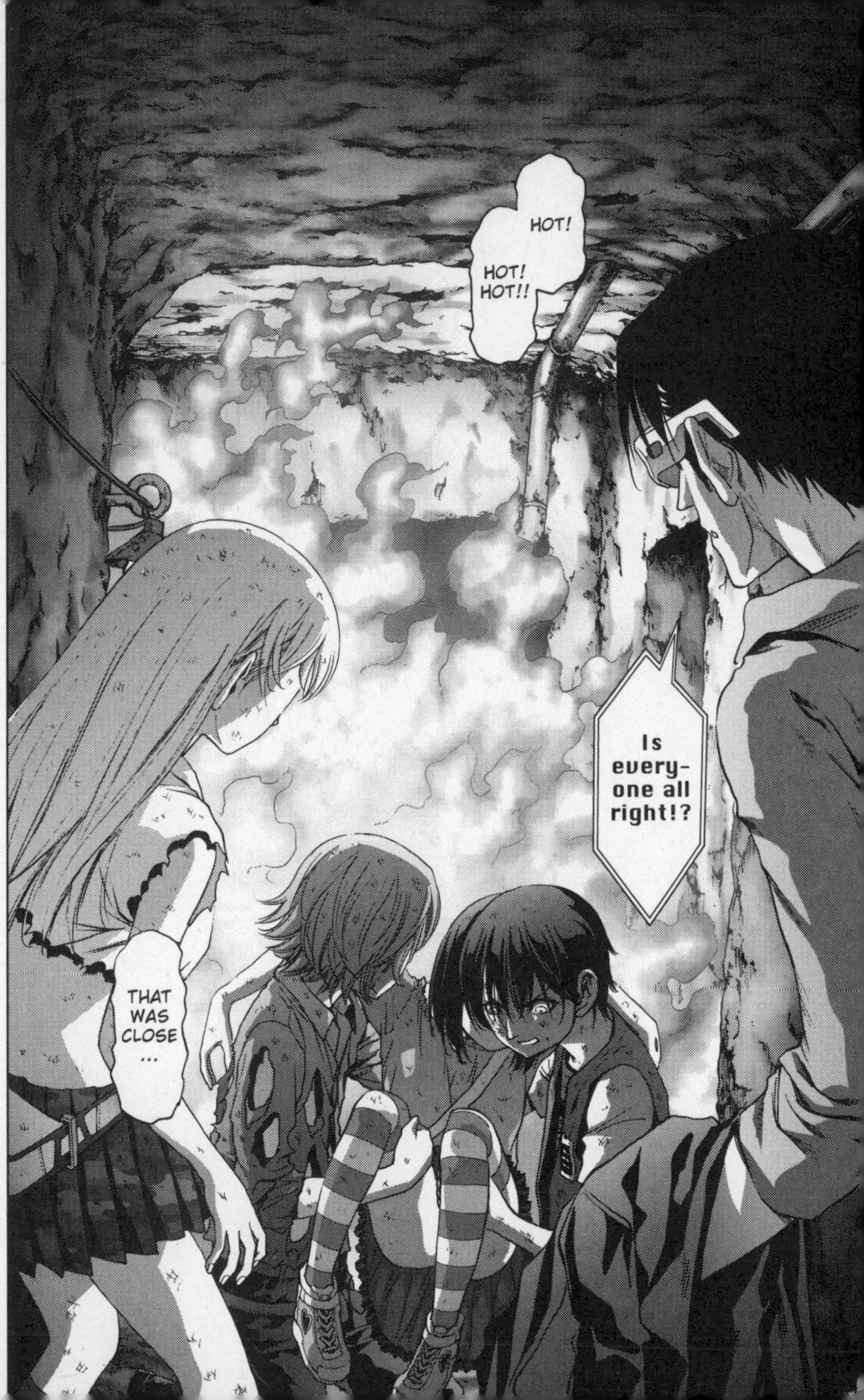
HOT! HOT! HOT!!
Is every-one all right!?
THAT WAS CLOSE...

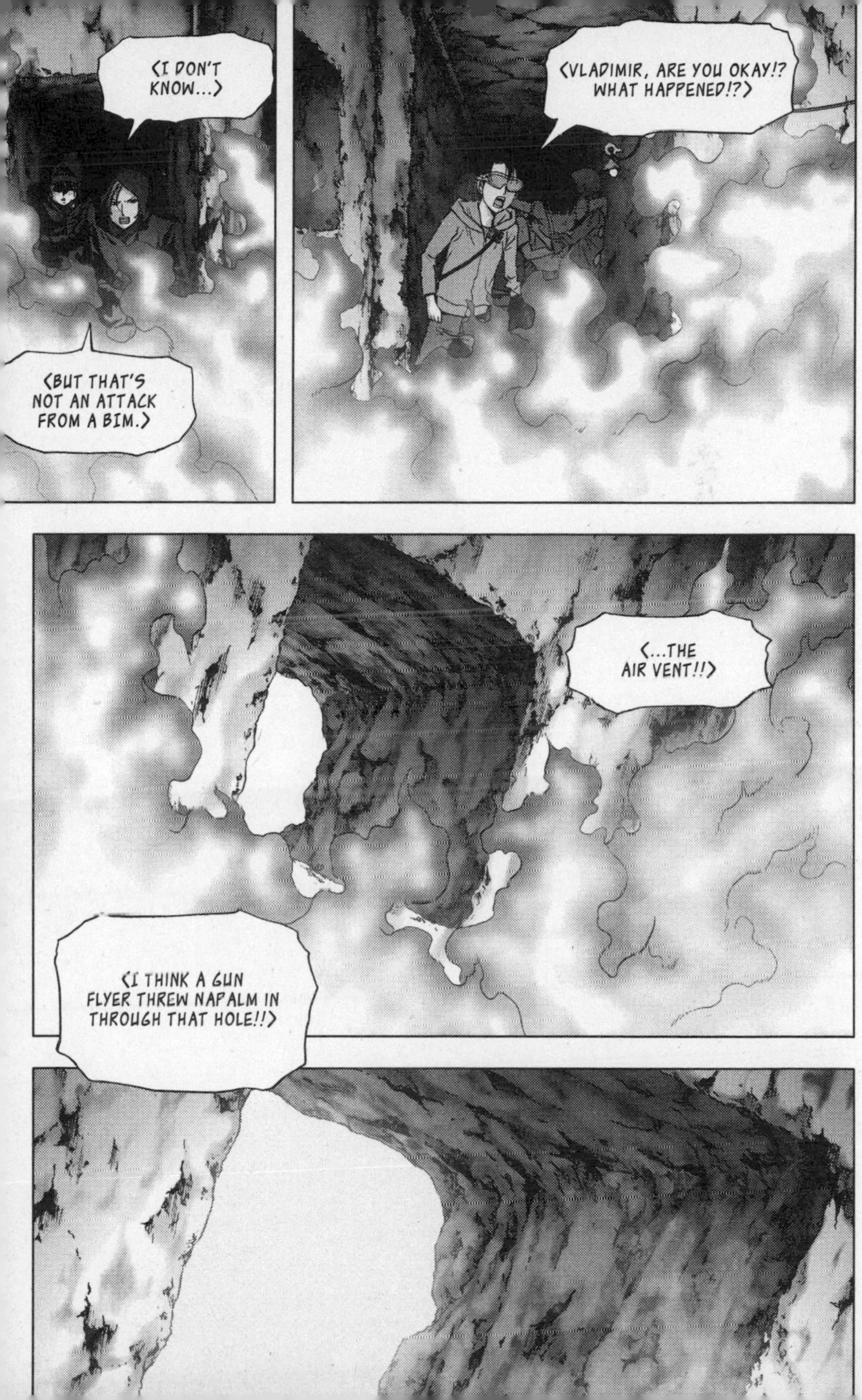
‹VLADIMIR, ARE YOU OKAY!? WHAT HAPPENED!?›
‹I DON'T KNOW...›
‹BUT THAT'S NOT AN ATTACK FROM A BIM.›
‹...THE AIR VENT!!›
‹I THINK A GUN FLYER THREW NAPALM IN THROUGH THAT HOLE!!›

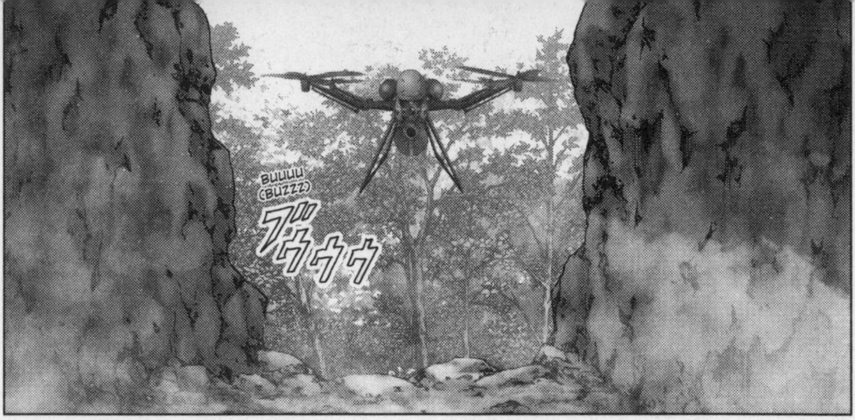
BUUUU
(BUZZZ)
ブウウウ
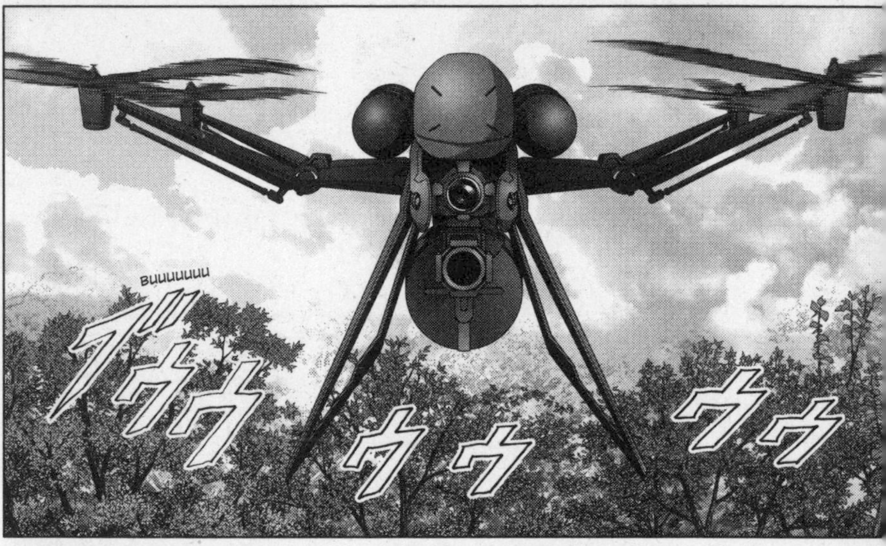
BUUUUUUUU
ブウウウウウウ
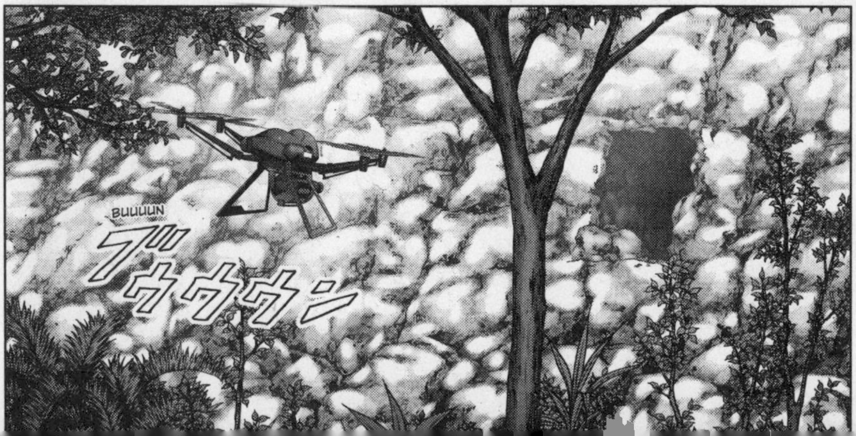
BUUUUN
ブウウウン

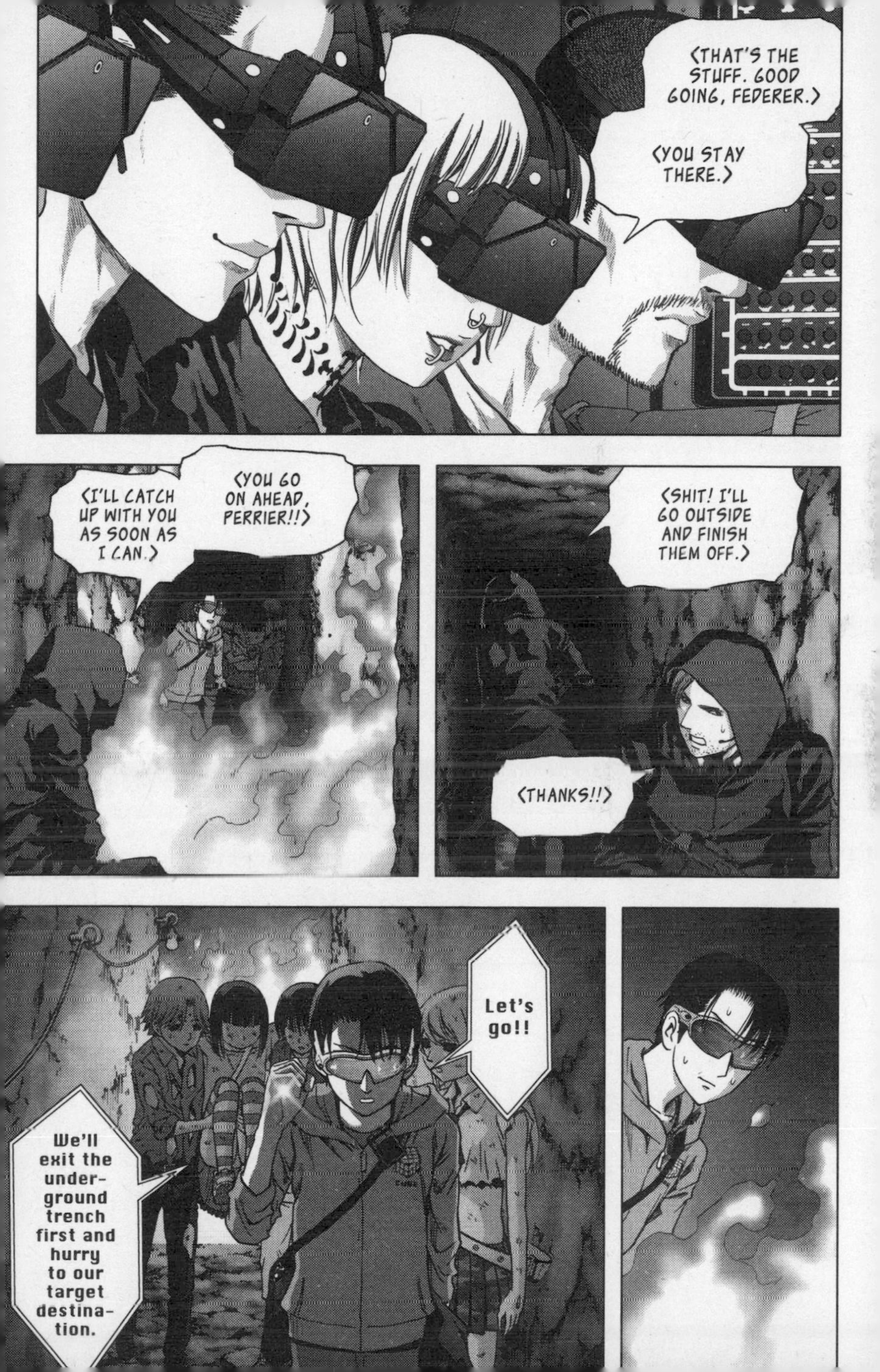
<THAT'S THE STUFF. GOOD GOING, FEDERER.>
<YOU STAY THERE.>
<SHIT! I'LL GO OUTSIDE AND FINISH THEM OFF.>
<THANKS!!>
<YOU GO ON AHEAD, PERRIER!!>
<I'LL CATCH UP WITH YOU AS SOON AS I CAN.>
Let's go!!
We'll exit the under-ground trench first and hurry to our target destina-tion.

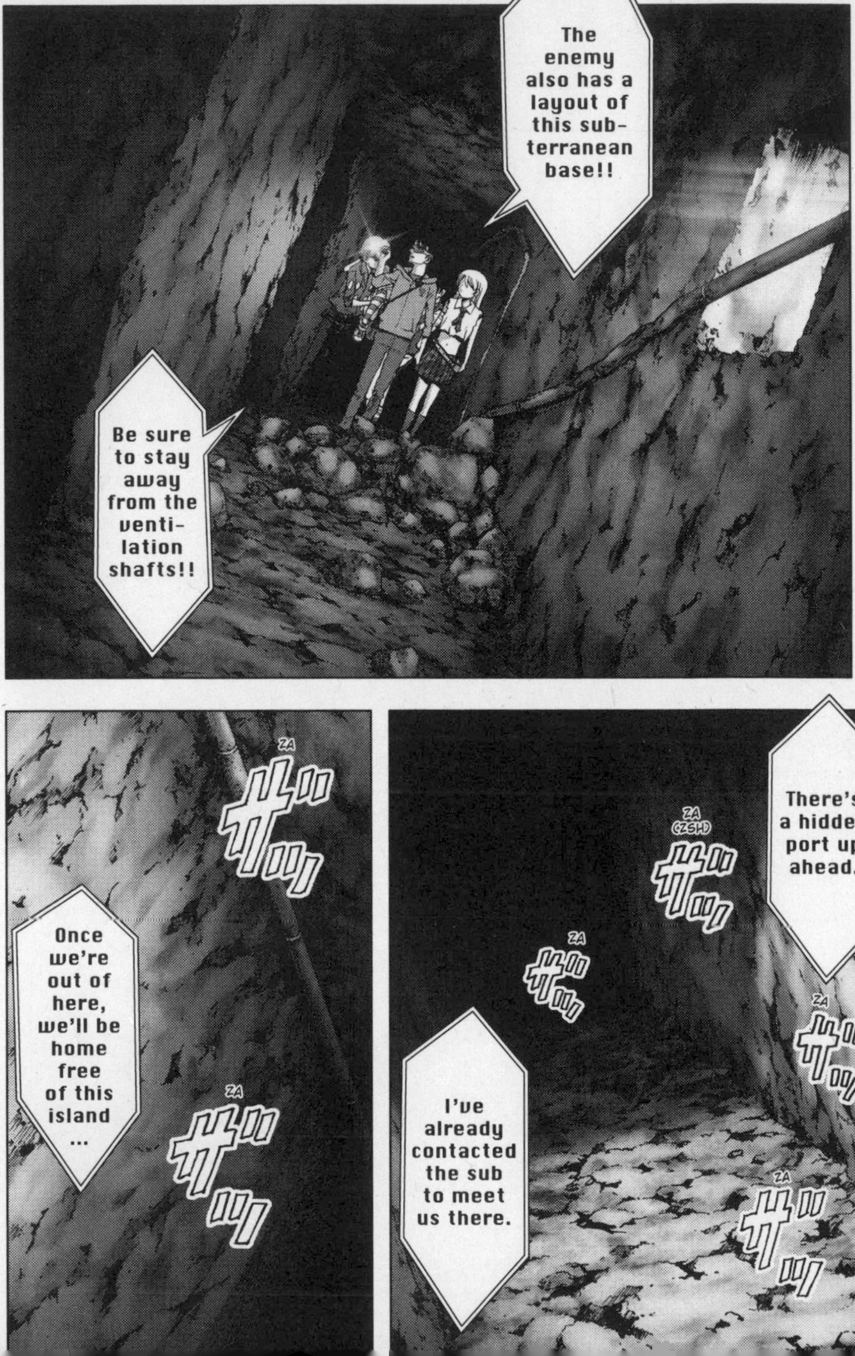
The enemy also has a layout of this sub-terranean base!!
Be sure to stay away from the venti-lation shafts!!
There's a hidden port up ahead.
ZA (ZSH)
ZA
ZA
I've already contacted the sub to meet us there.
ZA
ZA
Once we're out of here, we'll be home free of this island ...
ZA

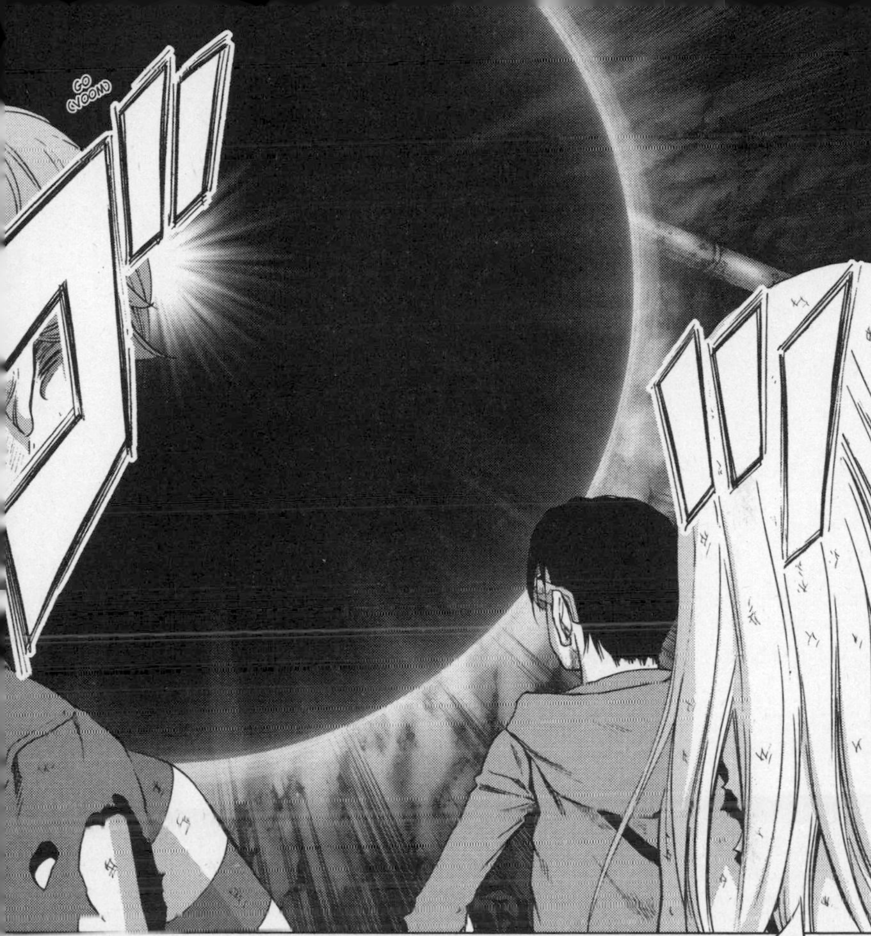
GO
(VOOM)

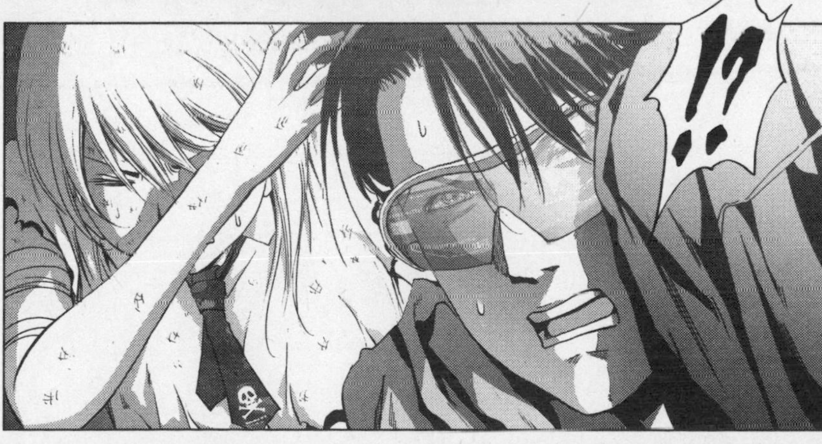
!?

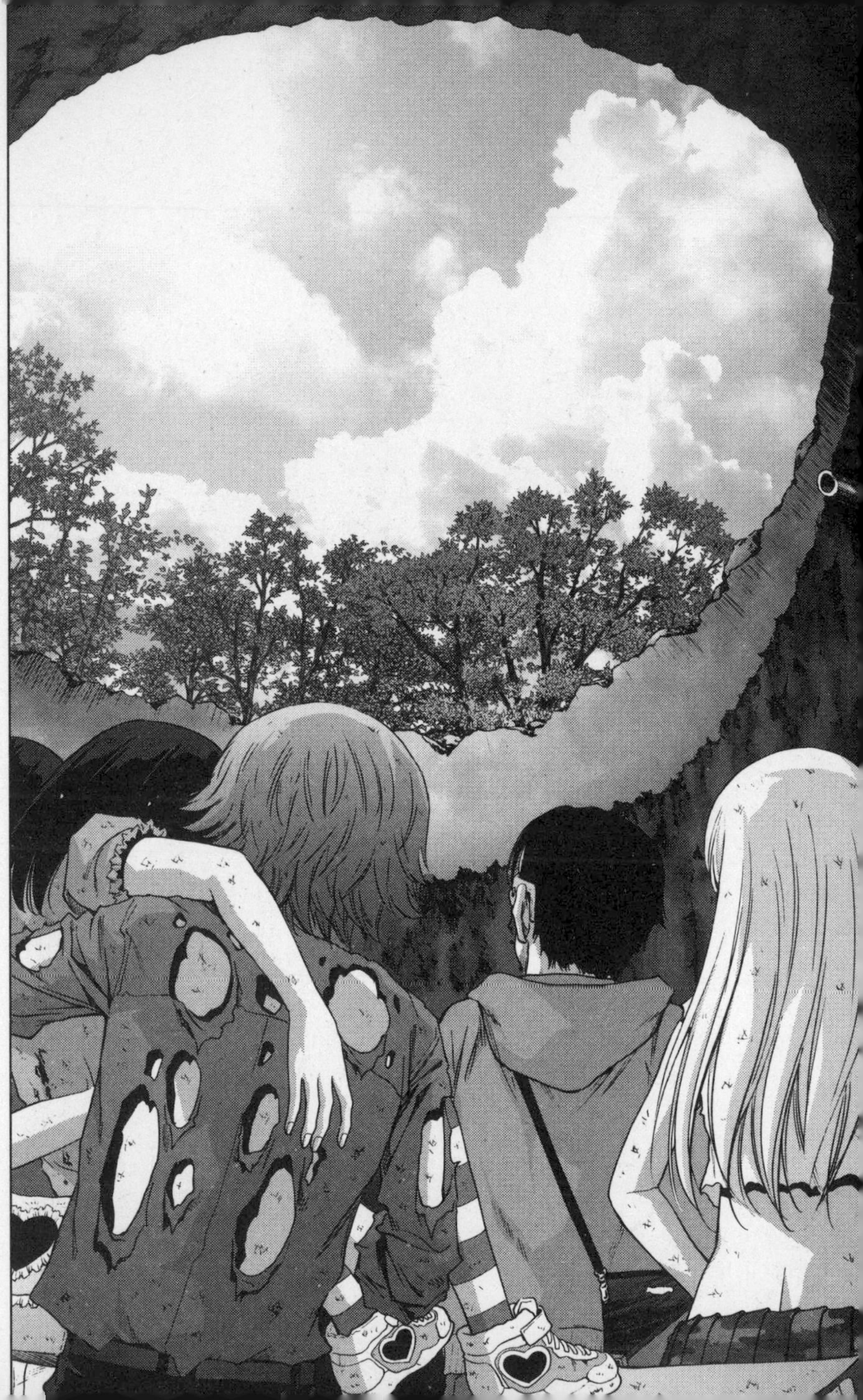

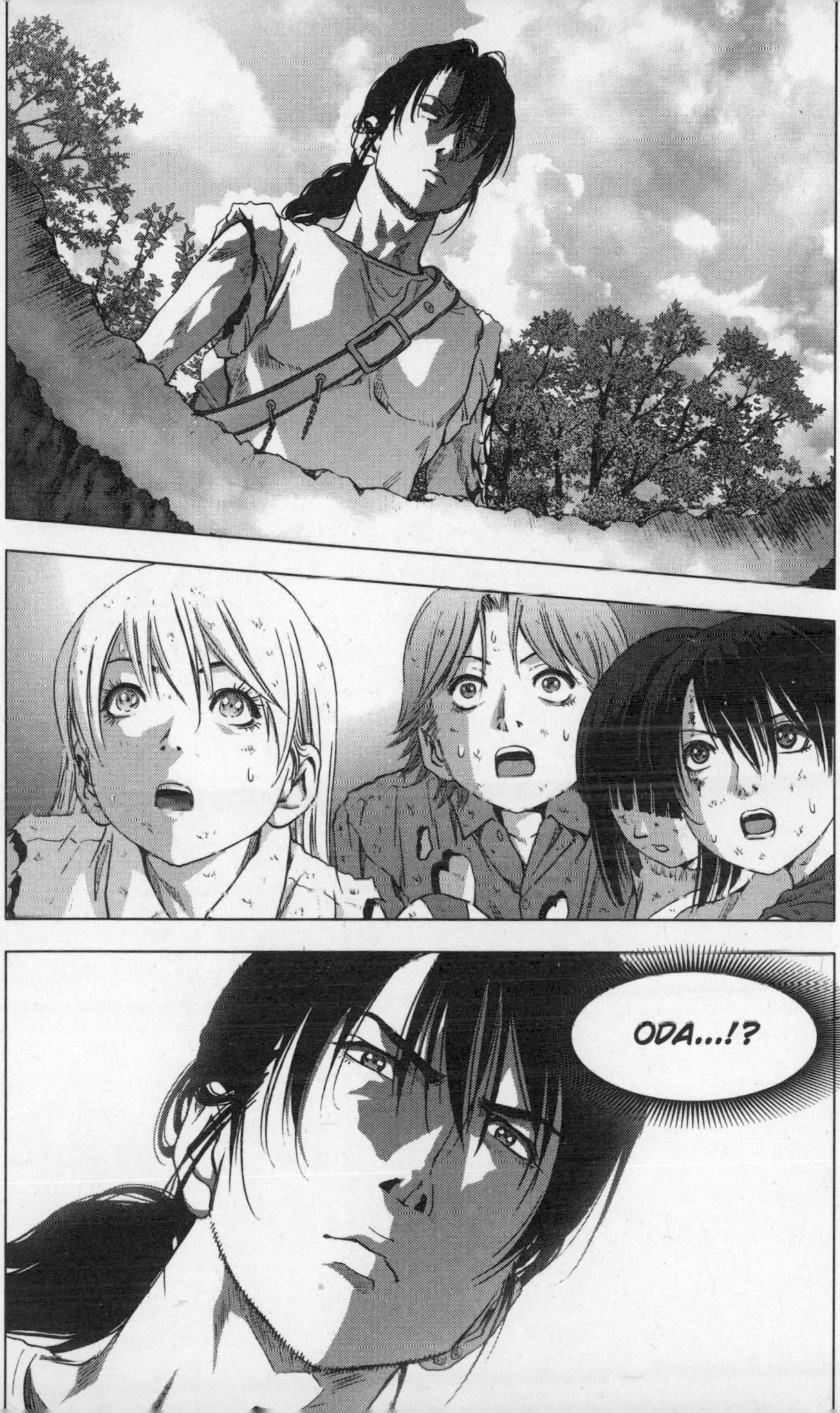
ODA...!?

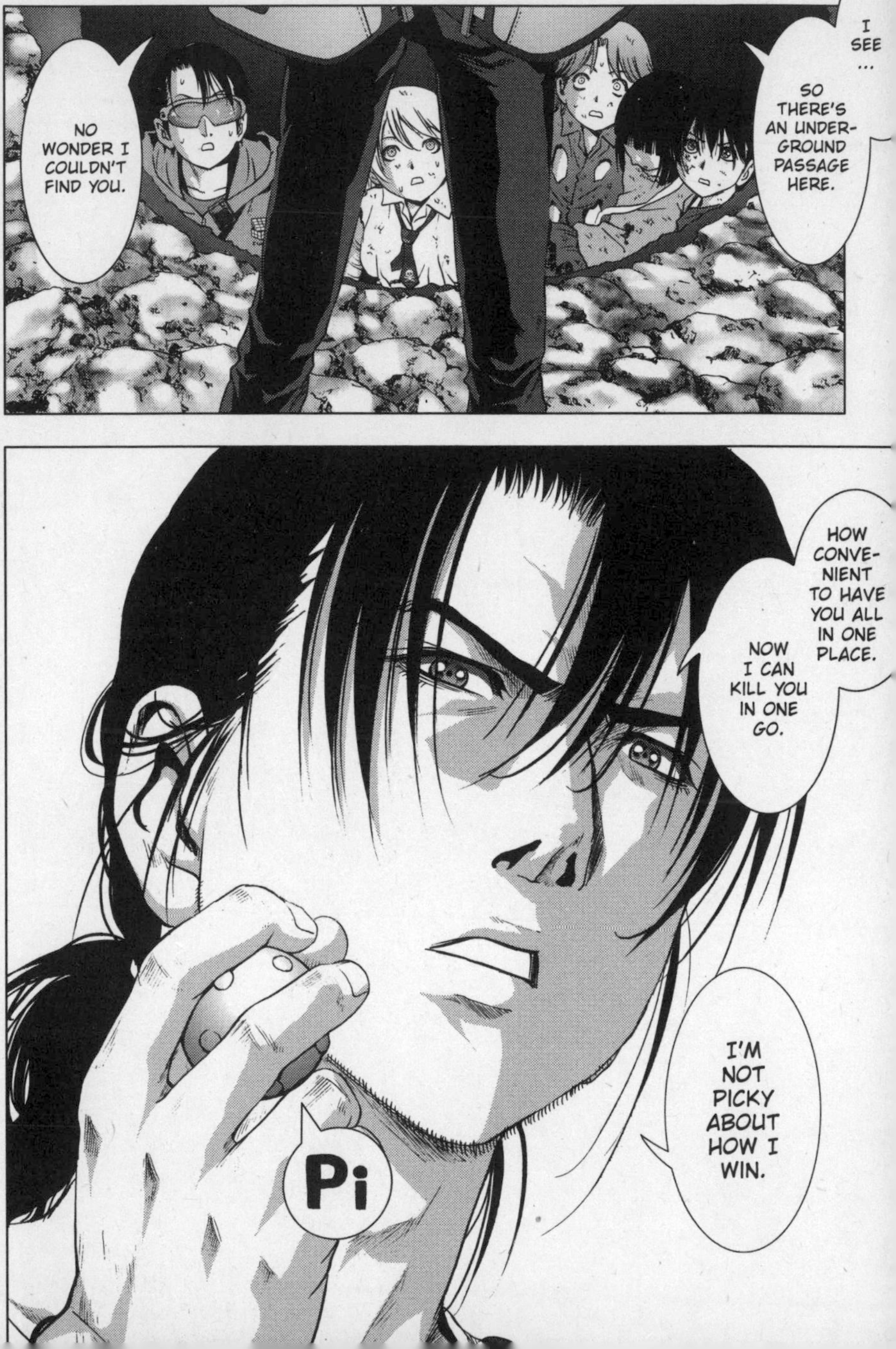
I SEE ...
SO THERE'S AN UNDER-GROUND PASSAGE HERE.
NO WONDER I COULDN'T FIND YOU.
HOW CONVE-NIENT TO HAVE YOU ALL IN ONE PLACE.
NOW I CAN KILL YOU IN ONE GO.
I'M NOT PICKY ABOUT HOW I WIN.
Pi

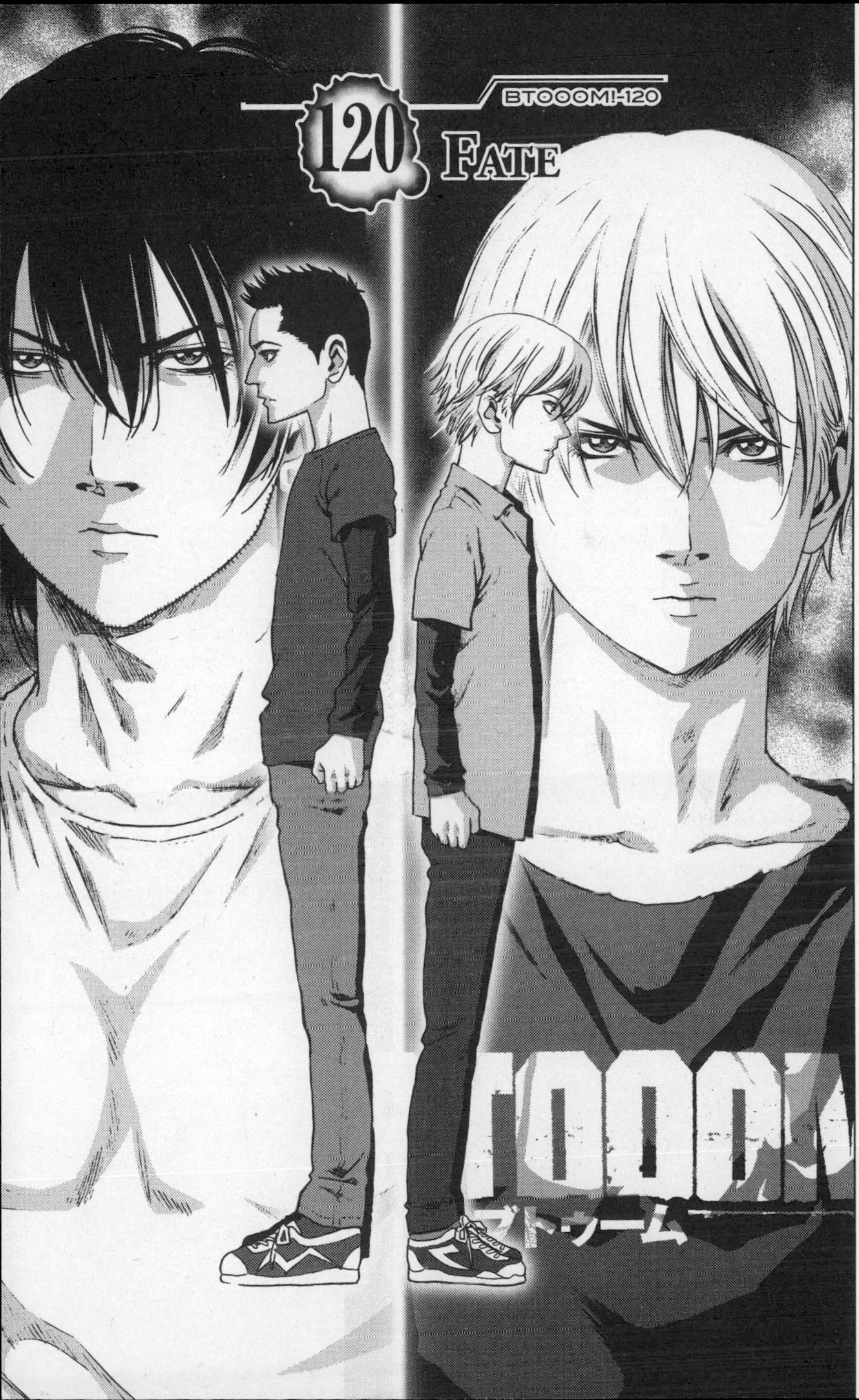
BTOOOM!-120
120
FATE

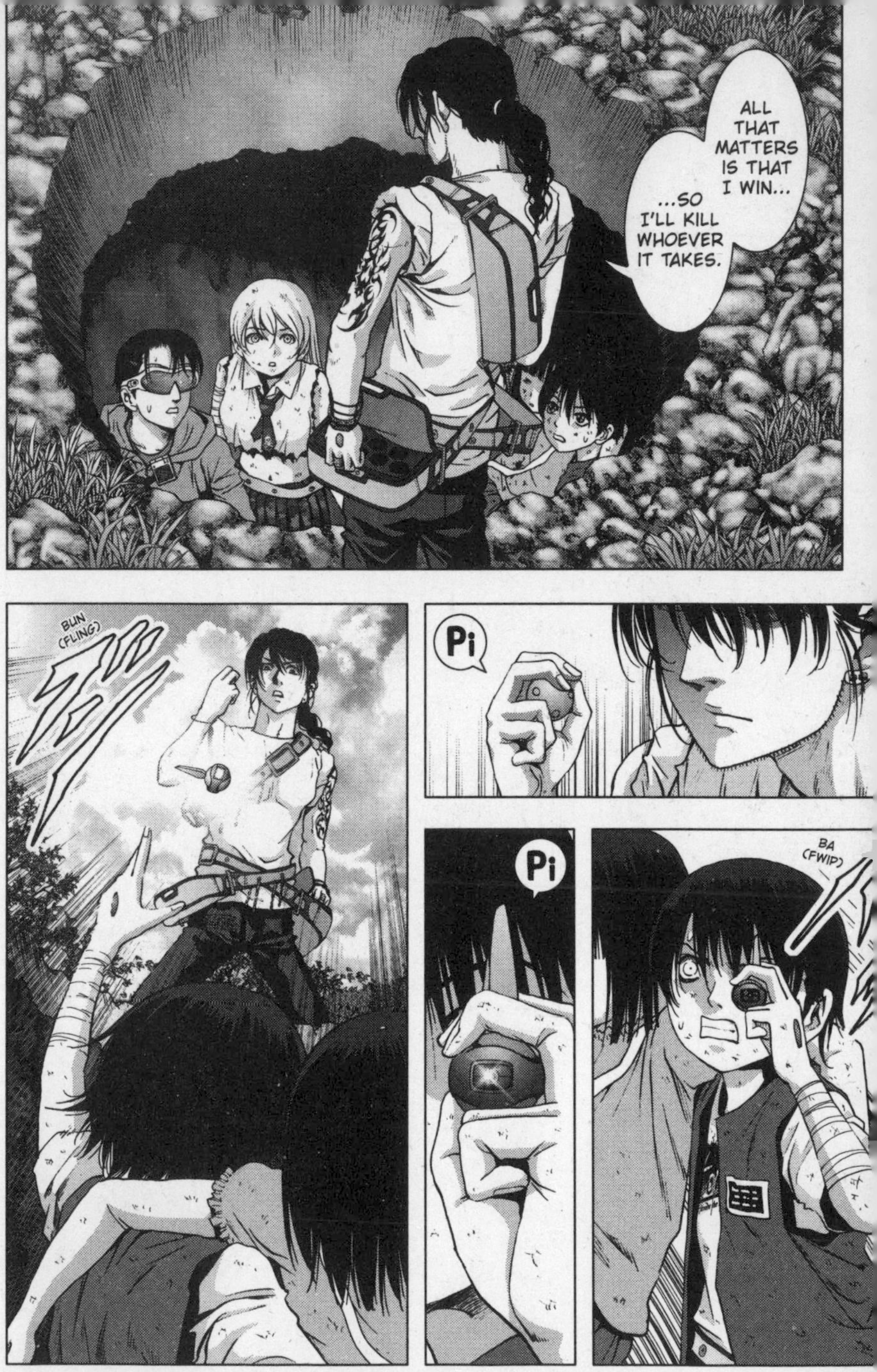
ALL THAT MATTERS IS THAT I WIN...
...SO I'LL KILL WHOEVER IT TAKES.
Pi
BUN (FLING)
BA (FWIP)
Pi

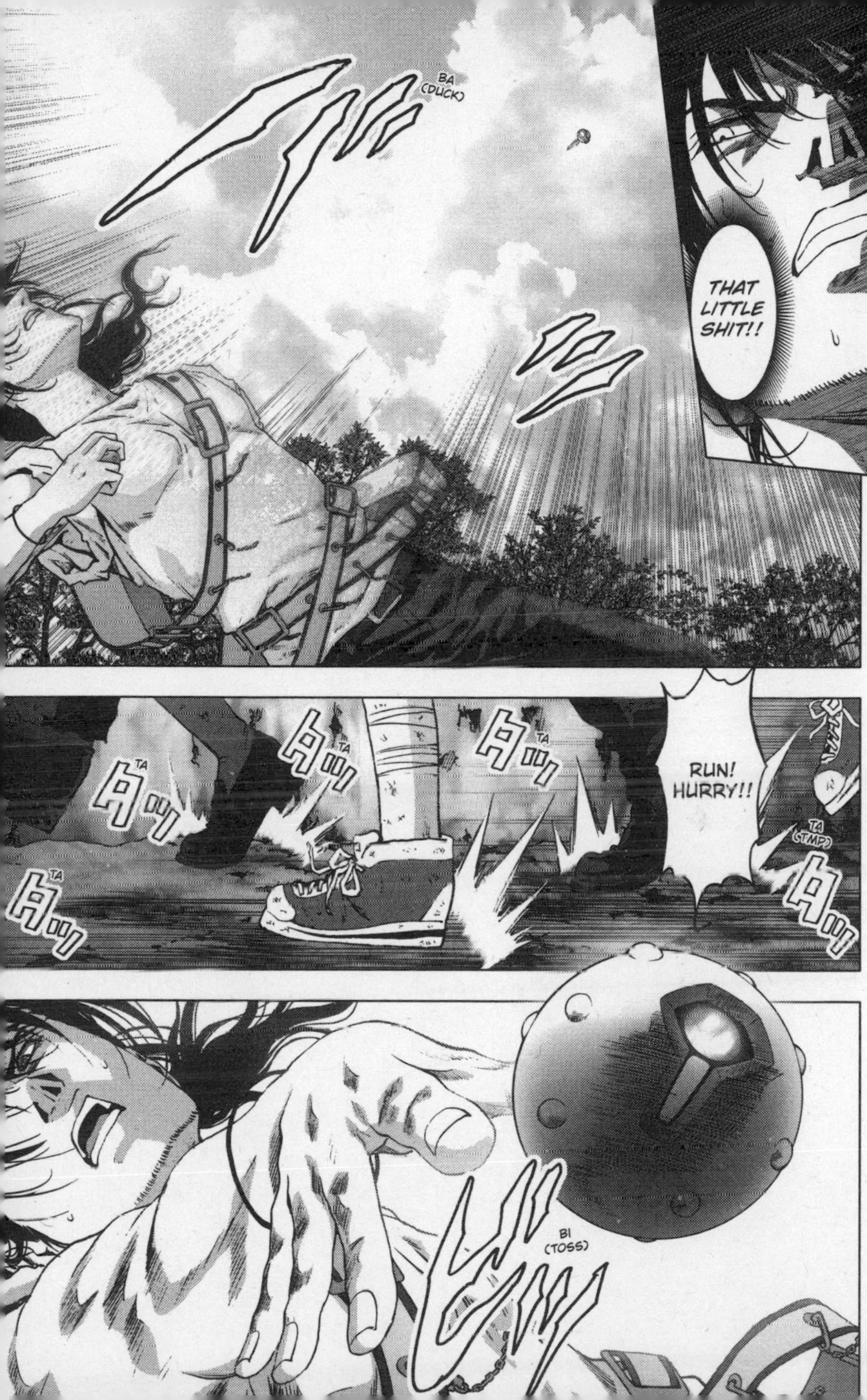
THAT LITTLE SHIT!!
BA (DUCK)
TA (TMP)
RUN! HURRY!!
TA
TA
TA
TA
BI (TOSS)

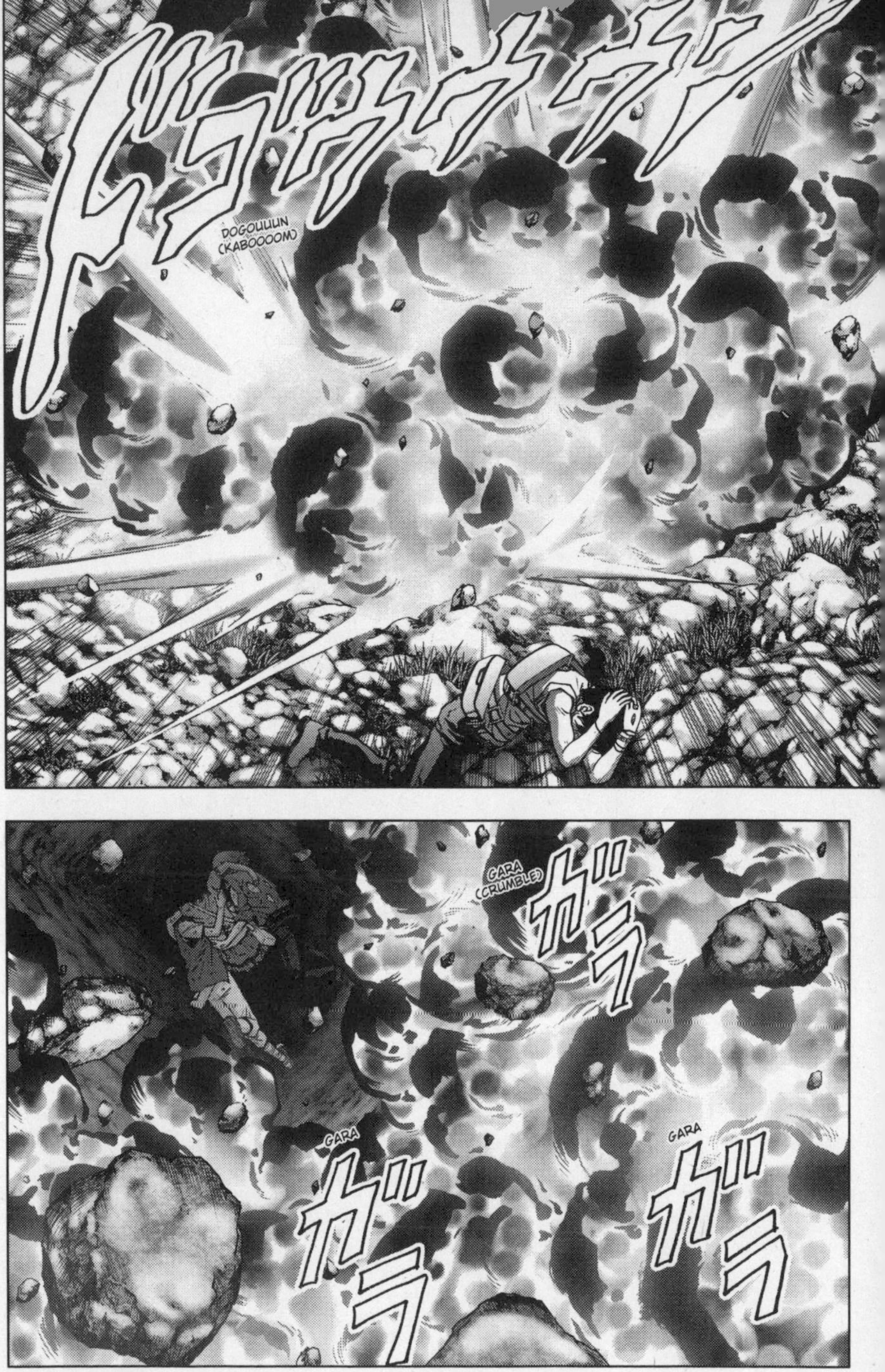
DOGOUUUN
(KABOOOOM)
GARA
(CRUMBLE)
ガラ
GARA
ガラ
GARA
ガラ

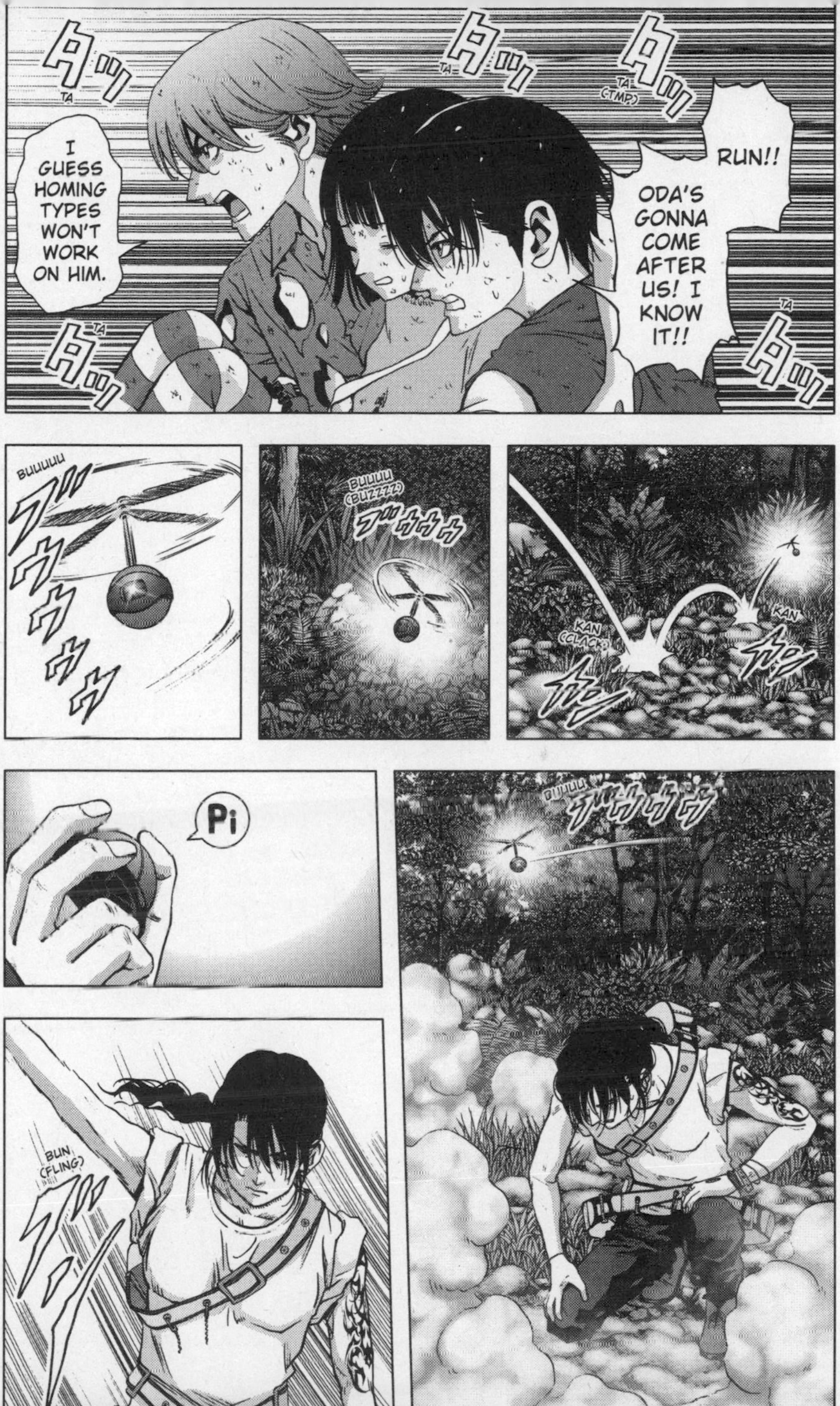
TA (TMP.)
TA
TA
RUN!!
ODA'S GONNA COME AFTER US! I KNOW IT!!
TA
I GUESS HOMING TYPES WON'T WORK ON HIM.
TA
KAN
KAN (CLACK)
BUUUU (BUZZZZ)
BUUUUU
BUUUUU
Pi
BUN (FLING)

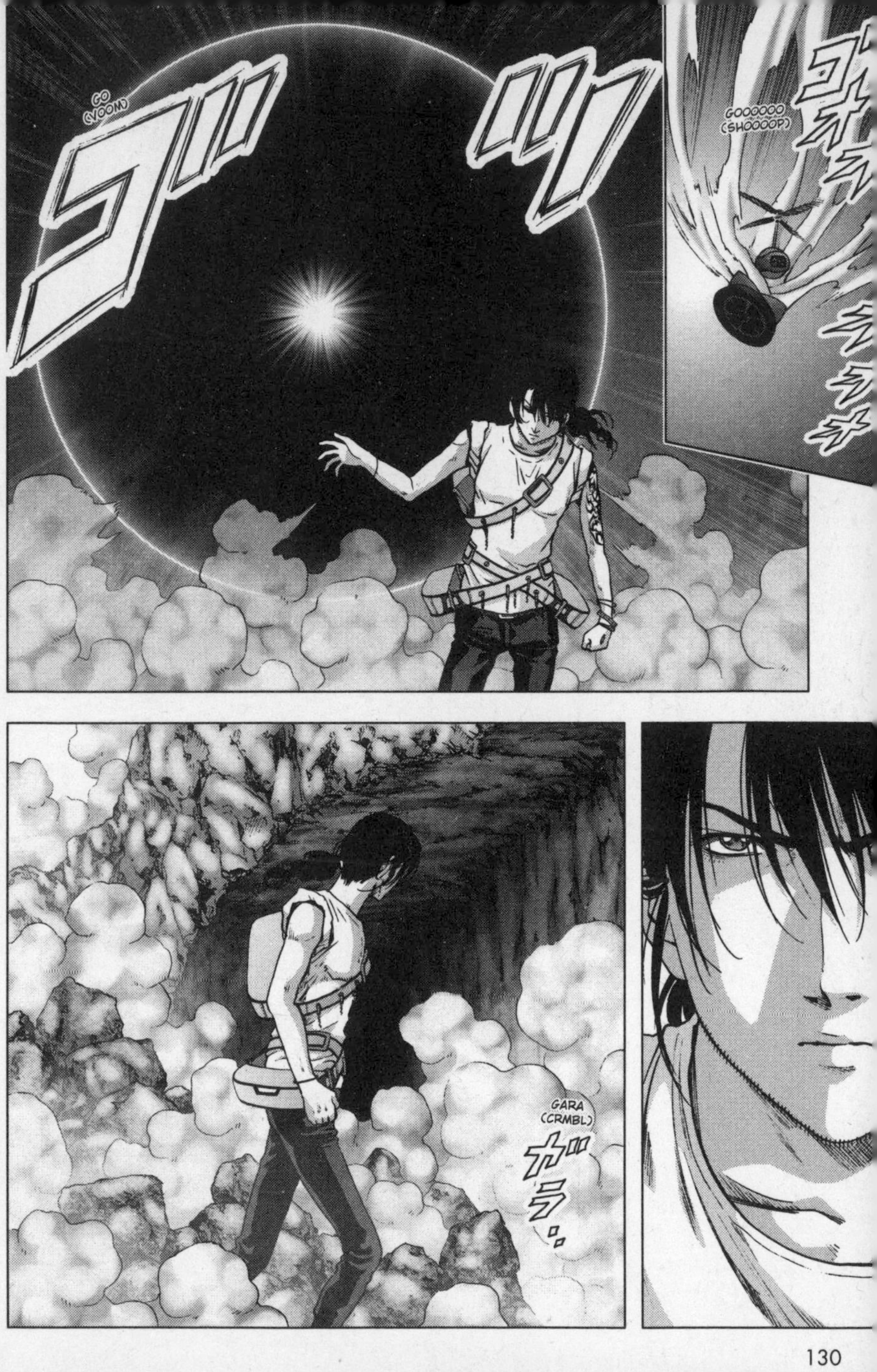
GOOOOOO
(SHOOOOP)
GO
(VOOM)
GARA
(CRMBL)

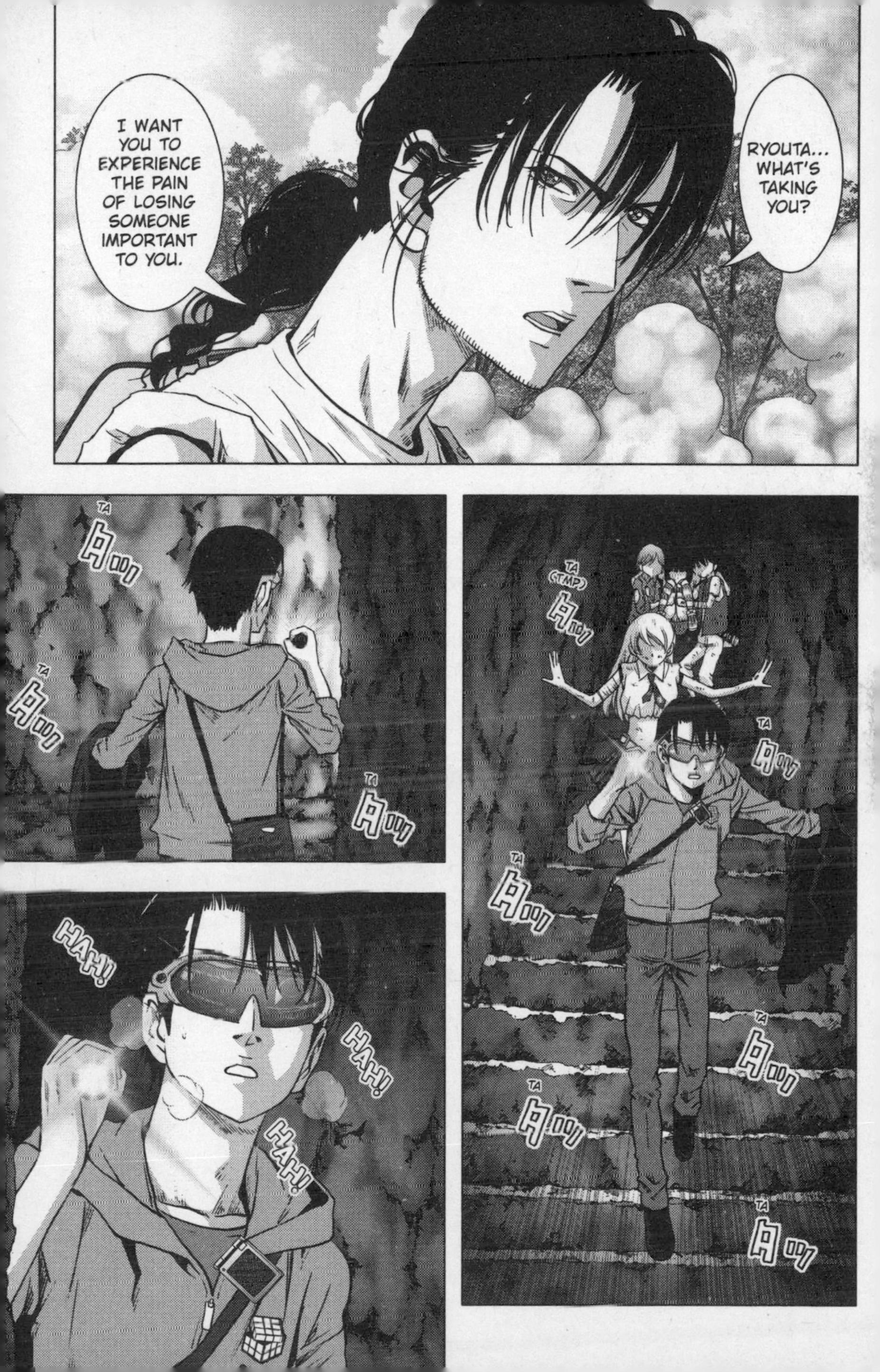
RYOUTA... WHAT'S TAKING YOU?
I WANT YOU TO EXPERIENCE THE PAIN OF LOSING SOMEONE IMPORTANT TO YOU.
TA (TMP)
TA
TA
TA
TA
TA
TA
TA
TA
HAH!
HAH!
HAH!

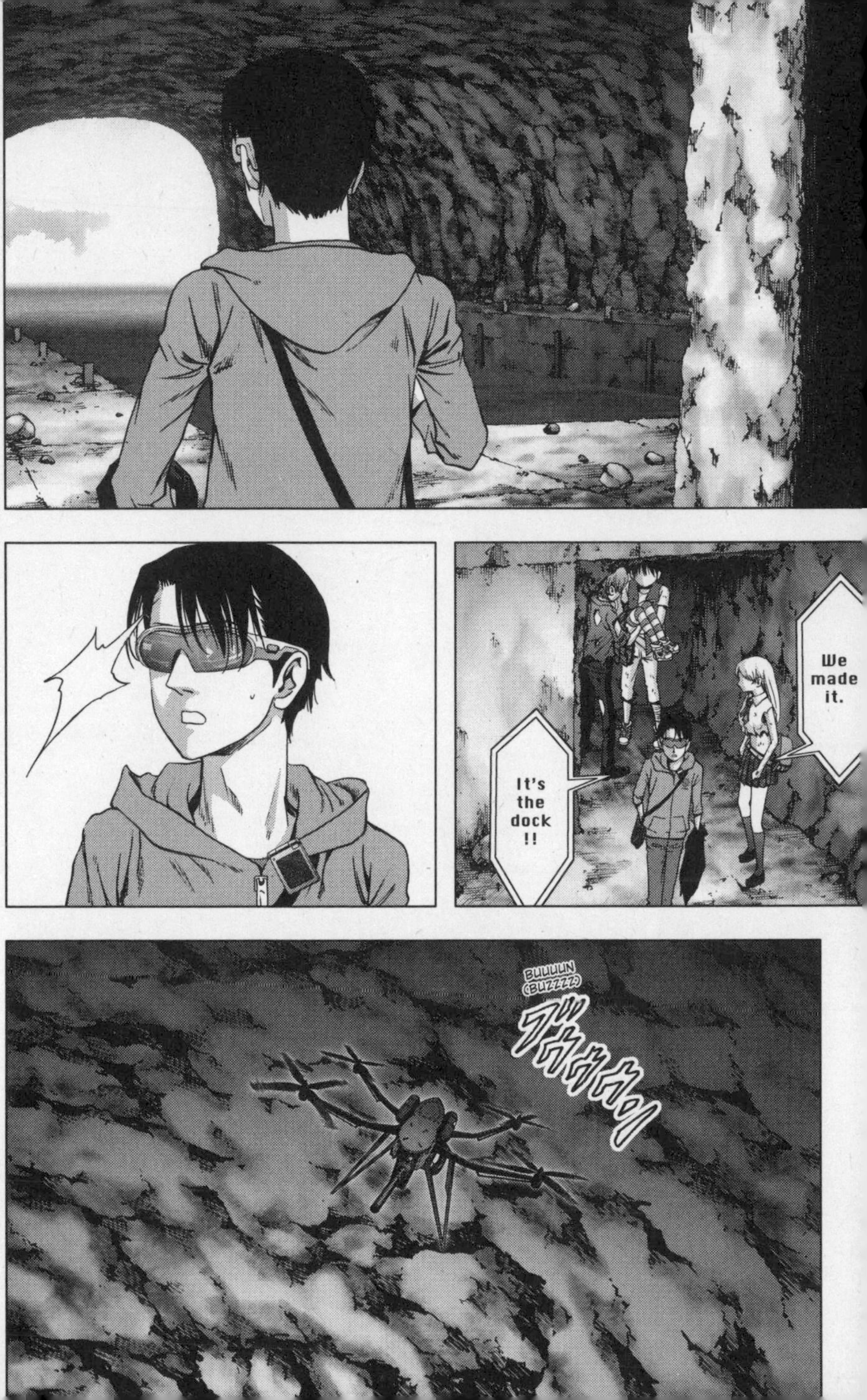
We made it.
It's the dock !!
BUUUUN (BUZZZZ)

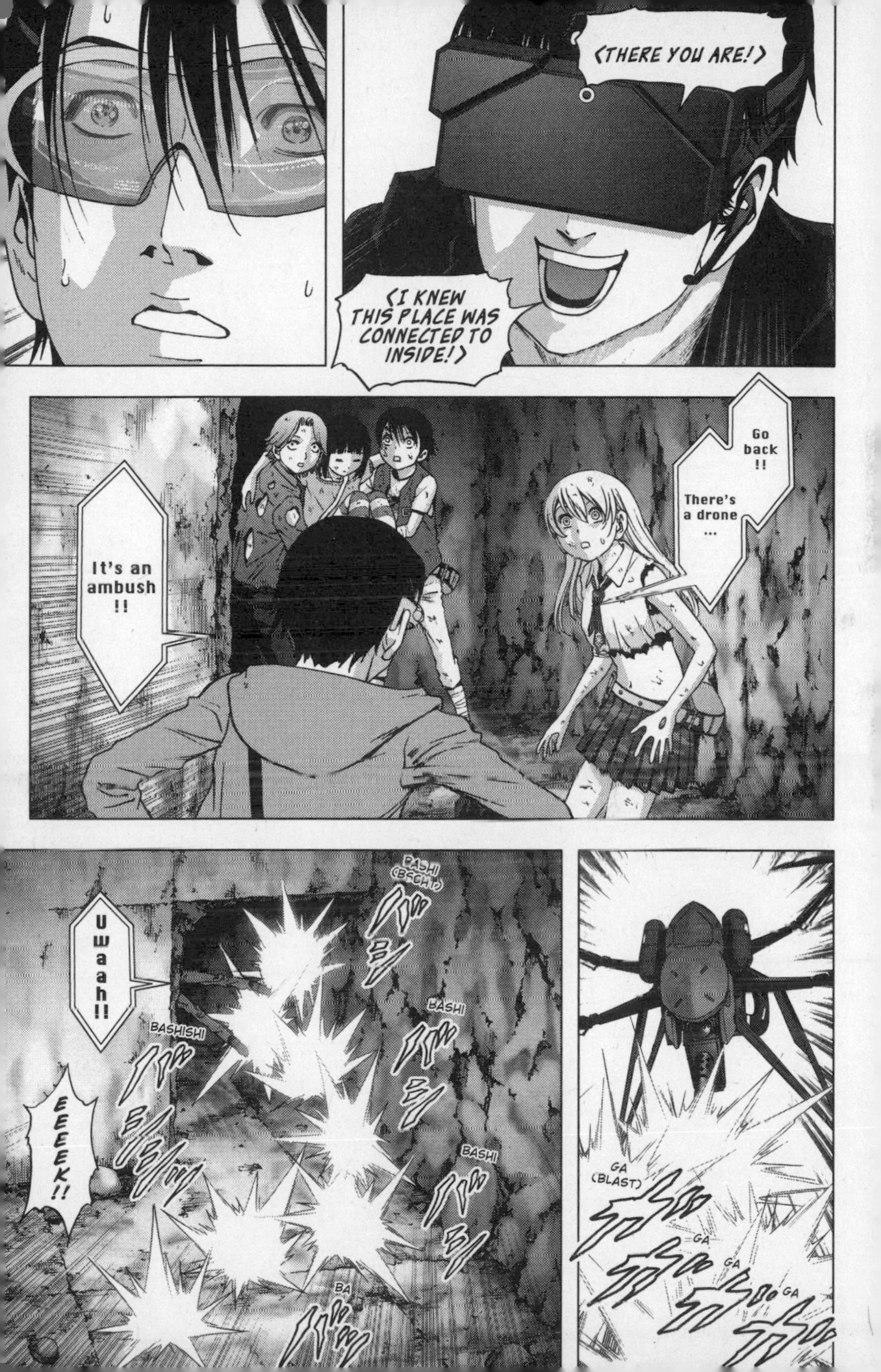
〈THERE YOU ARE!〉
〈I KNEW THIS PLACE WAS CONNECTED TO INSIDE!〉
Go back!! There's a drone...
It's an ambush!!
GA (BLAST)
GA
GA
GA
BASHI (BSCH!)
Uwaah!!
BASHI
BASHISHI
BASHI
EEEEK!!
BA

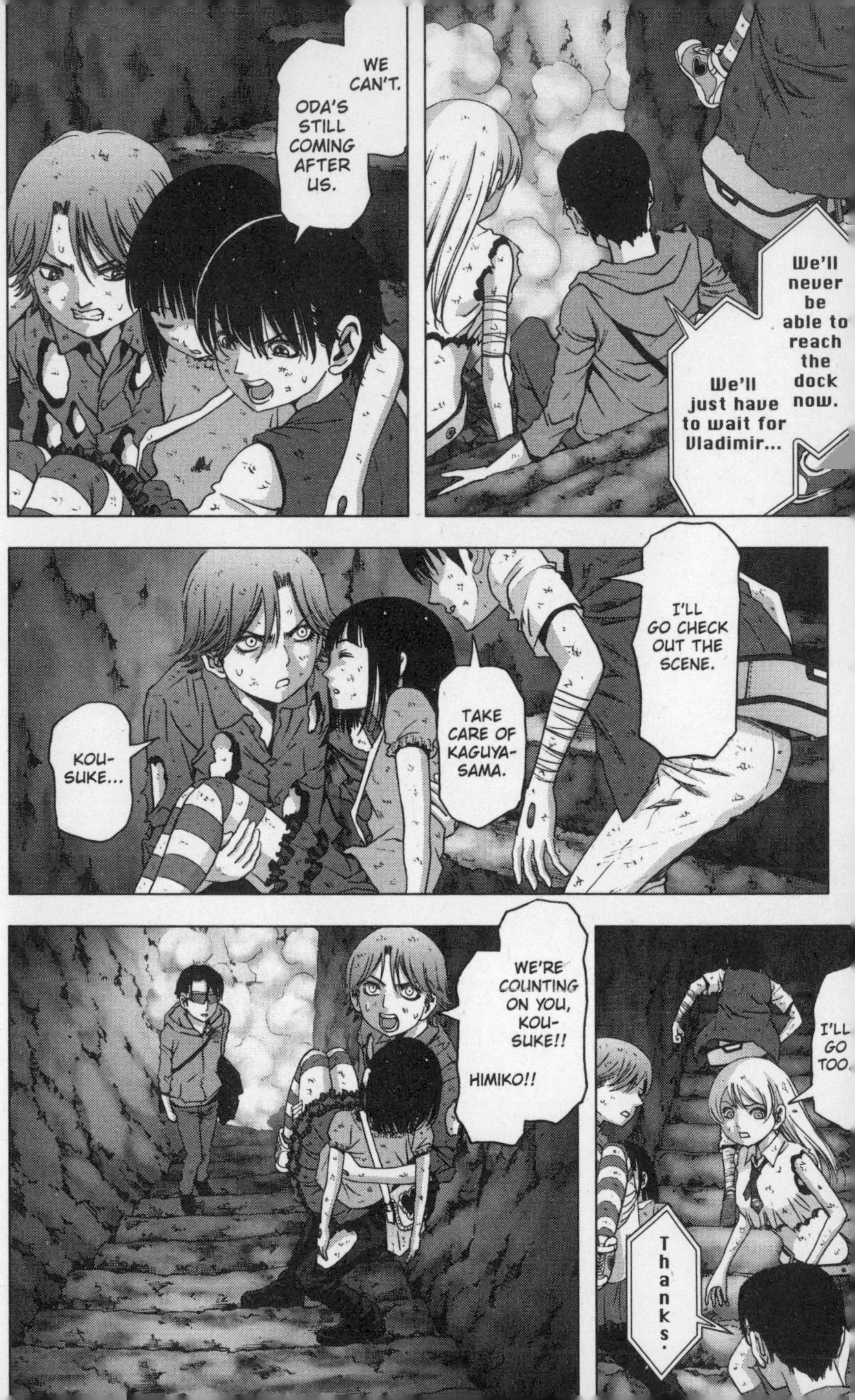
We'll never be able to reach the dock now.
We'll just have to wait for Vladimir...
WE CAN'T.
ODA'S STILL COMING AFTER US.
I'LL GO CHECK OUT THE SCENE.
TAKE CARE OF KAGUYA-SAMA.
KOU-SUKE...
I'LL GO TOO.
Thanks.
WE'RE COUNTING ON YOU, KOU-SUKE!!
HIMIKO!!

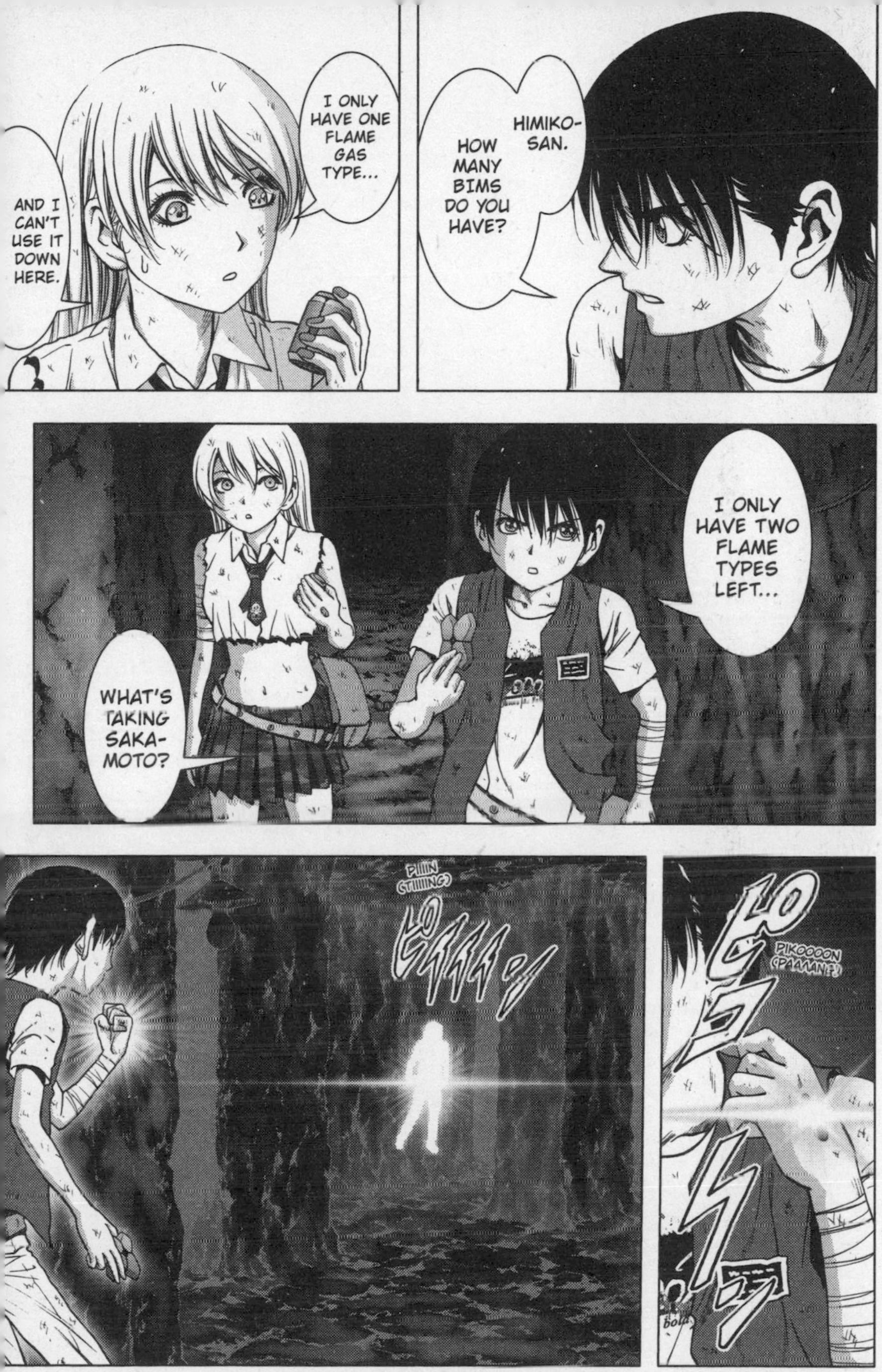
HIMIKO-SAN.
HOW MANY BIMS DO YOU HAVE?
I ONLY HAVE ONE FLAME GAS TYPE...
AND I CAN'T USE IT DOWN HERE.
I ONLY HAVE TWO FLAME TYPES LEFT...
WHAT'S TAKING SAKAMOTO?
PIKOOOOON (PAAAAN!!)
bota
PIIIN (TIIIIING)

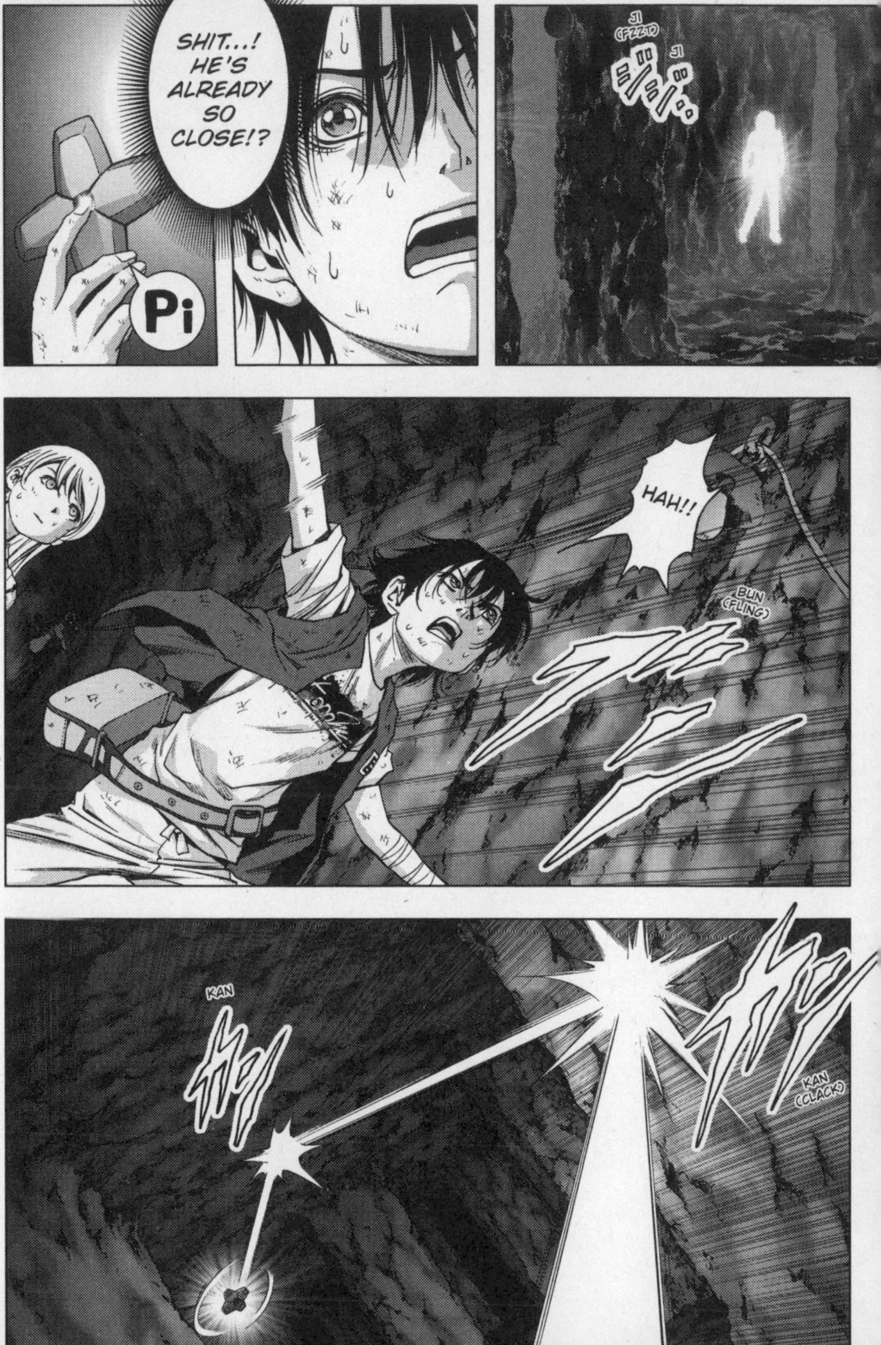
JI
(FZZT)
JI
SHIT...! HE'S ALREADY SO CLOSE!?
Pi
HAH!!
BUN
(FLING)
KAN
(CLACK)
KAN

BOOOO
(FWOOOOSH)

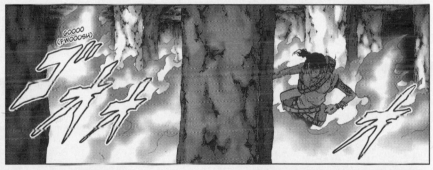

GOOOO
(FWOOOSH)

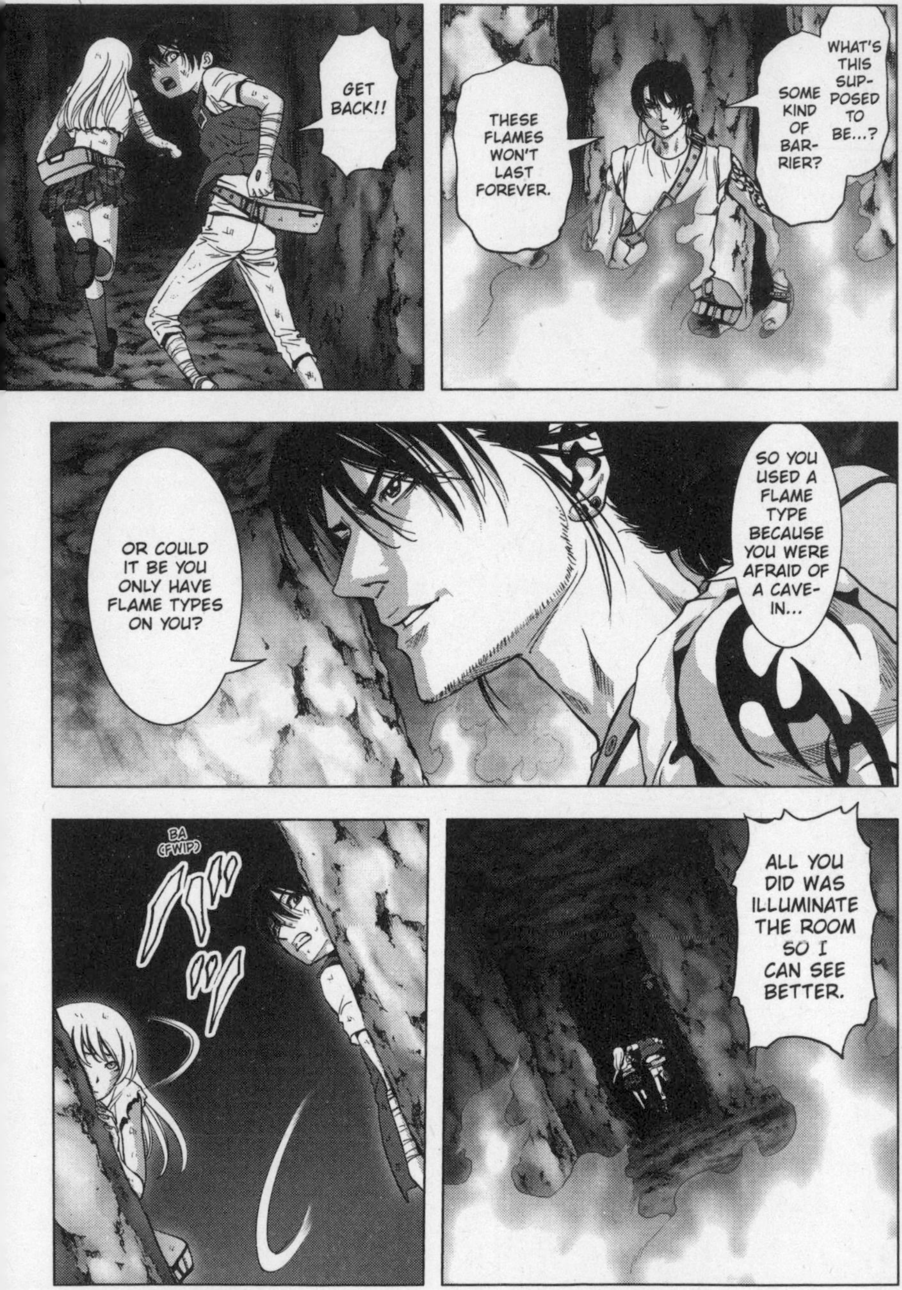
WHAT'S THIS SUPPOSED TO BE...? SOME KIND OF BARRIER?
THESE FLAMES WON'T LAST FOREVER.
GET BACK!!
SO YOU USED A FLAME TYPE BECAUSE YOU WERE AFRAID OF A CAVE-IN...
OR COULD IT BE YOU ONLY HAVE FLAME TYPES ON YOU?
ALL YOU DID WAS ILLUMINATE THE ROOM SO I CAN SEE BETTER.
BA (FWIP)

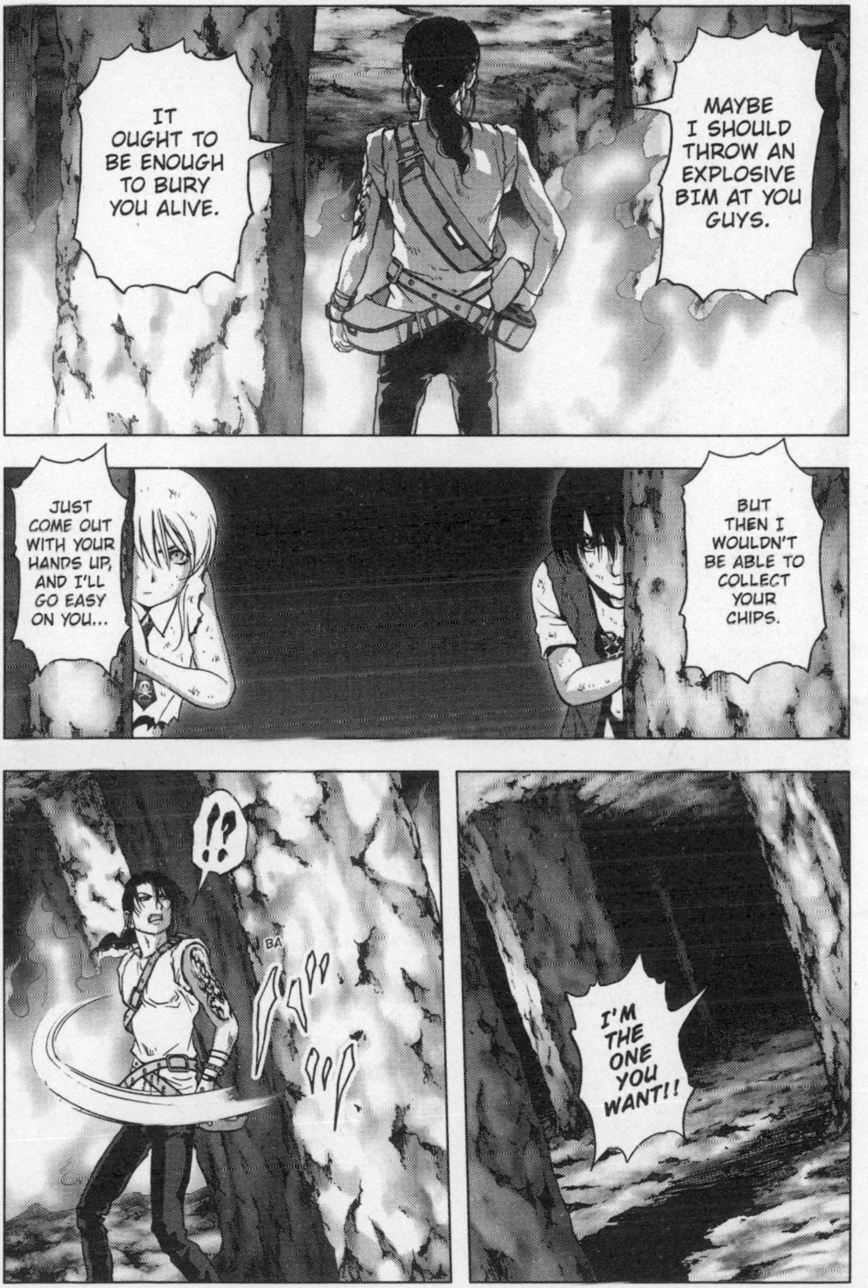
MAYBE I SHOULD THROW AN EXPLOSIVE BIM AT YOU GUYS.
IT OUGHT TO BE ENOUGH TO BURY YOU ALIVE.
BUT THEN I WOULDN'T BE ABLE TO COLLECT YOUR CHIPS.
JUST COME OUT WITH YOUR HANDS UP, AND I'LL GO EASY ON YOU...
I'M THE ONE YOU WANT!!
!?
BA

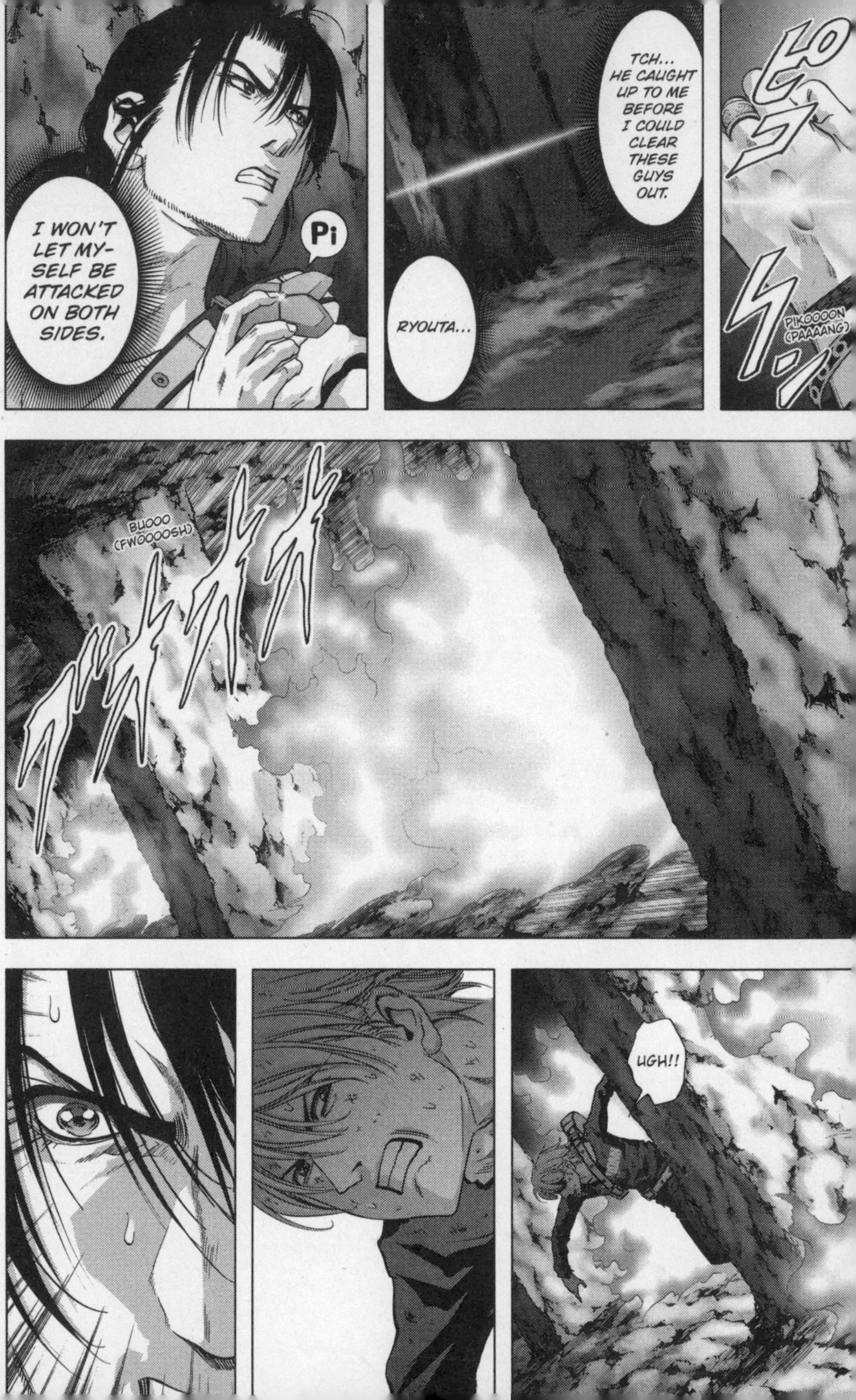
PIKOOOON (PAAAANG)
TCH... HE CAUGHT UP TO ME BEFORE I COULD CLEAR THESE GUYS OUT.
RYOUTA...
Pi
I WON'T LET MY-SELF BE ATTACKED ON BOTH SIDES.
BUOOO (FWOOOOSH)
UGH!!

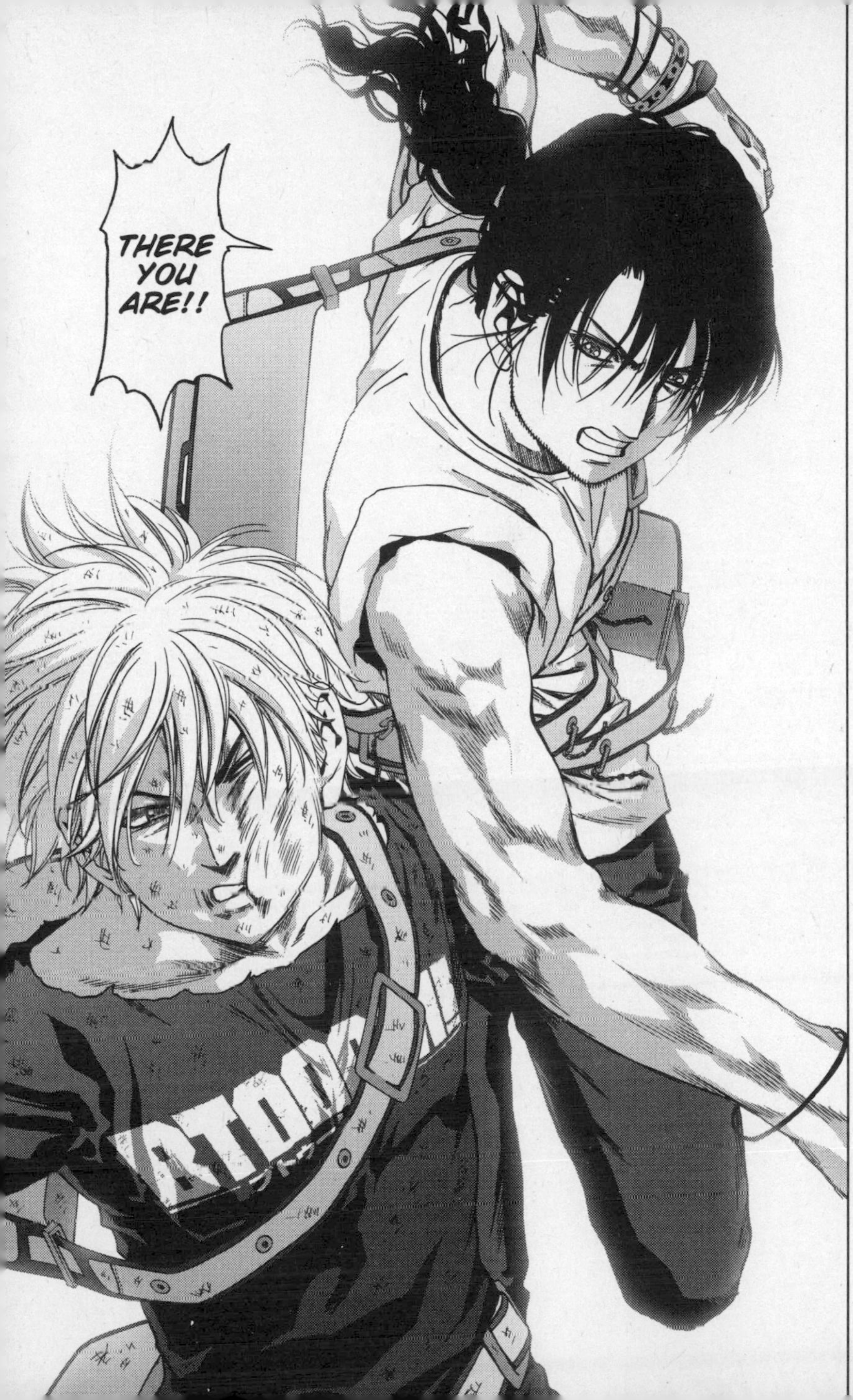
THERE YOU ARE!!

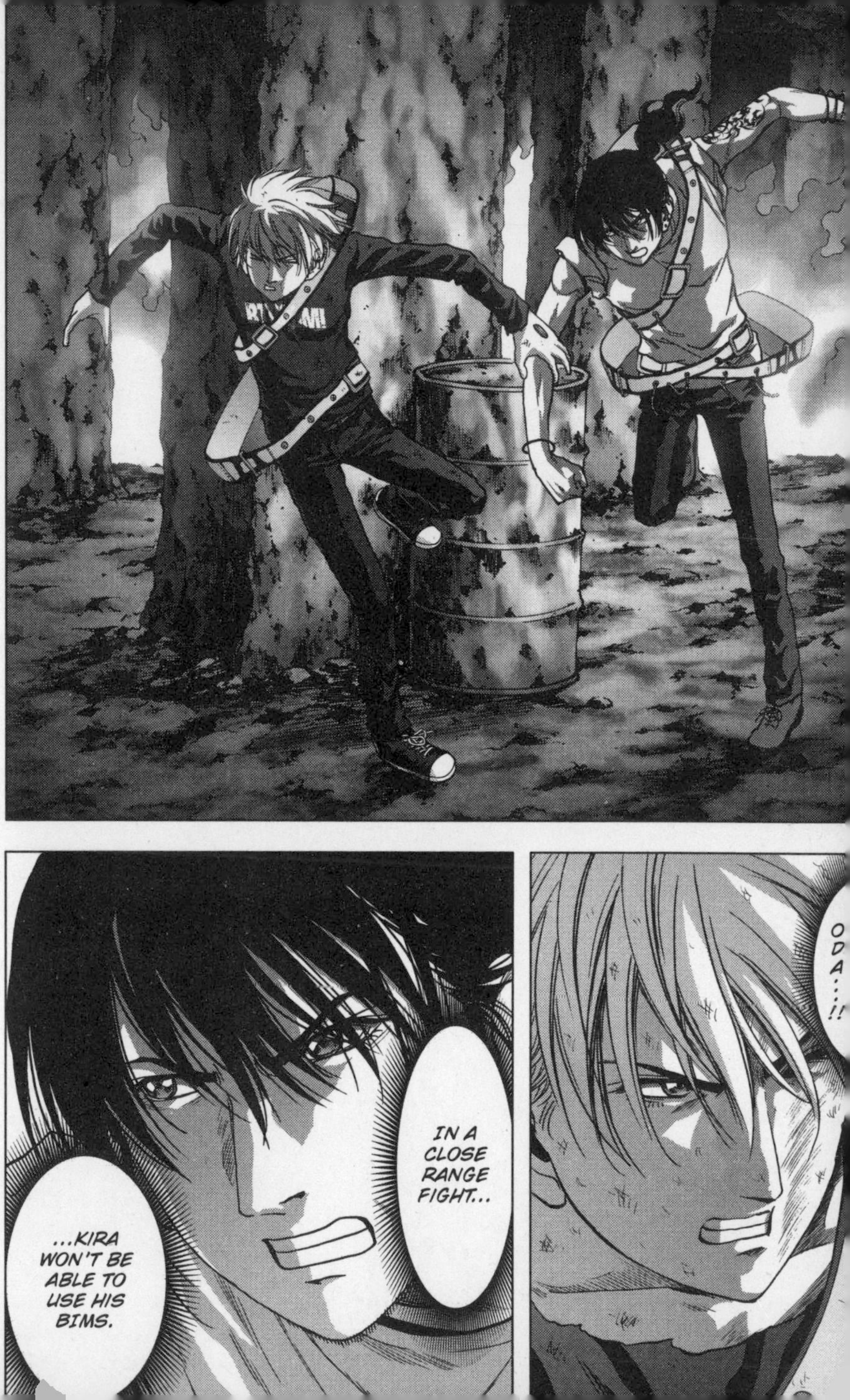
ODA...!!
IN A CLOSE RANGE FIGHT...
...KIRA WON'T BE ABLE TO USE HIS BIMS.

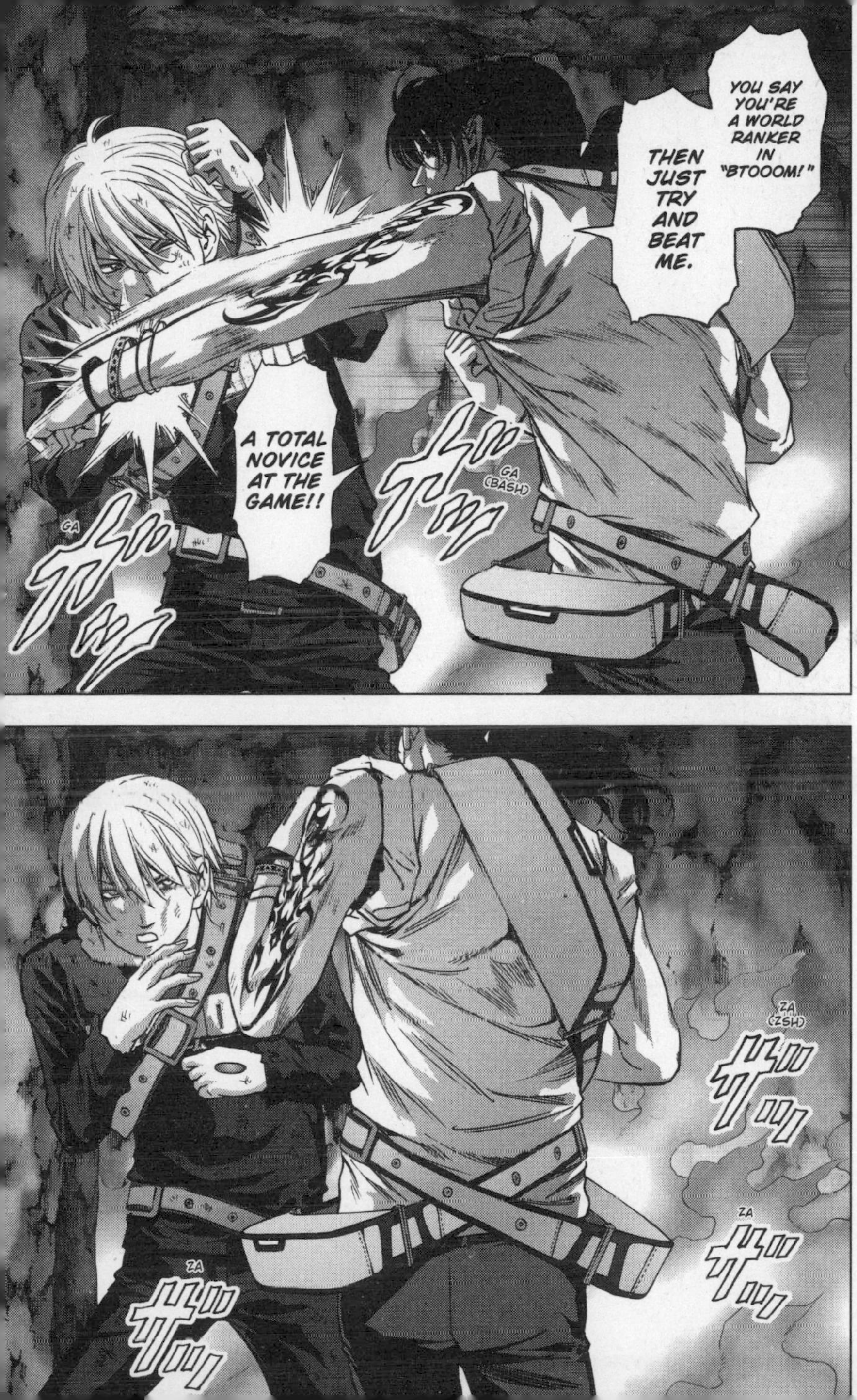
YOU SAY YOU'RE A WORLD RANKER IN "BTOOOM!"
THEN JUST TRY AND BEAT ME.
GA (BASH)
A TOTAL NOVICE AT THE GAME!!
GA
ZA (ZSH)
ZA
ZA

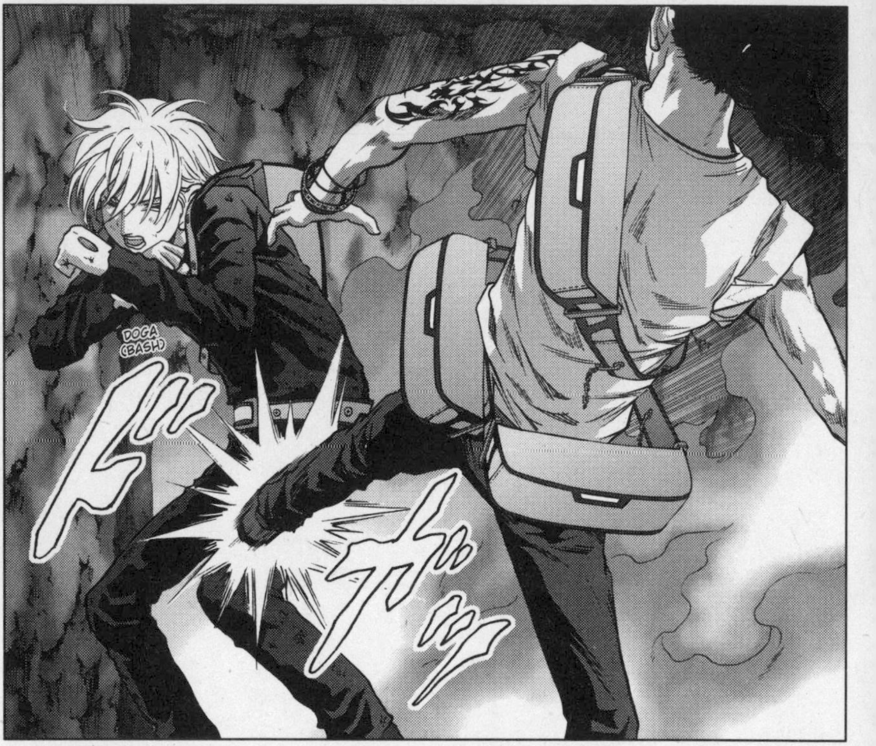
DOGA (BASH)
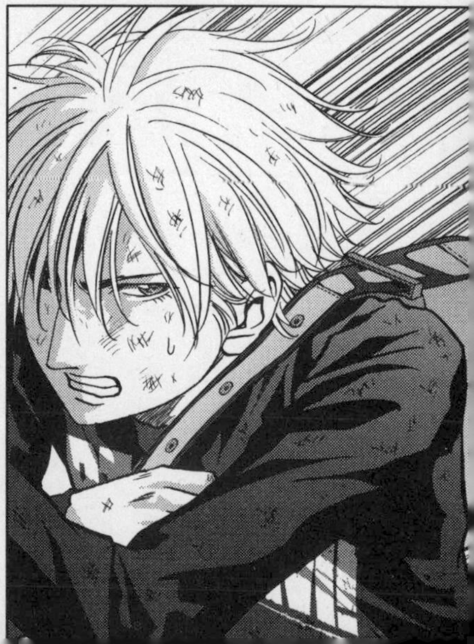
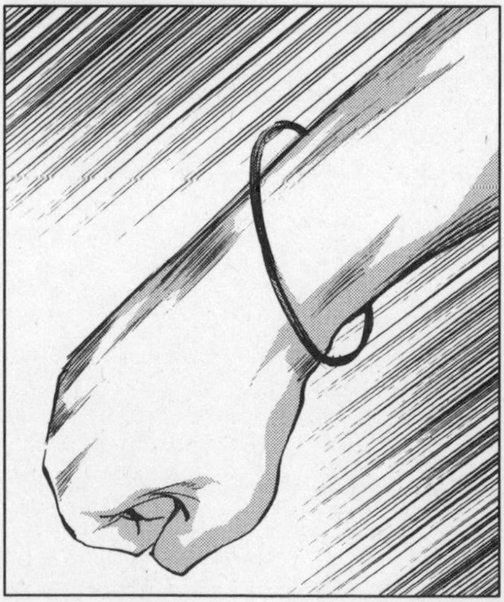

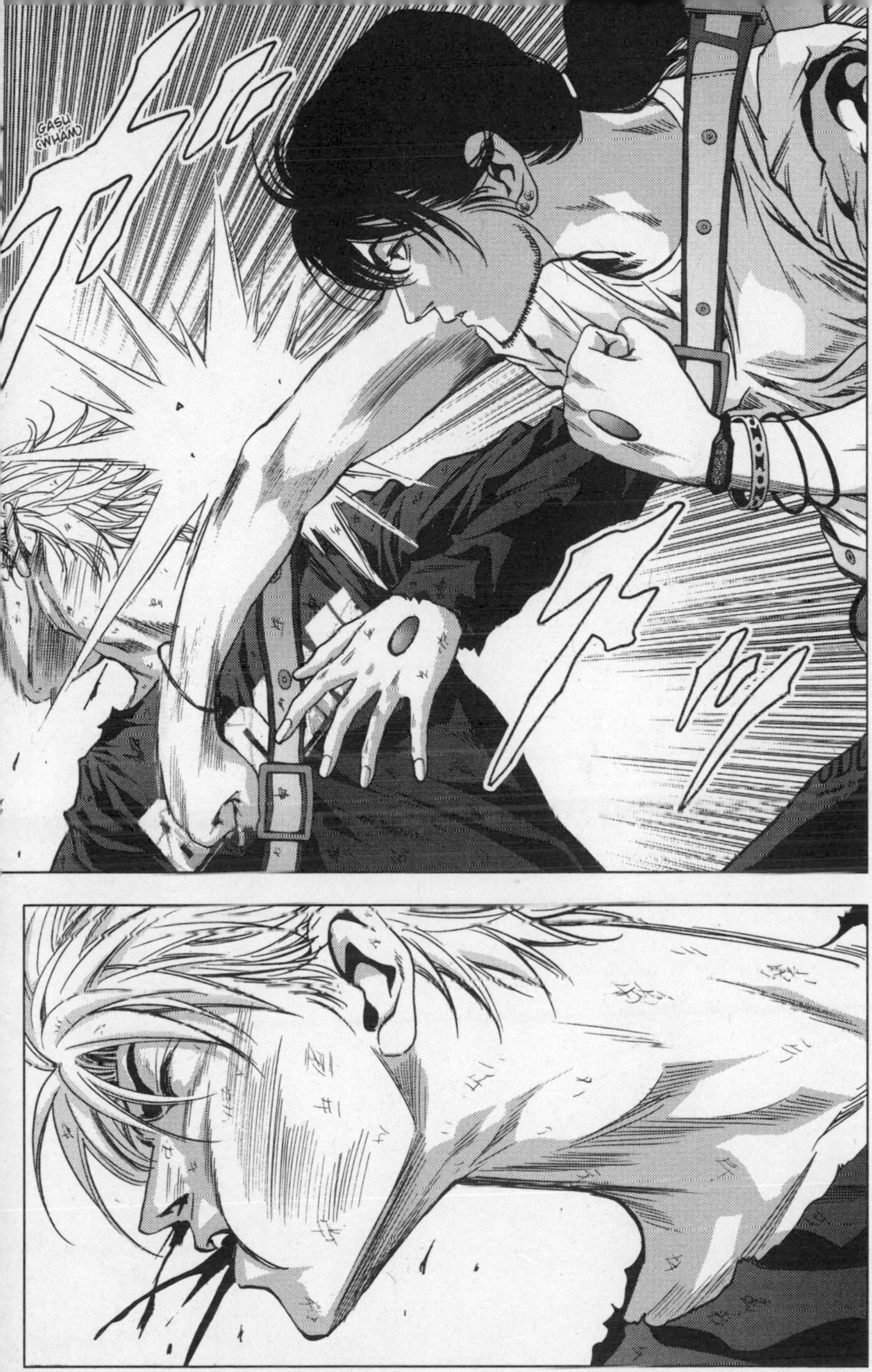
GASU (WHAM)

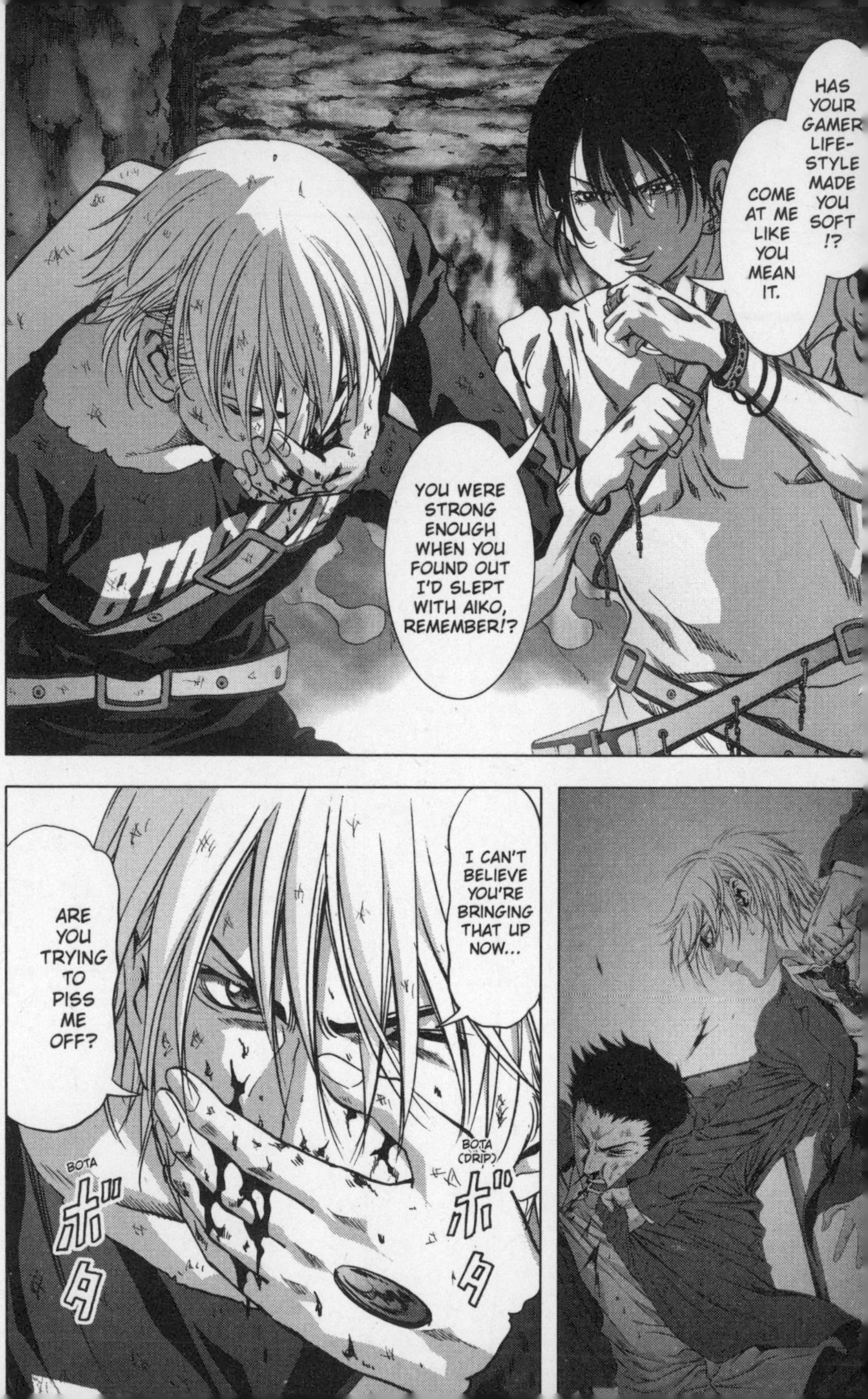
HAS YOUR GAMER LIFE-STYLE MADE YOU SOFT!?
COME AT ME LIKE YOU MEAN IT.
YOU WERE STRONG ENOUGH WHEN YOU FOUND OUT I'D SLEPT WITH AIKO, REMEMBER!?
I CAN'T BELIEVE YOU'RE BRINGING THAT UP NOW...
ARE YOU TRYING TO PISS ME OFF?
BOTA (DRIP)
ボタ
BOTA
ボタ

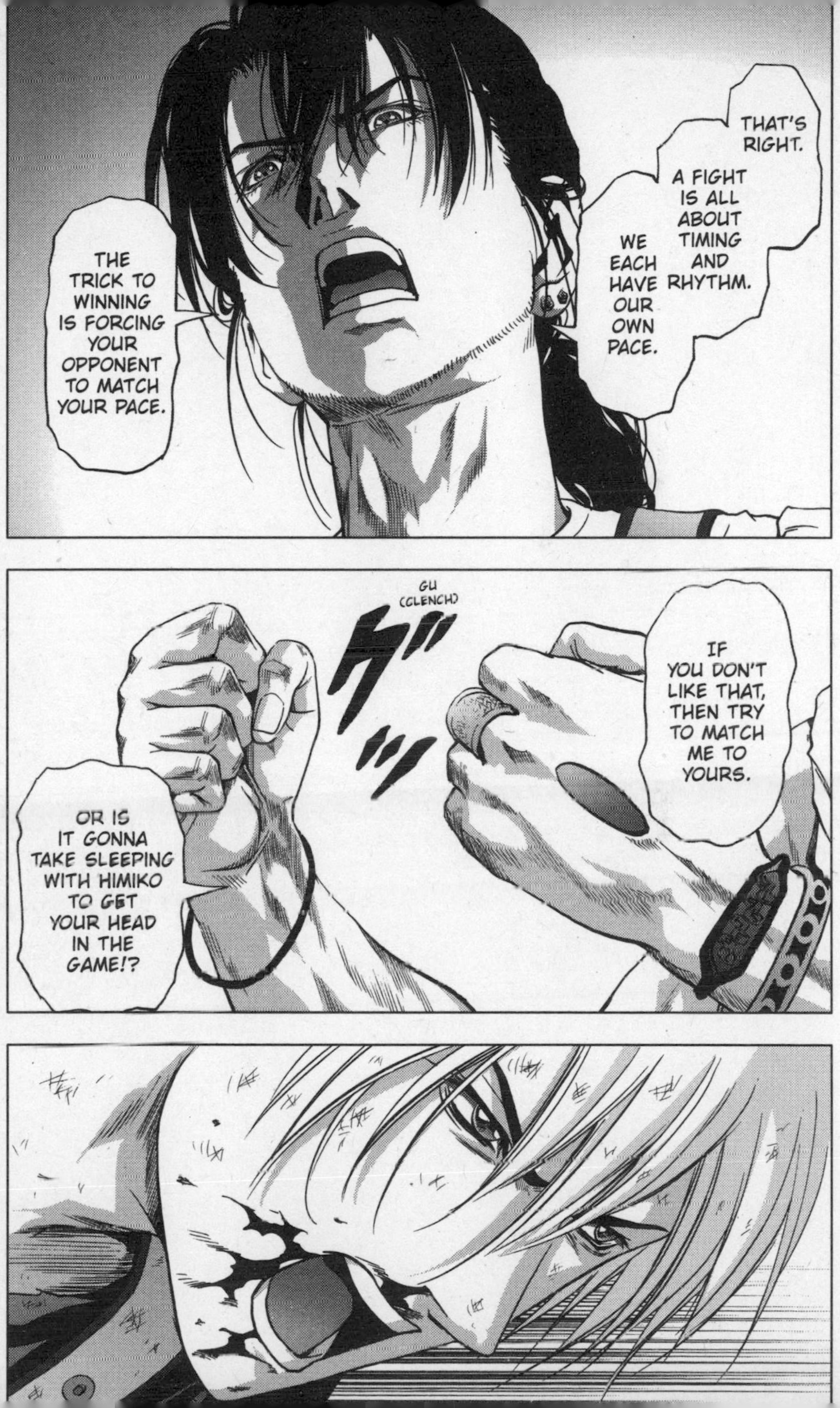
THAT'S RIGHT.
A FIGHT IS ALL ABOUT TIMING AND RHYTHM.
WE EACH HAVE OUR OWN PACE.
THE TRICK TO WINNING IS FORCING YOUR OPPONENT TO MATCH YOUR PACE.
GU (CLENCH)
IF YOU DON'T LIKE THAT, THEN TRY TO MATCH ME TO YOURS.
OR IS IT GONNA TAKE SLEEPING WITH HIMIKO TO GET YOUR HEAD IN THE GAME!?

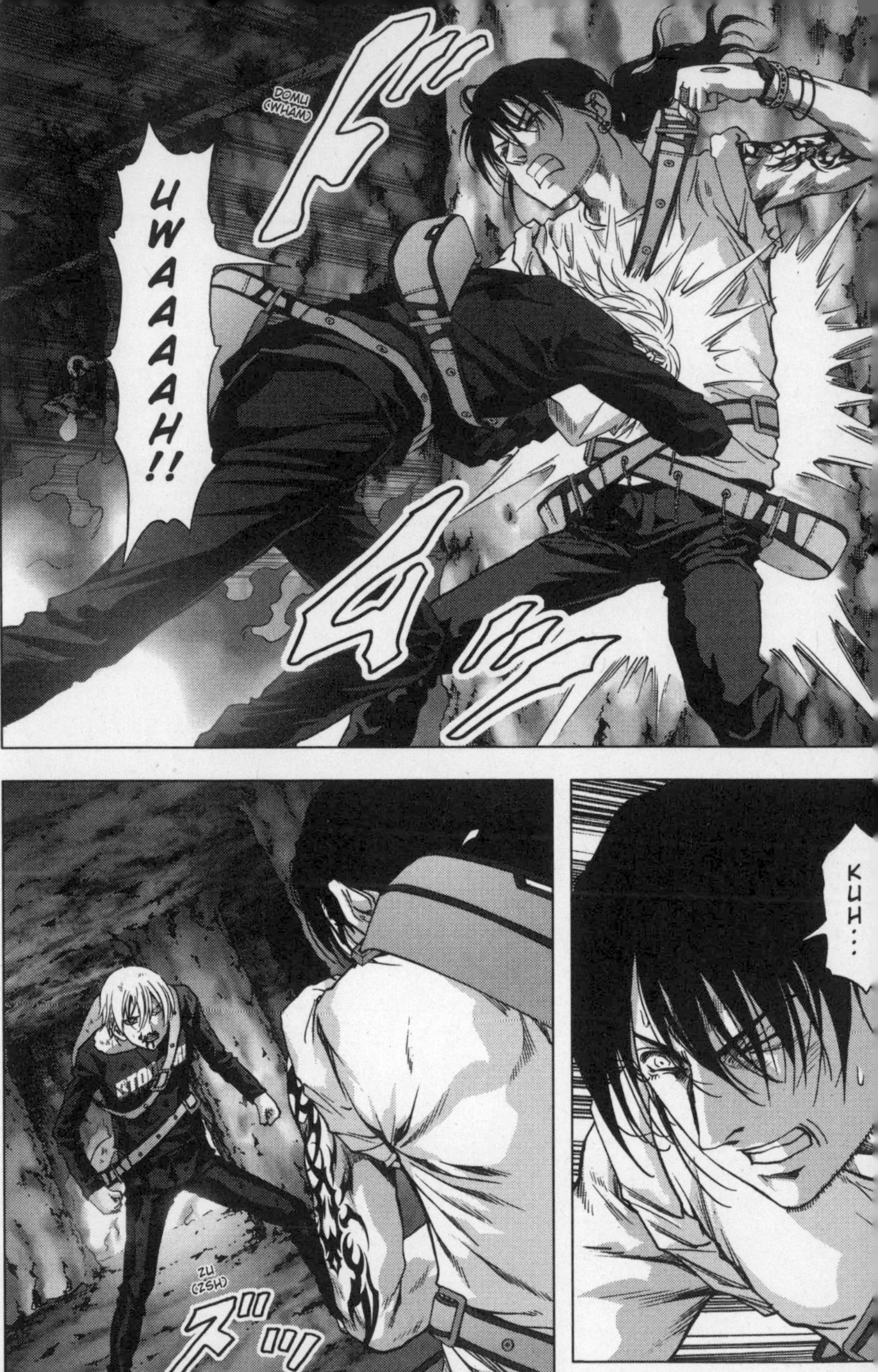
DOMU (WHAM)
UWAAAAAH!!
KUH...
ZU (ZSH)

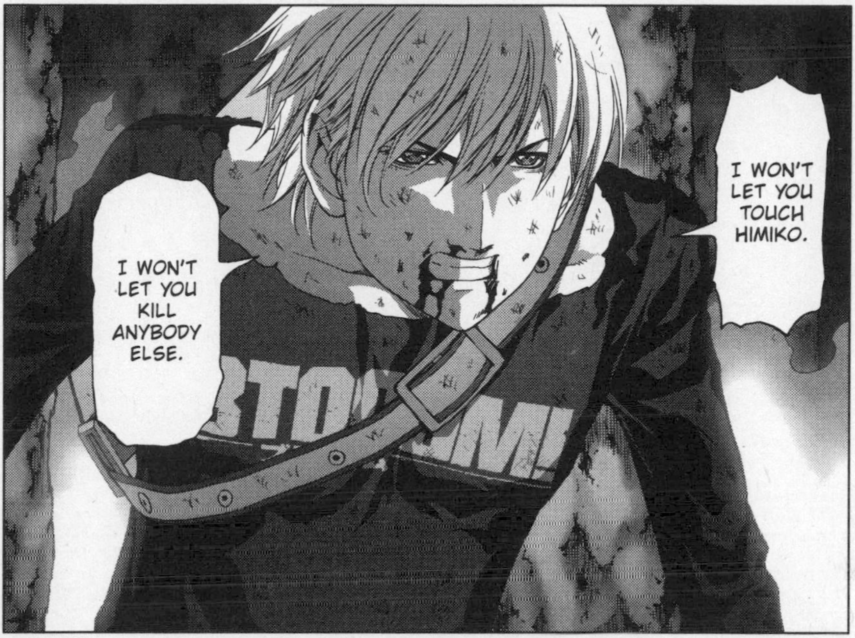
I WON'T LET YOU TOUCH HIMIKO.
I WON'T LET YOU KILL ANYBODY ELSE.

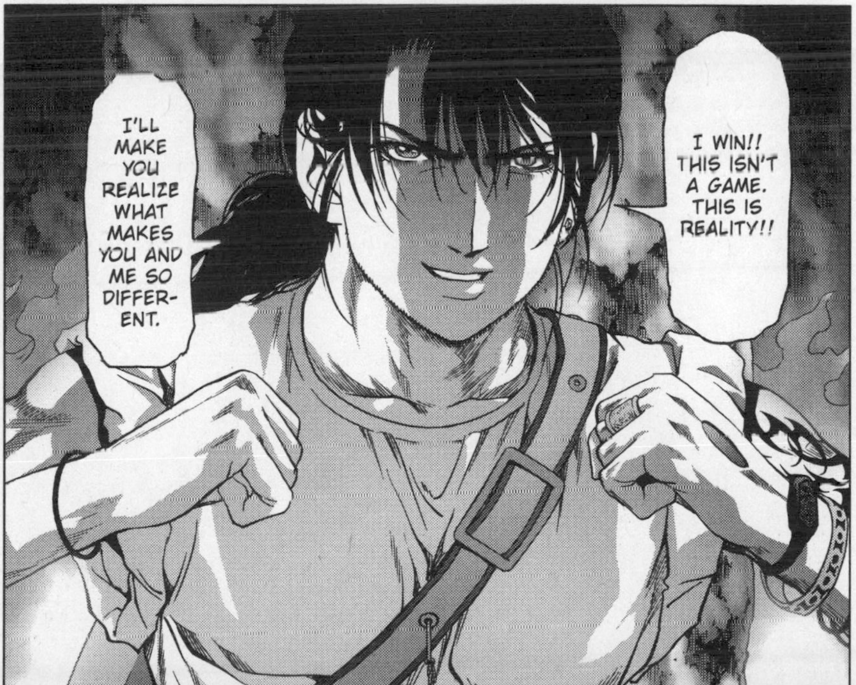
I WIN!! THIS ISN'T A GAME. THIS IS REALITY!!
I'LL MAKE YOU REALIZE WHAT MAKES YOU AND ME SO DIFFER-ENT.

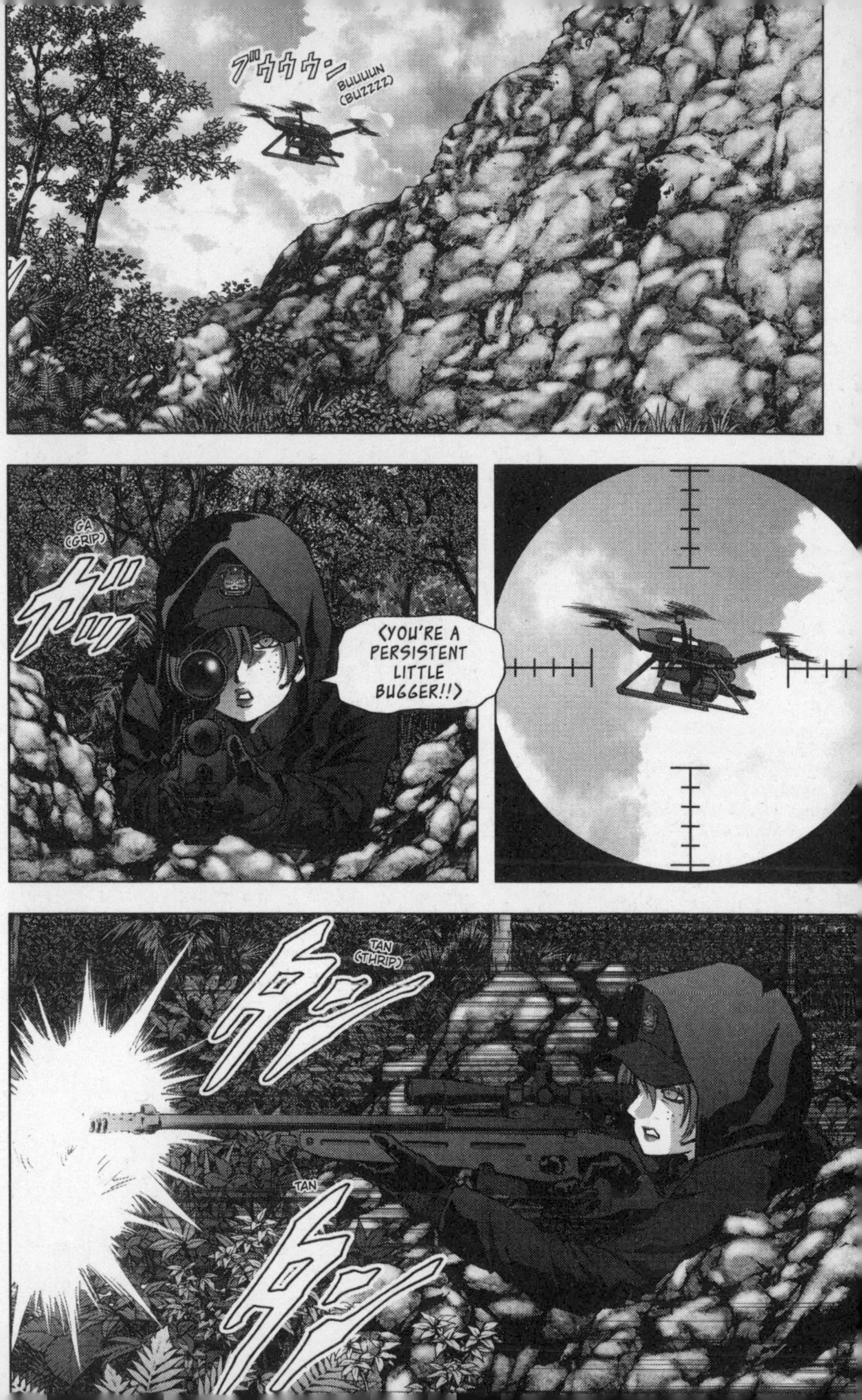
ブウウウン
BUUUUN (BUZZZZ)
ガッ
GA (GRIP)
〈YOU'RE A PERSISTENT LITTLE BUGGER!!〉
タン
TAN (THRIP)
タン
TAN

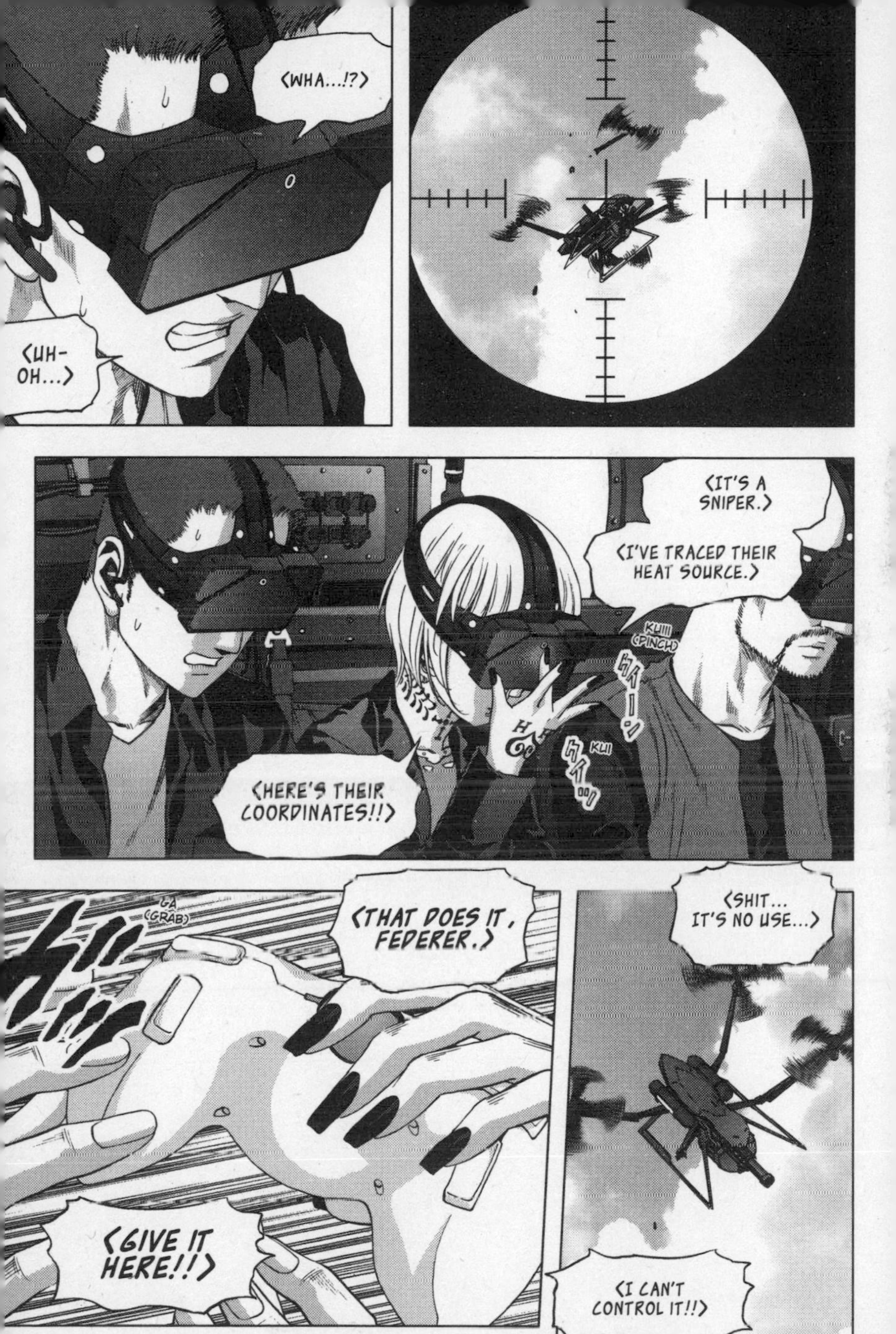
<WHA...!?>
<UH-OH...>
<IT'S A SNIPER.>
<I'VE TRACED THEIR HEAT SOURCE.>
KUIII (PINCH)
KUI
<HERE'S THEIR COORDINATES!!>
<SHIT... IT'S NO USE...>
<I CAN'T CONTROL IT!!>
GA (GRAB)
<THAT DOES IT, FEDERER.>
<GIVE IT HERE!!>

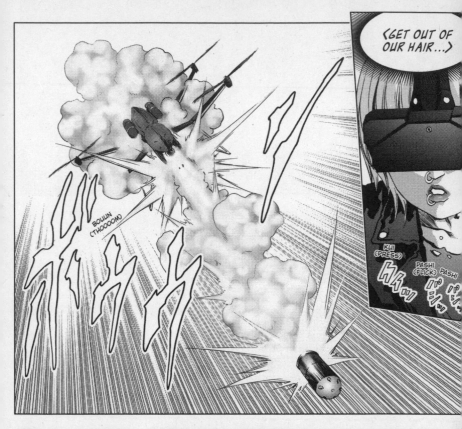

〈GET OUT OF OUR HAIR...〉

KUI (PRESS)

PASHI (FLICK) PASHI

BOUUN (CTHOOOOM)

BOGOUUUN (KABOOOOM)

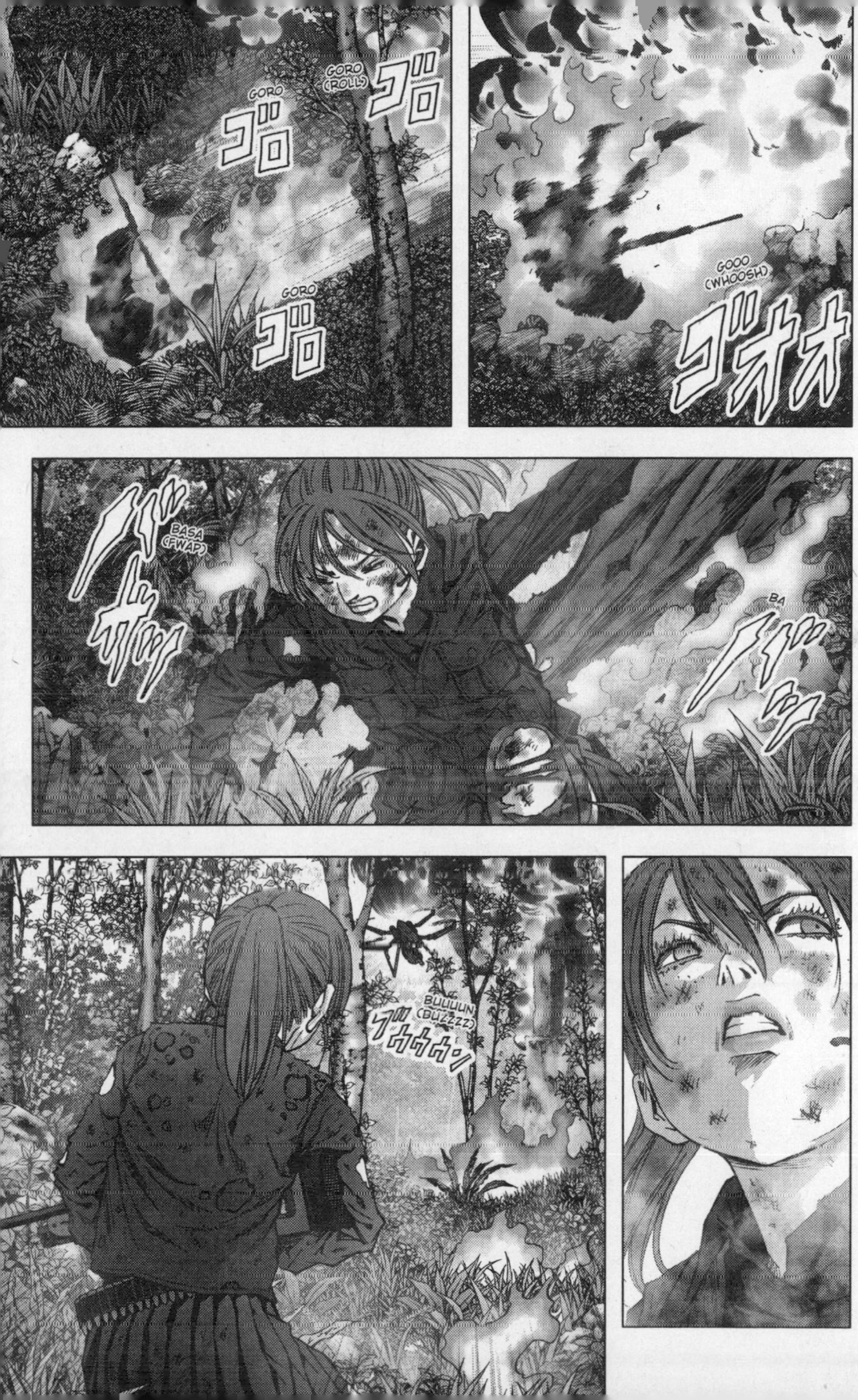
GOOO (WHOOSH)
ゴオオ
GORO (ROLL)
ゴロ
GORO
ゴロ
GORO
ゴロ
BA
BASA (FWAP)
BUUUUN (BUZZZZ)
ブウウウン

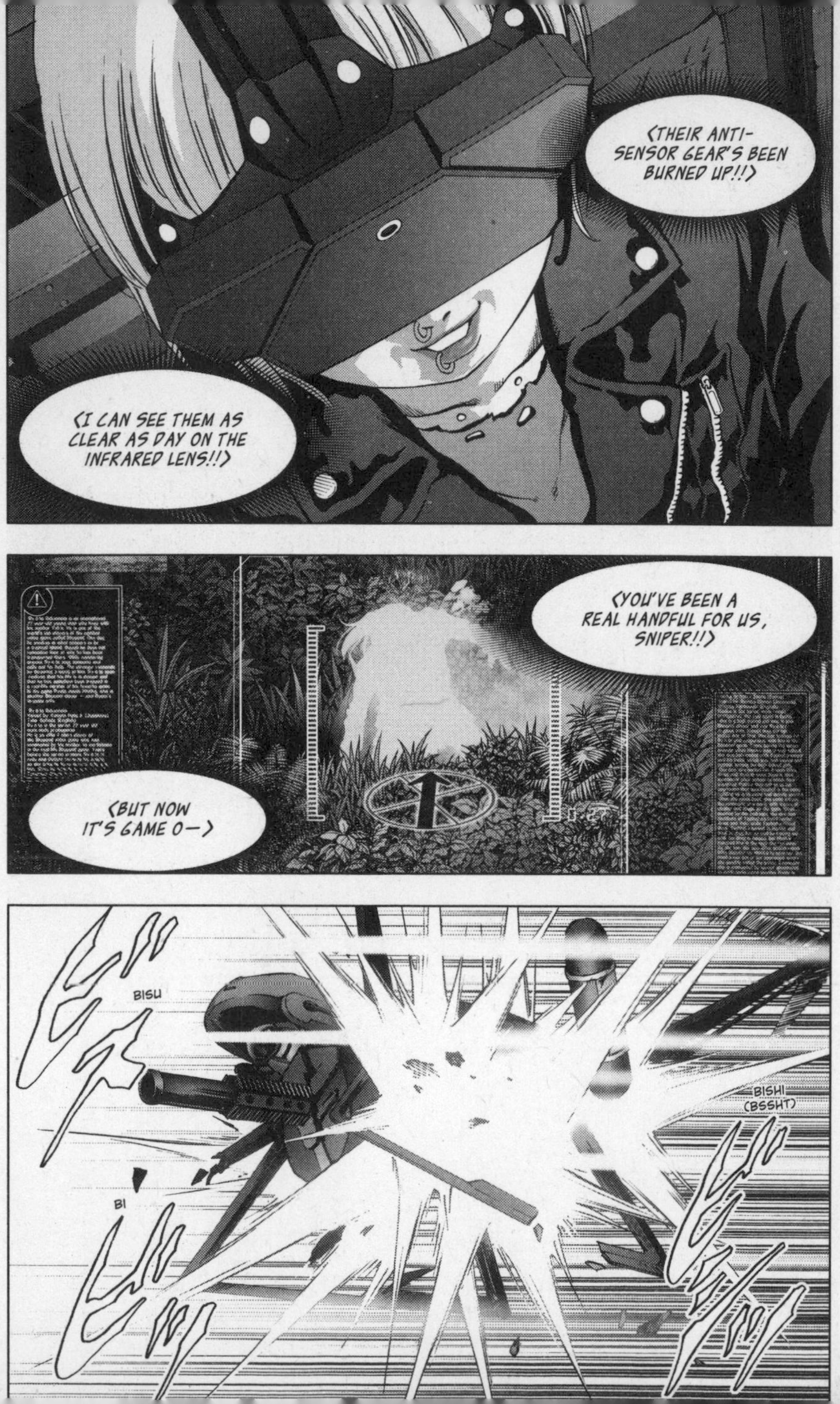
<THEIR ANTI-SENSOR GEAR'S BEEN BURNED UP!!>
<I CAN SEE THEM AS CLEAR AS DAY ON THE INFRARED LENS!!>
<YOU'VE BEEN A REAL HANDFUL FOR US, SNIPER!!>
<BUT NOW IT'S GAME O—>
BISHI (BSSHT)
BISU
BI

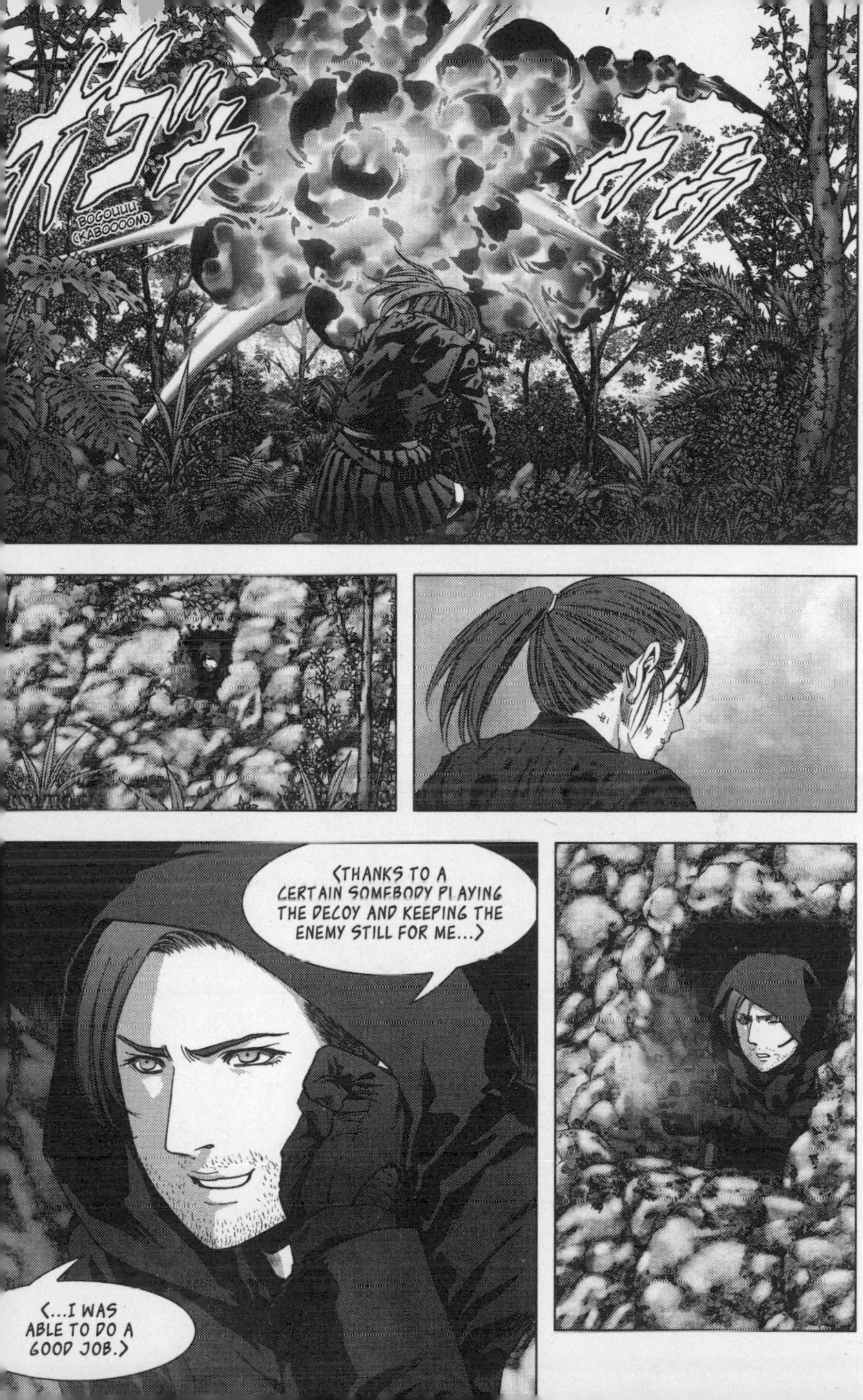
BOGOUUU (KABOOOOM)
<THANKS TO A CERTAIN SOMEBODY PLAYING THE DECOY AND KEEPING THE ENEMY STILL FOR ME...>
<...I WAS ABLE TO DO A GOOD JOB.>

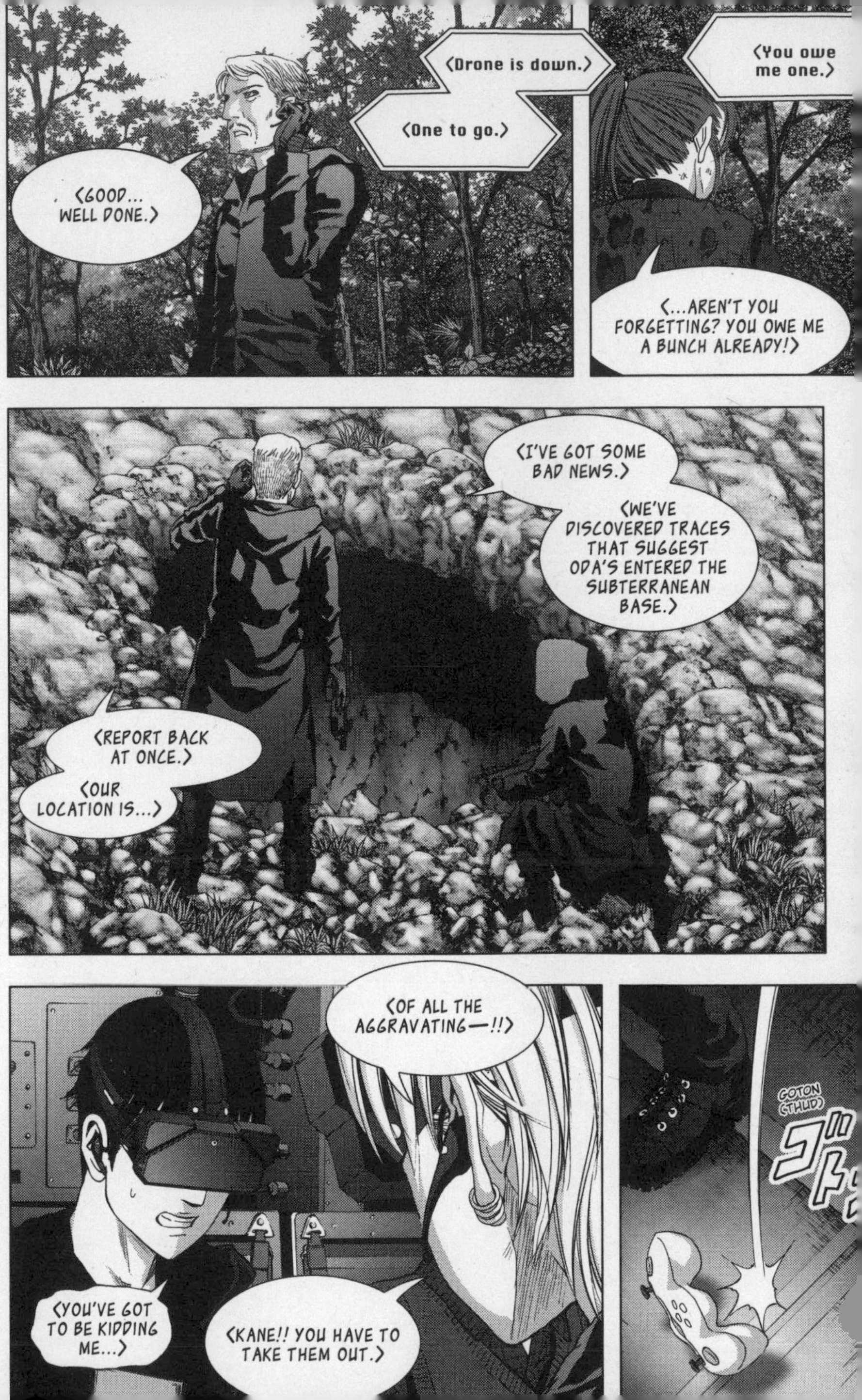
〈You owe me one.〉
〈...Aren't you forgetting? You owe me a bunch already!〉
〈Drone is down.〉
〈One to go.〉
〈Good... well done.〉
〈I've got some bad news.〉
〈We've discovered traces that suggest Oda's entered the subterranean base.〉
〈Report back at once.〉
〈Our location is...〉
GOTON (THUD)
〈Of all the aggravating—!!〉
〈Kane!! You have to take them out.〉
〈You've got to be kidding me...〉

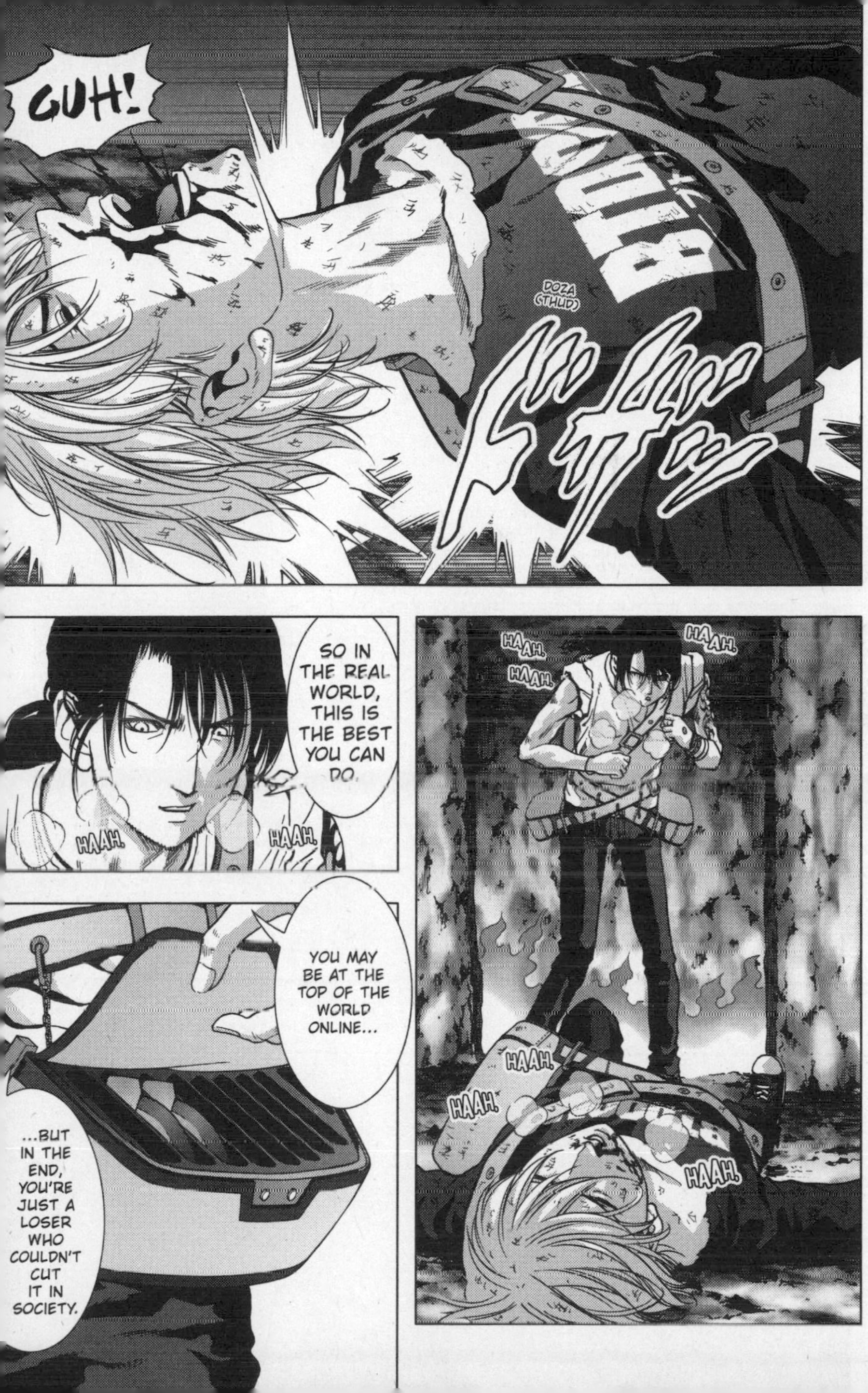
GUH!
DOZA (THUD)
HAAH.
HAAH.
HAAH.
HAAH.
HAAH.
HAAH.
SO IN THE REAL WORLD, THIS IS THE BEST YOU CAN DO.
HAAH.
HAAH.
YOU MAY BE AT THE TOP OF THE WORLD ONLINE...
...BUT IN THE END, YOU'RE JUST A LOSER WHO COULDN'T CUT IT IN SOCIETY.

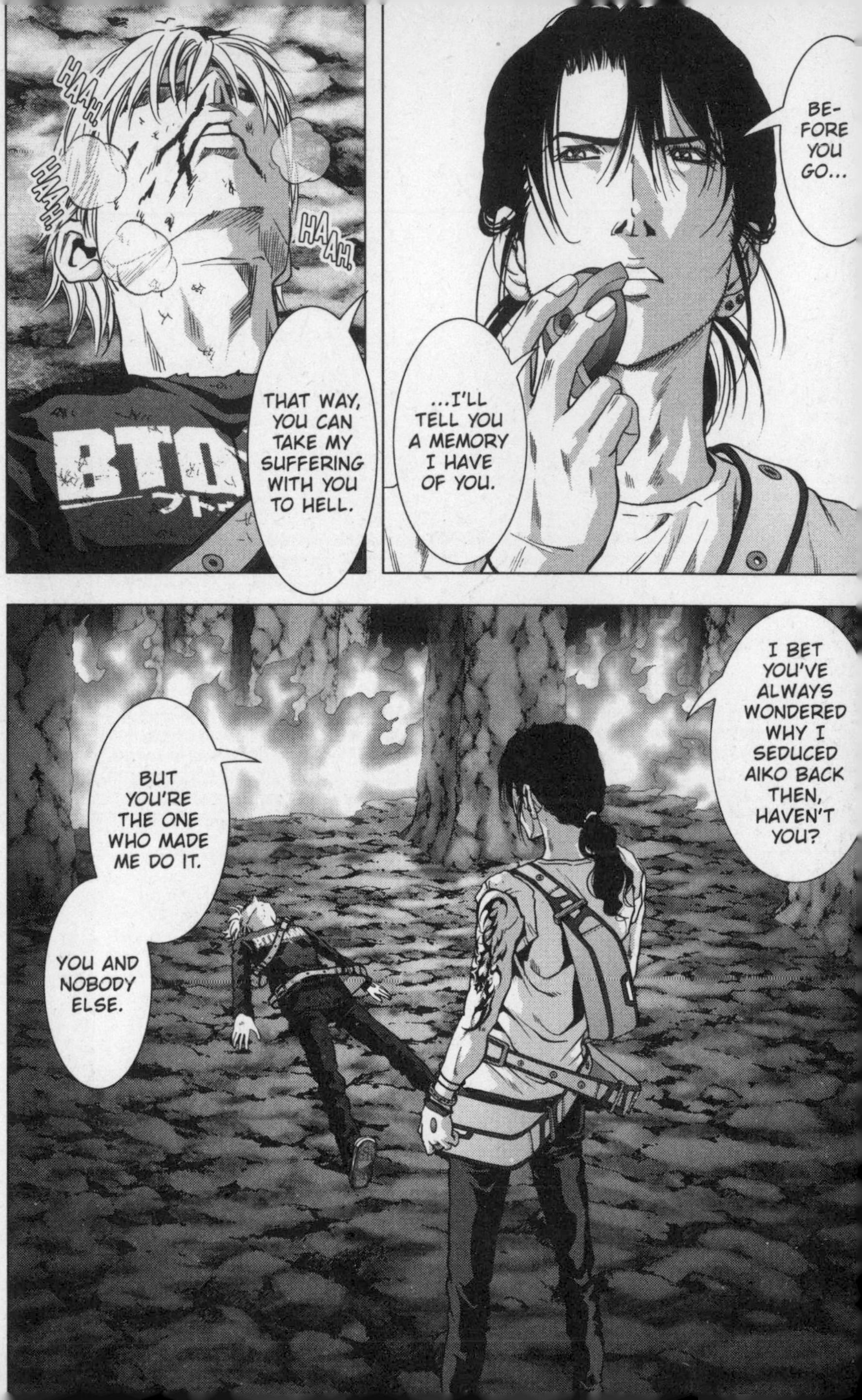
BE-FORE YOU GO...
...I'LL TELL YOU A MEMORY I HAVE OF YOU.
HAAH.
HAAH.
HAAH.
THAT WAY, YOU CAN TAKE MY SUFFERING WITH YOU TO HELL.
I BET YOU'VE ALWAYS WONDERED WHY I SEDUCED AIKO BACK THEN, HAVEN'T YOU?
BUT YOU'RE THE ONE WHO MADE ME DO IT.
YOU AND NOBODY ELSE.

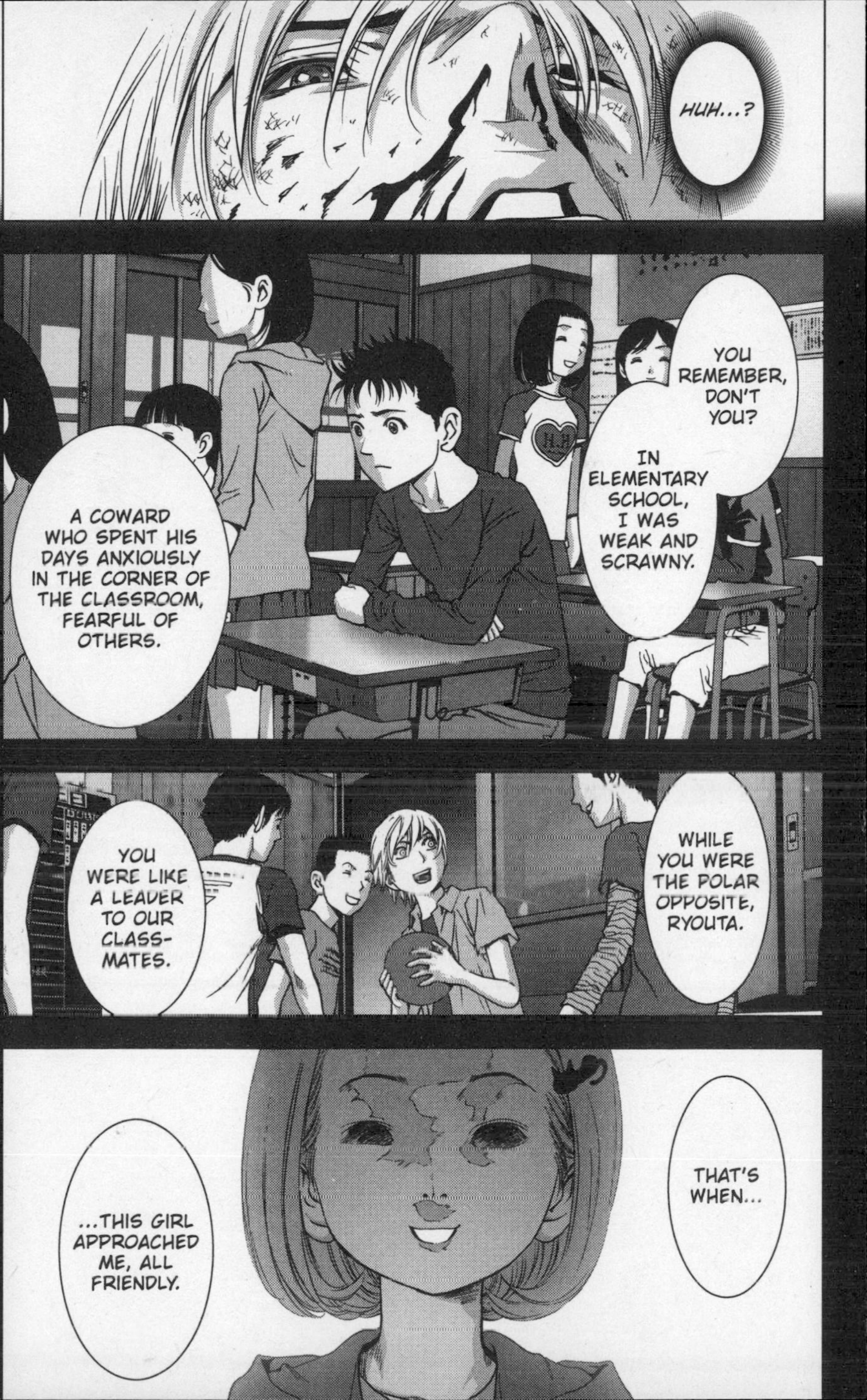
HUH...?
YOU REMEMBER, DON'T YOU?
IN ELEMENTARY SCHOOL, I WAS WEAK AND SCRAWNY.
A COWARD WHO SPENT HIS DAYS ANXIOUSLY IN THE CORNER OF THE CLASSROOM, FEARFUL OF OTHERS.
WHILE YOU WERE THE POLAR OPPOSITE, RYOUTA.
YOU WERE LIKE A LEADER TO OUR CLASS-MATES.
THAT'S WHEN...
...THIS GIRL APPROACHED ME, ALL FRIENDLY.

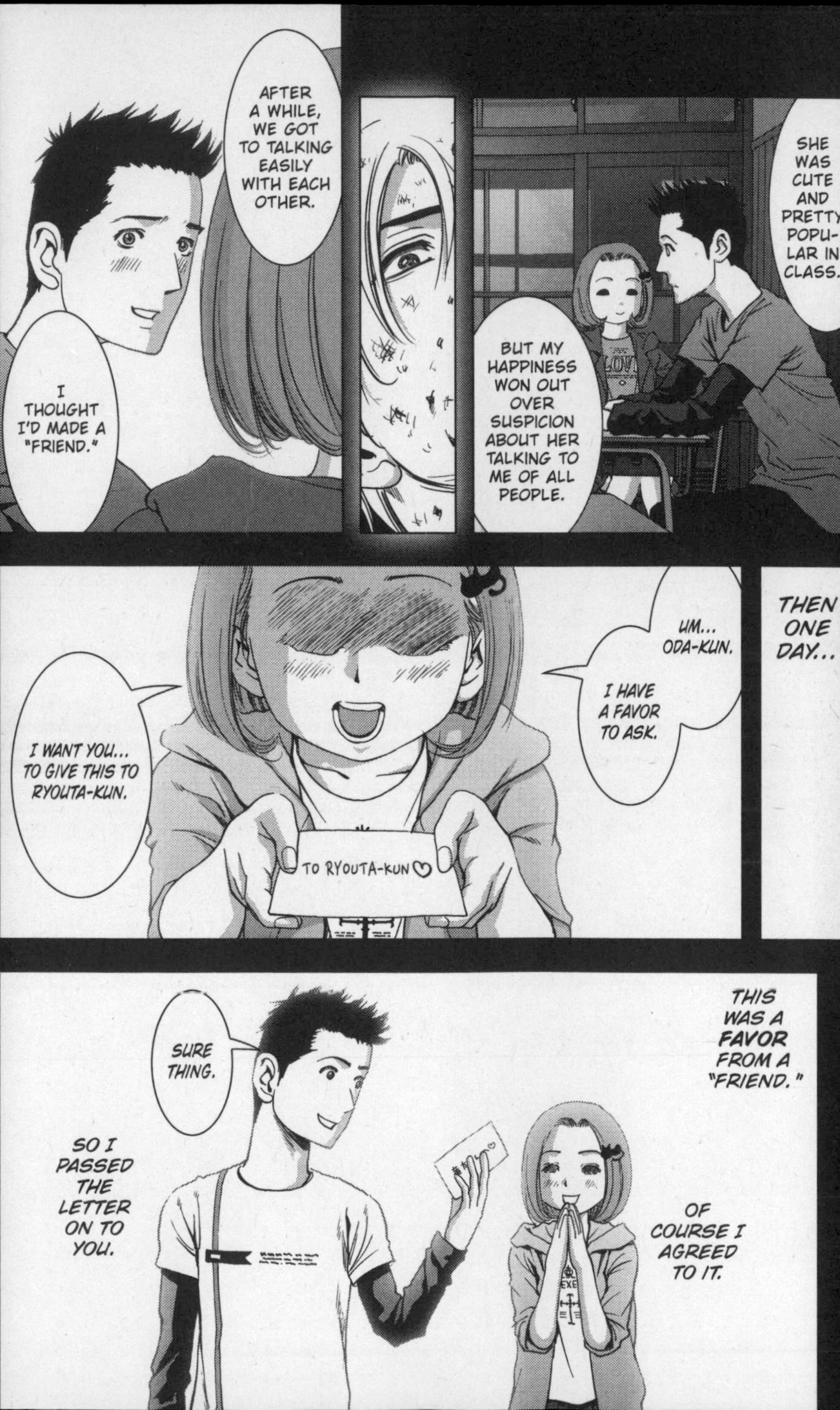
SHE WAS CUTE AND PRETTY POPULAR IN CLASS.
BUT MY HAPPINESS WON OUT OVER SUSPICION ABOUT HER TALKING TO ME OF ALL PEOPLE.
LOVE
AFTER A WHILE, WE GOT TO TALKING EASILY WITH EACH OTHER.
I THOUGHT I'D MADE A "FRIEND."
THEN ONE DAY...
UM... ODA-KUN.
I HAVE A FAVOR TO ASK.
I WANT YOU... TO GIVE THIS TO RYOUTA-KUN.
TO RYOUTA-KUN ♡
THIS WAS A FAVOR FROM A "FRIEND."
OF COURSE I AGREED TO IT.
SURE THING.
SO I PASSED THE LETTER ON TO YOU.

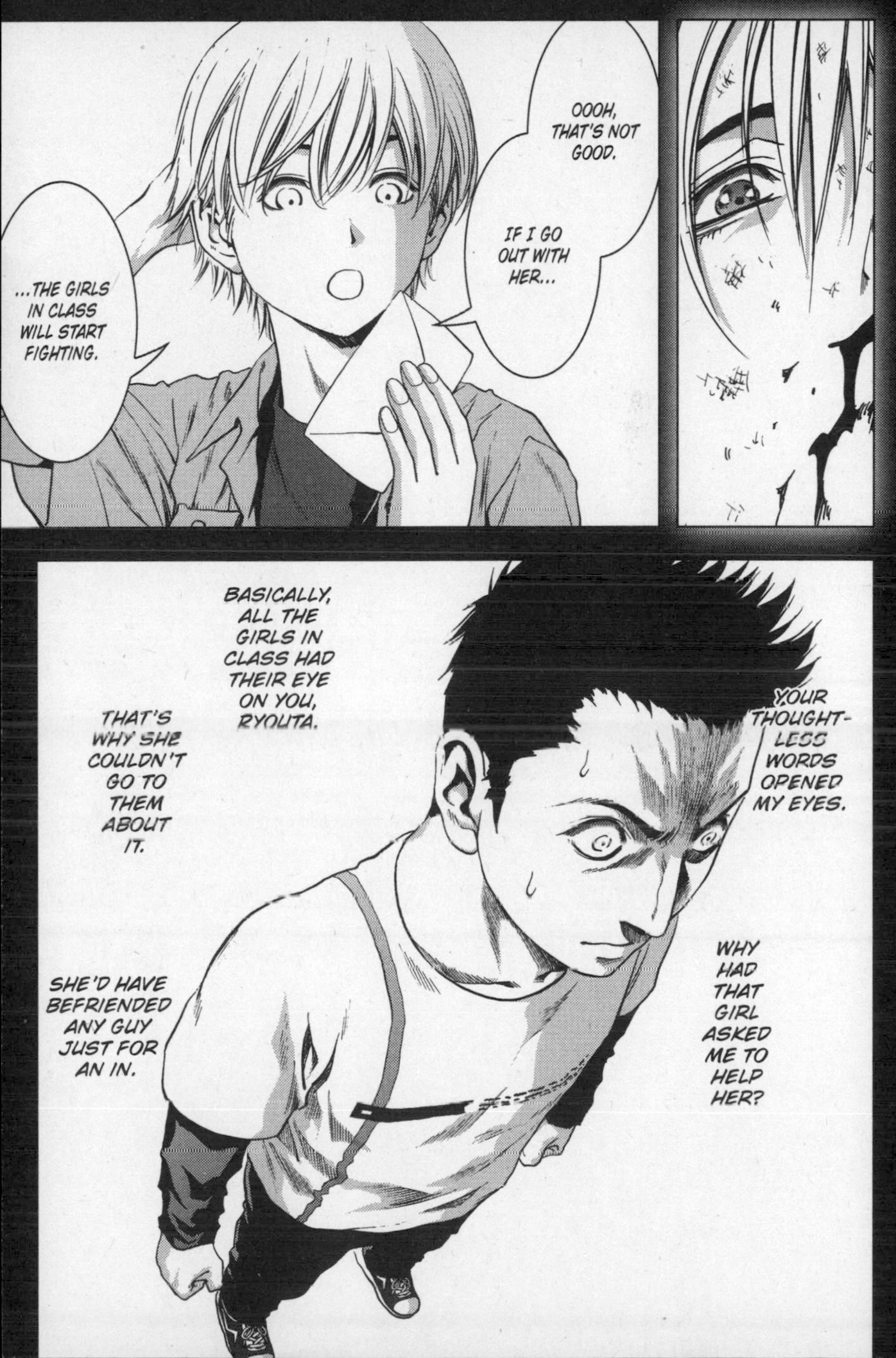

OOOH, THAT'S NOT GOOD.
IF I GO OUT WITH HER...
...THE GIRLS IN CLASS WILL START FIGHTING.
YOUR THOUGHTLESS WORDS OPENED MY EYES.
WHY HAD THAT GIRL ASKED ME TO HELP HER?
BASICALLY, ALL THE GIRLS IN CLASS HAD THEIR EYE ON YOU, RYOUTA.
THAT'S WHY SHE COULDN'T GO TO THEM ABOUT IT.
SHE'D HAVE BEFRIENDED ANY GUY JUST FOR AN IN.

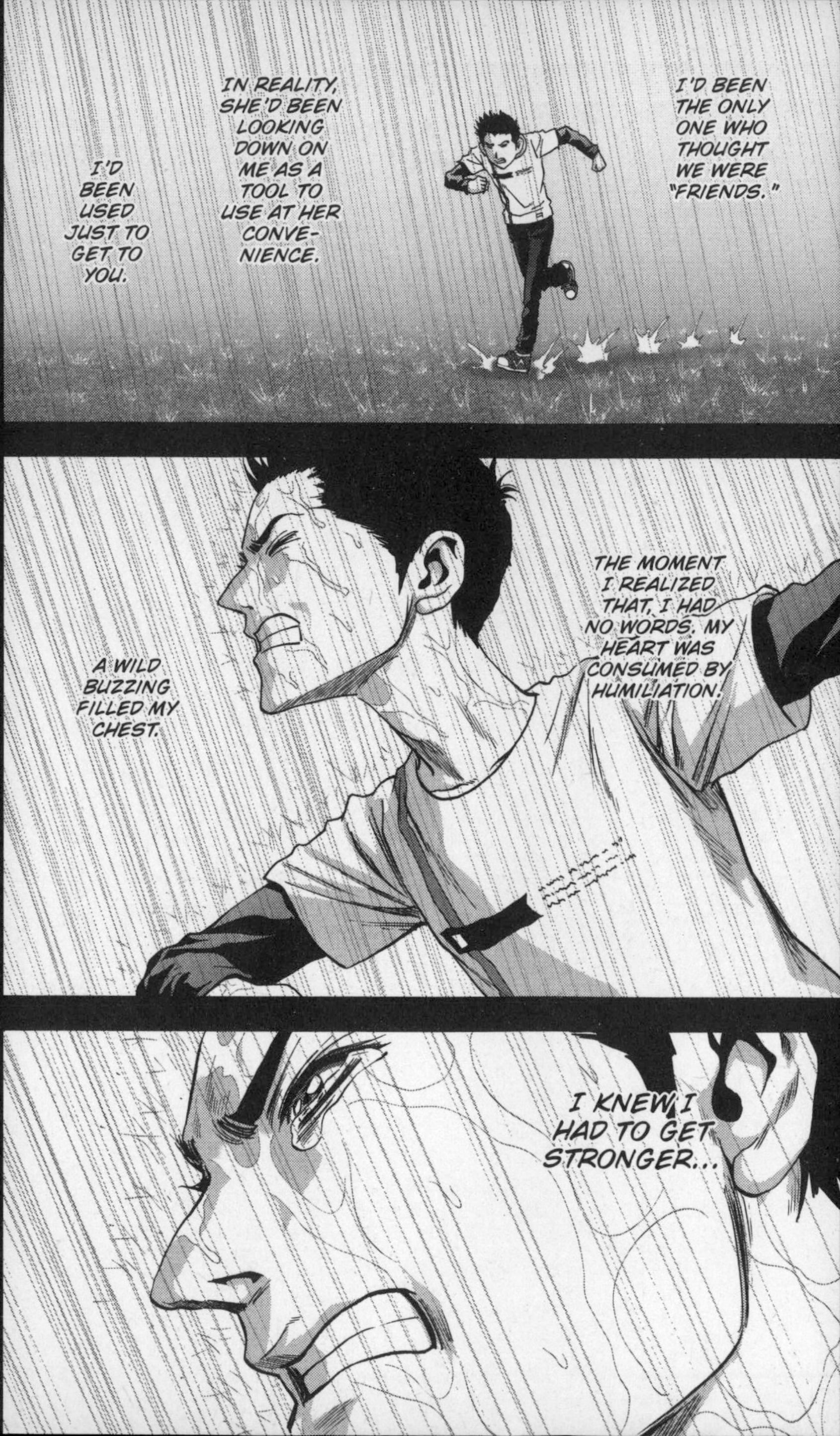
I'D BEEN THE ONLY ONE WHO THOUGHT WE WERE "FRIENDS."
IN REALITY, SHE'D BEEN LOOKING DOWN ON ME AS A TOOL TO USE AT HER CONVE-NIENCE.
I'D BEEN USED JUST TO GET TO YOU.
THE MOMENT I REALIZED THAT, I HAD NO WORDS. MY HEART WAS CONSUMED BY HUMILIATION.
A WILD BUZZING FILLED MY CHEST.
I KNEW I HAD TO GET STRONGER...

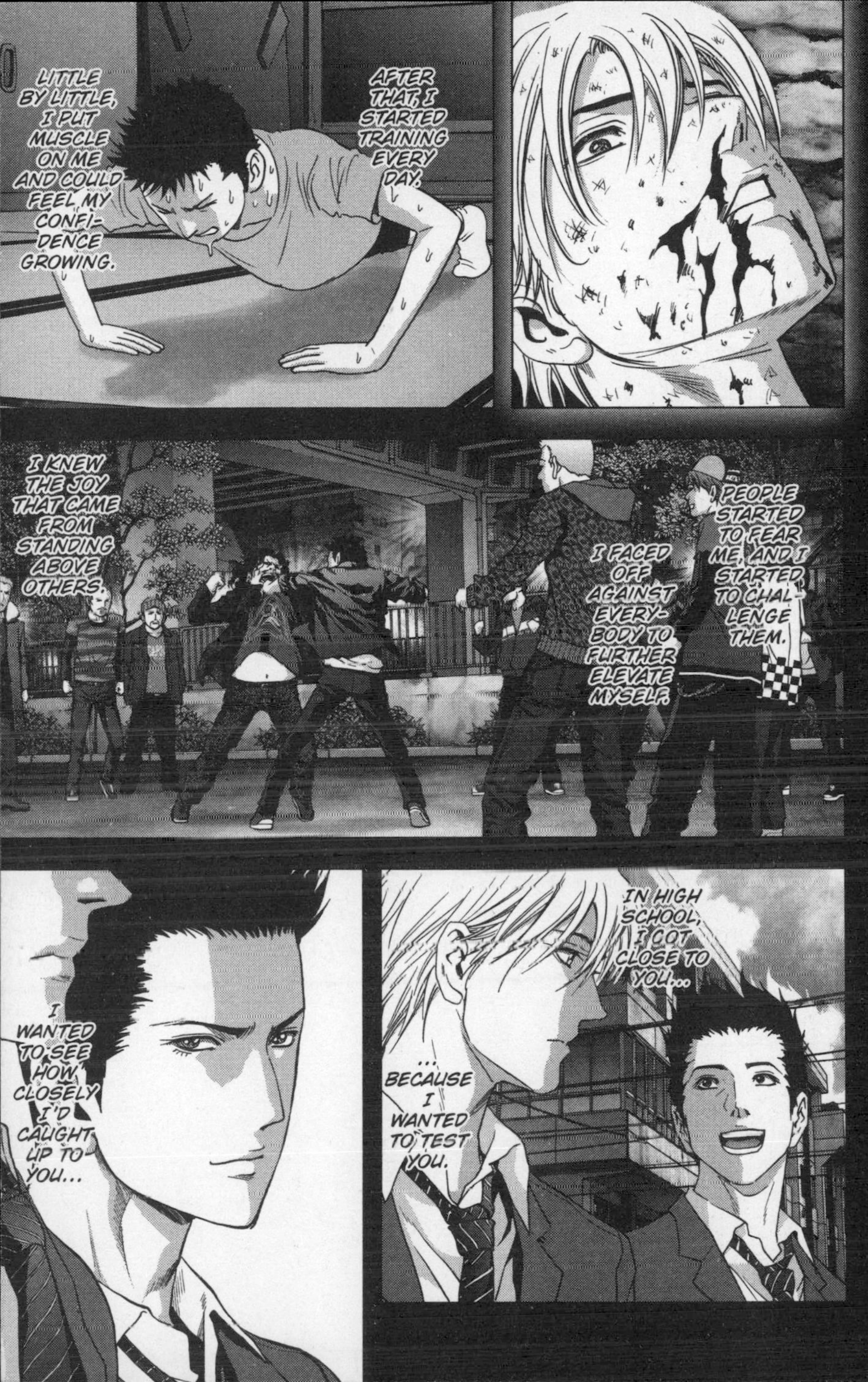
AFTER THAT, I STARTED TRAINING EVERY DAY.
LITTLE BY LITTLE, I PUT MUSCLE ON ME AND COULD FEEL MY CONFI-DENCE GROWING.
PEOPLE STARTED TO FEAR ME, AND I STARTED TO CHAL-LENGE THEM.
I FACED OFF AGAINST EVERY-BODY TO FURTHER ELEVATE MYSELF.
I KNEW THE JOY THAT CAME FROM STANDING ABOVE OTHERS.
IN HIGH SCHOOL, I GOT CLOSE TO YOU...
...BECAUSE I WANTED TO TEST YOU.
I WANTED TO SEE HOW CLOSELY I'D CAUGHT UP TO YOU...

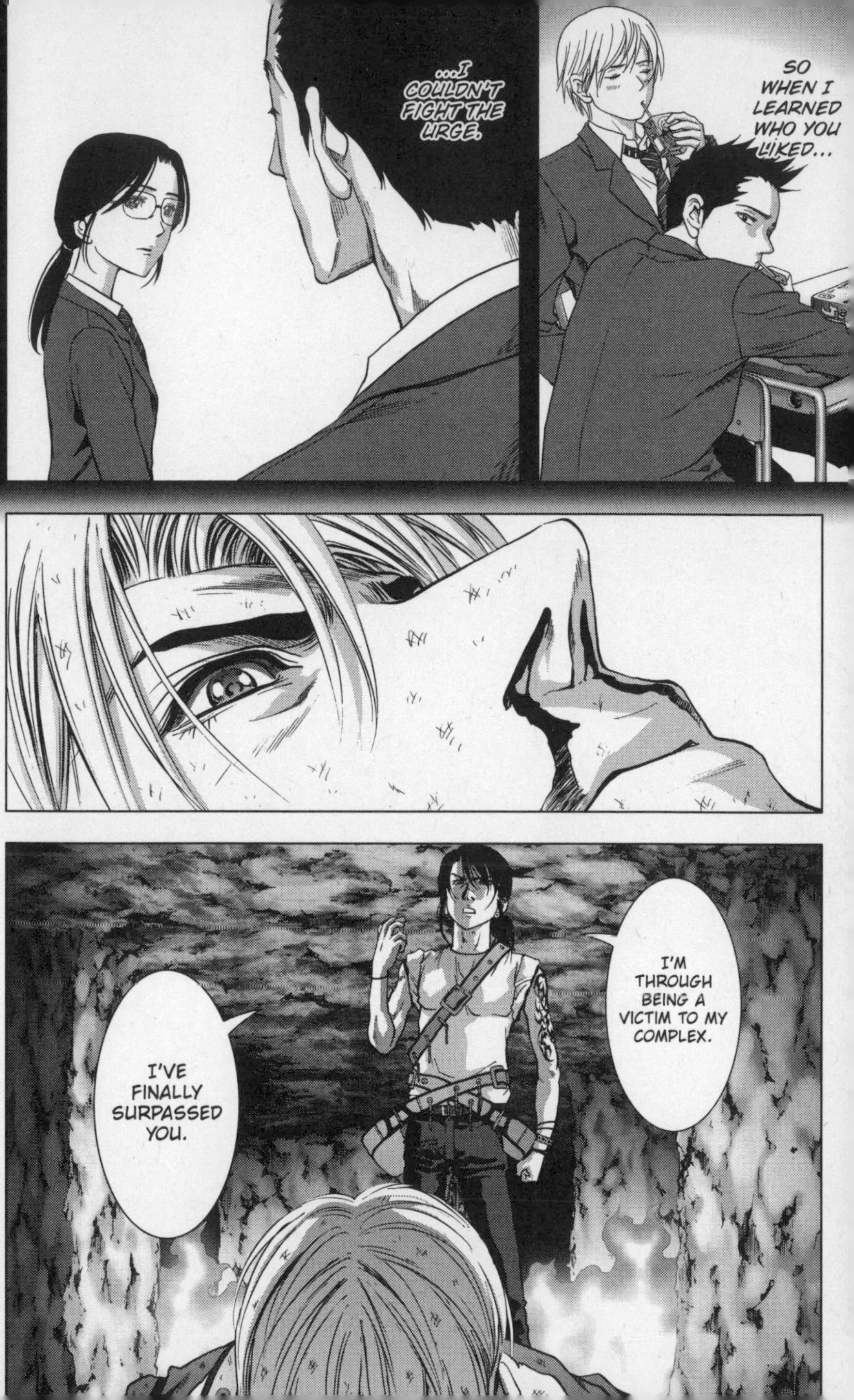
SO WHEN I LEARNED WHO YOU LIKED...
...I COULDN'T FIGHT THE URGE.
I'M THROUGH BEING A VICTIM TO MY COMPLEX.
I'VE FINALLY SURPASSED YOU.

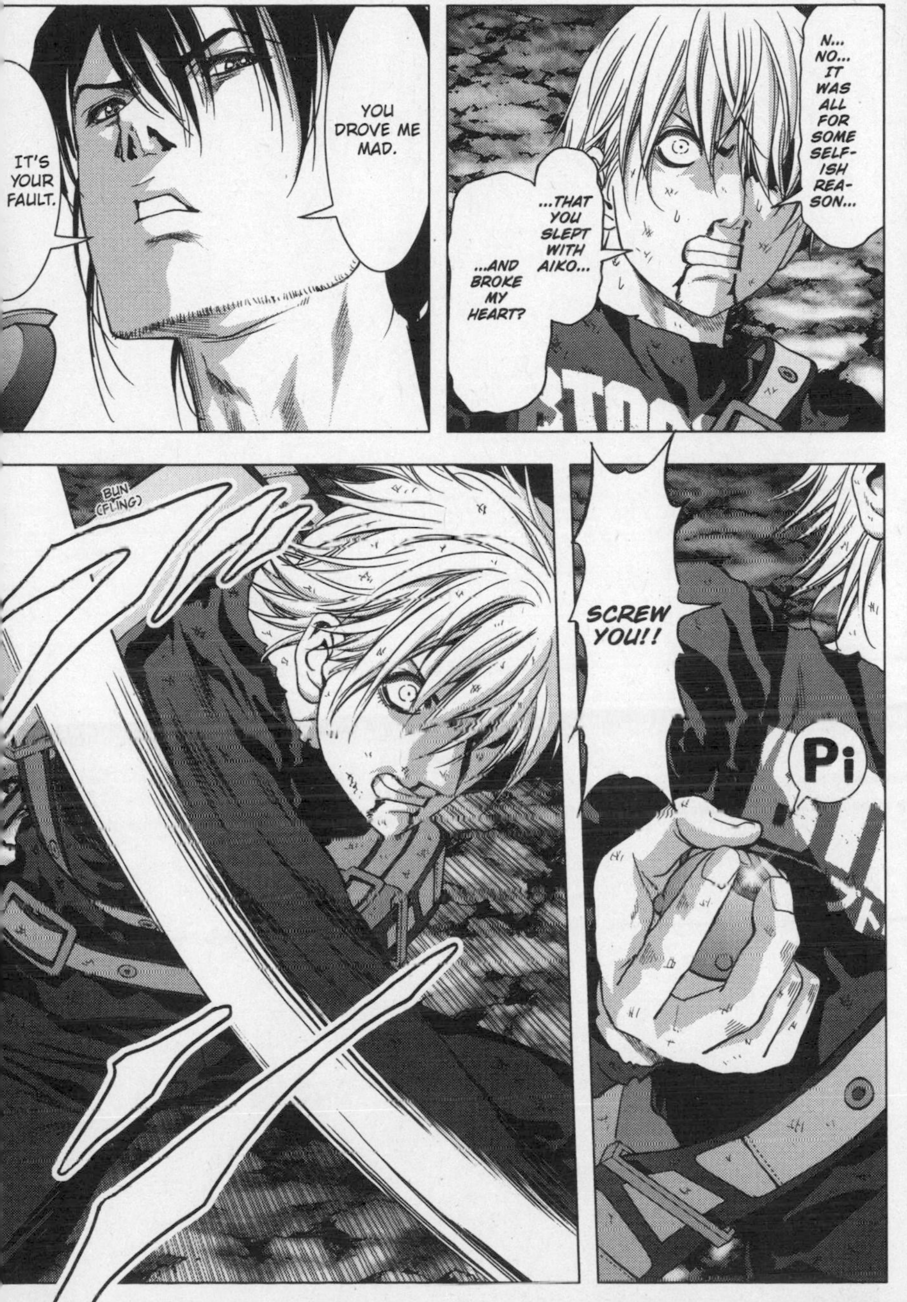
N... NO... IT WAS ALL FOR SOME SELF-ISH REA-SON...
...THAT YOU SLEPT WITH AIKO...
...AND BROKE MY HEART?
YOU DROVE ME MAD.
IT'S YOUR FAULT.
SCREW YOU!!
Pi
BUN (FLING)

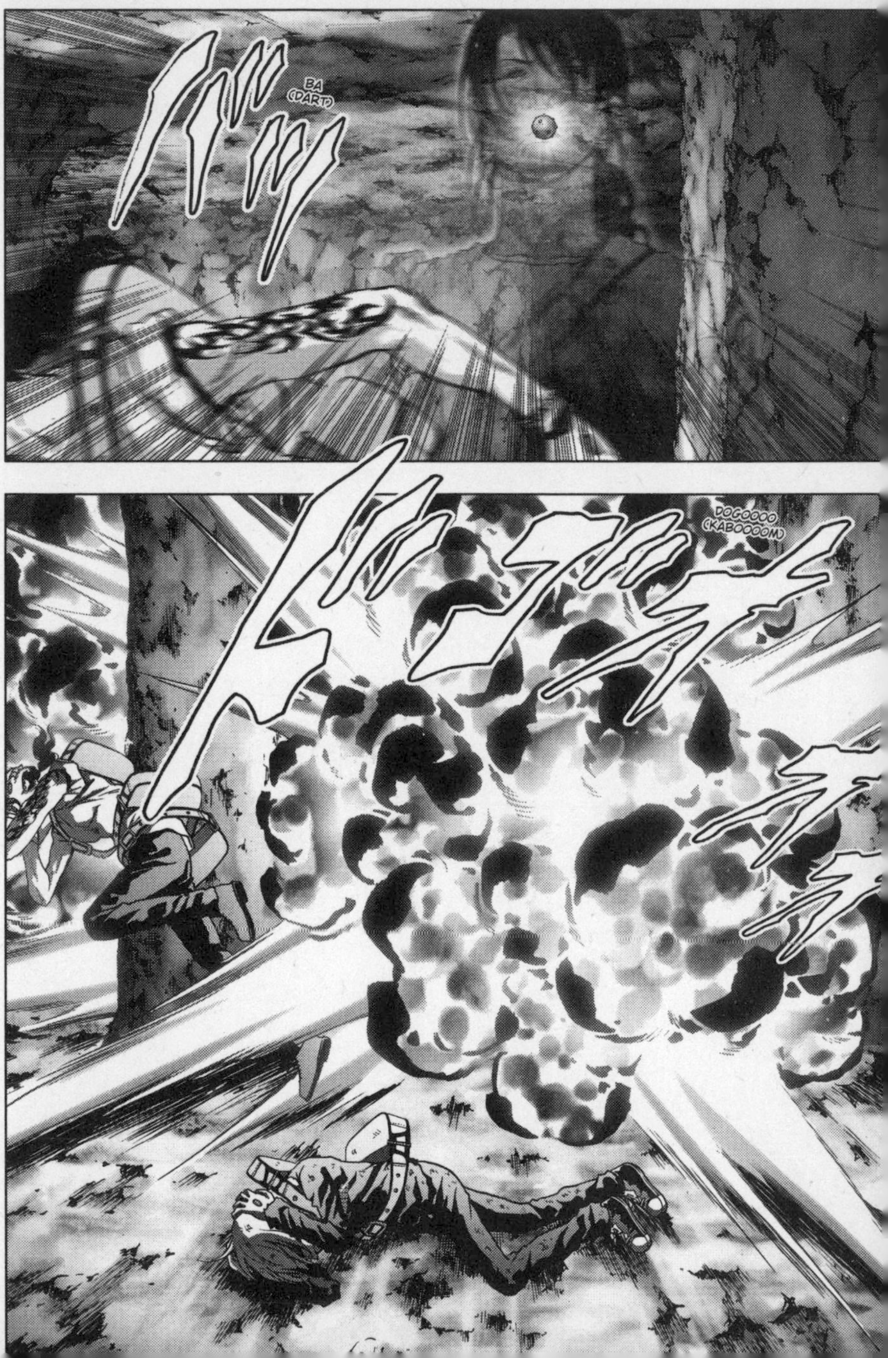
BA
(DART)
DOGOOOO
(KABOOOOM)

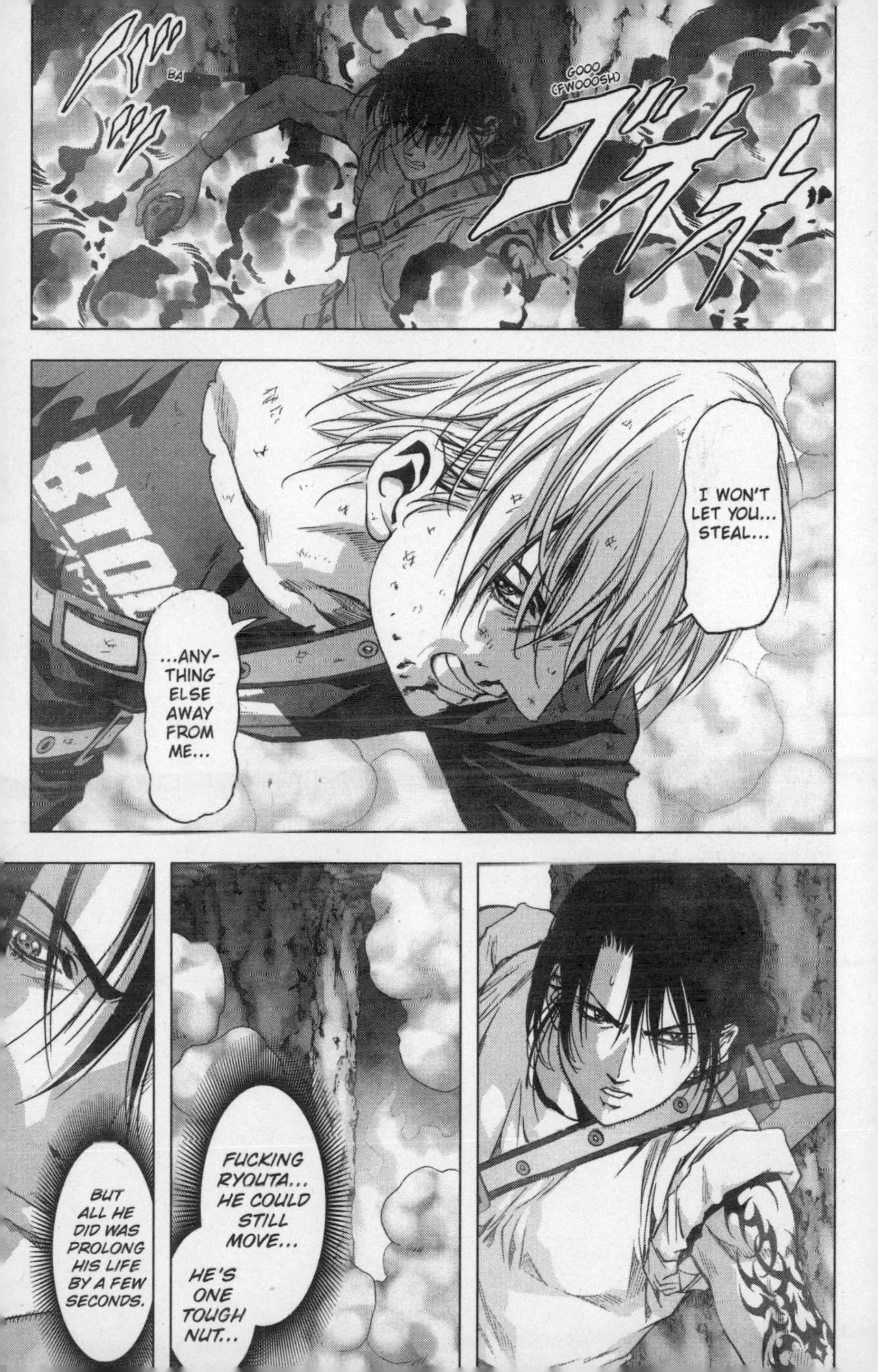
GOOO (FWOOOSH)
BA
I WON'T LET YOU... STEAL...
...ANY-THING ELSE AWAY FROM ME...
FUCKING RYOUTA... HE COULD STILL MOVE...
HE'S ONE TOUGH NUT...
BUT ALL HE DID WAS PROLONG HIS LIFE BY A FEW SECONDS.

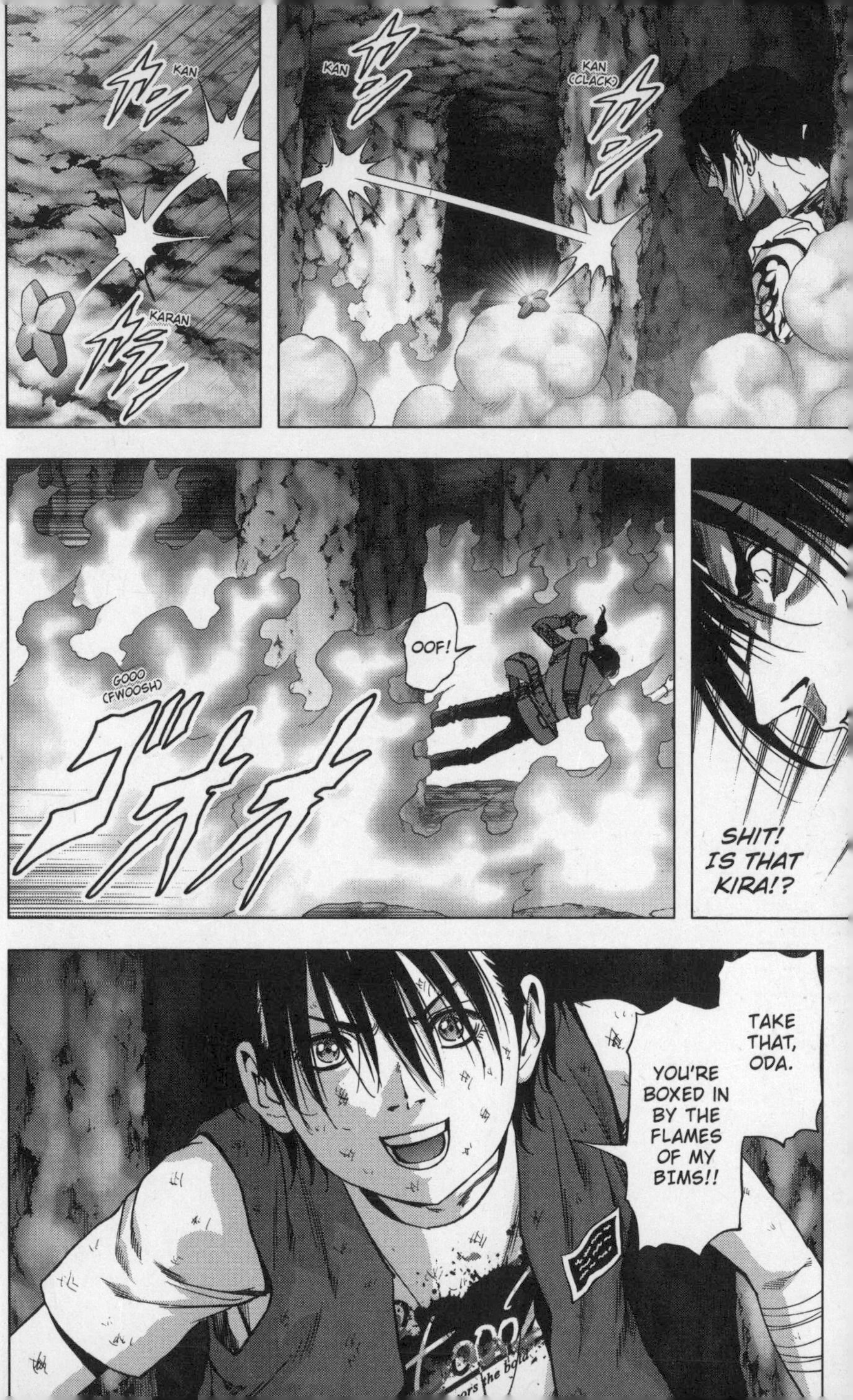
KAN (CLACK)
KAN
KAN
KARAN
SHIT! IS THAT KIRA!?
OOF!
GOOO (FWOOSH)
TAKE THAT, ODA.
YOU'RE BOXED IN BY THE FLAMES OF MY BIMS!!

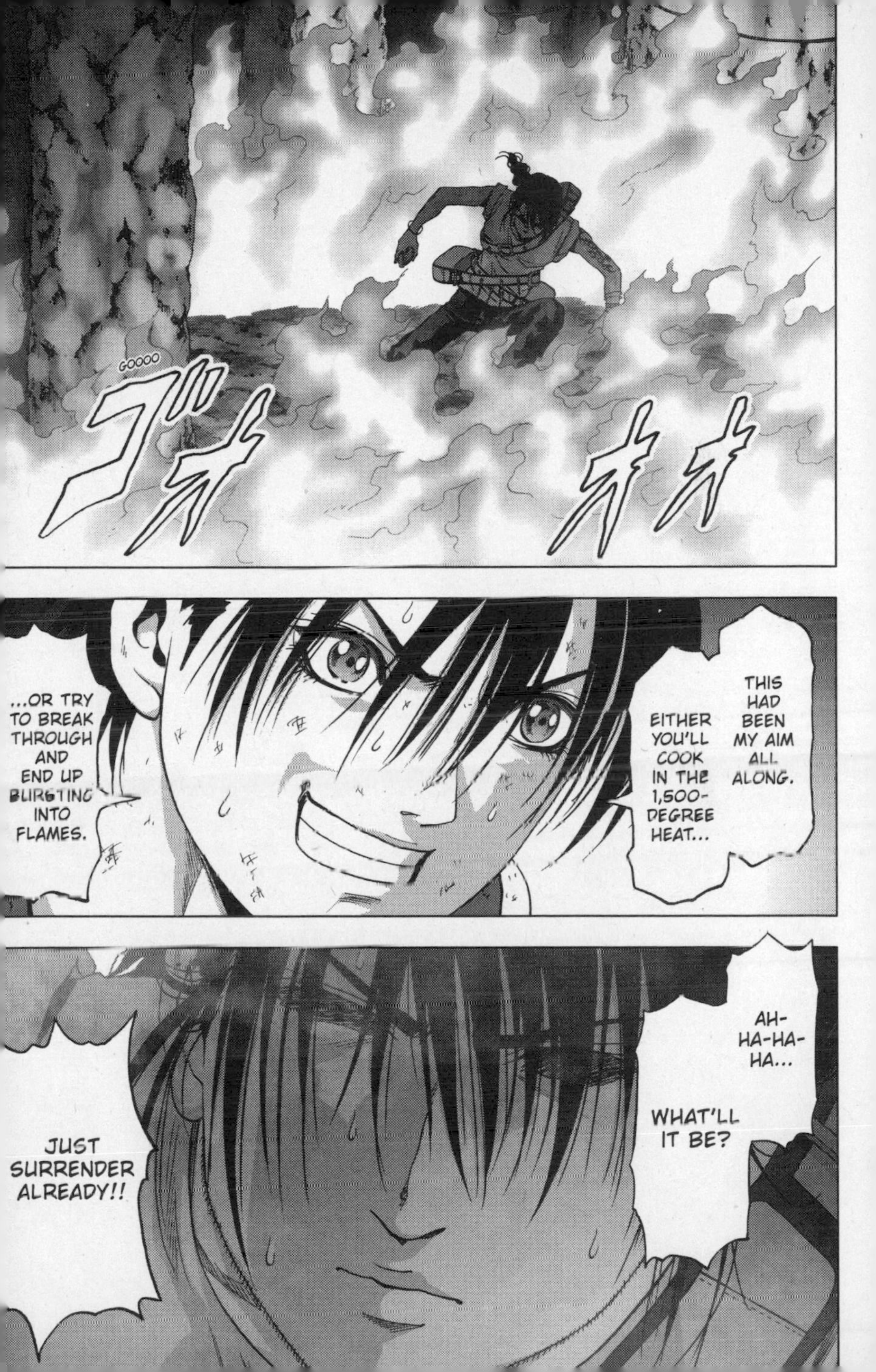
GOOOO
THIS HAD BEEN MY AIM ALL ALONG.
EITHER YOU'LL COOK IN THE 1,500-DEGREE HEAT...
...OR TRY TO BREAK THROUGH AND END UP BURSTING INTO FLAMES.
AH-HA-HA-HA...
WHAT'LL IT BE?
JUST SURRENDER ALREADY!!

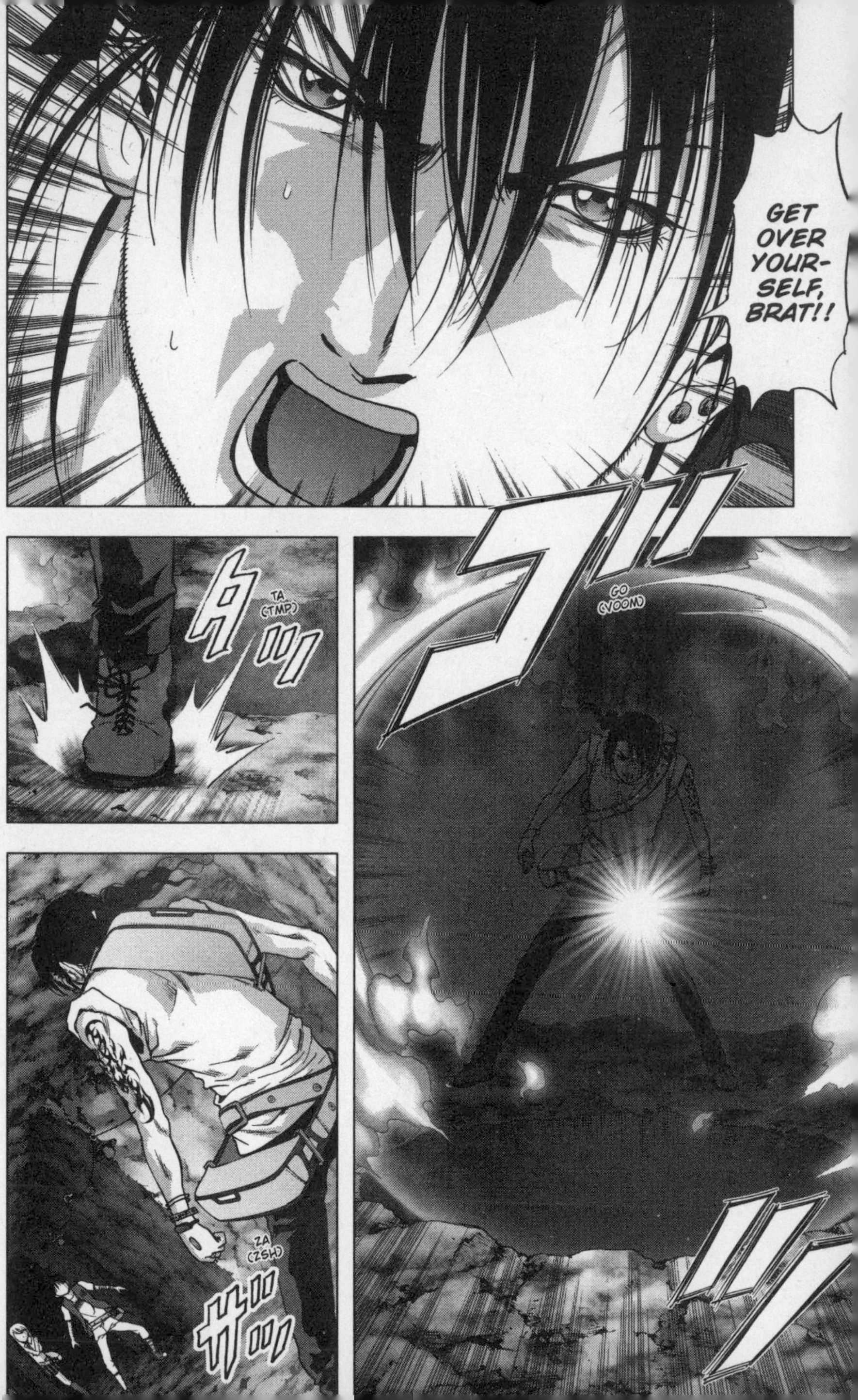
GET OVER YOURSELF, BRAT!!
ゴッ
GO (VOOM)
タッ
TA (TMP)
ザッ
ZA (ZSH)

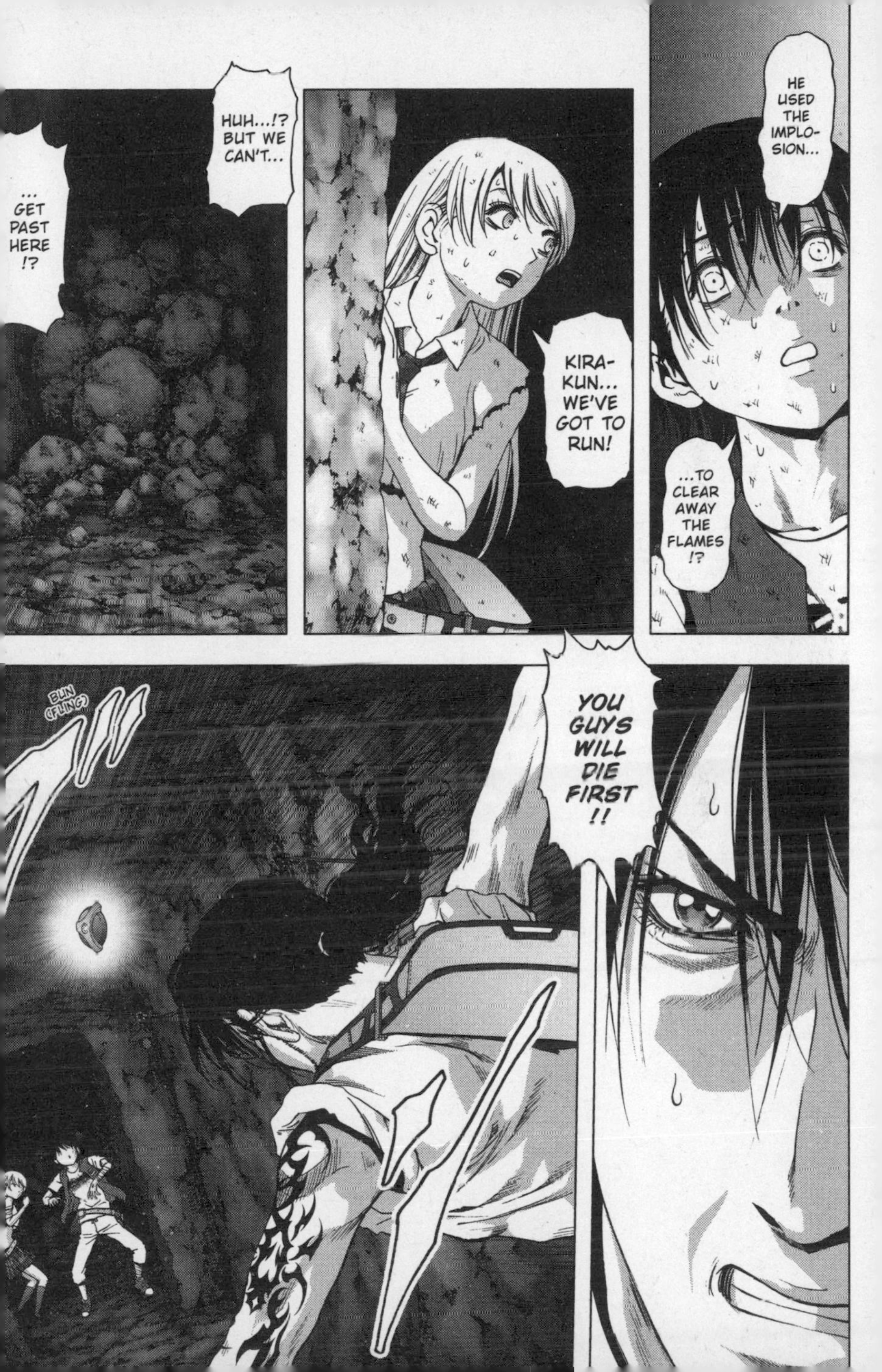
HE USED THE IMPLOSION...
...TO CLEAR AWAY THE FLAMES!?
KIRA-KUN... WE'VE GOT TO RUN!
HUH...!? BUT WE CAN'T...
...GET PAST HERE!?
YOU GUYS WILL DIE FIRST!!
BUN (FLING)

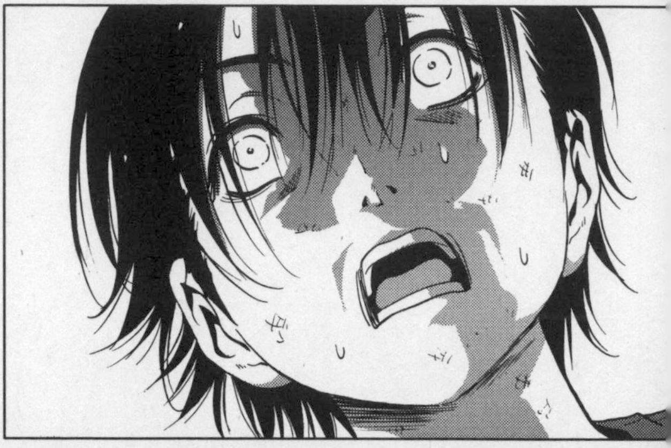

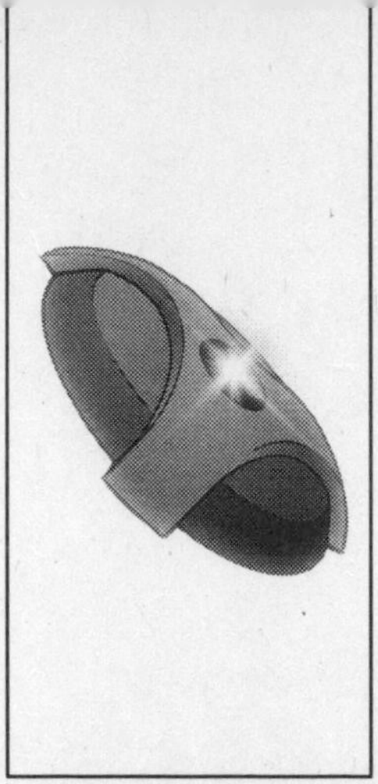

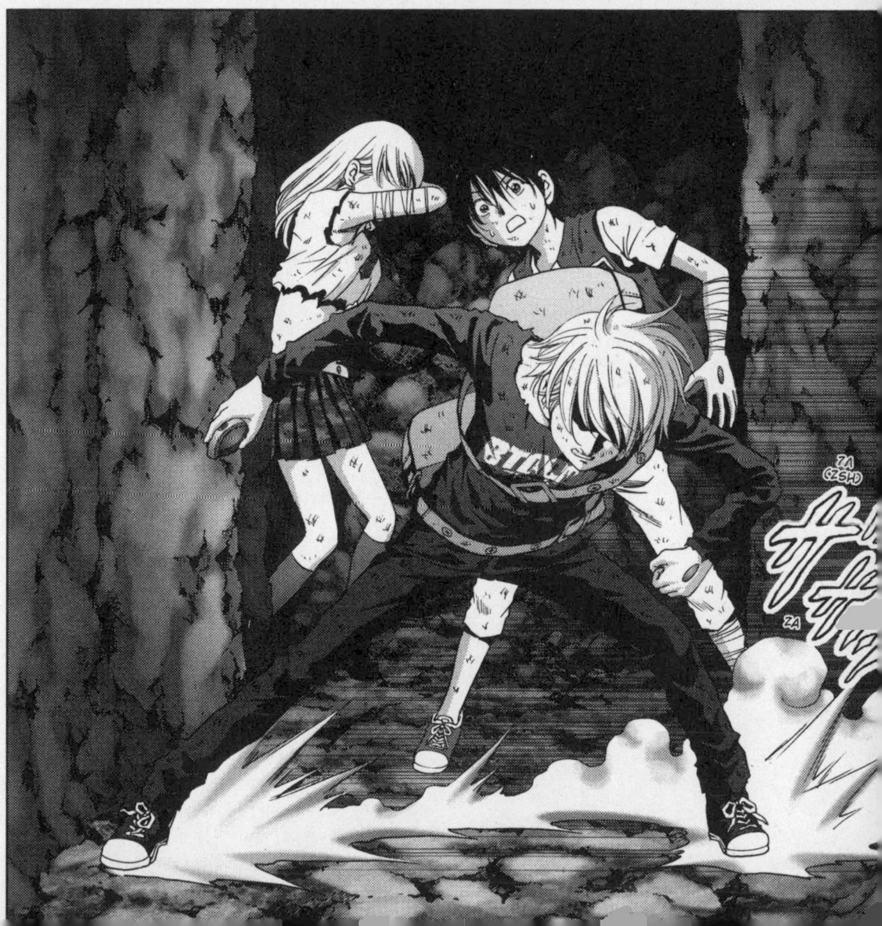
ZA (ZSH)
ZA

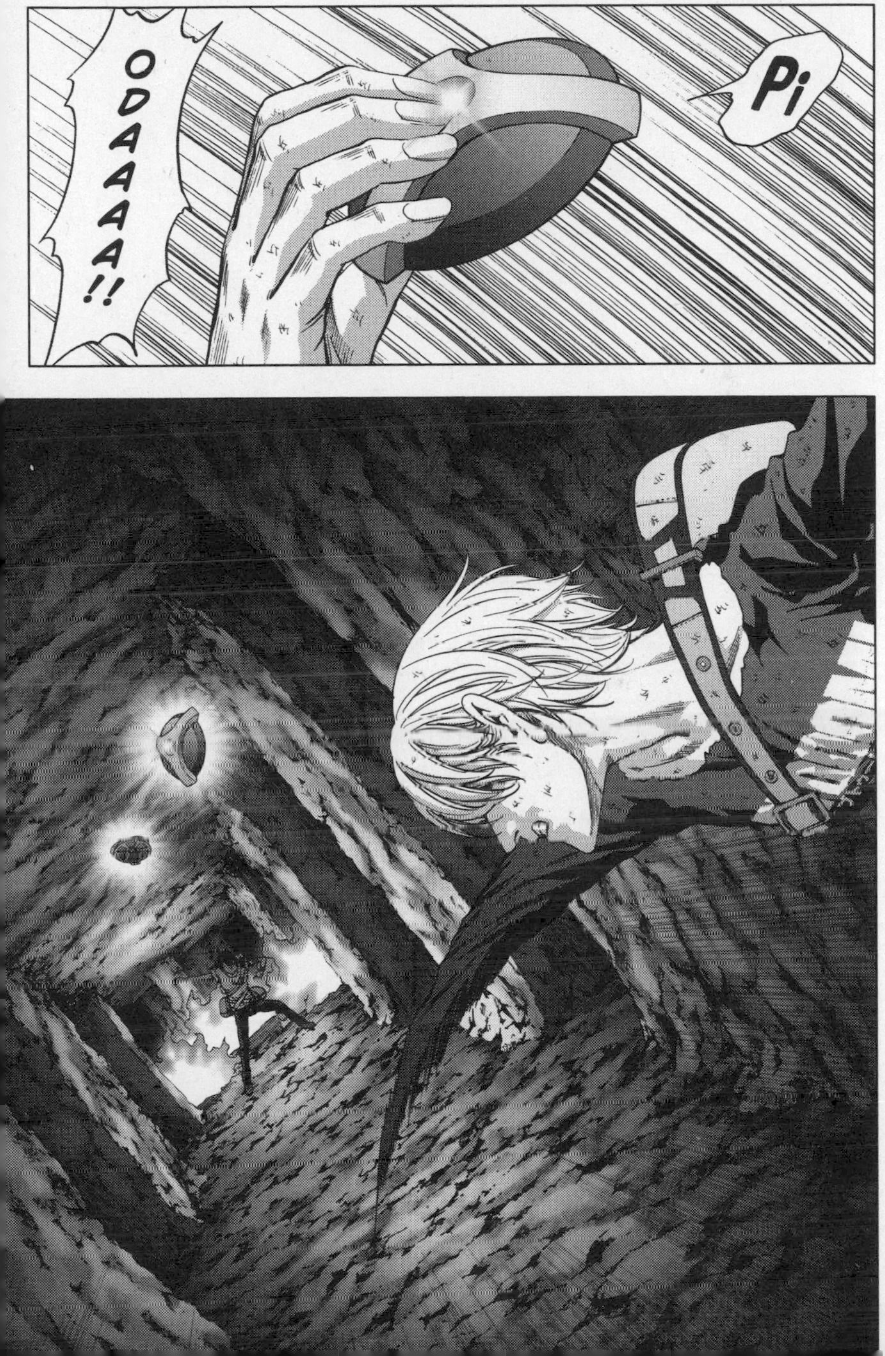
Pi
ODAAAAA!!

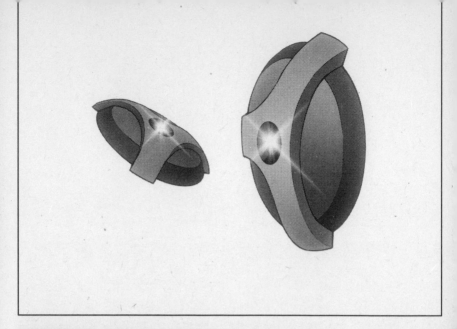

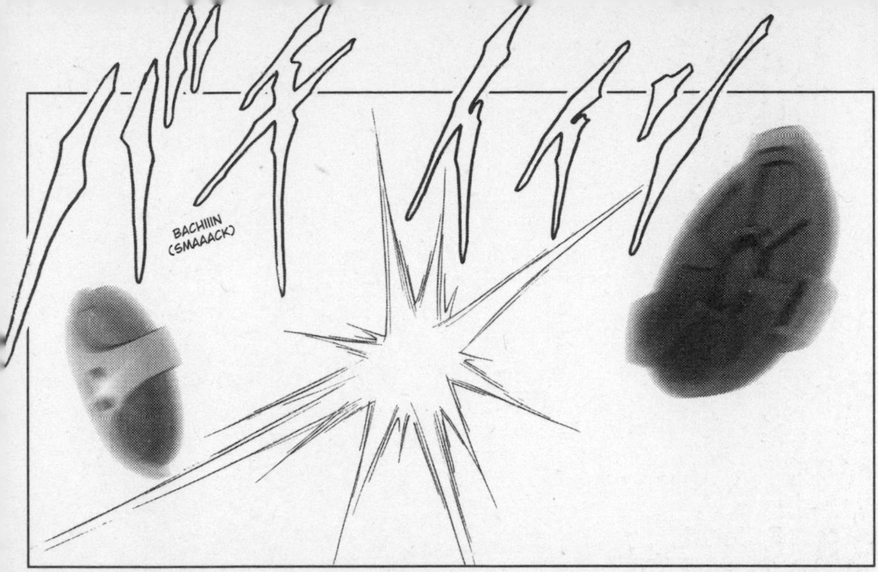
BACHIIIN
(SMAAACK)
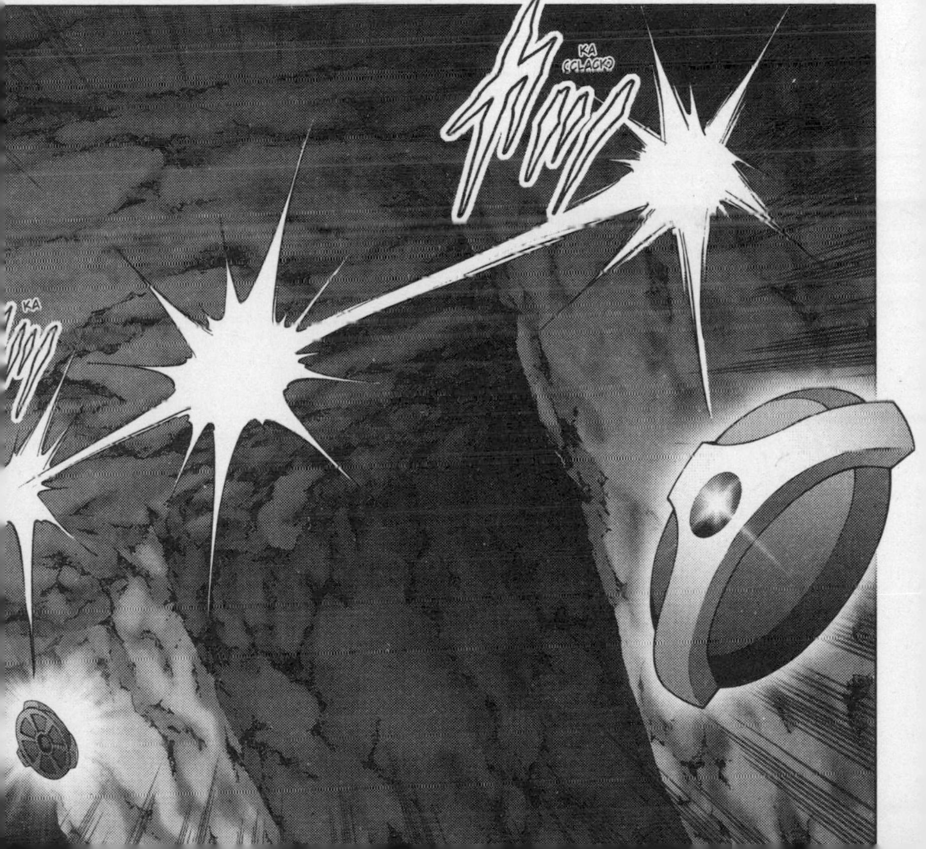
KA
(CLACK)
KA

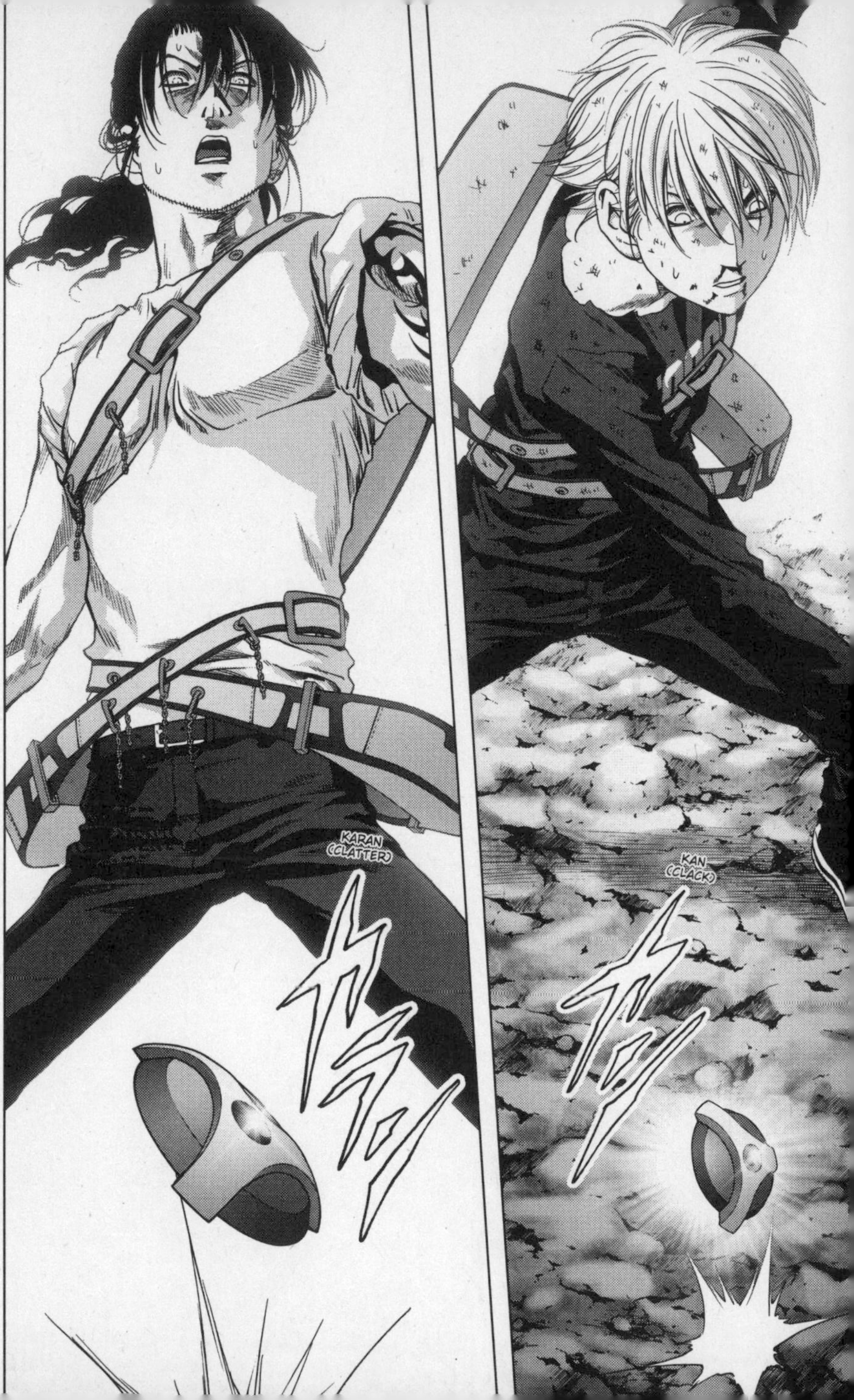
KAN (CLACK)
KARAN (CLATTER)

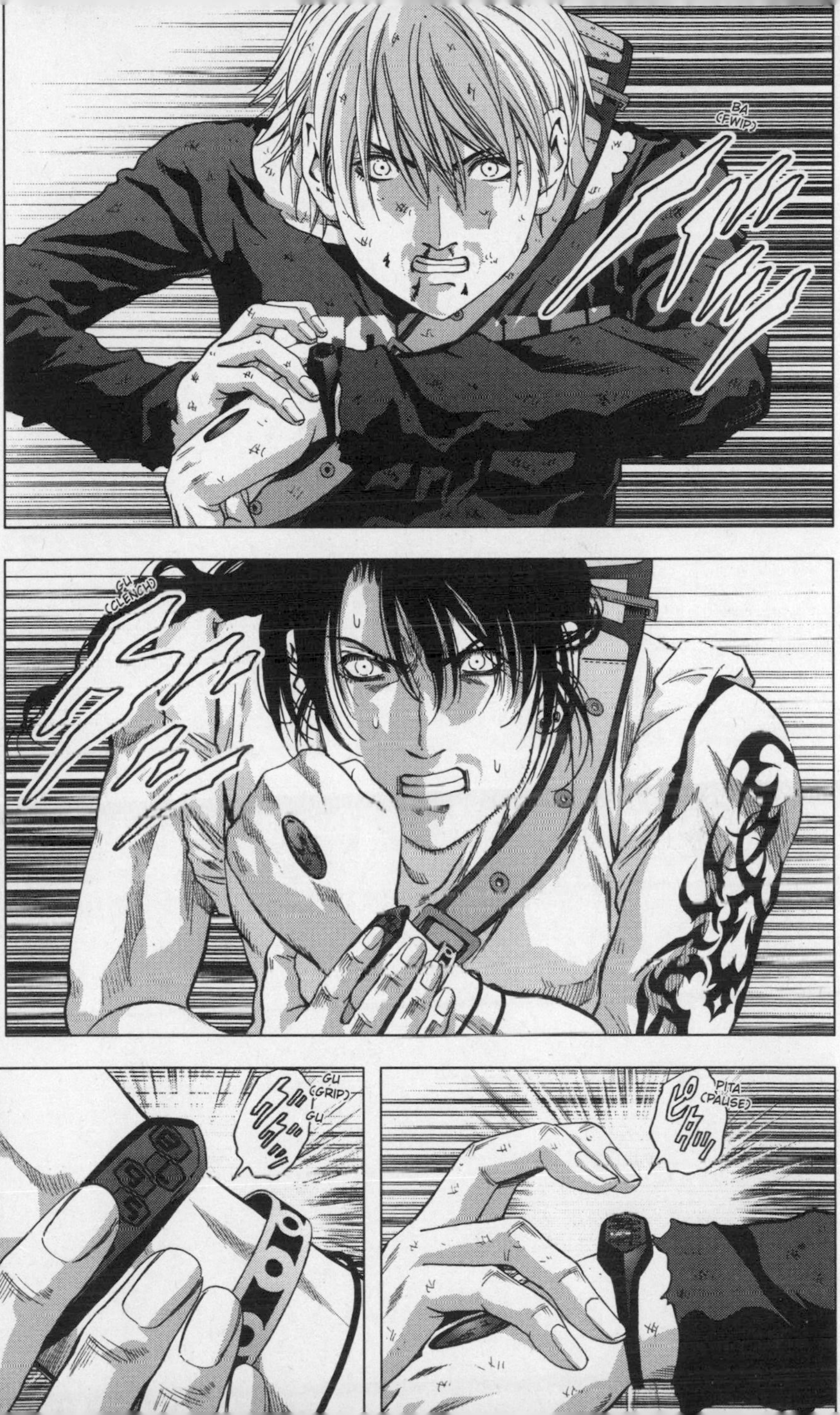
BA (FWIP)
GU (CLENCH)
PITA (PAUSE)
GU (GRIP) GU

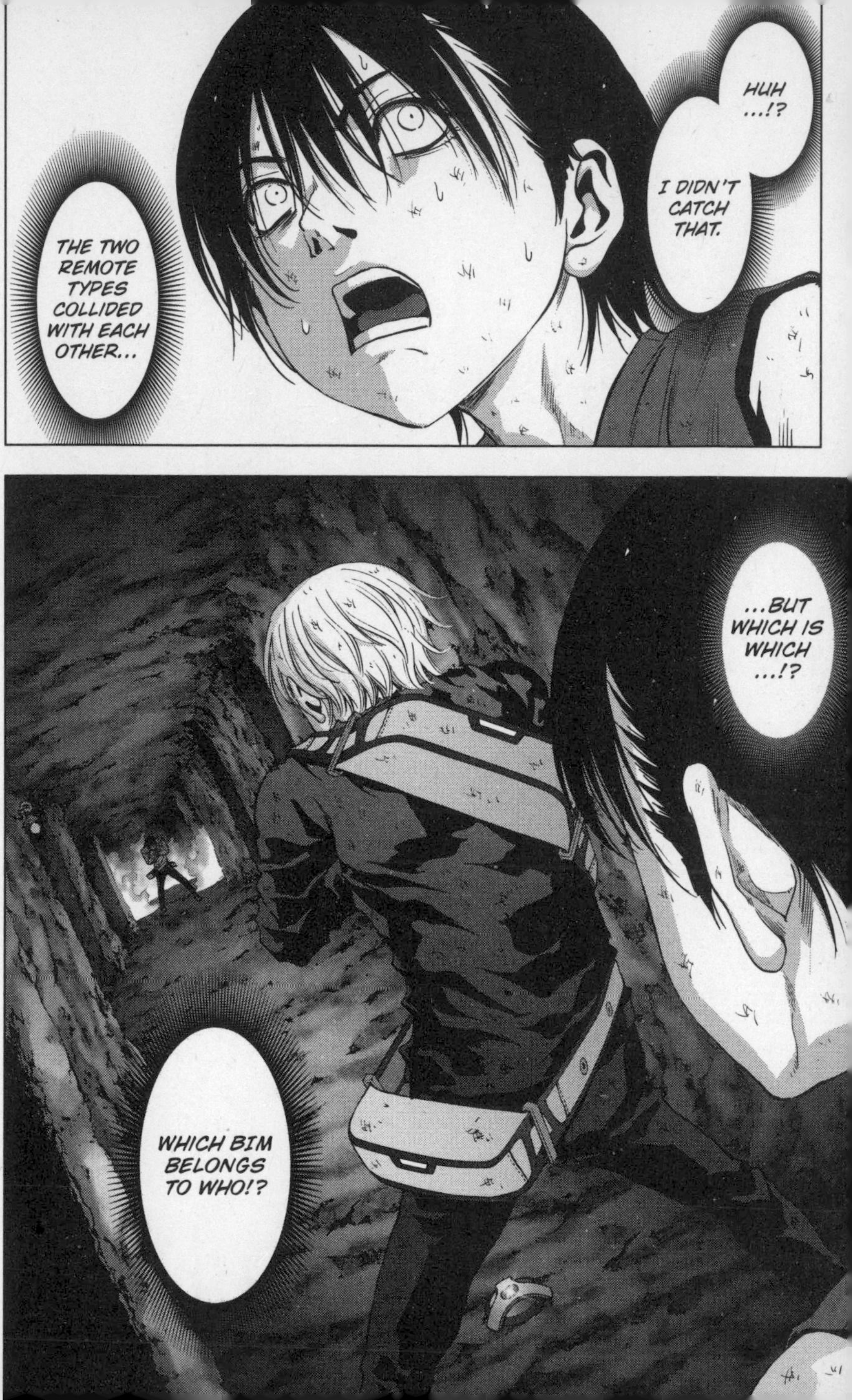
HUH ...!?
I DIDN'T CATCH THAT.
THE TWO REMOTE TYPES COLLIDED WITH EACH OTHER...
...BUT WHICH IS WHICH ...!?
WHICH BIM BELONGS TO WHO!?

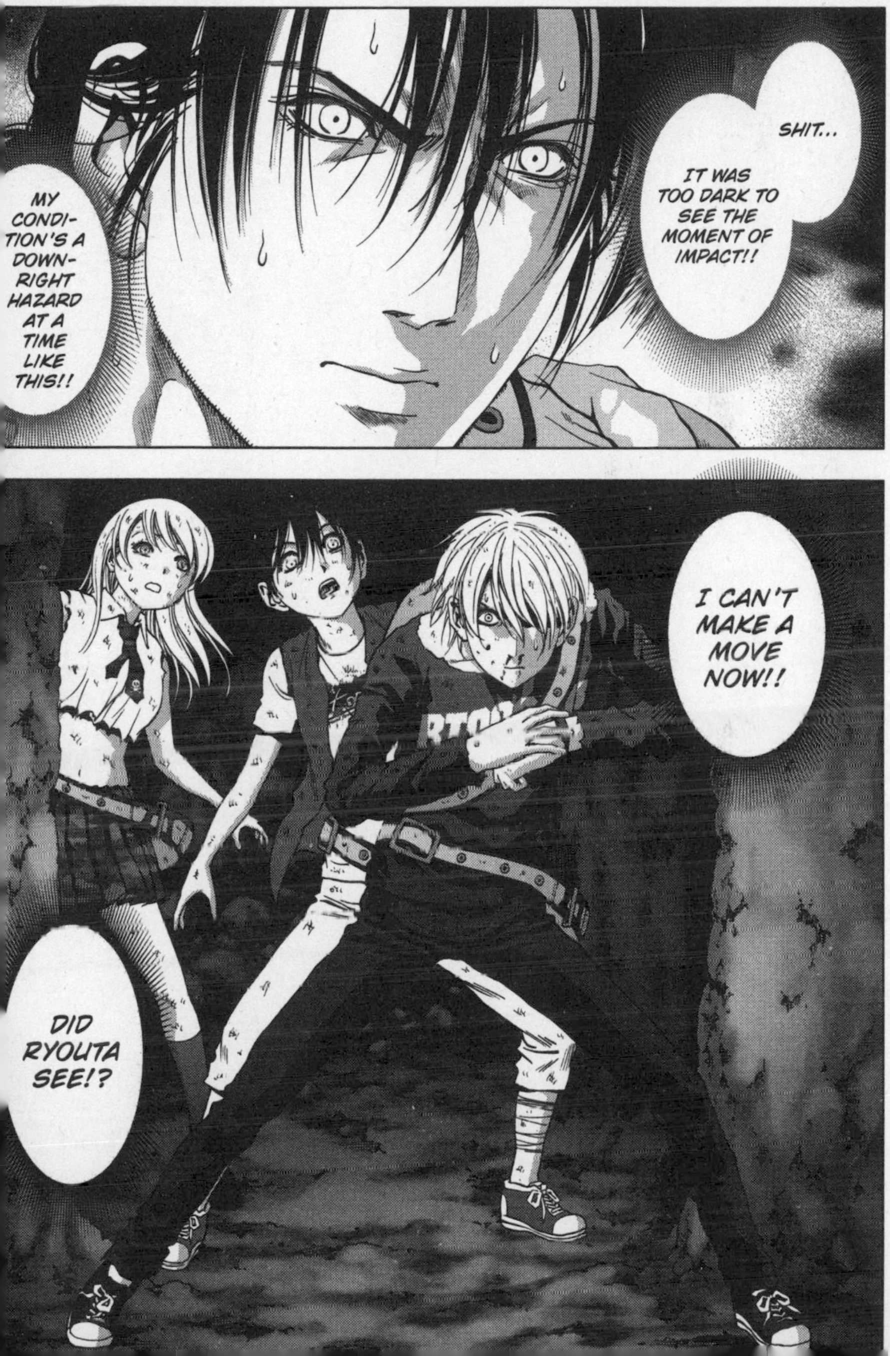
SHIT...
IT WAS TOO DARK TO SEE THE MOMENT OF IMPACT!!
MY CONDITION'S A DOWNRIGHT HAZARD AT A TIME LIKE THIS!!
I CAN'T MAKE A MOVE NOW!!
DID RYOUTA SEE!?

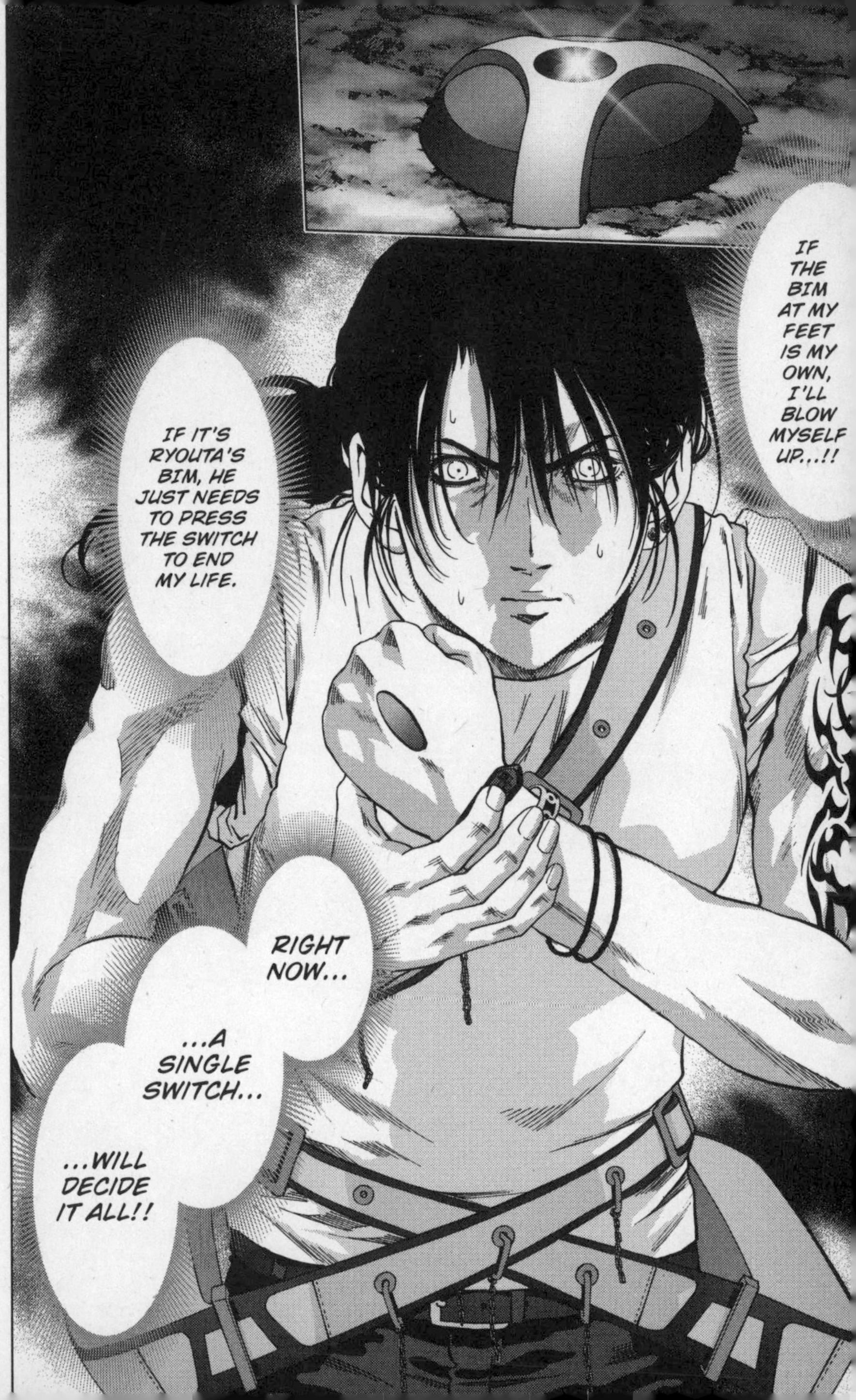
IF THE BIM AT MY FEET IS MY OWN, I'LL BLOW MYSELF UP...!!
IF IT'S RYOUTA'S BIM, HE JUST NEEDS TO PRESS THE SWITCH TO END MY LIFE.
RIGHT NOW...
...A SINGLE SWITCH...
...WILL DECIDE IT ALL!!

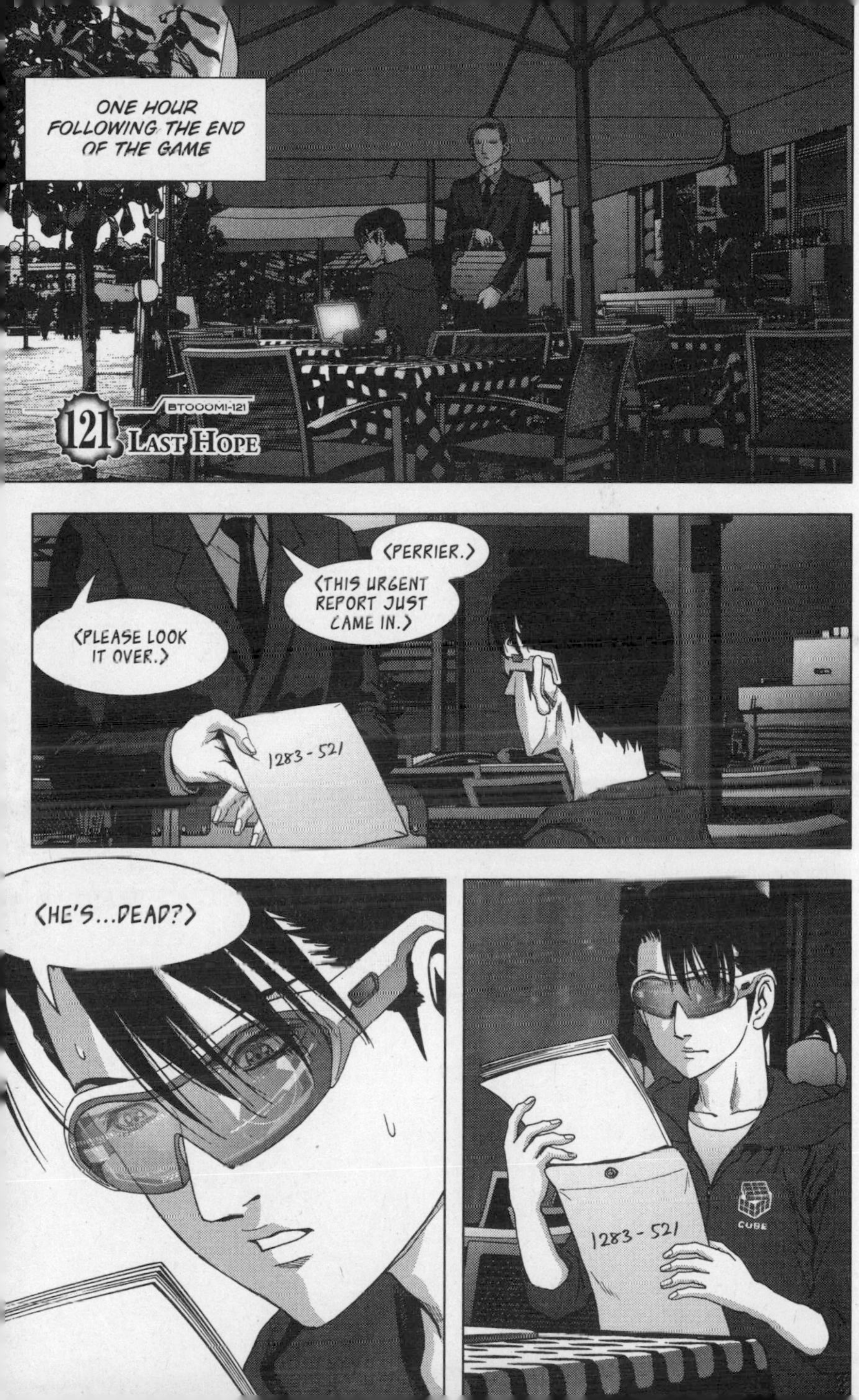
ONE HOUR FOLLOWING THE END OF THE GAME
BTOOOM!-121
121 LAST HOPE
<PERRIER.>
<THIS URGENT REPORT JUST CAME IN.>
<PLEASE LOOK IT OVER.>
1283 - 521
CUBE
1283 - 521
<HE'S...DEAD?>

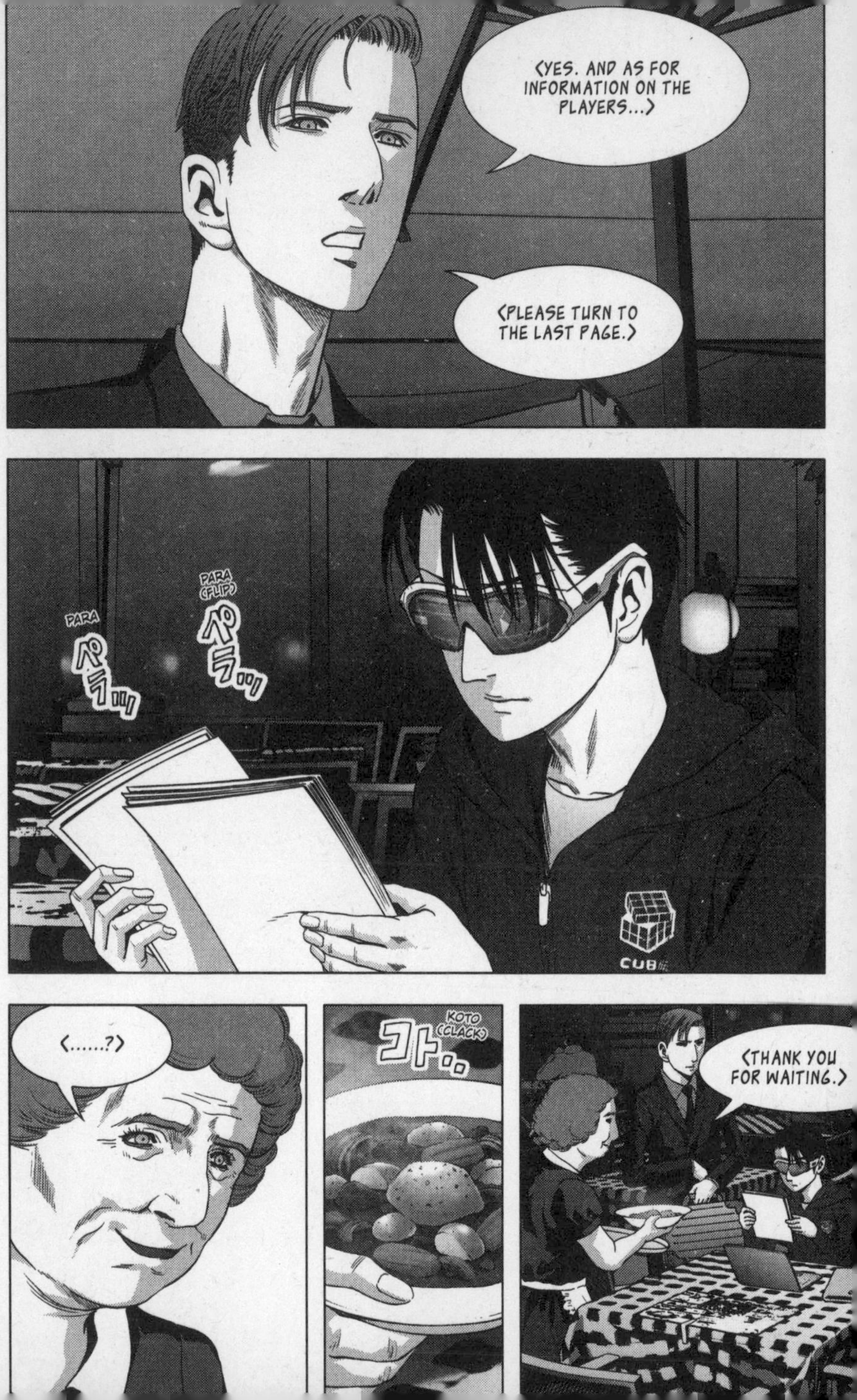

〈YES. AND AS FOR INFORMATION ON THE PLAYERS...〉
〈PLEASE TURN TO THE LAST PAGE.〉
PARA (FLIP)
ペラ…
PARA
ペラ…
〈THANK YOU FOR WAITING.〉
KOTO (CLACK)
コト…
〈......?〉

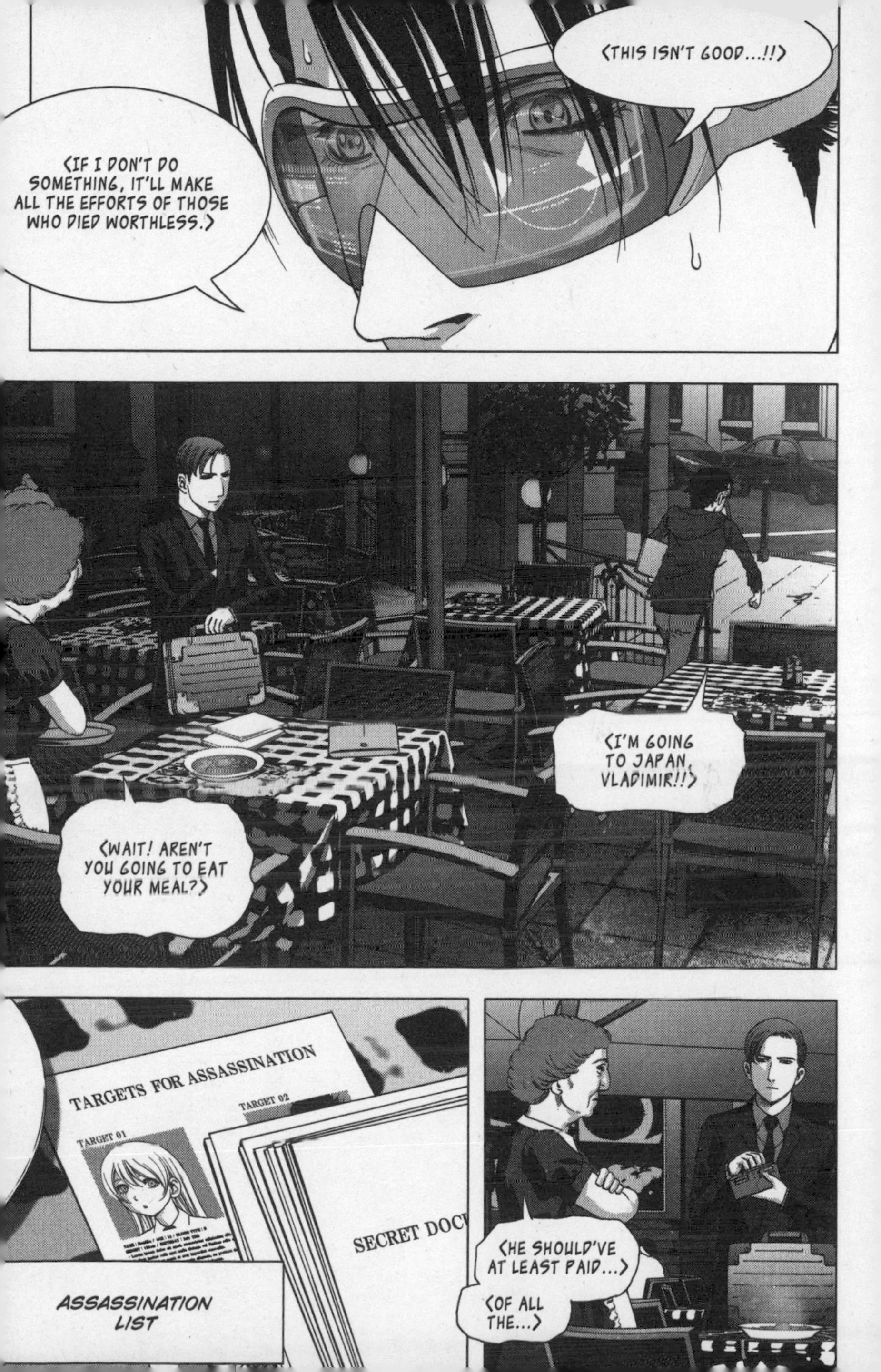
<THIS ISN'T GOOD...!!>
<IF I DON'T DO SOMETHING, IT'LL MAKE ALL THE EFFORTS OF THOSE WHO DIED WORTHLESS.>
<I'M GOING TO JAPAN, VLADIMIR!!>
<WAIT! AREN'T YOU GOING TO EAT YOUR MEAL?>
<HE SHOULD'VE AT LEAST PAID...>
<OF ALL THE...>
TARGETS FOR ASSASSINATION
TARGET 02
TARGET 01
SECRET DOC
ASSASSINATION LIST

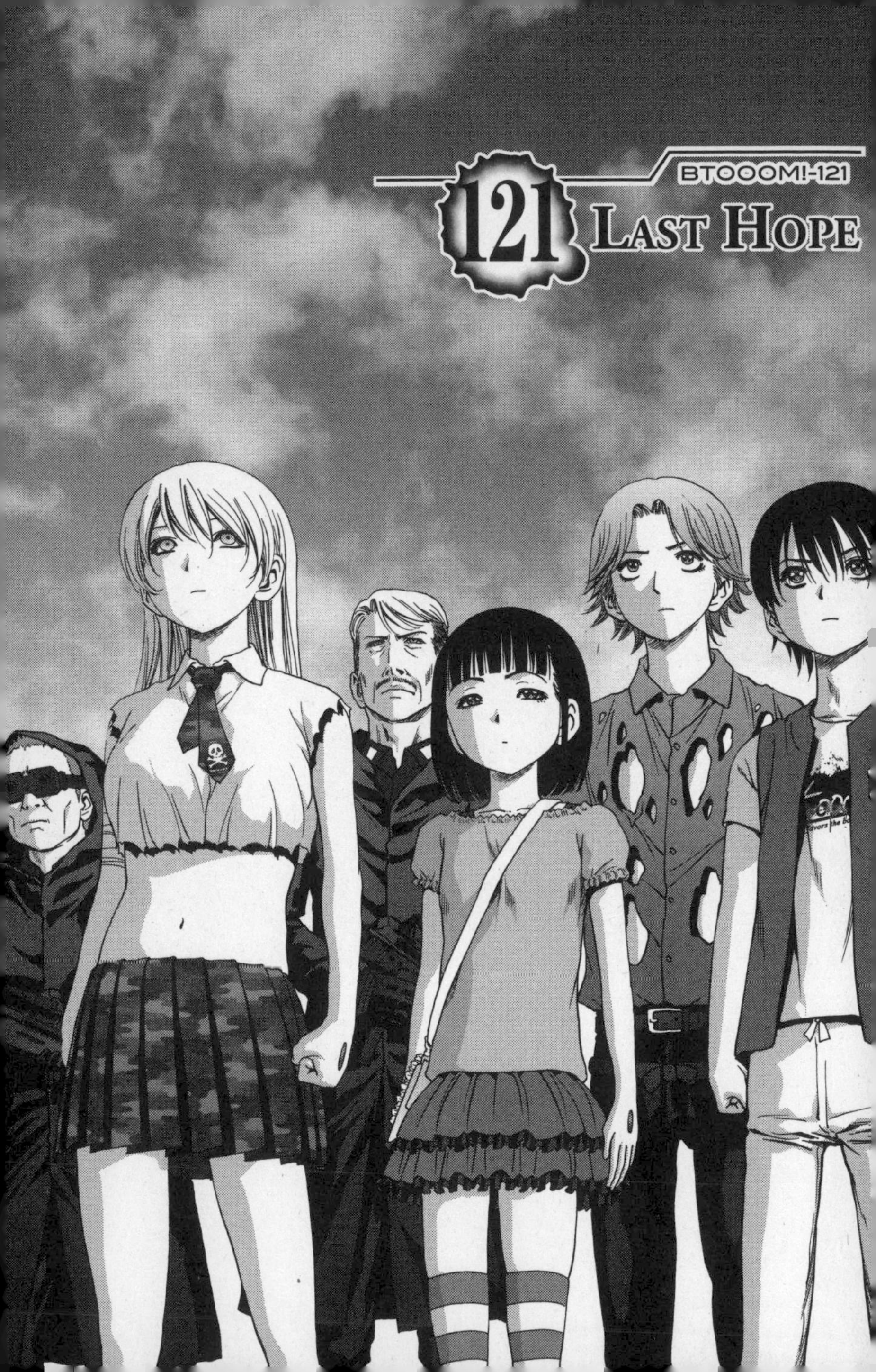
BTOOOM!-121
121
LAST HOPE

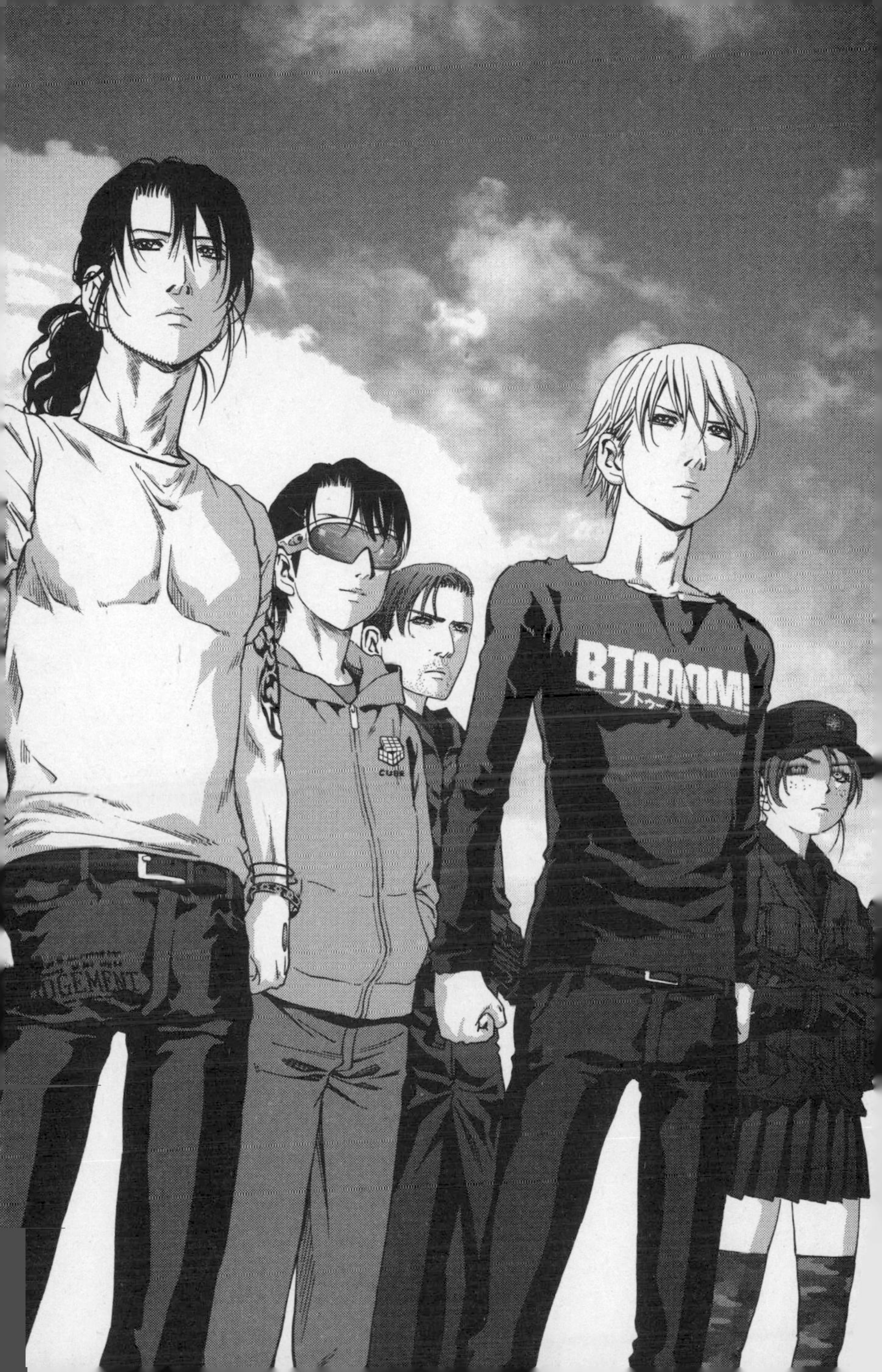
BTOOOM!
CUBE

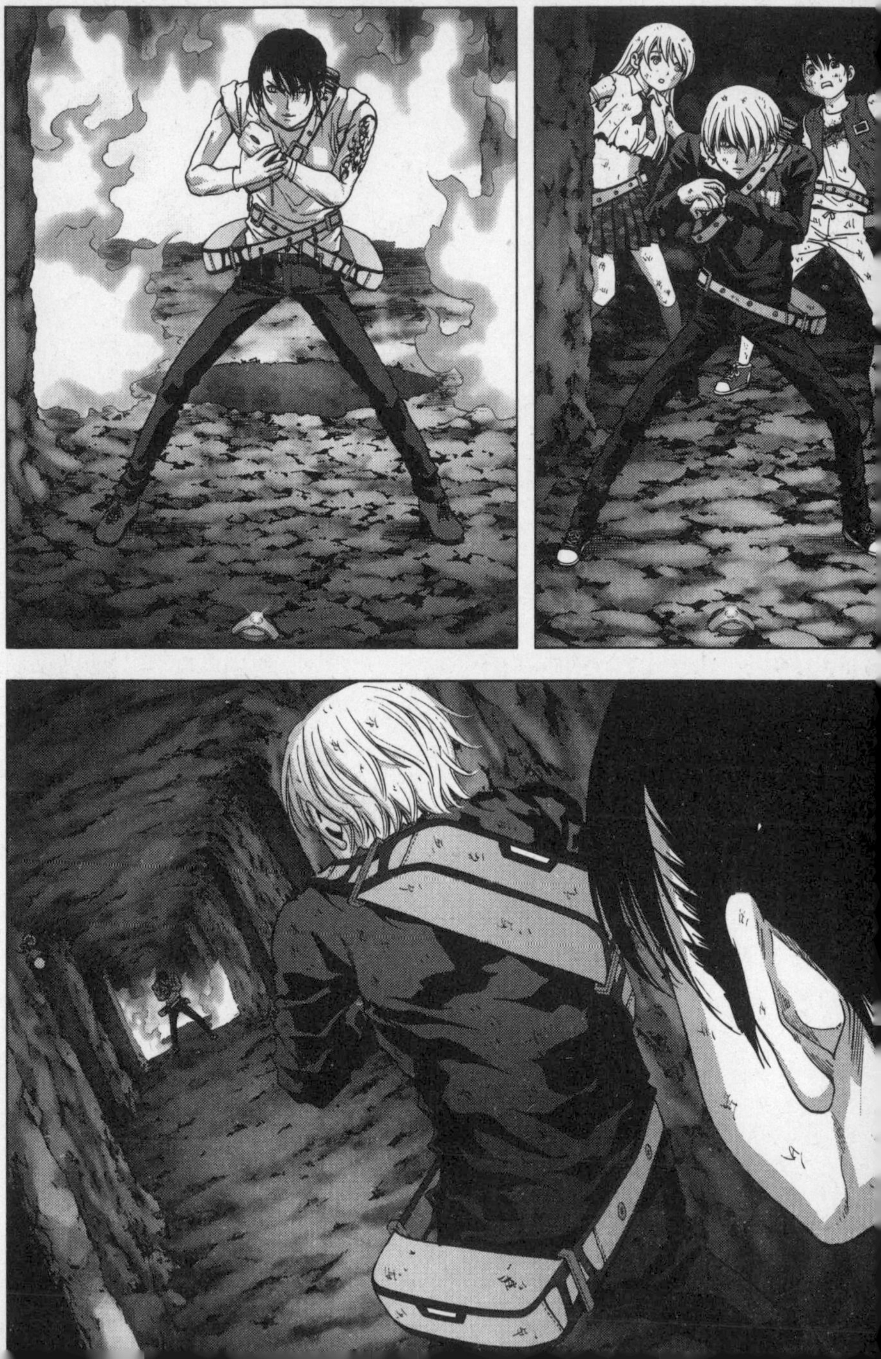

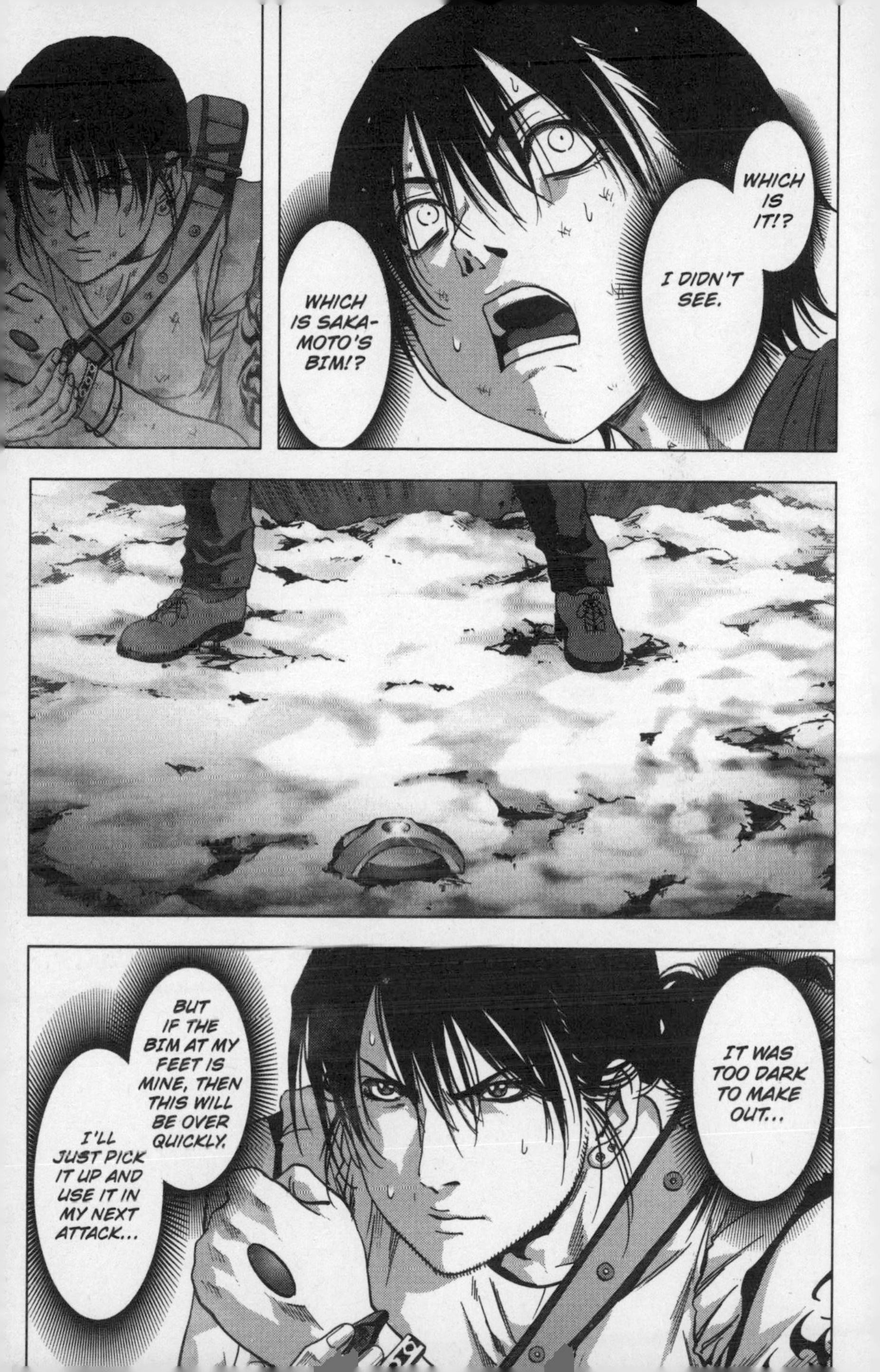
WHICH IS IT!?
I DIDN'T SEE.
WHICH IS SAKA-MOTO'S BIM!?
IT WAS TOO DARK TO MAKE OUT...
BUT IF THE BIM AT MY FEET IS MINE, THEN THIS WILL BE OVER QUICKLY.
I'LL JUST PICK IT UP AND USE IT IN MY NEXT ATTACK...

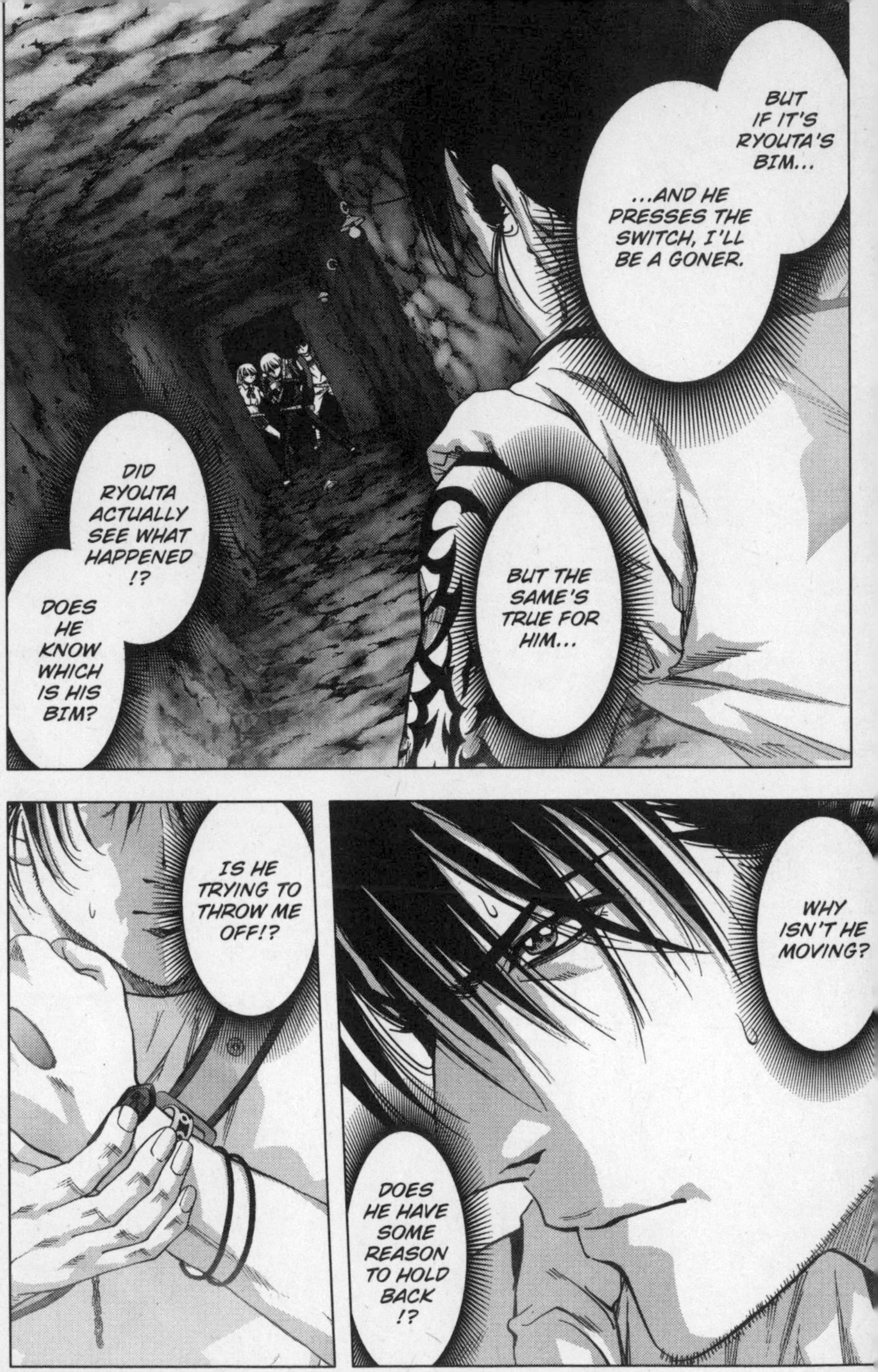
BUT IF IT'S RYOUTA'S BIM...
...AND HE PRESSES THE SWITCH, I'LL BE A GONER.
BUT THE SAME'S TRUE FOR HIM...
DID RYOUTA ACTUALLY SEE WHAT HAPPENED!?
DOES HE KNOW WHICH IS HIS BIM?
WHY ISN'T HE MOVING?
DOES HE HAVE SOME REASON TO HOLD BACK!?
IS HE TRYING TO THROW ME OFF!?

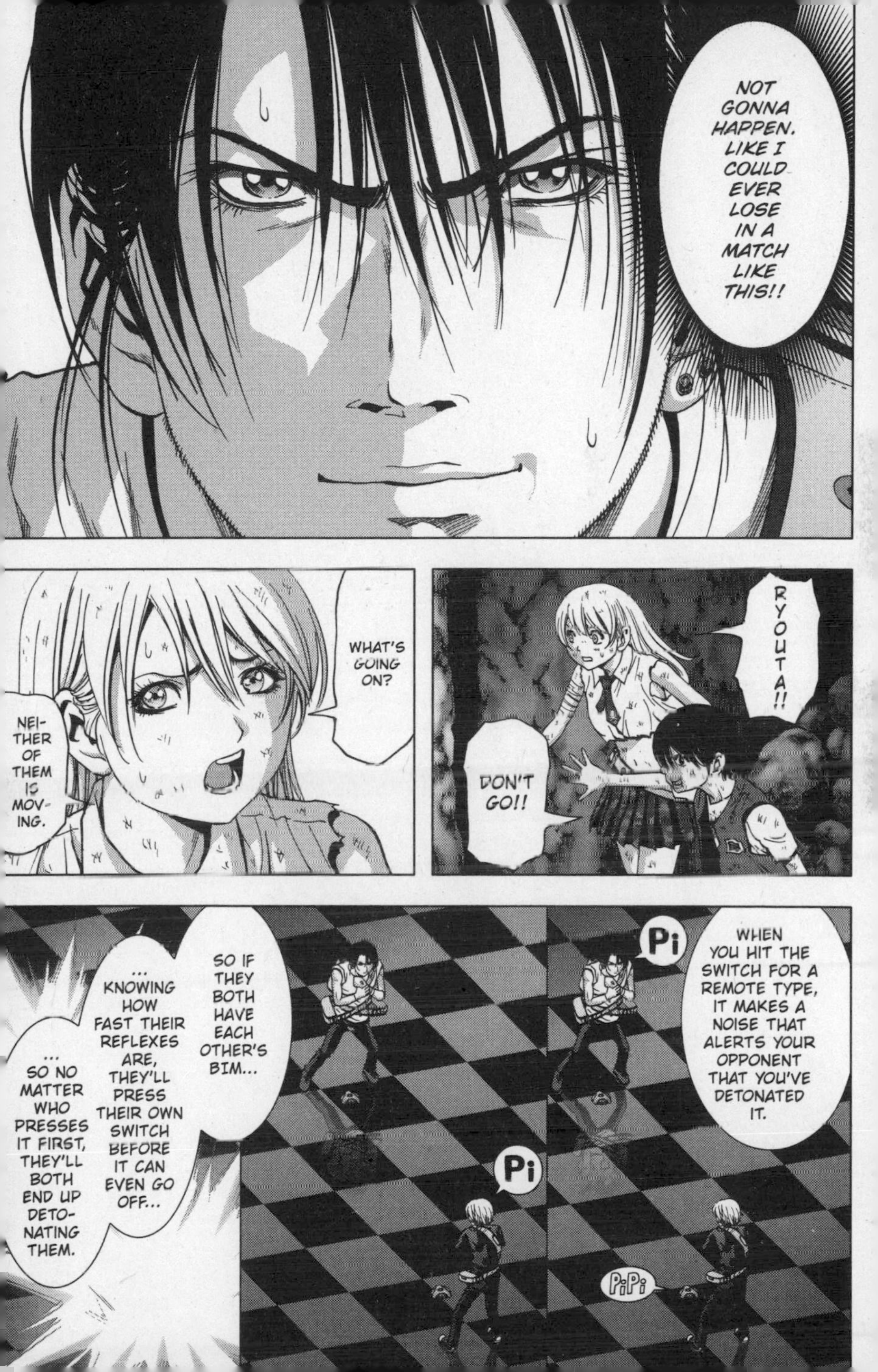
NOT GONNA HAPPEN. LIKE I COULD EVER LOSE IN A MATCH LIKE THIS!!
RYOUTA!!
DON'T GO!!
WHAT'S GOING ON?
NEITHER OF THEM IS MOVING.
WHEN YOU HIT THE SWITCH FOR A REMOTE TYPE, IT MAKES A NOISE THAT ALERTS YOUR OPPONENT THAT YOU'VE DETONATED IT.
Pi
PiPi
SO IF THEY BOTH HAVE EACH OTHER'S BIM...
...KNOWING HOW FAST THEIR REFLEXES ARE, THEY'LL PRESS THEIR OWN SWITCH BEFORE IT CAN EVEN GO OFF...
...SO NO MATTER WHO PRESSES IT FIRST, THEY'LL BOTH END UP DETONATING THEM.
Pi

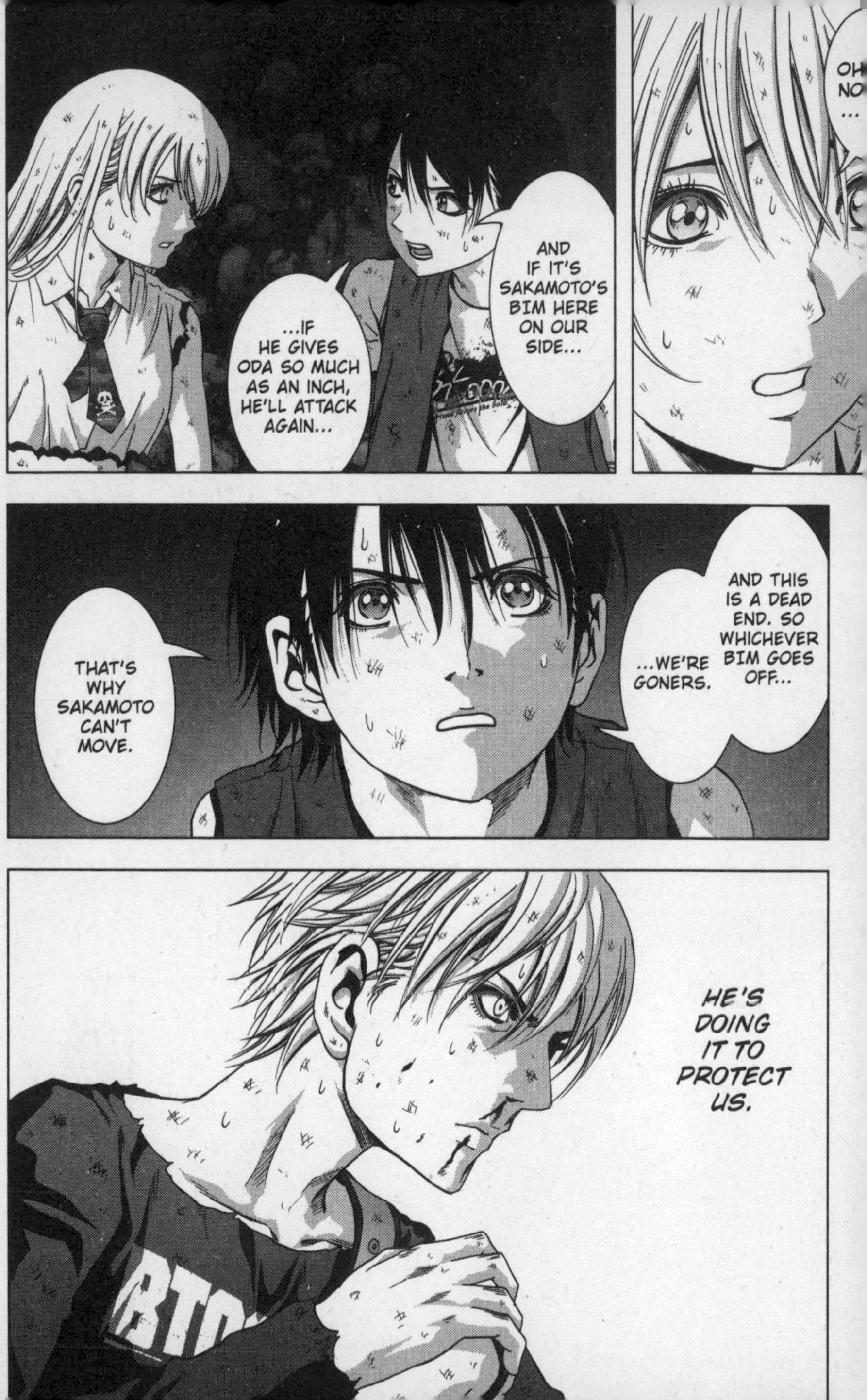
OH NO...
AND IF IT'S SAKAMOTO'S BIM HERE ON OUR SIDE...
...IF HE GIVES ODA SO MUCH AS AN INCH, HE'LL ATTACK AGAIN...
AND THIS IS A DEAD END. SO WHICHEVER BIM GOES OFF...
...WE'RE GONERS.
THAT'S WHY SAKAMOTO CAN'T MOVE.
HE'S DOING IT TO PROTECT US.

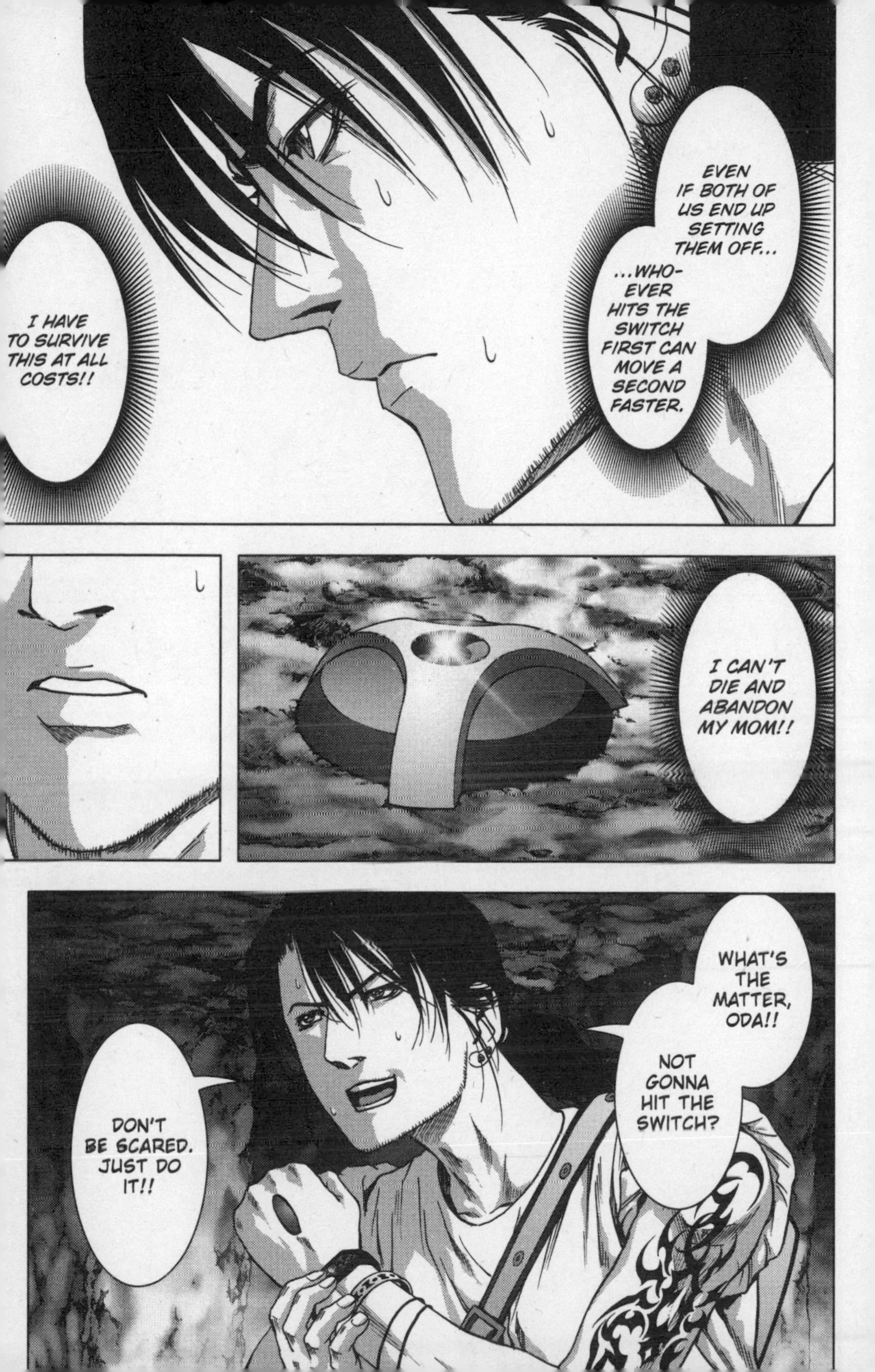
EVEN IF BOTH OF US END UP SETTING THEM OFF...
...WHO-EVER HITS THE SWITCH FIRST CAN MOVE A SECOND FASTER.
I HAVE TO SURVIVE THIS AT ALL COSTS!!
I CAN'T DIE AND ABANDON MY MOM!!
WHAT'S THE MATTER, ODA!!
NOT GONNA HIT THE SWITCH?
DON'T BE SCARED. JUST DO IT!!

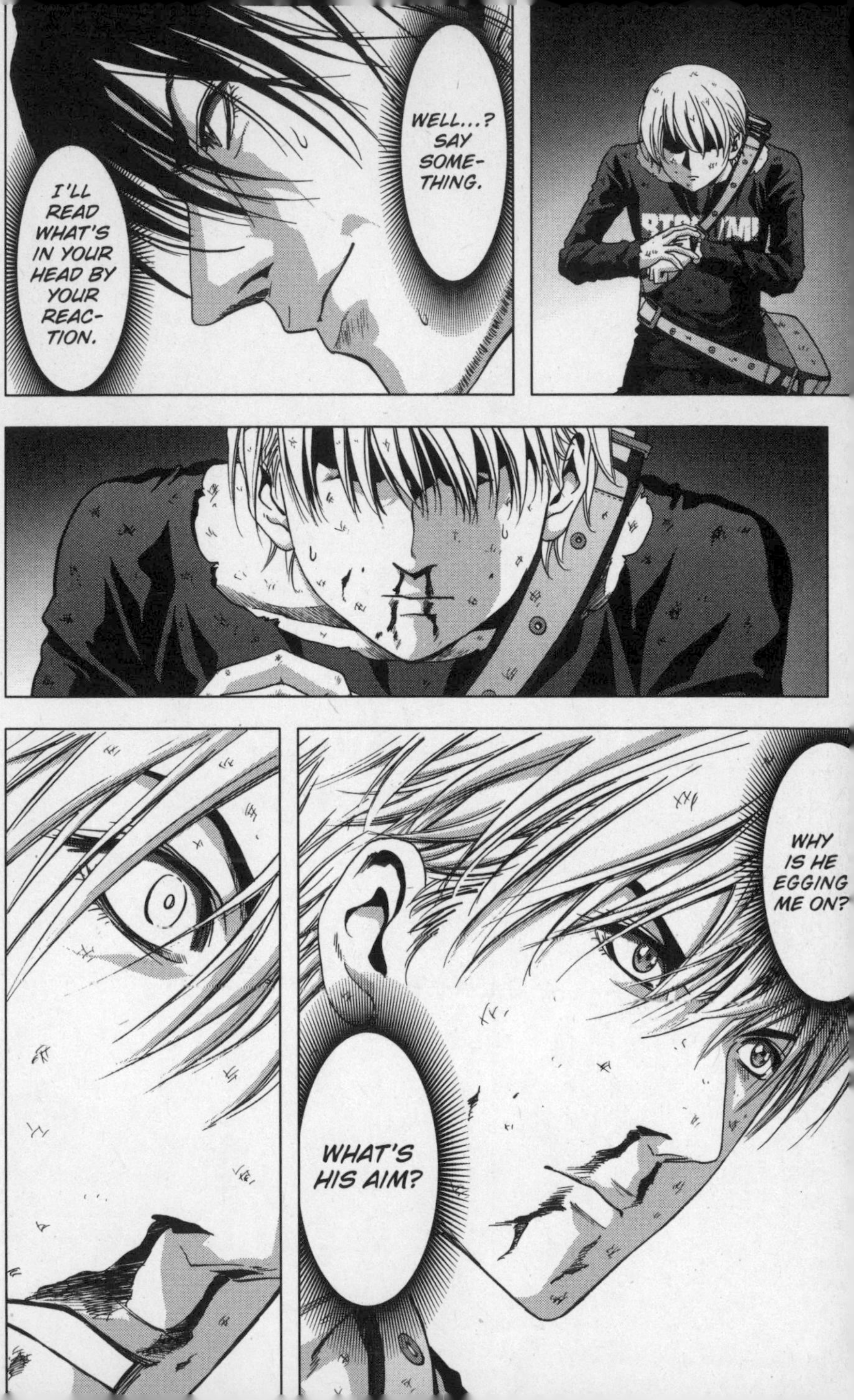
WELL...? SAY SOMETHING.
I'LL READ WHAT'S IN YOUR HEAD BY YOUR REACTION.
WHY IS HE EGGING ME ON?
WHAT'S HIS AIM?

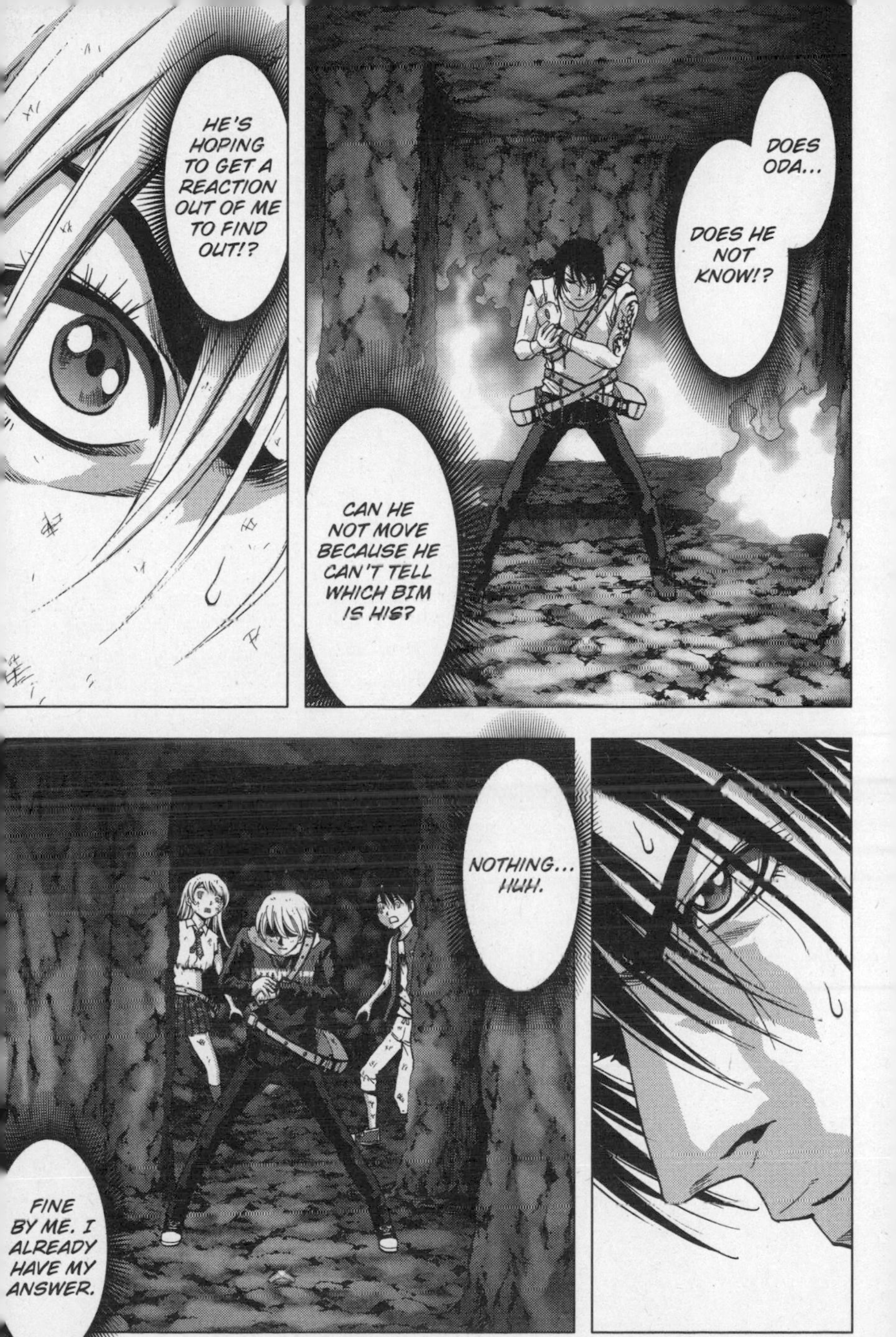

DOES ODA...
DOES HE NOT KNOW!?
CAN HE NOT MOVE BECAUSE HE CAN'T TELL WHICH BIM IS HIS?
HE'S HOPING TO GET A REACTION OUT OF ME TO FIND OUT!?
NOTHING... HUH.
FINE BY ME. I ALREADY HAVE MY ANSWER.

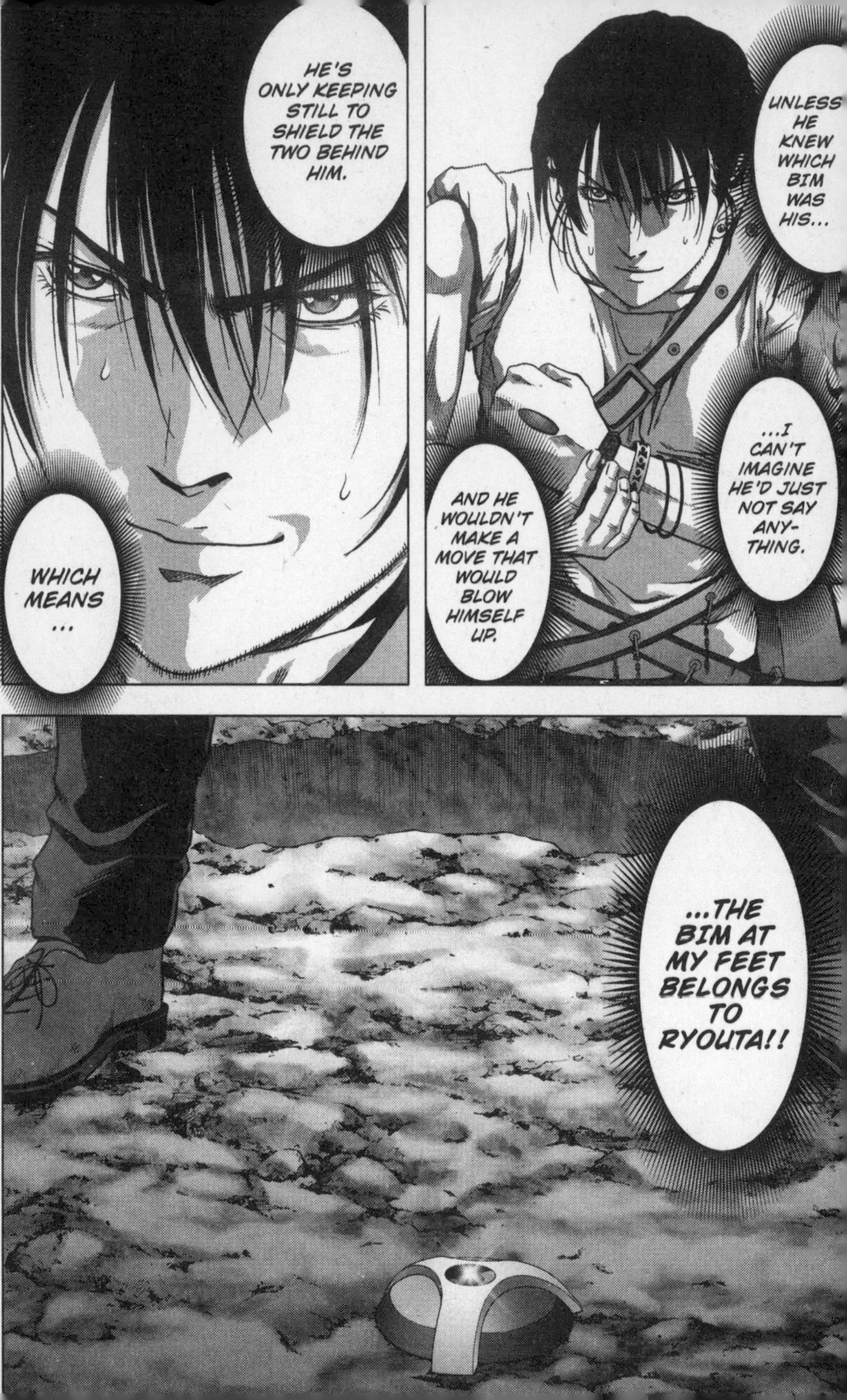
UNLESS HE KNEW WHICH BIM WAS HIS...
...I CAN'T IMAGINE HE'D JUST NOT SAY ANY-THING.
AND HE WOULDN'T MAKE A MOVE THAT WOULD BLOW HIMSELF UP.
HE'S ONLY KEEPING STILL TO SHIELD THE TWO BEHIND HIM.
WHICH MEANS...
...THE BIM AT MY FEET BELONGS TO RYOUTA!!

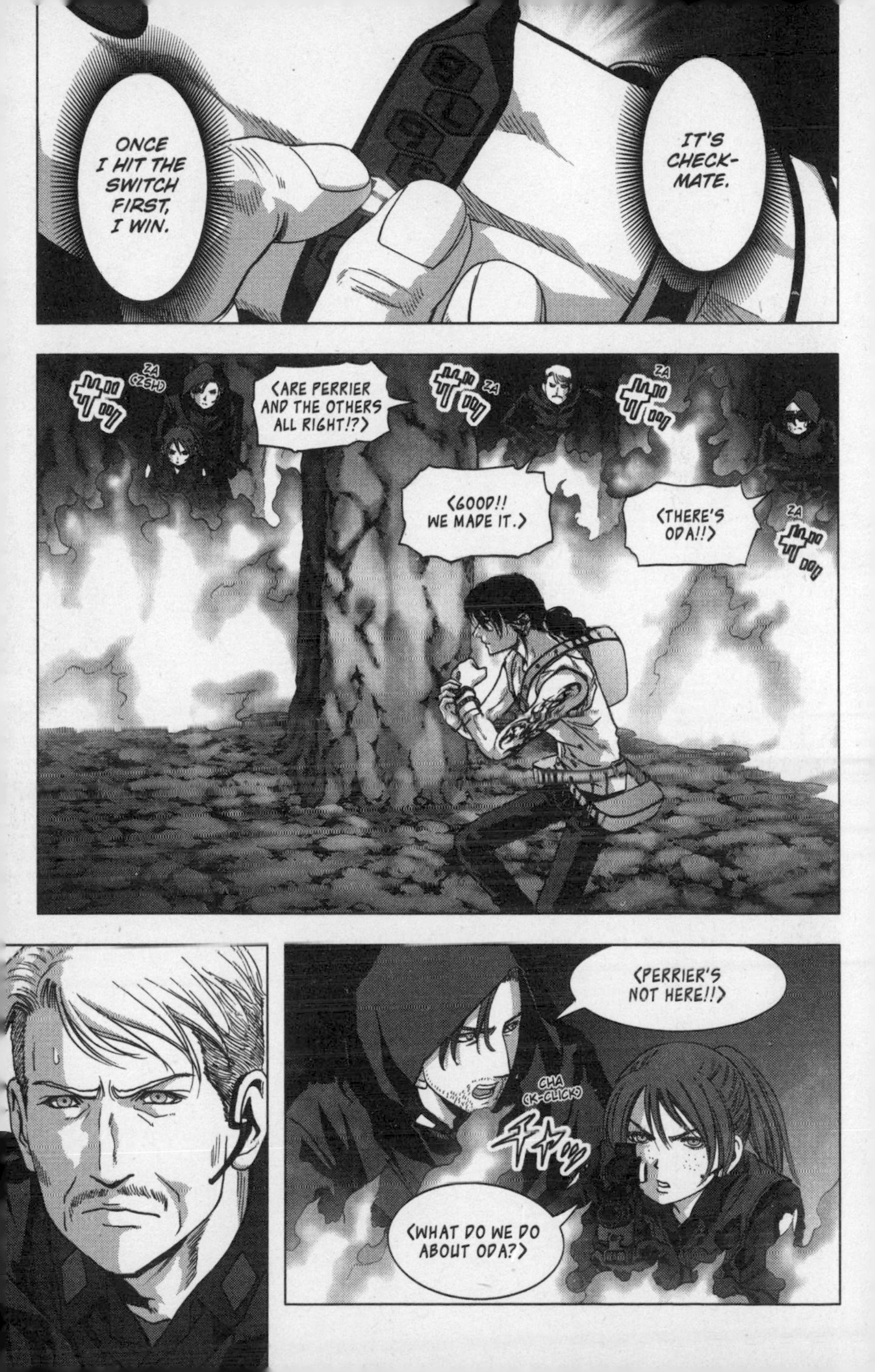
IT'S CHECK-MATE.
ONCE I HIT THE SWITCH FIRST, I WIN.
ZA
ZA
<ARE PERRIER AND THE OTHERS ALL RIGHT!?>
ZA (ZSH)
ZA
<THERE'S ODA!!>
<GOOD!! WE MADE IT.>
<PERRIER'S NOT HERE!!>
CHA (K-CLICK)
<WHAT DO WE DO ABOUT ODA?>

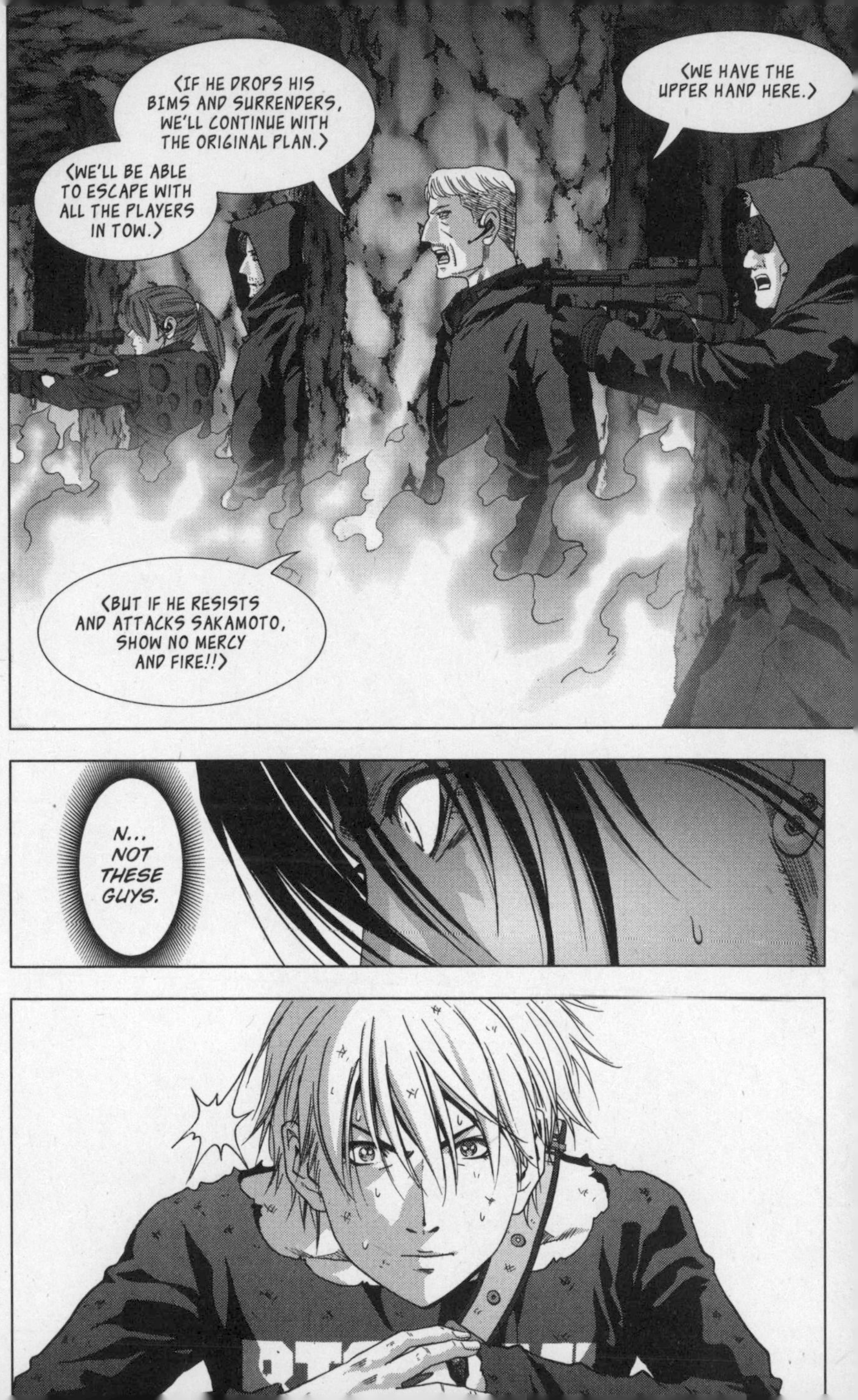

⟨WE HAVE THE UPPER HAND HERE.⟩
⟨IF HE DROPS HIS BIMS AND SURRENDERS, WE'LL CONTINUE WITH THE ORIGINAL PLAN.⟩
⟨WE'LL BE ABLE TO ESCAPE WITH ALL THE PLAYERS IN TOW.⟩
⟨BUT IF HE RESISTS AND ATTACKS SAKAMOTO, SHOW NO MERCY AND FIRE!!⟩
N... NOT THESE GUYS.

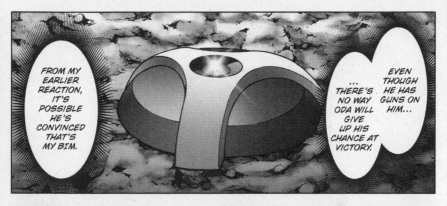

EVEN THOUGH HE HAS GUNS ON HIM...
...THERE'S NO WAY ODA WILL GIVE UP HIS CHANCE AT VICTORY.
FROM MY EARLIER REACTION, IT'S POSSIBLE HE'S CONVINCED THAT'S MY BIM.
EVEN IF HE GETS HURT, HE'LL CHOOSE SURVIVAL OVER ANYTHING.
ONCE THE FIRE FROM THE FLAME TYPES GO OUT...
...HE'S DEFINITELY GOING TO MAKE HIS MOVE...
IT'S NOW OR NEVER!!
I HAVE TO HIT THE SWITCH FIRST...

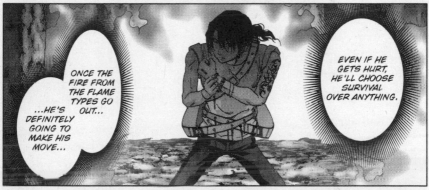

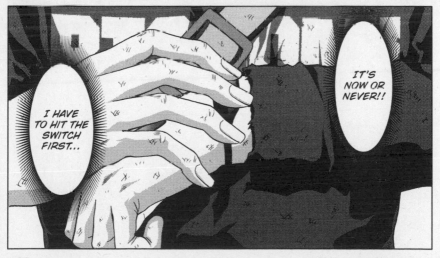

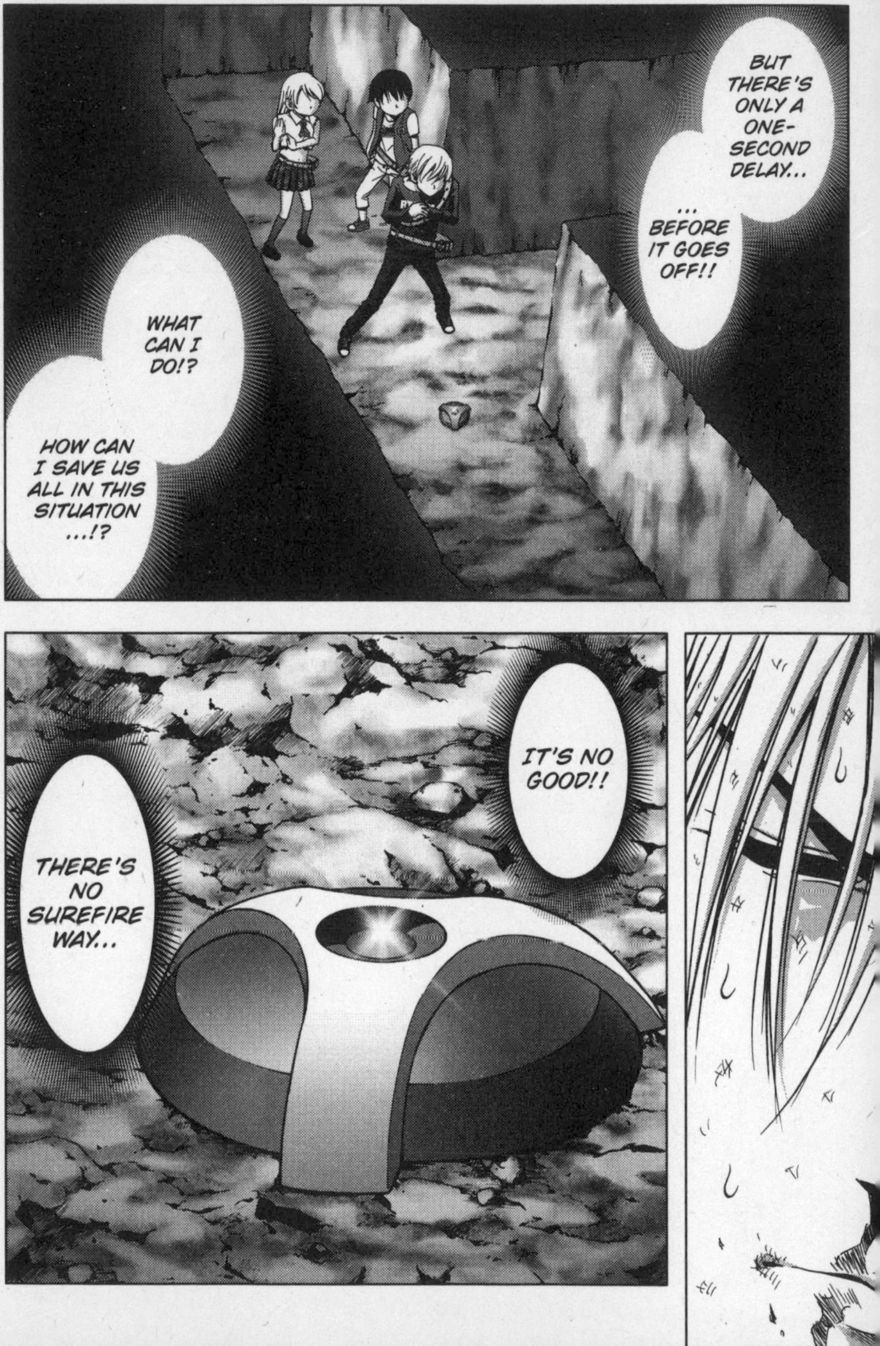
BUT THERE'S ONLY A ONE-SECOND DELAY...
...BEFORE IT GOES OFF!!
WHAT CAN I DO!?
HOW CAN I SAVE US ALL IN THIS SITUATION ...!?
IT'S NO GOOD!!
THERE'S NO SUREFIRE WAY...

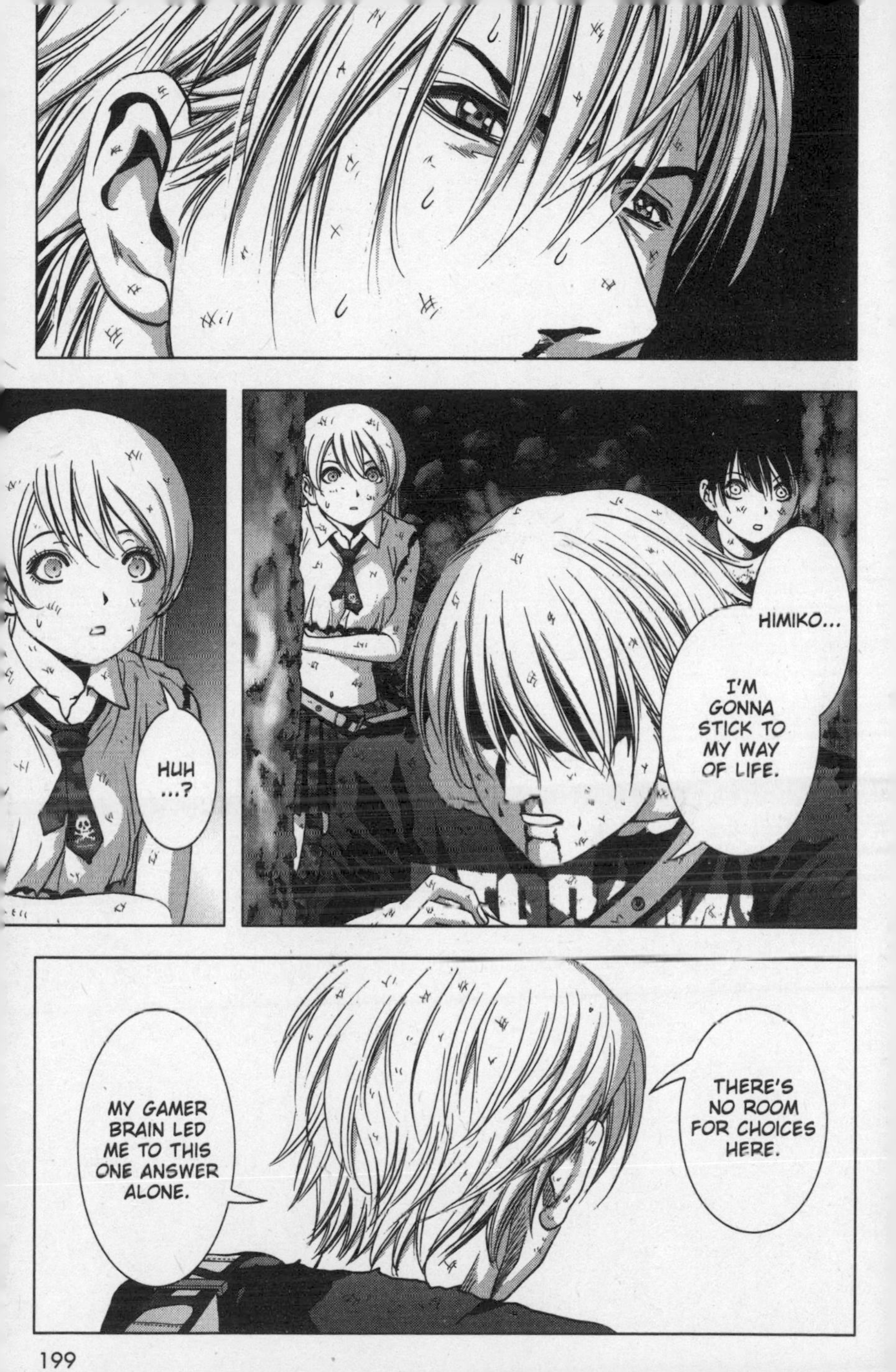
HIMIKO...
I'M GONNA STICK TO MY WAY OF LIFE.
HUH ...?
THERE'S NO ROOM FOR CHOICES HERE.
MY GAMER BRAIN LED ME TO THIS ONE ANSWER ALONE.

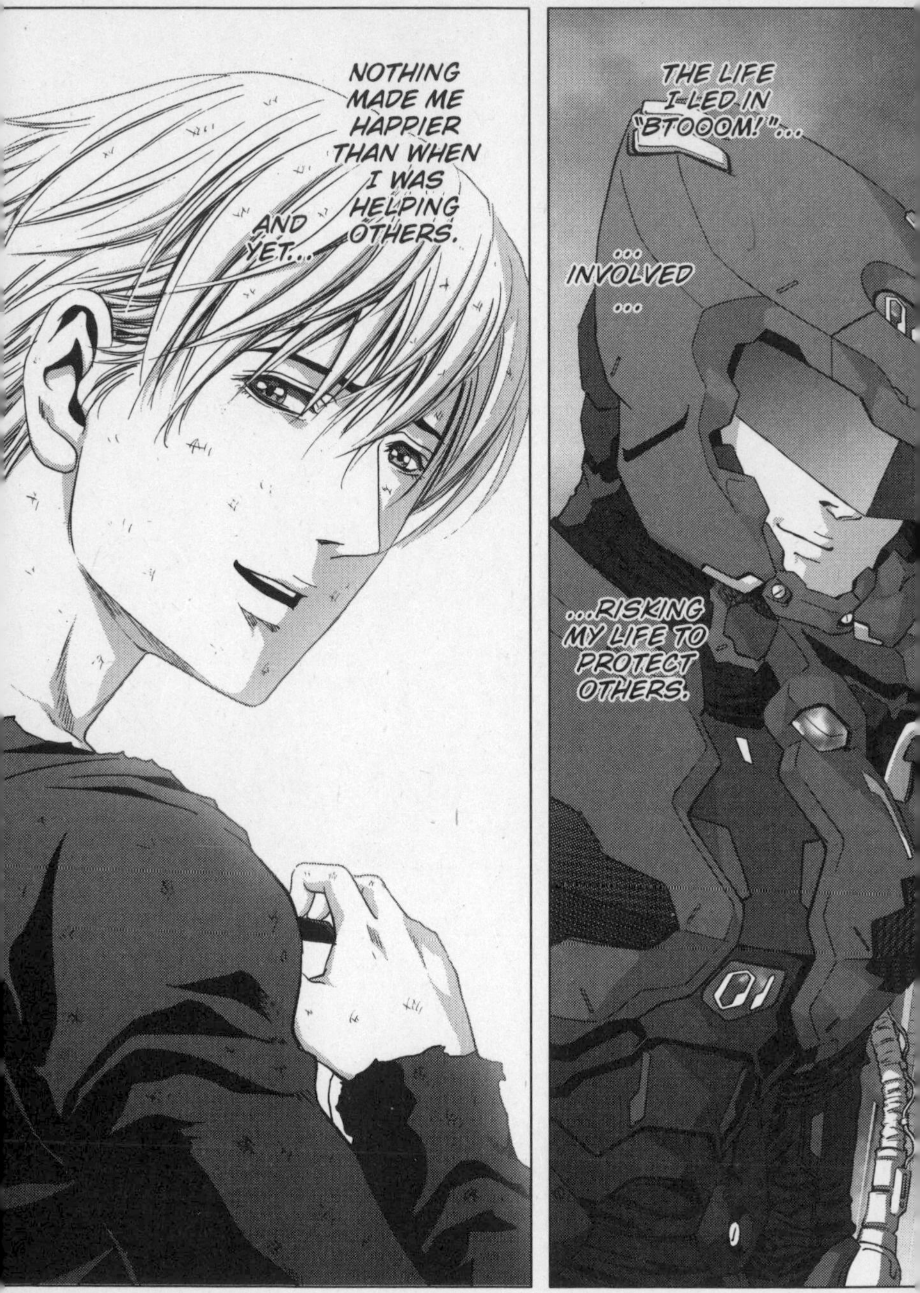
THE LIFE I LED IN "BTOOOM!"...
...INVOLVED...
...RISKING MY LIFE TO PROTECT OTHERS.
NOTHING MADE ME HAPPIER THAN WHEN I WAS HELPING OTHERS.
AND YET...

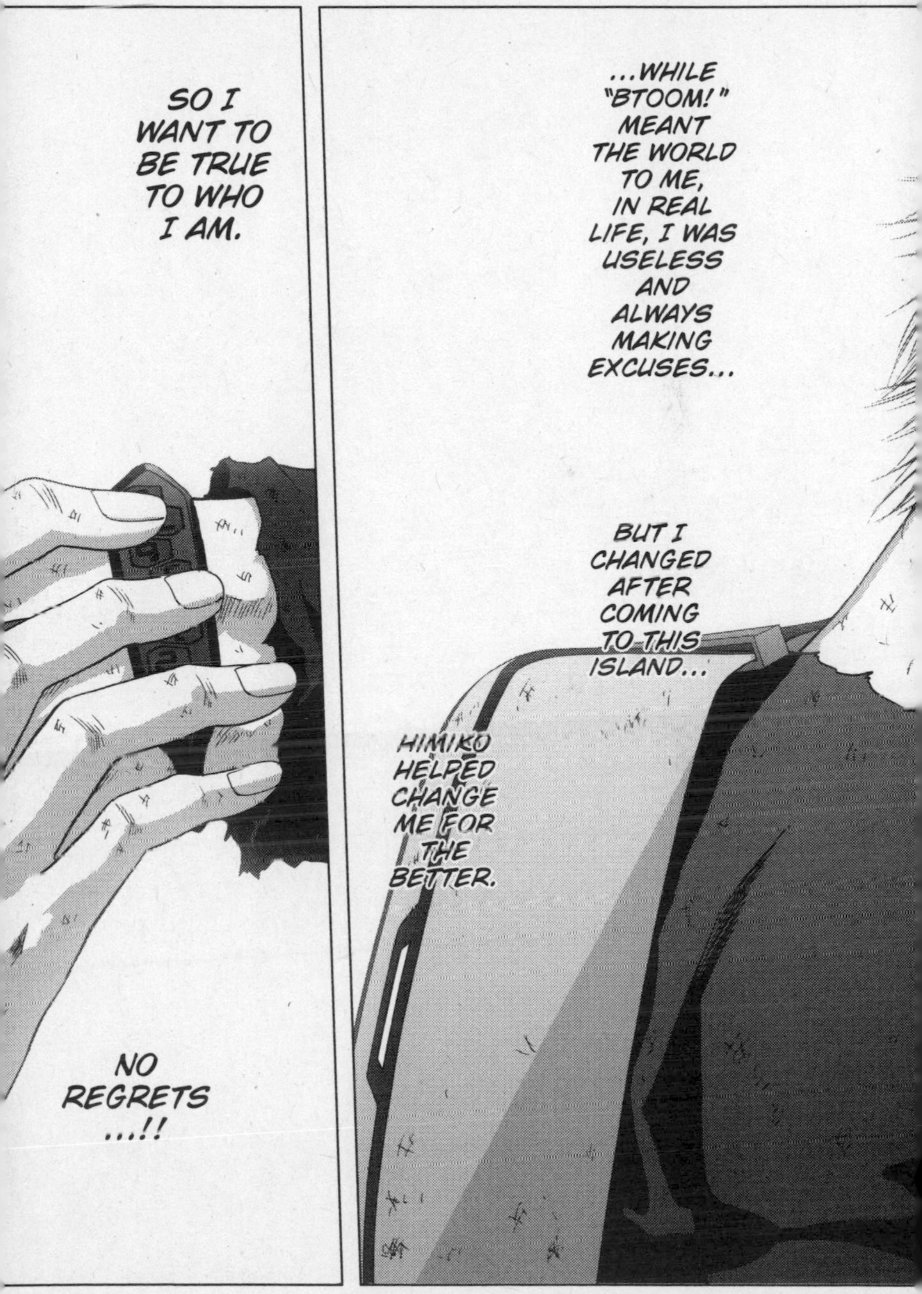
...WHILE "BTOOM!" MEANT THE WORLD TO ME, IN REAL LIFE, I WAS USELESS AND ALWAYS MAKING EXCUSES...
BUT I CHANGED AFTER COMING TO THIS ISLAND...
HIMIKO HELPED CHANGE ME FOR THE BETTER.
SO I WANT TO BE TRUE TO WHO I AM.
NO REGRETS ...!!

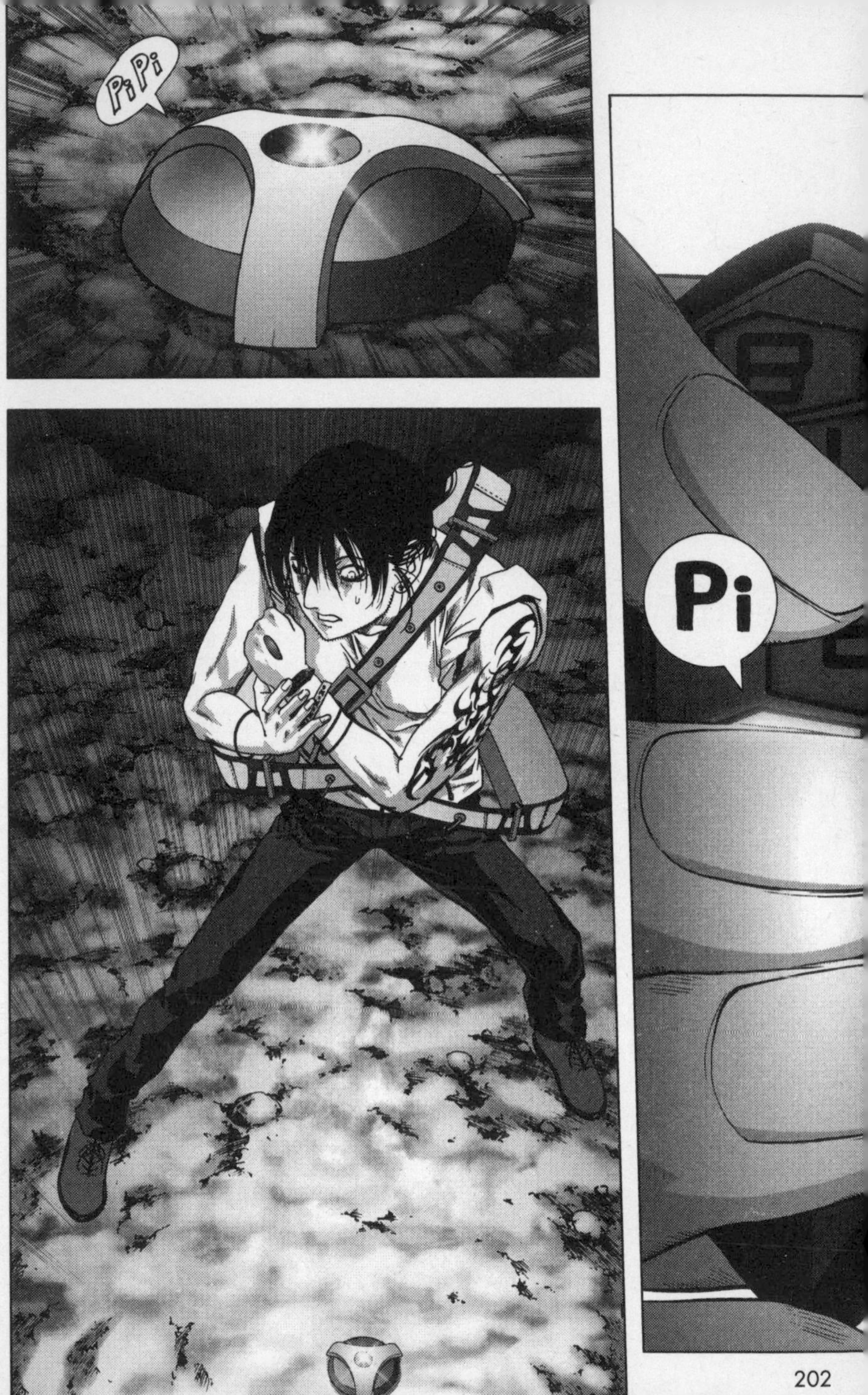
Pi
Pi Pi

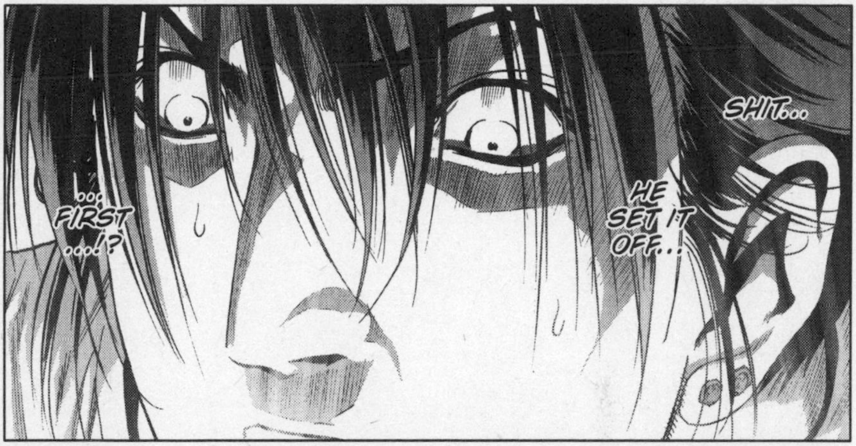
SHIT...
HE SET IT OFF...
...FIRST ...!?

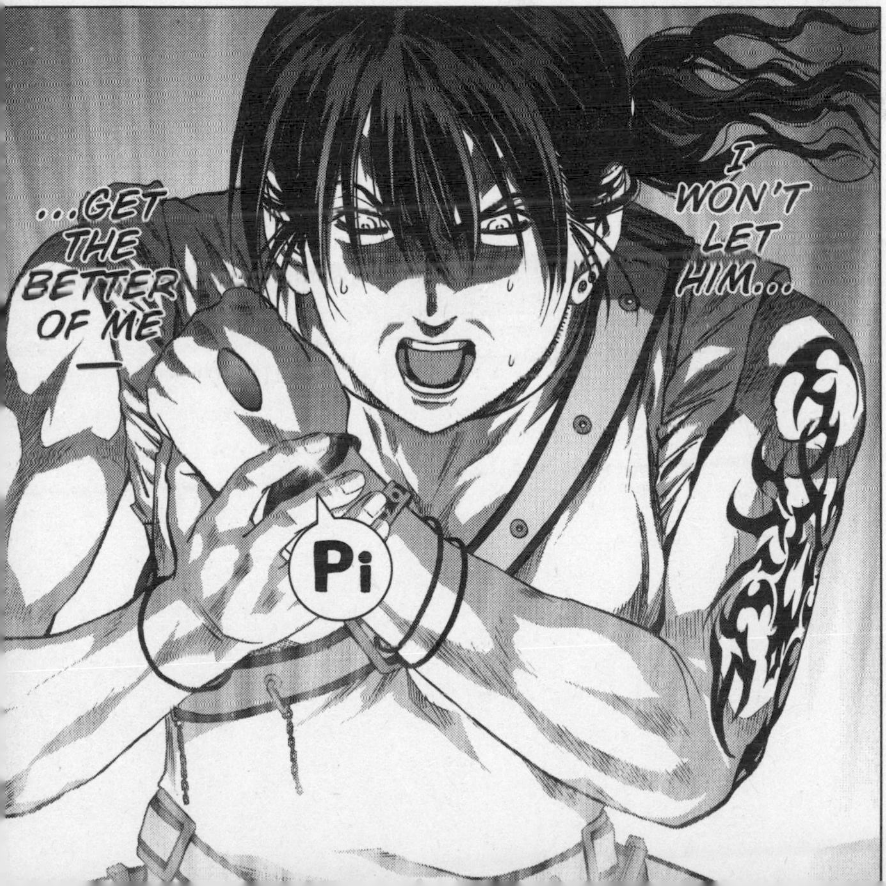
I WON'T LET HIM...
...GET THE BETTER OF ME—
Pi

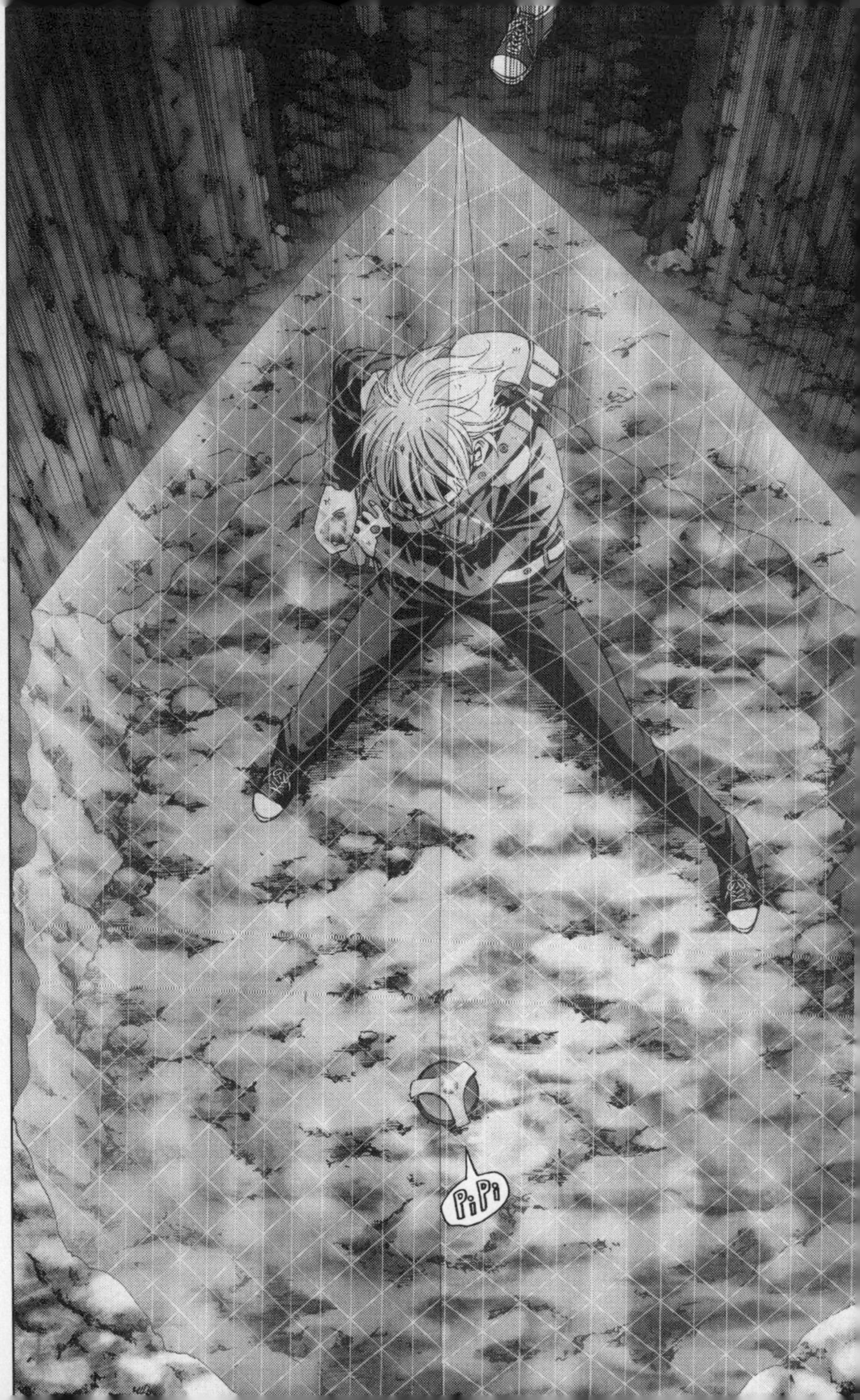
PiPi

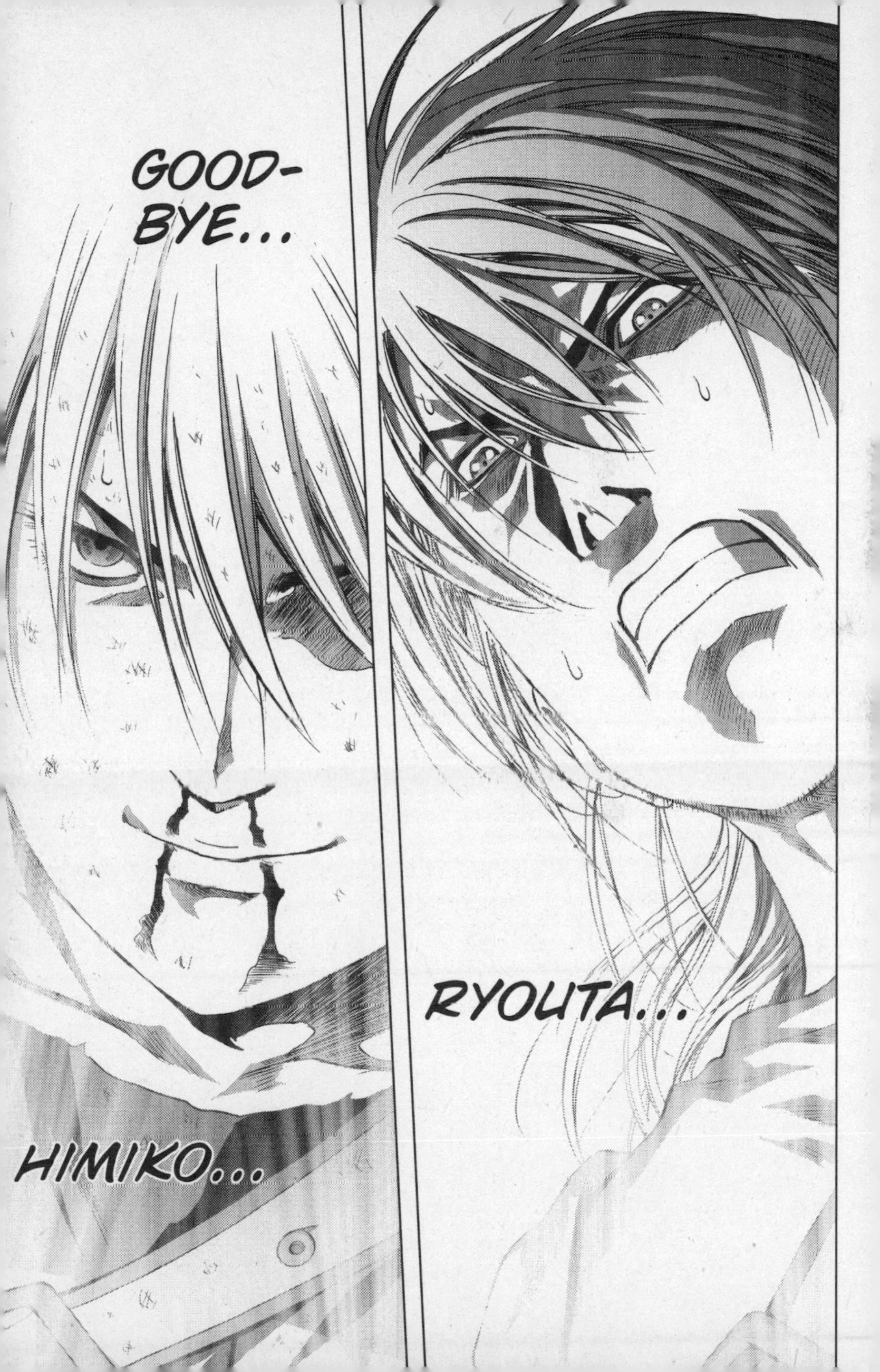
RYOUTA...
GOOD-BYE...
HIMIKO...

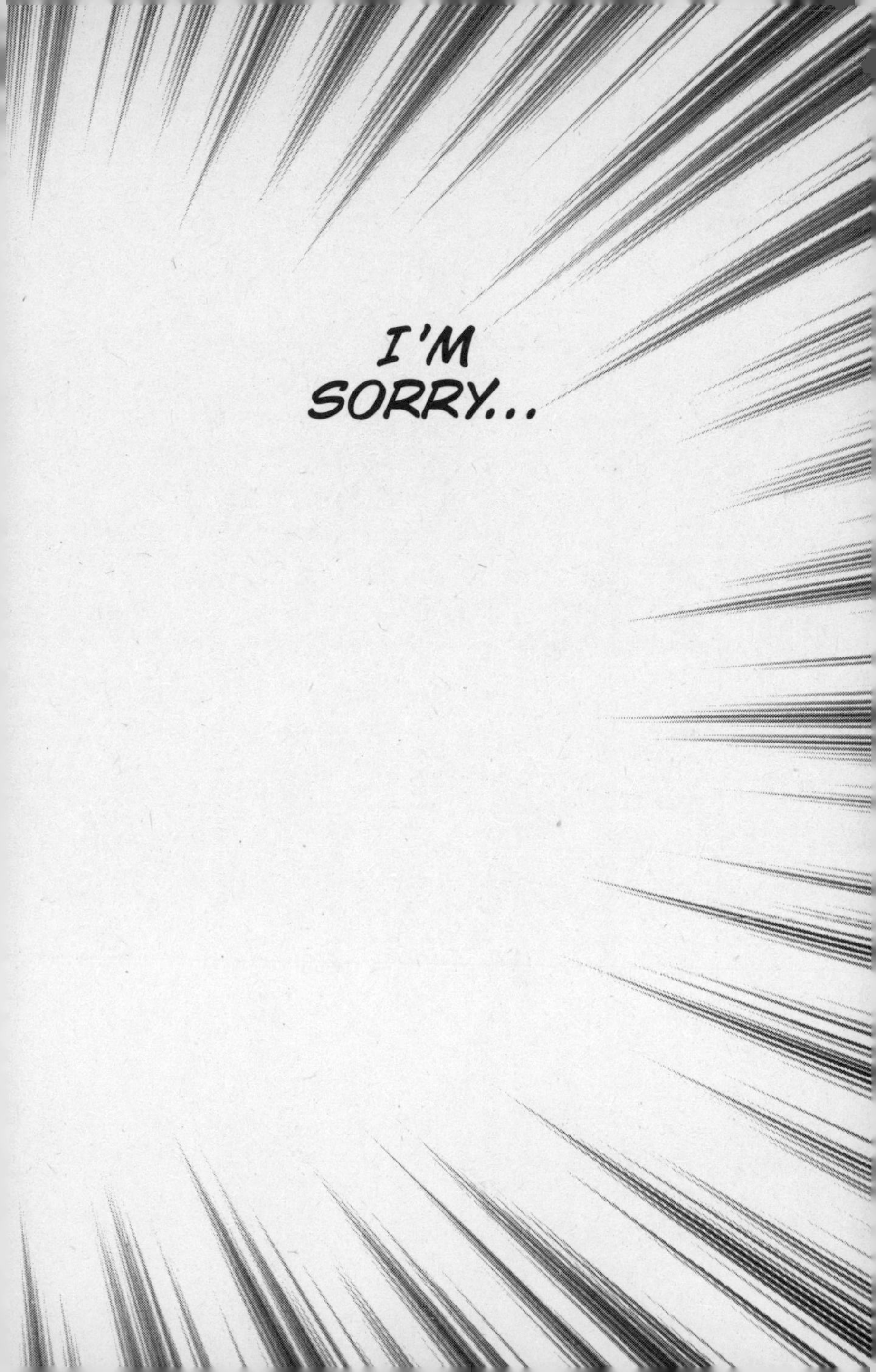
I'M SORRY...

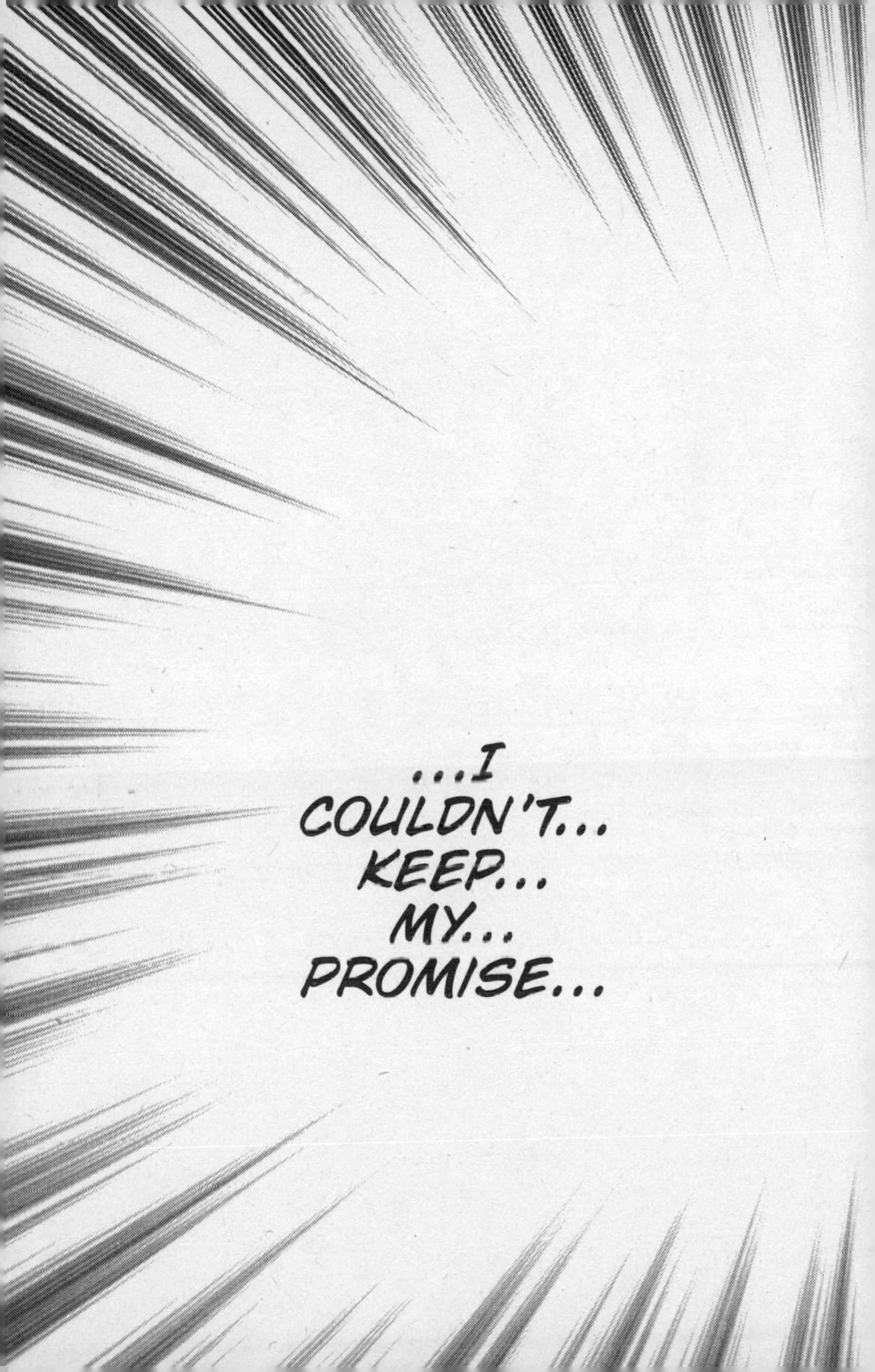
...I COULDN'T... KEEP... MY... PROMISE...

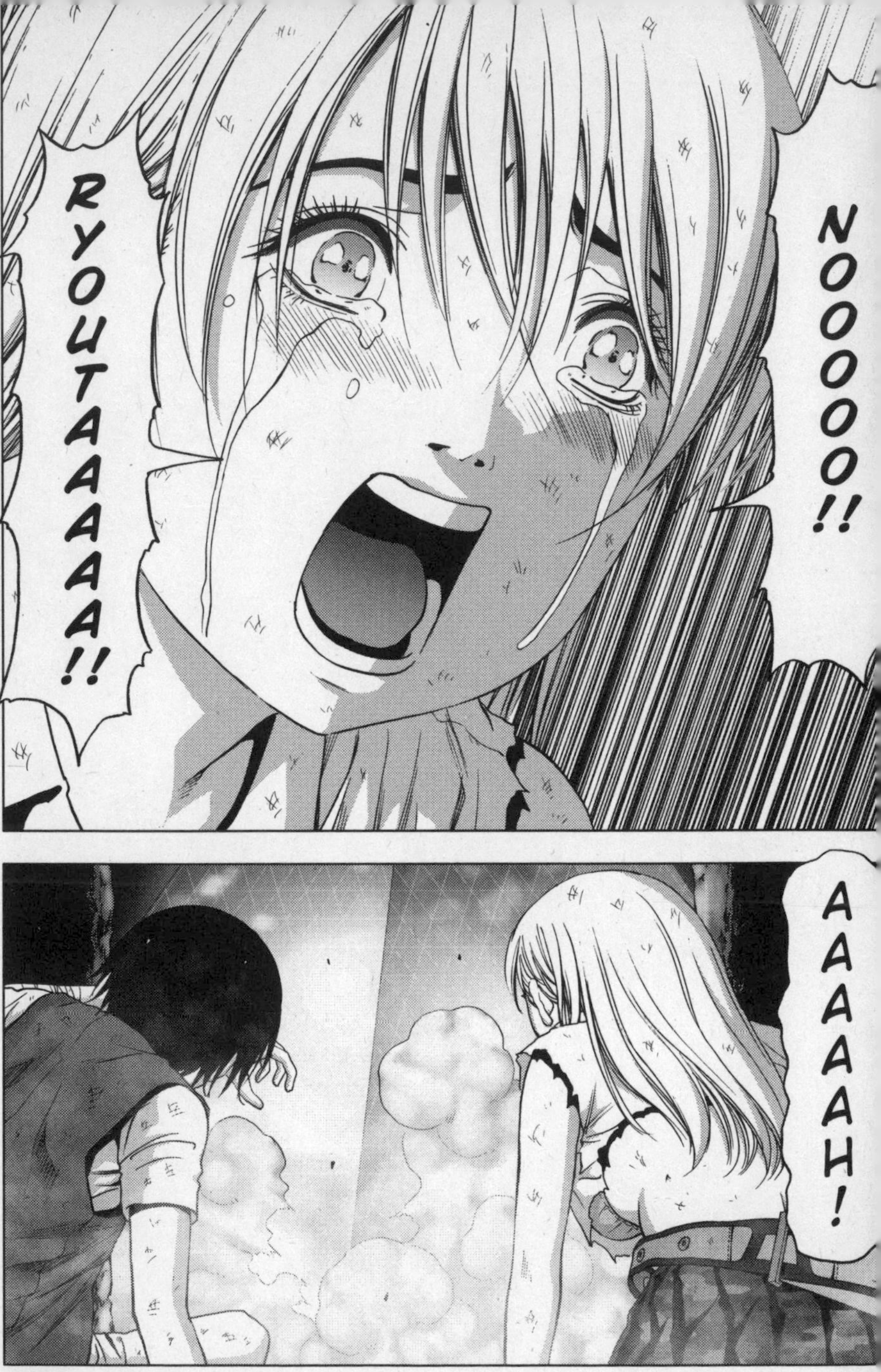
NOOOOOO!!
RYOUTAAAAAA!!
AAAAAAH!

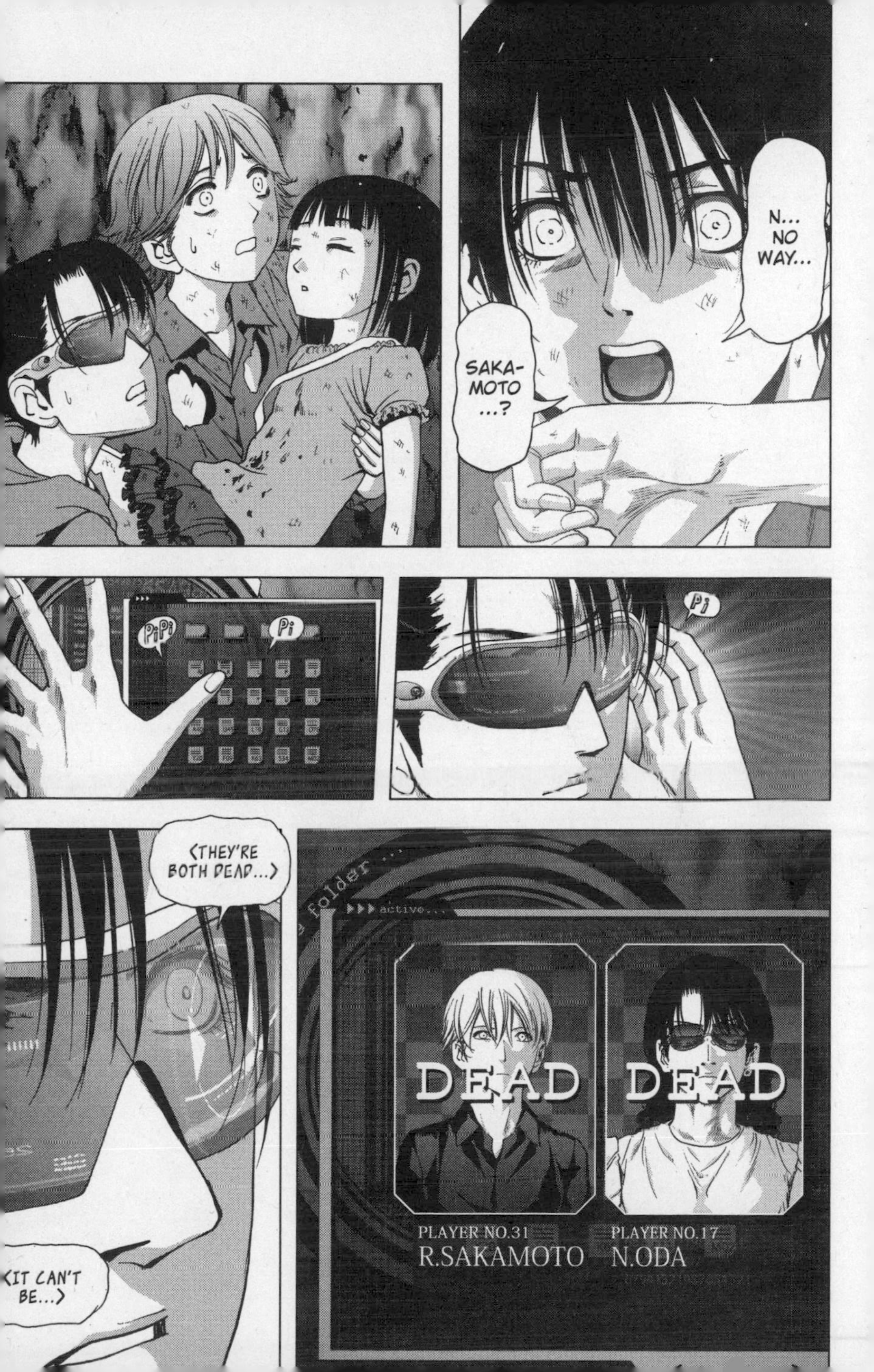
N... NO WAY...
SAKA-MOTO ...?
Pi
PiPi
Pi
folder
active...
DEAD
DEAD
PLAYER NO.31
R.SAKAMOTO
PLAYER NO.17
N.ODA
<THEY'RE BOTH DEAD...>
<IT CAN'T BE...>

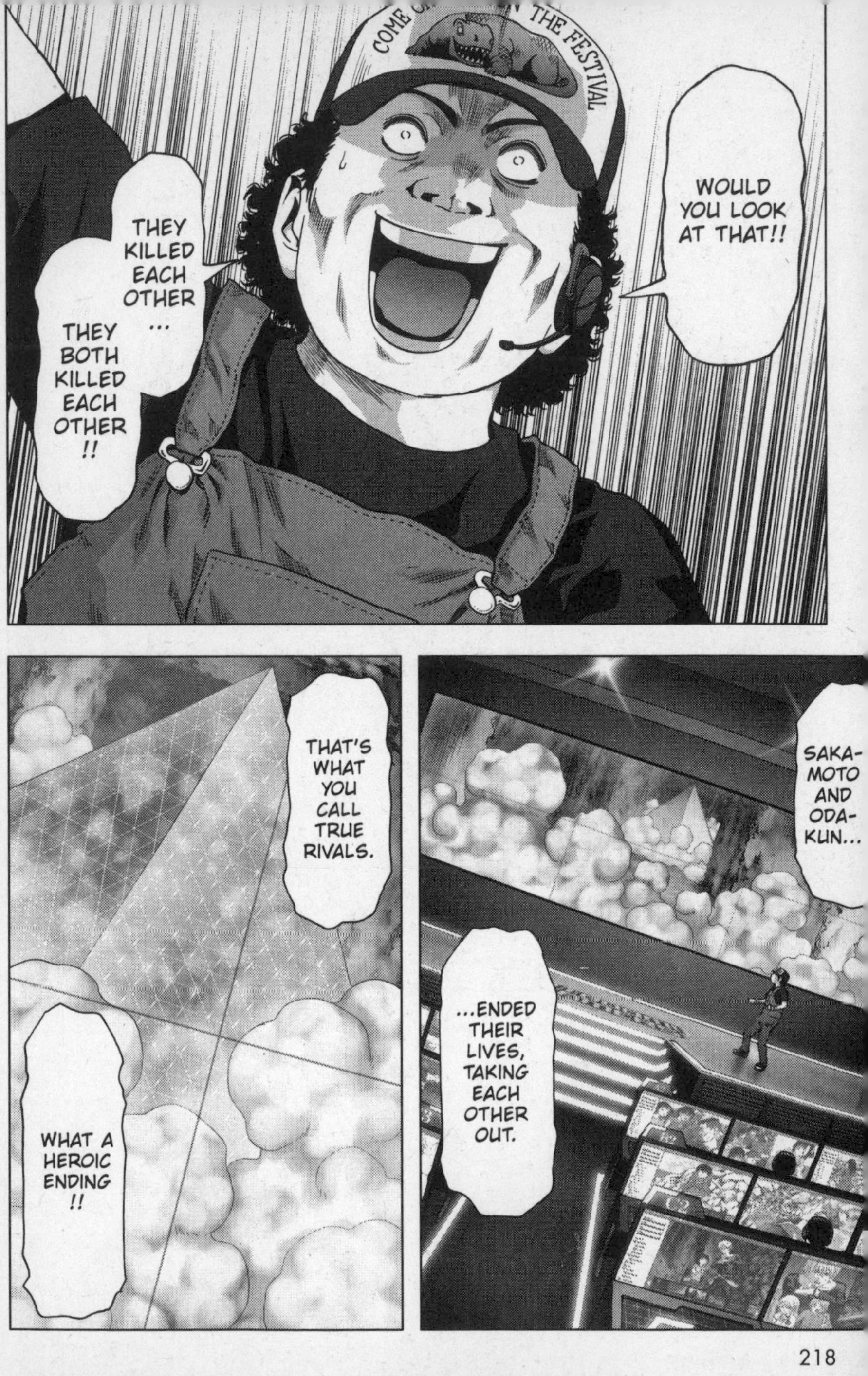
WOULD YOU LOOK AT THAT!!
THEY KILLED EACH OTHER...
THEY BOTH KILLED EACH OTHER!!
SAKAMOTO AND ODA-KUN...
...ENDED THEIR LIVES, TAKING EACH OTHER OUT.
THAT'S WHAT YOU CALL TRUE RIVALS.
WHAT A HEROIC ENDING!!

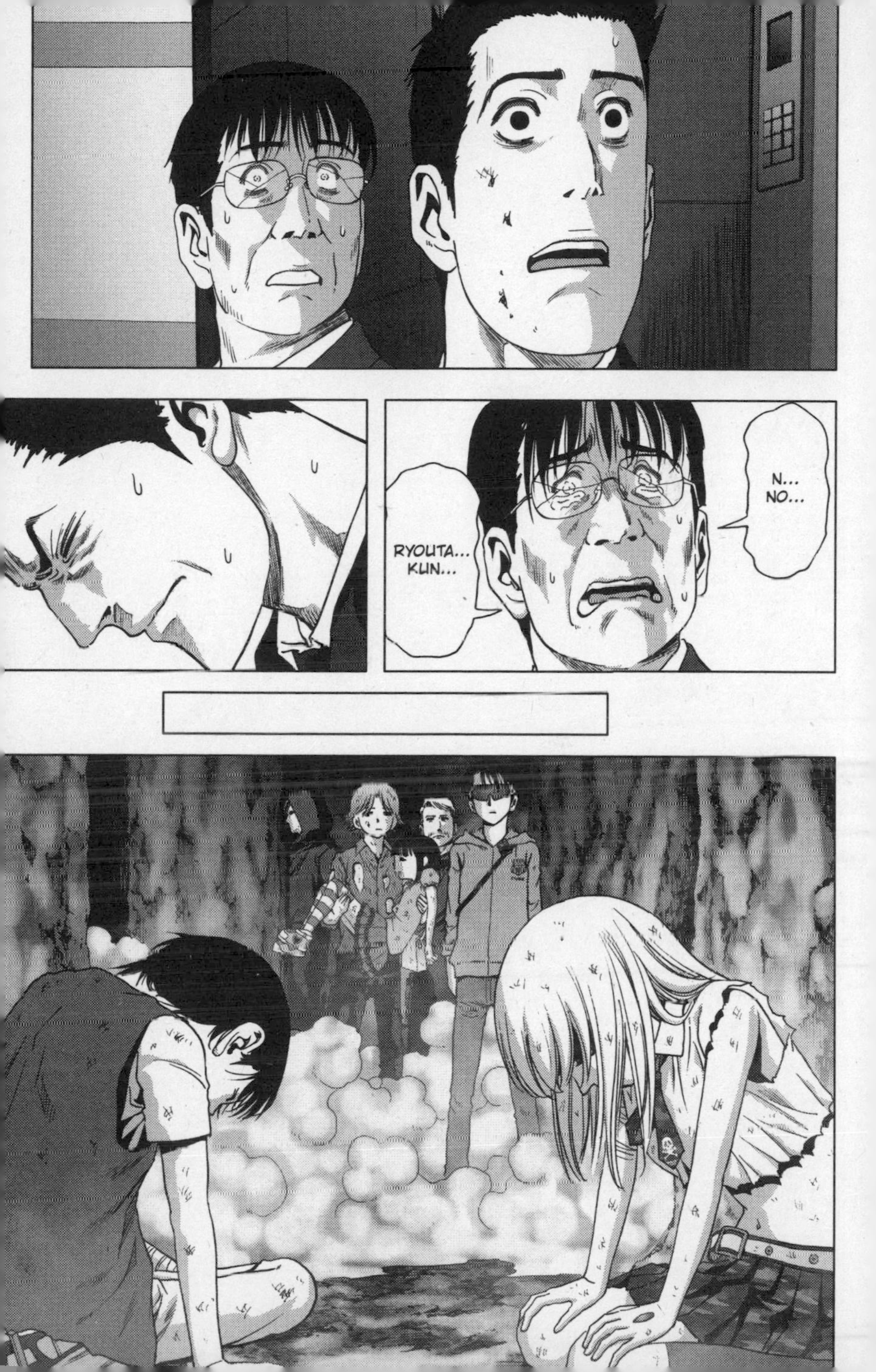
N... NO...
RYOUTA... KUN...

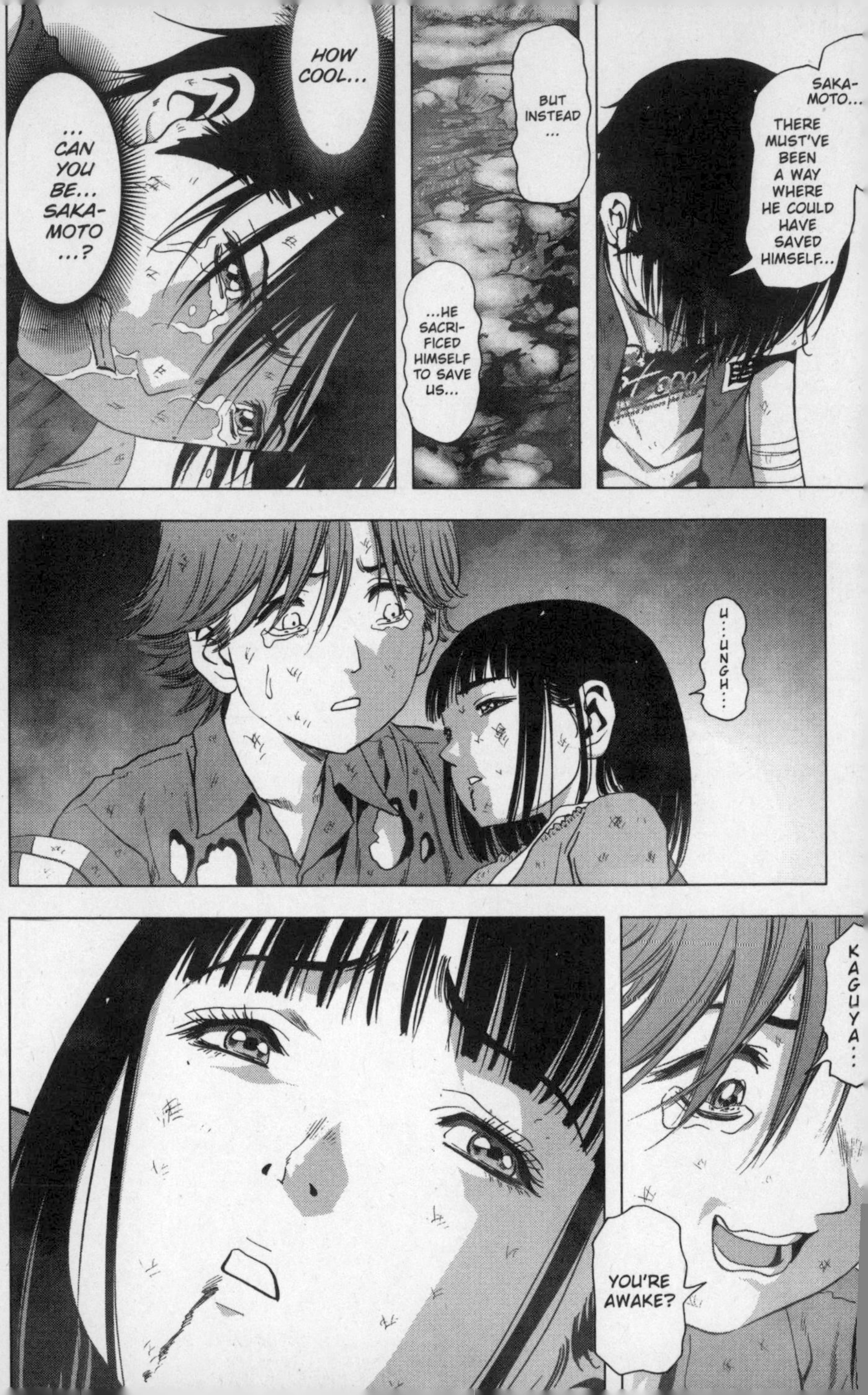
SAKA-MOTO...
THERE MUST'VE BEEN A WAY WHERE HE COULD HAVE SAVED HIMSELF...
BUT INSTEAD...
...HE SACRIFICED HIMSELF TO SAVE US...
HOW COOL...
...CAN YOU BE... SAKA-MOTO...?
U...UNGH...
KAGUYA...
YOU'RE AWAKE?

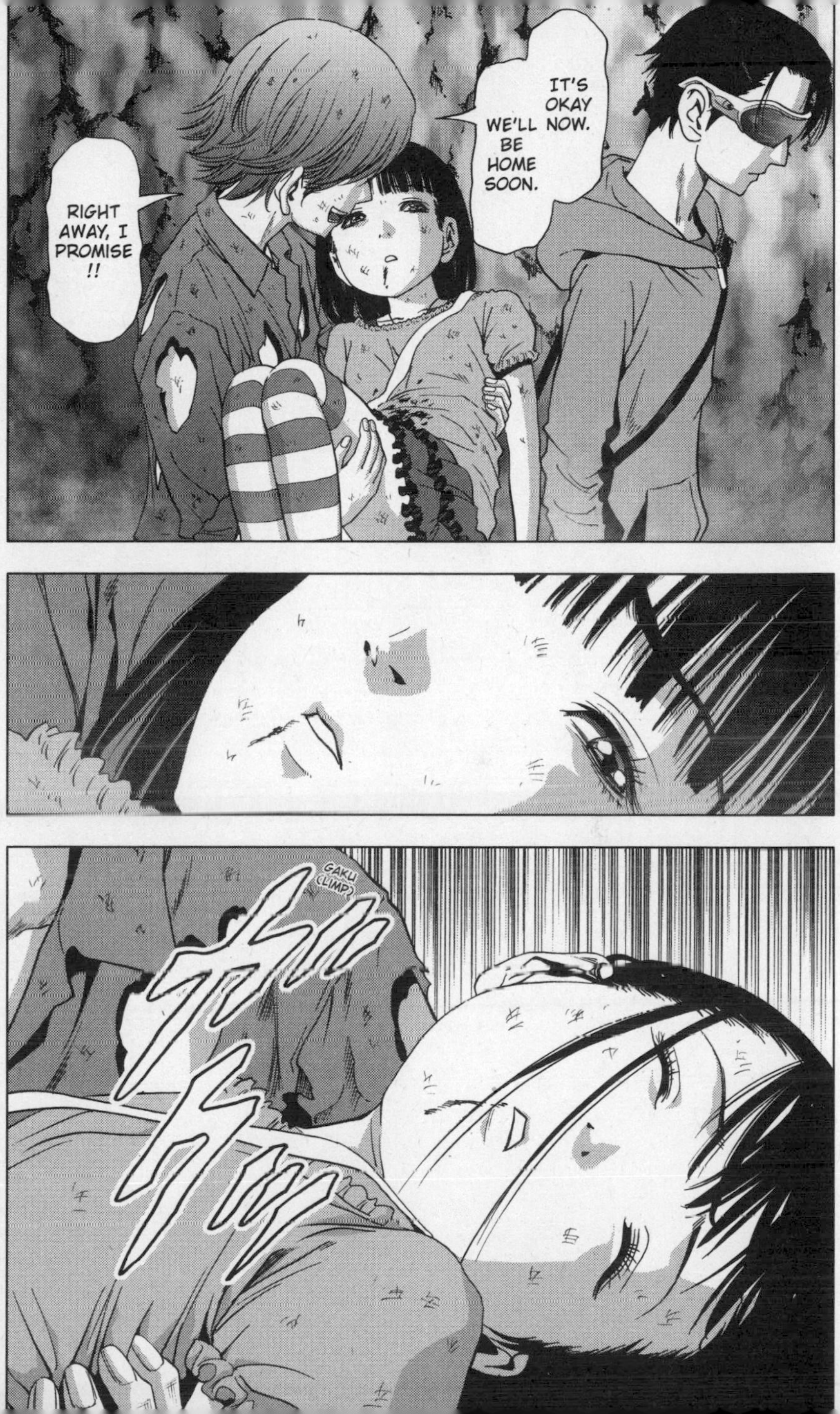
IT'S OKAY NOW. WE'LL BE HOME SOON.
RIGHT AWAY, I PROMISE !!
GAKU (LIMP)

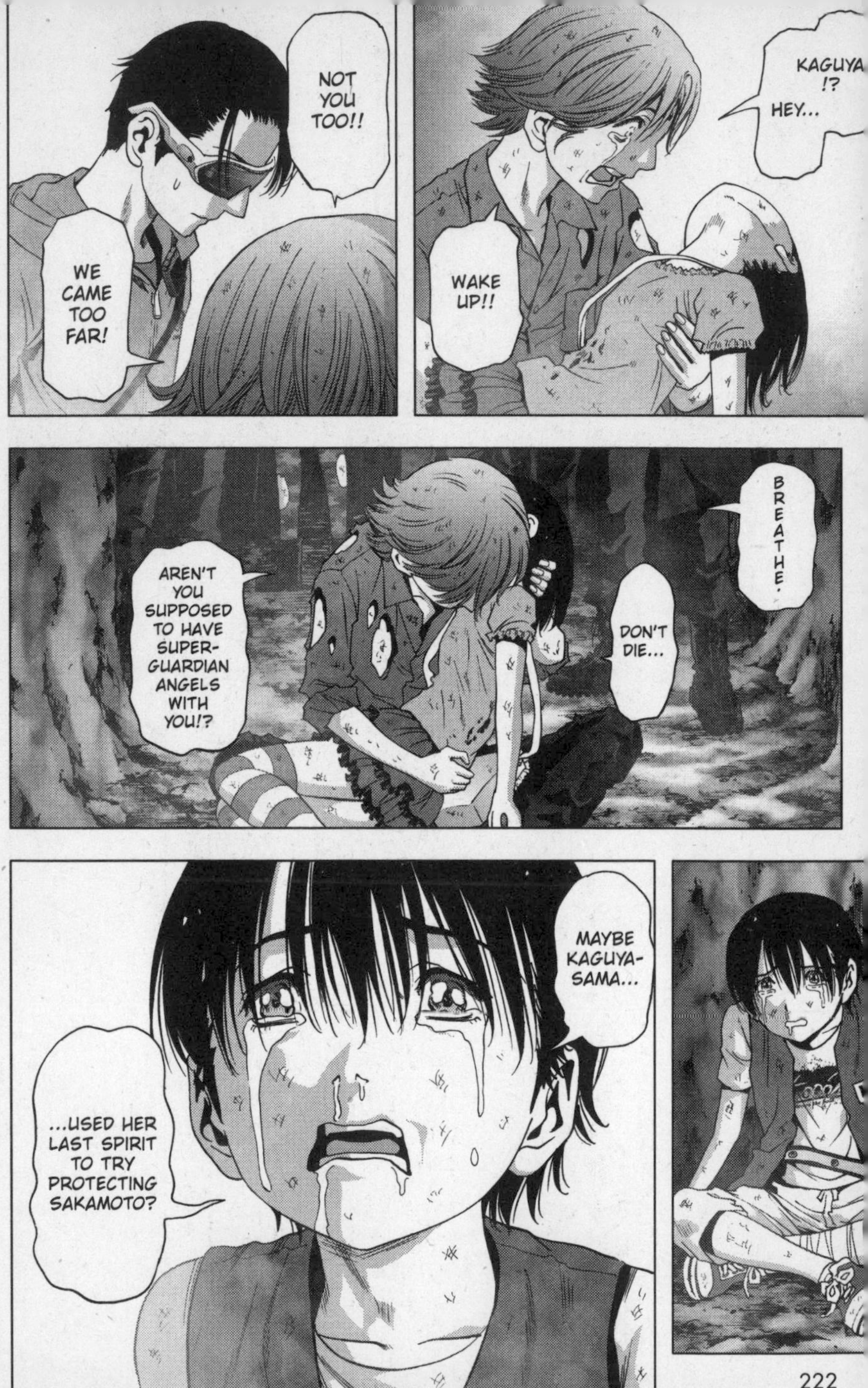
KAGUYA!? HEY...
WAKE UP!!
NOT YOU TOO!!
WE CAME TOO FAR!
BREATHE.
DON'T DIE...
AREN'T YOU SUPPOSED TO HAVE SUPER-GUARDIAN ANGELS WITH YOU!?
MAYBE KAGUYA-SAMA...
...USED HER LAST SPIRIT TO TRY PROTECTING SAKAMOTO?

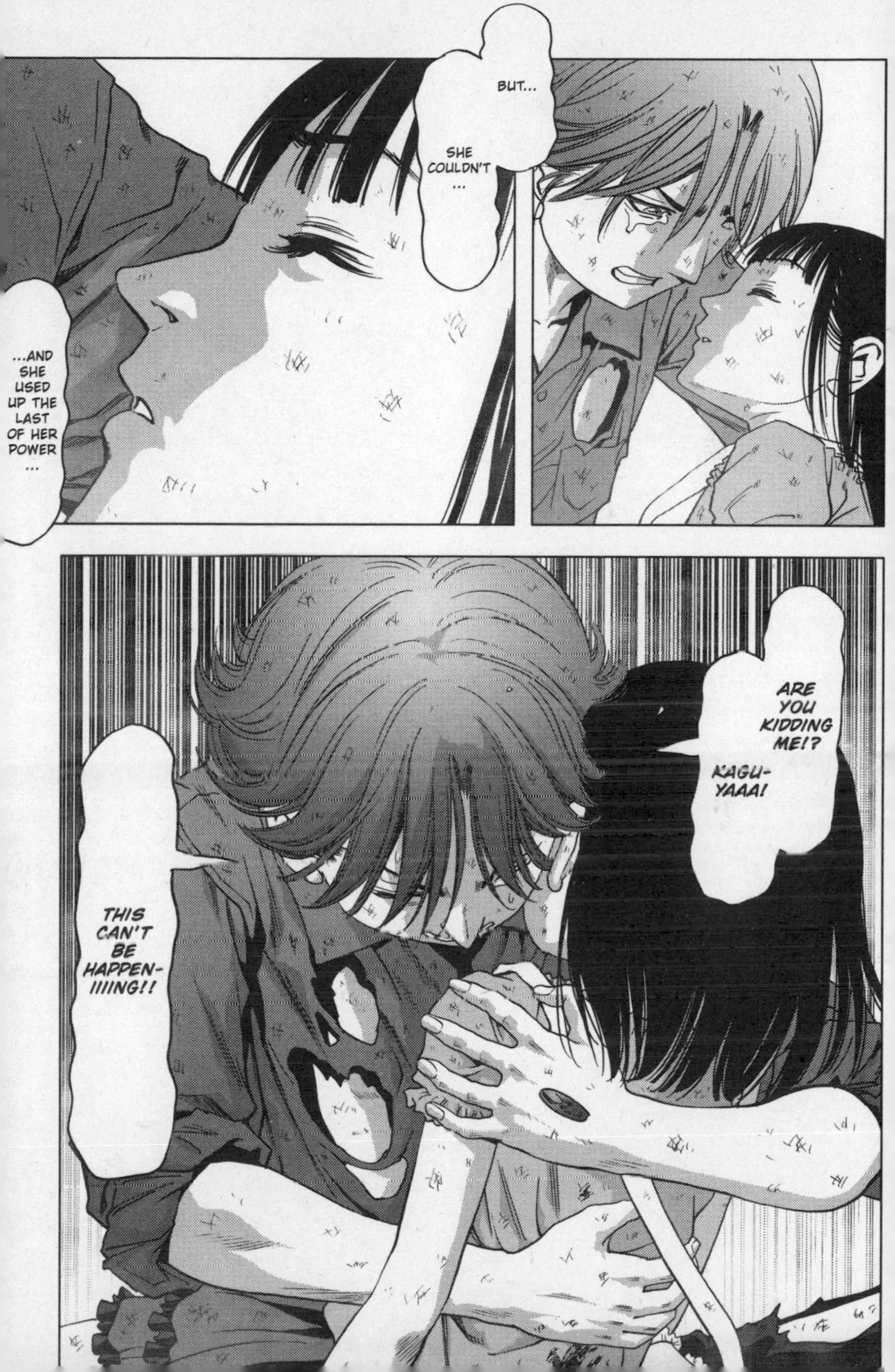
BUT...
SHE COULDN'T ...
...AND SHE USED UP THE LAST OF HER POWER ...
ARE YOU KIDDING ME!?
KAGU-YAAA!
THIS CAN'T BE HAPPEN-IIIING!!

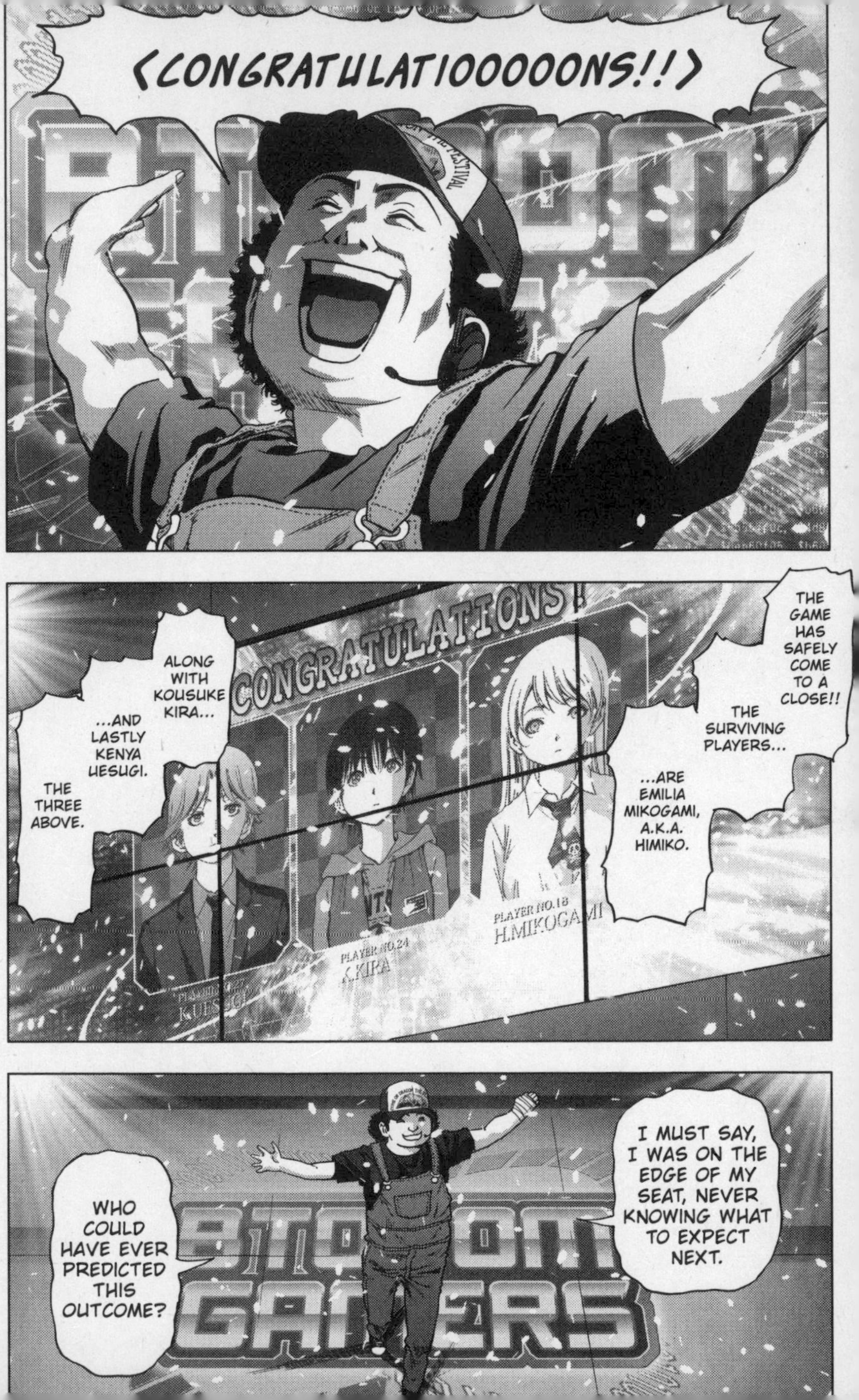
<CONGRATULATIOOOOONS!!!>
THE GAME HAS SAFELY COME TO A CLOSE!!
THE SURVIVING PLAYERS...
...ARE EMILIA MIKOGAMI, A.K.A. HIMIKO.
CONGRATULATIONS!
PLAYER NO.18
H.MIKOGAMI
PLAYER NO.24
K.KIRA
K.UESUGI
ALONG WITH KOUSUKE KIRA...
...AND LASTLY KENYA UESUGI.
THE THREE ABOVE.
I MUST SAY, I WAS ON THE EDGE OF MY SEAT, NEVER KNOWING WHAT TO EXPECT NEXT.
WHO COULD HAVE EVER PREDICTED THIS OUTCOME?

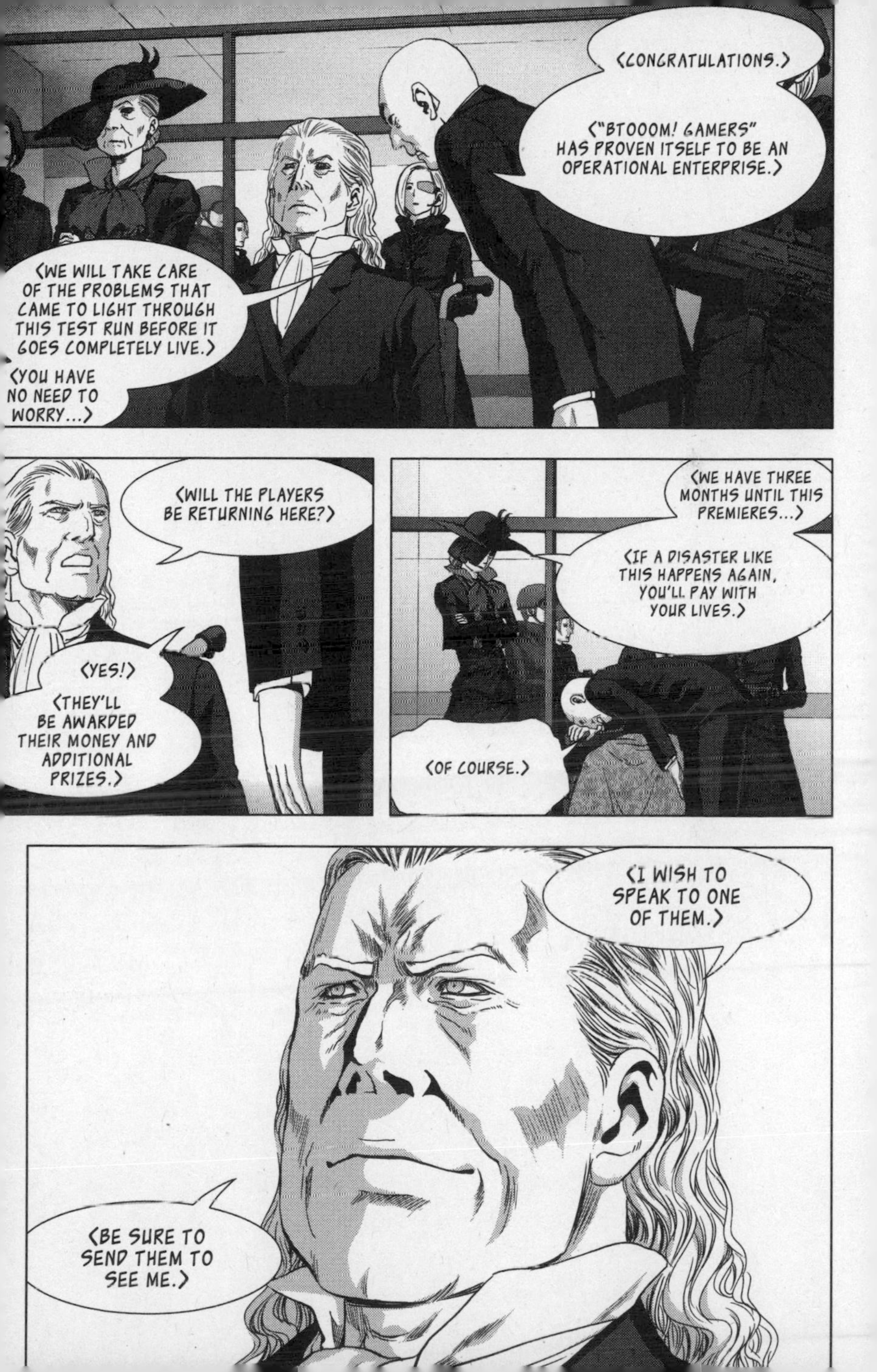
<CONGRATULATIONS.>
<"BTOOOM! GAMERS" HAS PROVEN ITSELF TO BE AN OPERATIONAL ENTERPRISE.>
<WE WILL TAKE CARE OF THE PROBLEMS THAT CAME TO LIGHT THROUGH THIS TEST RUN BEFORE IT GOES COMPLETELY LIVE.>
<YOU HAVE NO NEED TO WORRY...>
<WE HAVE THREE MONTHS UNTIL THIS PREMIERES...>
<IF A DISASTER LIKE THIS HAPPENS AGAIN, YOU'LL PAY WITH YOUR LIVES.>
<OF COURSE.>
<WILL THE PLAYERS BE RETURNING HERE?>
<YES!>
<THEY'LL BE AWARDED THEIR MONEY AND ADDITIONAL PRIZES.>
<I WISH TO SPEAK TO ONE OF THEM.>
<BE SURE TO SEND THEM TO SEE ME.>

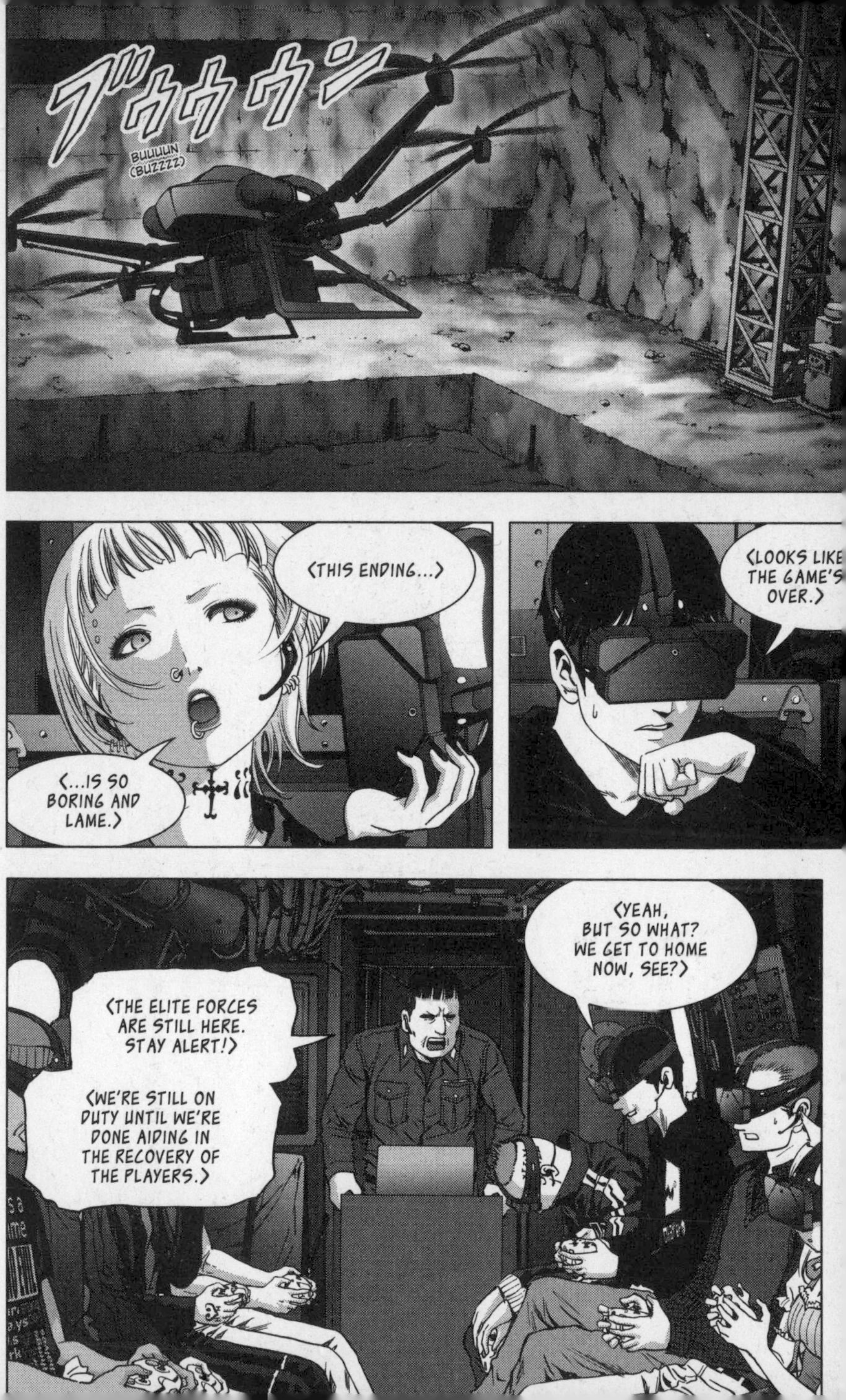
ブゥゥゥン
BUUUUN (BUZZZZ)
<LOOKS LIKE THE GAME'S OVER.>
<THIS ENDING...>
<...IS SO BORING AND LAME.>
<YEAH, BUT SO WHAT? WE GET TO HOME NOW, SEE?>
<THE ELITE FORCES ARE STILL HERE. STAY ALERT!>
<WE'RE STILL ON DUTY UNTIL WE'RE DONE AIDING IN THE RECOVERY OF THE PLAYERS.>

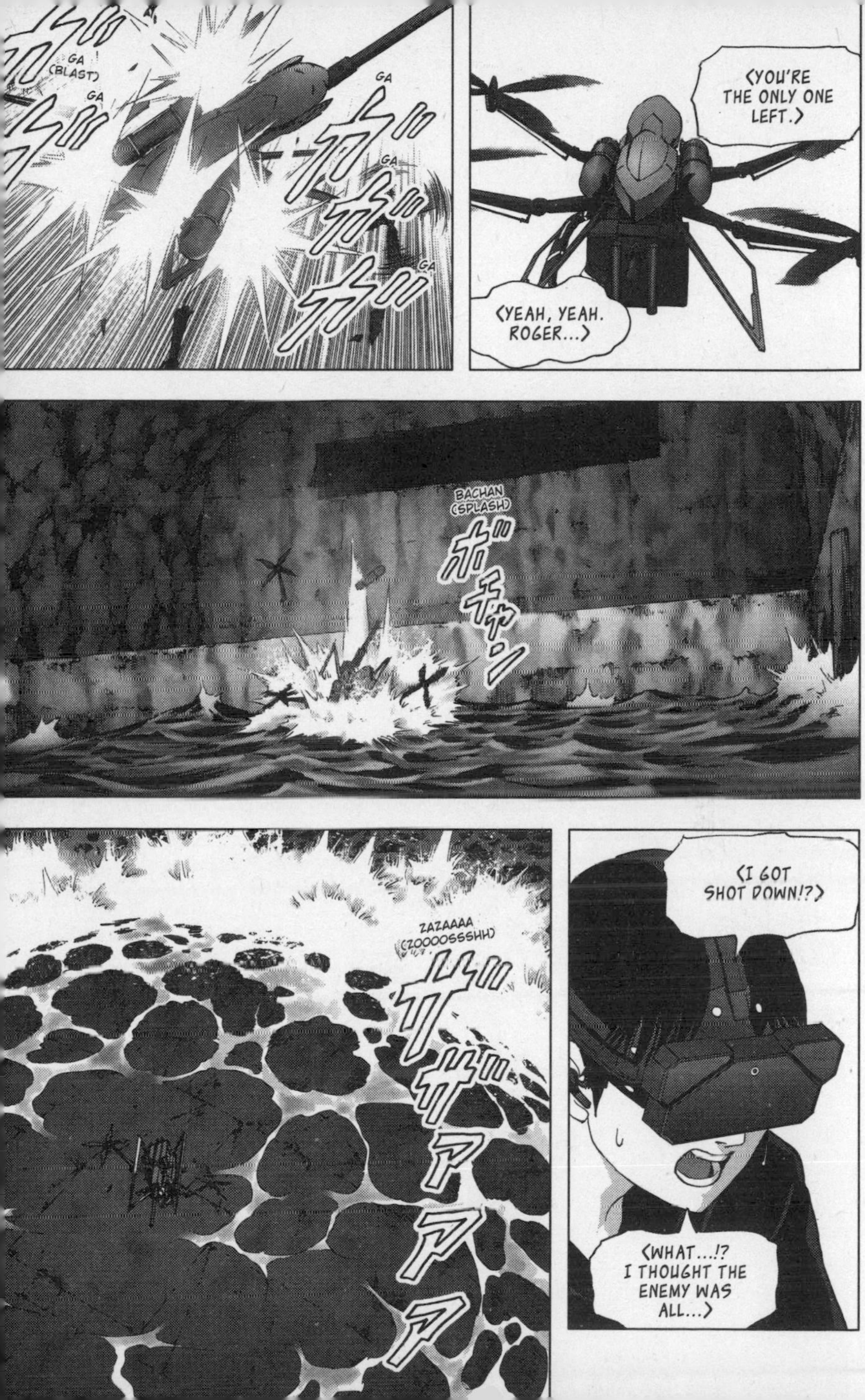
〈YOU'RE THE ONLY ONE LEFT.〉
〈YEAH, YEAH. ROGER...〉
GA (BLAST)
GA
GA
GA
GA
BACHAN (SPLASH)
〈I GOT SHOT DOWN!?〉
〈WHAT...!? I THOUGHT THE ENEMY WAS ALL...〉
ZAZAAAA (ZOOOOSSSHH)

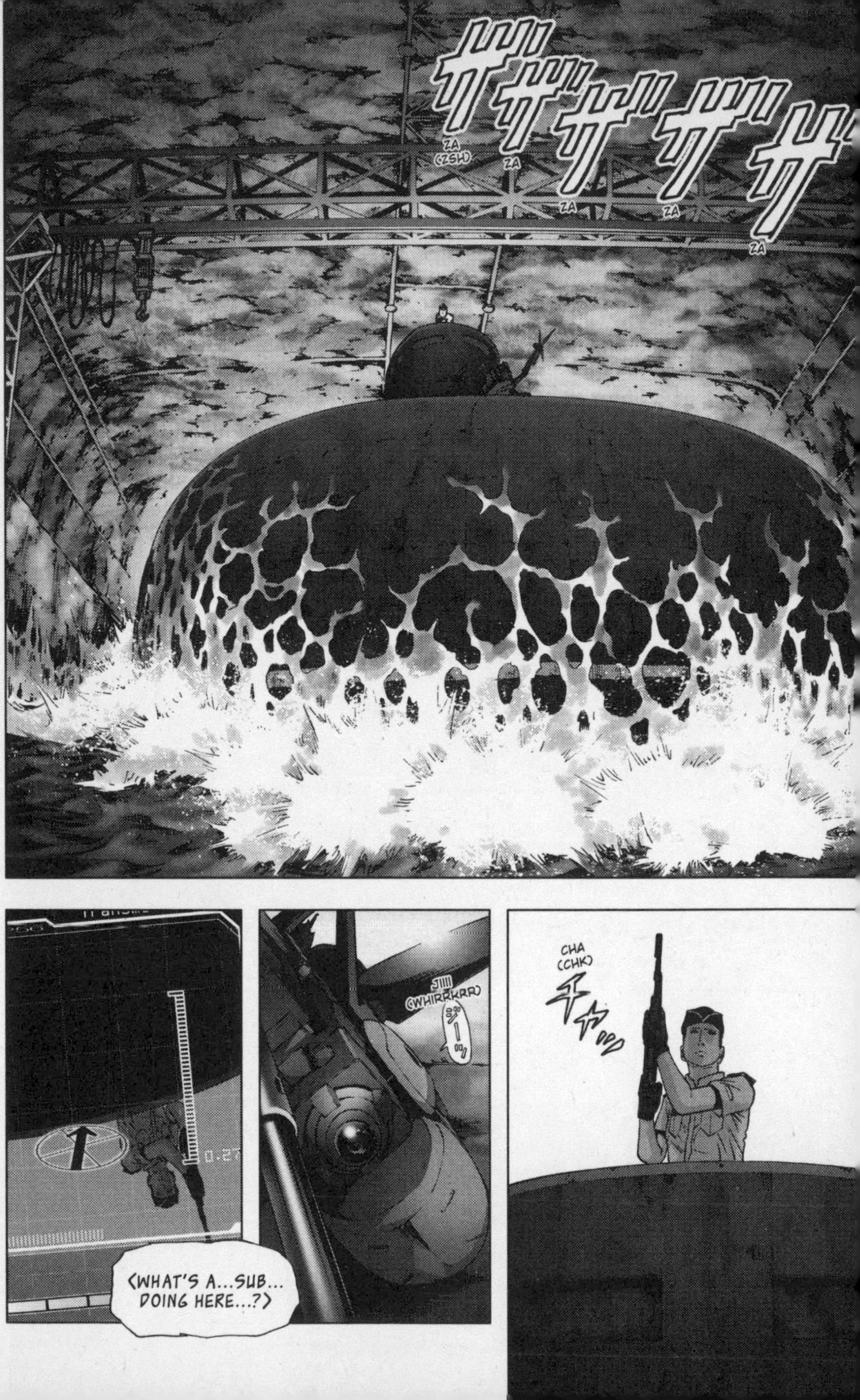
ZA
(ZSH)
ZA
ZA
ZA
ZA
CHA
(CHK)
JIIII
(WHIRRKRR)
<WHAT'S A...SUB... DOING HERE...?>

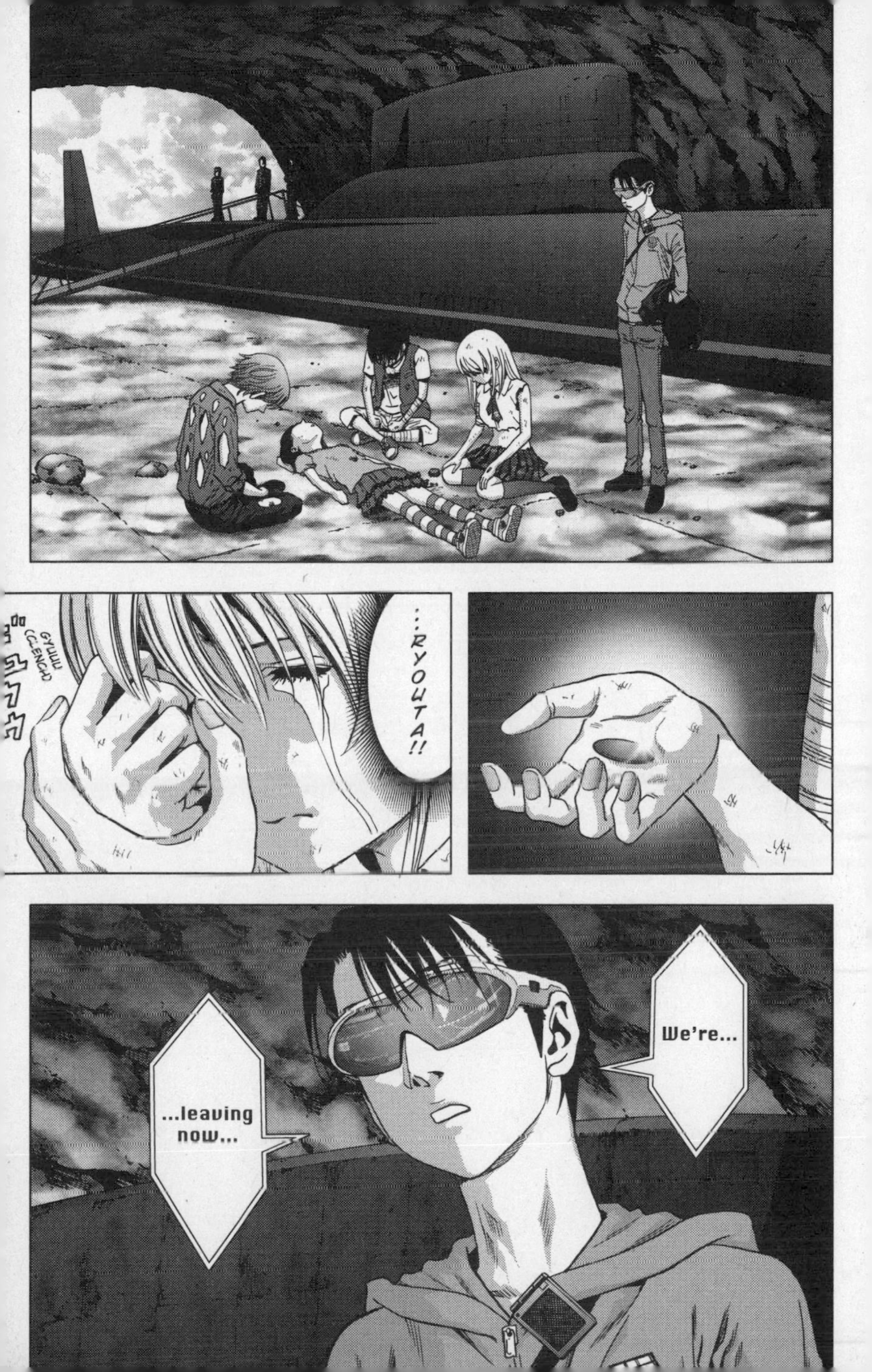
...RYOUTA!!
GYUUU (CLENCH)
We're...
...leaving now...

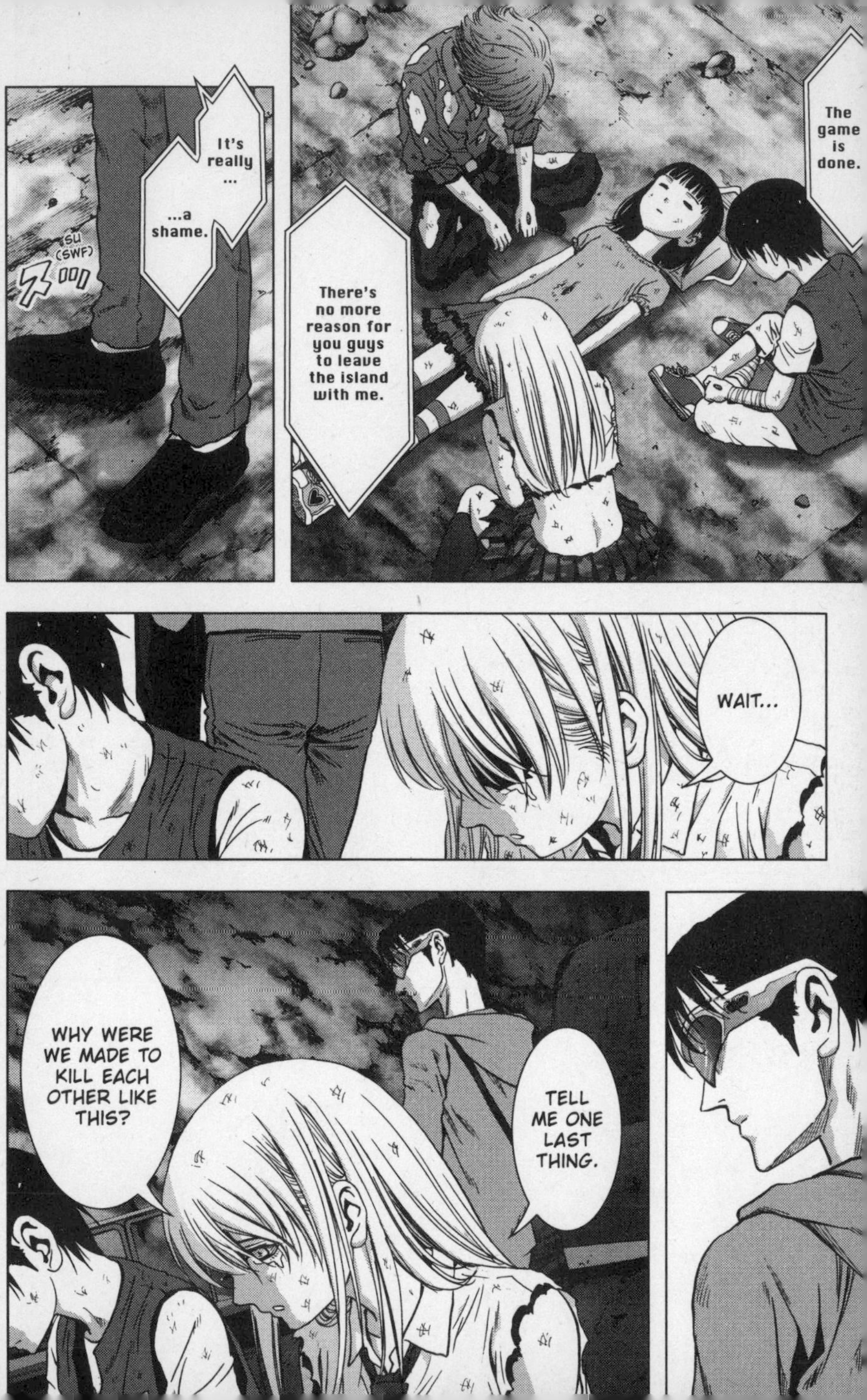

The game is done.
There's no more reason for you guys to leave the island with me.
It's really ...
...a shame.
SU (SWF)
WAIT...
TELL ME ONE LAST THING.
WHY WERE WE MADE TO KILL EACH OTHER LIKE THIS?

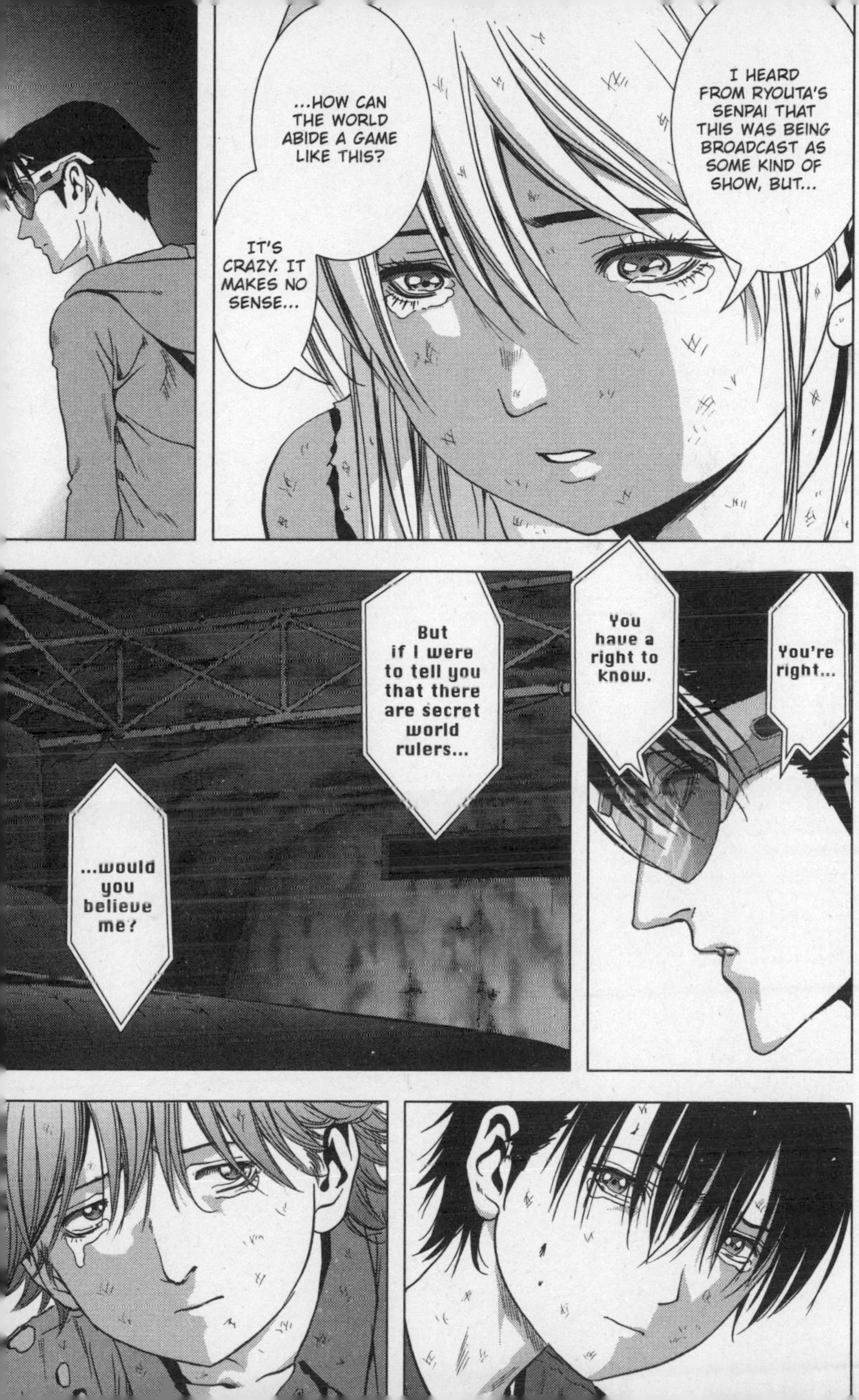
I HEARD FROM RYOUTA'S SENPAI THAT THIS WAS BEING BROADCAST AS SOME KIND OF SHOW, BUT...
...HOW CAN THE WORLD ABIDE A GAME LIKE THIS?
IT'S CRAZY. IT MAKES NO SENSE...
You're right...
You have a right to know.
But if I were to tell you that there are secret world rulers...
...would you believe me?

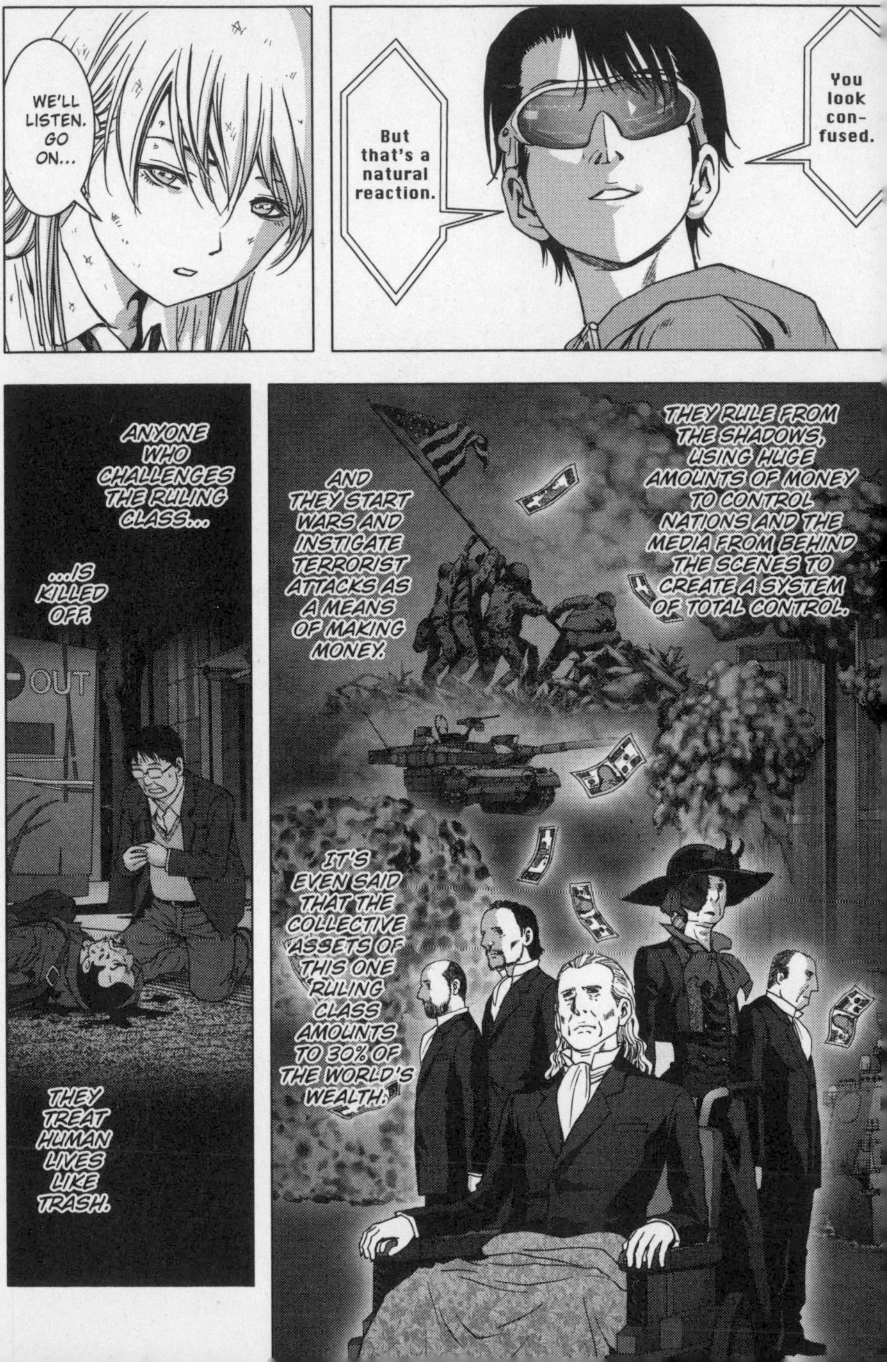
You look confused.
But that's a natural reaction.
WE'LL LISTEN. GO ON...
THEY RULE FROM THE SHADOWS, USING HUGE AMOUNTS OF MONEY TO CONTROL NATIONS AND THE MEDIA FROM BEHIND THE SCENES TO CREATE A SYSTEM OF TOTAL CONTROL.
AND THEY START WARS AND INSTIGATE TERRORIST ATTACKS AS A MEANS OF MAKING MONEY.
IT'S EVEN SAID THAT THE COLLECTIVE ASSETS OF THIS ONE RULING CLASS AMOUNTS TO 30% OF THE WORLD'S WEALTH.
ANYONE WHO CHALLENGES THE RULING CLASS...
...IS KILLED OFF.
OUT
THEY TREAT HUMAN LIVES LIKE TRASH.

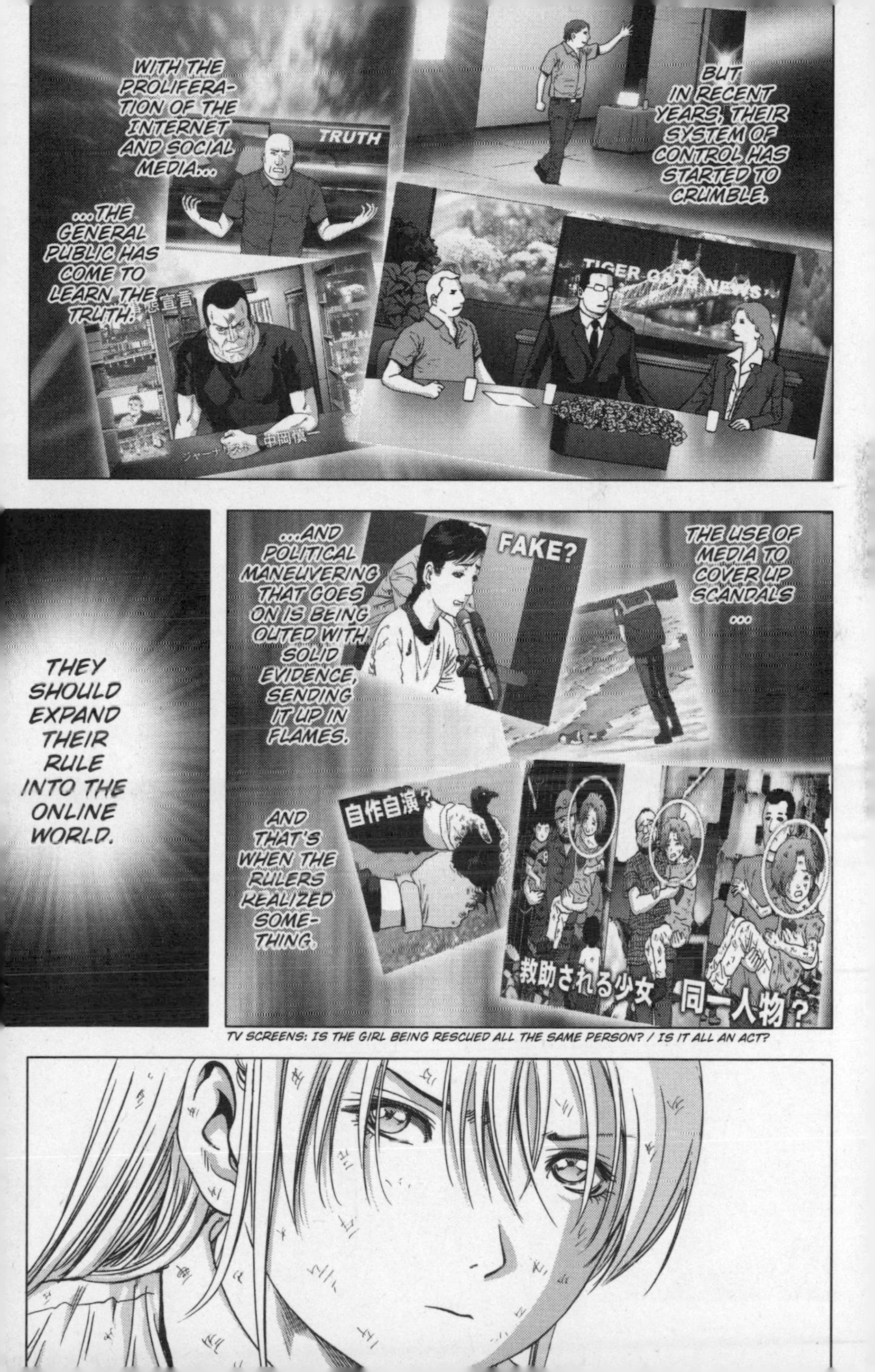
BUT IN RECENT YEARS, THEIR SYSTEM OF CONTROL HAS STARTED TO CRUMBLE.
TRUTH
WITH THE PROLIFERATION OF THE INTERNET AND SOCIAL MEDIA...
TIGER GATE NEWS
...THE GENERAL PUBLIC HAS COME TO LEARN THE TRUTH.
THE USE OF MEDIA TO COVER UP SCANDALS...
FAKE?
...AND POLITICAL MANEUVERING THAT GOES ON IS BEING OUTED WITH SOLID EVIDENCE, SENDING IT UP IN FLAMES.
救助される少女 同一人物？
自作自演？
AND THAT'S WHEN THE RULERS REALIZED SOMETHING.
THEY SHOULD EXPAND THEIR RULE INTO THE ONLINE WORLD.
TV SCREENS: IS THE GIRL BEING RESCUED ALL THE SAME PERSON? / IS IT ALL AN ACT?

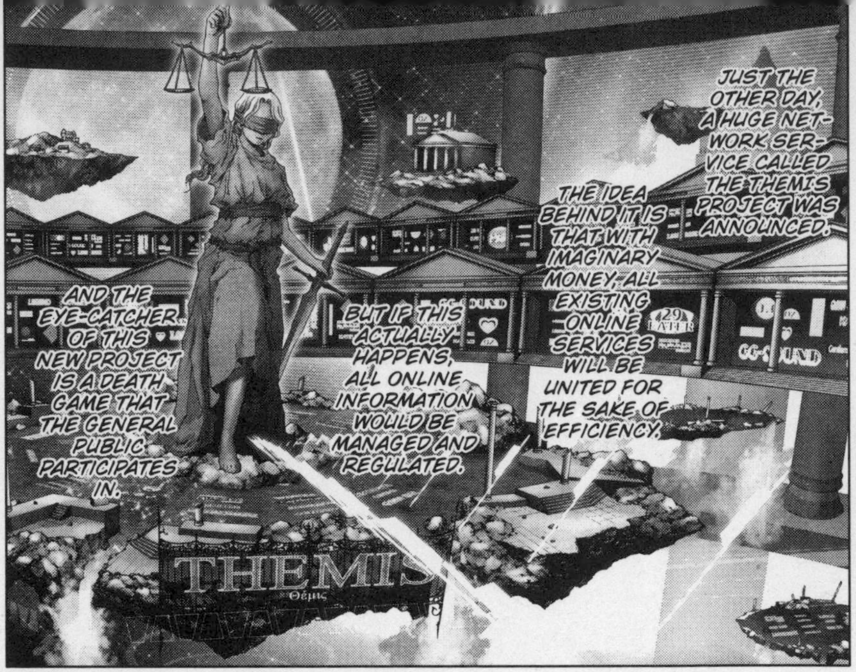
JUST THE OTHER DAY, A HUGE NETWORK SERVICE CALLED THE THEMIS PROJECT WAS ANNOUNCED.
THE IDEA BEHIND IT IS THAT WITH IMAGINARY MONEY, ALL EXISTING ONLINE SERVICES WILL BE UNITED FOR THE SAKE OF EFFICIENCY.
BUT IF THIS ACTUALLY HAPPENS, ALL ONLINE INFORMATION WOULD BE MANAGED AND REGULATED.
AND THE EYE-CATCHER OF THIS NEW PROJECT IS A DEATH GAME THAT THE GENERAL PUBLIC PARTICIPATES IN.
THEMIS

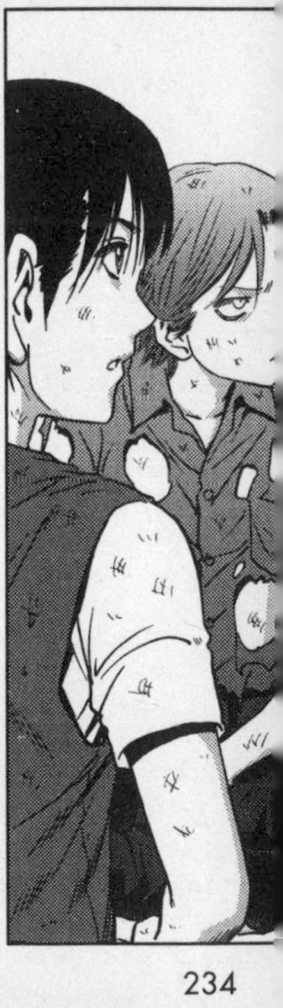

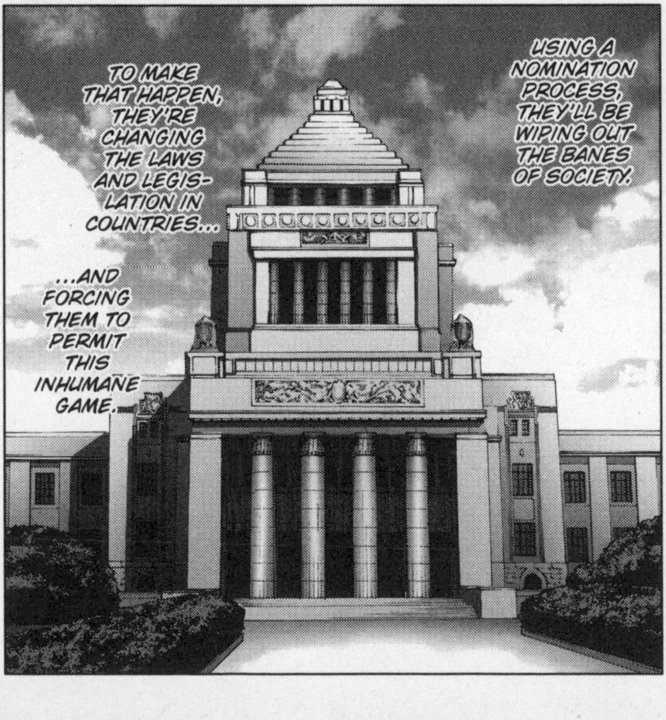
USING A NOMINATION PROCESS, THEY'LL BE WIPING OUT THE BANES OF SOCIETY.
TO MAKE THAT HAPPEN, THEY'RE CHANGING THE LAWS AND LEGISLATION IN COUNTRIES...
...AND FORCING THEM TO PERMIT THIS INHUMANE GAME.

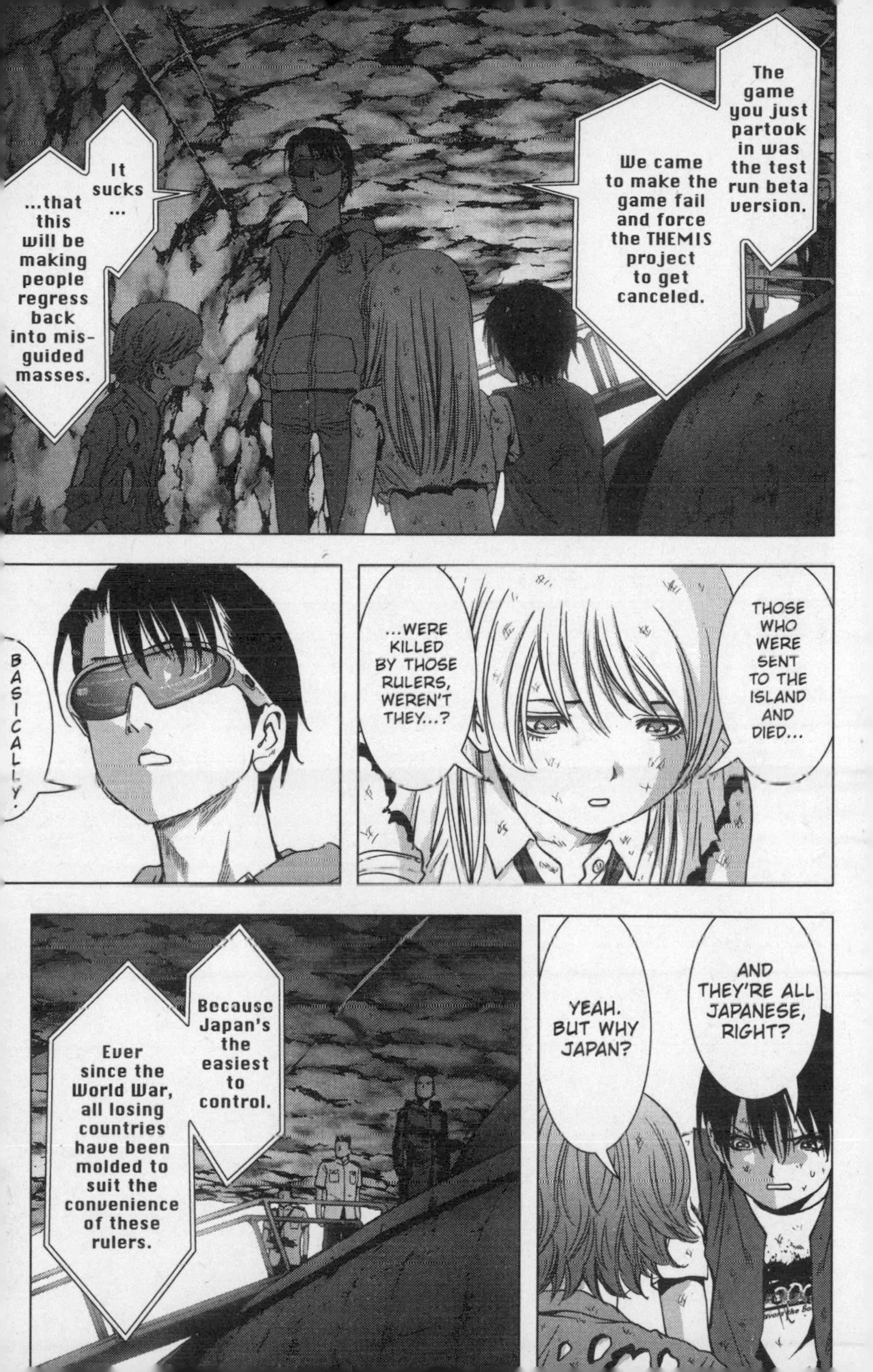
The game you just partook in was the test run beta version.
We came to make the game fail and force the THEMIS project to get canceled.
It sucks...
...that this will be making people regress back into mis-guided masses.
THOSE WHO WERE SENT TO THE ISLAND AND DIED...
...WERE KILLED BY THOSE RULERS, WEREN'T THEY...?
BASICALLY.
AND THEY'RE ALL JAPANESE, RIGHT?
YEAH. BUT WHY JAPAN?
Because Japan's the easiest to control.
Ever since the World War, all losing countries have been molded to suit the convenience of these rulers.

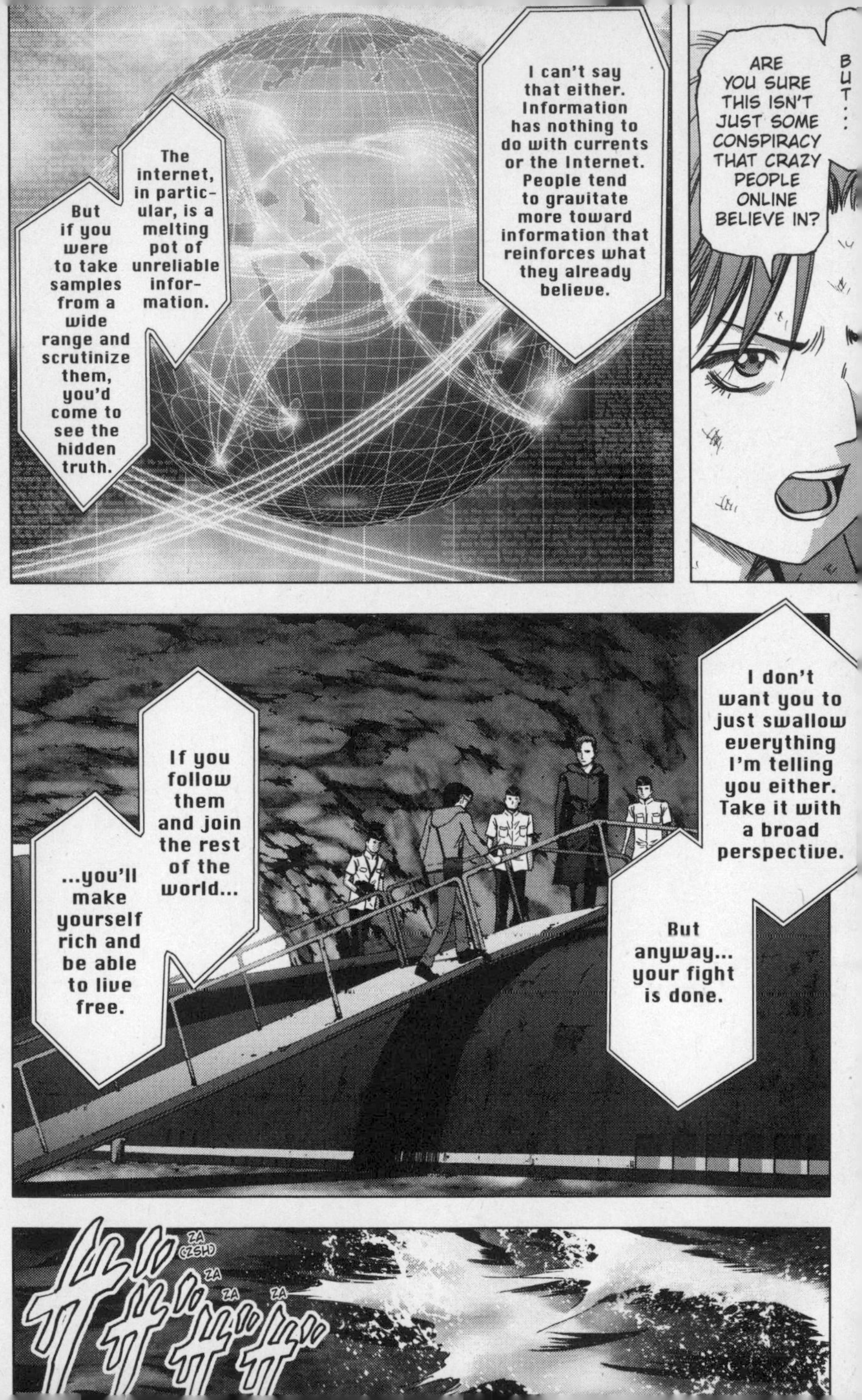
BUT...
ARE YOU SURE THIS ISN'T JUST SOME CONSPIRACY THAT CRAZY PEOPLE ONLINE BELIEVE IN?
I can't say that either. Information has nothing to do with currents or the Internet. People tend to gravitate more toward information that reinforces what they already believe.
The internet, in particular, is a melting pot of unreliable information.
But if you were to take samples from a wide range and scrutinize them, you'd come to see the hidden truth.
I don't want you to just swallow everything I'm telling you either. Take it with a broad perspective.
But anyway... your fight is done.
If you follow them and join the rest of the world...
...you'll make yourself rich and be able to live free.
ZA (ZSH)
ZA
ZA
ZA

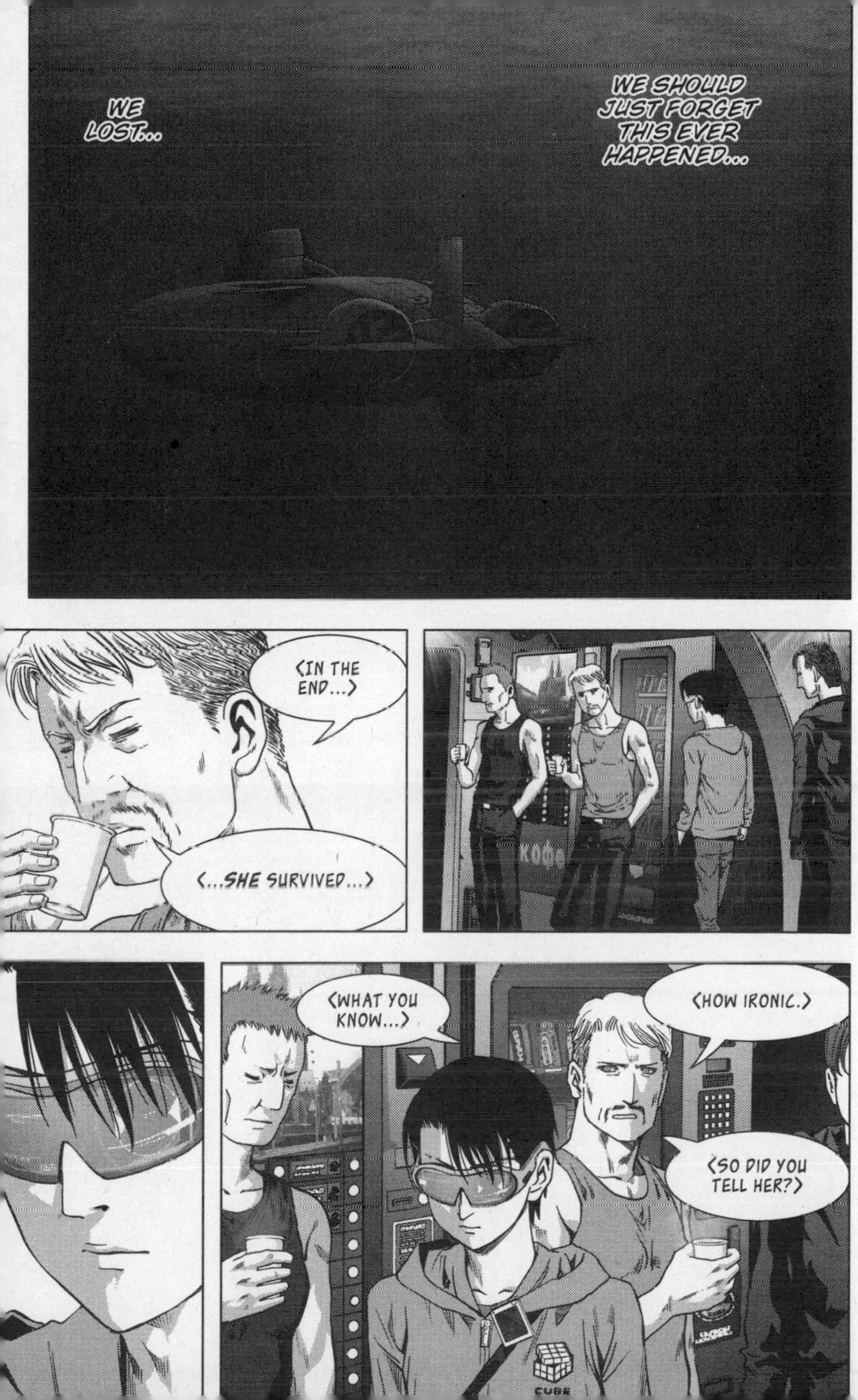
WE SHOULD JUST FORGET THIS EVER HAPPENED...
WE LOST...
<IN THE END...>
<...*SHE* SURVIVED...>
<HOW IRONIC.>
<WHAT YOU KNOW...>
<SO DID YOU TELL HER?>
CUBE

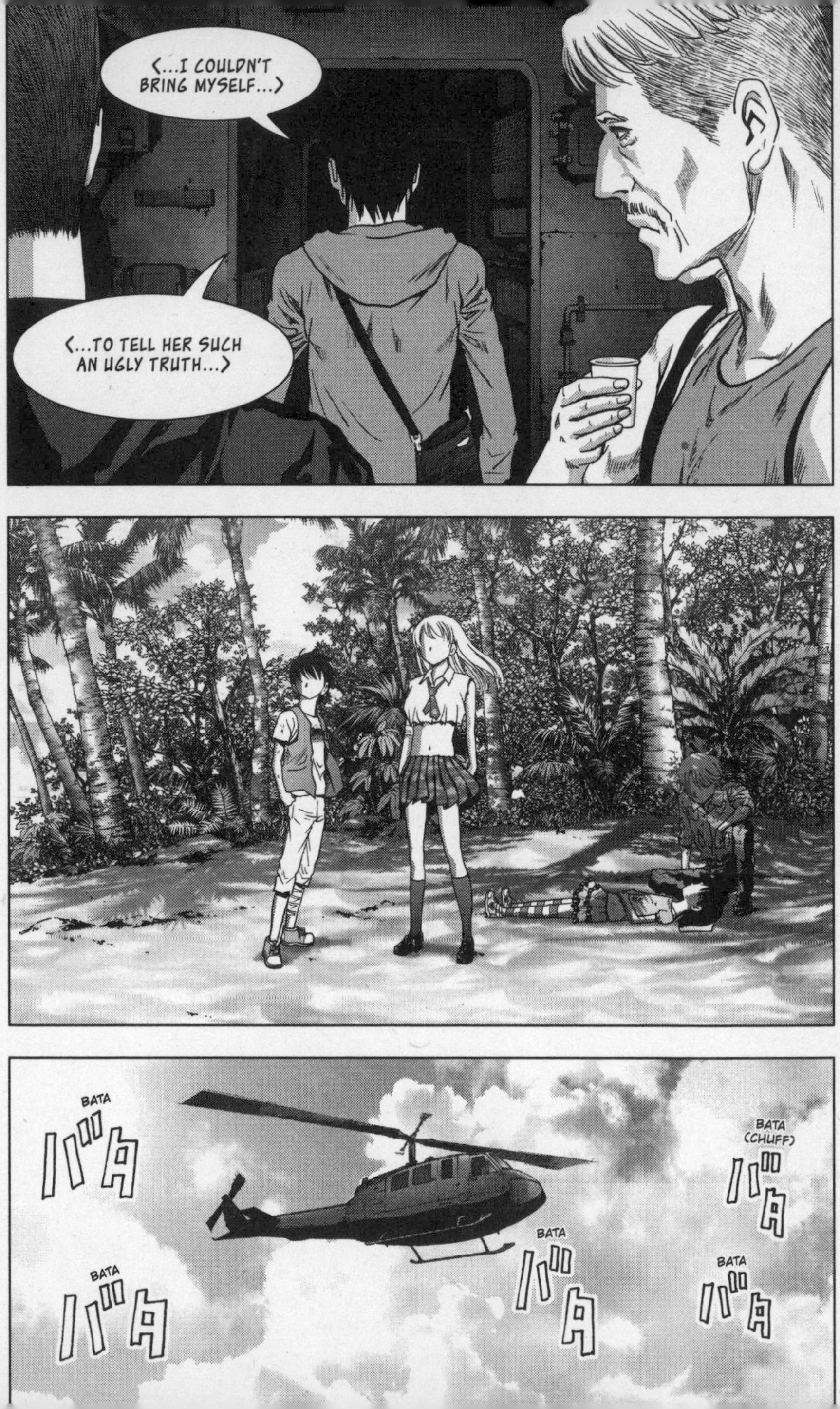
⟨...I COULDN'T BRING MYSELF...⟩
⟨...TO TELL HER SUCH AN UGLY TRUTH...⟩
BATA (CHUFF)
バタ
BATA
バタ
BATA
バタ
BATA
バタ
BATA
バタ

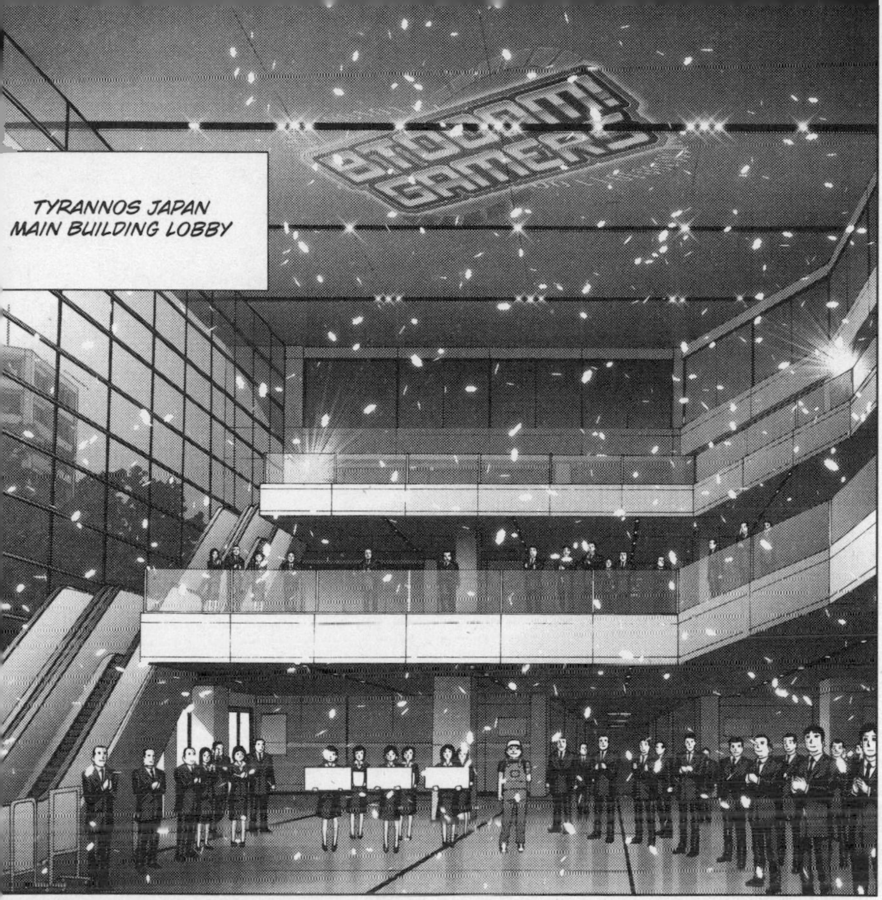
TYRANNOS JAPAN
MAIN BUILDING LOBBY

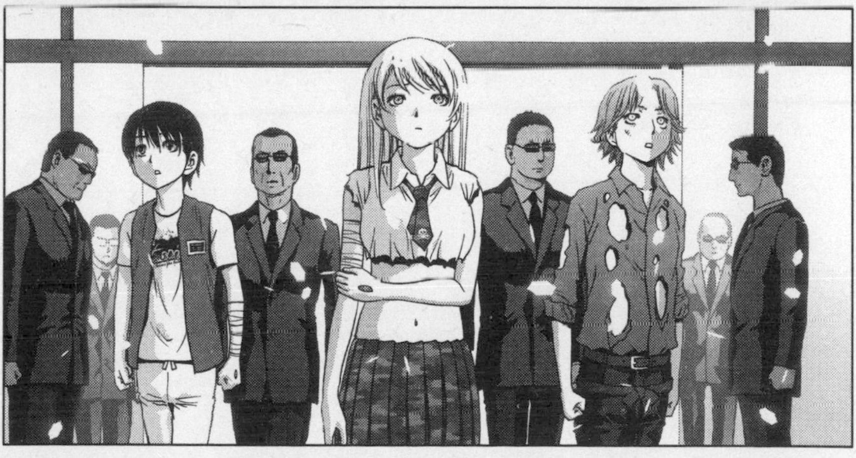

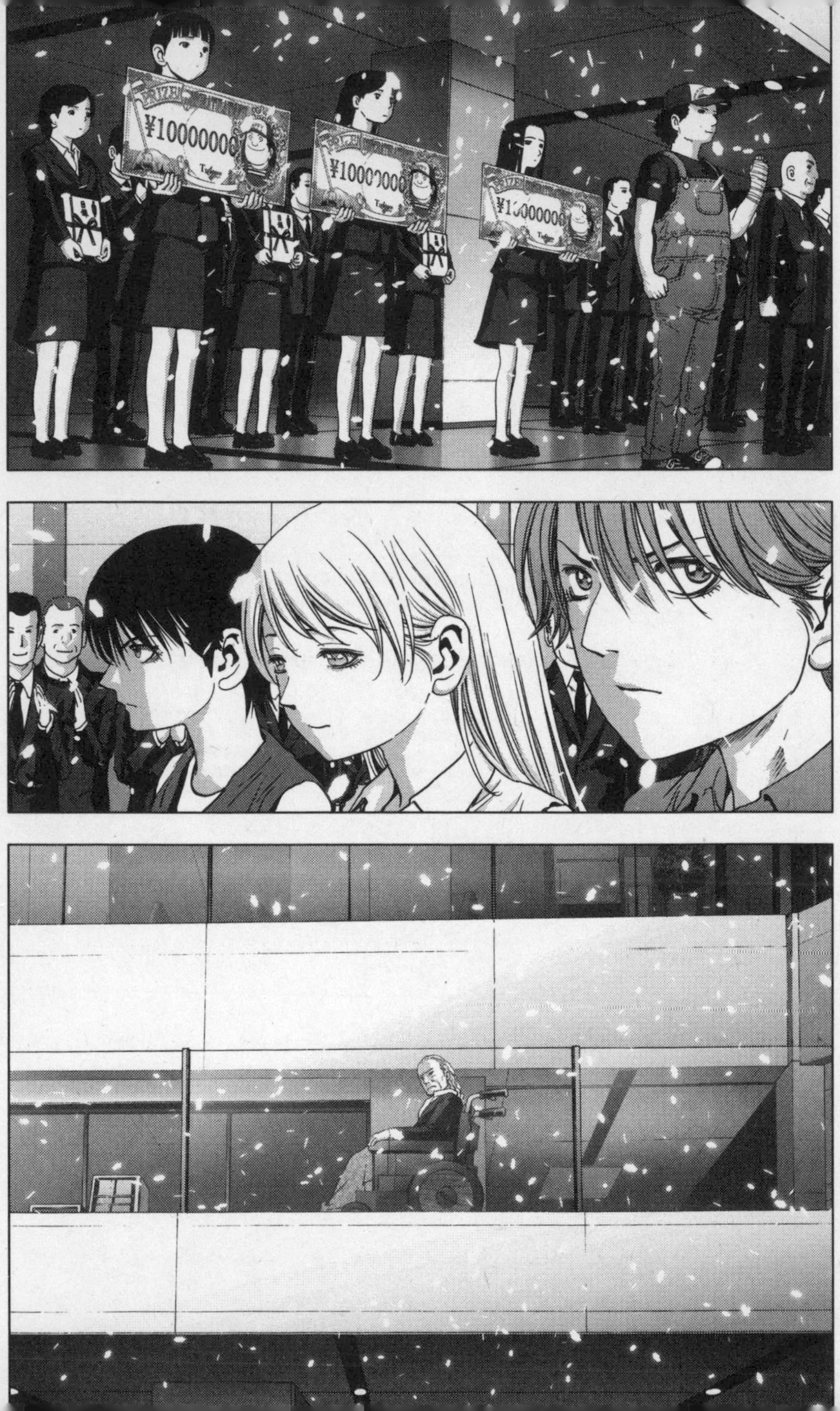
¥10000000

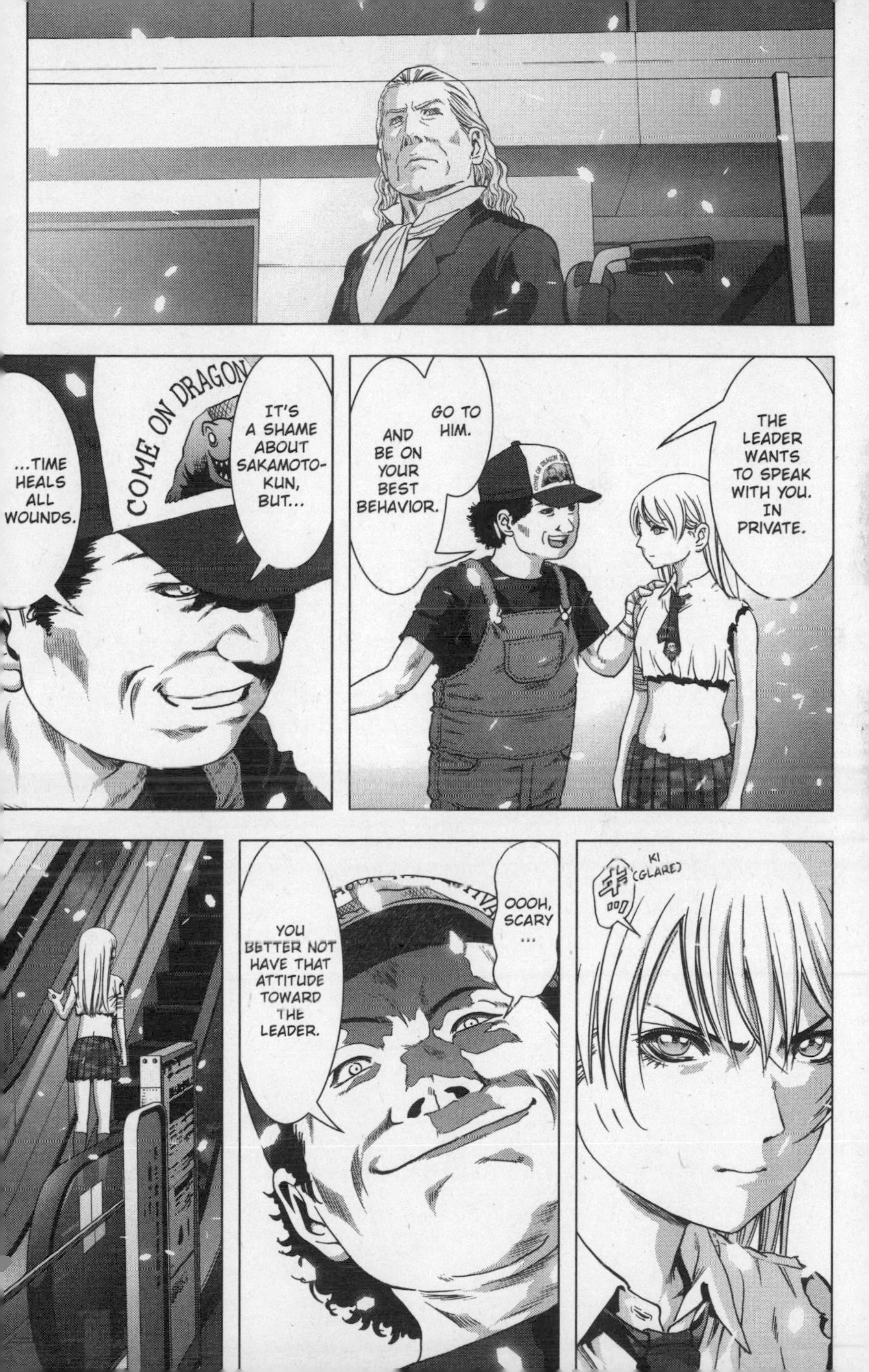
THE LEADER WANTS TO SPEAK WITH YOU. IN PRIVATE.
GO TO HIM.
AND BE ON YOUR BEST BEHAVIOR.
COME ON DRAGON
IT'S A SHAME ABOUT SAKAMOTO-KUN, BUT...
...TIME HEALS ALL WOUNDS.
KI (GLARE)
OOOH, SCARY ...
YOU BETTER NOT HAVE THAT ATTITUDE TOWARD THE LEADER.

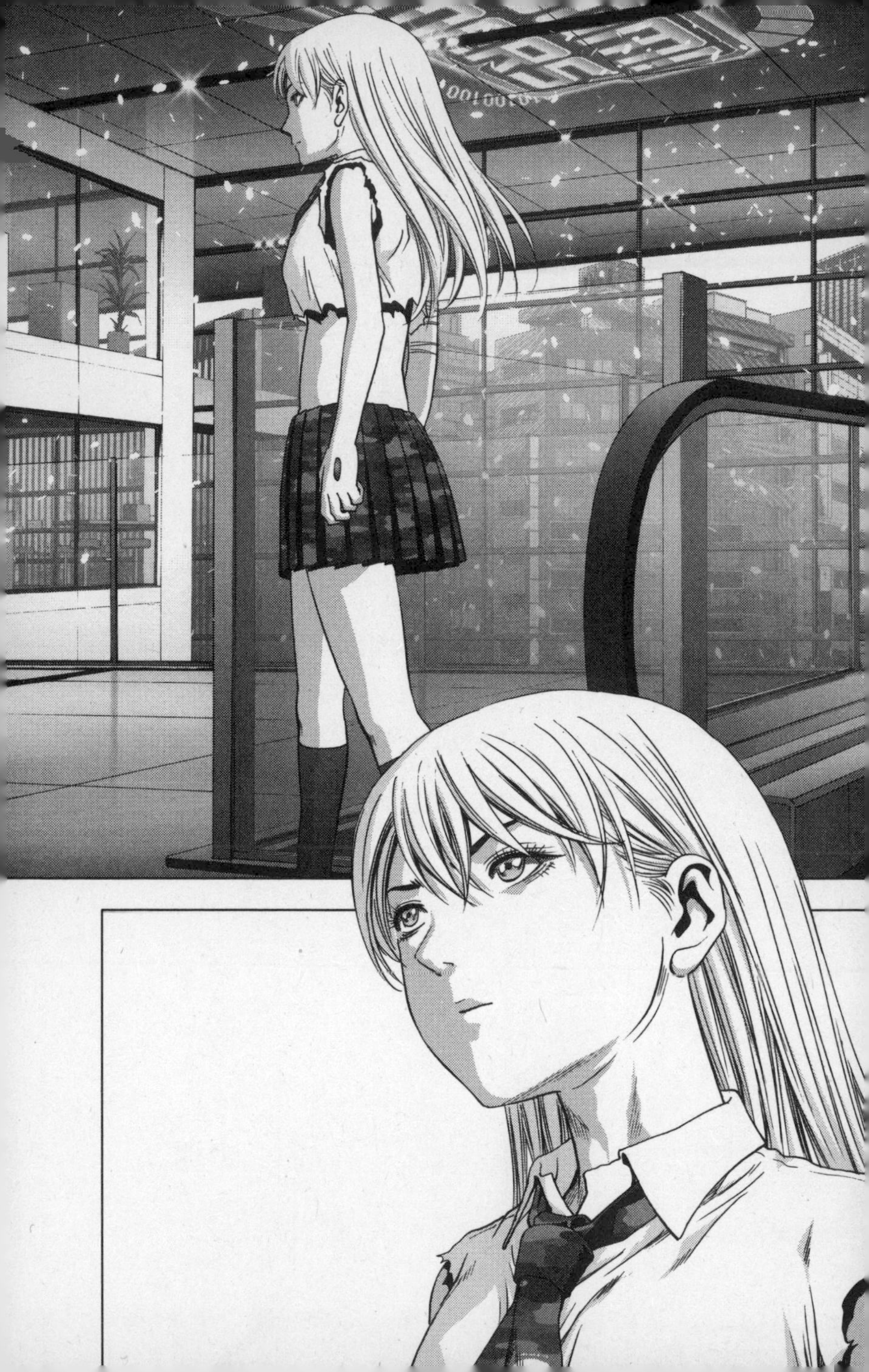

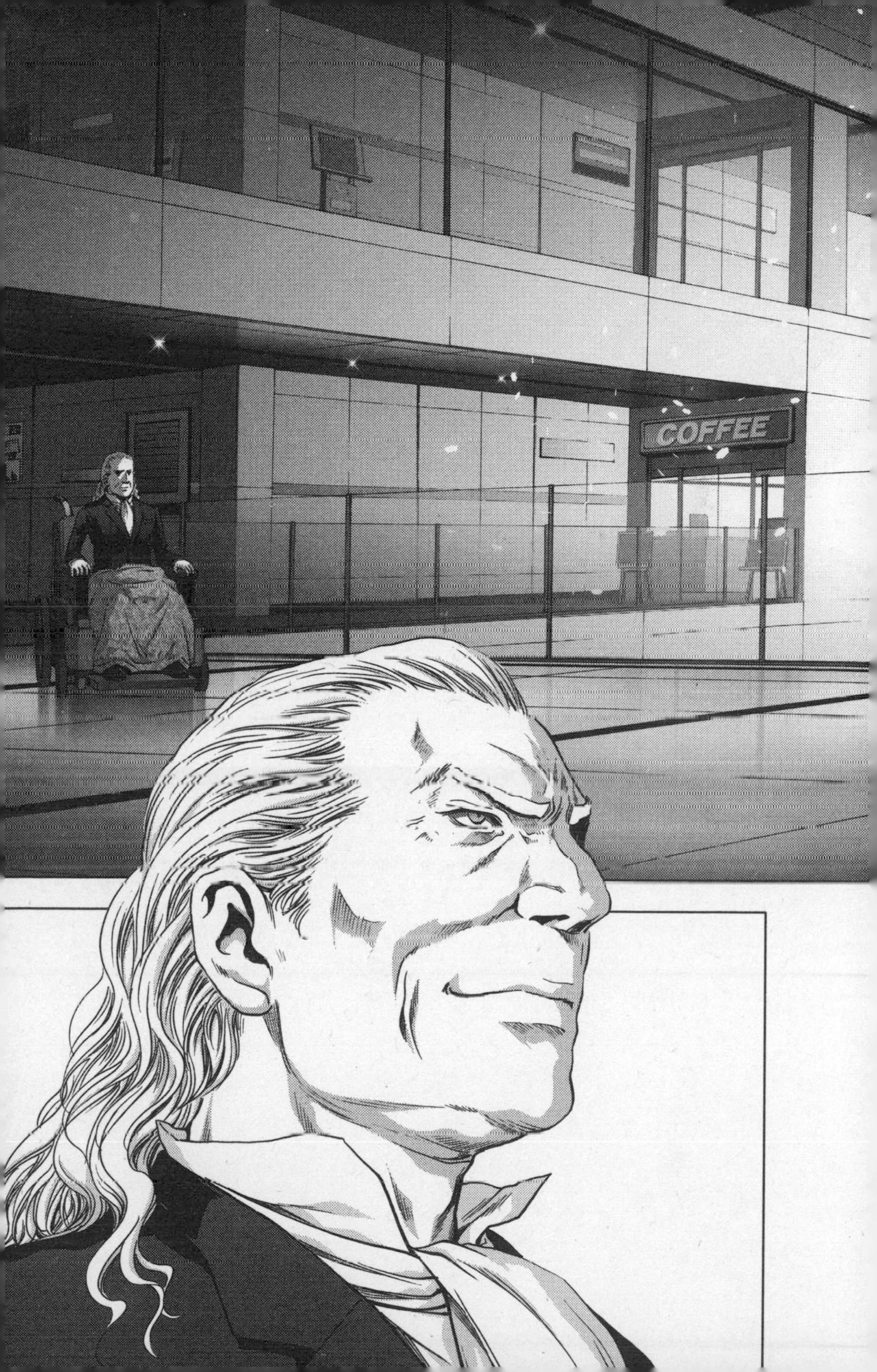
COFFEE

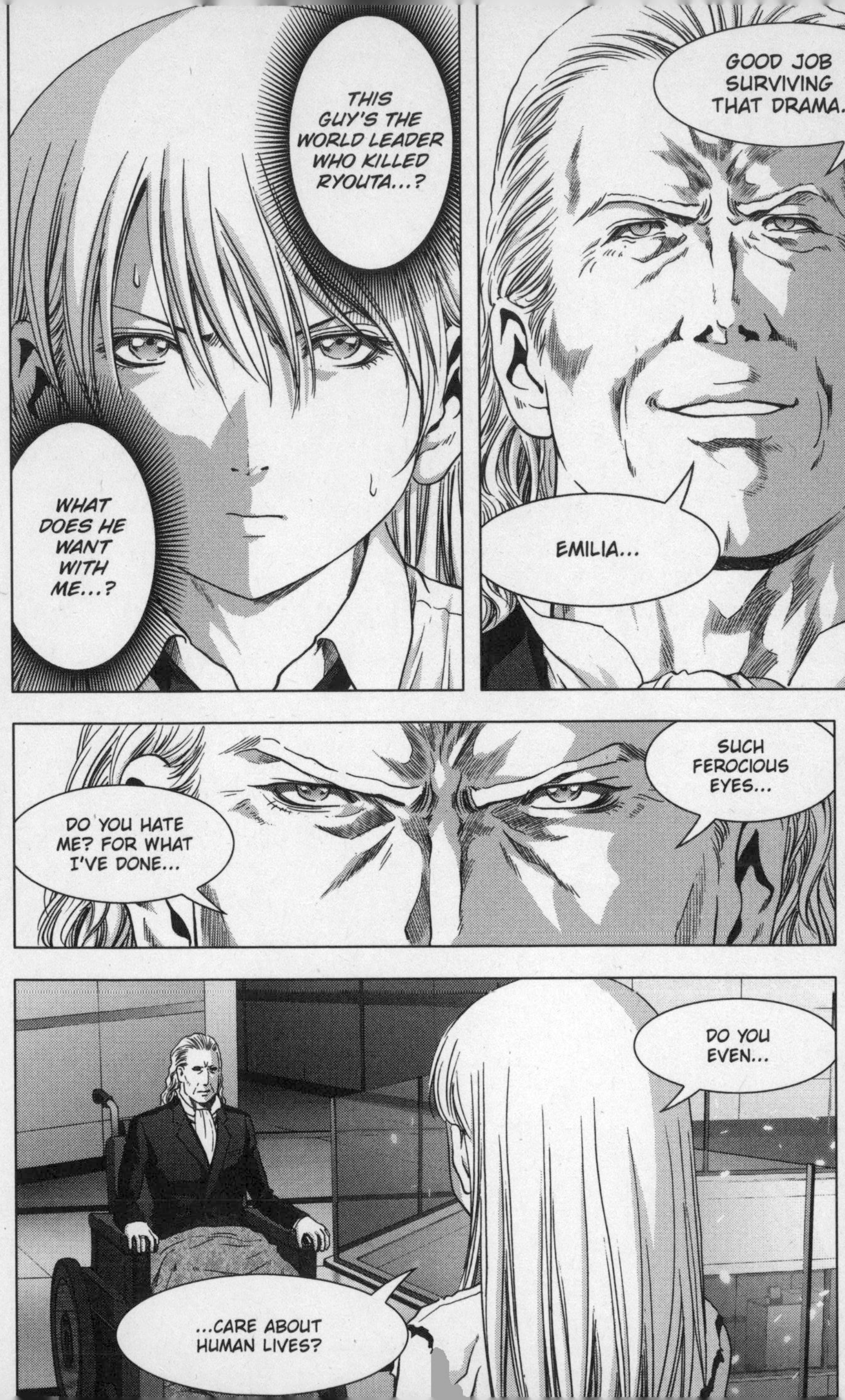
GOOD JOB SURVIVING THAT DRAMA.
EMILIA...
THIS GUY'S THE WORLD LEADER WHO KILLED RYOUTA...?
WHAT DOES HE WANT WITH ME...?
SUCH FEROCIOUS EYES...
DO YOU HATE ME? FOR WHAT I'VE DONE...
DO YOU EVEN...
...CARE ABOUT HUMAN LIVES?

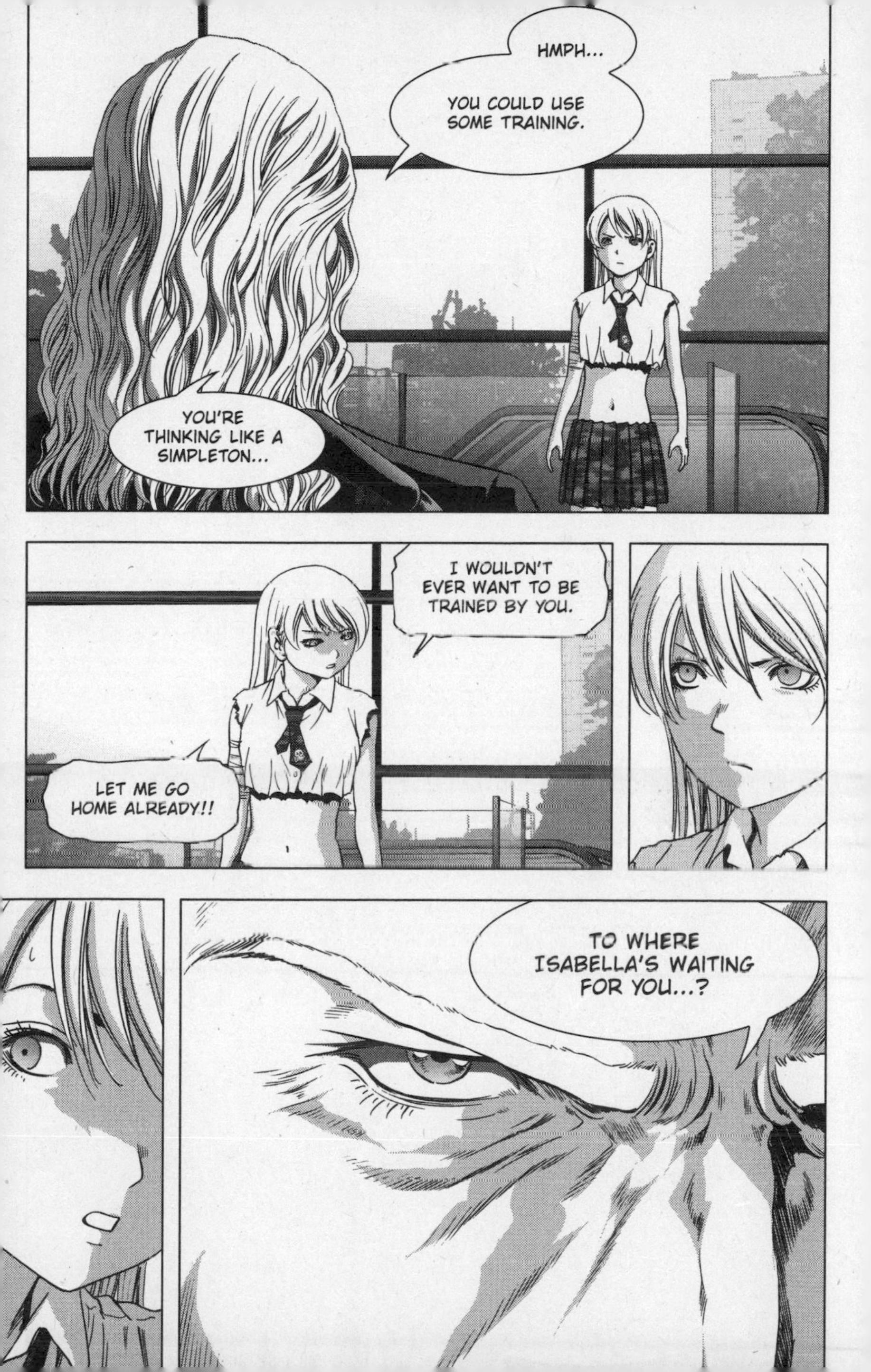
HMPH... YOU COULD USE SOME TRAINING.
YOU'RE THINKING LIKE A SIMPLETON...
I WOULDN'T EVER WANT TO BE TRAINED BY YOU.
LET ME GO HOME ALREADY!!
TO WHERE ISABELLA'S WAITING FOR YOU...?

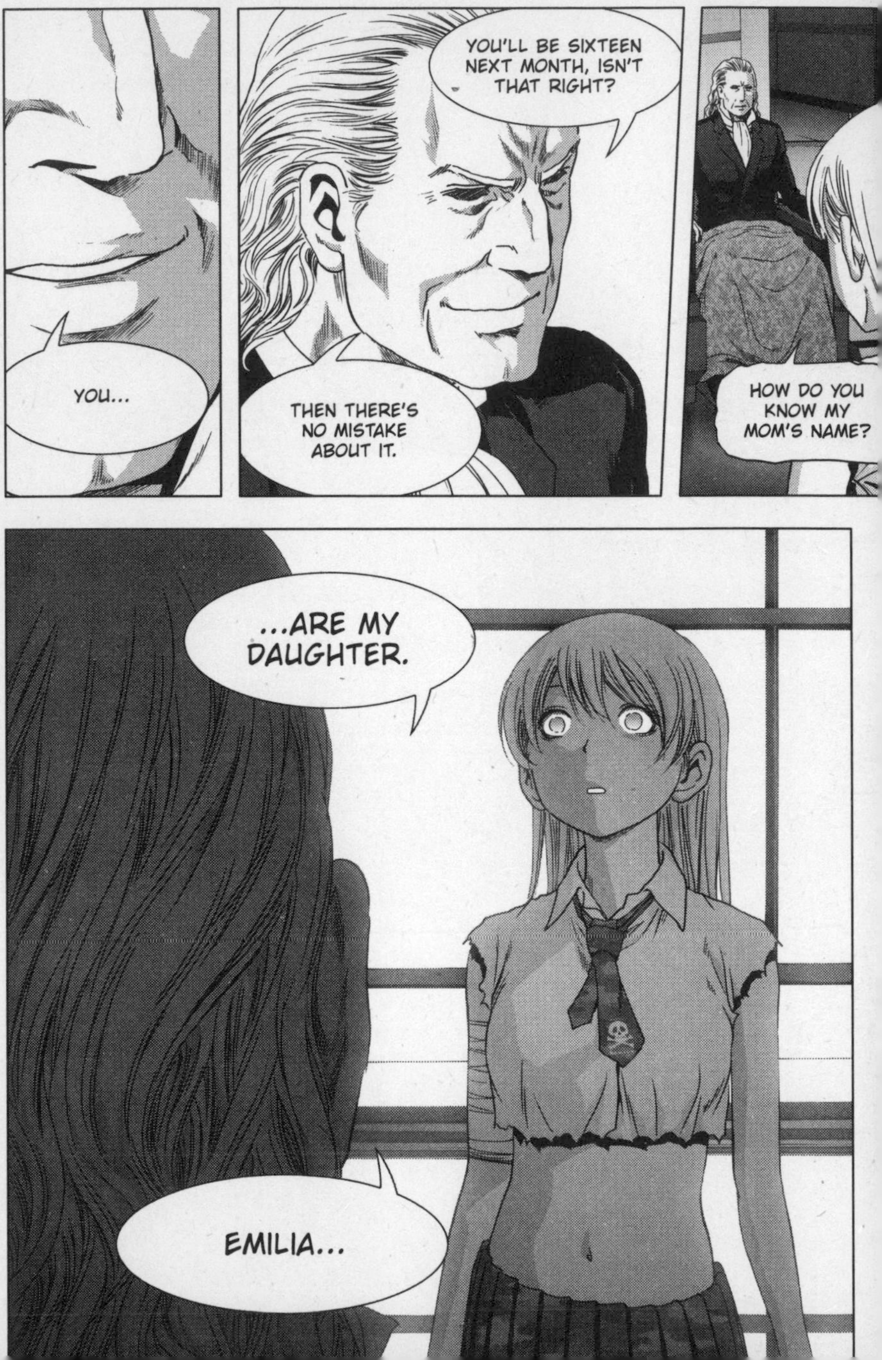
HOW DO YOU KNOW MY MOM'S NAME?
YOU'LL BE SIXTEEN NEXT MONTH, ISN'T THAT RIGHT?
THEN THERE'S NO MISTAKE ABOUT IT.
YOU...
...ARE MY DAUGHTER.
EMILIA...

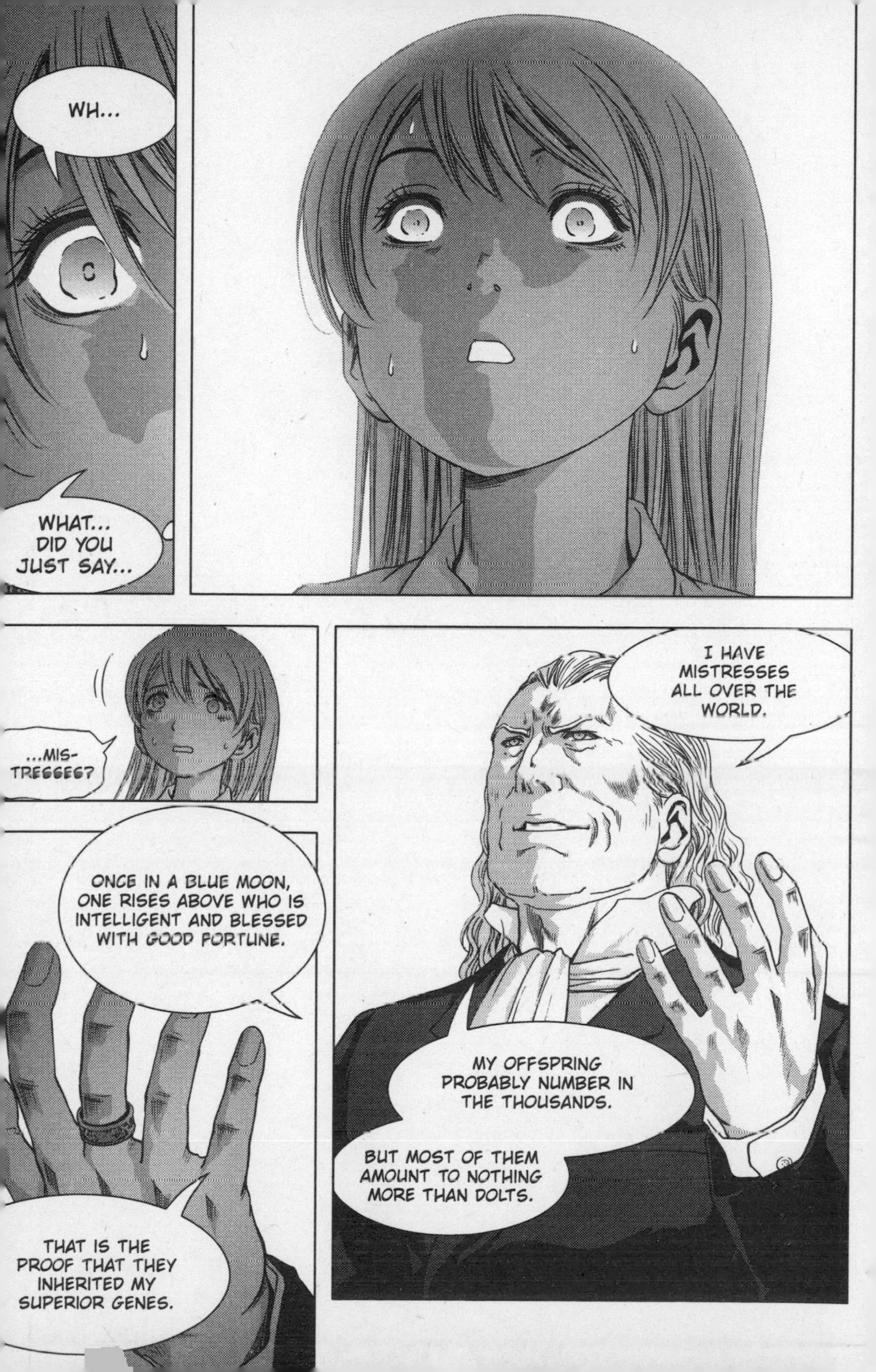
WH...
WHAT... DID YOU JUST SAY...
I HAVE MISTRESSES ALL OVER THE WORLD.
MY OFFSPRING PROBABLY NUMBER IN THE THOUSANDS.
BUT MOST OF THEM AMOUNT TO NOTHING MORE THAN DOLTS.
...MIS-TRESSES?
ONCE IN A BLUE MOON, ONE RISES ABOVE WHO IS INTELLIGENT AND BLESSED WITH *GOOD FORTUNE*.
THAT IS THE PROOF THAT THEY INHERITED MY SUPERIOR GENES.

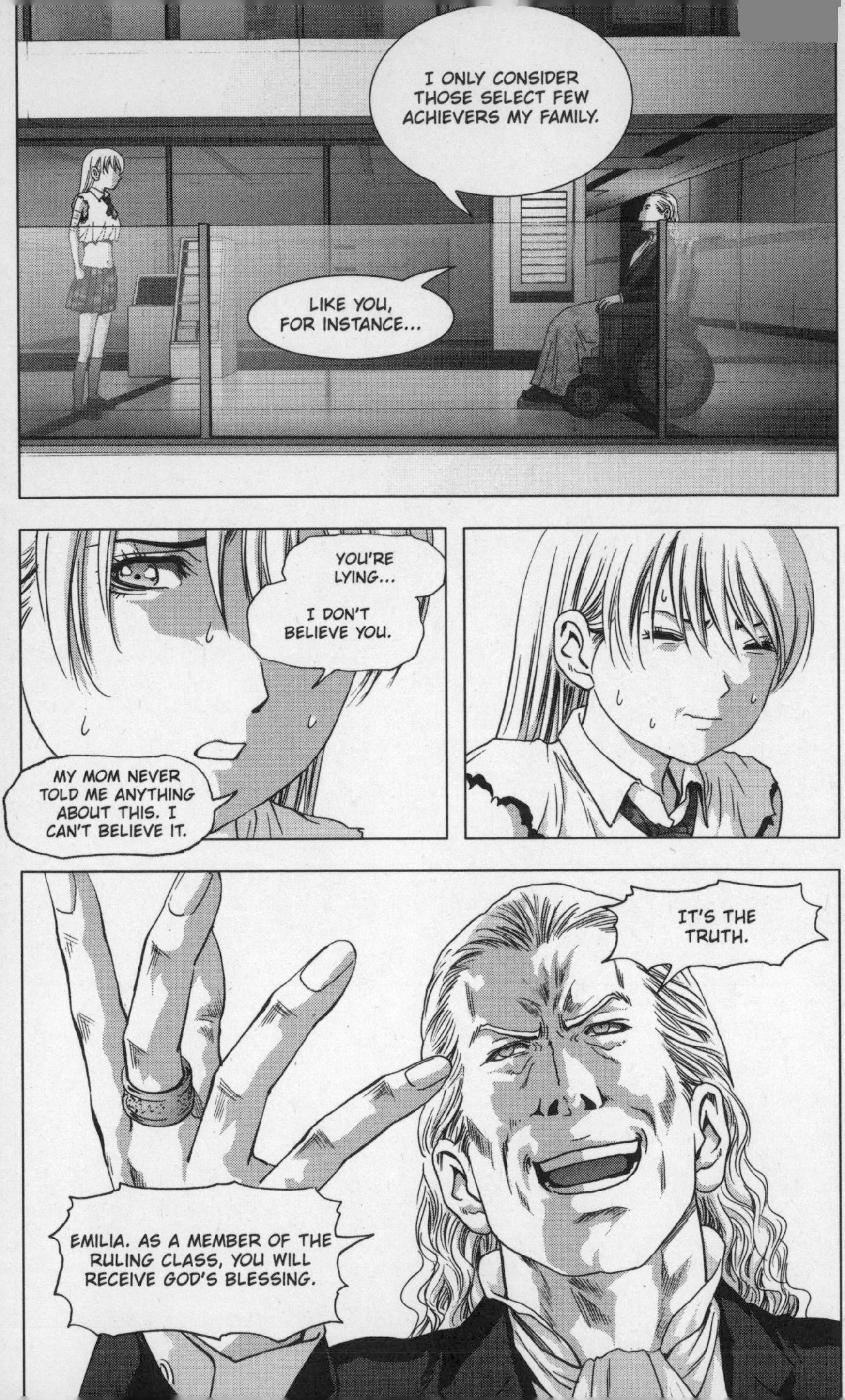
I ONLY CONSIDER THOSE SELECT FEW ACHIEVERS MY FAMILY.
LIKE YOU, FOR INSTANCE...
YOU'RE LYING...
I DON'T BELIEVE YOU.
MY MOM NEVER TOLD ME ANYTHING ABOUT THIS. I CAN'T BELIEVE IT.
IT'S THE TRUTH.
EMILIA. AS A MEMBER OF THE RULING CLASS, YOU WILL RECEIVE GOD'S BLESSING.

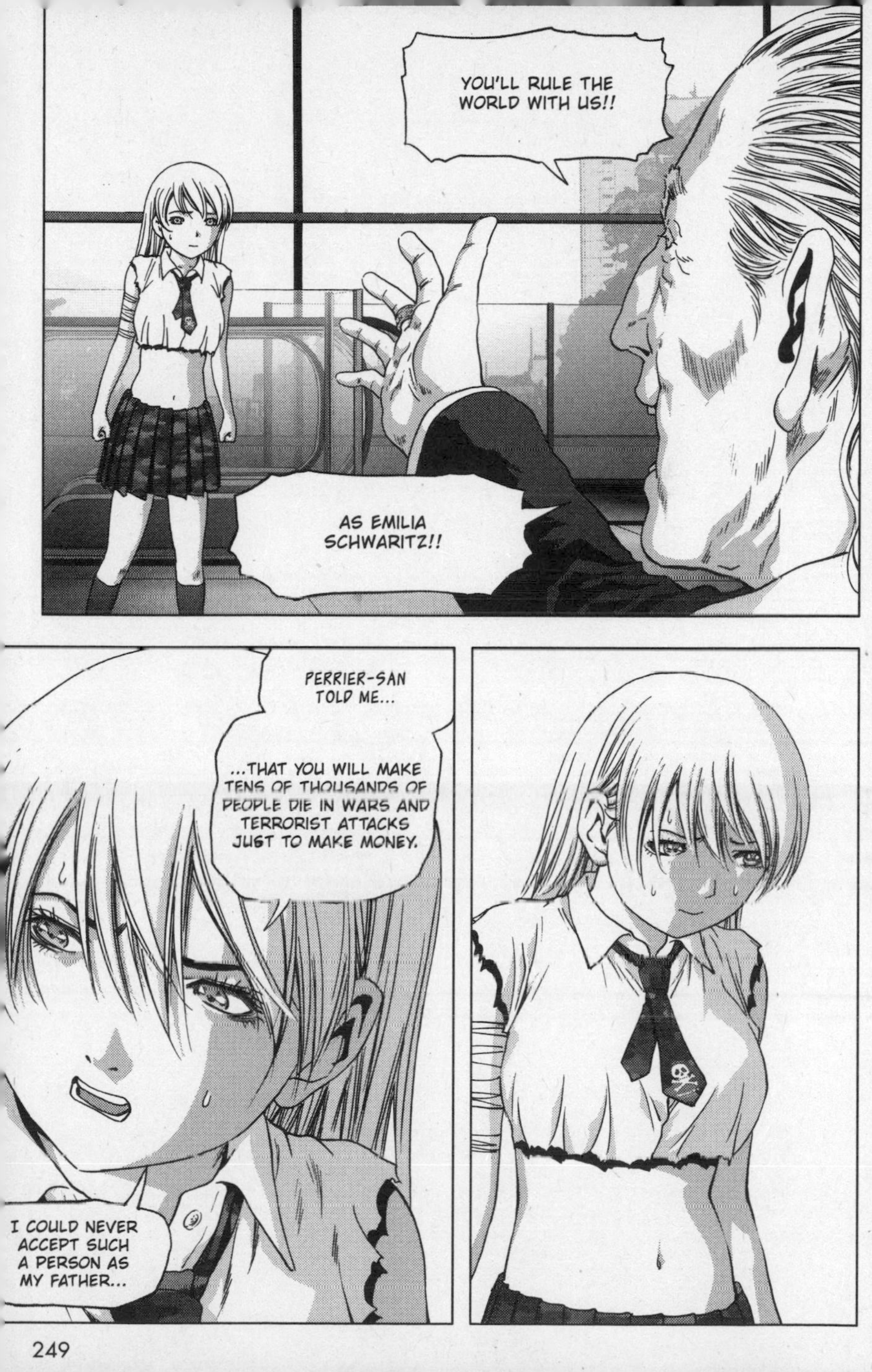
YOU'LL RULE THE WORLD WITH US!!
AS EMILIA SCHWARITZ!!
PERRIER-SAN TOLD ME...
...THAT YOU WILL MAKE TENS OF THOUSANDS OF PEOPLE DIE IN WARS AND TERRORIST ATTACKS JUST TO MAKE MONEY.
I COULD NEVER ACCEPT SUCH A PERSON AS MY FATHER...

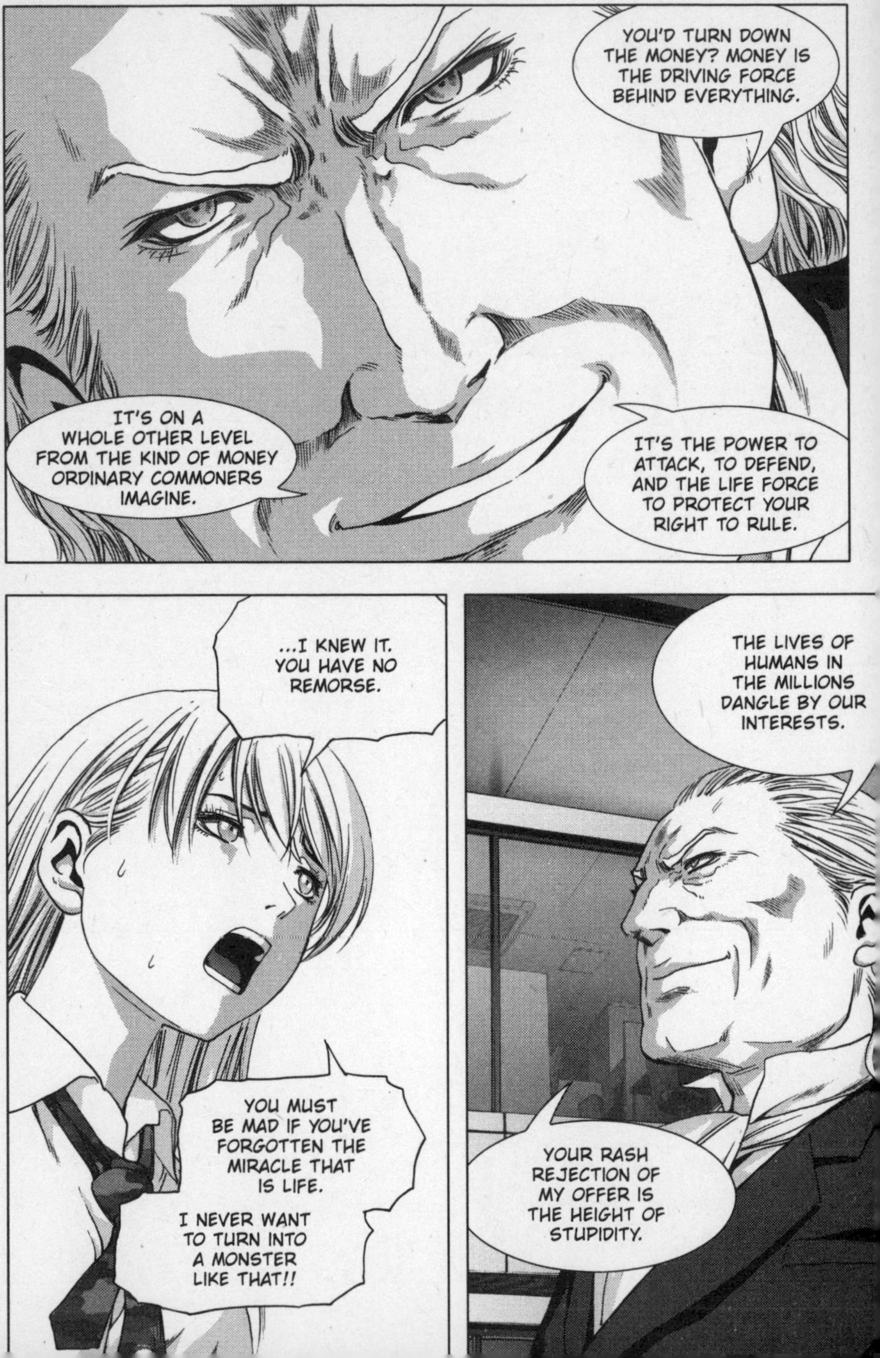
YOU'D TURN DOWN THE MONEY? MONEY IS THE DRIVING FORCE BEHIND EVERYTHING.
IT'S THE POWER TO ATTACK, TO DEFEND, AND THE LIFE FORCE TO PROTECT YOUR RIGHT TO RULE.
IT'S ON A WHOLE OTHER LEVEL FROM THE KIND OF MONEY ORDINARY COMMONERS IMAGINE.
THE LIVES OF HUMANS IN THE MILLIONS DANGLE BY OUR INTERESTS.
YOUR RASH REJECTION OF MY OFFER IS THE HEIGHT OF STUPIDITY.
...I KNEW IT. YOU HAVE NO REMORSE.
YOU MUST BE MAD IF YOU'VE FORGOTTEN THE MIRACLE THAT IS LIFE.
I NEVER WANT TO TURN INTO A MONSTER LIKE THAT!!

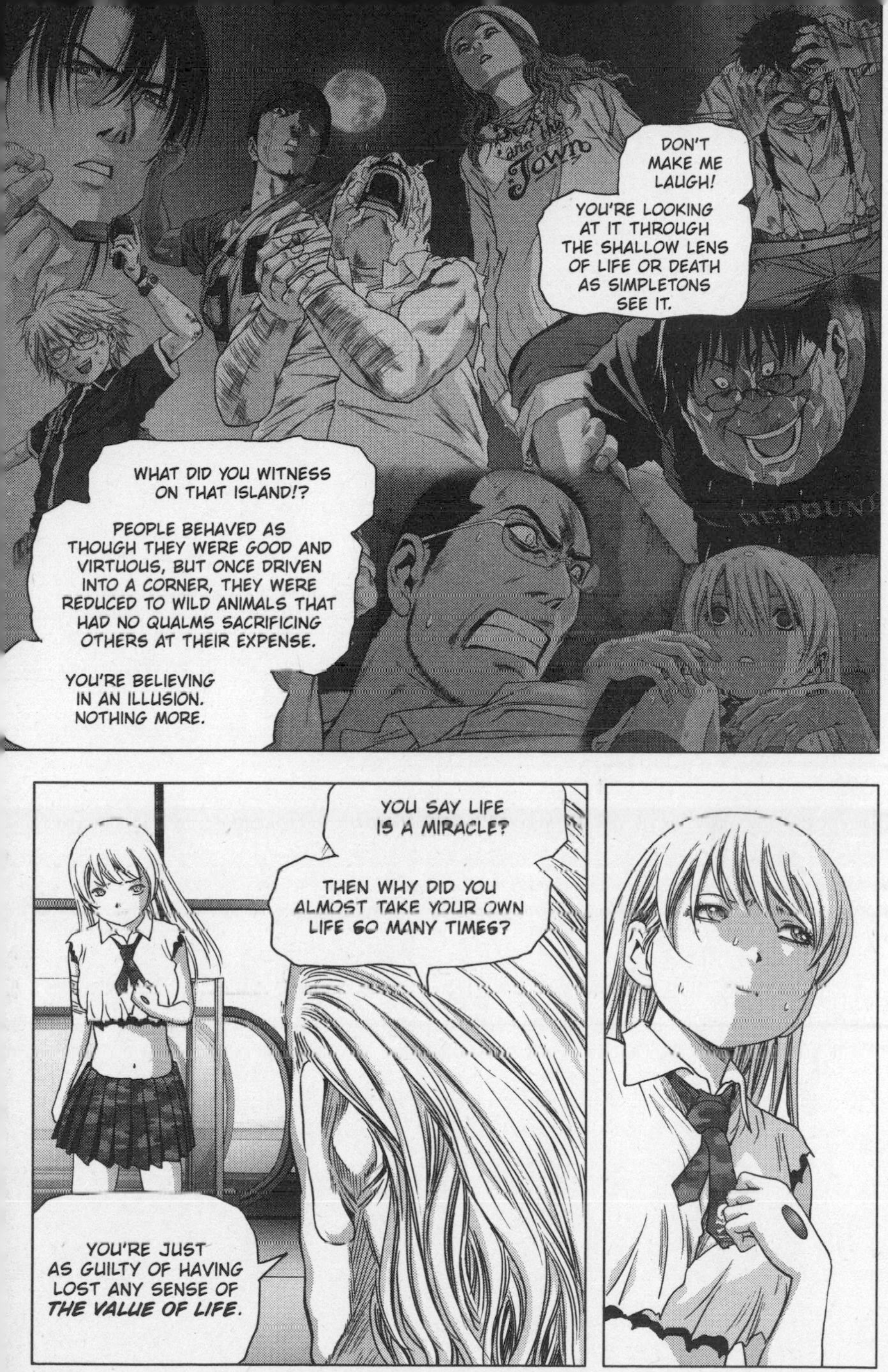
DON'T MAKE ME LAUGH!
YOU'RE LOOKING AT IT THROUGH THE SHALLOW LENS OF LIFE OR DEATH AS SIMPLETONS SEE IT.
WHAT DID YOU WITNESS ON THAT ISLAND!?
PEOPLE BEHAVED AS THOUGH THEY WERE GOOD AND VIRTUOUS, BUT ONCE DRIVEN INTO A CORNER, THEY WERE REDUCED TO WILD ANIMALS THAT HAD NO QUALMS SACRIFICING OTHERS AT THEIR EXPENSE.
YOU'RE BELIEVING IN AN ILLUSION. NOTHING MORE.
YOU SAY LIFE IS A MIRACLE?
THEN WHY DID YOU ALMOST TAKE YOUR OWN LIFE SO MANY TIMES?
YOU'RE JUST AS GUILTY OF HAVING LOST ANY SENSE OF *THE VALUE OF LIFE*.

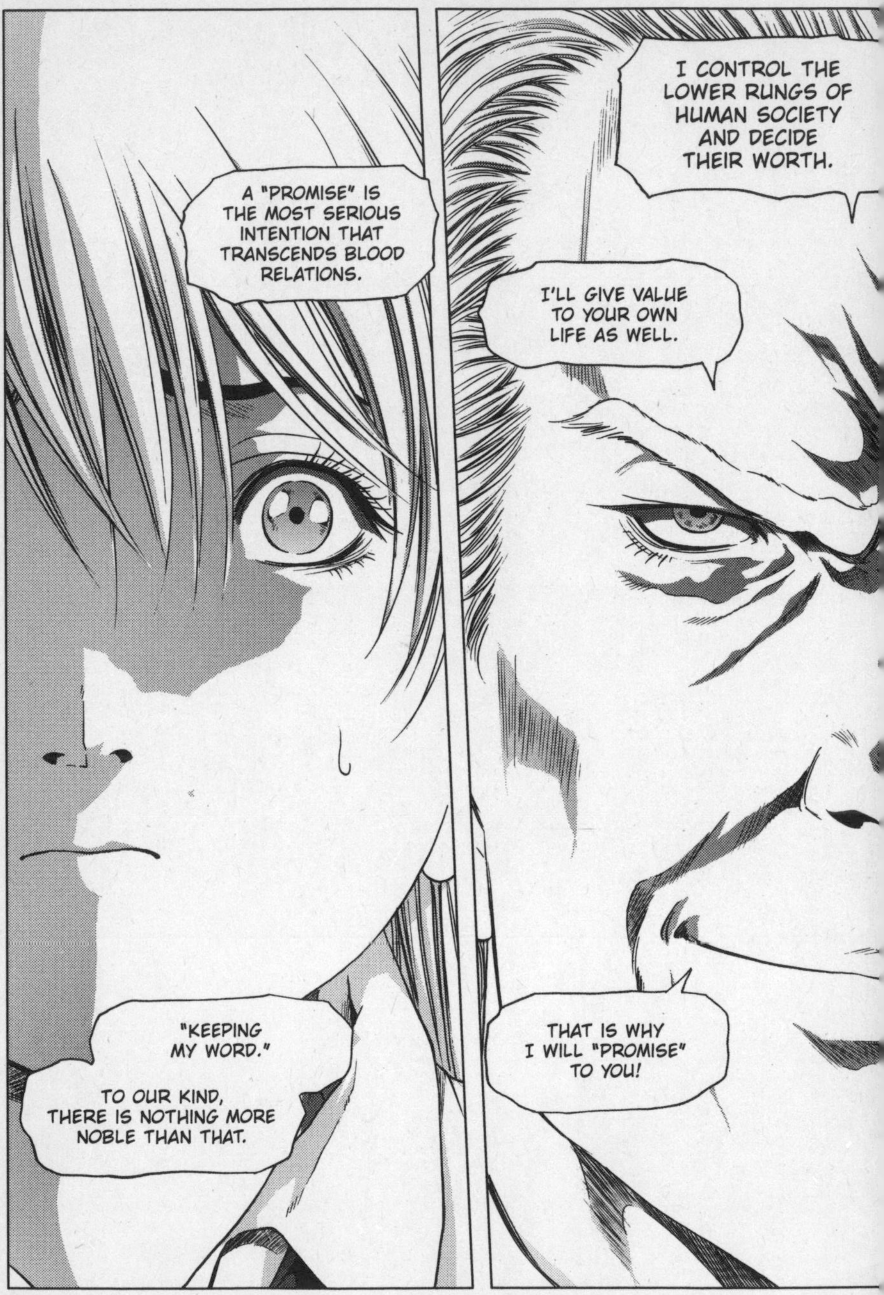
I CONTROL THE LOWER RUNGS OF HUMAN SOCIETY AND DECIDE THEIR WORTH.
I'LL GIVE VALUE TO YOUR OWN LIFE AS WELL.
THAT IS WHY I WILL "PROMISE" TO YOU!
A "PROMISE" IS THE MOST SERIOUS INTENTION THAT TRANSCENDS BLOOD RELATIONS.
"KEEPING MY WORD."
TO OUR KIND, THERE IS NOTHING MORE NOBLE THAN THAT.

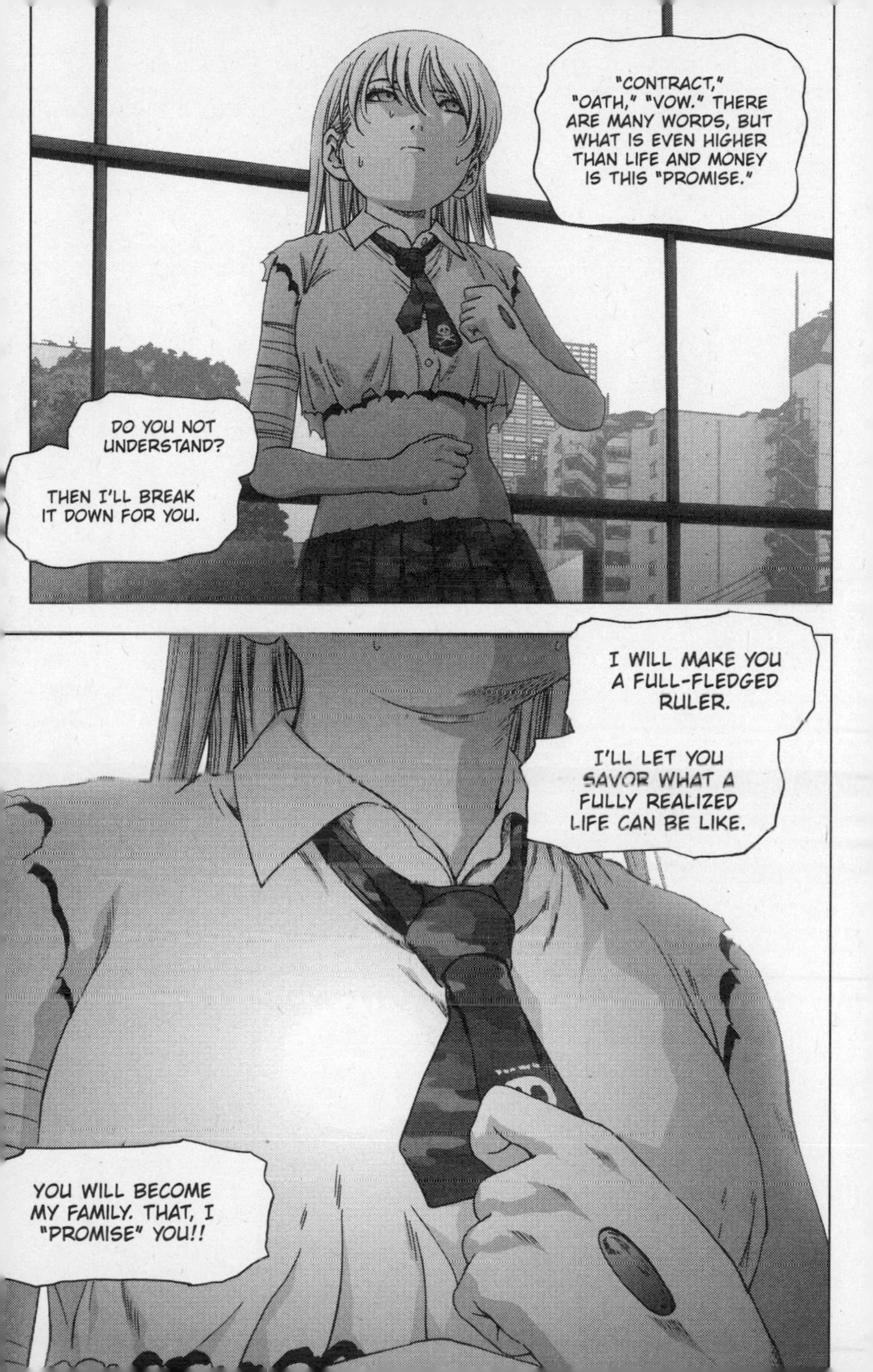
"CONTRACT," "OATH," "VOW." THERE ARE MANY WORDS, BUT WHAT IS EVEN HIGHER THAN LIFE AND MONEY IS THIS "PROMISE."
DO YOU NOT UNDERSTAND?
THEN I'LL BREAK IT DOWN FOR YOU.
I WILL MAKE YOU A FULL-FLEDGED RULER.
I'LL LET YOU SAVOR WHAT A FULLY REALIZED LIFE CAN BE LIKE.
YOU WILL BECOME MY FAMILY. THAT, I "PROMISE" YOU!!

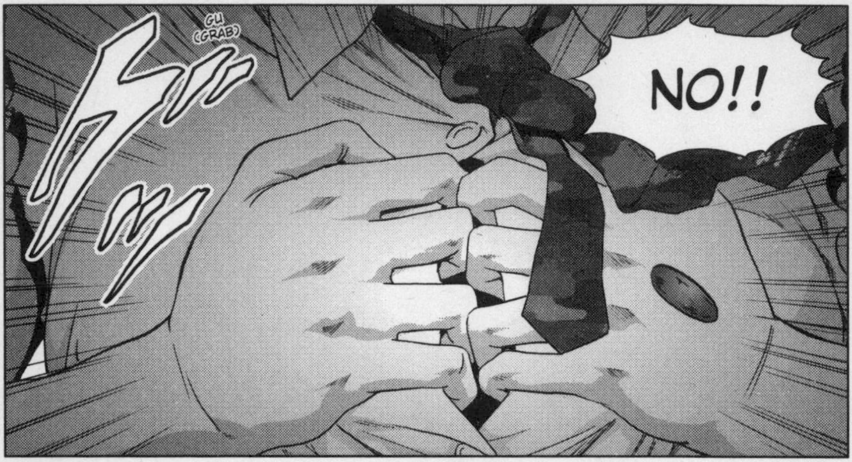
NO!!
GU (GRAB)
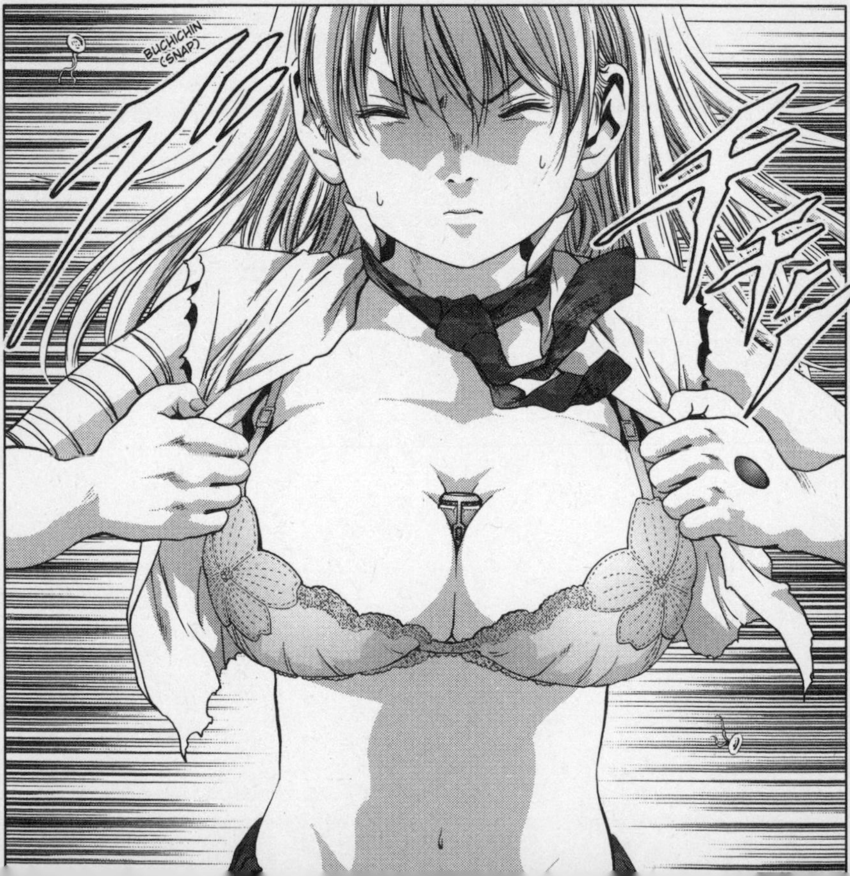
BUCHICHIN (SNAP)

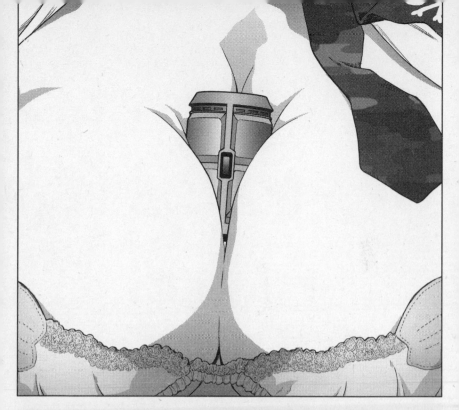

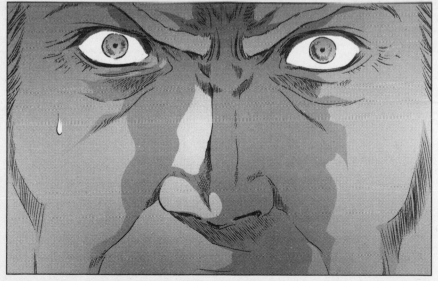

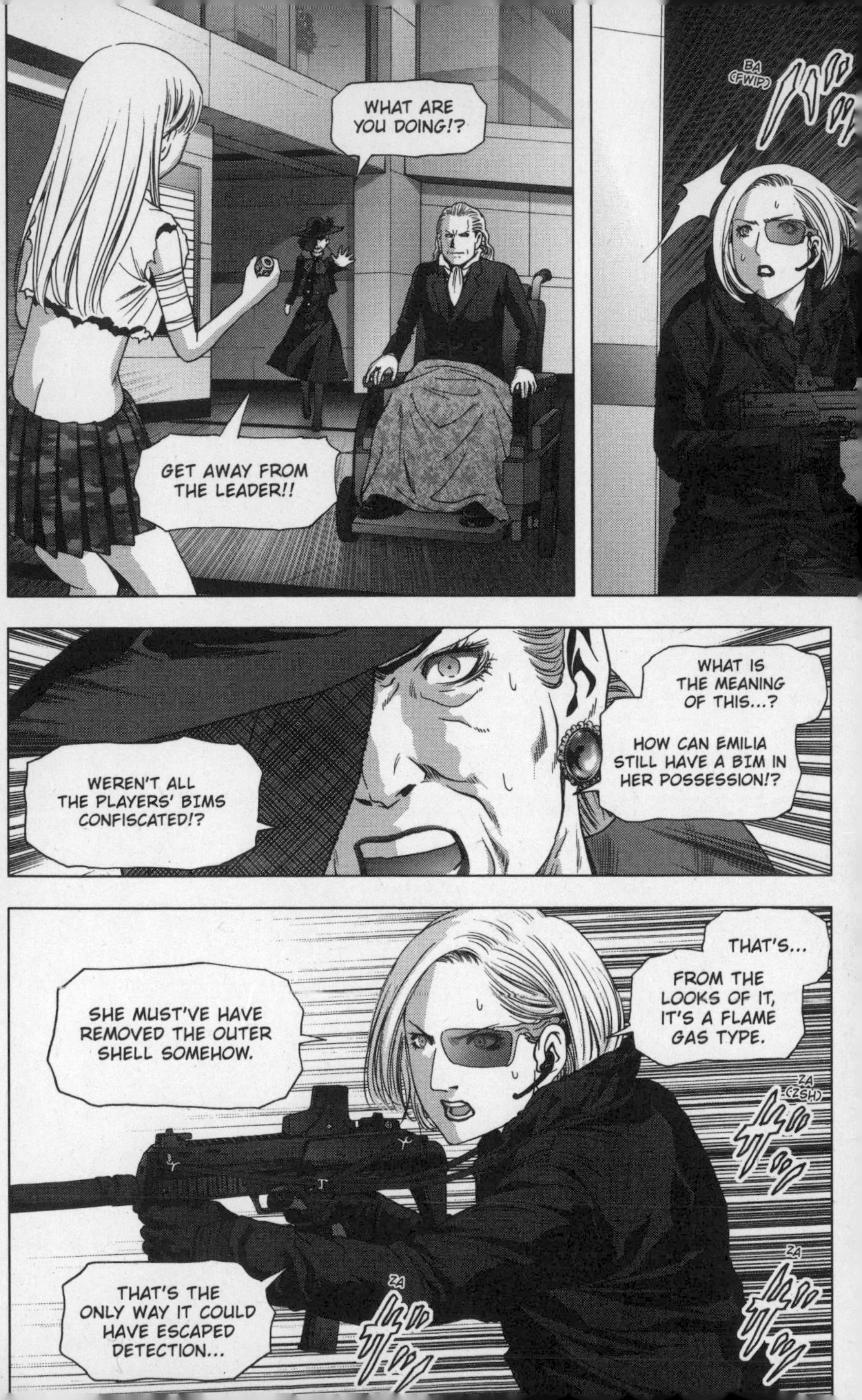
BA (FWIP)
WHAT ARE YOU DOING!?
GET AWAY FROM THE LEADER!!
WHAT IS THE MEANING OF THIS...?
HOW CAN EMILIA STILL HAVE A BIM IN HER POSSESSION!?
WEREN'T ALL THE PLAYERS' BIMS CONFISCATED!?
THAT'S...
FROM THE LOOKS OF IT, IT'S A FLAME GAS TYPE.
ZA (ZSH)
SHE MUST'VE HAVE REMOVED THE OUTER SHELL SOMEHOW.
ZA
THAT'S THE ONLY WAY IT COULD HAVE ESCAPED DETECTION...
ZA

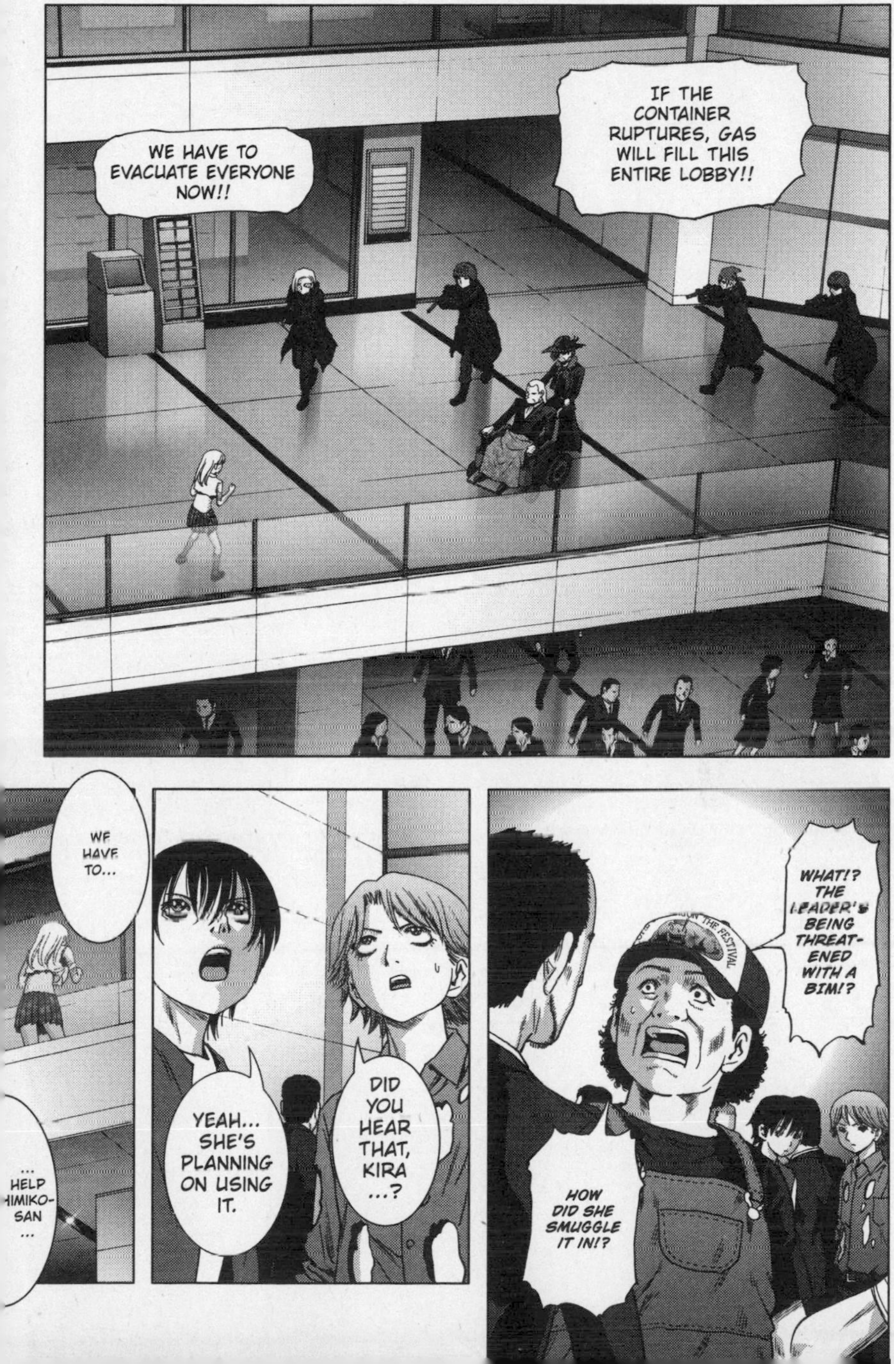
IF THE CONTAINER RUPTURES, GAS WILL FILL THIS ENTIRE LOBBY!!
WE HAVE TO EVACUATE EVERYONE NOW!!
WHAT!? THE LEADER'S BEING THREAT-ENED WITH A BIM!?
HOW DID SHE SMUGGLE IT IN!?
DID YOU HEAR THAT, KIRA ...?
YEAH... SHE'S PLANNING ON USING IT.
WE HAVE TO...
...HELP HIMIKO-SAN ...

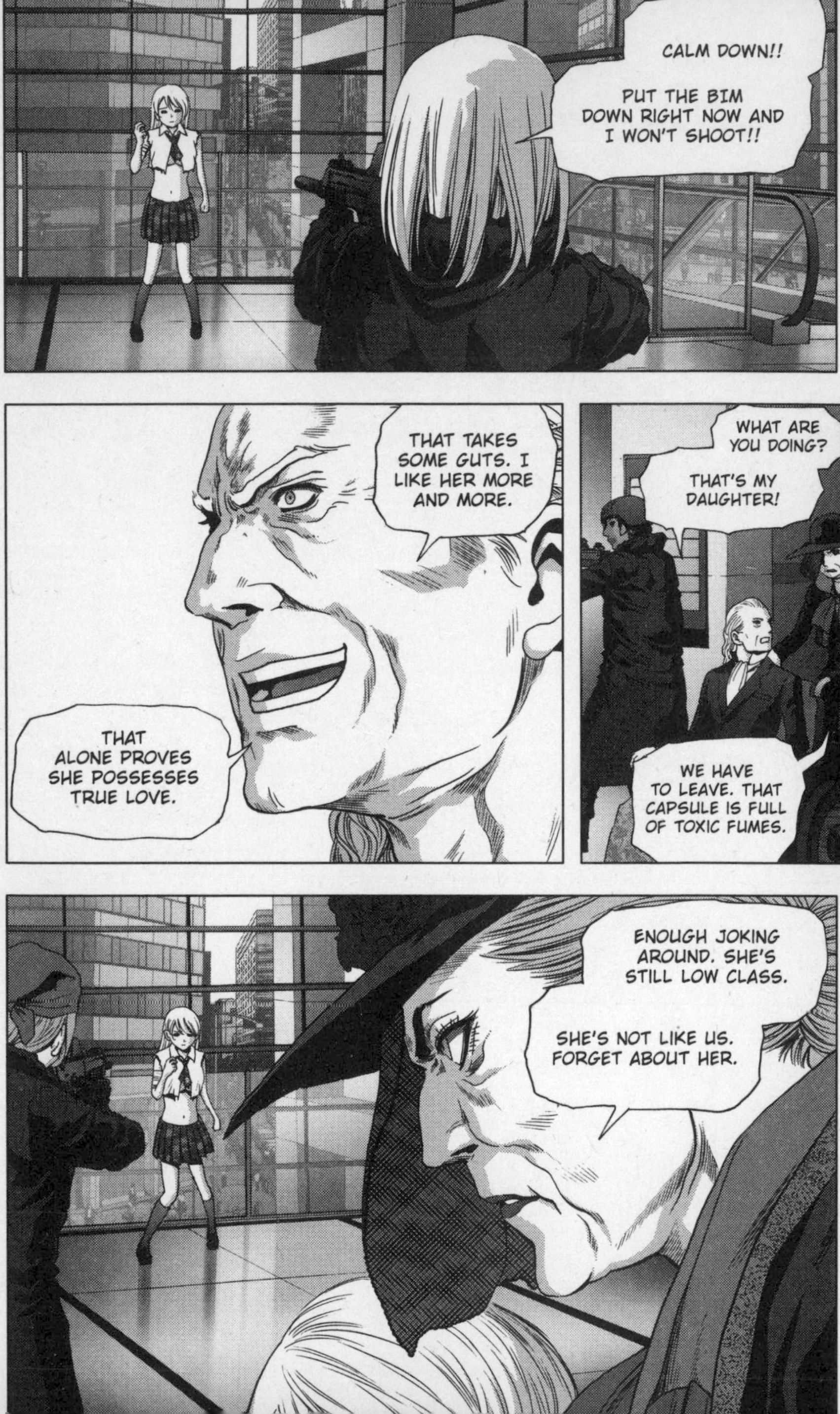
CALM DOWN!!
PUT THE BIM DOWN RIGHT NOW AND I WON'T SHOOT!!
WHAT ARE YOU DOING?
THAT'S MY DAUGHTER!
WE HAVE TO LEAVE. THAT CAPSULE IS FULL OF TOXIC FUMES.
THAT TAKES SOME GUTS. I LIKE HER MORE AND MORE.
THAT ALONE PROVES SHE POSSESSES TRUE LOVE.
ENOUGH JOKING AROUND. SHE'S STILL LOW CLASS.
SHE'S NOT LIKE US. FORGET ABOUT HER.

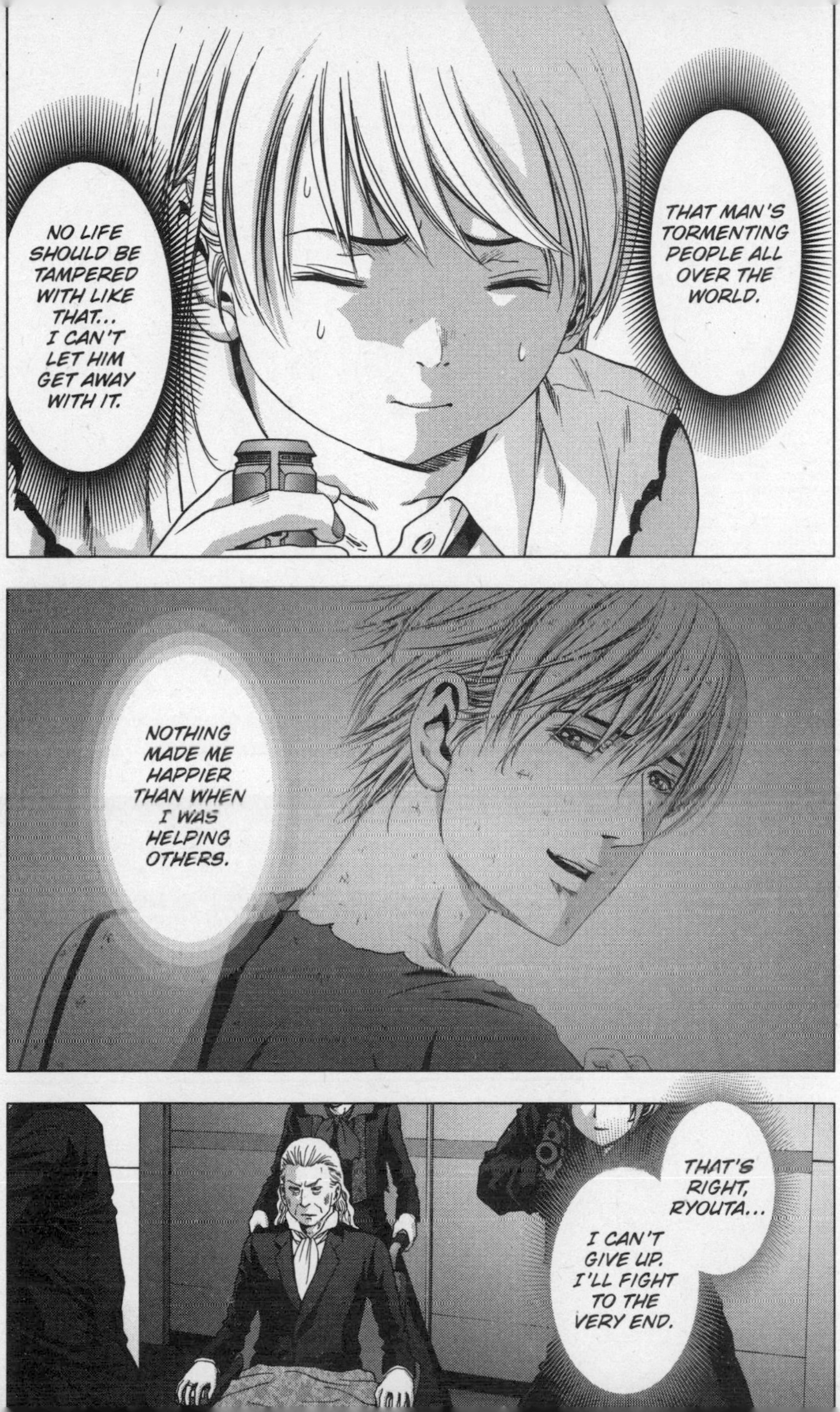
THAT MAN'S TORMENTING PEOPLE ALL OVER THE WORLD.
NO LIFE SHOULD BE TAMPERED WITH LIKE THAT... I CAN'T LET HIM GET AWAY WITH IT.
NOTHING MADE ME HAPPIER THAN WHEN I WAS HELPING OTHERS.
THAT'S RIGHT, RYOUTA...
I CAN'T GIVE UP. I'LL FIGHT TO THE VERY END.

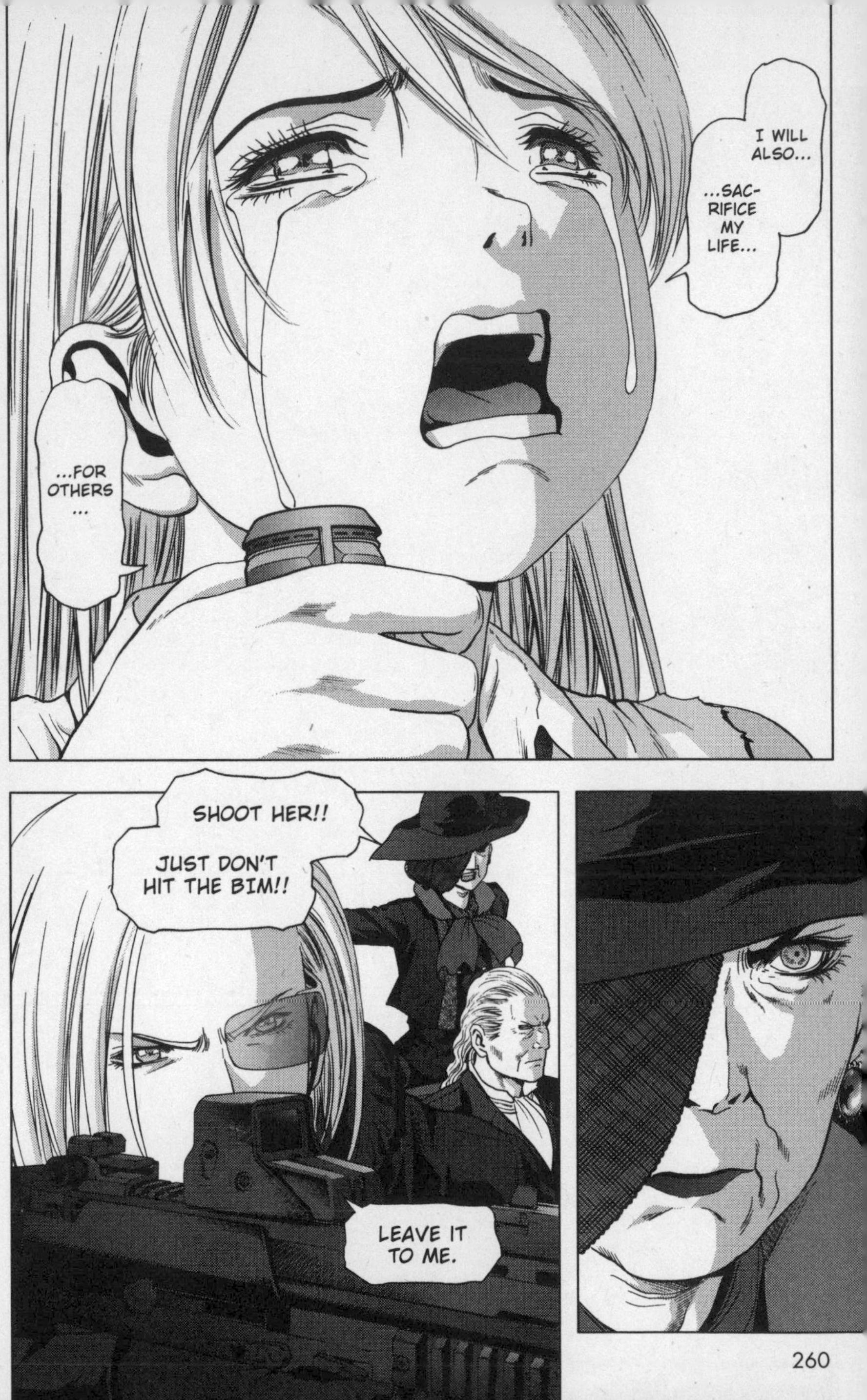
I WILL ALSO...
...SAC-RIFICE MY LIFE...
...FOR OTHERS...
SHOOT HER!! JUST DON'T HIT THE BIM!!
LEAVE IT TO ME.

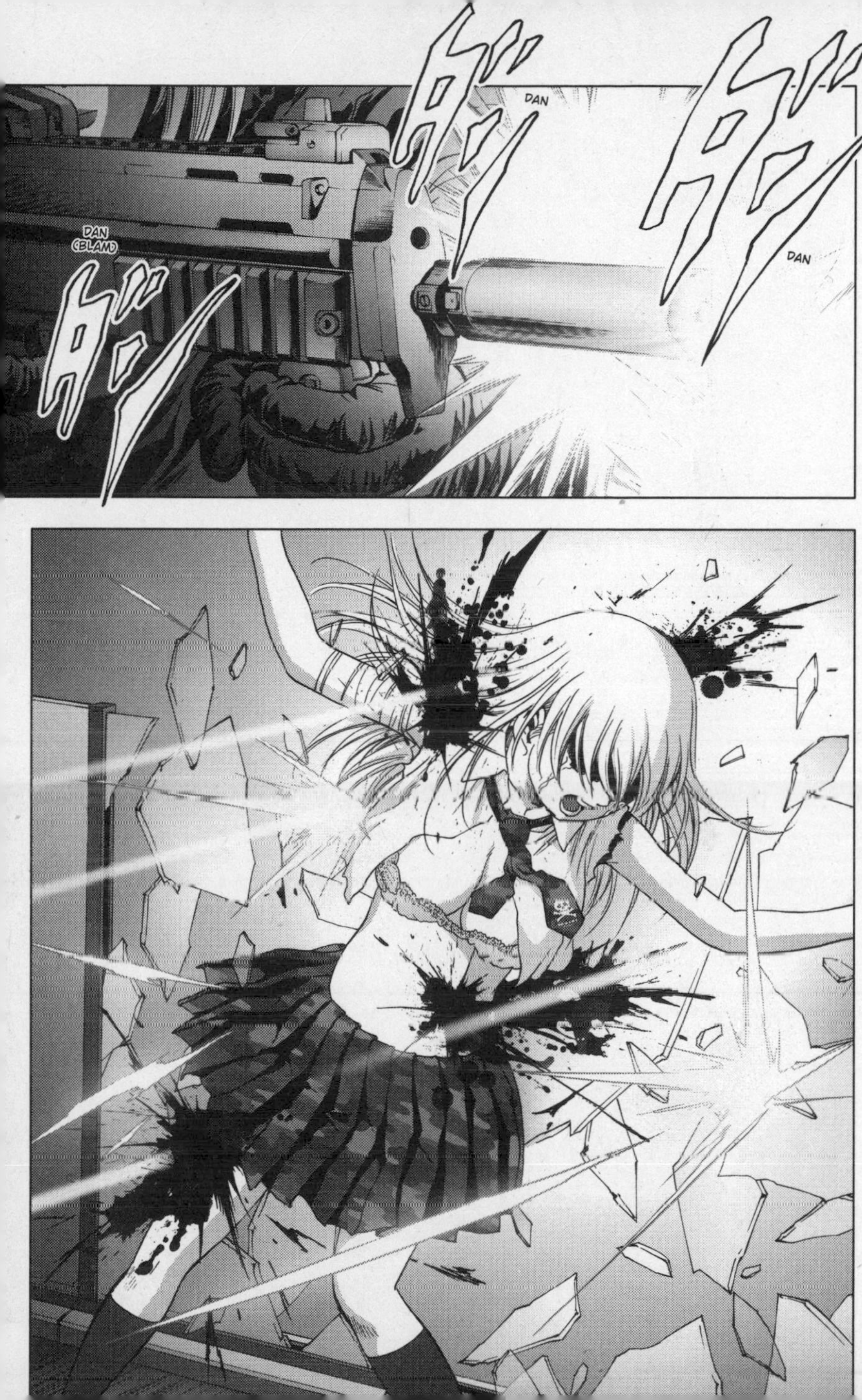
DAN
DAN
DAN
(BLAM)

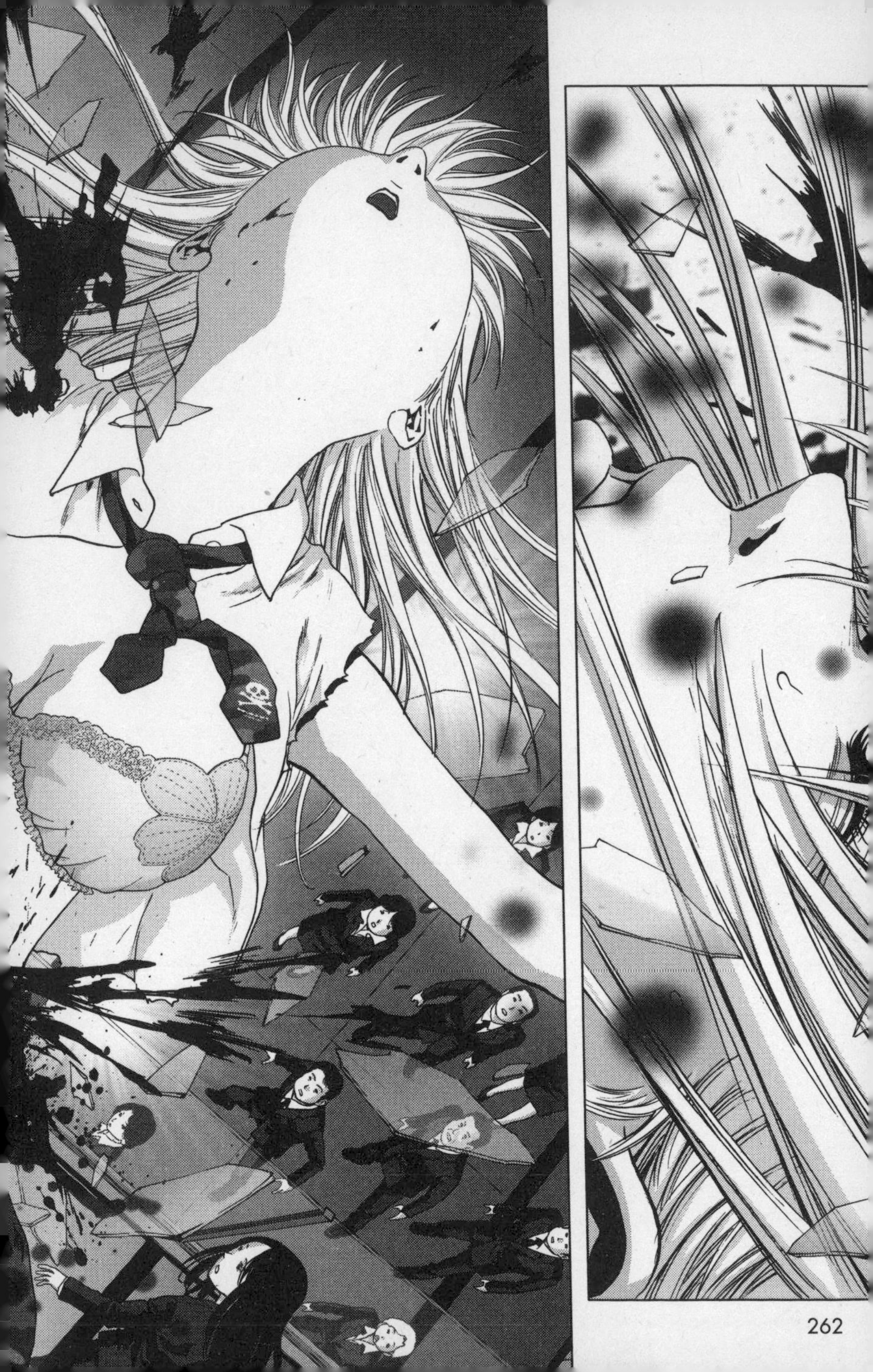

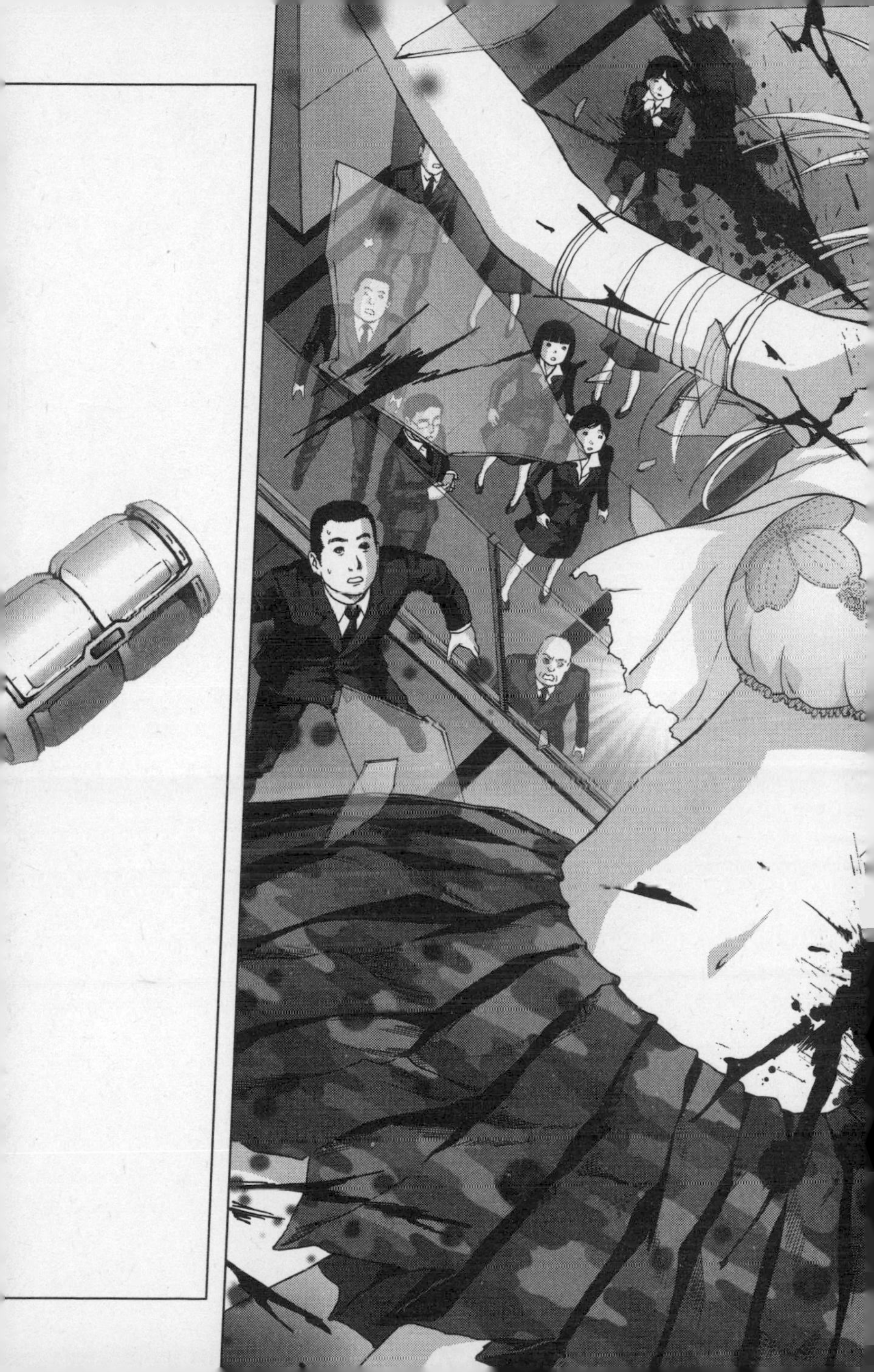

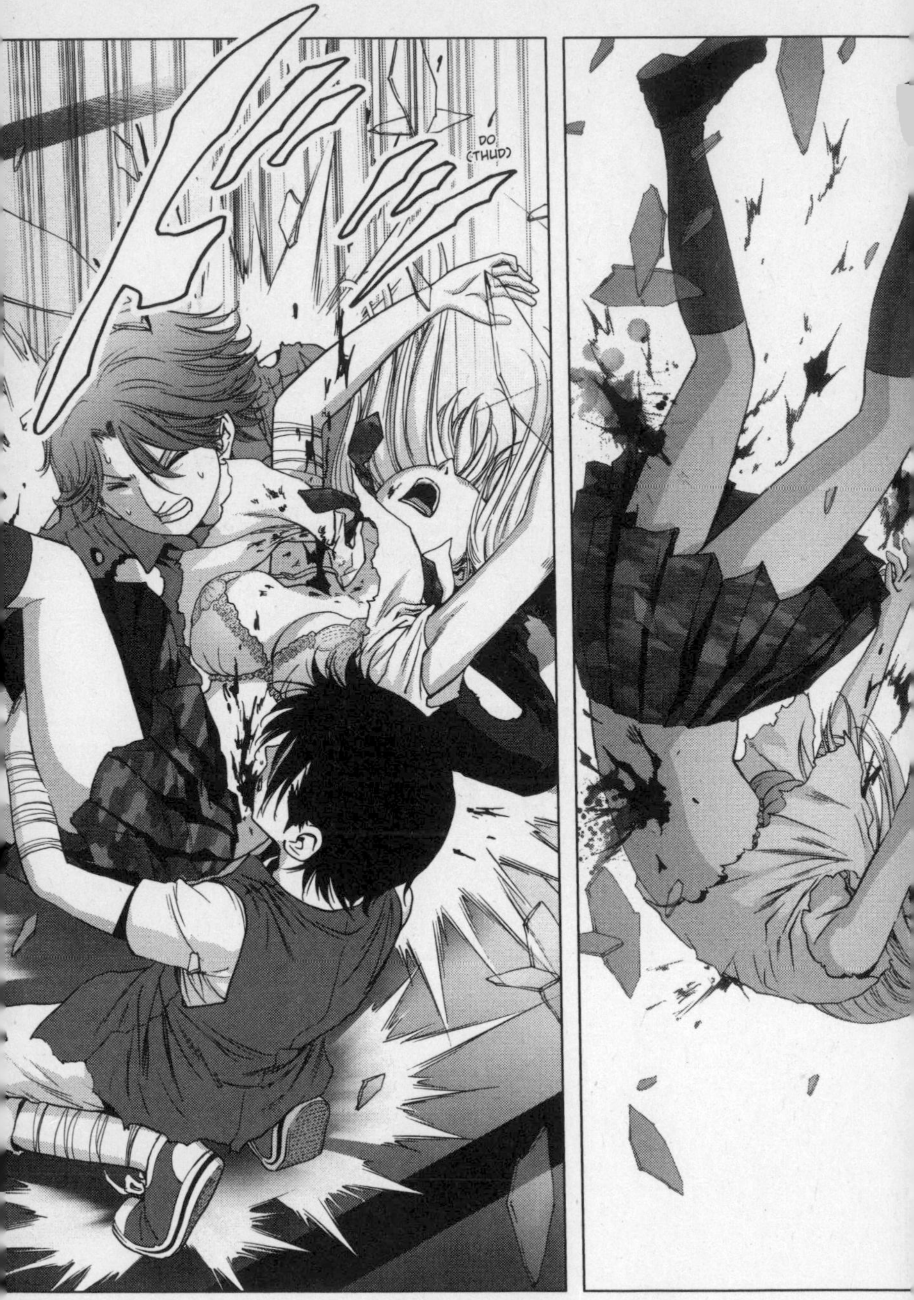
DO
(THUD)

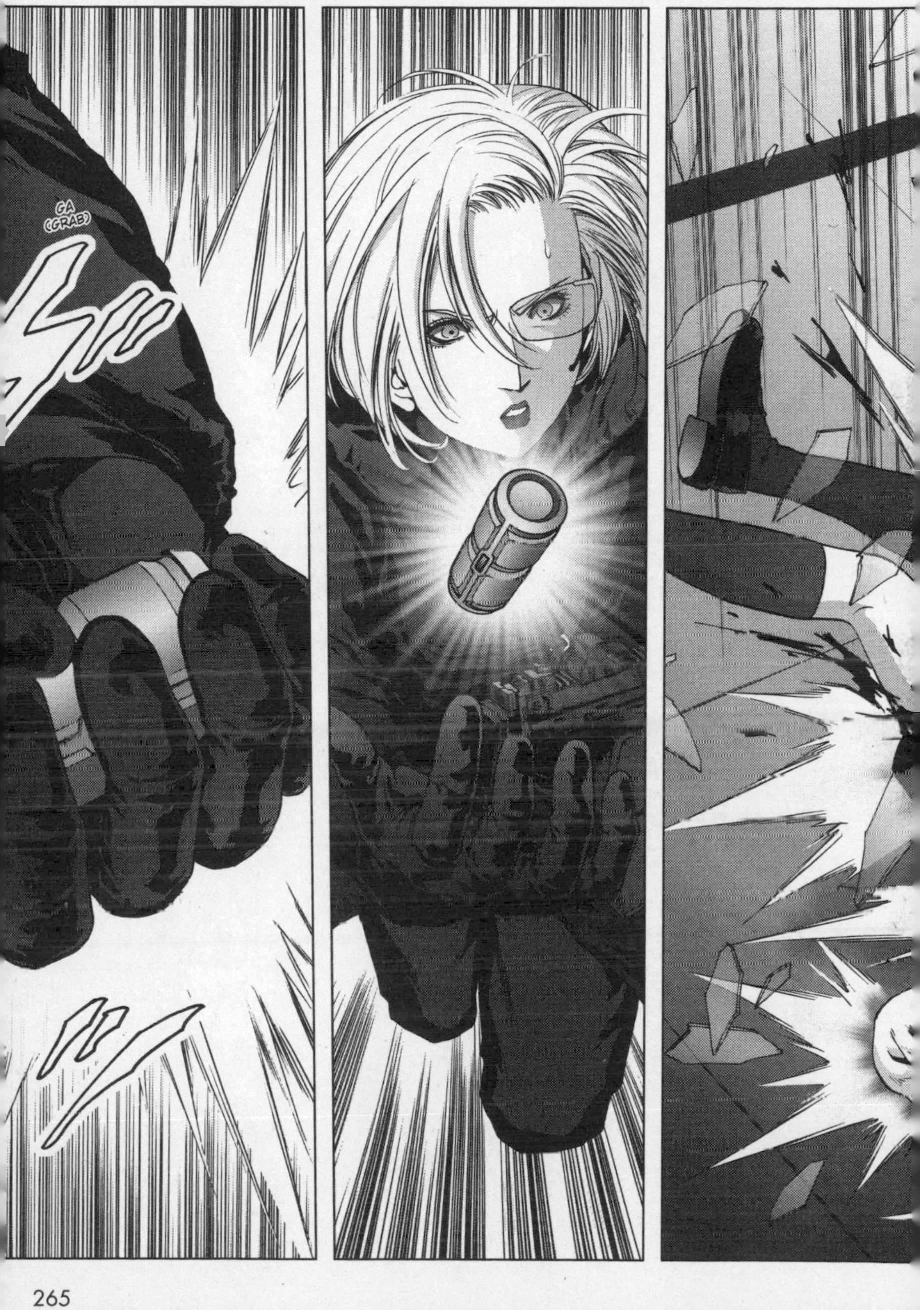
GA
(GRAB)

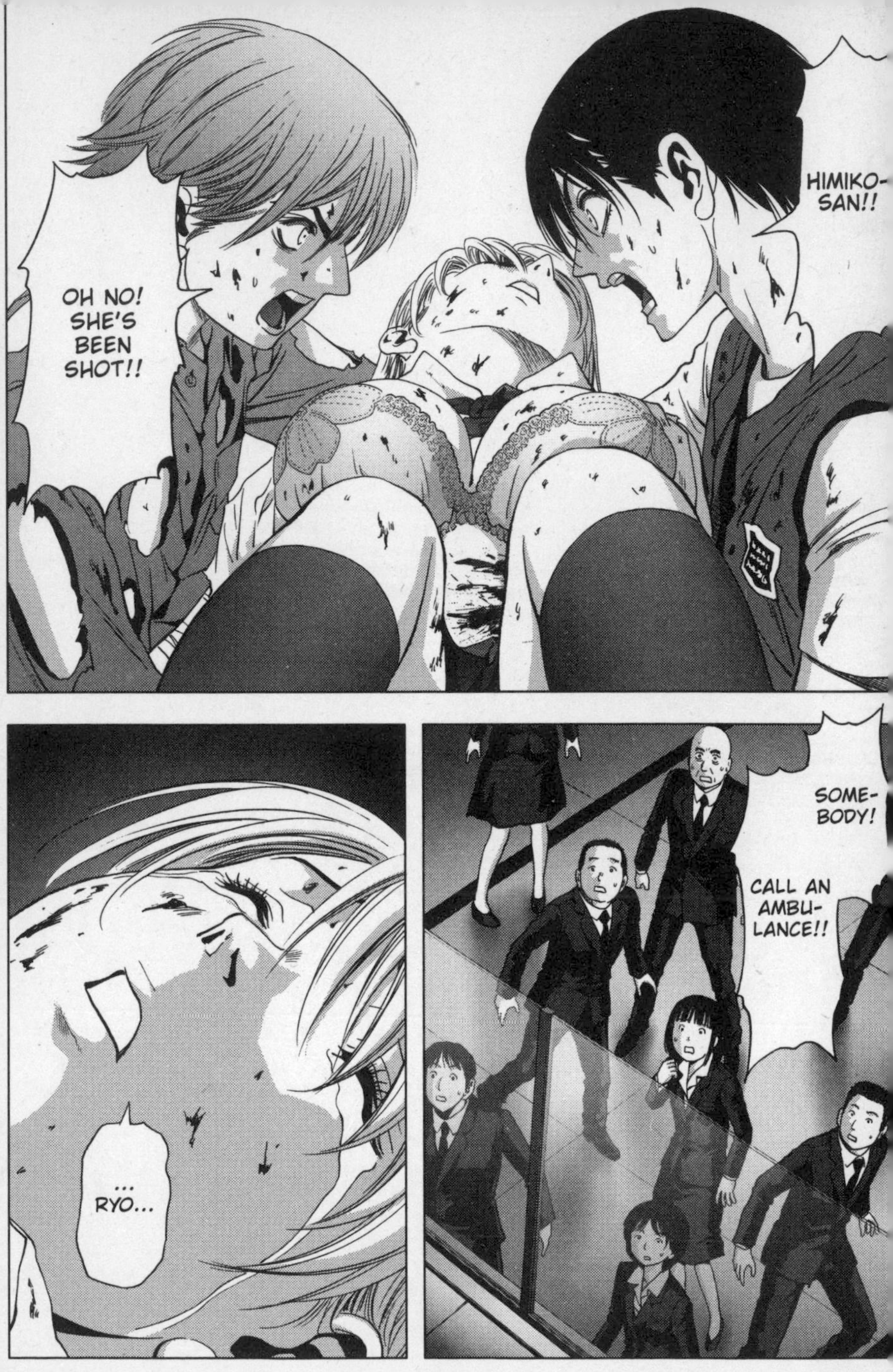
HIMIKO-SAN!!
OH NO! SHE'S BEEN SHOT!!
SOME-BODY!
CALL AN AMBU-LANCE!!
... RYO...

YOU KILLED HER...

I'M SORRY.

I SAW THAT SHE MEANT TO KILL HERSELF.

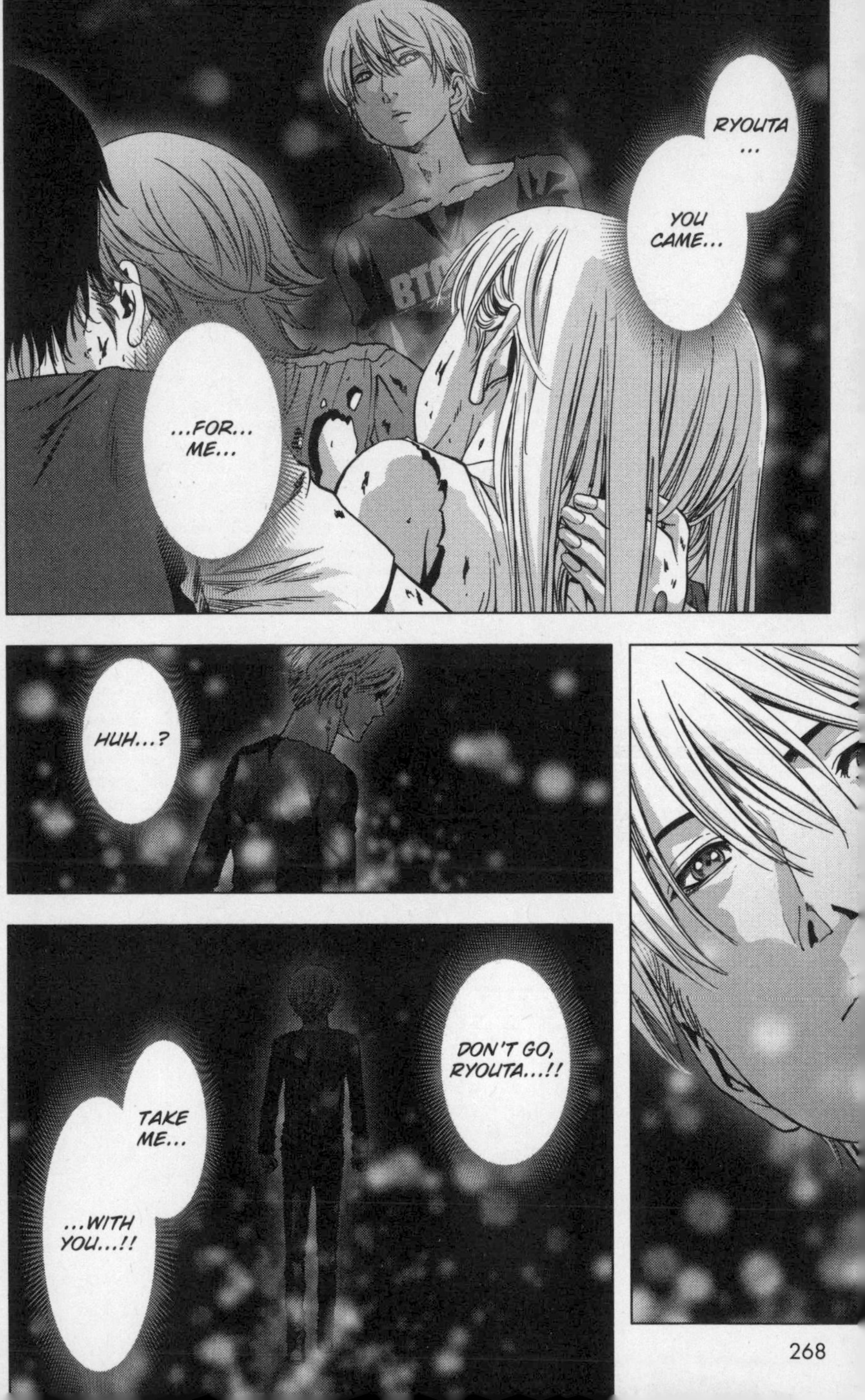
RYOUTA ...
YOU CAME...
...FOR... ME...
HUH...?
DON'T GO, RYOUTA...!!
TAKE ME...
...WITH YOU...!!

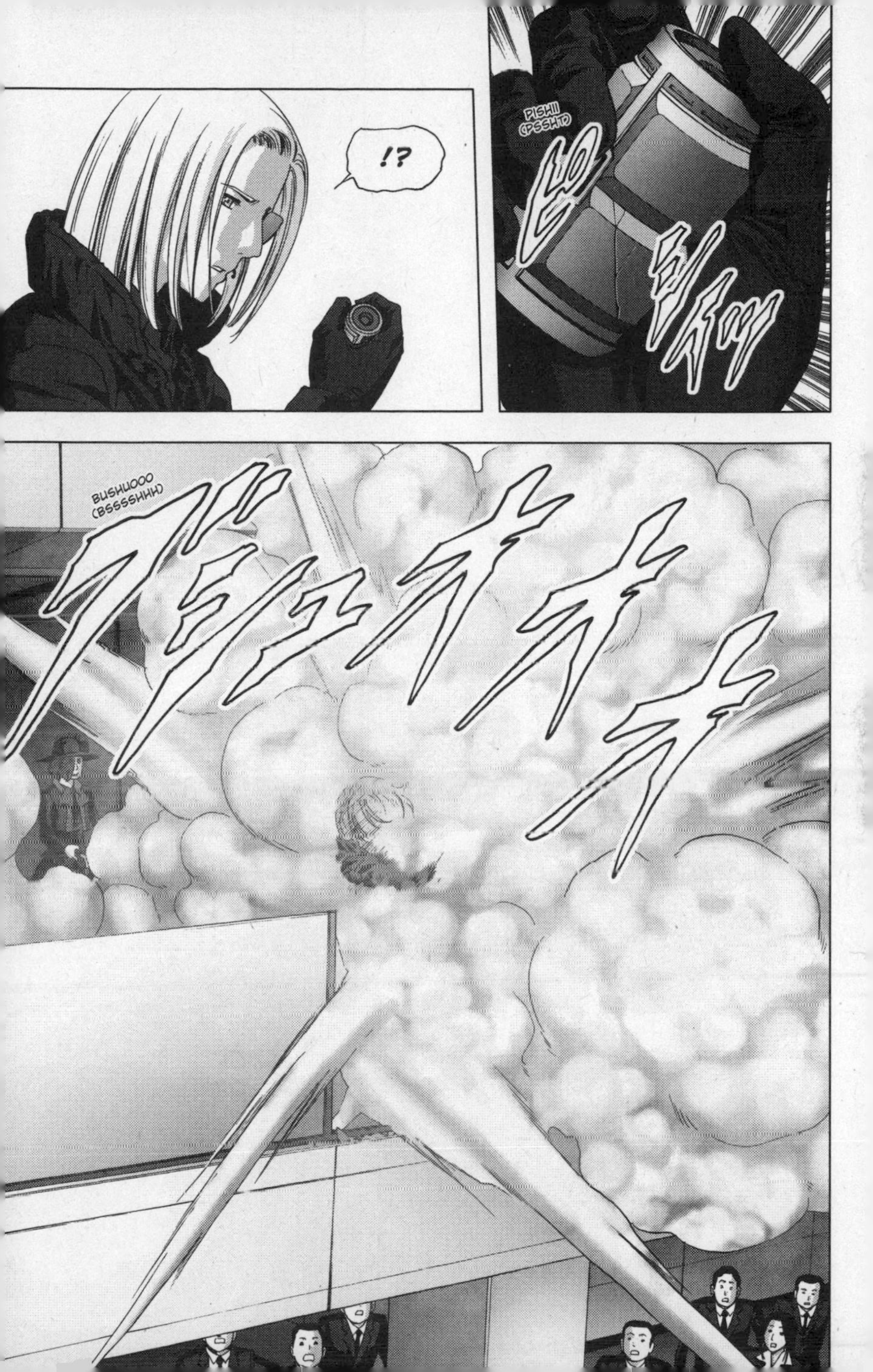
PISHII (PSSHT)
!?
BUSHUOOO (BSSSSHHH)

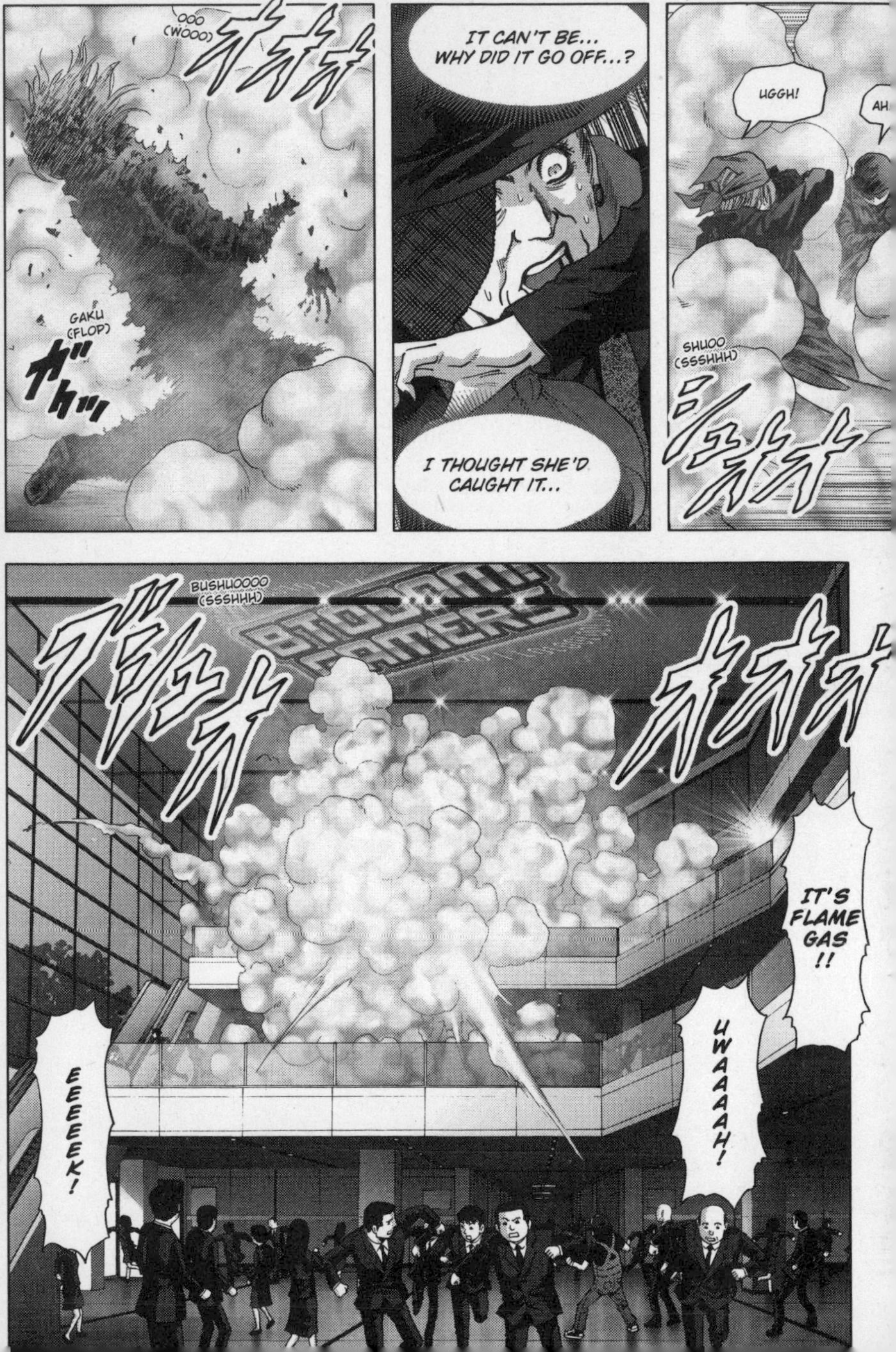
UGGH!
AH
SHUOO (SSSHHH)
IT CAN'T BE... WHY DID IT GO OFF...?
I THOUGHT SHE'D CAUGHT IT...
OOO (WOOO)
GAKU (FLOP)
BUSHUOOOO (SSSHHH)
IT'S FLAME GAS!!
UWAAAAAH!
EEEEEK!

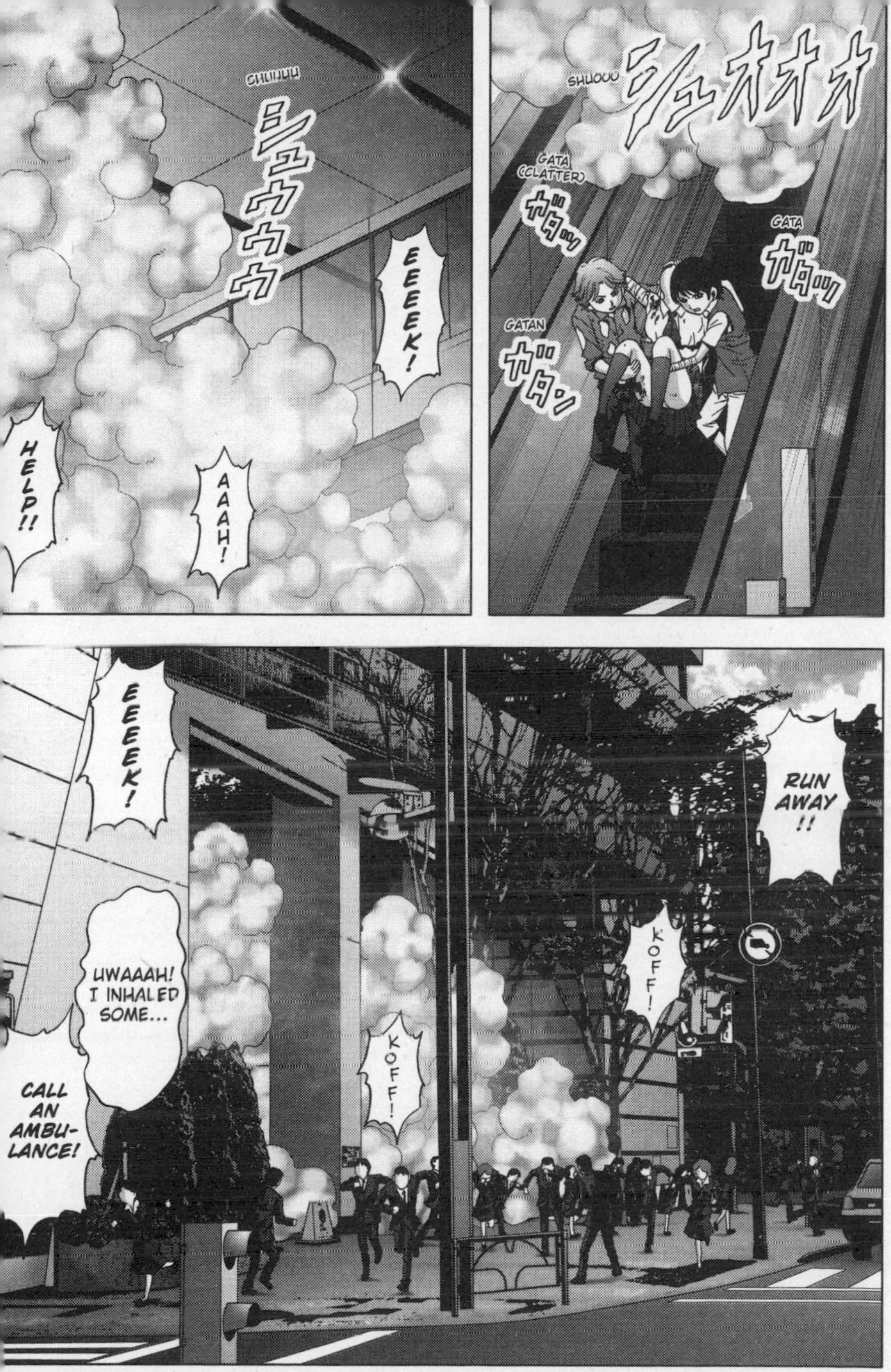
SHUOOO
シュオオオ
GATA (CLATTER)
ガタッ
GATA
ガタッ
GATAN
ガタン
SHUUUU
シュウウウ
EEEEK!
AAAAH!
HELP!!
RUN AWAY!!
KOFF!
KOFF!
EEEEK!
UWAAAH! I INHALED SOME...
CALL AN AMBULANCE!

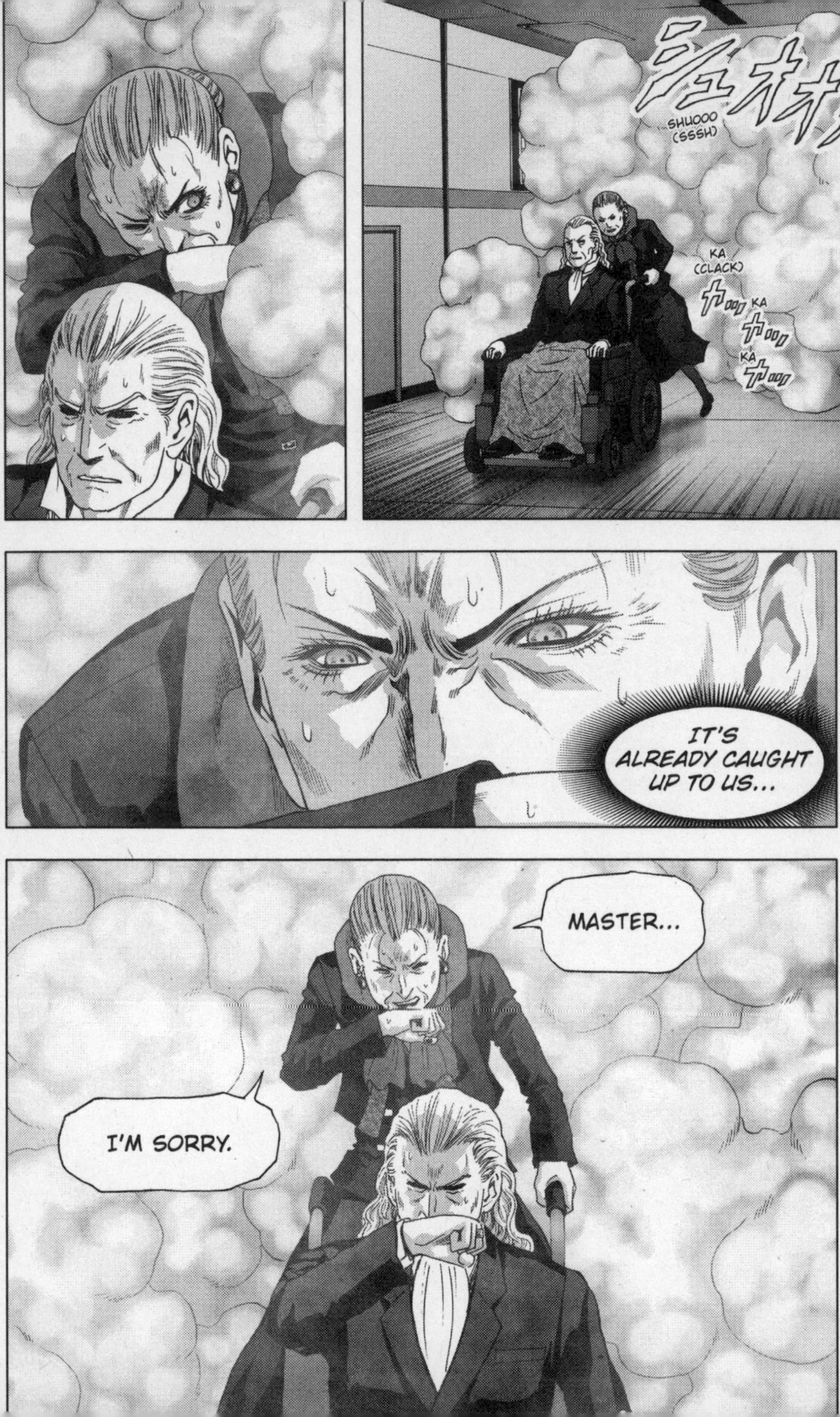
SHUOOO (SSSH)
KA (CLACK)
KA
KA
IT'S ALREADY CAUGHT UP TO US...
MASTER...
I'M SORRY.

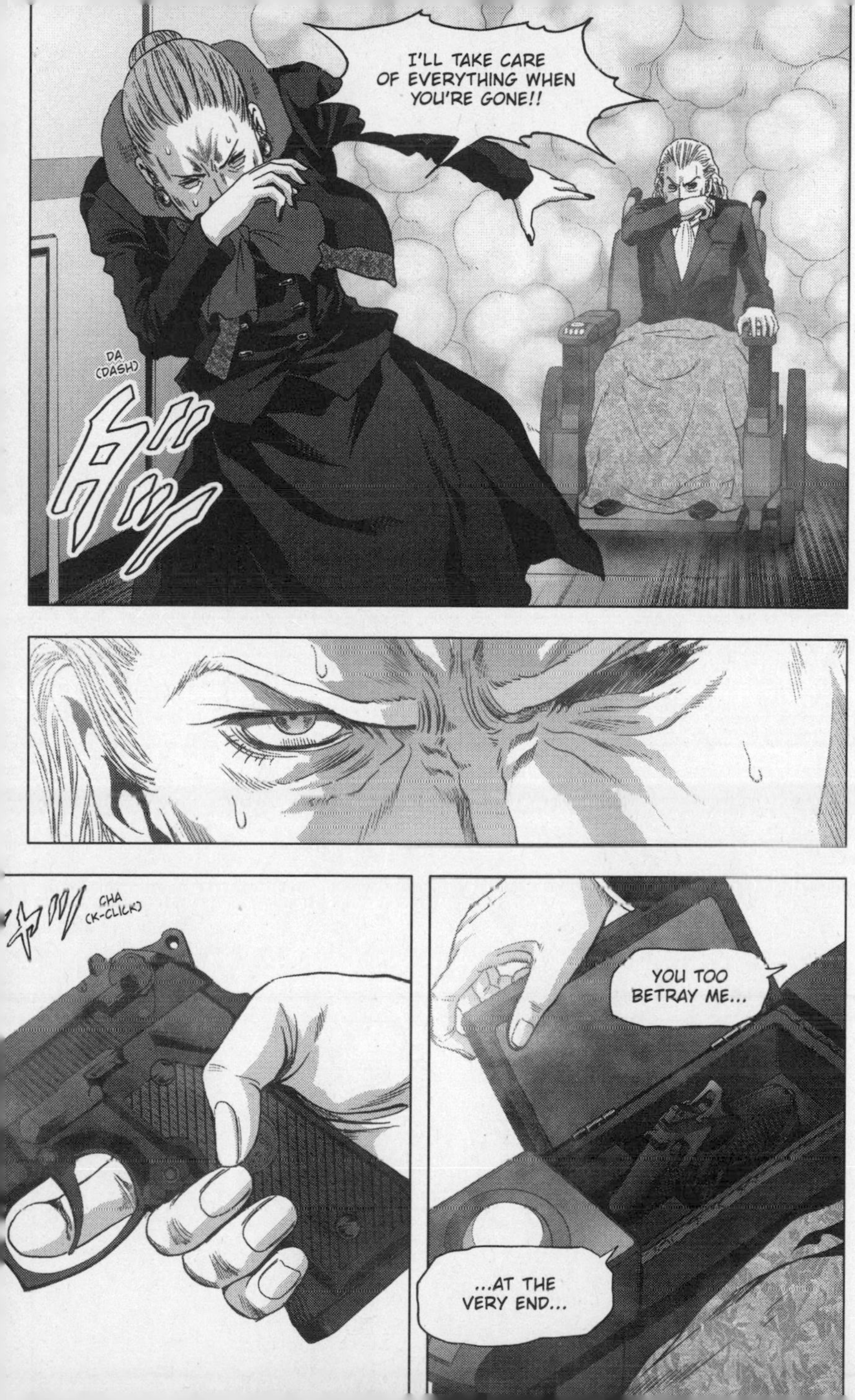
I'LL TAKE CARE OF EVERYTHING WHEN YOU'RE GONE!!
DA (DASH)
YOU TOO BETRAY ME...
...AT THE VERY END...
CHA (K-CLICK)

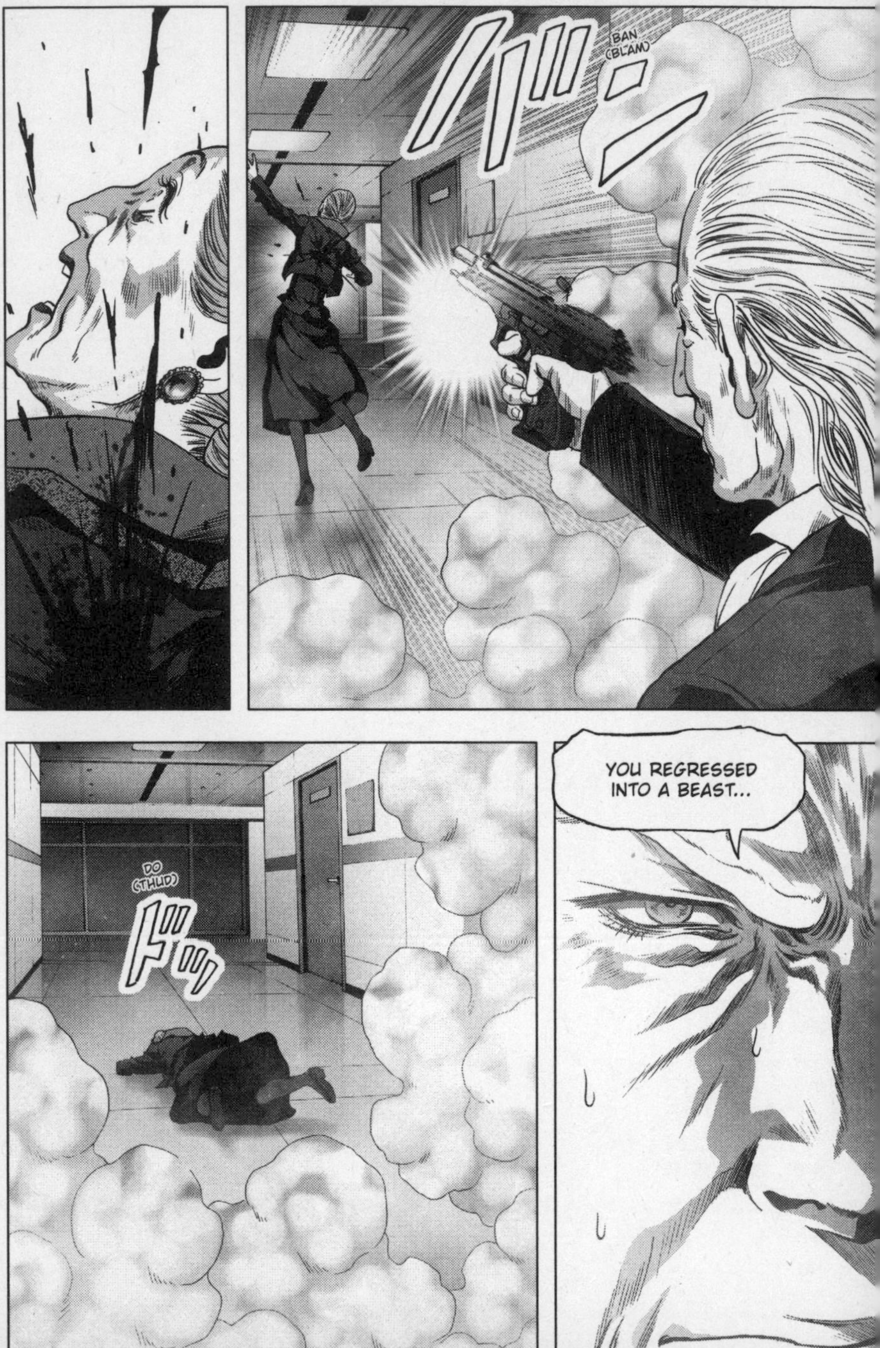
BAN
(BLAM)
DO
(THUD)
YOU REGRESSED INTO A BEAST...

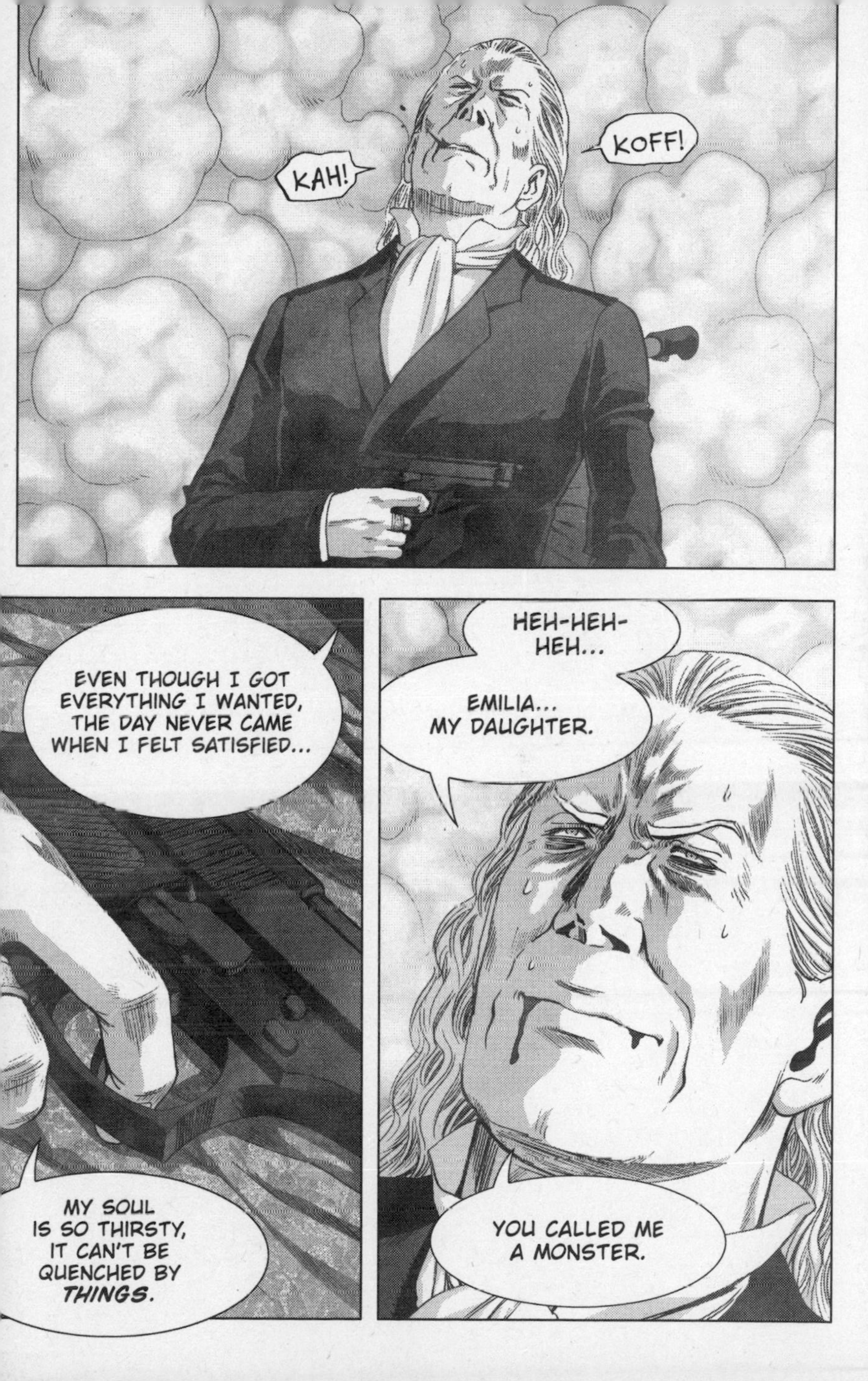
KOFF!
KAH!
HEH-HEH-HEH...
EMILIA... MY DAUGHTER.
YOU CALLED ME A MONSTER.
EVEN THOUGH I GOT EVERYTHING I WANTED, THE DAY NEVER CAME WHEN I FELT SATISFIED...
MY SOUL IS SO THIRSTY, IT CAN'T BE QUENCHED BY *THINGS*.

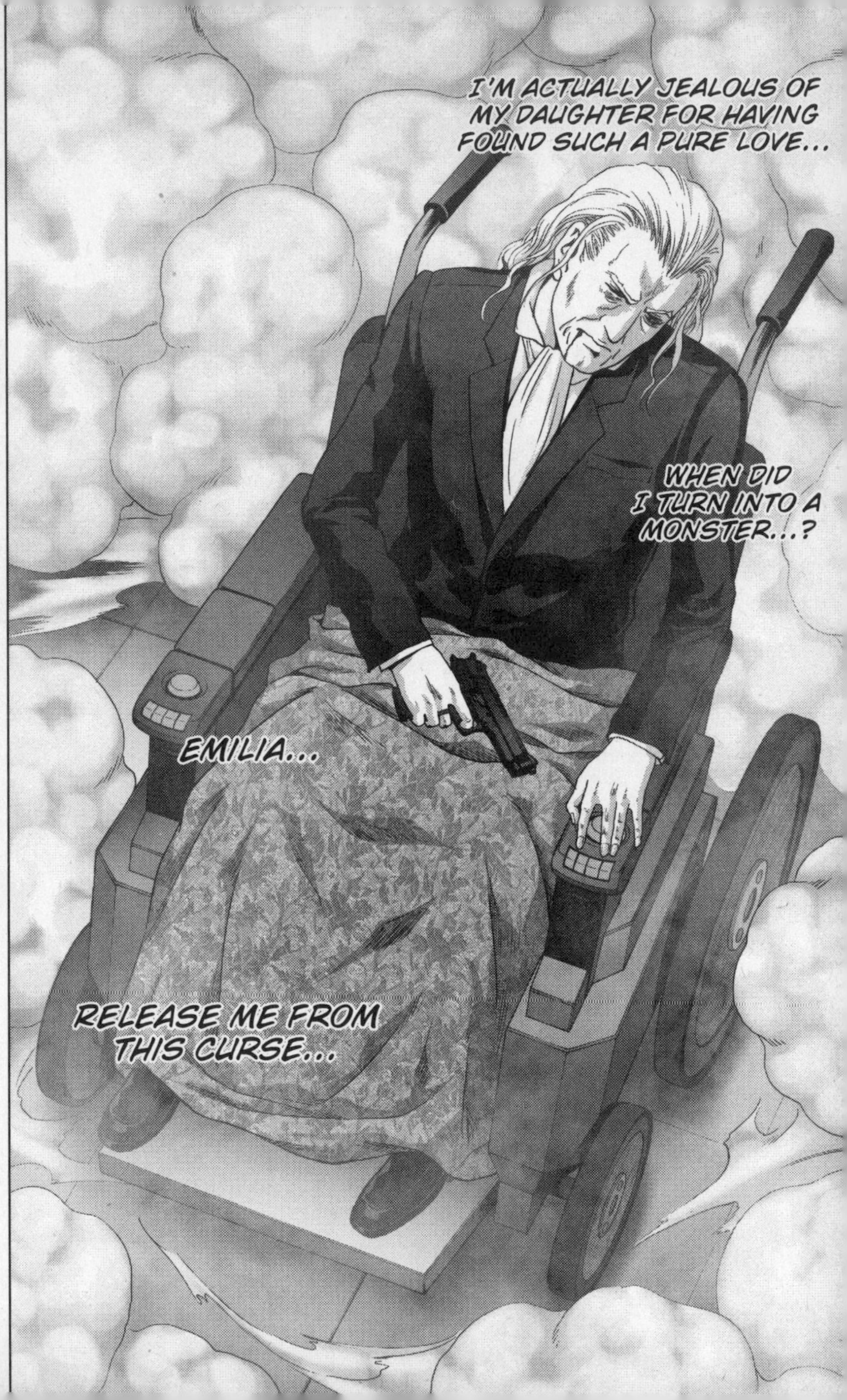
I'M ACTUALLY JEALOUS OF MY DAUGHTER FOR HAVING FOUND SUCH A PURE LOVE...
WHEN DID I TURN INTO A MONSTER...?
EMILIA...
RELEASE ME FROM THIS CURSE...

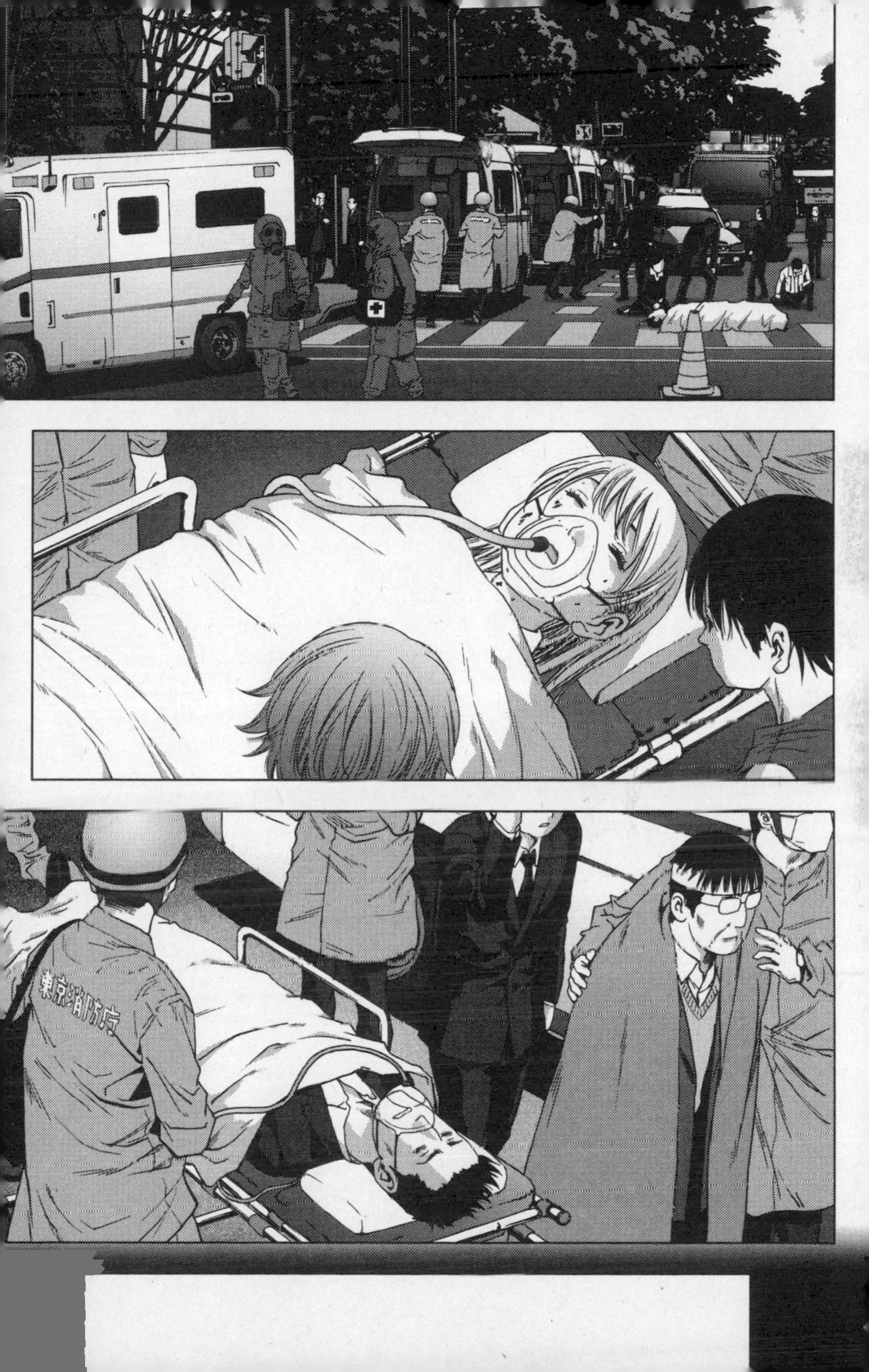
東京消防庁

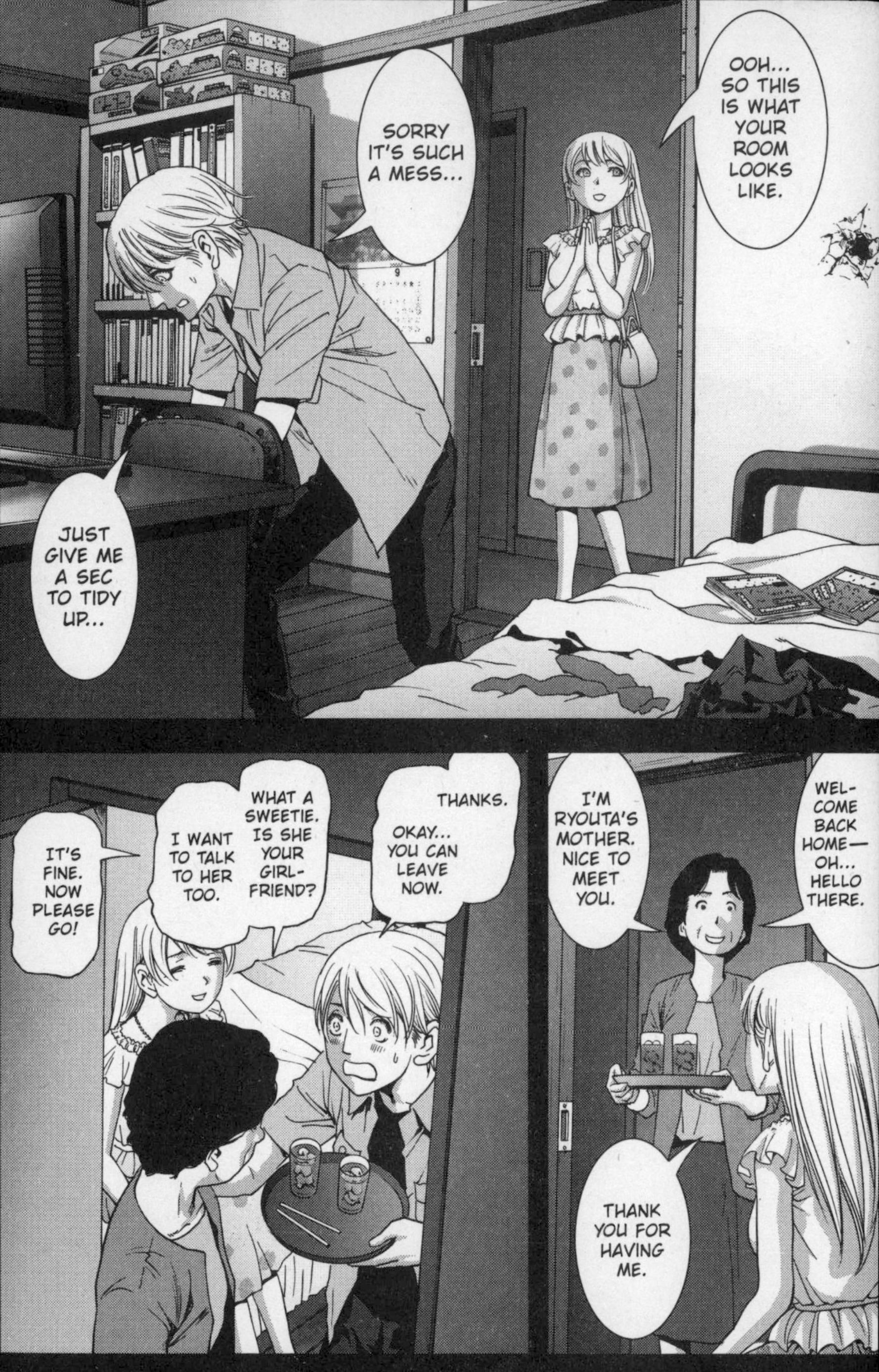
OOH... SO THIS IS WHAT YOUR ROOM LOOKS LIKE.
SORRY IT'S SUCH A MESS...
JUST GIVE ME A SEC TO TIDY UP...
WEL-COME BACK HOME—OH... HELLO THERE.
I'M RYOUTA'S MOTHER. NICE TO MEET YOU.
THANK YOU FOR HAVING ME.
THANKS.
OKAY... YOU CAN LEAVE NOW.
WHAT A SWEETIE. IS SHE YOUR GIRL-FRIEND?
I WANT TO TALK TO HER TOO.
IT'S FINE. NOW PLEASE GO!

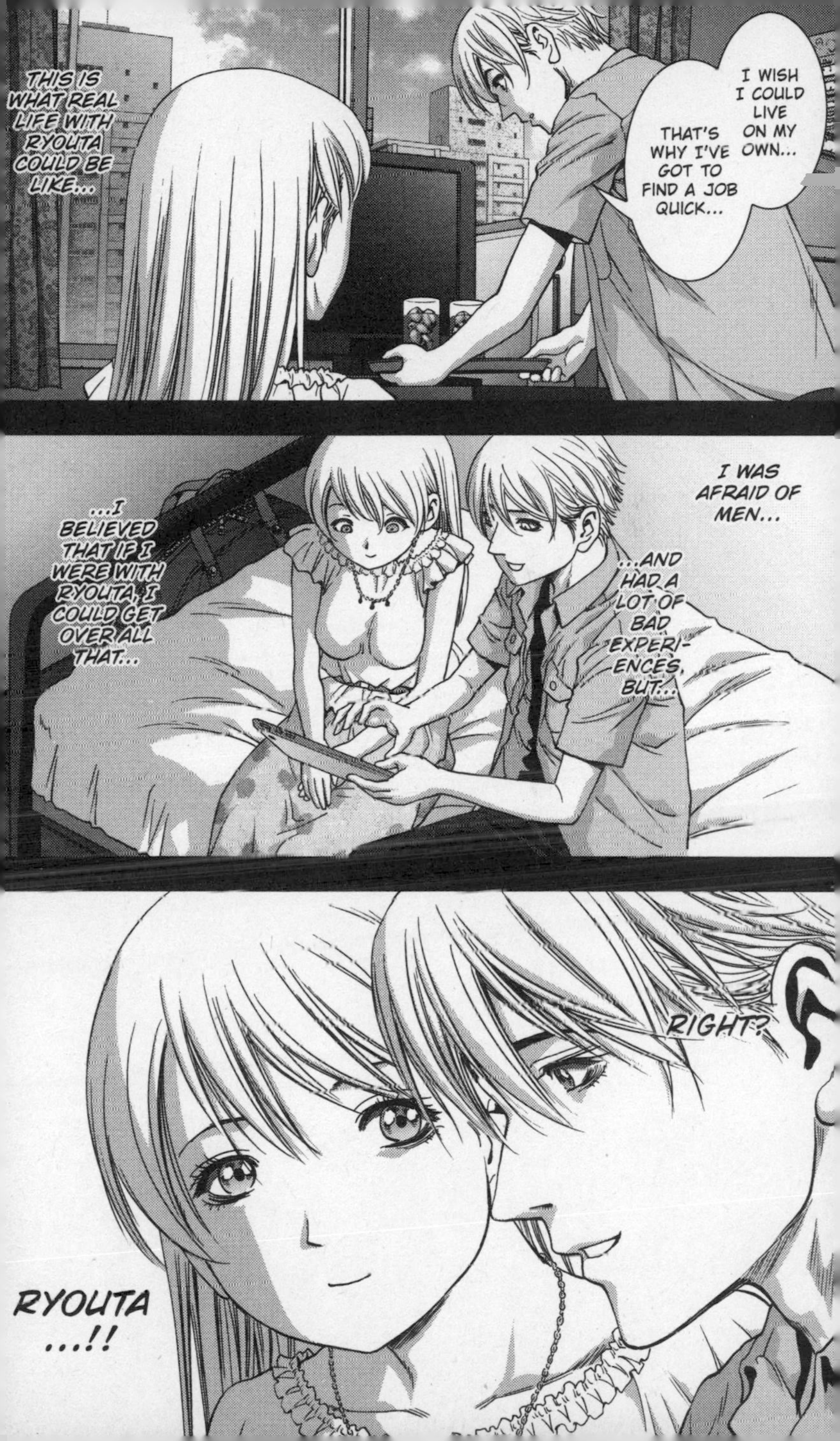
I WISH I COULD LIVE ON MY OWN...
THAT'S WHY I'VE GOT TO FIND A JOB QUICK...
THIS IS WHAT REAL LIFE WITH RYOUTA COULD BE LIKE...
I WAS AFRAID OF MEN...
...AND HAD A LOT OF BAD EXPERI-ENCES, BUT...
...I BELIEVED THAT IF I WERE WITH RYOUTA, I COULD GET OVER ALL THAT...
RIGHT?
RYOUTA ...!!

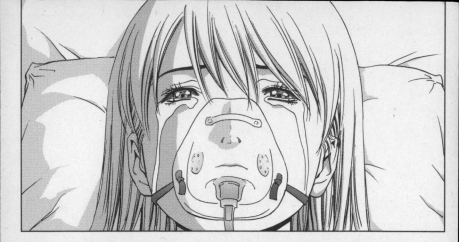

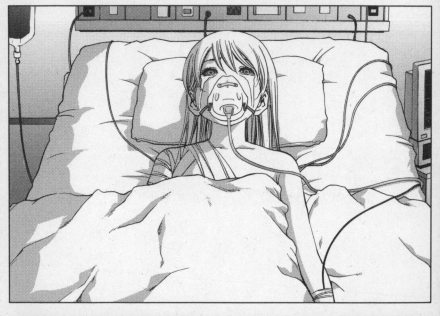

WHY DIDN'T YOU TAKE ME WITH YOU...?

TELL ME...

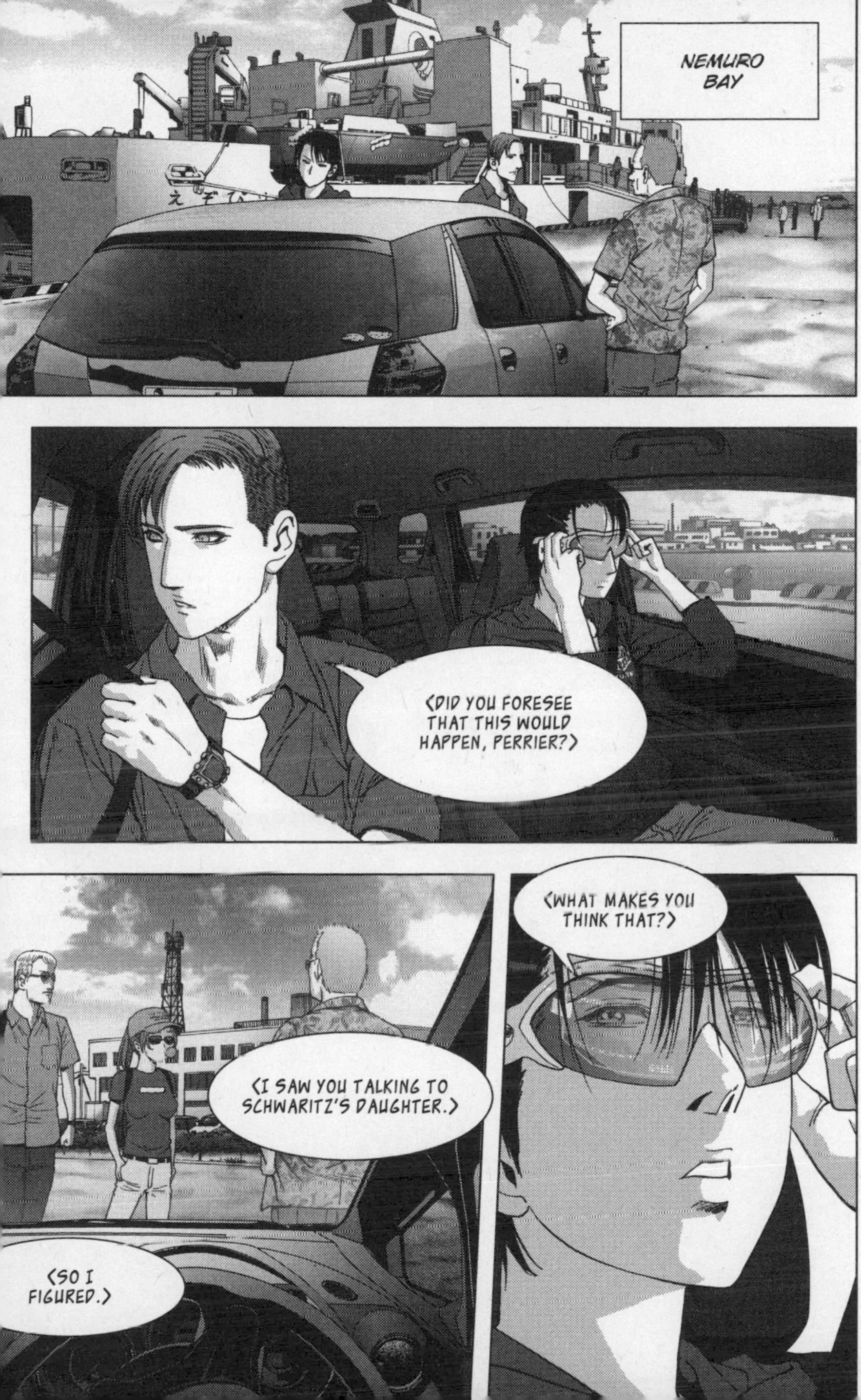
NEMURO BAY
<DID YOU FORESEE THAT THIS WOULD HAPPEN, PERRIER?>
<WHAT MAKES YOU THINK THAT?>
<I SAW YOU TALKING TO SCHWARITZ'S DAUGHTER.>
<SO I FIGURED.>

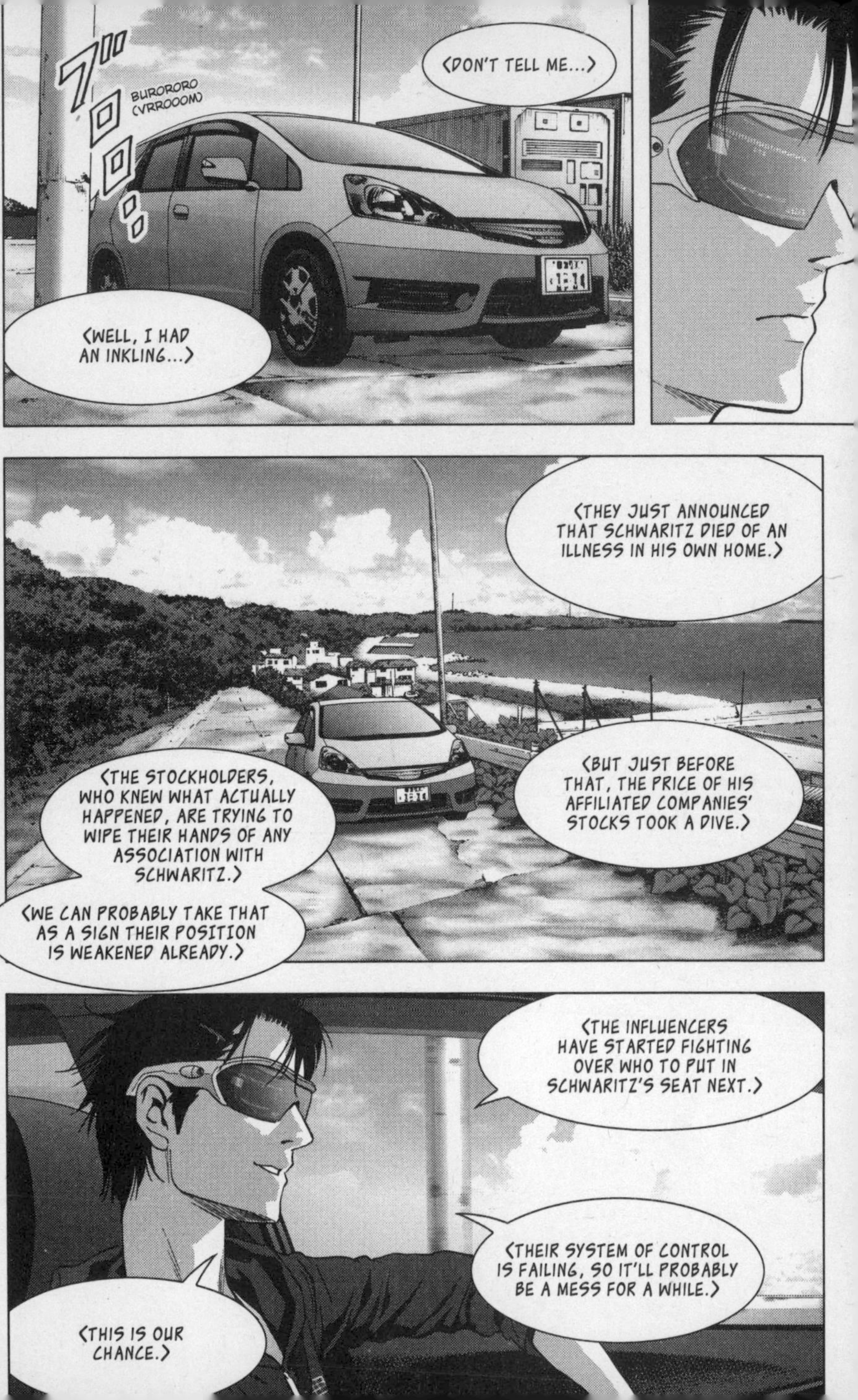
<DON'T TELL ME...>
BURORORO (VRROOOM)
<WELL, I HAD AN INKLING...>
<THEY JUST ANNOUNCED THAT SCHWARITZ DIED OF AN ILLNESS IN HIS OWN HOME.>
<BUT JUST BEFORE THAT, THE PRICE OF HIS AFFILIATED COMPANIES' STOCKS TOOK A DIVE.>
<THE STOCKHOLDERS, WHO KNEW WHAT ACTUALLY HAPPENED, ARE TRYING TO WIPE THEIR HANDS OF ANY ASSOCIATION WITH SCHWARITZ.>
<WE CAN PROBABLY TAKE THAT AS A SIGN THEIR POSITION IS WEAKENED ALREADY.>
<THE INFLUENCERS HAVE STARTED FIGHTING OVER WHO TO PUT IN SCHWARITZ'S SEAT NEXT.>
<THEIR SYSTEM OF CONTROL IS FAILING, SO IT'LL PROBABLY BE A MESS FOR A WHILE.>
<THIS IS OUR CHANCE.>

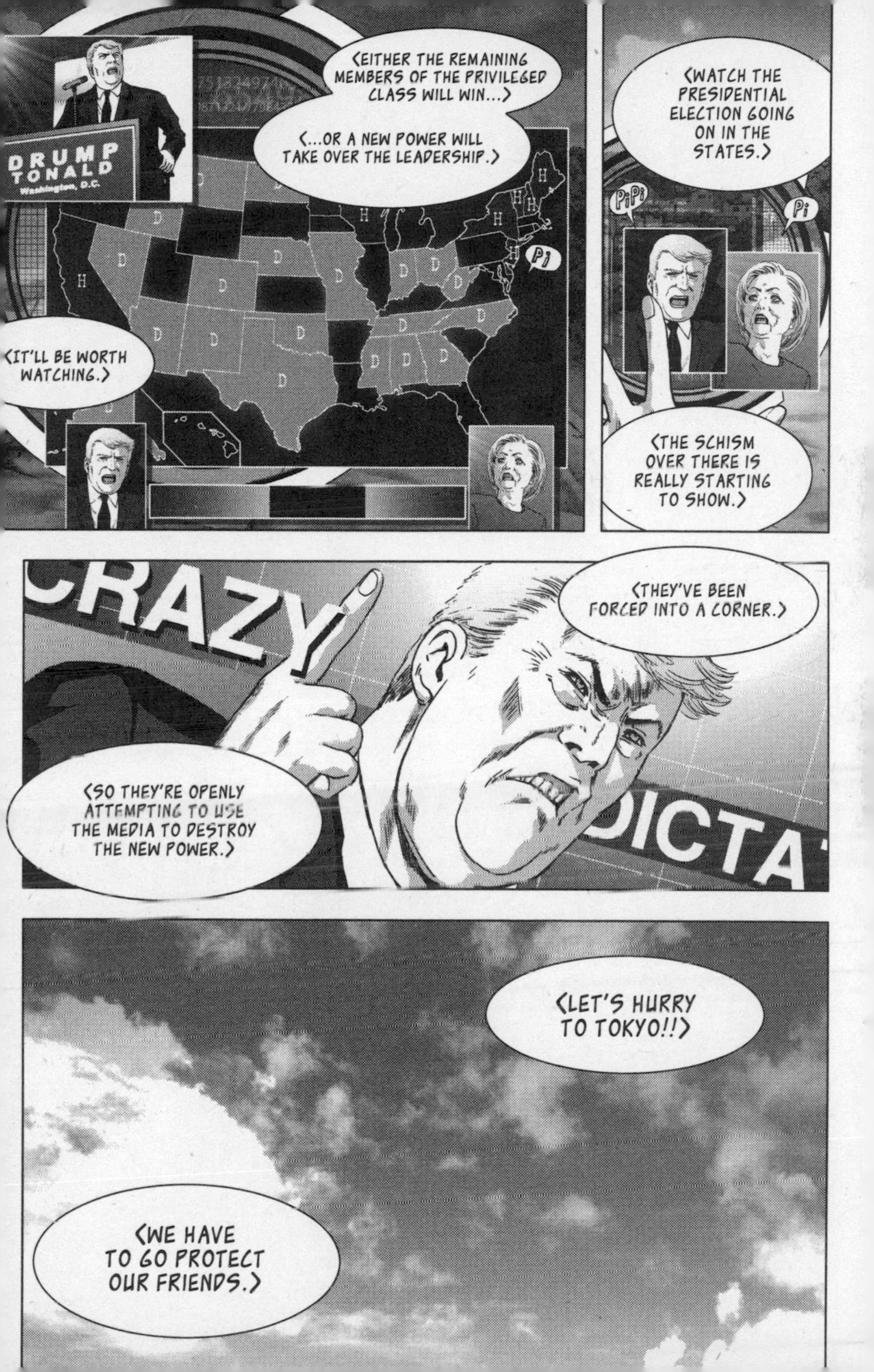
⟨WATCH THE PRESIDENTIAL ELECTION GOING ON IN THE STATES.⟩
PiPi
Pi
⟨THE SCHISM OVER THERE IS REALLY STARTING TO SHOW.⟩
⟨EITHER THE REMAINING MEMBERS OF THE PRIVILEGED CLASS WILL WIN...⟩
⟨...OR A NEW POWER WILL TAKE OVER THE LEADERSHIP.⟩
DRUMP TONALD
Washington, D.C.
Pi
⟨IT'LL BE WORTH WATCHING.⟩
CRAZY
⟨THEY'VE BEEN FORCED INTO A CORNER.⟩
⟨SO THEY'RE OPENLY ATTEMPTING TO USE THE MEDIA TO DESTROY THE NEW POWER.⟩
DICTA
⟨LET'S HURRY TO TOKYO!!⟩
⟨WE HAVE TO GO PROTECT OUR FRIENDS.⟩

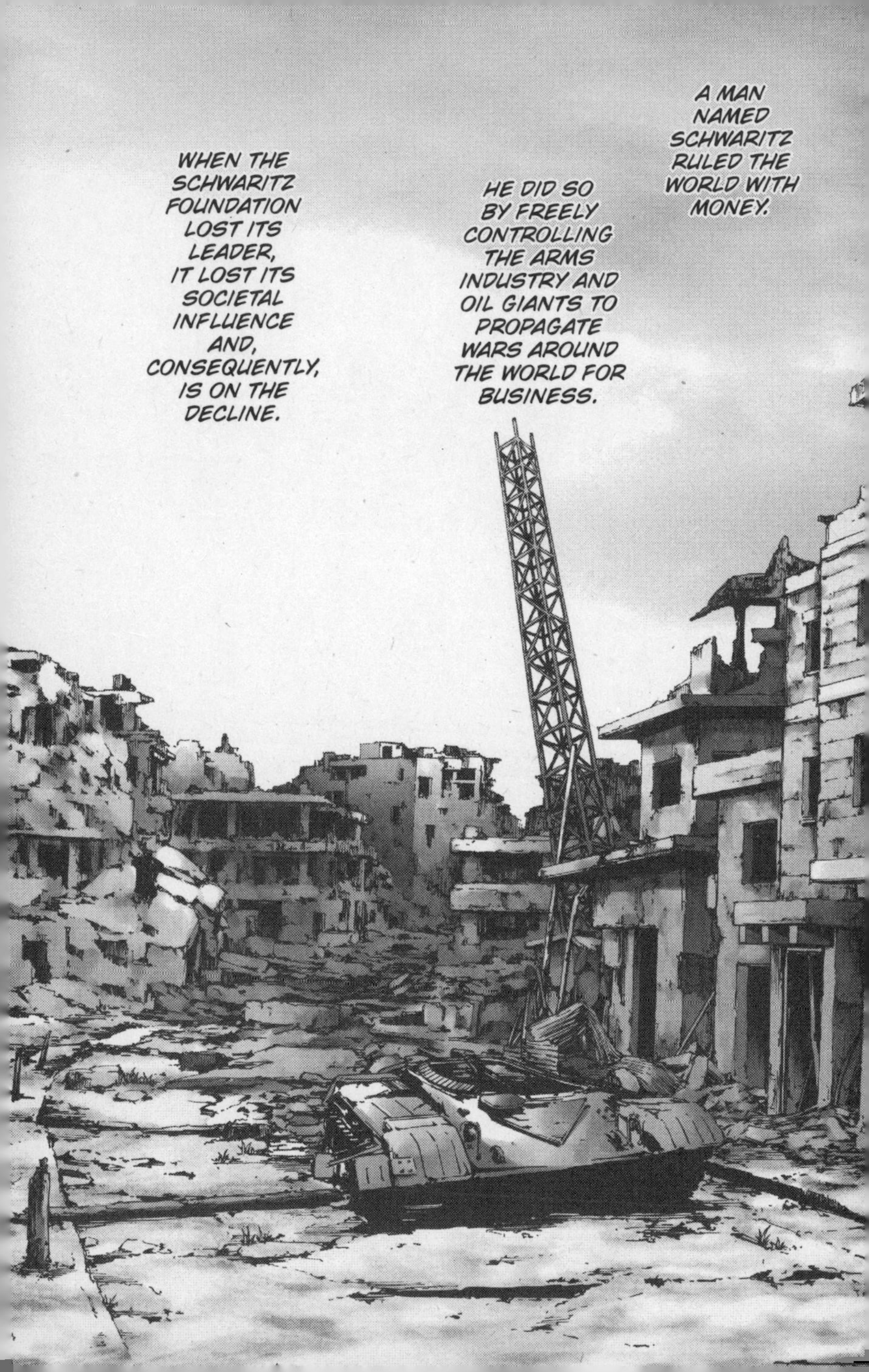
A MAN NAMED SCHWARITZ RULED THE WORLD WITH MONEY.
HE DID SO BY FREELY CONTROLLING THE ARMS INDUSTRY AND OIL GIANTS TO PROPAGATE WARS AROUND THE WORLD FOR BUSINESS.
WHEN THE SCHWARITZ FOUNDATION LOST ITS LEADER, IT LOST ITS SOCIETAL INFLUENCE AND, CONSEQUENTLY, IS ON THE DECLINE.

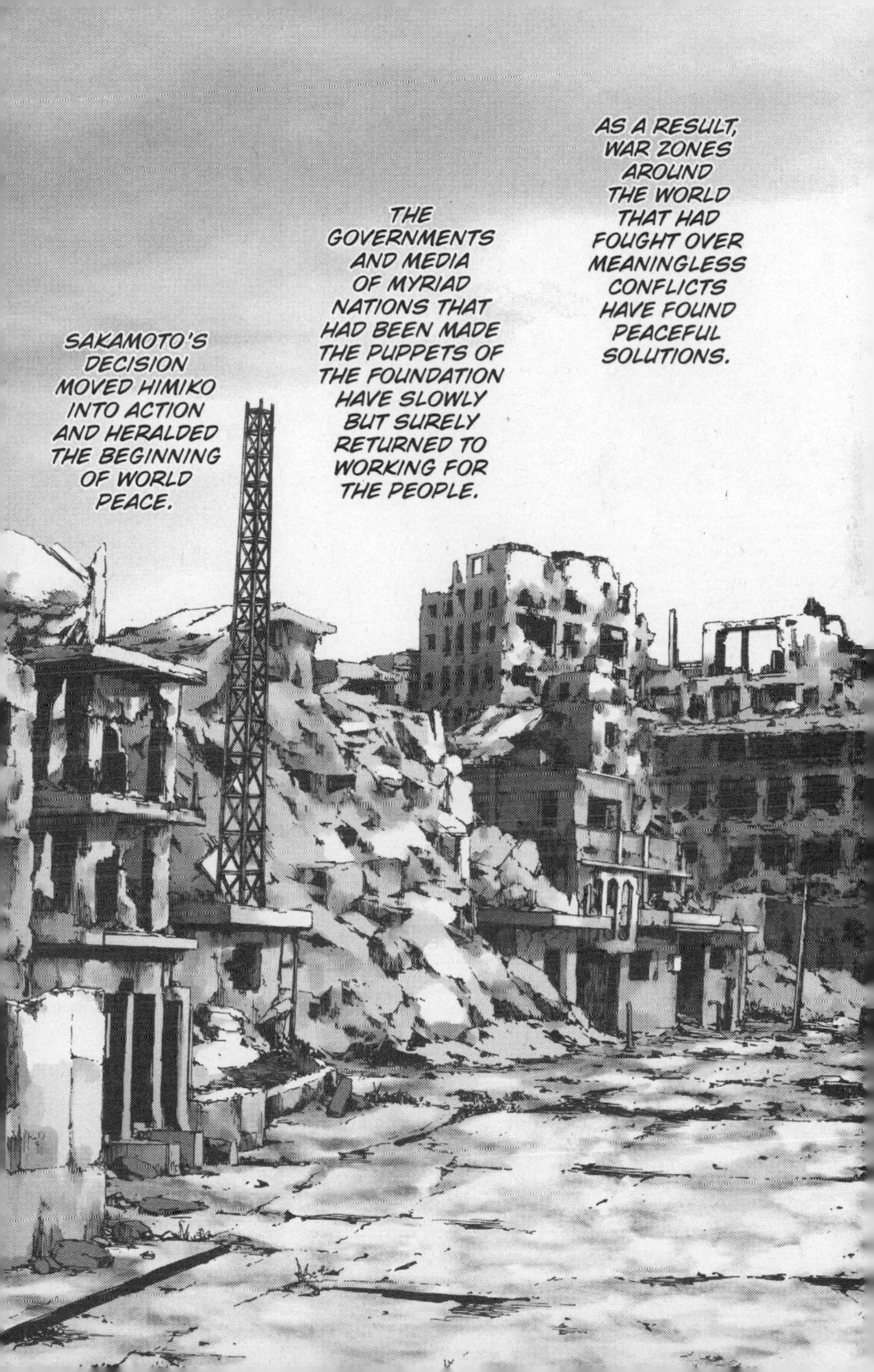
SAKAMOTO'S DECISION MOVED HIMIKO INTO ACTION AND HERALDED THE BEGINNING OF WORLD PEACE.
THE GOVERNMENTS AND MEDIA OF MYRIAD NATIONS THAT HAD BEEN MADE THE PUPPETS OF THE FOUNDATION HAVE SLOWLY BUT SURELY RETURNED TO WORKING FOR THE PEOPLE.
AS A RESULT, WAR ZONES AROUND THE WORLD THAT HAD FOUGHT OVER MEANINGLESS CONFLICTS HAVE FOUND PEACEFUL SOLUTIONS.

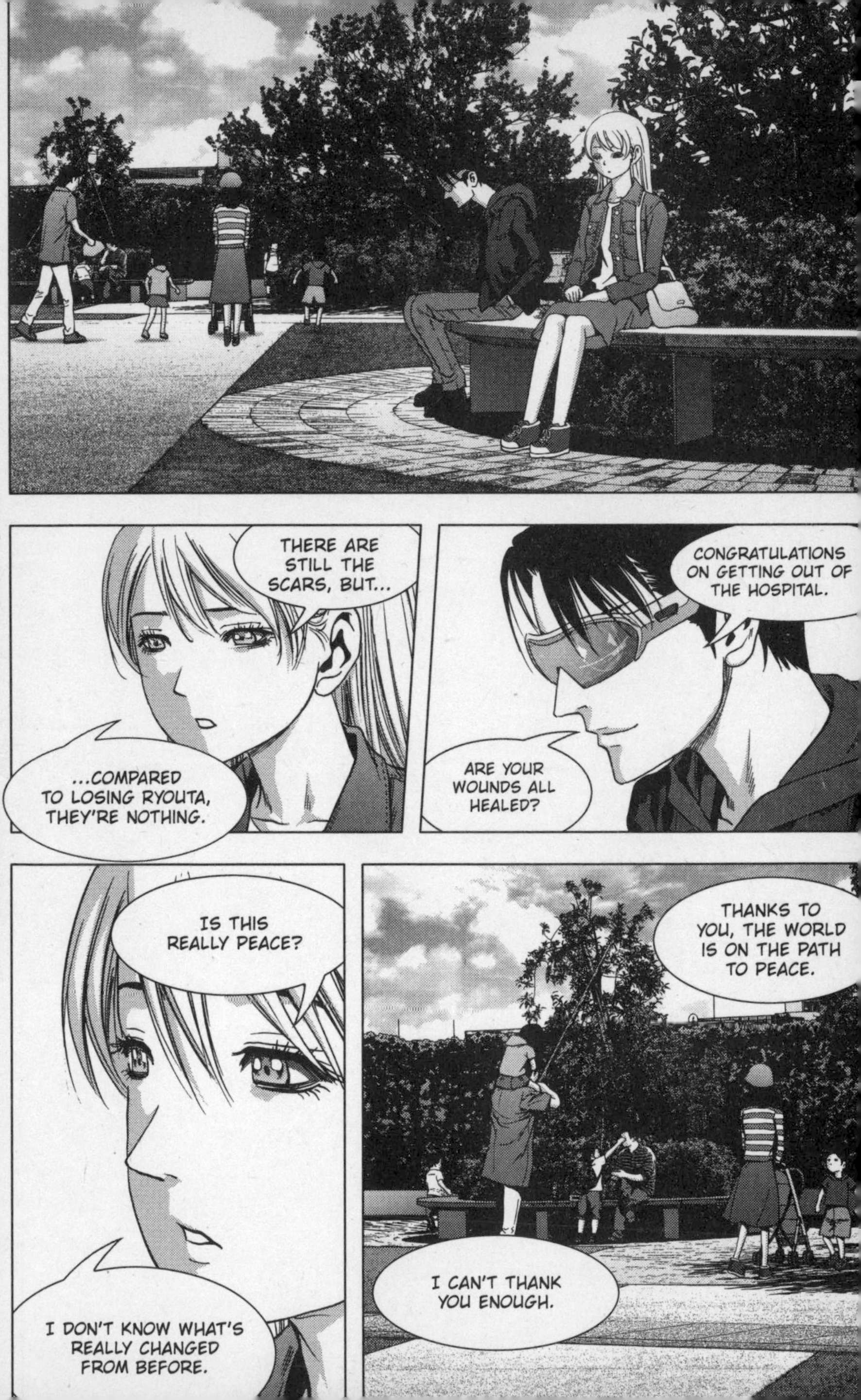
CONGRATULATIONS ON GETTING OUT OF THE HOSPITAL.
ARE YOUR WOUNDS ALL HEALED?
THERE ARE STILL THE SCARS, BUT...
...COMPARED TO LOSING RYOUTA, THEY'RE NOTHING.
THANKS TO YOU, THE WORLD IS ON THE PATH TO PEACE.
I CAN'T THANK YOU ENOUGH.
IS THIS REALLY PEACE?
I DON'T KNOW WHAT'S REALLY CHANGED FROM BEFORE.

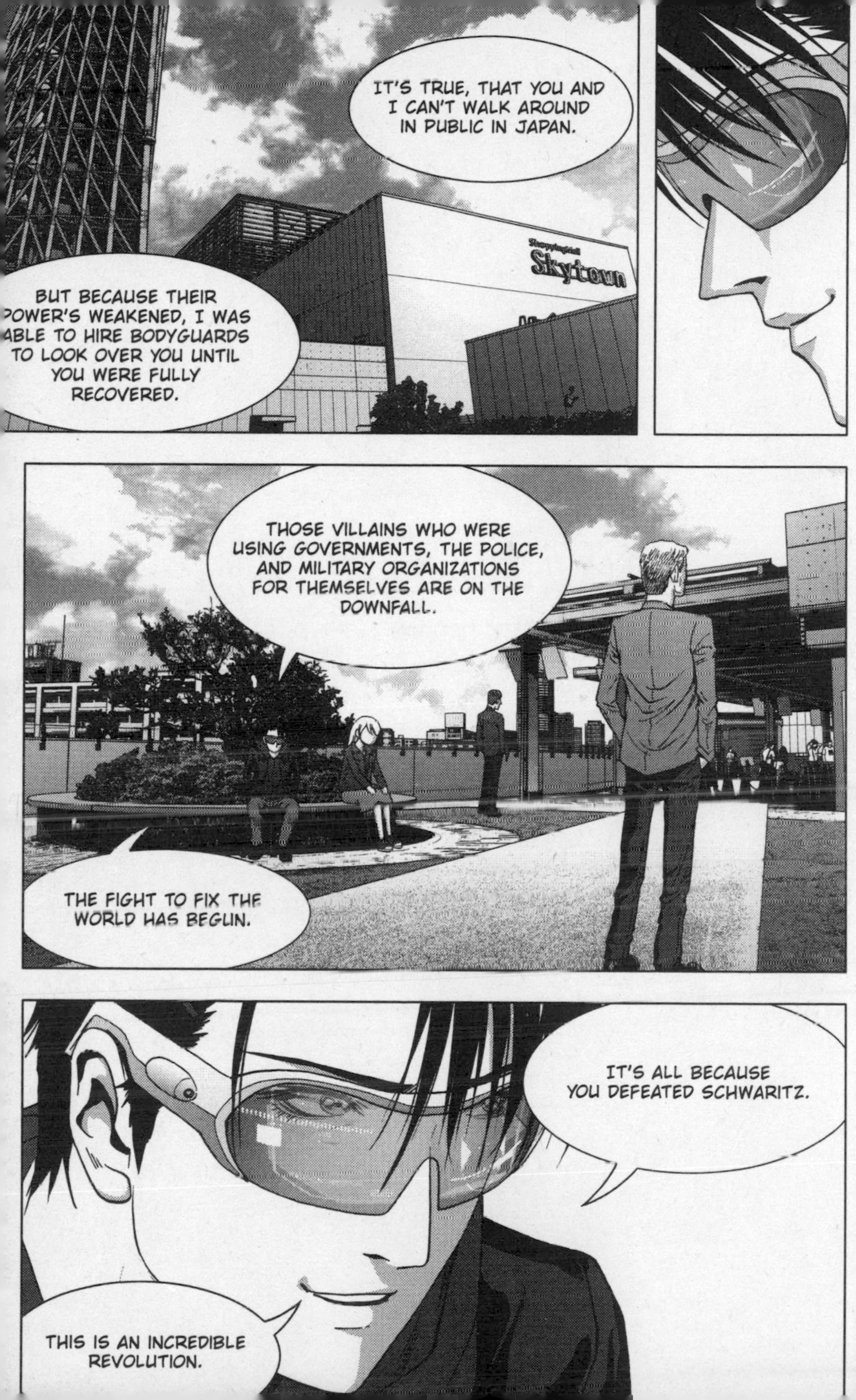
IT'S TRUE, THAT YOU AND I CAN'T WALK AROUND IN PUBLIC IN JAPAN.
Skytown
BUT BECAUSE THEIR POWER'S WEAKENED, I WAS ABLE TO HIRE BODYGUARDS TO LOOK OVER YOU UNTIL YOU WERE FULLY RECOVERED.
THOSE VILLAINS WHO WERE USING GOVERNMENTS, THE POLICE, AND MILITARY ORGANIZATIONS FOR THEMSELVES ARE ON THE DOWNFALL.
THE FIGHT TO FIX THE WORLD HAS BEGUN.
IT'S ALL BECAUSE YOU DEFEATED SCHWARITZ.
THIS IS AN INCREDIBLE REVOLUTION.

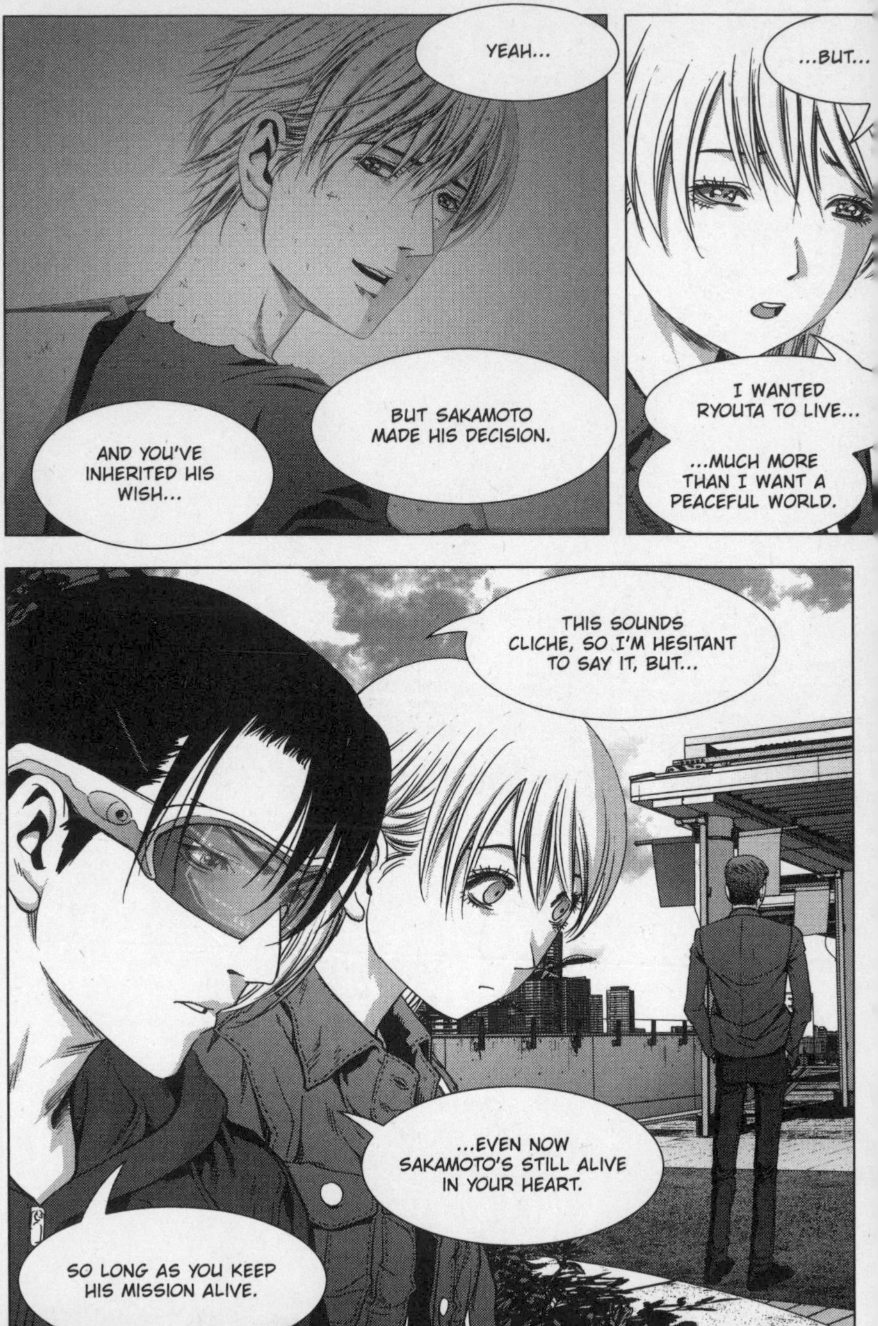
...BUT...
I WANTED RYOUTA TO LIVE...
...MUCH MORE THAN I WANT A PEACEFUL WORLD.
YEAH...
BUT SAKAMOTO MADE HIS DECISION.
AND YOU'VE INHERITED HIS WISH...
THIS SOUNDS CLICHE, SO I'M HESITANT TO SAY IT, BUT...
...EVEN NOW SAKAMOTO'S STILL ALIVE IN YOUR HEART.
SO LONG AS YOU KEEP HIS MISSION ALIVE.

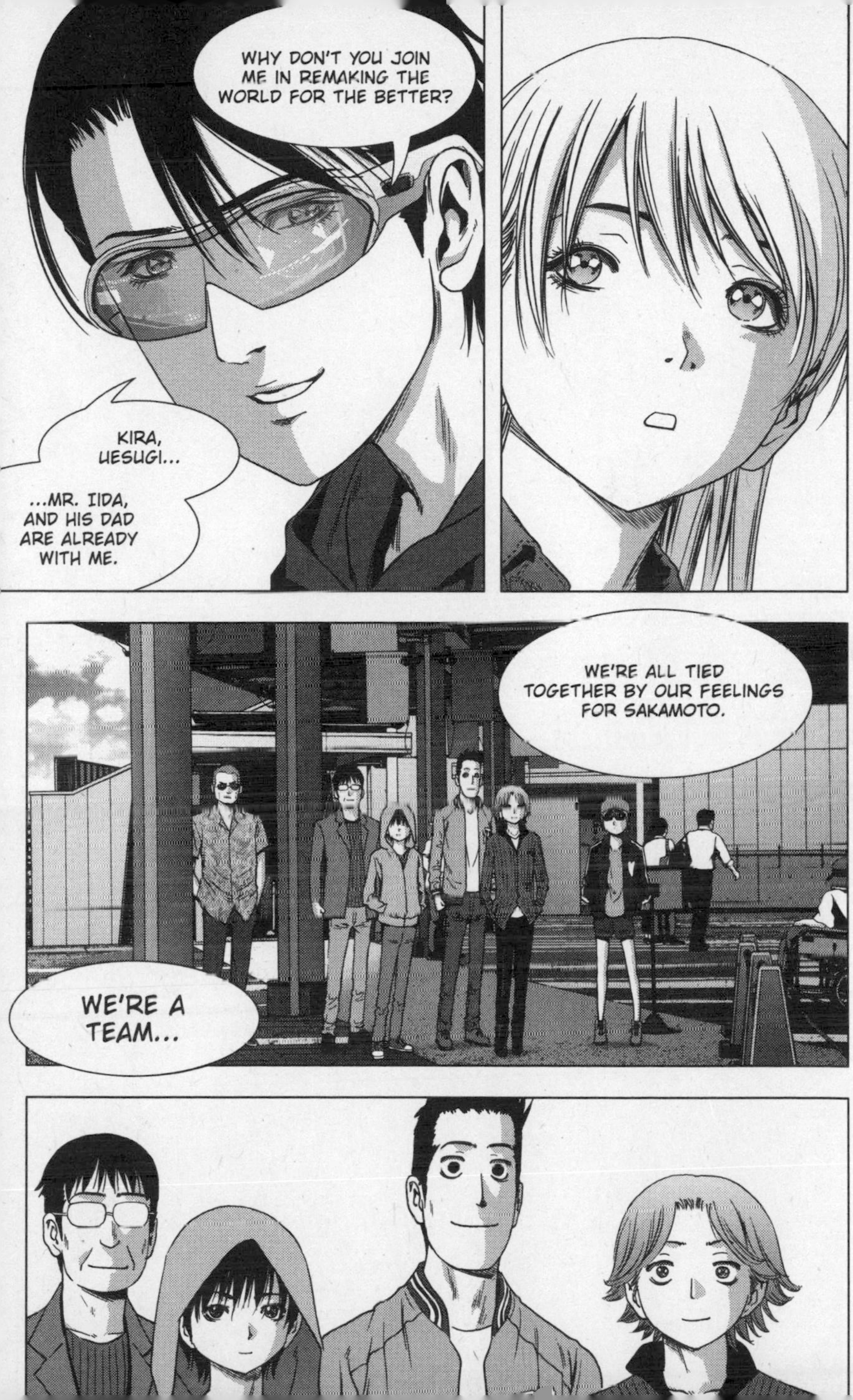
WHY DON'T YOU JOIN ME IN REMAKING THE WORLD FOR THE BETTER?
KIRA, UESUGI...
...MR. IIDA, AND HIS DAD ARE ALREADY WITH ME.
WE'RE ALL TIED TOGETHER BY OUR FEELINGS FOR SAKAMOTO.
WE'RE A TEAM...

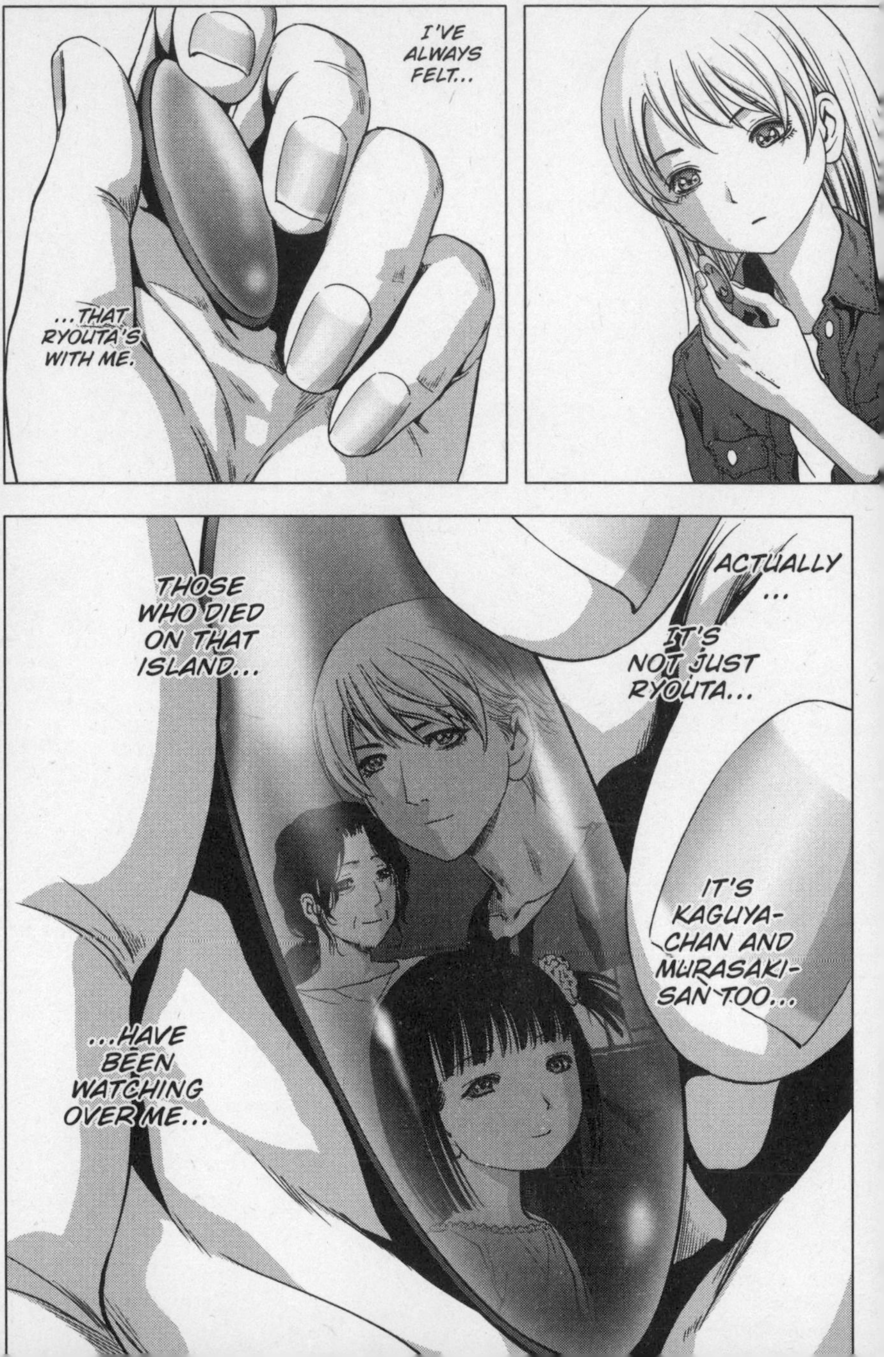
I'VE ALWAYS FELT...
...THAT RYOUTA'S WITH ME.
ACTUALLY...
IT'S NOT JUST RYOUTA...
IT'S KAGUYA-CHAN AND MURASAKI-SAN TOO...
THOSE WHO DIED ON THAT ISLAND...
...HAVE BEEN WATCHING OVER ME...

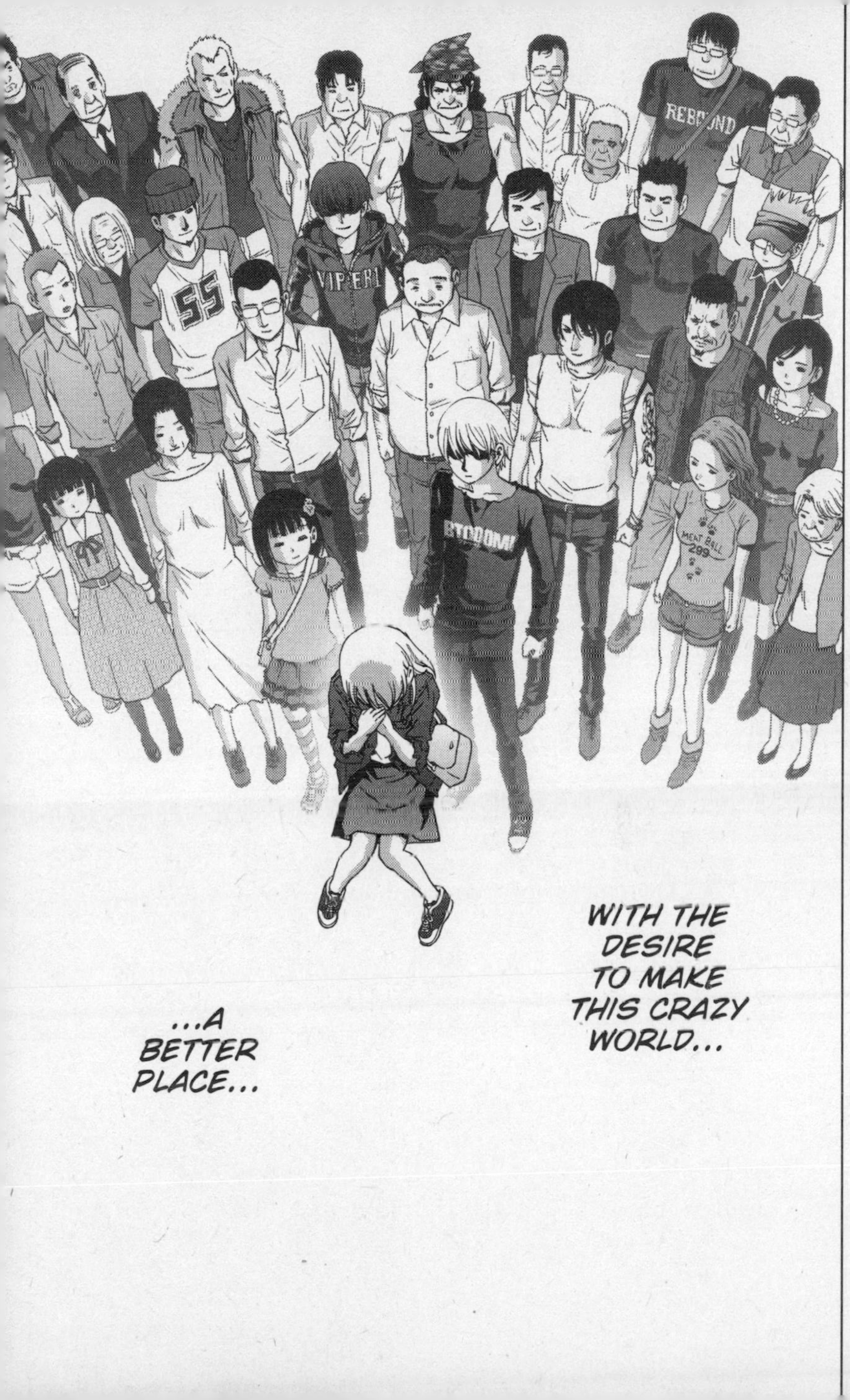
WITH THE DESIRE TO MAKE THIS CRAZY WORLD...
...A BETTER PLACE...

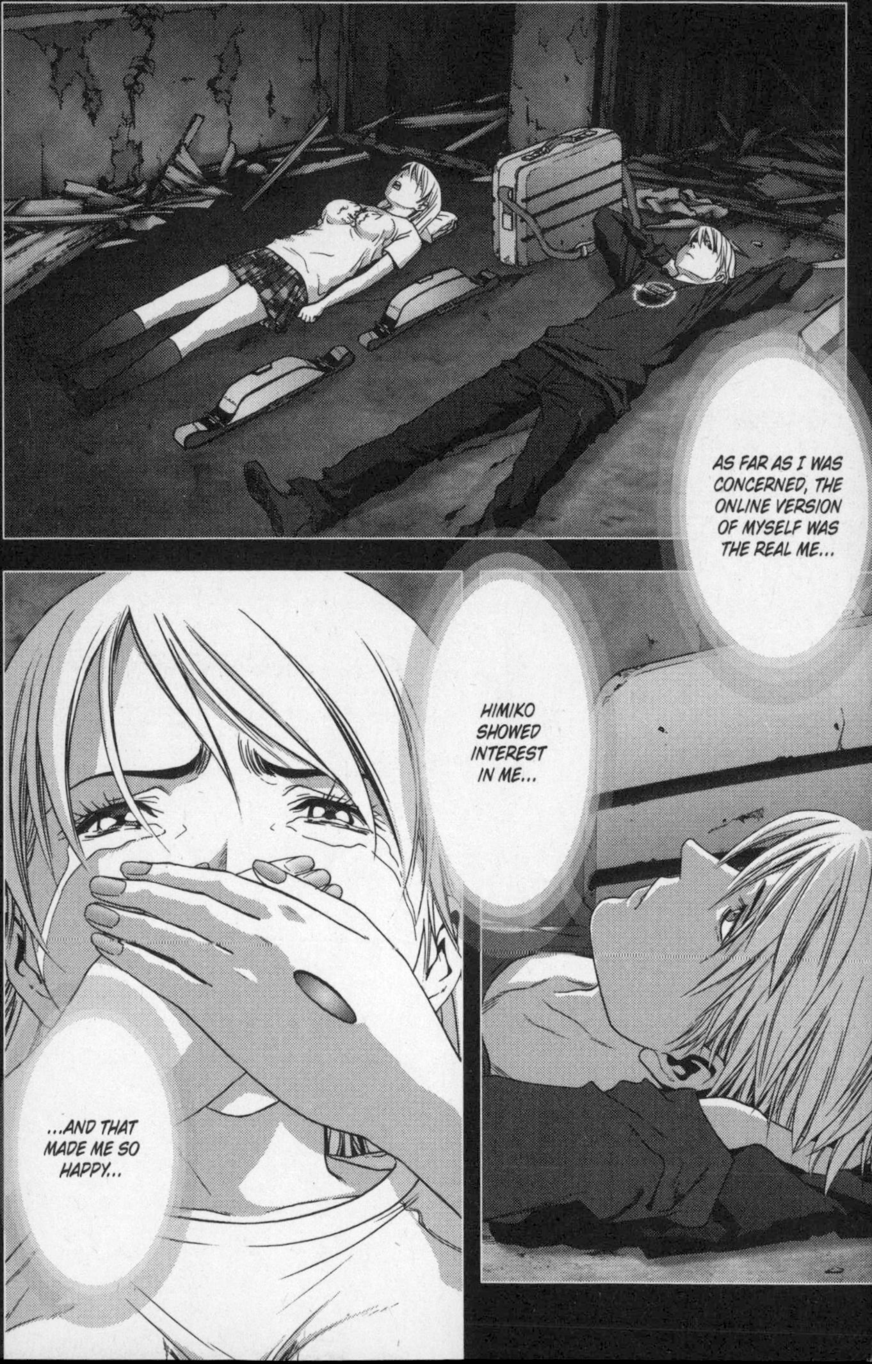
AS FAR AS I WAS CONCERNED, THE ONLINE VERSION OF MYSELF WAS THE REAL ME...
HIMIKO SHOWED INTEREST IN ME...
...AND THAT MADE ME SO HAPPY...

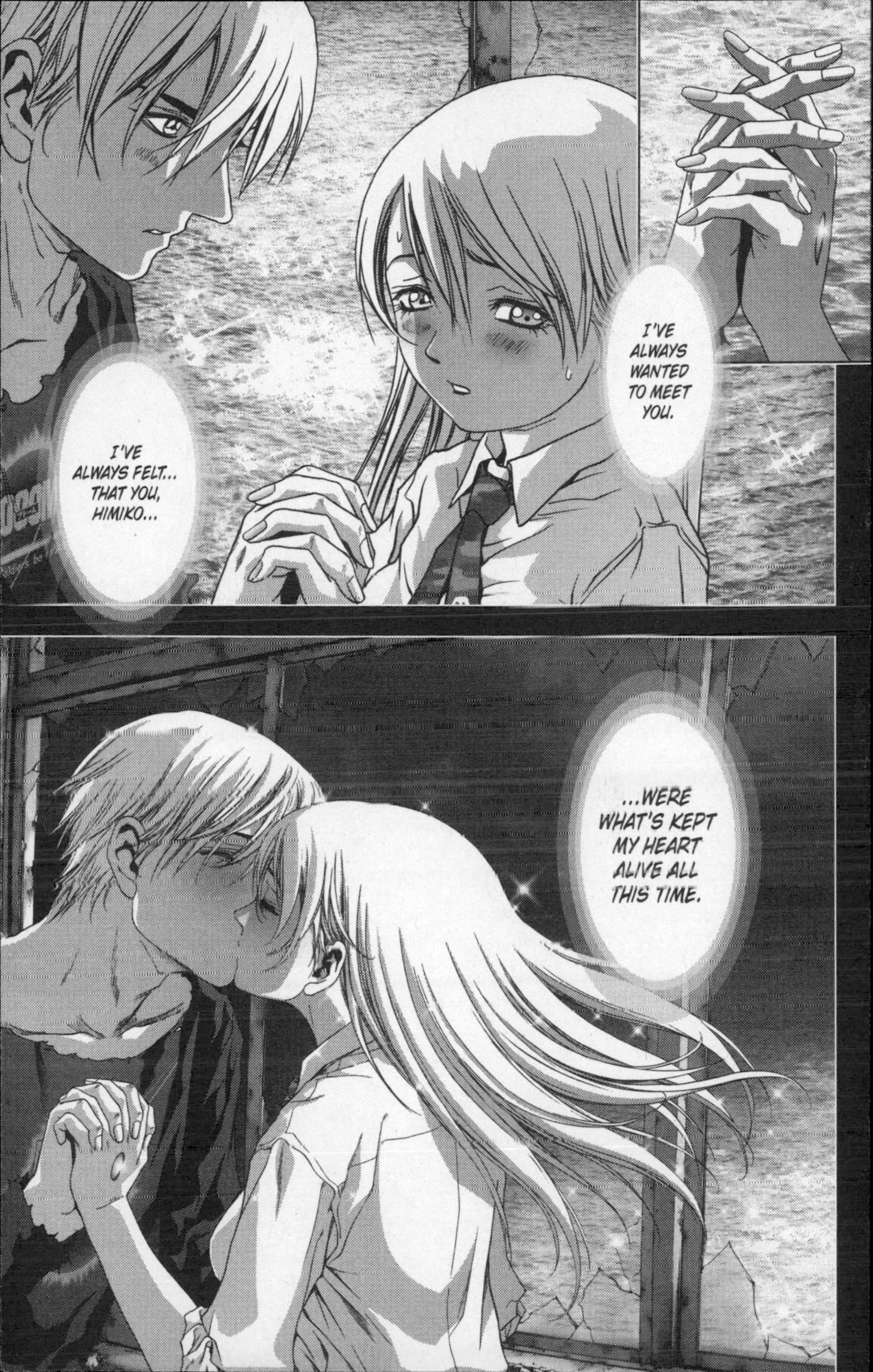
I'VE ALWAYS WANTED TO MEET YOU.
I'VE ALWAYS FELT... THAT YOU, HIMIKO...
...WERE WHAT'S KEPT MY HEART ALIVE ALL THIS TIME.

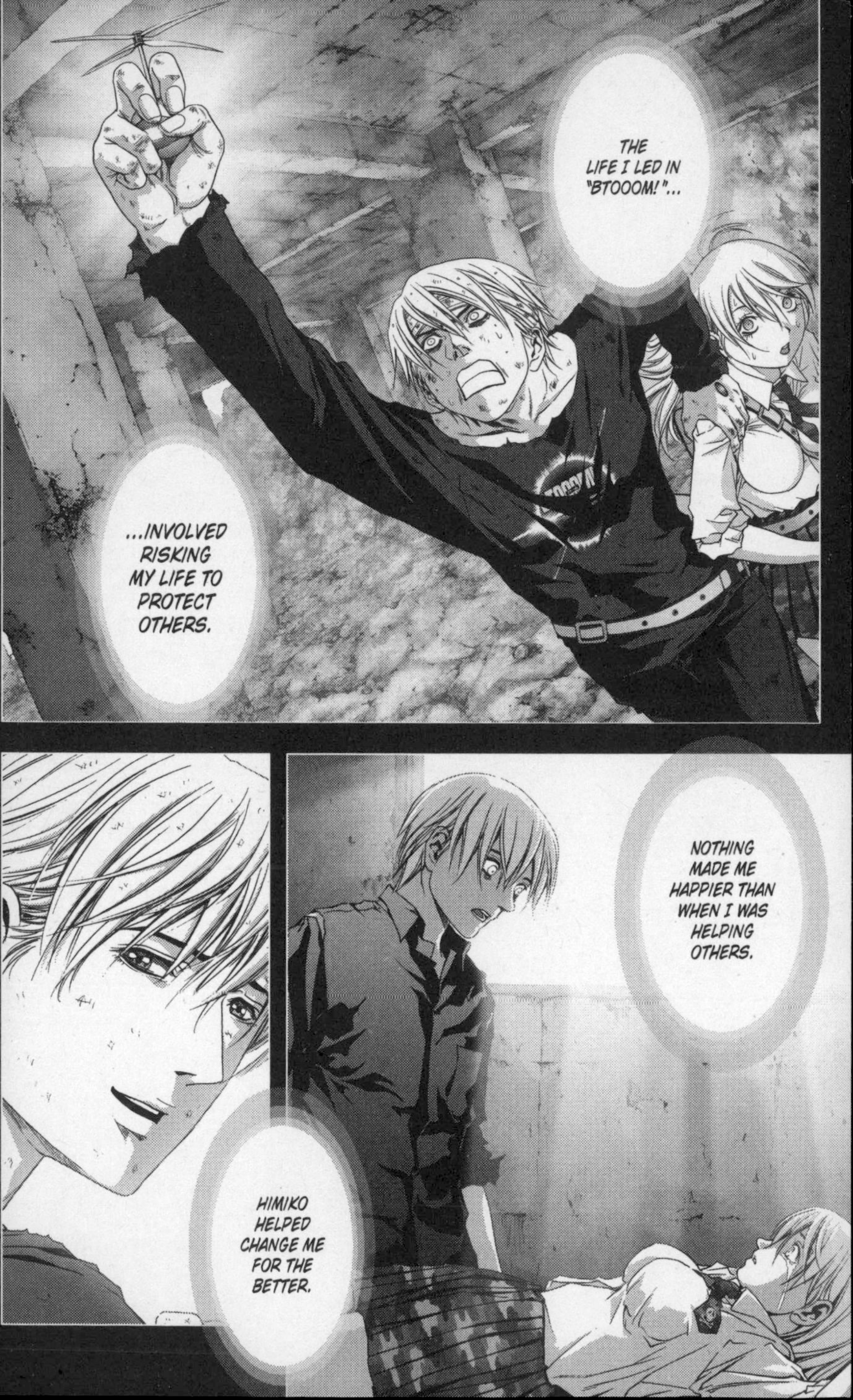
THE LIFE I LED IN "BTOOOM!"...
...INVOLVED RISKING MY LIFE TO PROTECT OTHERS.
NOTHING MADE ME HAPPIER THAN WHEN I WAS HELPING OTHERS.
HIMIKO HELPED CHANGE ME FOR THE BETTER.

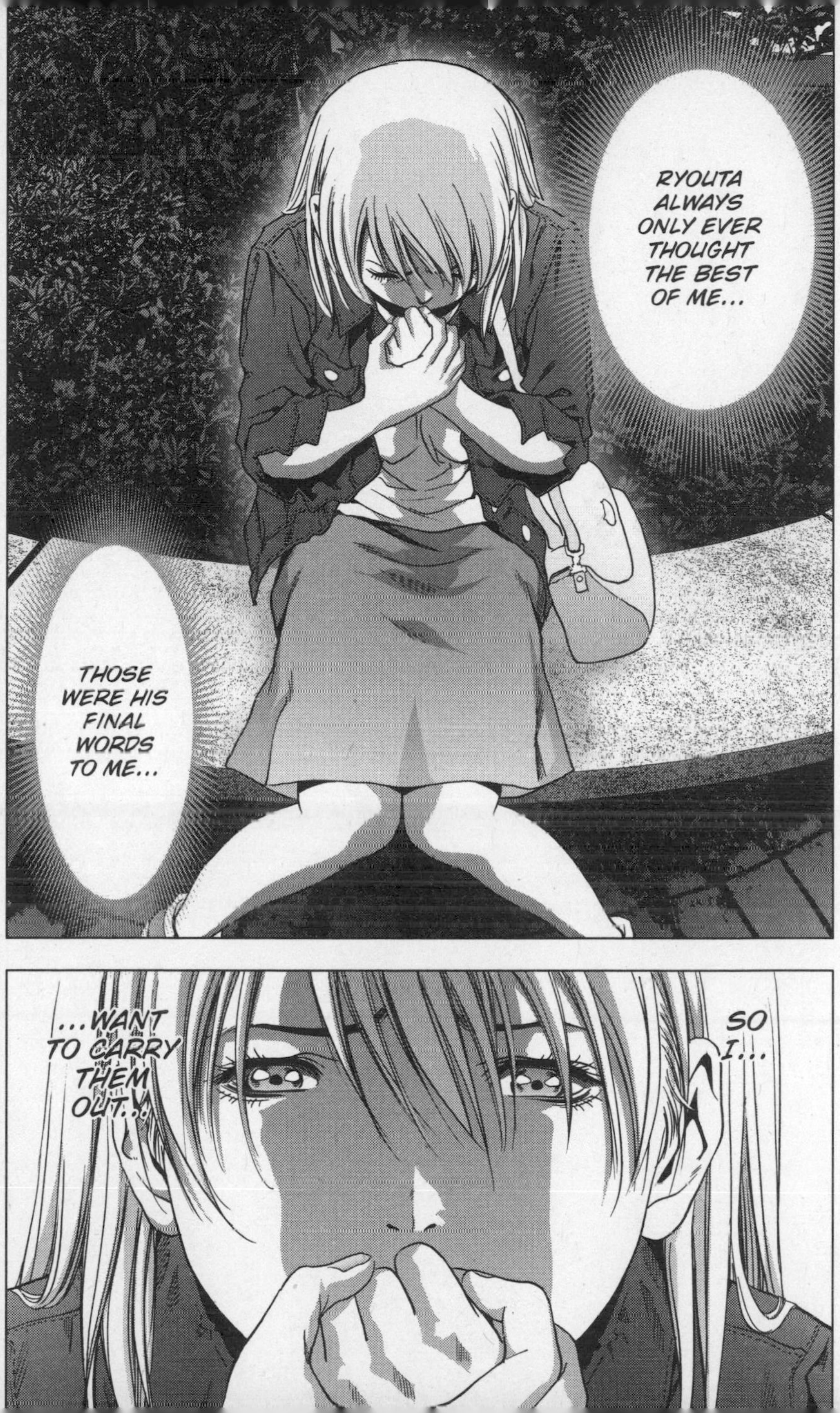
RYOUTA ALWAYS ONLY EVER THOUGHT THE BEST OF ME...
THOSE WERE HIS FINAL WORDS TO ME...
SO I...
...WANT TO CARRY THEM OUT...

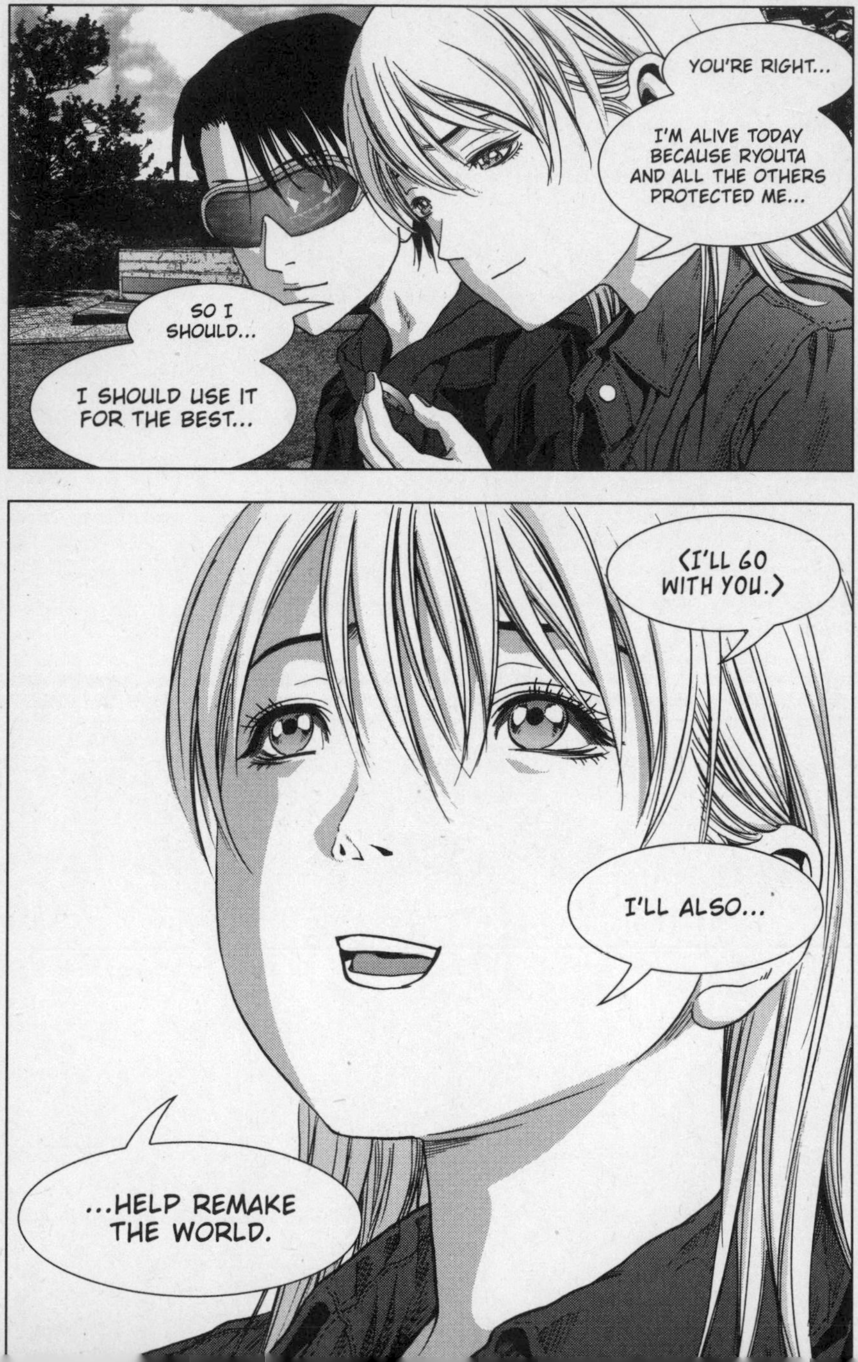
YOU'RE RIGHT...
I'M ALIVE TODAY BECAUSE RYOUTA AND ALL THE OTHERS PROTECTED ME...
SO I SHOULD...
I SHOULD USE IT FOR THE BEST...
<I'LL GO WITH YOU.>
I'LL ALSO...
...HELP REMAKE THE WORLD.

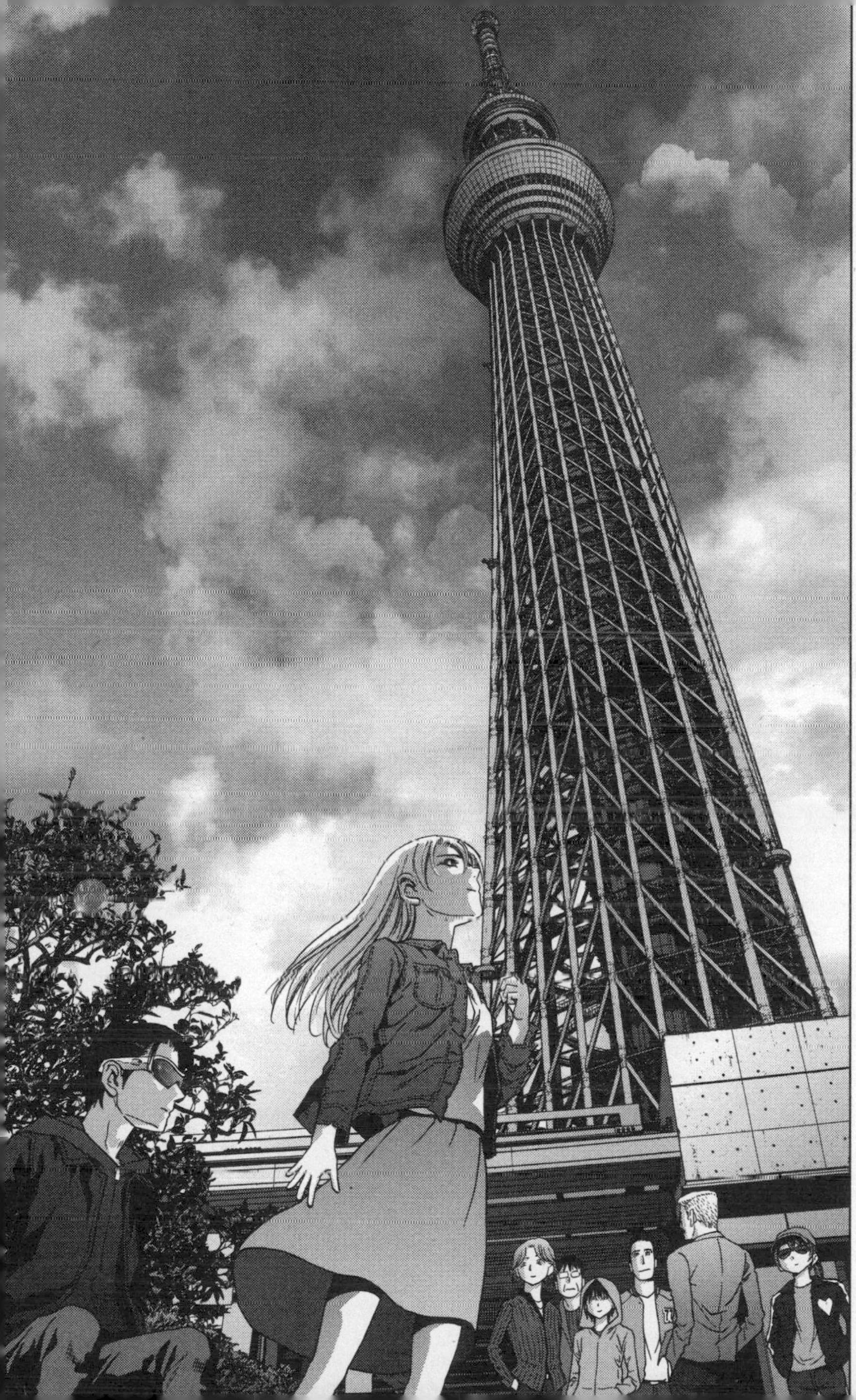

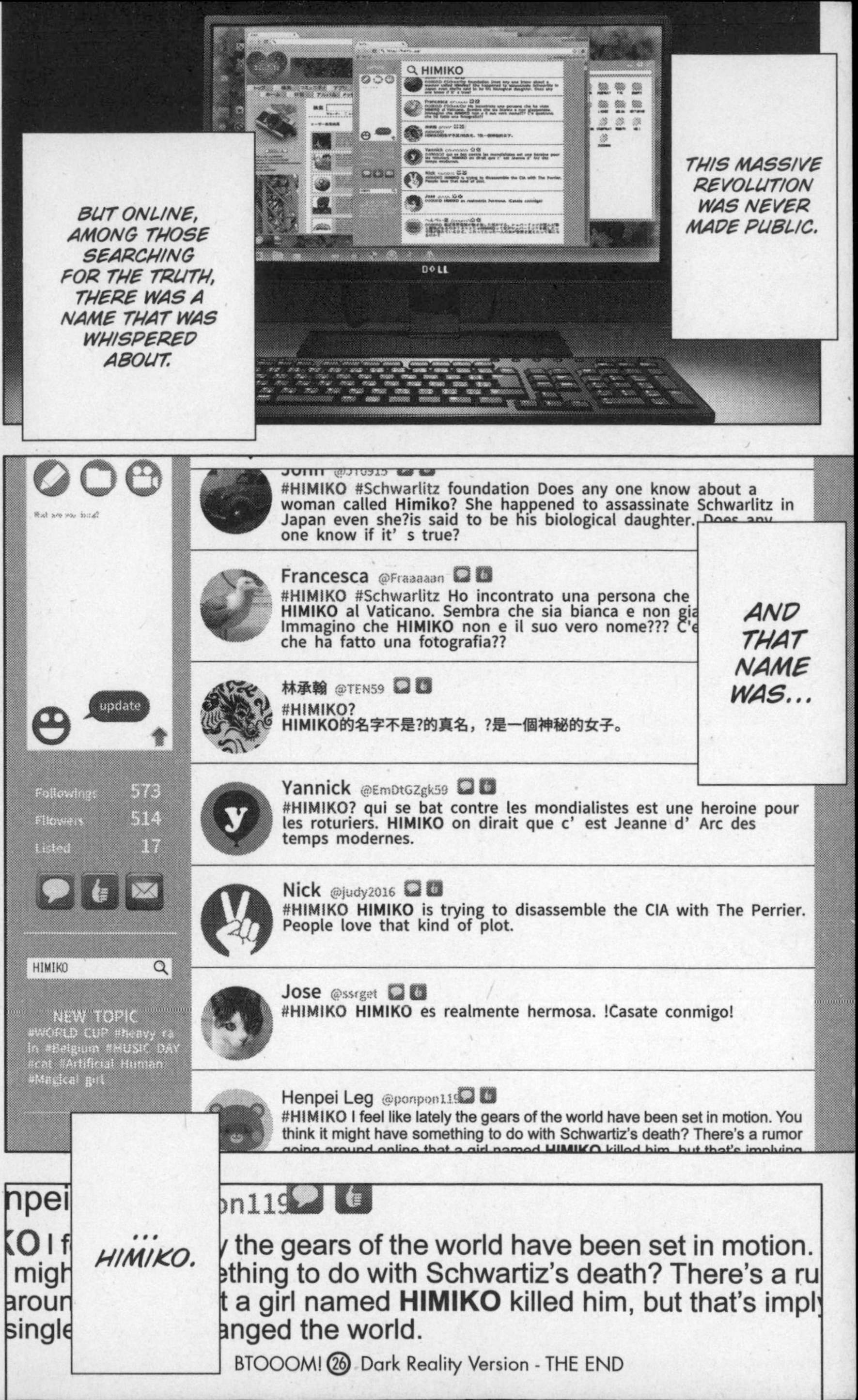

THIS MASSIVE REVOLUTION WAS NEVER MADE PUBLIC.

BUT ONLINE, AMONG THOSE SEARCHING FOR THE TRUTH, THERE WAS A NAME THAT WAS WHISPERED ABOUT.

AND THAT NAME WAS...

Followings 573
Flowers 514
Listed 17

update

HIMIKO 🔍

NEW TOPIC
#WORLD CUP #heavy ra
in #Belgium #MUSIC DAY
#cat #Artificial Human
#Magical girl

John @J10915
#HIMIKO #Schwarlitz foundation Does any one know about a woman called **Himiko**? She happened to assassinate Schwarlitz in Japan even she?is said to be his biological daughter. Does any one know if it's true?

Francesca @Fraaaaan
#HIMIKO #Schwarlitz Ho incontrato una persona che **HIMIKO** al Vaticano. Sembra che sia bianca e non già Immagino non e il suo vero nome??? C'e che ha fatto una fotografia??

林承翰 @TEN59
#HIMIKO?
HIMIKO的名字不是?的真名，?是一個神秘的女子。

Yannick @EmDtGZgk59
#HIMIKO? qui se bat contre les mondialistes est une heroine pour les roturiers. HIMIKO on dirait que c'est Jeanne d'Arc des temps modernes.

Nick @judy2016
#HIMIKO HIMIKO is trying to disassemble the CIA with The Perrier. People love that kind of plot.

Jose @ssrget
#HIMIKO HIMIKO es realmente hermosa. !Casate conmigo!

Henpei Leg @ponpon119
#HIMIKO I feel like lately the gears of the world have been set in motion. You think it might have something to do with Schwartiz's death? There's a rumor going around online that a girl named **HIMIKO** killed him, but that's implying

npei ... on119

HIMIKO.

KO I f ... y the gears of the world have been set in motion.
migh ... thing to do with Schwartiz's death? There's a ru
aroun ... t a girl named **HIMIKO** killed him, but that's imply
single ... anged the world.

BTOOOM! 26 Dark Reality Version - THE END